Praise for prior editions

"Finally, an accurate, well-researched, and insightful guide to the high-stakes law school admissions process. Richard Montauk asks the right questions, and he gets straight answers from the people who make decisions. Whether you're just getting started with the process or are simply looking for ways to fine-tune an application, this is great advice."
—Susan Palmer, Associate Dean for Admissions, University of Virginia School of Law

"This is a must-read for anyone thinking of attending law school! It not only has invaluable advice on how to navigate the admissions process, but is also the only resource that clearly describes the pros and cons of pursuing a JD and a legal career. I highly recommend it."
—Susan Robinson, Associate Dean for Career Services, Stanford Law School

"Finally a guide that clears up the misconceptions and takes the mystery out of the law school admissions process. Quite simply, this book is the most thorough resource available to those who intend to apply to the nation's top law schools. With solid advice from the admissions directors themselves on how to manage the admissions process and how to position and communicate your achievements, this book is a must-read if you want to maximize your chances and options."
—Don Rebstock, Associate Dean of Admissions and Financial Aid, Northwestern University School of Law

"Law school is a big investment; this guide is a must for those who want to invest wisely. Through a combination of his own insight (based on decades of admissions consulting) and in-depth discussions with the country's leading admissions and financial aid professionals, Montauk shows applicants how to maximize both their admissions and financial aid prospects. The best book on the subject."
—Rob Schwartz, Assistant Dean for Admissions, UCLA School of Law

"I highly recommend *How to Get Into the Top Law Schools*—it's unquestionably the best book ever written on the subject. Montauk has talked at length with all of the top schools' admissions directors, and they have been refreshingly candid in sharing their views of each aspect of the admissions process. The result is a comprehensive work that will help eliminate applicants' application anxieties. Absolutely required reading."
—Janice Austin, Associate Dean for Admissions, University of Pennsylvania Law School

continued . . .

"Anyone who aspires to being admitted to one of the nation's best law schools should take the application process itself very seriously. The preparation of the strongest possible application takes research and careful planning. *How to Get Into the Top Law Schools* contains very good advice from admissions professionals at highly competitive institutions that will help you to develop your application strategies as well as to determine which schools best match your interests."

—Kenneth Kleinrock, Assistant Dean for Admissions,
NYU School of Law

"Richard Montauk's book is a readable, comprehensive resource for individuals who are considering jumping into the law school admissions process. Through his well-established relationships with admissions deans at top law schools, Montauk has been able to compile accurate and honest information about how the law school admissions process really works. This book covers, in one source, all of the areas prospective students must investigate and consider—from selecting to which schools they will apply to figuring out how to finance their legal educations. I give Montauk's book an A+."

—Anne Richard, Associate Dean of Admissions and Financial Aid,
George Washington University Law School

"Montauk's information on law school admissions is virtually flawless and covers a broad range of topics with refreshing candor and unusual insight. This book not only contains very good advice directly from admissions deans, but also provides invaluable information and commentary aimed squarely at helping prospective lawyers manage the law school admission process effectively, maximize their options for law school, and choose paths that best fit personal interests and professional aspirations."

—Todd Morton, Assistant Dean and Dean of Admissions,
Vanderbilt University Law School

"Montauk analyzes each part of the application process and provides a wonderful roadmap to guide you as you assemble a coherent, persuasive application. Follow Montauk's advice and present yourself more effectively to the best law schools in the country!"   —Erica Munzel, Assistant Dean and Director of Admissions,
University of Michigan Law School

How to
Get Into
the
TOP LAW
SCHOOLS

4TH EDITION

RICHARD MONTAUK, J.D.

PRENTICE HALL PRESS

PRENTICE HALL PRESS
Published by the Penguin Group
Penguin Group (USA) Inc.
375 Hudson Street, New York, New York 10014, USA
Penguin Group (Canada), 90 Eglinton Avenue East, Suite 700, Toronto, Ontario M4P 2Y3, Canada
(a division of Pearson Penguin Canada Inc.)
Penguin Books Ltd., 80 Strand, London WC2R 0RL, England
Penguin Group Ireland, 25 St. Stephen's Green, Dublin 2, Ireland (a division of Penguin Books Ltd.)
Penguin Group (Australia), 250 Camberwell Road, Camberwell, Victoria 3124, Australia
(a division of Pearson Australia Group Pty. Ltd.)
Penguin Books India Pvt. Ltd., 11 Community Centre, Panchsheel Park, New Delhi—110 017, India
Penguin Group (NZ), 67 Apollo Drive, Rosedale, North Shore 0632, New Zealand
(a division of Pearson New Zealand Ltd.)
Penguin Books (South Africa) (Pty.) Ltd., 24 Sturdee Avenue, Rosebank, Johannesburg 2196, South Africa

Penguin Books Ltd., Registered Offices: 80 Strand, London WC2R 0RL, England

While the author has made every effort to provide accurate telephone numbers and Internet addresses at the time of publication, neither the publisher nor the author assumes any responsibility for errors, or for changes that occur after publication. Further, the publisher does not have any control over and does not assume any responsibility for author or third-party websites or their content.

PRINTING HISTORY
Prentice Hall Press trade paperback second edition / July 2004
Prentice Hall Press trade paperback third edition / August 2006
Prentice Hall Press trade paperback fourth edition / August 2008

Prentice Hall Press fourth edition ISBN: 978-0-7352-0429-4

The Library of Congress has cataloged the Prentice Hall Press second edition as follows:

Montauk, Richard.
    How to get into the top law schools / Richard Montauk.
      p. cm.
    Includes index.
    ISBN 0-7352-0376-8 (paper)
    1. Law schools—United States—Admission. I. Title.
KF285.M66 2001
340'.071'173—dc21   2001021691

PRINTED IN THE UNITED STATES OF AMERICA

10 9 8 7 6 5 4 3 2 1

Most Prentice Hall Press books are available at special quantity discounts for bulk purchases for sales promotions, premiums, fundraising, or educational use. Special books, or book excerpts, can also be created to fit specific needs. For details, write: Special Markets, Penguin Group (USA) Inc., 375 Hudson Street, New York, New York 10014.

Dedicated to three instructors, coaches, and role models who helped several generations of young people realize their potential:

Betty Edwards

Jack Edwards

Tom Gauerke

ACKNOWLEDGMENTS

I wish to thank those people who have been so helpful to the development and writing of *How to Get Into the Top Law Schools*:

First, the *admissions deans* at leading schools across the country who have been remarkably generous with their time and knowledge in discussing how admissions decisions are made at their schools. In particular, I would like to thank those I interviewed for this book and who have allowed themselves to be quoted throughout the text:

Elizabeth Rosselot (Boston College); Edward Tom (UC Berkeley/Boalt Hall); Rob Schwartz, Michael Rappaport, Andrea Sossin-Bergman (UCLA); Ann Killian Perry (Chicago); Nkonye Iwerebon, Venetta C. Amory, Jim Milligan (Columbia); Rick Geiger (Cornell); William Hoye, Dennis Shields (Duke); Anne Richard, Robert Stanek (George Washington); Andy Cornblatt (Georgetown); Joyce Curll (Harvard); Kip Darcy (Hastings); Sarah Zearfoss, Erica Munzel (Michigan); Kenneth Kleinrock (NYU); Don Rebstock (Northwestern); Renee Post, Derek Meeker, Janice Austin (Pennsylvania); Chloe T. Reid (Southern California); Faye Deal (Stanford); Monica Ingram, Shelli Soto (Texas); Todd Morton, Anne Brandt (Vanderbilt); Susan Palmer, Albert R. Turnbull (Virginia); and Megan Barnett and Jean Webb (Yale).

Second, the *financial aid deans and directors*, similarly generous with their time and knowledge regarding financial aid matters:

Dennis Tominaga, James Ausemus (UC Berkeley/Boalt Hall); Veronica Wilson (UCLA); Michael Machen (Chicago); Charles De Rubeis, Alice Rigas (Columbia); Karla Vargas, Jane Deathe (Cornell); William Hoye, Kochie Richardson (Duke); Tamara Devieux-Adams (George Washington); Charles Pruett III, Ruth Lammert-Reeves (Georgetown); Ken Lafler, Joyce Curll (Harvard); Katherine Gottschalk (Michigan); Joel Schoenecker, Stephen Brown (NYU); Don Rebstock (Northwestern); Anthony Henry, Derek Meeker, Janice Austin, Denise McGarry (Pennsylvania); Chloe T. Reid, Mary Bingham (Southern California); Faye Deal (Stanford); Monica Ingram, Linda Alba, Juan Zabala (Texas); Todd Morton (Vanderbilt); Cynthia Burns, Jerome B. Stokes (Virginia); Patricia Barnes, Louise DiMeo, and Zina Shaffer (Yale).

Third, the *career services and public interest program deans and directors*, for their insights regarding what employers value in recent law school graduates; what potential lawyers should know about law school, the profession, and themselves; and the current pay scales for different types of work in different locales:

Jean French (Boston College), Betsy Armour (Boston University), Jane Thomson (UC Davis), Catherine Mayorkas (UCLA), Karen Comstock (Cornell), Anna Akwari (Duke), Fred Thrasher (George Washington), Nancy Carver (George Washington), Abbie Willard (Georgetown), Ken Lafler (Harvard), Susan Guindi (Michigan), Susan Gainen (Minnesota), Irene Dorzback (NYU), Kimberly Reed (North Carolina), Lisa Patterson (Notre Dame), Jo-Ann Verrier (Pennsylvania), Susan Robinson (Stanford), Diane Chin (Stanford), Gloria Pyszka (Stanford), Kimberly Smith (Vanderbilt), Professor Susan Kay (Vanderbilt), Pam Malone (Vanderbilt), Steve Hopson (Virginia), Jane Heymann (Wisconsin), and Theresa Bryant (Yale).

Fourth, the *college pre-law advisors*, for an understanding of the challenges they confront in trying to help innumerable students interested in law school:

Verlaine Walker (Arizona), Julie Givens (Arizona State), Heather Struck (Binghamton), Don DeLeo (Boston College), Rita Callahan (Boston University), Catherine Bramble (Brigham Young), Suzanne Helbig (UC Berkeley), Albert E. Aubin (UCLA), Nicole Moran-O'Neil (UC San Diego), Lisa Harris (Cornell), Karen Whittet (Dartmouth), Gerald Wilson (Duke), Rodia Vance (Emory), Sara Mock (Florida), Michael Gabriel (George Washington), Leslie Adelman (Georgetown), Dena Rakoff (Harvard), Steven Shafer (Illinois), Mac Francis (Indiana), John Little (Iowa), Wendy Rohleder-Sook (Kansas), Greg Shaffer (Maryland), Janelle Larson (Minnesota), Donna Hanly (Missouri), Jeanne Ravid (Northwestern), Ava Preacher (Notre Dame), Barbara Rayman (Pennsylvania State), Lyon Zabsky (Princeton), Kathy Wright (Stanford), Tatem Oldham (Texas), Karen Severn (Texas A&M), Catherine Gillespie (Virginia), Nancy Hennes (Washington), Consuelo Lopez Springfield (Wisconsin), Kassian Kovalcheck (Vanderbilt), and Elayne Mazzarella (Yale).

Fifth, *my clients*, from whom I have learned a great deal, and particularly those who have allowed their work to be reproduced in this book.

Sixth, *my colleagues*, Rebecca Hulse and Krista Klein, whose expertise and hard work have contributed mightily to this volume.

—*Richard Montauk*

How to Benefit Most from This Book

Admissions deans at the country's top law schools admit that the hardest aspect of getting a degree from their schools is getting in. Getting through a top program may be demanding, but nearly 99 percent of the people who enroll get their degrees. At a school like Yale, however, only 6 to 8 percent of the people who apply are admitted. Of course, even more consider applying to the top schools than actually do so. Those who dream of the top schools, but do not ultimately apply, are discouraged by the difficulty of gaining admission.

The reason it is so difficult to get into these schools is clear. The value of a law degree from a top school is immense. Graduates of the top schools earn salaries that are, on average, double or triple (or more) of what graduates from lesser schools make. Increased salaries are not the end of the story. Greater career choice, increased job security, more interesting work, and numerous other benefits also result from a top law degree, so it is no wonder that so many people want to get into the best school they can manage.

Thus, it behooves you to do what you can to get into the school of your dreams. The first step is to make the best possible use of this book.

GETTING INTO A BETTER SCHOOL

The purpose of this book is to help applicants get into the best law school possible. Schools want candidates who will be successful lawyers of every stripe, legal journalists, administrators, and more. They assess a great deal of information to find them. Some of this is objective and quantifiable, such as a candidate's Law School Admission Test (LSAT) score; whereas much of it is not, such as what a candidate intends to do in the future. The objective elements of an application, which can be termed a candidate's credentials, are obviously important. The subjective elements, however, are ultimately at least as important.

Harvard could fill its class with candidates from the world's top universities—people who graduated in the top 10 percent of their classes, have scores in the upper 160s or better on the LSAT, and so on. Of course it accepts people who fit this profile, but it actually rejects as many of them as it accepts. The point is that the very top schools are looking for more in their candidates than just good scores.

Schools admit people rather than scores. Schools look for leaders as well as for brilliant analysts—people who work well as part of teams, who are determined to make an impact, and who have thought carefully about how they want their careers to progress. Given a certain baseline of achievement, they will look at far more than someone's grade-point average or LSAT score, because those are simply inadequate predictors of leadership, teamwork, and other critical skills. Grade-point averages and LSAT scores also reveal nothing about how a candidate can enrich the learning experience of classmates by virtue of his or her work experience, extracurricular interests, and so on.

Schools do consider objective credentials, but only as a part of the total picture of the person. They use all of the information they get, including the essays candidates write, the recommendations submitted on their behalf, and, increasingly, the results of application interviews, to determine whether someone will be a successful law student and lawyer. *Especially at the very top schools, the "who" is as important as the "what."*

In fact, the personal statements and other essays, recommendations, and interviews are doubly useful for the schools. They not only show these leadership and other qualities, but also show schools how to interpret the so-called objective data. A grade-point average of 3.5 on a 4.0 scale means different things in different contexts. If a student has to work 30 hours per week at a demanding job, that performance looks better. Similarly, if the person is a gifted engineer but chose to take a lot of writing courses to improve a weakness, that performance again looks better. The only way that schools know how to interpret a grade-point average, let alone someone's work experience or aspirations, is by hearing what the applicant (and the applicant's recommenders) say about it. In other words, the personal statement and other essays, recommendations, and interviews not only present new information but also "frame" the objective data.

How to Get Into the Top Law Schools shows you how to maximize the value of your credentials by presenting them in the best way. It does this in several ways:

■ It shows what leading law schools are looking for in their applicants and exactly how they interpret the different parts of the applicant's folder.

- It explains the nature of the admissions process, including showing who evaluates your application and how the final decisions are reached.

- It explains and illustrates how you can (and should) improve your own marketing efforts—via your application essays, recommendations, and interviews—to increase your chances of admission at the schools you most want to attend.

The key is to develop your own *personal marketing strategy*. This must be comprehensive, because a disjointed couple of essays or a recommendation that is at odds with what you say about yourself, is the kiss of death for your application. To maximize your chances, you must take advantage of every opportunity to show how professional you are, and why *you* should be admitted.

This book will show you how to prepare applications that distinguish you from the rest of the applicant pool and show you in your best light. Admissions directors routinely note that only 10 to 20 percent of applicants market themselves really well. This gives you a great opportunity to improve your chances by learning how to do a professional quality application.

WHO SHOULD READ THIS BOOK?

This book is geared toward people who want to get into the best law school they can. Although the text is weighted toward getting into the very top schools, frankly, anyone who wants to improve his or her candidacy to any school, in the top 25 or not, would benefit from a thorough understanding of application strategy.

UNIQUE FEATURES

How to Get Into the Top Law Schools provides a thorough explanation of how you can get into the best schools possible. It guides you through each step of the process, showing at each point how to develop your own marketing strategy. It analyzes and discusses each element in a thorough, detailed fashion. The unique features include:

- Advice from more than 20 admissions directors of the very top schools on every aspect of the applications process

  —Plus advice from the career services and financial aid directors, too

xii HOW TO BENEFIT MOST FROM THIS BOOK

- Nearly two dozen actual applicant essays representing:
  —Successful applications to each of the country's top schools
  —Applicants from a wide range of backgrounds, ethnicities, work experience, and colleges (and majors)
- An in-depth look at the strategies available to you to minimize the cost of law school
  —The focus is on strategy, not how to fill out the forms
- Detailed advice on how to write persuasive personal statements and other essays for maximum impact
- A first-of-its-kind analysis of law school interviews, an important feature of the admissions process at many of the top schools
- Solid advice on:
  —How to choose the right program for you
  —How to prepare for law school and how to get the most out of the program once you go
- A detailed timetable so you will know what to do when
- Complete explanations of what top schools look for in applicants, and how you can meet their needs
- Advice on what to do if you do *not* get into one of your top choice schools

HOW TO REALLY PROFIT FROM THIS BOOK

The key to maximizing the value of this book is to start the whole admission process early—earlier than you might believe necessary. As Chapter 6, "The Application Timetable," shows, it is ideal to begin the process more than a year before you expect to begin classes. Starting early, and using this book throughout the process, will allow you to complete strong, persuasive applications in the most efficient manner possible.

This book is designed to be used efficiently by people with radically different needs. Some will want to read it cover to cover; but many will want to dip into it for help on specific problems they face. Here are some suggestions for how to get the most out of the book, depending upon your own situation:

YOU ARE IN THE MIDST OF YOUR APPLICATIONS NOW

If you have applications due in just a few weeks, you should read several core chapters of the book immediately to avoid making terrible mistakes. Chapters 5 and 8 show you how law schools will evaluate your applications, Chapter 9 shows you the basics of how to market yourself, and Chapters 10 and 11 show you how to think about addressing your personal statement and other essays. You will also want to read the analyses of specific essay topics that you are going to write about. In addition, if you have yet to choose your recommenders, or if they have not yet sent in your recommendations, read Chapter 12 to see how you can improve what they say. Before your interviews, which presumably will not happen until after you have filed your applications, you will certainly want to read Chapter 13 on interviewing. When you have time, read the other chapters, or the executive summaries of them, to understand the application process more fully. Part III, which covers the post-application period, is important reading for you after you have finished your applications.

WHAT IF ONE OF YOUR APPLICATIONS IS DUE IN A WEEK?

Do not panic! This book can get you up to speed fast. Before going any further in your applications, be sure to read the executive summaries of each chapter and read Chapters 8 and 9 thoroughly. Then consult the relevant essay discussions (concerning any topics you are working on at the moment) in Chapter 11 and look through the discussion of how to write a strong and persuasive essay. Also be sure to read Chapter 12 on recommendations before giving the "go-ahead" to your recommenders.

YOU ARE GOING TO APPLY TO SCHOOLS IN THE NEAR FUTURE

If you intend to apply to schools in the next several months, you will probably want to get an overview of the applications process by reading the executive summaries of each chapter now, plus Chapters 8 and 9, which will explain the fundamentals of what you want to demonstrate in your applications. Read Chapter 6 to be sure that you do not miss the starting dates for important activities. Then read each chapter as it becomes relevant to your efforts, starting with Chapters 10 and 11, which will show you how to prepare for your essays.

YOU WILL NOT APPLY UNTIL SEVERAL YEARS FROM NOW

If you are not going to apply to schools for another two or three (or more) years, read Chapters 8 and 9 now. These will show you how best to ready yourself for admission, while you still have the opportunity to improve your credentials dramatically. Then read Chapter 6, "The Application Timetable," to determine when to start the process for keeps. Later on you can read the executive summaries of each chapter (about 15–18 months before you intend to go) to prepare for the application process itself.

YOU ARE NOT SURE THAT LAW SCHOOL IS FOR YOU

Read two chapters to start your assessment process. Chapter 1, "Why Go to a Top Law School?" discusses appropriate and inappropriate reasons for attending law school, as well as some of the steps that all applicants should take to be sure that law makes sense for them. Chapter 2, "Looking at Law School," gives an overview of the law school experience, thereby offering you a chance to see in advance what you might be in for.

A FINAL NOTE: THE APPLICATION PROCESS MAY PROVE HELPFUL (AS WELL AS PAINFUL)

Many applicants look upon the task of producing hundreds of details about their pasts, writing essays about intimate or obscure topics, securing recommendations from old professors and current bosses, and enduring interviews as a modern form of "death by a thousand cuts." They feel that it is trial enough simply to research the schools and figure out which ones would be appropriate for them, let alone to have to manage the data-, paper-, writing-, and time-intensive application process.

If that is your view, keep in mind that the application process, however imperfect it may be, encourages applicants to think seriously about where they want to go in their careers and in their lives, and how they are going to get there. Too few people do this at any point, let alone at this most appropriate of times. Applicants to law schools, whether they are still in college or have been in different careers for a dozen years, are highly likely to be right at the point where sensible decisions about these matters can yield a lifetime of benefits, and a failure to consider their options carefully can result in opportunities missed, opportunities that will not be offered again. Confronting such important career decisions might open doors you never even realized existed.

ABOUT DEGREE OF DIFFERENCE

Founded by Richard Montauk in 1991, Degree of Difference is a consulting firm that provides quality one-on-one service to individuals applying to professional schools (especially law and business), colleges, and other educational institutions. We help many hundreds of individuals each year plan their educational careers and complete successful applications to the top programs worldwide.

Degree of Difference provides a full menu of services for law school applicants.

OUR INDIVIDUALIZED CONSULTING

MATCHING APPLICANTS WITH LAW SCHOOLS

We begin the consulting process by learning about your past—your background, education, extracurricular interests, work experience, and the like—and your ambitions for the future. We help you to select the law schools that will be most appropriate for your needs and desires, and also ensure that your final list of target schools includes an adequate number of "stretches," "possibles," and "likelies."

- *Note, too, that we help clients who are uncertain about whether law is their best option.* Some people are better off not going into law, either because law is not a good fit for them or because something else is simply a better fit than law would be. We urge such clients to explore their career options and help them to do so.

    We also help clients determine which area (or areas) of law will be a good fit for them.

STRATEGIZING

We help you develop a coherent strategy to follow during (as well as before and after) the law school application process.

- We advise you on when to apply to school. Some candidates, for example, can improve their chances of getting into a top school dramatically with an additional year of interesting and substantive work, or well-planned community or civic activity. We advise you regarding what you could do to maximize your chances for whenever you will apply.

- We help you develop a comprehensive positioning strategy. We show you how to market your strengths, account for or overcome your weaknesses, and best position yourself to enhance your candidacy.

- We teach you how to tailor your applications to each individual school.

- We help you make decisions regarding joint degree programs (and help you apply to the other, non-law program, as appropriate).

INTERVIEWING

Evaluative interviews are a relatively new part of the law school application process, yet they are being used by more and more of the top schools. We teach you how to approach your interviews with confidence and make a positive impression.

- We help you understand both your own candidacy—including how you compare with other applicants in a given school's applicant pool—and the schools to which you are applying.

- We show you what to expect in your interview and how to handle the most likely questions.

- We coach you on successful interviewing techniques, providing assistance not only regarding what to say but also regarding how to say it, what to wear, and how to act in a variety of formal and informal settings.

- We provide mock interviews and consequent feedback sessions.

SOLICITING RECOMMENDATIONS

Getting the most from recommenders is often one of the most difficult—and one of the most overlooked—tasks in the law school application process.

- We teach you how to look at your application in its entirety in order to determine what is most needed from your recommenders to fill in the gaps, enhance your strengths, and compensate for your weaknesses.

- We provide advice on how to approach recommenders tactfully, and how best to provide them with the information you would like conveyed in your letters of recommendation.

- We also assist your recommenders (if desired) to develop high-impact letters of endorsement.

COMPLETING APPLICATIONS

A sloppy or uninformative application will do you no good. We are happy to review any and all of your written materials to ensure that all the necessary information is well communicated and error-free.

- We review all of the written work that a client wishes reviewed, including application data forms; listings of extracurricular activities, community service write-ups, and job descriptions; and responses to short-answer and essay questions.
- We help you to write a clear, professionally formatted résumé.

ESSAY WRITING

Writing personal statements and other essays is the area of greatest concern for many of our clients.

- We help you determine what subjects should form the basis of your personal statement(s). We also help you understand what should be communicated in addenda rather than in the main essays. We help you get the most out of your experiences and strengths.
- We help you craft themes in order to make your entire set of essays (and the rest of your application) convey a set of consistent, appropriate messages.
- We provide advice on essay structure and form, yet strive to do so in a way that retains a client's own voice, style, and personality. In addition, we edit essays down to the finest points of grammar, word choice, and so on.

Please note that we do not write essays for our clients under any circumstances.

MANAGING YOUR CAREER

Given that few applicants to law school are extending their current careers, rather than entering their first career or changing careers, it is unsurprising how few are ready to get the most out of their law school years from a career perspective. We help you evaluate and plan your law school "career," including choice of courses, student organizations and journals, bar and industry association involvement, internship and pro bono efforts, professional research, writing for outside journals, and so on.

MY WORKSHOPS

For several years I have been offering one-day intensive workshops in various parts of the country. They cover the critical aspects of the application "game" in a very hands-on, interactive fashion. The examples are drawn largely from the participants. (Thus, participants are encouraged to provide draft personal statements and résumés in advance so that I can assess and use them as real-life teaching vehicles in the workshops.) These workshops provide participants with:

- The understanding and tools necessary to do wonderful applications
- Encouragement to push ahead and get their applications done
- A reality check regarding where they stand

Most of the attendees are committed to applying to law school, but some come to assess whether or not they should apply, as well as when to do so. Similarly, some parents of applicants choose to attend (with or without their children) in order to understand what their children will face and how best they can help in the process.

For further information about these workshops, please consult our website (www.degreeofdiffence.com) or call us at (415) 273-1782.

HOW TO INITIATE A CONSULTING RELATIONSHIP
WITH DEGREE OF DIFFERENCE

If you are interested in our consulting services, please contact us to discuss your current situation and goals—and how we can best help you. Some of our most successful clients sign up for our services one or more years in advance of actually applying for law school, in order to discuss long-term strategy and goals that should be addressed long before applications are put together. This way you will be best prepared to market yourself when the time comes.

On the other hand, plenty of clients come to us at a later stage in the game—at the beginning of the application "season" or even in the midst of doing applications. We are prepared to help you at any point in your application work and encourage panicked applicants who find themselves behind schedule to contact us for immediate assistance.

Please contact us at one of our primary locations:

Degree of Difference, Inc. (USA)
Tel. (415) 273-1782
www.degreeofdifference.com
info@degreeofdifference.com

Degree of Difference, Inc. (UK)
126 Aldersgate Street
Barbican, London EC1A 4JQ
United Kingdom
Tel. (44) 20 76 08 18 11

CONTENTS

Part II APPLYING TO LAW SCHOOL

---

13 Interviews—341

Part III ON THE ROAD TO LAW SCHOOL

14 Responding to Wait-Listing, Denial, and Other Disappointments—393

Part V   APPLICATION ESSAY EXAMPLES

Index—553

Part I

INTRODUCING LAW SCHOOL

1

Why Go to a Top Law School?

— EXECUTIVE SUMMARY —

If you wish to go to law school, go to the very best one you can.
—The rewards of attending a top law school are compelling.

But do not go to law school until you have thoroughly analyzed:
—Yourself
—Law school
—Law as a profession
—Legal specialties and practice types that would fit you

Consider waiting to attend law school until you
have worked for several years.
—It is difficult to understand your fit with the world of work
absent full-time work experience.

Once upon a time, a high school diploma was a sufficient credential to get a good executive job. Then, as more and more people went to college, a high school diploma was no longer enough to land an executive position. A college degree sufficed for a time, but as more and more people got JDs and MBAs, even a college degree was no longer sufficient to get most high-powered jobs. That was the case in the 1970s. Since then, the number of people getting such degrees has increased to the point that simply having such a degree is insufficient to get plum jobs; the *quality* and reputation of the law program have become determinative.

If you decide law school is for you, you should go to the best school you can manage.

THE VALUE OF GOING TO A TOP SCHOOL

As the number of JD holders in the world increases, so does the importance of getting a top-quality JD, keyed to your needs, rather than just any law degree.

CAREER CHOICE

Some parts of the legal profession are virtually off-limits to graduates of lesser law schools. These include the major corporate law firms and high-profile government jobs as well as public interest organizations. The most desirable employers to work for, such as the major firms, would no more think of recruiting at "Acme" Law School than they would of giving this year's profits to the Flat Earth Society. These firms look to hire the best and the brightest and they know that the best and the brightest are to be found at the world's leading law schools. The same is true in other legal fields, too. For instance, in a profession that is notorious for snobbery (regarding which law schools people attended), arguably the snobbiest employers of all are the public interest organizations.

STATUS

This category nearly speaks for itself. Whether for personal or business reasons, being a graduate of Yale conjures up entirely different impressions and reactions among people you encounter than does being a graduate of Acme Law. Status is partially related to the other items listed here, such as salary, but it also reflects the fact that Yale admits only people who are highly regarded to begin with.

CAREER FLEXIBILITY

The top law schools offer substantial geographic mobility to their graduates. Whereas lesser schools place few of their graduates outside their city or region, the top schools invariably send many of their graduates to firms across the country (and the world).

The benefits of going to a top school are not limited to your initial job upon graduation. If you decide to change employers, or even to change fields, the quality of your education will be one of the determining factors in your ability to make the switch successfully: It will determine how other people rate your chances (and whether they will risk hiring you). The alumni network, and your own personal network from law school, will also be important determinants of your ability to switch. With a strong network willing to help you, your chances are automatically better.

INCREASED PAY

The better the reputation of a school, the more its graduates earn. For example, the graduates of Harvard who enter the private sector will, in their first year, have median earnings exceeding $135,000. First-year graduates from the top dozen or two dozen schools can expect, on average, to earn 50 percent to 100 percent more than graduates from schools ranked nearer to number 50. This pay gap increases dramatically as one goes further down the rankings to those schools near the bottom of the 200 or so that grant law degrees in the United States.

It is important to note that the median salary of lawyers in the U.S. is approximately $95,000. Graduates of the top schools, however, earn more than that from the moment they start in private practice. In fact, lawyers at the leading firms have been making at least $160,000 in their first year out of law school.

INTANGIBLES

Many of the benefits of attending a top law school are intangible. For example, you will be spending three years of your life interacting with faculty and fellow students; you might well value having the smartest, most motivated group of faculty and fellow students you can. Indeed, given that many of the friendships and professional relationships you form at law school will continue for many years after school, you will derive pleasure from attending a top school long after graduation. By the same token, you will have the opportunity to work with and compare yourself to some of the finest minds in the country.

FINANCIAL CONSIDERATIONS

Getting a law degree represents an extremely large investment of money, as well as time and effort. The tuition alone for a three-year program may be $120,000 or more, and your income forgone may be even greater. Books, computer, travel to and from the program, and other assorted expenses will add thousands more.

Is a law degree worth this large sum? Although not everyone will be financially better off from getting a JD, those attending the top programs are highly likely to be. The payoff to attending a top school is partly a matter of increased earnings. It is also a matter of increased career options, increased confidence that one can do a given job extremely well, increased security (no matter what happens there are jobs available for people from top schools), and increased status. It is therefore probably a mistake to view the decision to get a JD on a purely financial basis, despite the sums involved.

SHOULD YOU GO TO LAW SCHOOL?

This book is dedicated largely to the issues of helping you determine which schools would be best for you and showing you how to maximize your chances of gaining admission to them. A much more important question, however, is whether you should go to law school at all. The rest of this chapter is devoted to this issue.

> Do not go to law school unless you are quite certain that you want to be a practicing lawyer (and you know the one or two fields that will best suit your needs) or you want to do something intimately related to legal practice, such as legal journalism.

A LAW DEGREE IS NOT A GENERAL PURPOSE DEGREE

A JD has long been considered the most flexible of degrees insofar as it will prepare you to do almost anything. This is utterly wrong. A law degree does nothing but teach you about practicing law. It does not teach you how to administer, nor does it teach you how to start a business (except in the narrow sense of how to file incorporation documents). The true multipurpose degree of today is the MBA, the skills from which would indeed help you in most fields.

IS LAW SCHOOL FOR YOU?

There is some correlation between those who most like law school and those who enjoy practicing law, just as there is between those who dislike law school and then dislike practicing law. The correlation, however, is not as strong as one might like. As a result, it makes sense to evaluate both law and law school independently.

Therefore, separate your decision into two parts: Consider first whether you are going to like law school. If you decide that the three years you will spend at law school will be the best three years of your life to date, then you need not have so high a degree of certainty that you will love the practice of law because at least the process of getting there will be enjoyable. On the other hand, if you determine that law school is likely to be a misery, you need to be dead certain that the practice of law is indeed right for you.

You can readily determine what law school will be like by spending time in law classes. You probably live near a law school. Approach the admissions department with a request to sit in on classes, or simply ask a professor for permission. Then follow one or two classes for an extended period. Do not just drop in once or twice. Instead, do the required reading and prepare for the class as if your grade (and life) depended upon it. Be sure to talk with other students about what they think of the process. (Note that the better the quality of the law school, the more representative and valuable this effort will be for someone who is potentially headed to a top school. Lower-tier law schools teach law in a different way, for a different purpose, and to a different group of students than do top schools.)

If you are unable to access an appropriate law school's classes, try to follow the readings for two or three courses that interest you. Course syllabi are increasingly available on law school websites.

You might think you already have a fair idea of what law school will be like because you took political science or pre-law courses in college. Such courses, however, hardly resemble true law school courses, so do not take your enjoyment of these as a sign that you will like law school.

Do not rely, either, on what is written or filmed about law school. You need to investigate it for yourself. If you do not go to this small amount of effort because you deem it to be too much trouble, you will deserve whatever you encounter later on!

IS LAW FOR YOU?

Law is not a single, unitary field; there are many different specialties within it, just as there are many different employers. Although there are certain personality traits that seem to fit most comfortably within law, the range is substantial. How, then, you might ask, can you sensibly investigate the field? Note, first of all, that you need to do two things. You need to understand your own interests, skills, and needs. You also need to understand what is on offer in law, and see whether the two provide a suitable match.

This book is avowedly not a career planning manual. It is important to note, though, that you should put yourself through the exercises that such manuals—and sophisticated consultants—require. The following is meant simply to sketch out (albeit extremely briefly) what types of analysis you will need to do and to provide you with a guide to the resources likely to help you.

UNDERSTAND YOUR OWN INTERESTS, SKILLS, VALUES, AND GOALS

It is important that you choose a career that matches your needs as fully as possible. It may be that no job will be perfect for you—giving you everything you might wish for, and fulfilling you completely—but ending up with one that is not at least a close fit inevitably leads to trouble. The way to avoid feeling miserable in your career is to analyze your needs *before* you enter the field.

One starting point is to ask yourself and those who know you (family, friends, colleagues) what is likely to be most important to you in a career. What are your *interests*? Do you like to write, ride horses, travel, fiddle around in a laboratory? What do you have no interest in? You are, of course, most likely to enjoy a career that keeps you in touch with whatever areas or activities you enjoy.

What do you do well? Your inventory of *skills* is important for numerous reasons, one being that you will tend to enjoy whatever you do well, and vice versa, so entering a field that allows you to utilize what you do well is a good bet.

What are your *values*? At one level, this asks you to identify what causes you support—free speech, unfettered capitalism, environmentalism, and so on. At another level, this asks how you wish to live your life. Do you value time with your family more than being the highest paid associate in the office, for example? Both types of values should have a major effect upon your choice of career (and how you pursue your career).

What are your *goals*? What do you hope to accomplish in life, whether in the short term or the long term?

The resources listed below will provide you with a starting point for your self-analysis. Do not overlook the possibility of using a professional career counselor, but make sure it is someone who has substantial experience dealing with lawyers or would-be lawyers.

IT TAKES MANY YEARS TO GET OUT OF LAW (ONCE YOU ARE IN)

Deciding to go to law school is a risky decision that is surprisingly hard to reverse. Many people attend law school for lack of anything better to do or despite major misgivings. They do not drop out at the top schools, despite the fact that a fair-sized minority dislike law school itself. (Harvard's attrition rate is typically under 1 percent.) Those who dislike law school and those who are unsure of whether they are going to like practice (having not enjoyed their summer employment between years of law school) nonetheless enter practice. They console themselves in the first years of practice that the reason they dislike it is because they are simply at the bottom of the totem pole, learning necessary skills and establishing credibility. They assume that matters will improve. For those who find themselves still unhappy after three or more years, the natural instinct is to switch practice areas within the firm (if they enjoy their colleagues) or to switch firms (if they do not particularly care for their colleagues). This guarantees another few years of hoping that matters will improve.

Those who enter law are generally too goal-oriented to opt out; they will leave only when forced. It is only after half a dozen or more years that such lawyers will finally admit that they made the wrong career choice. *Thus, law represents a decade's commitment, or more.* They tell themselves that a law degree has at least prepared them to do anything. Unfortunately, they discover how untrue that notion really is. They talk with friends in other fields, headhunters who help lawyers find other employment, and so on. They learn that they will have to cut their salaries by two-thirds and be willing to start at the bottom of another field, unless they find a job closely related to law. (If they take a job closely related to law, such as being the executive director of a public interest organization, they still have to accept a substantial salary cut.) Given that many lawyers will still owe $80,000–$125,000 in law school loans, changing professions may not be feasible. Even if they are willing and able to take the massive salary cut involved in starting over—that is, they can give up their long-held professional identity (and their pride can handle no longer being a "professional"), despite their friends' and family's comments that they are wasting their degree—they find that the barriers to doing so are massive.

Employers value legal training only in lawyers. High-tech firms, traditional companies, and everyone else in business (and in innumerable other areas as well) do not believe that lawyers, uniquely, have been "taught how to think." Nor do they find that lawyers have necessarily acquired nonlegal skills worth paying for. Indeed, employers view lawyers as overly contentious, not very team-oriented, and very narrowly focused. Employers grant that lawyers (from top schools, at least) are probably pretty smart and willing to work hard. However, they also consider them to be damaged goods. They figure that such lawyers are running away from law rather than toward something else in particular. They may also figure that because lawyers have so little background of relevance to choosing another field, they are likely to make another poor career decision the next time around, just as they did in entering law.

For those lawyers who wish finally to get the true multipurpose degree, an MBA, the outlook is also discouraging. The only lawyers able to get into top business schools are those who have had very substantial business experience along the way. Business schools value experience much more highly than do law schools, but they do not value a knowledge of product liability law, federal jurisdiction, or the like. Thus, lawyers with top GPAs and GMAT scores flop in the business school admissions game because they have wasted (by business school standards) their last eight or ten years.

This is not a pretty picture. The way to avoid it is simple: Learn in advance whether law and law school are for you.

AN M.A. IN LAW?

It is a pity that law schools do not do what doctoral programs in other fields have long done: give an intermediate degree along the way. If you wish to do a Ph.D. in economics, for example, but stop before completing your thesis, you will still get a master's degree. Law schools could do something similar, giving a master's in law after one or one and a half years, which would be a good point at which you could assess whether law really made sense for you. Those who opted out of law would nonetheless have a fine-looking degree for their résumés, but would no doubt find it easier to leave at this point than to continue to invest heavily in a field that they might well already sense was not going to be what they had hoped.

CAREER SERVICES DEANS DISCUSS SELF-ASSESSMENT

It's extremely beneficial if a person has made some sort of self-assessment, looked inward and self-assessed his or her skills, interests, and values. It is important that these three coalesce. *Fred Thrasher, George Washington*

Choose jobs, including part-time and summer jobs, as well as internships, to give you as much information as possible about yourself, the profession, or the world. Analyze important aspects, positive and negative, of all the experiences you've had. What did you like about being treasurer of a club, for example? Did you like preparing a financial statement each month, or analyzing the data, or did you just like the title? *Irene Dorzback, NYU*

Most of us old-timers were pretty pathetic in our own self-assessment and knowledge of careers, but we muddled through. Unfortunately, muddling through can be a painful experience, with lots of career frustrations, poor fits, and disappointment. The best way I know of to minimize this is to realize that finding a great career requires effort, and the effort will probably extend over years of your life. Students should definitely begin to assess their interests, goals, and skills, and gain knowledge of careers, in college, in summer jobs, in post-graduation employment, and in law school. *Theresa J. Bryant, Yale*

Ideally you should explore an area or type of job that interests you. If you're interested in policy, for instance, work on Capitol Hill or in a think-tank. See whether there is a career path that makes sense; then ask whether law school is necessary to do what you love. *Susan Robinson, Stanford*

Guidance programs in high school and college could do more to help students evaluate what they've done, what they've liked, and why certain activities appealed to them so that students have a frame of reference for determining their skills, interests, and values. *Irene Dorzback, NYU*

WITHOUT FULL-TIME WORK EXPERIENCE, YOU CANNOT PROPERLY ASSESS YOUR NEEDS

It is very difficult to get sufficient understanding of what you do and do not like, let alone what the world of work is all about, without substantial work experience. Although you can eliminate some fields of endeavor as possible choices on the basis of your college and part-time work experiences, you are unlikely to get very far toward making a final choice. (Knowing that you dislike science does eliminate medicine from your future, but it does not help you choose among journalism, investment banking, and law.) Your early- to mid-twenties are the ideal time to sample the world of work, so take advantage of the opportunity.

    You (and/or your parents) may be unwilling to take the risk that you will be unable to get into a worthwhile, rewarding, or prestigious position. As a result, you (or they) may feel the need to get into law school as soon as possible. This is wrong-headed for two reasons. First, your chances of getting into a good law school increase with real-world experience. (This is explored in detail throughout the rest of this book.) Second, the greatest risk is that you will have entered the wrong field and be unable to get out of it successfully. Therefore, do not rush into law school. Work for at least two years, in one or more serious jobs, after college. Make sure law school is an affirmative rather than a default choice.

CAREER SERVICES AND ADMISSIONS DEANS
DISCUSS THE VALUE OF LIFE AND WORK EXPERIENCE

THE VALUE OF WORK EXPERIENCE BEFORE LAW SCHOOL

Get a sense of what you like and dislike in a work environment—what you really need from a job. Do you need to be out and about? Do you like to write, including spending the hours alone in your office crafting your material? (Or do you agonize over your writing and hate to be isolated at your computer for long stretches?) Do you prefer team strategy sessions? Are you a last-minute adrenaline-driven person or someone who plans all the details in advance? *Susan Robinson, Stanford (Career Services)*

Work experience is the most valuable way to learn about yourself and a potential career. Students should definitely do all they can to get summer, term time, and post-graduate employment (volunteer or paid) in fields that interest them so they can try out their tentative career plans.   *Theresa J. Bryant, Yale (Career Services)*

Having had real experience helps students make more informed career choices; they have more realistic expectations of what the world is like. *Jane Heymann, Wisconsin (Career Services)*

If all the top schools agreed not to accept applicants unless they had three-plus years of experience, it would probably work out better for everyone. The work experience would benefit applicants, who would better understand what they want with a law degree. As a result, it would really help career services directors, too. None of us wants to sit across from broken dreams, or a perception of law that was never checked out. *Irene Dorzback, NYU (Career Services)*

WAITING TO APPLY

Someone with a weak undergraduate record is well advised to wait to apply; the rule of thumb is about five years. Many require some time out to grow up as well as to accomplish something. They need to develop a sense of focus, time management skills. *Elizabeth Rosselot, Boston College (Admissions)*

Take the time to figure out what you want to do in life. The biggest mistake I see is people saying, "I'll figure it our later." The sooner you do so the better. Going to law school is too often a means of apparently moving forward while still avoiding the self-assessment that is necessary to figure out where you should be headed. That postponement costs three years and $150,000 or more. *Susan Robinson, Stanford (Career Services)*

Whether or not any individual student should proceed directly to law school or take several years off to work, really depends on them . . . their maturity, readiness, previous job experience, and confidence that law school is the right path to take. *Theresa J. Bryant, Yale (Career Services)*

It's never a bad idea to take time off before law school. You might find something that's your life's work or a wonderful adjunct to a law career. Or it might function just as a necessary break. We'll still be here, and a legal career lasts for a very long time, so there's no need to rush. *Rick Geiger, Cornell (Admissions)*

From a purely career development standpoint, I don't know anyone who should go straight from college to law school. I don't know how it can hurt you to wait, but I do see many people who go straight through, and all they figure out in the process is that they don't want to practice law. *Susan Robinson, Stanford (Career Services)*

There is absolutely not a "penalty" for waiting some years after graduating college to apply. A lot of students face wonderful internship or work opportunities at graduation, such as Teach for America. Being successful at any of them will only make their law school applications stronger when they do apply. *Monica Ingram, Texas (Admissions)*

Too many people apply to law school for lack of other ideas of what to do. You don't have to go to law school right out of college. I'm pleased that more applicants wait longer to apply now; they work for a few years on average and determine where they're headed. The older students tend to be more focused and are better able to handle the stresses of law school. *Faye Deal, Stanford (Admissions)*

Anyone who has any reservations whatsoever about pursuing law or law school should definitely wait before starting the process—particularly if he or she is being pressured by someone else to attend law school but has his or her own reservations about doing so. Take the opportunity to gain professional experience while determining whether law and law school are good choices for you. *Renée Post, Penn*

It's a very individual decision as to whether to work (or do something else) before law school. That said, those who have worked for a few years beforehand tend to be more committed to the law school enterprise because they know it's right for them. In addition, they often have much to contribute to the classroom discussions by virtue of their experience. *Todd Morton, Vanderbilt*

Older, more experienced students seem to do better in class. They are often more dedicated and focused regarding why they are in law school. They have gained discipline and organizational ability, and are able to tackle school work more efficiently and well. *William Hoye, Duke (Admissions)*

Students who've taken a break often are more motivated to take on the rigors of studying. They're usually excited about being back in an academic environment. *Kenneth Kleinrock, NYU (Admissions)*

Most people who go to law school after time out are glad they took time out. Senioritis at college can be a real problem. You don't know what you want to do, which is frightening. You figure that you might as well hedge your bets, so you take the LSAT. If you do well, you apply to law school. If you get into a good school, you probably go. After all, it relieves the career uncertainty you've felt. Once you go, you commit yourself to finish. After you graduate—and almost everyone does—you'll end up practicing law for the next fifty years. The consequences to having senioritis are pretty serious. *Joyce Curll, Harvard (Admissions)*

HOW MUCH WORK EXPERIENCE IS PREFERABLE?

There are a couple of reasons that work experience before law school is such a good thing. In terms of introspection and self-understanding, those with work experience are typically further along. Also, employers like to see a couple years of real-world experience. *Jo-Ann Verrier, Penn (Career Services)*

Employers look very favorably on work experience, especially if you've accomplished something. Three to four years is a good length of time between college and law school. It's enough time that employers will really take the experience into account and assume that you've gotten to know an area well. In fact, you can have a lower GPA and still be very marketable to top firms if you have significant work experience. *Susan Robinson, Stanford (Career Services)*

THE EFFECT OF WORK EXPERIENCE UPON YOUR MARKETABILITY

The average age of our entering students is going up, and those with real-work experience are at an advantage in the job search. *Betsy Armour, Boston University (Career Services)*

Interpersonal skills are crucial to success. Employers like to see that you've worked with a team, preferably in a professional setting. *Susan Guindi, Michigan (Career Services)*

POOR REASONS TO ENTER LAW

Your parents want you to be a lawyer. Live your own life. If you are still being influenced to this extent by your parents, you are by definition not yet mature enough to choose a career.

You like to argue. Get married instead.

You are afraid to enter the workforce. Get a grip. Starting a first job is not nearly so difficult as starting college was. In fact, the consequences of failure are much less, too. If you are bounced by your first employer after a month, this need never even show up on your résumé.

You do not know what else to do. If you are still at college or recently graduated, look at the career literature, discuss matters with friends and a high-quality career counselor, and shadow people working in jobs that sound as if they might fit you. Do not worry that you might make a mistake. Your early twenties are made for sampling. If you are substantially older, do all of the above, but focus your efforts on some in-depth career counseling, starting with an assessment of your needs and interests. In either case, do not feel you need to choose the exact right career immediately. Each job you have should allow you, with suitable reflection and analysis, to understand better how you fit into the world of work.

You want to help people. This is a fine starting point, but practicing law is hardly the only way to help others. You should still want to find a career that will fit you; you will not be much use to others if you hate your career, in spite of being of benefit to others. (As is discussed below, most of those who enter law school intending to pursue public interest law careers do not actually do so. Thus, you may find yourself going in a different direction from that which you intended; this is not a bad thing, per se, but it does undercut the initial reason for going.)

You want to increase your options. Unfortunately, a law degree tends to close many non-law options rather than open them (see the discussion above).

You want a glamorous field. Law may sound glamorous to those who do not know much about it, but it is actually a matter of very hard work, attention to detail, and working at the behest of others (partners, clients, et al.).

You want to enter a genteel profession rather than a business. Law is no longer an exclusive club whose members are guaranteed a good living without having to jostle one another and outsiders, too. Instead, it has become a cutthroat business. Firms go out of business, partners (not just young associates) are fired for not producing enough revenue—just like in any business. And, as in any business environment, lawyers need to manage their careers actively. (Check with some lawyers to find out when they last revised their résumés in case they need to seek new employment.)

You want to make a lot of money. It is not terribly difficult to make money in law if you go to a top school and then enter a corporate practice. (Of course, it is not clear whether you are getting paid for one job or two, given the number of hours you will log.) Having said this, however, you risk failure if you find that you do not enjoy practicing law (or a type of law that pays particularly well). You also risk personal troubles if you force yourself to do something you dislike (especially for 80 hours a week). In addition, there are other ways to make a lot of money. In sum, this is a perfectly reasonable rationale for going to law school, but only if law will be a good fit for you in other regards.

You need another degree. There are some pretty interesting and valuable degrees other than JDs available.

GOOD REASONS TO AVOID LAW SCHOOL

You tend not to finish things. Dropping out in the middle of law school is likely to saddle you with $60,000 or more of debt (and no degree).

You don't enjoying reading and writing. Reading and writing are the stuff of law school, and of most types of legal practice.

You dislike details. Law is one of the most fault-intolerant of all professions.

You are not the sort of person whose judgment is trusted by those who know you. Lawyers are first and foremost counselors to their clients, so if people are disinclined to look to you for advice you are in for a hard time.

You do not have a strong desire to counsel and aid the perplexed. In other words, you don't readily understand and empathize with those less expert in law than yourself (who are otherwise known as clients).

You dislike having to present an argument in front of others. In law school and legal practice, you will constantly be presenting arguments in front of various people, some of whom will oppose you and all of whom will evaluate you.

You cannot analyze a situation dispassionately. Viewing a situation from more than one side, without letting your personal feelings overwhelm you, is one of a lawyer's core responsibilities.

CAREER SERVICES DEANS DISCUSS POOR REASONS FOR ATTENDING LAW SCHOOL

Law school is the default option for those who are bright and don't know what to do.   *Theresa Bryant, Yale*

Law school is the refuge for the liberal arts majors. They don't see a clear career path, so they opt for law school, believing that it will broaden their opportunities. That is definitely not the case.   *Susan Robinson, Stanford*

WHAT ELSE COULD YOU DO WITH THREE YEARS AND $175,000?

Law school will take three years of your life and a lot of money. Before you commit to this, consider what else you might do. Here is just one possibility (there are an infinite number of others). Start by going to Central America to learn Spanish. If you live in a private home and are tutored individually for five hours a day, you should go from zero knowledge to absolute fluency within a year. (*Price:* about $900 per month, including room, board, and tuition.) After that, do a three-month cooking school course in Italy during the summer. (*Price:* about $12,000 for an expensive course, room and board included.) Then, do a master's degree in economics at The London School of Economics and Political Science. (*Price:* about $50,000, including room, board, and tuition.) Next, spend a summer as a tour guide cycling through France. (*Price:* you get paid for your effort.) Last, do another master's degree, perhaps in politics (The Fletcher School of Law and Diplomacy, for instance), perhaps in management (at HEC, the leading French business school, for example). (*Price:* Fletcher, about $47,000; HEC, about $36,000).

The net result of this odyssey: three years of exploring the physical world (Latin America, England, France, Italy); three years of exploring the intellectual world (fluency in Spanish, knowledge of Italian cooking, an outstanding master's degree in economics, and an outstanding degree in politics or marketing). *The price:* about $110,000–$120,000, minus any earnings along the way. (Note the savings this represents compared with the total tab for law school.) If your parents are going to sponsor your law school effort, by the way, perhaps you should have them read this and consider what they could buy you for a lot less than law school might cost them. Whoever pays, are you sure that going into law—and working hard for three years at law school as a preliminary to working very hard as a lawyer—is your only option?

UNDERSTAND WHAT IS ON OFFER IN LAW

You can start your research by talking with lawyers you know or by examining books, such as those listed later, that describe law as a career. Once you have an overview of the field, however, you need to get beneath the generalities.

First, you need to investigate legal specialties (insofar as virtually no one is a generalist in law anymore). After your initial research, focus on two to four practice areas that appeal to you. Learn what personality types fit best with each area, what skills (general, such as public speaking, and specific, such as an ability to draft complex debt covenants) are necessary, what types of work fill up the day, and what are considered the best (and worst) aspects of the field. Read several of the professional journals in the field, cover to cover, for several months at a time. Once you have narrowed your interests to one or two fields, talk with a number of practitioners in each. Ask for permission to spend several days "shadowing" them, literally spending full workdays at their side, to learn what their work life is truly like. Be sure to ask, too, whether what you have seen is typical of their practices.

Note how many legal fields require a facility with numbers. It is not just tax lawyers and the like who benefit from an understanding of accounting, finance, statistics, and so on.

Second, understand what employment possibilities there are in the field. Examine the different types of employers (large firms, small firms, government agencies—municipal, state, federal—nonprofit organizations, and so on) for lawyers in the one or two specialties you have chosen. Learn the basics about each type:

- The focus of the work (at each level)
- Where they are located
- What hours are worked, and when (five days per week, on-call 24/7?)
- What the pay is at each level
- What it takes to advance to each level, and what percentage make it
- What those who leave end up doing
- How risky the employment is
- What the work environment is like (competitive, stressful, relaxed, dynamic?)
- The nature of one's colleagues (age, interests, training, skills, values, goals)
- The clients or interests represented

Compare and contrast the different employer types for whichever field interests you.

By the time you have gone through this exercise, you should know, for example, that criminal defense trial work and criminal appellate work may look nearly identical from the outside but are virtually unrelated in real terms. For instance, different personality types are attracted to each: Criminal defense lawyers like the courtroom action and derive some pleasure from being in touch with the more sordid aspects of humanity, whereas criminal appellate lawyers relish the intellectual challenges of their work but like to avoid the hurly-burly of direct contact with clients and the messiness of trials. The differences in how they get clients, how they charge, their reputations in the legal community, and a whole host of other matters are just as great.

One way to learn about law, of course, is to work as a paralegal in a law firm or other legal environment. You get a close-up view of lawyers going about their daily business; you also may perform some tasks that involve learning about legal research, writing, courtroom performance, and the like. Note, however, that firms often assign paralegals highly repetitive tasks that do not necessarily expose them to much of the firm's operations or let them see a variety of lawyers in action. If you choose to work as a paralegal, be sure that the firm you choose gives its paralegals a suitable exposure to the world of law (and then make sure you take full advantage of the opportunity).

PUTTING IT ALL TOGETHER

Once you have really explored one or two specialties and several employment options for each, compare the results with your analysis of your own skills, interests, values, and goals. Reconsider your options if the fit is not a close one.

FEW ENTERING LAW STUDENTS DO SUFFICIENT CAREER RESEARCH

It is often claimed that students entering law school now do a pretty fair job of evaluating themselves and their career options. A quick look at one piece of data should dispel this notion. One of the truisms of law school admissions at the top schools is that half of those entering believe they will enter a public interest field, yet not even 5 percent do so. In fact, at most top schools the percentage entering public interest law is well *under* 5 percent. This means that over 90 percent of those who figured they were going into public interest law had done insufficient research about themselves and their career choices.

WHAT ELSE COULD YOU DO IF YOU DO NOT ENTER LAW SCHOOL?

The career literature regarding what jobs are on offer is nothing if not voluminous. If you are smart enough, and hardworking enough, to get into a top law school, you also have what it takes to get a job in another field or in a related field, if it turns out law is not the right field for you.

Be an analyst at an investment bank or a research associate at a corporate strategy consulting firm. Be a reporter for a small-town newspaper. Choose something that appeals to you on its own, or because it will allow you to see close-up the legal field you might wish to enter. If you like the field, and like what lawyers do in it, you will have learned something very valuable. If you do antitrust consulting work as an economist, for example, you may prefer to do what the antitrust lawyers do. On the other hand, you may stay on the economics side, or move on to something else entirely.

CAREER DISSATISFACTION

Major surveys done of lawyers in recent years—whether by the American Bar Association, the University of Michigan Law School, *California Lawyer* magazine, or others—have revealed that a substantial minority are unhappy that they became lawyers. This is in stark contrast to the results of studies of all workers, such as one by Rutgers University and the University of Connecticut, which found that 91 percent were unhappy with their work. (What, one wonders, would the percentage have been had they not included lawyers?) In some cases, the most important reason for the dissatisfaction has been the lack of a suitable quality of life (long hours, the need to be available to clients year-round, and so on); in other cases, it has been the nature of the work itself (dull, overly detail-oriented).

An interesting feature of the legal scene of recent years has been the publication of literally dozens of books cautioning people about the true nature of legal practice and the development of a mini-industry that helps practicing lawyers determine what they really want to do in life and another that helps them transition to other fields. The following books will give you a taste of this work:

Deborah Arron, *Running from the Law: Why Good Lawyers Are Getting Out of the Profession*

Amiram Elwork, *Stress Management for Lawyers: How to Increase Personal and Professional Satisfaction in the Law*

CAREER SERVICE DEANS COMMENT ON LAWYER DISSATISFACTION

The number of websites, studies, and support groups regarding lawyer dissatisfaction is extraordinary. This is very predictable because many of those people did not know why they attended law school in the first place. They did not do, on the front end of the process, the kind of self-evaluation that was called for. *Irene Dorzback, NYU*

A person cannot survive in this stressful profession without having an enthusiasm for law. *Susan Robinson, Stanford*

CONCLUSION

Law is a fine field, but it is not for everyone. The cost of law school and the difficulty of getting out of the profession once you are in it should propel you to do substantial investigation before entering it. If you choose law as a default choice, because you lack the common sense to try something else or the nerve to enter the work world after college, you are setting yourself up for real trouble in the future.

If you do decide to enter law, learn as much as you can about the legal field you intend to enter. As other parts of the book explain, this will help you to determine which law schools will be best for you; it will also help you to get the most out of your law school experience, both in the classroom and outside. Last, make sure you get into the best quality schools that you can. For help in that regard, read the rest of this book (or call for consulting assistance).

INDIVIDUAL CONSULTING AND WORKSHOPS

I routinely consult to clients who want the extra admissions edge that is possible through *individualized assistance*. I also help those who are trying to figure out whether law represents the right career path for them and, if so, which aspect of it would best suit them. Those desiring individual consulting are welcome to contact me through my website (www.degreeofdifference.com) or at (415) 273-1782.

I also offer small-group *workshops* that some readers will find to be attractive alternatives or supplements to individualized consulting. These are described briefly on p.xviii in the introduction, or in more detail on my website (www.degreeof difference.com).

ADDITIONAL RESOURCES

CONTEMPLATING LAW AND LAW SCHOOL

Richard W. Moll, *The Lure of the Law: Why People Become Lawyers and What the Profession Does to Them*

Mark Byers, et al., *Lawyers in Transition: Planning a Life in the Law*

Scott Turow, *One L: An Inside Account of Life at Harvard Law School* (Overblown and out of date, but still amusing.)

Edward Levi, *An Introduction to Legal Reasoning*. Classic exploration of what it means to "think like a lawyer."

EXPLORING SPECIFIC AREAS OF LAW

American Bar Association Career Series: includes books on Admiralty, Civil Litigation, Entertainment, Government Jobs for Lawyers, Labor, Sports, etc. (Note, however, that these tend to be rather rah-rah endorsements of their respective fields.)

Lisa L. Abrams, *Guide to Legal Specialties*. Describes some 30 different legal fields.

Steve Bogin, *Courtroom 302: A Year Behind the Scenes in an American Criminal Courthouse*

Gary Delsohn, *The Prosecutors*. A reporter's behind-the-scenes look at what a prosecutor really does, based on a year's close observation.

Clifford Ennico, *Business Lawyer's Handbook*. Explains what business lawyers (i.e., those who do not litigate) actually do, as well as the skills required of them.

Ronald Fox, *Lawful Pursuit: Careers in Public Interest Law*

Bradley M. Bittan, *The Public Defender Experience*

The National Association for Public Interest Law (www.napil.org). Good links to other public interest sites.

Harvard Public Interest Site (www.law.harvard.edu/students/opia). Excellent information about public interest law, plus good links to other public interest sites.

BEGINNING PRACTICE

Suzanne B. O'Neill and Catherine Gerhauser Sparkman, *From Law School to Law Practice*. A fine guide to what a new associate must do (well) in the first years of practice.

Mark Simenhoff, *My First Year as a Lawyer*. Lawyers in different types of law discuss their initial experience in practice.

Gary A. Munneke, *The Legal Career Guide: From Law Student to Lawyer*

Jeffrey R. Simmons, ed., *Flying Solo: A Survival Guide for the Solo Lawyer*

Carroll Seron, *The Business of Practicing Law: The Work Lives of Solo and Small-Firm Attorneys*

To get further information about the books described above, along with other appropriate readings, consult my website, www.degreeofdifference.com, which also makes purchasing them easy.

**ADDITIONAL COMMENTS FROM CAREER
SERVICES AND ADMISSIONS DEANS**

Knowing Why You Want to Attend Law School Is Critical

You should enter law school not because you are fascinated with law, but with the *practice* of law.   *Gloria Pyszka, Stanford (Career Services)*

Students are always stunned when they get to law school to learn that they need to think about how they want to practice law. They thought they had already made a career choice in coming to law school, and we inform them that choosing "law" was just the tip of the iceberg. Public interest, private sector, business, or academia? Litigation, transactional, negotiation, policy? Labor law, family law, corporate law, environmental law? Corporate clients, individual wealthy clients, needy clients, criminal clients, government clients? The decisions keep coming.... Knowing where you are heading allows a student to choose classes and summer jobs wisely, to further explore an area of tentative interest, and to prepare for it. This experience and education will help in their post-graduation job search. *Theresa J. Bryant, Yale (Career Services)*

I talk to a number of prospective students whose reasons for wanting to attend law school are so ethereal. I want to say, "Take a deferral. . . . Go and *do* something."   *Gloria Pyszka, Stanford (Career Services)*

Imagine what it's like to feel stuck at the end of year one (of law school), knowing you're so in debt that you have no way out except to finish and get the best-paying job you can.   *Irene Dorzback, NYU (Career Services)*

People shouldn't head to law school unless they like serving—being in a position working with and for others, not for themselves—and actually want to practice law.   *Steve Hopson, Virginia (Career Services)*

We conduct a workshop at Admitted Students' Day to help prospective students explore a career in the law. We discuss what a law career entails . . . and integrating one's interests and passions into the decision to attend law school. We find that many don't necessarily want to practice law, so we discuss deferring their attendance until they have had the opportunity to engage in a more thorough self-assessment.   *Irene Dorzback, NYU (Career Services)*

Working as a Paralegal

Those who work as a paralegal for a year or two often end up just as naïve about the practice of law as those who've never been inside a law firm. Maybe they're so convinced they want to go to law school that they're blind to the realities of practice. As a result, they tend not to learn whether lawyering is right for them. *Susan Robinson, Stanford (Career Services)*

A paralegal position is not the job that will make you the most marketable to law firms as a law student. Often, major employers put more value on experience earned outside of the big law firms. For example, firms hiring intellectual property lawyers like to see that someone has worked in an engineering or science environment. It's very helpful to see what is involved in actually developing an idea, something that is not readily captured in a book. Corporate departments like to see prior work in management consulting or banking. *Susan Robinson, Stanford (Career Services)*

Being a paralegal does not add much to your application—we see many, many applicants with the same experience. On the other hand, working as a paralegal can help the applicant decide whether law firm practice is the right field for him or her. *Megan A. Barnett, Yale (Admissions)*

Working as a paralegal can be very useful if you see law practice up close and personal, although for many the experience may include more time in the copy room than in the court room. *Todd Morton, Vanderbilt (Admissions)*

Many applicants are paralegals. Paralegal jobs are not designed to prepare one for law school—nor do these jobs give a student a tactical advantage in law school—sometimes, however, paralegal jobs give you the opportunity to observe firsthand the work of a lawyer in a specific area; similarly, you might get a sense of what is required of an associate in a law firm. *Kenneth Kleinrock, NYU (Admissions)*

Exploring Law as a Career

If you want to learn whether you should become a lawyer, it's not a bad idea to do paralegal work. You might also shadow a lawyer for however long you can, or volunteer at a legal clinic, law firm, or government office. Take advantage of any resources on-campus. Sit in on law school courses. Go to panel discussions at law schools when alums speak about what they do. Talk with law school alumni who volunteer to help prospective lawyers or law students. *Faye Deal, Stanford (Admissions)*

Students should have more than an inkling that they actually want to practice law, if not, preferably, some real exposure to it. The student who comes by default may question his or her decision—if not during law school, then after. Attending law school is not a "career" decision. *Fred Thrasher, George Washington (Career Services)*

The greatest problem I've seen is that students think, "I know that I'm only going to work in a big firm for a few years and then I'll figure out what I *really* want to do." That is the worst possible plan. *Susan Robinson, Stanford (Career Services)*

No conductor ever asks if you want to be on his train. Unless people step off, ask themselves questions, interact with alums, take stock of the field, see whether it fits their specific needs, and so on, they may not ever figure out whether it's the right train to be on (or at least not for years and years). The first time people do this is when they go to work. Ten to twelve weeks of summer employment during law school, for example, is seldom sufficient. It takes time to sort out whether the source of dissatisfaction is the specific practice area, the city, the firm, the environment, or law as a profession. *Irene Dorzback, NYU (Career Services)*

Try to take a job in the field, read the *NALP Guide to Legal Specialties* and other books on practicing law, and most important, talk to lawyers. If you do not know any lawyers, you probably know someone who knows someone who is a lawyer. Your undergraduate career services office may be able to hook you up with attorney alumni, and may have further materials and self-assessment tools for you as well. It is very flattering to have someone come to you for advice, and with the slightest connection most lawyers would be happy to talk with you about their work. *Theresa J. Bryant, Yale (Career Services)*

2

LOOKING AT LAW SCHOOL

— EXECUTIVE SUMMARY —

■

Both full-time and part-time programs are available.
—Yet there are relatively few top-quality part-time programs.

■

The first year of the JD program is largely fixed,
but the second and third years offer flexibility.

■

Law schools use four basic types of instruction:
—Case Method; Lecture; Seminar; Clinical Study

■

The workload is generally heavy, especially for the first year and a half.
—But note that you are the one who determines how much work to do.

■

Law schools offer highly flexible programs.
—You can specialize in any of several dozen fields.
—You can take (a few) courses in other parts of the university.
—You can do a joint degree.

■

Law school is not just about classes.
—Numerous social activities and publications beckon.

Law school has been a prerequisite for admission to the bar for approximately a century now. The initial assumption was that it was to provide training for someone without prior law study, so it was made a three-year degree, with the first year providing an introduction to the fundamentals of law. Although there have been innumerable changes in the typical program, it retains certain core characteristics. It is still, almost without exception, a three-year program (if done full-time). It has a set of core courses that are required for all students. And it demands hard work.

In the last two or three decades, however, law schools have dramatically changed certain elements of their programs. For one thing, they have established clinical programs aimed to give students hands-on experience in the "practice" of law. This trend, harkening back to the informal apprenticeship method of law clerks in past centuries, provides needed balance to what are otherwise heavily theoretical curricula. For another, schools have followed the trends in legal practice to incorporate a more international focus, allow students to specialize in a particular area, and promote an interdisciplinary perspective.

Although the top law schools vary in the range of courses, clinics, and specialized programs they offer, they share a common approach to training lawyers. First-year students generally study seven subjects:

- Civil Procedure
- Constitutional Law
- Contracts
- Criminal Law
- Property
- Torts
- Legal Research and Writing

During the second and third years, the courseload in most law programs is entirely elective, with the possible exception of an independent writing project, Professional Responsibility course, or one of the core courses listed above (if it is given in the second year rather than the first). Despite this freedom, most schools expect that their students will select courses that require them to develop their research and writing abilities as well as substantive knowledge of major legal subject areas. During their second and third years, students also have the opportunity to gain academic credit through work done in a variety of clinical programs and internships.

This chapter is designed to give you a feel for what law school will be like in a full-time program. Part-time programs are similar in most regards, with the obvious differences caused by the fact that students are not spending all of their time in school. As a result, the first year is not so overwhelming and their social lives tend not to revolve around school.

**FULL-TIME VERSUS
PART-TIME PROGRAMS**

In recent years, approximately 17 percent of law students have been enrolled in part-time programs. Among the top programs, however, part-time law degrees are not commonly offered. The few examples, with the percentage of the student body enrolled in the part-time program, are:

Fordham	25%
Georgetown	22%
George Washington	21%
Wisconsin	6%

PROGRAM STRUCTURE

The structure of a part-time JD does not differ significantly from that of a full-time JD. The same core courses are generally required, although they may be taken in a slightly different sequence due to the scheduling difficulties that result from students' proceeding through the program at varying speeds. The number of courses that must be completed in order to graduate will almost invariably be the same.

ADVANTAGES

➤ Part-time programs are somewhat easier to get into than are full-time programs at the same schools.

➤ If you are uncertain whether or not law school is the right move for you, you can sample law school without having to disrupt your life entirely. If you dislike it, you can quit. It you enjoy it, you can continue in the program or transfer to another one. (For more information regarding the transfer decision, see Chapter 15.)

➤ By maintaining your job, you can continue to receive a salary throughout the three-year program.

➤ You do not have to relocate for your studies.

➤ If your current work is related to the career you intend to pursue after law school graduation, you can often employ what you learn in law school on the job as you go. (Your studies may even be tax deductible—see the discussion in Chapter 18.)

➤ Ongoing relevant work experience may be drawn upon to enhance your performance in the law program.

DISADVANTAGES

➤ Part-time programs carry somewhat less prestige than do top full-time programs.

➤ You will not be able to commit yourself to your studies and to your classmates the way you could if you attended school full-time. The result is that you will probably feel you have not gotten as fully to grips with many of your courses as you would have had you been a full-time student.

➤ Although you may be welcome to join student journals and other organizations, you may find it logistically difficult to do so, especially if they meet at times when you are meant to be working.

➤ The demands made by the combination of a full-time job and part-time study tend to be overwhelming, causing people to feel they are doing neither of these activities well. The possibility of handling both well, plus a rewarding personal life, is remote.

➤ Your job performance may suffer so much, due to the effort you must make for your classes, that you will not increase your responsibilities or salary as you would if you could devote yourself more fully to your job.

➤ Your company may not be pleased about your planning to subordinate your work effort for four to six years of school.

The bottom line is that a part-time course may make sense to the extent that your current job is very attractive to you and is of a type that would permit you to pursue a part-time program, and you are fortunate enough to have a top quality part-time JD program available in your area.

TYPICAL REQUIRED COURSES

Nearly all schools traditionally require the following courses:

Civil Procedure focuses on the rules that structure federal and state civil litigation.

Constitutional Law provides a general introduction to the U.S. Constitution's allocation of power among the branches of the federal government and to the limitations on the substantive powers of the government.

Contracts explores the nature and enforceability of promises and bargains, and the remedies available for nonperformance.

Criminal Law examines the general principles of criminal liability, the rules for enforcing punishment against those accused of criminal acts, and the rights guaranteed to those charged with crimes.

Property examines the philosophical and economic origins of property rights, the rules that govern the acquisition and transfer of property rights, and private and public means of regulation.

Torts explores the policies and rules of the private law system that provide compensation for injuries or damage to persons and property.

Legal Research and Writing introduces students to legal discourse through problem analysis, legal research, writing, oral skills, and legal citation. Students are introduced to the contexts for and processes involved in legal problem-solving and communication.

Some leading schools now require courses in international or comparative law, legislation and regulation, and complex problem solving. Expect other schools to follow suit in the near future.

TEACHING METHODS

CASE METHOD

Most courses are taught via the case method in the first year of law school. (Some courses will be taught this way in the second and third years, whereas others will be taught via lecture, small group discussion, or clinic.) Your reading for these courses will consist almost exclusively of a series of appellate cases, some long, some short. There will be no text—no book that gives an overview of the field and highlights what is most important within it. Instead, you will be expected to piece together the nature and structure of the field by reading a series of cases that focus on one legal point (or occasionally two). These points will not be aggregated for you. Thus, you must learn how to see the forest for the trees.

The accompanying classroom method requires substantial student participation. Instead of sitting back and taking notes on what the professor says, as you probably did in college, you will need to be alert to the direction the professor is taking. She will call upon students to answer highly specific questions about the required reading; she may also ask about the economic, political, societal, or other significance of the rules under discussion. If this is an aggressive attempt to grill students, it will be termed the "Socratic Method."

The Socratic Method is a misnomer when used in this context. Socrates asked his students questions to get them to understand and recognize the truths that they already had in their minds; inherent truths, if you will. The law school version of this has been distorted out of all recognition, focusing on not-yet-learned concepts rather than inherent truths. In the past, professors grilled students mercilessly on new or foreign concepts. (To see not altogether fanciful versions of this, watch *The Paper Chase* or read Scott Turow's *One L*.) There are still a few unreformed Socratic Method types who "cold call" students—call on students who have not raised their hands or otherwise volunteered to answer—and seemingly delight in making them squirm. Most professors, however, have toned this down. The most common form of the still-feared Socratic Method involves professors warning a few students that during an upcoming class they can expect to be called on, giving them plenty of advance notice (and incentive) to prepare the assigned cases well.

The form of the questions has not changed much over the years. The first student called upon regarding a given case is likely to be asked to give an overview of it: to state the court, parties, facts, issues, holding, and rationale behind the holding. The follow-up questions may start by asking about the specifics of this case, but will soon venture afield into hypothetical matters. The professor will twist the facts of the case to determine what causes you to believe, for instance, that the court was right in its decision. "If the bus had not contained a bunch of convicts being taken away for execution but instead a group of nuns, would you still claim that the driver who rammed into it, killing three, should not be held liable?" "What if the driver was drunk at the time?" "What if the driver had not had a driver's license?" And so on.

One of the differences between this and the college-style lecture courses to which you are probably accustomed is that it is harder to take useful notes in such a class. Learning what is relevant for mastering the subject—and what will help you to ace the exam—is part of the first-year education process.

LECTURE

Many second- and third-year classes resemble the traditional lecture classes familiar to any American college student. (The general rule is that subjects depending more upon case law than statute are likely to be taught by the case method, whereas so-called statutory courses are more likely to be taught in a lecture format.) Lecture classes are less burdensome than case method courses insofar as there is less fear that the professor will call upon a student to grill him. Note-taking is also easier than in the case method classes, where one needs to be following every little nuance to be ready to answer highly specific questions. Instead, one can listen for major points and note them down, without fearing that he has missed the last thing said while writing a note, placing him in jeopardy.

SEMINARS

All of the leading law schools offer a wide range of seminars (usually defined as classes with twenty or fewer students, and involving substantial student participation). These are generally devoted to advanced topics rather than introductory ones. As is true of college seminars, the teaching approach can range from professorial introduction of the day's subject, followed by student and professor discussion, to student presentations with only muted professorial involvement.

CLINICAL STUDIES

The relatively recent utilization of clinical courses within law school curricula is an attempt to bridge the gap between theoretical instruction and the everyday work of lawyers. As "situation-based" teaching, clinical courses place students in actual or simulated circumstances that require them to address a client's problems.

Another, unspoken goal is to keep students involved in school and their classes through graduation. Most students in regular law classes have become bored and complacent by sometime in their second years; the change of pace offered by clinical education is one means of combating the problem.

The format of schools' clinical programs varies widely. Often, schools will have both "in-house" clinical programs and externship opportunities. The in-house clinics are more likely to be heavily supervised by faculty and administered in conjunction with a specific course. Clinical facilities centered outside the confines of the campus are supervised by staff attorneys and generally give students a bit more authority. Schools also offer "field placement programs," in which students receive academic credit for working in public interest organizations or governmental agencies under the supervision of a practicing attorney.

WORKLOAD

Top JD programs demand a remarkable amount of work. During the first year of a program (and particularly the first semester), the demands are especially great. There are several reasons for this. The first is that the schools are trying to teach critically important areas of law, plus an understanding of legal research and writing. There is a large amount to learn in such a short time, so the workload is inevitably high. (The second and third years are less intense, both because students have learned how to play the law school "game" and because they are taking elective courses suited to their interests and strengths.)

Another important reason for the time pressure is that the workload of a practicing attorney can be grueling. The JD program is structured to simulate that workload, so that students can be prepared for it later on. The excessive amount of work forces students to learn how to manage their time, one of the key skills a lawyer must acquire. Thus, a student will almost certainly have to learn to prioritize—to determine how to learn in the most efficient way.

YOUR WORKLOAD IS LARGELY UP TO YOU

For the average student, the first three semesters involve much more effort than the last three. Sometime during the middle of the second year, the average student opts out of the game—emotionally and academically. There are, of course, notable exceptions to this generalization. Those who are trying to make Order of the Coif, given to the top 10 percent of the class, may well keep pushing for top grades. The same is true for those whose employment fate will not be determined until (or after) the end of law school. Those who wish to teach law at a leading law school, for example, are likely to be given their first jobs elsewhere (perhaps clerking for a federal judge, working in a government agency, or teaching at a lesser law school). When it comes time for them to try to scale the heights of a top-tier law school, their law grades for each year of school are likely to be examined closely.

Students are in charge of their fate, of course, and can choose (within some limits) how much to study, but most do not recognize this until after the fact. As Chapter 17 discusses in detail, there are many ways to "do" law school. It is by no means necessary to read and brief every case, for instance, yet many students try to do so—at least during the first year. The level of uncertainty students face, given that almost none of them know enough about law school to be sure they can buck the crowd, means that a "groupthink" born of panic causes most students to put in very long hours. Much of this work is actually a waste of effort. To confirm this, ask students in their last semester what amount of the work they did in their first year was truly worthwhile.

GRADING

The difference between college and law school is nowhere more marked than in the grading. Most college courses involve at least a mid-term and a final exam; some involve a mid-term, a final, and a paper. Other courses involve multiple papers, multiple exams, or both. In nearly all first-year law school courses, however, the grade is based solely upon the single end-of-term exam. This exam is typically three or four hours long; it requires that you analyze a hypothetical case (or two or three) or a recently decided "real" case.

Despite the nerve-wracking aspects of preparing for class each day, class participation is seldom graded. (Consequently, it is not worth torturing yourself over classroom performance. It is useful to impress fellow students and professors, but the most important means of impressing people is through your grades.)

Basing the entire grade upon one exam results in a great deal of anxiety for law school students. This is particularly true during the first year, of course, before students have adjusted to taking such exams, learned to study for them, and gained confidence that they will survive them. One wonders when a law school (not run largely by and for its faculty) will seek to gain a substantial competitive advantage by giving first-term students quizzes or mid-term exams as well as finals, thereby attracting applicants who would prefer to avoid the traditional first-term panic.

CURRICULAR ORGANIZATION OF THE TRADITIONAL JD PROGRAM

The First Year

The first year is likely to be overwhelming unless you have had very good preparation for it, meaning that you have already had experience in a law related profession, or that you have taken the preparatory measures recommended in Chapter 16. There is so much work to do, so many new concepts to learn, that you are likely to feel you are drowning. Not only do you have a great deal to learn, you also have to learn *how* to learn. As time goes on, however, you will figure out how to cut through the massive amounts of case reading and detail and to focus on the key aspects. Most students feel that the first year (particularly the first semester) is infinitely more difficult than anything that follows.

The Second Year

The second-year curriculum is almost entirely elective, allowing students to tailor their courseload to fit their interests. The second year is hardly relaxed, however, due to the fact that students are spending serious amounts of time looking—and interviewing—for a summer job. They may also be lucky enough to be slaving away for law review or another school publication, or working part-time.

The Third Year

The third year is more of a breeze. Many students are too occupied with part-time jobs or extracurricular interests to attend many of their courses. A large number of students will find comfort in the fact that they have been offered jobs by the firms at which they spent their summers working. The result of so many students tuning out of course work is that those who remain engaged find it much easier to get good grades.

There is still a great deal of truth to the old law school adage that "in the first year they frighten you to death, in the second year they work you to death, and in the third year they bore you to death."

SPECIALIZATION

Just as the world of legal practice has become ever more specialized, so, too, have law schools tried to offer multiple courses in every popular (and not so popular) specialty. Whether this means traditional specialties such as labor law, or new ones such as any of the various corporate transactional areas, schools have tried with varying degrees of success to keep pace with the market. Some schools offer formal concentrations, akin to majors in college, but whether or not a school formalizes its offerings matters less than the availability of the appropriate courses and professors.

COURSES OUTSIDE LAW SCHOOL

Law schools have recently recognized that law is increasingly tied to other fields. This has been reflected in the increase in joint-degree programs they offer as well as the law schools' increased recruitment of professors with doctorates in other fields (in addition to their JDs). Unfortunately, these same schools are extremely ungenerous in the number of courses they permit law students to take for credit in other parts of the university. Thus, in law schools requiring approximately thirty courses in total, generally no more than two (or three, in some schools) may be taken elsewhere in the university.

This parochialism is particularly unfortunate in view of the way these same schools market themselves. Law schools routinely brag about all of the marvelous courses on offer throughout the university of which they are a part and make it sound as though it is a simple matter for one of their students to take advantage of these course offerings. Unfortunately, the reality fails to live up to the rhetoric. This is a policy sorely in need of modernization.

JOINT DEGREES

Joint-degree programs offer students the opportunity to study law and another field, more or less at one and the same time. A typical program, the JD–MBA, has students do their first-year at the law school (following the usual first-year law curriculum), their second year at the business school (following the usual first-year business curriculum), and their last two years taking a mixture of law and business courses. The time required to get the two degrees is four years, one fewer than would be required if the student did each degree separately. This saving of a year in study time is typical for joint programs, not just the JD–MBA. The integration of programs leads to this saving of time.

Most of the top law schools now offer a host of joint degrees, at both the master's and the doctoral levels. Duke, for instance, offers more than twenty joint degree programs, with fully a quarter of law students pursuing one or another. Yale offers joint degrees with the schools of Forestry and Environmental Studies, Divinity, and Medicine, in addition to the more common arrangements with the School of Management and the Graduate School (meaning the usual departments such as economics, history, and the like). The University of Pennsylvania offers joint programs in business administration and other commonly pursued fields; it also offers joint programs in such unusual fields as bioethics, city planning, communications, and Islamic studies.

Although only a relatively small number of students pursue any of these programs (apart from the JD–MBA), the variety of programs on offer across the whole set of leading schools is truly impressive. In addition, some schools offer a chance to design an individualized joint-degree program. Not every school offers a JD–MS Forestry or JD–MA Islamic Studies possibility, of course, so it is essential to research the specific degree options at each school.

A relatively new development is the opportunity to get two law degrees. Cornell, for instance, offers a chance to get both a JD and a Maîtrise en Droit (French) or an M.LL. (German) degree at an affiliated European university. Students spend two years at Cornell followed by two years at the respective European university. NYU provides an option closer to home: a two-plus-two program with Canada's Osgoode Hall Law School.

There are, of course, some potential disadvantages to doing a joint degree. Joint degrees generally require more time (and money) than a single degree. Any sort of joint degree is also likely to limit the number of courses you can take that are totally unrelated to the two fields.

PUBLICATIONS

The top law schools have anywhere from a handful to a dozen and a half publications that are edited by students. Georgetown, for instance, publishes the *Georgetown Law Journal*, *American Criminal Law Review*, *Georgetown Journal on Poverty Law & Policy*, *Georgetown Journal of Gender and the Law*, *Georgetown Immigration Law Journal*, *Georgetown International Environmental Law Review*, *Georgetown Journal of Law and Public Policy*, *Law & Policy in International Business*, *Georgetown Journal of Legal Ethics*, and *The Tax Lawyer*. Despite the impressiveness of this listing, it is by no means inclusive of all of the many fields such journals cover.

The "law review" (called the "Law Journal" in Georgetown's case) is the flagship publication of each law school. It features articles by professors and practitioners, edited by second- and third-year students. Membership of the law review is immensely prestigious; being the editor-in-chief is extraordinarily so. At some schools, membership is determined by first-year grades: those with the highest grades are invited to join. At other schools, membership is determined solely through a writing competition: Prospective members write lengthy articles, with the best writers being invited to join. At still other schools, membership is determined by a combination of these two methods.

Being an editor of the law review involves as much hard work as it does prestige. Editors commonly put more time into their law review efforts than they do preparing for classes. The checking of citations ("cite-checking," in law school parlance), copyediting, and editing for substance combine to provide a formidable training in legal analysis and writing. Employers are by no means unaware of this. Indeed, many firms and agencies recruit primarily from law review ranks.

The other publications offer similar opportunities for learning, but at somewhat less rarefied levels. The competition to become an editor at these other publications tends to be much less intense than for the law review; the degree of competition varies according to the place of the specific journal in the clear, if informal, pecking order of the journals. Subject-specific journals, such as a labor law journal, offer the additional prospect of gaining subject-specific knowledge. As a result, the competition to gain prestigious and influential positions on them will likely be limited to people intending careers in those fields.

STUDENT BODY

The student body at the top schools has changed considerably over the years. The ratio of men to women now approximates one-to-one. The percentage of minority students has almost tripled in recent decades. The percentage of international students, although still low, has increased dramatically in the last decade. Students come from a number of different educational and professional backgrounds. The percentage of students with work experience has overtaken that of the "traditional" applicant, the recent college graduate. Columbia, for instance, lists its entering class as containing: professional dancers and theater managers; Peace Corps, VISTA, and military veterans; physicists, engineers, biochemists; management, computer, website, trademark, and environmental consultants; professional musicians; editors and publishers; university professors and high school teachers; accountants and financial analysts; and human rights advocates.

Much of the learning experience in a high-quality program comes from your fellow students, who can give real-life insights into problems, based upon their recent experiences. The range of different jobs, industries, and educational backgrounds makes for a rich mixture of relevant experience to bring to bear in classroom discussions and study-group sessions. Whatever their work backgrounds, the different students have several things in common. They are invariably highly motivated as well as quite intelligent, and have been extremely successful in whatever they have done so far.

These are not just people you will work with, and compete with, during your time together in law school. You will form lifelong friendships with some of them and may well work for the same firm with some, too. Your law school colleagues represent your future network of contacts, the people who will be your clients and partners and sources of job information.

SOCIAL LIFE

Some suspect that the only way law students manage to have any social life at all is by sleeping very little. There is a lot of truth in this. The time pressure inherent in demanding programs ensures that only the energetic can manage a thorough-going social or family life in addition to their studies (at least during the first half of the program).

Social life differs greatly from one program to the next. At all schools, however, student clubs and organizations will be the focus of substantial time and effort. Many of these are pre-professional clubs designed to educate students about the fields. An environmental law society, for example, may hold forums at which participants in major disputes discuss their experiences and argue their points of view. In addition, it will help members get jobs in environmental law by inviting speakers and recruiters to visit and discuss the field—and their respective firms—with interested members. The leading schools tend to have a magnificent range of such clubs, covering everything from Criminal Law to Internet Law.

Not all student clubs are an extension of the job search. Many sports and activities can be found on a typical campus. These are likely to be open to spouses and even children. Like the pre-professional clubs, these offer the opportunity to demonstrate leadership and other desirable attributes, as well as energy and love of a given activity. Unsurprisingly, many campuses have an In Vino Veritas or equivalent club, although Georgetown may be unique in offering a Gilbert & Sullivan Society. Advocacy and action groups also abound. Examples include Civil Liberties Unions, Prison Legal Assistance Projects, and Volunteer Income Tax Assistance Programs. Special interest and affinity groups—not just law school Democrats and Republicans—also exist in great numbers.

Of course, not all student social life revolves around clubs. Student parties fortunately are a staple of law programs, with the excuse for holding one varying from the need to get away from studying when the pressure is greatest to the need to take advantage of the opportunity when the pressure is lowest. In addition, students find innumerable ways to enjoy informal activities with their fellow students and outsiders, although the more isolated campuses make interaction with nonstudents rather problematic.

3

HOW TO CHOOSE THE RIGHT SCHOOL FOR *YOU*

— EXECUTIVE SUMMARY —

The first step in choosing a school is to know well what you
want from a law degree.

Researching the schools is a time-consuming, involved process.
—Start with the recommended guidebooks,
then investigate specific schools in depth.
—Consult the relevant rankings, but do not regard them as gospel.

Your search will not be complete until you:
—Visit the most likely choices.
—Check out these schools with leading employers in your chosen field.

Apply to an appropriate number and range of schools.

Your selection of a school should be driven by two actions: (1) analyzing your-self and your needs well enough to determine what programs will be most ap-propriate for you, and then (2) getting into the highest quality, best reputed of these programs.

It is essential that you really get to grips with both sides of this equation. Your reasons for getting a JD will help pinpoint which schools are right for you. You are likely to opt for the right program if you carefully analyze your own needs. By the same token, you are likely to choose the wrong program if you do only a cursory analysis of the different programs, depending largely upon their slick websites or the one-size-fits-all rankings.

KNOW YOURSELF—AND WHAT YOU WANT FROM A LAW DEGREE

Your decision to go to law school represents a milestone, and few decisions will equal this one in significance. You want to get it right. The starting point is knowing what you want to accomplish by getting a JD. Chapter 1 discusses some of the more common reasons for getting a JD. What are yours? Do you want to become the ACLU's leading appellate lawyer? Do you hope to become a specialist in New York Stock Exchange rules and regulations, as well as secu-rities law, so as to help countries adopting American-style stock exchanges? Do you want to be a commercial litigator for a major law firm? Do you want to be in-house counsel at a biotech firm?

Your reason for getting a JD will color your choice of schools. Your relative ability—your strengths and weaknesses where law schools are concerned—will also help you narrow your choices. If you are among the country's top 5,000–10,000 candidates, you will probably focus your attention on the top 20 or 30 schools.

RESEARCH THE SCHOOLS

The process of choosing schools is likely to be an iterative one. As you under-stand better what you are looking for in a JD program, you will be able to choose programs that better meet your needs. As you research schools and learn what they have to offer, you may also change what you are looking for from a JD and thus what you will demand in a program.

STEP 1: DEVELOP GENERAL KNOWLEDGE ABOUT JD PROGRAMS

Before narrowing your search to a handful of schools, you should become acquainted with what the various JD programs have to offer.

1. Examine this chapter's discussion of several dozen possible criteria for choosing a school. This will introduce you to the wide range of factors that might be relevant to your choice of schools.

2. Read several of the publications devoted solely to the question of which school to choose. The best of the guides are listed at the end of this chapter, along with a brief description of their contents. These publications provide better overviews of the quantitative elements of the programs (such as the number of students and types of courses offered) than the subjective (such as what the schools do best).

3. You should also read the rankings produced by such publications as *U.S. News & World Report* to get a rough approximation of the reputation of the different schools. See Chapter 4 for more information on the different rankings.

STEP 2: START GETTING INFORMATION ABOUT SPECIFIC SCHOOLS

Your initial efforts should have generated a preliminary list of schools that might be appropriate for you. Now you should start to investigate these schools more seriously.

1. Start to determine which criteria are most important to you. Two criteria should weigh heavily in your thinking at this point. *What type of learning environment is best for you?* Some people need to get their adrenaline flowing through competition and fear. If so, there are a number of programs that should be ideal. For other people, these programs would be disasters because they learn best in collegial, supportive environments. If one of these environments would be much better than the other for you, be sure you know which schools fall in which category. *What subject(s) do you intend to focus on?* If you intend to focus on civil litigation, you may be safe going to any leading school, since they all offer numerous courses in it (although some of the leading schools are more famous for it than are others). If you intend to focus on international taxation, however, some schools will offer many relevant courses whereas others will offer one or none. In addition, you must *consider what additional criteria are particularly important for you.* The most likely criteria include location, size, teaching quality, mission, and cost.

2. Get information from the schools themselves. Have each send you its brochures, which will explain the school's philosophy, what it seeks in applicants, and what makes it noteworthy. (Do not, however, believe all that you

read.) Visit the school's website to gather further information. Either the brochure, the website, or both should list what courses are currently on offer as well as detailed information about each member of the faculty.

3. Learn when you can meet the schools' representatives. They will travel to law school forums, which are gatherings held at cities around the United States and the world at which schools set up booths and relay information about their programs. The forums are convenient affairs for meeting representatives from a large number of schools, but they are sometimes too crowded and hectic to provide good opportunities for lengthy questioning of any one representative. Schools also send their representatives around the country, especially to leading undergraduate colleges, to do "dog-and-pony shows" to sell the programs to potential applicants. These sessions are often less hurried than the law school forums, thereby providing the opportunity to question representatives at greater length.

STEP 3: FOCUS ON THE SCHOOLS YOU FIND MOST APPEALING

By the time you have finished the first two steps, you should have a good understanding of which schools are most likely to meet your needs. It is now time to investigate these schools carefully.

1. Talk with each school's alumni to learn more about the schools. Schools are generally glad to give you the names of alumni living near you who have volunteered to discuss the respective programs. Recent alumni, in particular, can be good sources of information about the atmosphere of the school, its academic strengths and weaknesses, the ease with which they did (or did not) get a job in their chosen field, and the types of students who seem most pleased by their selection of this school.

2. Talk with a school's competitors to learn what the weak aspects of a school might be. (Take these comments with at least one grain of salt.)

3. Visiting the school is an important part of your research. There are a host of things you are unlikely to find out in any other way. Schedule your visit with the admissions office. They will make it possible for you to sit in on classes and meet students. You should by all means do this.

You should also talk with a representative group of students. If you attend this school, you will soon be spending all of your waking hours with people just like them, so be sure they are people with whom you would be comfortable. Do not limit yourself to those students the admissions office arranges for you to meet, because those who volunteer to do so may not be entirely representative of the student body. You can meet plenty of students just by going to the school's cafeteria and joining a group of students who will certainly remember when they were going through the same process, making it quite likely that they will spend whatever time they can with you. (For more about visiting schools, see Appendix II in this chapter.)

4. Most important, if you know what field you intend to enter, contact the leading employers in it. Be sure to include the organizations you would most like to work for: Ask their human resource people (those responsible for hiring) which are the schools where they actively recruit. Have them explain why they choose these schools, their impressions of strengths and weaknesses of the respective programs, what types of people they choose from each (to the extent that this differs by school), and how many individuals they generally hire from each school. Ask them from which other schools they would be particularly

---

WHAT TO DO IF YOU WILL BE UNABLE TO GET INTO THE RIGHT LEVEL OF SCHOOL

Your analysis of the appropriate schools for you, given the type of employer you favor, may reveal something distressing. You may not be able to get into the schools from which these employers recruit, effectively foreclosing the possibility of working for them. For instance, a leading New York private firm (or public interest firm) may recruit actively only at Columbia, NYU, Harvard, and Penn, and accept résumés only from the remaining "top ten" schools. The reason for not visiting other top schools for on-campus recruiting may be that it has never been able to get enough serious applicants from them to warrant the expense involved. (This is particularly true for a small, distant school such as Stanford.) You have several choices:

➤ Revise your employment goals. Maybe you are being unrealistic about your talents in general. Maybe you are trying to please someone else who wants you to have the most prestigious employment possible, whereas you may not actually value it. Be sure to examine your own motivations in real depth.

➤ Take another job upon graduation from law school and hope to move laterally after several years. Perhaps your chosen employers hire people not just straight from law school but also laterally (with some years of experience). If so, your best bet may be to get a job with an appropriate feeder organization. If you excel there, you can hold out hope of making the jump to whichever employer you most value.

➤ Go to a slightly "lesser" school and hope. You can always try to excel at a school with a reputation just below those at which your chosen employers recruit in hopes that a sterling résumé will be enough. This is highly risky, however, and sets you up for a long period of anxiety—and potential disappointment.

➤ Go to a lesser school in hopes of transferring to one of your target schools after your first year.

> ➤ Wait to apply to law schools. You can improve your marketability dramatically if you excel in a demanding and interesting job or jobs over the next few years, as much of the rest of this book discusses.

happy to receive résumés. (They might not recruit at some schools for logistical reasons, but would be glad to hear from students at those schools. Similarly, they might be glad to hear from the best students at certain schools that they feel produce strong graduates, but in too small a number to warrant proactive recruiting efforts.)

This is a critical step to finding the right school for yourself, but the one most frequently skipped because it involves a bit of honest effort. By the way, the connection you make with these firms' human resource people should be viewed as an advance marketing effort, so treat these folks well and keep in touch with them.

Do not start your law school research efforts with the human resource professionals, because you will be imposing upon their time as it is, and to do so without knowing anything about schools will prove embarrassing. Approach them for such a favor when you have some reasonable idea of what's what in JD programs and can thus use their time efficiently.

5. Do not overreact to the on-line chat room discussions in which applicants discuss their concerns and opinions. The ratio of ignorant statements and misconceptions to helpful comments is very high.

DETERMINE HOW MANY SCHOOLS TO APPLY TO

Some people want to go to a specific school and would not even think about going to one of its rivals—perhaps due to geographic constraints, such as a spouse attending medical school in the location of the law school. Those who feel this way do not face any problem in determining how many schools they should consider. On the other hand, you may be content to attend one of a number of schools. If so, you must consider how many applications to file. This will depend upon several factors:

■ Are you determined to go this year? If so, you must apply to enough (safety) schools to be sure of getting into at least one of them.

■　What are your chances at the schools you favor? If your credentials are better across the board than those of the average student accepted at these schools, and you can present yourself very well, you need not do a great number of applications. (Do not limit yourself to consideration of just the quantitative credentials, though. As Chapters 5, 8, and 9 discuss, consider, too, the rest of what you have to offer, including in particular your career experience and success to date.) If your credentials are not superior, however, be prepared to do more applications.

■　How many applications can you do without sacrificing the quality of essays, the visiting of schools, the interviewing opportunities, and so on? Note, by the way, that there is a large fixed cost to starting the application process, but additional applications tend to take less and less time. Conscientious applicants who prepare for the first application by gathering the necessary information about themselves and establishing how to market themselves effectively generally find that the first application takes about the same time and effort as the next five or more applications altogether.

Many serious applicants apply to about six to ten schools. For all but the very strongest candidates (who will apply only to the most demanding programs), it is appropriate to spread your applications across a range of schools. Thus, you can apply to one or two "likely" schools, several "possible" schools, and a number of "stretches." "Likelies" are schools to which you are likely to be admitted. These are schools at which admittees have substantially lesser credentials than you possess. For example, your LSAT score is four to five points higher than the school's average, your undergraduate grade-point average is 0.3 points higher, your undergraduate college and curriculum more demanding, and your career more interesting and successful than others of similar age. "Possibles" are schools where your credentials are about equal to the average for those admitted. "Stretches" are the flip side of "likelies": Your credentials are substantially lower than those of the average person admitted.

CHOOSING A PART-TIME PROGRAM

Choosing a part-time JD program is necessarily somewhat different from choosing a full-time program. Your choice of program will probably be limited to those within your immediate area. Therefore, some of the criteria used for determining the most appropriate full-time program, such as available housing, will no longer be relevant because you will probably not be moving. Some of the other criteria may be less important than would be the case if you were to attend a full-time program. The career services office may be unimportant for you if you intend to remain with the same employer after you complete your degree. Other criteria are likely to become more important. A program's schedule may not fit within your own, thereby eliminating it as a possibility.

In spite of these differences, choosing a part-time program still resembles the selection process for a full-time program. The courses must be of value to you, with an academic atmosphere suited to your desires. When you are choosing among several schools that offer what you want, reputation is still likely to be the most important criterion. (Remember, of course, that a part-time program often does not command the same reputation as the school's full-time program.)

Why separate schools into these three categories and apply to some in each category? If you apply only to schools in one category, you are likely to miss out on an opportunity. If you do not apply to some "stretches," you may not get into the highest quality school possible. If, on the other hand, you do not apply to a "likely" or two, you risk not getting into any school at all.

AVOID THE LIKELY PITFALLS IN CHOOSING A SCHOOL

Some warnings to keep in mind as you go through the search process:

- Start the process early. You need to gather a lot of information and you should give yourself time to reflect on what you learn at each step.

- Do not take the rankings too seriously. They are no better than rough proxies for a school's quality and reputation. (See Chapter 4 for more on the limitations of law school rankings.) They obviously do not take account of your specific set of key criteria. Look for high-quality programs that will satisfy your needs.

- Be wary of schools with learning environments that are not hospitable to you. Do not put yourself through months of hell and the disappointment of performing poorly due to a bad match between you and a school's learning environment.

■ Be aware that your interests may change as you go through both the self-evaluation and search processes. You can alter what you want to do and better understand what would help you. As a result, your criteria for schools should change to reflect your changed interests.

■ Do not be swayed by spiffy school brochures or websites. The quality of a school is not directly related to the quality of the pictures in its publications.

■ Do not be swayed by warm (or cold, or inefficient) admissions people. They are not the ones who will be teaching you or helping you to get a job upon graduation.

■ Do pay attention to the quality of the careers service. Your job fate can be dramatically improved by a top-notch department.

■ Remember: Eliminate schools that do not offer the program you need.

—Eliminate those with inappropriate learning atmospheres.

—Eliminate those with other important negatives for you, such as an unsuitable location and size.

—Include the highest quality schools you believe you can get into (and, yes, pay attention to the consensus views of the rankings).

■ Ultimately, any number of schools can give you a great learning experience and help your career prospects dramatically, but it is up to you to take advantage of the opportunities afforded you.

THE LOCAL ADVANTAGE

If you know where you'd like to practice, apply to accessible schools there. The major firms (and other key employers) lean heavily on the leading local schools. Even in cities with major law schools, lesser-ranked schools place many graduates at elite employers. Yes, in Boston, Harvard dominates—but Boston University and Boston College do very well. Just try to find a leading Boston law firm that does not have a substantial number of partners from each. This is doubly true in cities without a top fifteen or twenty school, such as San Diego, New Orleans, Miami, Kansas City, and so on.

The more certain you are of where you would like to practice, the more weight you should give local schools. Of course it is still likely to make sense to go to a Harvard, Yale, or Stanford if you can get in, rather than to a lower-tier local school. On the other hand, it probably will not make sense to attend a distant school that is only of marginally higher quality (or ranking) than your local school, unless there is a substantially better fit with your interests (or pocketbook).

Those who are uncertain of where they would like to practice gain geographic flexibility (as well as the chance to delay their choice of location) by attending a national school, which, by definition, is able to place graduates in jobs across the country. Those who are unable to get into such schools, however, can benefit by considering local hiring conditions. Thus, someone who finds Ohio and Arizona equally attractive places to live and practice should favor attending law school in Arizona. After all, it is invariably harder to get attractive employment in a slow-growing (let alone shrinking) economy than in a rapidly growing one.

FINAL-DECISION CRITERIA

The most important criteria for each applicant will, of course, differ substantially. Some applicants will be greatly cost-constrained, leading them to choose schools that have lower tuition or offer financial aid. Others will choose schools only in a given area. Others will look for the school with the best course offerings on taxation they can get into.

No matter which criteria are relevant to you, it would be highly appropriate to determine which schools will give you the courses you most want, in an atmosphere in which you think you could thrive (collegial versus competitive, faculty open door versus isolated, etc.), and in a location that is appropriate to your current circumstances and future goals. Having taken account of these and the other criteria most important to you, the final choice will often come down to the school's reputation. If you were intending to do international corporate law and were admitted to both NYU and Miami, for instance, it would be peculiar to choose Miami. Although Miami is a fine school with a substantial international program, it is not generally regarded as one of the top half dozen or dozen schools in the country, as is NYU. Reputation is not everything, but among schools that do not differ dramatically in their ability to deliver what you are looking for, reputation will ordinarily be a critical factor.

READINGS

Unfortunately, there are no books equivalent to the best college guides, which capture relevant statistics about schools but also go beyond the numbers to capture the nature of a school, its students, and the sorts of experience on offer. The following is the best of a very weak field:

ABA-LSAC Official Guide to ABA-Approved Law Schools. Provides basic data regarding: employment (by geography, type of employment), financial aid, informational and library resources, student body and faculty ethnicity and sex, and curriculum. The curriculum description includes the typical first-year section size; number of courses offered for second- and third-year students; number of seminars offered, and number of positions available in the seminars (along with the number filled); number of positions available in simulation courses (and the number filled); number of positions available in faculty-supervised clinical courses (and the number filled); and the number involved in field placements and law journals.

Of less value is the nonstatistical description of schools, which reads like a purposely dull press release from the school itself. It recounts, in a dutiful fashion, each school's location, a description of its facilities, its research centers and institutes, and so on.

(U.S. News & World Report) Ultimate Guide to Law Schools. Another decidedly misnamed guide book, which provides much the same information as the ABA-LSAC book, albeit with some helpful lists, such as average debt levels of graduates. It is, at least, lighter and cheaper than the *Official Guide*.

Do not expect anything as sophisticated as a listing of the number of real estate courses, seminars, or clinics from either of these sources. Thus, they will be of very limited value in your search.

ADMISSIONS DEANS DISCUSS CHOOSING THE RIGHT SCHOOL

Determining Your Own Needs

There are some applicants for whom academics will be most important, others for whom publications, student groups, and a host of other activities will be. *Joyce Curll, Harvard*

It's especially hard for younger applicants to know the right questions to ask in order to choose the right school. To get a broad range of perspectives about what is really important in a law school, ask a variety of people—some current students, some recent graduates, and some mid-career lawyers—what aspects of law school were important to them and what they would have changed if they could. Then analyze what will matter most to you.   *Megan A. Barnett, Yale*

Applicants should look at schools that excel at the specific fields in which they hope to practice (if they have already made that choice), but most of all, they should also look very closely at a school that will best prepare them to address the vagaries and complexities that they will encounter in the practice of law. *Nkonye Iwerebon, Columbia*

Your future success depends upon how well you do in law school. Therefore, selecting a law school where you'll be happy and thrive is obviously in your best interest. *Rob Schwartz, UCLA*

The first thing is to do a self-assessment of what matters to you: curriculum, faculty, location, employment opportunities, costs, and so on. Then use a matching process; look at different schools to see which have strengths in areas that matter most to you. *Chloe T. Reid, USC*

It's critically important, even before applying, to visit schools. Explore, preferably in person, or at least on the Web, the scope of the law school. Read what they say about themselves. Think about how you learn best and work best. Do you take the initiative and thrive on finding things out for yourself, choosing among a wide variety of options, or do you want to have a set menu of what you can do put in front of you? *Joyce Curll, Harvard*

The local environment matters a lot. For instance, urban versus country—which one is a plus for you? The kind of person who's happy at a rural school may be the kind of person who relieves stress by going out to visit a waterfall; at an urban school it'll be someone who does so by enjoying the nightlife, for example. *Joyce Curll, Harvard*

Begin with a self-evaluation. You can make some broad cuts regarding the type of geographic setting you want, etc. The top schools differ somewhat in geography, size, culture, and mission or philosophy. Some key questions are: Where will you feel comfortable; who is at the school; where is the school located? The number of volumes in the library is irrelevant. The way to get at this is to visit the school, sit in on a class, perhaps come to an open house, information session, or admitted students day. At a minimum you should at least access the relevant websites, CD/ROMs, and the like. Personally, I cannot imagine investing three years and so much money without at least visiting the school. *Kenneth Kleinrock, NYU*

ADMISSIONS DEANS DISCUSS THEIR OWN SCHOOLS

At each of the top schools you expect a superbly qualified faculty, a comprehensive range of coursework, bright, engaged, and committed students, and superb job placement opportunities. What sets UVA apart is the incredibly collegial and cooperative student body. The students are competitive, but not cutthroat. Working as part of a team and supporting one another are part of the experience here. Not only does this make for a sane and enjoyable three years, but it also makes you a better lawyer. Solving problems in a team and developing interpersonal skills—including the ability to listen—make you better prepared for practice. *Susan Palmer, Virginia*

Admitted applicants generally choose to enroll at that law school where they believe they will feel most "comfortable." Well, admitted students choosing Columbia are men and women who are most comfortable when they are uncomfortable—when they are engaging a community of classmates who are quite different than themselves—in terms of their backgrounds, perspectives, experiences, and developing professional ambition. With one of the very largest percentages of students of color, the largest percentage of international students in our JD student body (and by integrating our LLM students, 80 percent of whom are international lawyers), by attracting students from an extraordinary range of professions and careers, by enrolling entering classes the majority of whom realistically aspire to international careers, Columbia is truly, wonderfully diverse. . . . Our students are somewhat older and more experienced than those at peer schools. We try from the get-go to look for diversity of experience. This makes for a better education for everybody, including the faculty. *Jim Milligan, Columbia*

Our school has the advantages of its size and location. We don't have a lot of bureaucracy; there is a true sense of community; and no one is likely to feel anonymous. We're not in a big city, which makes us attractive to those favoring a low-key lifestyle while attending law school. Housing, safety, and commuting tend not to be hot issues here.

   The school itself features a faculty that is incredibly dedicated to teaching; there is no tension here between teaching and scholarship. And even though we're not in a major city, we have a very well-known international legal program, excellent clinical opportunities, and the largest legal non-profit website in the world. Being part of a large research campus also provides rich opportunities beyond the law school. *Rick Geiger, Cornell*

There are a number of things that are different about Michigan Law. We're in the heart of a vibrant, albeit smallish city. It's an excellent town to be a student in—everything is very accessible. Many people love the sports scene here, of course, but it doesn't color the environment unduly. The career service is almost unique: because we're in the middle of the country, without any single city taking a large percentage of our graduates, you can keep your options open. We have over 700 employers come for on-campus interviewing, with large numbers from all major cities. Also, we have full-time faculty teaching legal writing, which means our students end up better prepared to write than do graduates of many other schools. The culture here is very open; professors are extraordinarily accessible. Drop in when you want, invite them to lunch, stay in touch after graduation. This is a major advantage for those intending to teach law, given that professorial recommendations are critically important. *Sarah C. Zearfoss, Michigan*

A number of programs set us apart from other leading schools. We offer four specializations—that appear as such on your transcript: public interest and policy, entertainment and media law (taking advantage of our LA location), business law (with over sixty courses each year), and critical race studies (which is the only program of its kind). In addition, we have a history of innovative clinical offerings, with more than two dozen courses on offer—and an environmental law center that is a leader in addressing global climate change. *Rob Schwartz, UCLA*

George Washington is a large, national law school located in the heart of the nation's capital. Being large gives us the ability to offer more of everything: a large (and distinguished) faculty, innumerable course offerings, and unparalleled opportunities for networking and internships—whether at large or small firms, government agencies, nonprofits, or with judges. GW is the oldest law school in Washington, DC. We have 21,000 living alumni across the globe—a large and strong network. Also, this is a teaching school. Despite the fact that our faculty publish a great deal, the first emphasis is on teaching. The collegiality within the school, and the involvement of faculty with students, is superb. *Anne Richard, George Washington*

The Penn Law experience is unique due to our cross-disciplinary approach to legal education and the Penn Law culture. The Law School and the University as a whole embrace cross disciplinary learning. This is reflected in our faculty, at least half of whom have Ph.D.s (in addition to the law degree) and teach in other departments at the University. This is an ideal place for those wishing to do more than just learn a trade—to pursue academic interests.

   The Penn Law community is collegial and supportive where a true work life balance exists. Law school is ordinarily thought of as very competitive, but this is not the case at Penn. Academic rigor and collaboration exist here. *Renée Post, Penn*

The small size of the class (190–200 enter each year) means that people know each other well. Due partly to that, but partly to tradition and other factors, this is a very respectful and collaborative environment. That is as true of relations between faculty and students as it is of relations between students. The law school environment is nicely balanced by what is available in Nashville. It's big enough to have an outstanding opera and symphony, great restaurants and cheap eats, as well as the well-known entertainment options—yet it is small enough that these things are readily available. It's also big enough to provide an array of opportunities to gain valuable experience in large or small firms, state or federal courts and agencies, non-profits, or corporations, and Vanderbilt is ideally situated in the legal community. It's an unusual school in terms of the balance between the smallish, supportive, but energetic academic environment and the city around it. However high people's expectations when they come here, the quality of the intellectual environment at the school coupled with the quality of life afforded students always impress. *Todd Morton, Vanderbilt*

First, being in the midst of the second largest legal market in the country provides enormous opportunities for students while they are here, whether they are interested in nonprofit, government, or private firm work. And with Los Angeles being the entertainment capitol of the world, it provides an exciting backdrop for those interested in entertainment and media law. The law school's well-connected alumni, experienced faculty, and strong curriculum prepares and supports students to pursue any area of law. Secondly, students interact in very powerful and meaningful ways with the community that surrounds the school. They can get involved in service-learning that makes a difference in real peoples' lives. Third, being on the campus of a large research institution, rather than on a satellite campus, means students can explore and pursue other graduate coursework as well as engage fully in one of the most rich and diverse student bodies in the U.S. Fourth, experiencing 300-plus days of sunshine per year is hard to beat. *Chloe T. Reid, USC*

Our faculty is pretty amazing—remarkable scholars who nonetheless are here to teach. Our students enjoy interacting with them in and out of the classroom. And, of course, the fact that we're a small school makes for a particularly close-knit community. *Ann Killian Perry, Chicago*

I would find it hard to put together as diverse and interesting a group of people if the class were much smaller. *Joyce Curll, Harvard*

We're a larger law school, allowing us to offer a lot of courses, seminars, lectures, and extracurricular activities. On the other hand, if you cannot handle choice, this is probably not the right place for you. *Kenneth Kleinrock, NYU*

INVESTIGATING SCHOOLS

Look at schools' websites, visit them, and discuss them with current students and graduates. . . . There is no substitute for the personal visit; the web picture of the campus may not be representative. Meet the people and get a sense of the environment. Make sure you could be happy there for three years. *Rob Schwartz, UCLA*

The best way to investigate law schools is to explore the school's website and publications, which usually provide comprehensive information about the various facets of that institution. In investigating schools, applicants should examine curricular offerings, faculty scholarship, institutional resources, and post-law school opportunities. Ultimately, if able, there is no substitute for visiting the school and attending a class and taking a tour. *Nkonye Iwerebon, Columbia*

Start with the ABA/LSAC Official Guide to ABA-Approved Law Schools, which has a wealth of information about each school. Once you've narrowed down your choices, you should plan a visit to the schools. Get a sense of whether there are people who look and think like you to gauge whether you'd fit in. *Chloe T. Reid, USC*

It's unfortunate, but the reference books are often quite out of date. *William Hoye, Duke*

Don't be lazy when it comes time to choose one from the set of schools that have accepted you. For example, don't simply assume that all big schools are more impersonal or competitive than smaller ones are. I strongly recommend that you visit the schools to see how you are treated by the admissions office and by the rest of the administration. Talk with current students to see how they feel about the school and whatever you care most about. In general, make your own decision about which school will best meet your needs rather than relying on what *U.S. News* says or on the outdated view of an alum who graduated fifteen or twenty years ago. *Andy Cornblatt, Georgetown*

You have to visit schools and talk to students. Students are brutally honest about their schools. Internet chat groups don't substitute for these visits: The threads take on lives of their own, not closely connected to the realities of the schools. *Elizabeth Rosselot, Boston College*

How Different Are the Schools?

You should visit every school you apply to, or at least those you are admitted to. Top schools tend to feature identical salaries and placement statistics, strong professors, etc. Thus the nonquantitative factors are especially important. These include whether a school is urban or rural, large or small, competitive or not. The result can be very different atmospheres at the various top schools. Ask yourself how you want to develop as a person over three years. Similarly, where the school is headed is critical. What changes are planned? What changes have recently taken place? What is the attitude of the school regarding adapting to change? *Don Rebstock, Northwestern*

They are very different. The nature of the communities, interaction with faculty, course offerings, and locations (on a campus, in a city, etc.) differ markedly. They're all much more than a simple numerical rank. *Rob Schwartz, UCLA*

Some schools have started to specialize in one or another specific field, but sometimes that's more a matter of marketing than of substance. *William Hoye, Duke*

Some law schools are continuations of undergraduate experiences: They have a small-town atmosphere and most of the students are straight out of college. On the other hand, some applicants may want something very different than what they wanted or liked in college. *Jim Milligan, Columbia*

Students should select a law school where they feel they will get the best general legal education. It is not necessarily a good strategy to select a school solely based on one specialization which the school may be marketing. Your interests may very well change in law school. *Kenneth Kleinrock, NYU*

Appendix I

CRITERIA FOR ASSESSING SCHOOLS

Few people will consider all of the following criteria to be important, but they are listed here to spur your thinking about what you would most like in a program. The most important criteria will depend upon your specific needs, but on average they include course offerings, school reputation, location, academic and - political atmospheres, school size, facilities, and teaching quality. The two items applicants tend not to weight heavily enough are the learning atmosphere, for reasons discussed in the body of the chapter, and the quality of the career services function, because schools of equal quality and reputation tend to have very different rates of success in placing their graduates in desirable positions.

GENERAL

Reputation. Is the school considered one of the best schools in the country? Is it particularly well known and respected where you would most like to work? Is it highly regarded in your chosen specialty? Are professors in that specialty highly regarded? As Chapter 4 discusses in detail, the various school rankings should not be considered definitive. Pay at least as much attention to the opinions of those in charge of hiring at employers of the type for whom you wish to work.

Size. Smaller schools often engender a friendly, family atmosphere, with relatively close contact between professors and students. Large schools, on the other hand, are able to provide large numbers of elective courses, activities, and publications.

Location. What part of the country would you prefer to be in for three years? New York is exciting, but expensive and no one's idea of charming. Charlottesville is charming and inexpensive, but not exciting. Do not ignore the fact that you are about to spend three years of your life in law school; try to spend it somewhere you will appreciate.

The location of a school helps determine its social environment. Schools in large cities tend not to foster the degree of social bonding among classmates that schools in small towns do, largely due to the lack of other entertainment options in the latter.

Where do you intend to practice? A "national" school, of course, is termed national because it is well known across the country and able to place its graduates around the country. This does not, however, gainsay the benefits of attending school where you wish to practice. A school will tend to do very well placing its graduates in local firms and agencies. (For any given quality of school, it is easier to get a job in the nearby region than elsewhere.) More than that, you will have the chance to get to know the local legal scene well. Local practitioners will be frequent guest speakers at classes, colloquia, and brown-bag lunches devoted to various employment options. You and your classmates will share knowledge about local employers based upon summer and part-time work for them. This will afford you an understanding of the local scene far beyond what you could get from a distant school, however good it might be. The value of networking, moreover, will be greatest for those intending a very local practice. (Family law specialists need to know, and be known by, the judges and other practitioners in their jurisdiction whereas international corporate lawyers do not.)

Do not be concerned about where you will take the bar exam. You do not need to be at an Illinois law school simply because you intend to take the Illinois bar exam. The top law schools do not teach the laws of their home state, so you will be equally prepared (or unprepared) for Illinois's bar exam after attending Columbia or NYU rather than Chicago or Northwestern.

The school's location will have a major impact upon your spouse's (or significant other's) employment options. A corporate strategy consultant will have a relatively easy time finding appropriate employment in a major city but not in a small town. Similarly, your spouse's educational options are likely to be greatest in a city with numerous major universities rather than in a one-university town. By the same token, your children might have a tougher time socially and educationally in a large city than in a small town, or vice versa.

One additional locational factor to consider: How important is it to be close enough to your former home to allow easy visits?

Safety. Related to the location issue is the question of safety. Be sure that the school environment is, and feels, safe. In assessing safety, make sure you see the school and its environs (wherever students spend time), and do not assume that what appears safe at noon will also be safe at midnight. Discuss the matter with school officials, of course, but do not take their comments on faith. Be sure to discuss your concerns with students physically most like you. (Your notion of a safe environment will not necessarily be the same as that held by a 250-pound world karate champion or a tiny, fragile arthritis sufferer.)

Facilities. Check to be sure the library and computer facilities are top-notch. In particular, note whether they are comfortable for extended work efforts.

Housing. Housing can be a major concern, especially in your first year. Look at the law school dorms and apartments (where married students are generally housed). Examine the price and availability of off-campus housing. Note what transportation options you will have (and their safety implications).

Mission. Schools vary in the extent to which they wish to educate legal generalists versus legal specialists, those who will actually practice law versus those who will use legal training as a springboard for another profession, and those who will practice in private law firms versus those who will work in the public interest sector. These differences can have a major effect upon your fit with a program and the students who have chosen to attend it.

PROGRAM

Term length. Long semesters lift the pressure of constant examinations and papers, but quarters make it possible to sample a wider variety of courses.

Program length and timing. Several schools offer the chance to take sufficient courses during summers that it is possible to graduate in just over two years. Michigan offers the chance to start in late May and finish at Christmas (rather than in late spring). Northwestern offers an extended, four-year program for those whose family obligations make a three-year program too intensive.

Courses in other departments. Those studying many different fields of law can benefit from courses in related areas. Thus, someone studying antitrust law might wish to take courses in economics; someone studying taxation might wish to take accounting courses; family law, psychology and finance; and so on. In some cases, this might call for doing a joint degree, but often the needs can be met through just a handful of courses, rather than adding a year or more to one's program. The problem is that many law schools permit only two, perhaps three, courses to be taken elsewhere in the university. (Penn and Michigan are rarities in allowing four courses to be taken elsewhere in the university.) Some schools, however, have brought many such courses within their own program. Thus, some offer multiple courses in accounting, economics, finance, statistics, and so on as part of the regular law school program, thereby obviating the need to take as many courses outside the law school itself. If you will want to take such courses, check to see how many are offered within the law school itself. If you will need other courses, check to be sure that they are open to law students, and that you will be allowed (by the law school) to take the number you need (and be given law school credit for doing so).

Joint degrees. The number and variety of joint-degree programs on offer at the top schools is spectacular. If you want a joint law and forestry degree, contact Yale; law and information science, Michigan; law and bioethics or city planning, Penn; law and industrial relations, Cornell. The most popular option remains the JD–MBA, which accounts for nearly half of those doing joint degrees. Joint law and master's degree programs generally require four years of study, thereby decreasing the amount of time that would be required to do each degree independently by one year. (An exception to this is Northwestern's JD–MBA program, which can be completed in three calendar years rather than four.) Joint law and doctoral programs operate similarly, cutting about one year from the required study time.

The reputation of the other degree program may be vitally important down the road. If you intend to teach law and economics in an economics department, for example, the quality of the economics degree you get may matter

---

DO NOT RUSH INTO A JOINT-DEGREE PROGRAM

Some employers cherish those having joint degrees. Thus, law schools love to hire professors with both a JD and a Ph.D. and many Wall Street firms love JD–MBA holders. In some cases, though, the value of a joint degree will not manifest itself for some time. If you are headed into a corporate legal practice, for example, the full value of the MBA may not be apparent until you are advising clients on complex matters (rather than researching issues at the behest of the partner in charge of the client relationship) or managing some aspect of the practice.

Before opting for a joint degree, however, consider whether your needs could be met simply by taking a few courses in the relevant department (or in the law school). Given that law school, at three years, is longer than most knowledgeable observers consider necessary, and most law students tune out from their studies by the end of the second year, it is not clear that adding another year of study makes a lot of sense. Indeed, adding a year of study for a master's degree is going to be worthwhile for only a modest percentage of those who first contemplate it.

Conversely, you may not need to get a law degree, either. For example, if you intend to open your own business (one unrelated to law), it would be silly to think you should get a law degree so as to eliminate the need for lawyers to help you incorporate, negotiate with your "employees," and so on. Even if law school were free, the extra two years you would spend in school to pursue a JD as well as an MBA would be too high a price to pay. In fact, if you did do a law degree, your failure to practice in the profession on a daily basis would mean that your knowledge and skills, far from improving, would atrophy. As a result, even with a law degree in your pocket, you would find yourself calling in lawyers nearly as often as you would without a law degree. A better solution is to take one or two law courses in the business school aimed at people in your position; then, as appropriate, consider taking another one or two in the law school.

more in your job hunt than does the quality of the law degree. For a JD–MBA, the MBA portion will weigh more heavily if your intended employers are in the business, rather than the legal, sector. Note that although many top law schools are ranked at approximately the same level as their affiliated MBA programs, there are some prominent exceptions. Yale's MBA program is ranked significantly lower than its law program (the same is true for NYU), whereas Northwestern and Penn have higher-ranked MBA programs.

ADMISSIONS DEANS DISCUSS
JOINT-DEGREE PROGRAMS

The JD–MBA is really of benefit to them later in their careers, when they are at partner level in a firm, for example, or when they set up their own businesses. The JD/Ph.D. in social sciences is mainly for future law school professors. *Don Rebstock, Northwestern*

Candidates should have a real sense of purpose when applying for a joint degree program. They should be able to articulate what they are going to do with each degree. My advice is to talk with as many people as possible regarding the value added of the additional degree including: current joint degree students, alumni of the program, and career services professionals. *Renée Post, Penn*

You apply to each one separately. You only gain a slight advantage if you've been admitted to one and then apply to the other. *Rob Schwartz, UCLA*

Everyone seems to be interested in joint degrees, but I encourage you to consider them carefully. You may be able to satisfy your interests by taking courses elsewhere in the university (for law school credit) without spending the time and money to get a second degree. One good way to decide whether you really need a joint degree: find two or three people with your dream job. Find out whether they have a joint degree and whether they consider one necessary—or even helpful—to their work. *Megan A. Barnett, Yale*

People wanting to do a joint degree generally apply to both programs together (although it is possible to apply to one school while in the first year of the program at another). For example, those applying for a JD–MBA apply using just the Kellogg (business school) application, which requires more essay-writing and thus shows more about them. Kellogg processes them, then we jointly arrive at a decision. If one of us doesn't want them, the other can accept them, but it's usually all or nothing. *Don Rebstock, Northwestern*

The JD–MSFS is our most popular joint degree. Admissions decisions for each are made separately, although getting into the MSFS might help a little bit in getting into the law school. *Andy Cornblatt, Georgetown*

Internationalization. Law has become a strikingly more global profession in recent years. Law firms in Europe and the United States are merging; other firms are working hand in glove across continents. These developments mirror the needs of businesses and individuals whose affairs are increasingly international. In most practice areas you can now expect to have an international dimension that would not have existed 20 years ago. Most of the top schools, though, have adapted only partially to this new environment. Therefore, if your field has (or will have) such an international dimension, look at schools' programs carefully. Do not just look to see whether some courses on international law are offered. Instead, examine whether courses devoted specifically to the international aspects of your field are offered. Examine, too, whether regular courses (i.e., those not labeled "international") include an international component.

Depending upon your interests, you might wish to do an exchange abroad (see below) or go a large step further and get an American law degree and a foreign degree, too. For instance, Cornell offers the opportunity to do two years of study in the United States, followed by two years of study in France or Germany, resulting in both a JD and Maîtrise en Droit (France) or M.LL.prax. (Germany).

Exchange programs. Those interested in an international dimension to their practice might benefit from a term at a top foreign school, one that offers the opportunity to study in another language or pursue a specialized topic in greater depth. Consider the number and quality of exchanges on offer at a given school, but also make sure your particular interests are catered to. For instance, if you intend to practice international tax law, with a specialization in French taxation, make sure the school has an exchange with a leading French law school. Make sure, as well, that you will have access to the appropriate tax courses in that program. A school like Duke has established relations with more than a dozen programs abroad. Some other leading schools, in contrast, have few established exchange programs.

Languages. Despite the globalization of legal practice, virtually no law schools have taken the initiative to provide serious language training to their students. The University of Denver is an honorable exception, offering a set of legal courses such as "International Business Law in Spanish" and "Immigration Law in Spanish." It also offers extensive internships in Spain and Latin America for students to develop the full range of legal skills—researching, writing, interviewing, negotiating, and so on—in Spanish.

CURRICULUM

First-year courses. Nearly all schools require that you take civil procedure, constitutional law, contracts, criminal law, property law, and torts. These are normally taken in the first year, although some schools require that constitutional law be taken in the second year, instead; this difference is not meaningful.

Several schools, however, are experimenting with the first-year curriculum, largely to provide a more meaningful context for the study of law. Students have often been mystified at the start of law school insofar as the only overall perspective they have on the study of law, its role in American life, and lawyering in general will have come from the odd political science course they may have taken or the reading they have happened to do on their own. Schools are to be commended for their efforts to dispel these problems. Georgetown, notably, has a special section of its first-year class pursue an alternative approach, examining the economic, historical, and philosophical foundations of laws. (Its "Curriculum B" is available to students, but by no means compulsory.)

Electives. Make sure the school offers sufficient electives in your chosen field. Note, too, whether the course offerings reflect recent developments in the field. Be sure courses listed in the catalogue or on the website are given annually. Some schools list all the courses they have given at some point in recent years, or hope to give, rather than those that will indeed be offered. (Virginia is an honorable exception, showing clearly on its website when in each of the last three years a course has been given.) Be sure, too, that more than one professor provides them, so that your education will not be savaged by one professor choosing to take a sabbatical during your third year.

Note that some schools have definite specialties (and reputations to match). For example, Tulane is famous for its admiralty and maritime law program, NYU for taxation, Berkeley for law and technology, Columbia for international and comparative law, Chicago for law and economics—and Harvard for too many items to mention.

Clinical courses. Clinical courses offer the opportunity to develop practical lawyering skills and learn what it is like to work for real clients. Internal clinics feature clients coming to the law school for help, with a faculty member on hand to supervise student efforts. External clinics are held away from the law school; a faculty member may or may not directly supervise work done there. In place of a faculty member, the attorneys who regularly work at the institution may be charged with supervisory responsibilities. Mock sessions are the rule in simulated clinics. Sessions are often videotaped, followed by debriefing with a faculty member. Clinical courses are extremely helpful in some fields, such as litigation and family law. In other fields, they are likely to prove useful rather than vital. Check the *ABA-LSAC Official Guide to ABA-Approved Law Schools* for the number of positions available and filled in each type of clinical course. Check the school's website for listings of the courses on offer for each subject.

Soft skills and law firm management courses. There are many skills essential to successful legal practice that are not learned in a traditional, substantive legal course. Negotiating, public speaking, and other "soft" skills are often critical to success, but some schools offer few opportunities to develop them in a structured class environment (rather than developing them on your own through student organizations and the like). This is a pity. Examine your chosen schools' offerings in areas important to your chosen specialty. For example, if you intend to develop a family law practice on your own, or with one or two others, you may wish to promote yourself by giving speeches to local groups. Public speaking and presentation skills will be important to your success. So, too, will be your knowledge of how to run a practice. Some schools offer courses on law firm management that can be invaluable for you. (If such courses are not on offer, they should be. It is astounding that despite the fact that the business of law has become extremely important, few schools prepare their students for the business side of practice. As a rough and ready substitute, look at the business school's offerings, but be aware that they will not focus on the law firm environment.)

Internships. Nonpaying positions can range from working for a judge to working for a national public interest organization. These placements often offer opportunities that are not readily available via classroom or proper work experiences. As with any good job placement, you have an opportunity to learn about a job at the same time as you are learning how to do it. You can make substantial contacts in your field and your firm or agency. Such placements tend to be particularly important for those not going the standard corporate law firm route. Those headed toward public interest law, for example, will find that an appropriate internship will help them demonstrate their commitment to public interest work (which is critically important in gaining paid employment in this sector).

Externships. Schools increasingly provide real-world placements for which course credit is granted. You can be placed in a private firm, nonprofit organization, government agency, the judiciary, and so on. UCLA, for instance, offers externships at organizations ranging from the Earthjustice Legal Defense Fund to the Directors Guild of America.

Technology. Whether in formal workshops or via assistance in student labs, the school should provide you with ample opportunity to become a proficient user of new technologies.

PEDAGOGICAL ISSUES

Teaching quality. Even apart from the question of what would be the best method for teaching a given subject, quality is remarkably uneven and hard to assess (especially from a distance). It varies mightily from school to school and professor to professor, yet few students take enough courses at multiple law schools to be able to render a judgment about the relative merits of the schools' teaching. As a result, the best way to gauge a school's teaching is by examining the ways in which it promotes good teaching. Kellogg (Northwestern University's business school), noted for good teaching, has a number of procedures in place to facilitate good teaching: "Professors are held to high standards in the classroom. Each new faculty member attends an orientation, is assigned a mentor, and is invited to a session on teaching techniques especially designed for Kellogg. New faculty do not teach in their first quarter, so that they may observe more senior colleagues and become familiar with the Kellogg environment. Every class is evaluated by students, and the evaluations are posted publicly. Tenure and promotion decisions are partially based on teaching quality." Compare each law school's efforts against this standard—but expect to be disappointed.

Workload. All of the top schools require substantial work, but there is still a large disparity between the load at the least and the most demanding schools. This is partly a function of the degree of competition (see below) at the school rather than the actual demands of professors. To this extent, it is under your control; you do not have to work 100-hour weeks simply because people around you are doing so. In fact, as Chapter 17 shows, you can do well in courses (in terms of learning the material and getting good grades) without putting in the ridiculous number of hours many students do.

Still, the more easygoing the academic atmosphere, the less hard you will need to work for a given rank-in-class or possibility to be on law review. Be careful in assessing workload, by the way, because even asking admissions people may mark you as someone insufficiently determined. Pay close attention, instead, at school information sessions when someone else is silly enough to inquire about it. When visiting a school, ask students how hard most people work (and note how many people are still in the library or computer rooms at midnight), but do not take their replies at face value since students love to complain about how hard they have to work.

Class size. During the *first year*, most classes will be quite large, but their exact size is of little consequence. There is little difference between a class of 80 and a class of 125 in terms of the learning experience. In order to provide a more personal, intense learning experience, without blowing the budget, schools generally have one class per term split into smaller sections (with each still taught by a professor). The size of this section can range from about 20 to 50. This size differential can have an impact upon your learning, so prefer schools that have a smaller first-year section size.

During the *second and third years*, classes taken by most students—such as corporations, evidence, and individual taxation—will generally be very large. Other, more advanced or less popular subjects will be taught to much smaller numbers. It is valuable to have available seminars in your field, not just for the in-class attention you can get from professors, but also for the opportunity to get to know professors in your field out of class. (In some fields, such as litigation, the availability of small classes will be less important than the availability of clinics with appropriate professorial supervision.)

Professors. The ideal professor would combine three related activities. She would be dedicated to teaching, and would always be available in her office for conversations and assistance. She would also be a famous lawyer (or consultant on her subject), hired in all manner of controversies. (She might also be a prominent television commentator.) The ideal professor is, moreover, someone who devotes substantial energy to research and publishing, to increase her fame and that of the school.

Although it is impossible to square the circle and have professors both be readily available and be practicing law in important cases *and* be prolific authors, a school can foster an open-door policy that encourages professors to be on campus and readily available to students for at least some portion of each week. Students routinely prefer teachers who teach well over those who do high-quality research at the expense of quality teaching. Some schools have student evaluations of professors printed for student use. You are unlikely to be sent a copy if you request this by mail, but on a school visit you should be able to get a copy from the bookstore or an individual student. Look at this to determine how students really feel about teaching quality at the school. Similarly, some schools, such as Texas, have a course/instructor survey conducted online. The results can only be accessed by Texas faculty, staff, and students, in the case of Texas. In such circumstances, consider having a friend who already attends the school access the results for you.

It is important that a school have full-time professors in your field, not just adjunct professors or lecturers whose full-time occupation is actually practicing in the field. Such adjunct faculty can provide a wonderful view of current issues and the realities of practice, but they are less likely to remain at a school for an extended period (thereby risking leaving you high and dry) and may not be available on campus for out-of-class discussions.

The greatest danger exists for someone who chooses a school because of one or two famous professors. He may be unable to get a class with either of them—perhaps due to their taking a sabbatical year or leaving the school altogether. Or he may change his specific field of interest, negating the value of having these professors at the school. It is also unlikely that a student will develop substantial relationships with these kinds of professors, though there are always exceptions.

To learn about individual professors, consult school websites, which increasingly give detailed information about professors' teaching experience, publications, current research interests, testimony to Congress, education, honors and awards, activities, and so on.

SOCIAL ISSUES

Politics. The political leanings of professors can have a major impact upon your experience. Do you want Marxist professors who believe that law is a means of keeping the oppressed people down? Do you want a professoriat that pooh-poohs public interest work in the belief that serious lawyers work in the corporate sector? Most schools have professors representing different points on the political spectrum and, of course, some professors are better than others at keeping their political views from determining how they treat students holding different opinions.

The same is true of the *student body*. Nonetheless, some schools are notably more conservative or liberal (radical?) than others. To get a reading on the political climate, examine the course catalog (are there more courses on corporate taxation than feminist views of the legal process, or vice versa?), check the biographies of the professors (noting whether they have served in Republican or Democratic administrations, the subjects about which they choose to write, and so on), and talk with students at the school.

Even if you are not a particularly political person yourself, a school's political scene can affect you. It can determine what courses are offered, what student groups are active, and whether you will easily make good friends. It can also determine whether you will find professors of like mind with whom you will work closely (and from whom a recommendation will be necessary if you hope to get a judicial clerkship or go into teaching). At its most extreme, a school can be torn apart, as Harvard was in the 1980s, by the battle between left and right.

Student body. The composition of the student body will have a major effect upon your learning experience, your enjoyment of the program, and even your ability to get desirable jobs in the future. The intensity of the law school experience guarantees that much of your time, particularly in the first year and a half, will be spent discussing legal (and societal) issues with other students. You risk being isolated and miserable if you do not fit in with the typical students at a school. Spend some time with current students or those who have recently graduated to make sure you will feel comfortable at a school.

You can determine a lot about the nature of a school by looking at the makeup of its student body. Some aspects that might be of interest are the types of jobs people have held before law school; the age range (and, for instance, the percentage of people over 30 or the percentage of married students); the percentage of women students, international students, gay students, and minority students (perhaps including specific minority groups); and the percentage of students coming straight from college. In general, the more experienced the students, the more you stand to learn from them. Conversely, the more students who have come straight from college, the more the school will resemble an extension of college rather than a professional school.

It is, of course, one thing to have a number of students who are like you in some aspect you regard as critical. It is another to see how such people are treated. If you are foreign, for example, you should check to see whether foreigners are well integrated into campus life rather than being a distinct sub-group that mixes little with others.

Competition. Although most students would prefer an atmosphere that emphasizes cooperation more than competition, that is not true for everyone. Some people are inspired to work harder and perform better in a competitive environment. In assessing schools, note that five factors tend to determine the degree of competitiveness among students. Schools that have a high percentage of old-style Socratic method professors are prone to a high degree of competition. On the other hand, the more work that is done in teams (and graded on a team basis), the less competitive the atmosphere is likely to be. If students' grades and class rank are displayed to the class and to potential employers, the atmosphere is likely to be more competitive. The use of a mandated grading curve inspires competition, since an improvement in one student's grade means another's must suffer. Last, the number of students who are flunked out of the school has a large impact. Many, but by no means all, schools try to retain every student they enroll, thereby easing student fears.

Student–faculty relations. The student–faculty ratio, at the extremes, can have an effect upon the relations between the two groups. Thus, at a school with a 20:1 ratio, getting to know professors may be more difficult than at one with a 7:1 ratio. But this simple ratio is likely to conceal as much as it reveals. For one thing, most publications consider only full-time faculty when calculating this ratio, thereby ignoring a potentially substantial number of adjunct faculty. In addition, the relative numbers of students and professors tend to have less impact upon relations between the two groups than do other factors. Most important is the attitude professors have toward students. Some schools have a traditional closeness between students and faculty; faculty routinely invite students around for coffee or drinks, join them for lunches, and so on. At other schools, professors do little more than hold periodic office hours. One determinant of the tradition is the school's geographic situation. Schools that are isolated tend to have closer faculty–student relations than those in the midst of major cities. Another determining factor is the size of the law school. Smaller schools tend to have closer relations between faculty and students than large schools have.

Quality of life. Student lifestyles may vary a great deal, of course, depending upon both the program and the student. A program in New York City may influence a student's life less than one in the country. At a school like Duke, in a small city, most student socializing is done with other students, both because the students tend to get on well with one another and because Raleigh-Durham offers limited enticement to pull students away from the law school.

Note that some schools treat spouses and families much better than do other schools. Some allow spouses to sit in on courses as a routine matter, whereas others have never heard of the idea. Again, some but not all schools include families in the school's social life and go to great lengths to help them find jobs, whether in the law school (or university) or in the surrounding area.

Be sure that your favorite activities (including those typically organized as a law school society or club, as discussed below) are available, whether at the school itself or nearby.

JOURNALS AND SOCIETIES

Law review. "Making law review" is important to many people, whether for the prestige it confers or the improved job prospects that result. For those headed into the teaching of law or work at a major law firm, making law review can be critically important. (The law review is invariably the most prestigious of a school's journals.) Law reviews select members on the basis of grades, a writing competition—candidates are given, say, five days to produce an article on an assigned topic—or a mixture of the two. (Several schools permit writing an article on any subject that might prove publishable.) If you are determined to get onto law review and are a particularly strong writer, you might favor a school that uses a writing competition to select members.

Subject-specific journals. The top law schools publish student-edited journals on a wide variety of subjects. Editing such a journal provides you with an opportunity to develop both your writing skill and your knowledge of the field. Some topics are routinely the subject of journals (environmental law, international law), whereas others are quite rare (criminal law, for instance). Even Harvard, with twelve journals, does not cover all fields.

Student societies. A rich and varied offering of student organizations can make law school a fine learning *and* socializing experience. As Chapter 17 discusses, these organizations offer you a chance to develop your skills and legal knowledge, make important contacts, contribute your newfound skills to worthy causes, and have a good time. Remember, of course, that if a certain organization does *not* exist at a target school, you can always plan to take the bull by the horns yourself and create it.

JOBS

Jobs. The more highly employers regard a school's graduates, the more job offers will flow. Specific offers depend upon more, however, than just a school's general reputation. If you intend to practice labor law, for instance, you will certainly want to choose a school that offers numerous courses in the field and has several highly regarded professors who specialize in it. You will also want to make sure other students will be entering the field; otherwise, you can be left out in the cold. A labor law firm will not travel across the country to recruit at Chicago, in spite of its high regard for Chicago graduates, if it suspects that few if any will venture into labor law.

Check whether people get jobs that you would like to have. In addition, check what credentials they had. In general, distinguish between the job prospects of those at the top of the class and those at the middle and the bottom. The top graduates of the national schools can be expected to get highly desirable jobs. The differences between schools become more marked as you work your way down their class rankings. Those at the bottom of the class at a Harvard or a Columbia, for instance, tend to do quite well, getting jobs at well-known firms and other highly desirable employers. At less highly regarded schools, this is by no means necessarily the case.

To assess whether a school's degree "travels" to whatever area is of interest to you, consider both where recruiters come from and where graduates end up working. Similarly, to assess the school's overall success in placing graduates, consider not just which jobs graduates take, but also the nature and number of recruiters pursuing graduates (and summer hires). Precise calculations, such as the number of recruiters per student, should not be taken as definitive, just suggestive of the school's success.

SCHOOLS ARE NOT ALL THE SAME

Despite the apparent similarity of the leading law schools, in terms of their curricula and what they say about themselves, a quick look at the jobs taken by recent graduates of UC Berkeley (Boalt Hall), Cornell, Northwestern, and Yale suggests how different the schools can be, at least in terms of job placement:

	UC BERKELEY (BOALT HALL)	CORNELL	NORTHWESTERN	YALE
Law firms	69%	70%	70%	37%
Business and industry: legal	2%	2%	1%	0%
Business and industry: other	0%	1%	8%	3%
Government	2%	4%	4%	3%
Public interest	13%	3%	3%	6%
Judicial clerkship	14%	13%	14%	51%
Academia	0%	3%	0%	2%
Unknown/other	0%	4%	0%	0%

Career services. A good career services department will provide in-depth assistance to you at each stage of the career assessment and job search process. Essentially all such departments now offer an opportunity to assess your own skills and interests, but the depth and quality of these assessments are not uniform at even the very top schools. The same is true regarding the following stages: determining precisely in which field, then at which type of employer, you will first work; mastering the résumé and cover-letter writing, interviewing, and "callback" interviewing processes (including those specific to your chosen field, such as public interest); sorting through job offers and negotiating for the best deal; and learning how to succeed in the first months (years) on the job.

Good departments offer presentations—and extensive one-on-one assistance—regarding each step of the process. They also offer brown-bag lunches, for instance, where you can hear from graduates about practice in large firms versus small firms, job opportunities in a given practice area, or how to apply for judicial clerkships. They should have a database of alumni that can be easily searched by location, graduating class, function or specialty, nature of employer, and so on. (Alumni, as discussed below, are potentially highly valuable in your career assessment and search as well as your career success later on.) These services should be available to alums, too, because you may need them more when you are out of law school than when you are in.

To assess a career services department, compare the programs it offers for each of the aspects mentioned above. Note what is available only on a group basis and what is available one-on-one with career service professionals. Good departments will have specialists devoted to each major employment sector. Thus, there will be counselors who deal only with the public interest, the corporate, or the government sector. Discuss the effectiveness of the various programs, and the availability and professionalism of the staff, with a variety of students.

Alumni. Alumni can be useful in providing pointers to jobs, or indeed jobs themselves. They can also mentor students while the latter are still in school, offering advice and contacts that can help establish them in their careers. In addition, alumni affect the ranking of the school by virtue of their degree of career success and also by the amount of money they raise for the school. The value of alumni thus resides in their number and their dedication to the school. It is easy for you to determine the number of alums—the bigger the school, the more alums it has. To determine their dedication to the school, look at the amount of money they raise, the percentage of alums who donate, their willingness to come back to the school to sit on panels offering advice to current students, and so on.

Local connections. Schools tend to do very well in placing their graduates in nearby firms. If you are sure of where you want to practice, consider the extent to which a local school's connections may balance the appeal of a slightly more prestigious but distant rival. Check with the local employers you most value to help you analyze this.

FINANCES

The following provides just a quick glance at key financial issues. See Chapter 18 for an in-depth discussion of these and other financial considerations.

Your costs. Tuition rates vary dramatically from school to school. Public schools charge less than private schools, even for nonresidents. Tuition rates vary across public schools, too, whether for residents or nonresidents. In some states it is relatively easy to become a resident by the second year (or in advance of the first), making the differential in tuition—compared with private schools—all the greater. The cost of living also varies dramatically from school to school. Living in a major city tends to cost almost 50 percent more than living in a small city or rural area.

The cost of attending a school also includes the opportunity cost of what you (or your spouse) might otherwise do during the three years. In other words, you forgo income and other opportunities during this time. If your spouse is unable to work at his or her profession, or must take a poorly compensated position, the differential in salary and career advancement is effectively a cost of the program. This differential will vary according to the location of schools, with those in major urban centers generally offering the best employment possibilities for spouses.

Part-time work. Much of the sting can be taken out of the cost of law school through summer employment (between years of law school) and part-time work during the second and third years of law school. You can expect to gross some $25,000–$35,000 for a summer at a top firm. The better the school and the better your grades (and other credentials), the better your chances of landing such a summer job.

Part-time work during law school is different from summer employment insofar as it can only be done near the campus. Whereas you can travel from California to New York for a summer job, if you are in law school at UCLA you can do part-time work only in the greater Los Angeles area. The salaries on offer for such part-time work vary dramatically from one location to another. In rural areas, you might not be able to earn more than $10 or $15 per hour. In the major legal centers, such as New York, District of Columbia, Chicago, Los Angeles, and Silicon Valley, you might earn $30 to $60 (or even more) per hour. Consequently, your choice of school can have a dramatic effect on the amount of money you can earn during law school. In addition, many schools will ignore what you earn during the school year and not, therefore, alter your financial aid package due to your unexpectedly large yearly earnings. Chat with the career services director, as well as second- and third-year students, to get a sense of the availability of part-time work at local firms, the "going rate" in effect, and the school's treatment of term-time earnings.

Debt load. Calculate the law school debt you will carry upon graduation for each of your chosen schools. Factor in the financial package offered to you, plus your expected summer and term-time earnings.

An average debt figure is $75,000–$125,000. If you borrow $100,000 for 10 years at 9 percent interest, you will sacrifice about $24,000 per year of pre-tax earnings to debt repayment in the decade after law school.

The amount of debt you will carry upon graduation can constrain your actions thereafter. If you have a massive debt load, you may need to work in a field, or for an employer, that you would otherwise avoid. (This can be every bit as constraining upon your career options as would be the case if you went to a lesser school.) If you intend to practice corporate tax law, you may not be concerned if your financial obligations push you toward working for a major firm. If, on the other hand, you want to do education law for a (low-paying) foundation, you might resent being forced to take a high-paying job doing corporate litigation instead.

Appendix II

VISITING LAW SCHOOLS

Visiting a law school is an extremely important part of your research. The visit brings to life a school that has heretofore been only an imaginary place fashioned by rumors, hearsay, website information, guidebook and brochure blurbs, and statistics. In addition to partaking in the usual tours and information sessions, you should attempt to understand both what daily life is like for students and whether the academic experience is what you seek. Law school visits also offer opportunities to improve your admissions chances: Knowing well the school to which you are marketing yourself, and showing yourself as interested enough in it to have undertaken a substantial visit, are two ways in which you can distinguish yourself.

WHEN TO VISIT

It is best to visit a law school when it is in session so that you can get the right feel for student and academic life. If at all possible, visit when classes are in session, but not during exam period. Attending when school is in session will give you an opportunity to interact with students, who are the best reflection of a school and what it is all about. At exam times, however, students will have little interest in discussing the school (or anything else) with you, so you will be unable to gain an in-depth understanding of the school.

Try to visit a campus on a weekday in order to get the best sense of the school. Weekday visits will allow you to see students interacting and to attend several classes. Visiting Monday through Friday will also ensure an opportunity to visit with admissions staff. Even if the school does not conduct formal interviews, you may be able to leave a favorable impression with admissions officers, which can work to your benefit. (See Appendix VII for a discussion of "hidden" interviews.)

It is not particularly important that you visit immediately before applying. Even if you visit a year (or two) beforehand, your understanding of the school will stand you in good stead as long as your key criteria for selecting a school have not changed substantially in the interim. By the same token, it is not a bad idea to revisit schools you are seriously considering after you have been accepted in order to arrive at a final decision.

BEFORE THE VISIT

Plan to visit a range of law schools. This is extremely important if you are not certain what you are looking for. Visiting different kinds of schools is a smart move even for those who think they know what they want. You might be certain, for example, that you want to attend a small, suburban law school because you had a good experience at just such a college. Upon visiting a range of schools, however, you might find that you now would be better served by a much larger environment, both law school and city. Visit small and large, public and private, urban and rural schools. Also, be sure to visit schools that represent a range of selectivity. You need to visit not just your "stretches," but also your "possibles" and "likelies."

Note that you will learn about law schools—and about law school visits—as you tour schools. After you have visited several schools, you will know what items are most crucial for you to investigate as well as how best to gather the information you need. Therefore, do not plan to visit your likely top two choices first. Instead, try to visit several schools that may or may not make your final list as a means of familiarizing yourself with the visiting process.

Keep these additional guidelines in mind when planning your itinerary:

- Familiarize yourself thoroughly with the law schools you will be visiting. (See this chapter for specific information sources.) You should be familiar with all the basic facts about a school before getting to the campus, where your job is to refine your impressions and conduct a more detailed investigation—not to learn the absolute basics. Start a law school file in which you record your data.

- Visit no more than one school per day. The amount you need to do on campus necessitates a full day, not just two or three hours. The more you value a given school, the longer you should plan to spend at it.

- Arrange meetings with individuals in areas of interest to you, whether professors, career service professionals, or financial aid officers.

- Arrange for a formal interview (if this is part of the admissions process for that school).

- Compile a list of the questions you intend to ask at each school, along with any that are specific to this school. (See page 81 for suggestions.)

WHILE ON CAMPUS

Your visit can include general information-gathering and efforts targeted at specific areas of interest or concern to you. Thus, you can take a campus tour or spend time talking with each administrative law professor. The time you have available is likely to determine much of what you do. If you have very little time, a great need for financial aid, a keen interest in corporate taxation, and you have already visited a number of other schools, you would be silly to spend most of your time taking a general campus tour. Instead, you would probably want to spend time with a financial aid officer, talk in depth with several tax professors, and discuss the school and the tax department with several students. Given sufficient time, you might want to meet with the career services department as well as sit in on several corporate tax courses.

THE CAMPUS TOUR

You can take a general tour of the university or, perhaps, a tour of just the law school. The former is likely to last up to an hour, whereas the latter is likely to be much shorter. These tours are a pleasant way to get your bearings; they can also give you the chance to size up the atmosphere of the campus. The students who lead such tours are, of course, salespeople for the school, so do not expect to get a forthright perspective on the school's strengths and weaknesses from them.

INFORMATION SESSION

A group information session is essentially a school's sales pitch. It is, however, a useful tool for gaining basic information about a school. These sessions generally give an overview of the school's tradition and philosophy as well as the multitude of academic, extracurricular, and other opportunities available there.

Although admissions officers often lead these sessions, this is seldom a time to try to stand out from the crowd in order to impress them. Those who try to dominate sessions or gain attention with too many questions that are not of interest to other applicants are frowned upon by admissions officers. If you are lucky enough to be one of only a couple attendees, however, keep in mind that your efforts may improve your admissions chances (as the next section discusses).

THE ADMISSIONS OFFICE

At many schools, you can visit the admissions office and ask to speak with an admissions officer, even if you have not arranged an interview. (Do not expect to be given a formal interview, however, unless you have arranged one in advance.) An officer might be willing to give you a few minutes of his or her time to answer questions and address concerns. Express your interest in the school and ask questions that show you to be serious.

You have the chance to impress the admissions officer in a way that might benefit you. Be on your best behavior and be sure your questions and comments show your overall knowledge of the school, your general intelligence, and your poise. Even at schools that do not conduct formal interviews, it is common for admissions officers to make notes of any substantive interactions with applicants. (For more about "hidden interviews" see Appendix VII.)

THE FINANCIAL AID OFFICE

If you intend to seek financial aid, you are likely to have numerous questions about how this school handles financial aid matters. Arrange in advance to speak with a financial aid officer; 20 to 30 minutes is likely to be enough time if you are well organized. See Chapter 18 for a discussion of what you will need to know about financial aid.

THE CAREER SERVICES DEPARTMENT

Relatively few applicants pay sufficient attention to the value a good career services department can add to a school—and to their own career prospects. Visiting the career services department at each school you visit will quickly show you which are the most able where your interests are concerned. Take 20 or 30 minutes to discuss what they offer (in light of the discussion on prior pages of what a good career services department can do).

CLASSES

Upon contacting the admissions office to arrange a visit, ask about the possibility of sitting in on classes. This is your opportunity to get a feel for the professors, students, and the nature and quality of teaching at the school. If you have time, try to sit in on a variety of classes. Consider sitting in on a first-year (core) course as well as an advanced course in a subject of particular interest to you. Try to sit in on a course for which the admissions office does not make the arrangements. Given that the admissions officers want to sell their school, you can expect them to try to route you to the best instructors. To see what an ordinary professor is like, ask students for a suggestion in your chosen field. Then approach the professor of the course and see whether he or she will permit you to sit in. Most will accommodate you without hesitation.

BE AWARE OF YOUR PREJUDICES

Many things can skew your impressions of a school for better or for worse, thereby affecting your ability to evaluate it. Therefore, pay attention to these points:

- Do not let your like or dislike of a single person (admissions officer or other administrator, student, professor) influence your overall impression of a school.

- Bear in mind that weather is a transitory matter and you might be visiting a school on the rare sunny (or rainy) day.

- Depending upon when in the term you visit (i.e., at the beginning of the term or during midterm or final exams), students may be more or less enthusiastic about their choice of school—and about spending time with you. This can vary dramatically from first- to second- to third-year students, by the way, given that each is facing a very different set of factors that will influence their views of life, law, and school.

- If you sit in on an advanced class, do not be surprised if the material and the class discussion are beyond your comprehension. (On the other hand, if the material seems extraordinarily dry, do not be afraid to reexamine whether law school is the right choice for you.)

- Remember that school officials are more likely to try to sell you than are students. Try to talk with as many different types of people as possible to build the most complete and accurate picture of the school.

- Pay particular attention to those students who most resemble you in terms of their background and goals. Whenever you encounter someone who reminds you of you, dig in. Pump her, and all of her friends, for as much information as you can get regarding what she thinks the school does and does not do well.

- Appreciate and observe the school for what it is rather than obsessing about your chances of admission there. If you focus too much on the latter, you will limit your ability to assess the school.

- Keep in mind that even though a school might have a prestigious name, it is not necessarily the best school or the best school for you. As you carry on your visit, keep in mind the criteria you have established for determining the best school for *you*.

- Remember that choosing a law school is an iterative process—as you visit and examine schools, you should learn more about your own needs; and as you learn more about your own needs, you will refine your criteria regarding which schools are best for you.

THINGS TO NOTE ON YOUR CAMPUS VISIT

- ➤ Are the students happy or glum? Engaged or apathetic? (Remember, though, that the timing of your visit can affect the ways students are acting.)

- ➤ Do different ethnic and racial groups interact? On campus and off?

- ➤ Do professors interact with students? (Look outside of classrooms, especially in cafeterias, the student union, and local watering holes.) Do professors, especially older ones, seem weary and bored with their material—and the prospect of teaching mere law students—or are they energetic and uplifting?

- ➤ What is the atmosphere like in the classes you sit in on? Are students afraid or engaged?

- ➤ Are the library and computer facilities well-used? Comfortable? Are there sufficient private carrels and areas for group meetings? Is the atmosphere conducive to studying? (Note that some students work best in absolute quiet, whereas others like to be surrounded by a buzz of noise and activity. Check that the school's facilities meet your own personal requirements for effective study space.)

- ➤ What is the pulse of the law school? What sorts of activities and events are advertised on bulletin boards? What issues are important to students? (You can discover the latter by talking to students, listening to conversations in eating facilities, and reading the school newspaper.) What is the overall "feel" of the school?

- ➤ Is there a student course evaluation booklet available?

- ➤ Where do most law students live? Are there housing options that will fit your needs?

- ➤ How much interaction is there with other departments and schools of the university? With the surrounding town?

- ➤ Does the area feel safe, both during the day and the night?

- ➤ How readily available are restaurants, cafés, bars, theaters, and the like?

- ➤ Are the athletic facilities of good quality? Available at useful times?

UPON LEAVING CAMPUS

RECORD YOUR IMPRESSIONS

Keep detailed notes of the law schools you visit. During the course of your visits, note what you can. Be sure not to let the day of a visit end without completing your written record. If you visit multiple schools on a single trip, failure to complete your notes on one school before you visit the next will almost surely cause you to forget important things about the first or muddle together your impressions of the various schools.

QUESTIONS TO ASK WHILE ON CAMPUS

Do not be merely a silent observer of a law school scene. Instead, ask the people you encounter whatever questions are important to you. Asking the same question of a variety of people will often give you different perspectives on an issue.

➤ What do you particularly like, and what do you particularly dislike, about the school? What do you see as its benefits and shortcomings?

➤ If you could change one thing about your school, what would it be? (This question is especially useful in gauging the honesty—and grip on reality—of the person responding. If the respondent cannot think of anything that she would like to change, assume that you are dealing with a shill for the school or a Pollyanna. In either case, you would do well to spend your precious time questioning others.)

➤ Which professors do essentially no teaching?

➤ Which professors are excellent teachers? Terrible teachers?

➤ How much Socratic Method teaching is there? How strict a version is employed?

➤ Is it common for students to have close relationships with their professors? What opportunities exist for students to foster such relationships?

➤ What are the most popular courses? Which courses are difficult to get into?

➤ What are the strongest and weakest fields?

➤ What are the most popular student societies and clubs?

➤ How competitive are the students?

➤ What do students do for fun?

➤ What campus, legal, and world issues are most important to students?

➤ How political are the students? What is the normal range of political opinion?

➤ What do you consider the strengths of this school relative to its competitors? (For students only: Why did you choose this school over others?)

➤ How many students work part-time off campus? What is the usual pay?

➤ What is the quality of the career services department? Are there career services professionals who specialize in (your area of interest)? (Ask the career services people what their backgrounds and specialties are.)

QUESTIONS NOT TO ASK

- ➤ Avoid asking questions about admissions requirements or any other questions to which you can find answers on your own by simply reading admissions brochures and websites.
- ➤ Avoid grilling anyone only about the school's weaknesses. Asking about weaknesses shows that you are doing serious investigative work and that you are appropriately concerned about your future, but remember also to be positive and ask about strengths as well.

SEND THANK-YOU NOTES

Send thank-you notes (or e-mails) to key people with whom you interacted. This can include students, interviewers, financial aid officers, professors, or other faculty who took time to chat with you. It is not necessary (or worth your time and effort) to send notes to people who conducted large information sessions or tours—these people are not likely to remember you and there is no reason to send a note to thank someone for this kind of routine group treatment. It is the individualized treatments that need to be addressed with letters of appreciation.

Be sure to note the names, titles, and addresses of individuals while on your visits—and be sure to get all the spellings correct. If you are unsure of any spelling details, you can always call the admissions department (for the names of admissions officers), the financial aid office (for the names of financial aid officers), the student telephone directory (for the names of students), or academic department offices (for the names of faculty or administrators) to make sure you are correct. Although sending thank-you notes will not guarantee your admission, it is nevertheless a nice gesture and will be appreciated by the recipients.

4

HOW TO USE
THE RANKINGS

— EXECUTIVE SUMMARY —

▪

Schools are routinely ranked by various authorities (and dilettantes).

▪

The rankings provide handy guides to the reputations of different programs,
but are subject to many qualifications.

▪

Consult them, but do not rely on them.

▪

Recognize their limitations
as well as their strengths.

▪

Devise your own rankings to suit your needs.

For years, the annual ranking put out by *U.S. News & World Report* has been the most important in the field. The decisions of applicants, recruiters, and even the law schools themselves are heavily influenced by the results of the annual *U.S. News* rankings. Consequently, this chapter devotes considerable attention to its strengths and weaknesses. In addition, it explores other rankings as well as data that can be used to rank law schools in various ways.

USING THE RANKINGS

The ranking of law schools is a very uncertain science. Organizations and individuals undertaking these rankings are confronted by daunting methodological problems. From an immense amount of information, a few factors must necessarily be singled out and calculated—all in order to provide "scores" that allow readers to differentiate among schools that have performed almost identically. For example, how important is it to have a library of 5,000,000 volumes rather than 600,000 volumes, and how does that compare with having a student body LSAT average of 168 rather than 171? Is the school with 5,000,000 volumes and a LSAT average of 168 better than the school with 600,000 and 171, respectively? Or is it equal to it, or worse? It is not obvious how the two schools should be compared, even when two relatively simple quantitative measures are employed. The problem is made infinitely more complicated when numerous other factors are considered, especially because many of these are inherently subjective rather than easily and objectively quantifiable.

Several bypasses are available to the ranking organizations. They can examine the opinions of those doing the hiring at major firms, taking the likely employers of JDs as the ultimate arbiters of worth. (To an extent this is correct, of course, insofar as JDs tend to view the value of their degree in large measure as a matter of what employment doors it opens.) Another possible shortcut is to examine the earnings of the graduates of each school, relying again on the market as the arbiter of the value of the JDs from the various schools. Unfortunately, these shortcuts also suffer from limitations. Some are due to the fact that an overall ranking for a school does not distinguish between how its private-practice graduates do and how its public-interest graduates fare. Nor does it take account of the fact that its graduates may do very well locally but not in another region (or country). Thus, if a school is rated highly because its graduates make a lot of money in private practice, but you intend to work as a public defender, this school may not boost your salary—or employment options—more than another school would.

SOME WARNINGS

Rankings are useful as a very rough guide to the reputation and quality of different programs. Most people take them far too seriously, however, when considering where to apply. It is inappropriate to take the latest *U.S. News* ranking and limit yourself to the top five schools in the list. The schools differ enough in their goals, programs, and atmospheres that a person who will be well served by one may be poorly served by another. To take an obvious example, a person who is determined to study tax should probably be looking at Georgetown rather than Texas (unless he or she intends to practice in Texas). Both are superb, but their missions and offerings are quite different. Georgetown offers dozens of tax courses and an LLM in tax, whereas Texas offers only a handful of tax courses.

Chapter 3 lists several dozen criteria that are relevant to choosing the right program. Not all are equally significant, and it is undeniable that reputation is critically important. But it would be foolish to opt for a school ranked fourth by *U.S. News*, rather than one ranked sixth, solely because of these rankings—if the first had an unsuitable atmosphere, had few electives in the field of law you want to enter, or suffered from one of a number of other defects that may also be important to you. There is no precision to these rankings; the same publication may reverse the rankings of these same schools next year! The imprecision and variability of the rankings is one reason for being cautious in using them; another reason for caution is that one school will be able to offer you a program geared to your needs whereas another will not.

These concerns give rise to some guidelines for using rankings:

1. Look at as many rankings as possible and consider the consensus rather than any one ranking.

2. Consider even this consensus view as only an approximation of the appropriate tier for a school. Thus, a school ranked about tenth to fifteenth in various rankings should be regarded as a very fine school, to be taken very seriously, but whether it should be ranked in the top 5 or merely the top 20 is not determinable.

3. Because you should be looking for the best program to meet your specific subject and other needs, with an atmosphere in which you will thrive, the rankings have only a modest part to play in helping you to find this program. They have little to say about which school will provide the courses that will be most useful, the connections that will matter most for the job and region in which you wish to be employed, the academic and social environments at each school, and other key factors.

4. More important than the rankings will be the research you do concerning the details of specific programs, which is discussed in detail in Chapter 3.

THE RANKINGS

The seven rankings charted below cover a total of 33 out of the 191 law pro-grams currently accredited by the American Bar Association. The starting point was to consider the top schools according to *U.S. News*, then see how those same schools fare from other perspectives. The various rankings are explained and discussed later in the chapter.

	US NEWS OVERALL	MEDIAN SALARY	PEER ASSESS.	LSAT SCORES	BERKELEY MATCHING	TEXAS MATCHING	SUPREME CT. CLERKS
Yale	1	2	1	1	x	x	1
Harvard	2	2	2	2	x	x	3
Stanford	2	1	3	6	x	x	4
NYU	4	2	4	5	x	x	10
Columbia	5	2	4	3	x	x	5
Chicago	6	2	4	4	x	x	2
Penn	6	2	10	7	x	x	14
UC Berkeley (Boalt Hall)	8	2	8	14	N/A	x	9
Michigan	8	2	7	11	x	x	7
Duke	10	19	11	12	x	x	12
Virginia	10	18	8	7	x	x	6
Northwestern	12	2	14	7		x	8
Cornell	13	2	11	12	x	x	21
Georgetown	14	2	11	7	x	x	16
UCLA	15	16	14	16		x	17
Southern California	16	13	17	14			22
Vanderbilt	16	21	17	16			15
Texas	18	24	14	19		N/A	13
Washington U. (St. Louis)	19	16	19	22			
Boston University	20	13	22	22			
Minnesota	20	29	19	19			
Emory	22	27	22	26			
George Washington	22	13	22	22			19
Iowa	24	31	22	31			
Fordham	25	26	31	19			24
Illinois	25	23	22	29			18
Washington & Lee	25	30	22	22			23
Boston College	28	20	28	26			
Notre Dame	28	21	28	16			11
Univ. of Washington	28	32	33	30			
William & Mary	31	24	31	26			
Ohio State	31	33	28	31			20
Wisconsin	31	28	19	33			

There is little agreement as to which school is the fourth best, or which is the nineteenth best. There is reasonable agreement, however, as to which of those schools are viewed as the elite. Considering four sets of rankings (median salary, peer assessment, LSAT score, and Supreme Court clerks), the following schools were ranked in the top 5 or 10 at least three times:

RANKED IN TOP 5	RANKED IN TOP 10
Chicago	UC Berkeley (Boalt Hall)
Columbia	Michigan
Harvard	Northwestern
NYU	Pennsylvania
Stanford	Virginia
Yale	

Other schools were ranked in the top 15 or 20 at least three times:

RANKED IN TOP 15	RANKED IN TOP 20
Cornell	UCLA
Duke	Southern California
Georgetown	Texas
	Vanderbilt

These rankings considered widely disparate data, yet a reasonably clear picture emerges when the whole set of rankings is considered. Eleven schools were routinely ranked in the top 10 and another seven were ranked in the top 20 multiple times.

U.S. NEWS & WORLD REPORT

Methodology. The *U.S. News & World Report* magazine rates law schools each spring. Its methodology is purported to be quite comprehensive: Each factor considered in the ranking is broken down by score for the reader to examine. These factors, which are divided into several subcategories, are: "quality assessment," formerly termed "reputation" (counting for 40%); student selectivity (25%); placement success (20%); and faculty resources (15%).

Advantages of this approach. The virtues of this approach are clear. By measuring each school on a number of bases, *U.S. News* can claim to have achieved a depth and breadth that no other ranking has. Furthermore, the ratings that *U.S. News*'s methodology produces are reasonably stable over time, with few extreme jumps and falls in individual rankings year-on-year. This is presumably a reflection of reality, as it is rather unlikely that the quality of many law schools would change dramatically in a short period of time.

Limitations of this approach. The *U.S. News* ranking suffers from two problems that face any such survey. For one, innumerable factors that might be highly relevant to you are not included in this (or any other) ranking. Thus, there is no direct measure, for instance, of the actual quality of teaching or of faculty accessibility at each school.

For another, different applicants want different things in a school. For example, George may prefer a small school with extensive student-faculty interaction and plenty of environmental law courses. Lisa, on the other hand, may prefer a large school in which she can be relatively anonymous and have plenty of electives in intellectual property. Producing one ranking, based upon whatever weighting of these two factors is chosen, cannot do justice to the needs of both George and Lisa. (In point of fact, the *U.S. News* rankings are arbitrary in the weights assigned to the various factors.)

Some of *U.S. News*'s categories are clearly relevant to ranking schools but are hard to calculate in a sensible fashion. Other of its categories can be calculated fairly easily but fail to produce useful information.

Thus, school **quality** is highly relevant to the ranking of schools and to candidates' decision-making. The problem is in measuring it. *U.S. News* uses two separate surveys—a poll of law school deans and professors ("peer assessment"), and a poll of judges and lawyers—and combines the responses. Each person polled is asked to rank (on a scale of 1 to 5) the reputation of each of the 190 or so schools. It is highly unlikely, however, that even a well-informed law school dean will know the operations of other schools so thoroughly that he or she can accurately rate many of them. This is likely to be more true of judges and lawyers, who are not even in the education business. The probable effect of this is that both groups might tend to overrate schools in their region, schools that are already famous, or those that make the biggest splash—or even those they themselves attended. *U.S. News* surveys only large firms, which gives a boost to schools with large graduate populations in New York City.

A potentially larger problem is that one critical group is somewhat overlooked: employers are not asked about their hiring practices.

The **selectivity** measure depends heavily upon the median undergraduate grade-point average of incoming students. This statistic is, remarkably, unadjusted in any way. This assumes that a grade is a grade, regardless of circumstances. At a large number of colleges the median grade point is 3.3–3.6, whereas at the military academies it is below 3.0. The rigor of courses at a community college should hardly be compared with that of courses at CalTech, but for the purposes of *U.S. News*'s rankings, a GPA is a GPA no matter where it was earned. The difficulty of getting top grades in hard sciences is generally far greater than that encountered in the liberal arts, yet the rankings do not take this into account. By the same token, a student who took only introductory or low-level courses would be considered on equal footing with someone else who did advanced course work in physics, philosophy, and ancient Greek.

Consider, too, what this measurement completely ignores. Many law schools now accept a substantial number of transfer students, but their undergraduate grades are not considered in this measure. Neither are the graduate results for those who have gone beyond undergraduate studies prior to attending law school.

THE GPA MESS

The *U.S. News* treatment of undergraduate GPAs, described in the text, is roughly analogous to the following treatment of LSAT scores:

➤ Applicants from some schools (especially the least rigorous) are given a 4-point bonus.

➤ Applicants (from all schools) taking the fewest credits and easiest courses get a 3-point bonus.

➤ Students in some fields (arts, humanities, social sciences) receive a 5-point bonus, whereas those in other fields (mathematics, hard sciences) receive a 3-point penalty.

Combining the resulting LSAT scores would produce a complete muddle, of course, but no more so than currently exists with the GPA statistics.

The measure of so-called **faculty resources** (the expenditures per student for instruction, library, and student services) is relatively straightforward; the problem is that it is of extremely dubious value. Let's consider two schools, Acme Law School and Garage College of Law. Acme charges $40,000 annual tuition, whereas Garage charges $20,000. If Acme gives $20,000 of financial aid to each student whereas Garage gives no financial aid, students at both schools will pay precisely $20,000 each. Acme, however, will be considered to have "spent" money on its students and Garage will not, resulting in Acme being given a higher ranking in this category.

Some law schools are silly enough to let the overall university administration pay their utility, maintenance, and other bills. Other law schools make sure that they are "billed" by their universities for these expenses. The latter schools are considered to have "spent" more money on their students, thereby raising their rankings. Presumably some smart law school deans are considering getting their universities to charge them mega-rents for their buildings so as to bolster their *U.S. News* rankings.

The problem does not end with how to calculate what a law school really spends on its students. An even greater problem arises from the fact that schools are ranked according to how much they spend, not according to the value they get for their expenditures. For example, throughout the 1990s Japan spent a higher percentage of its national income on business investment than did any other developed economy, but spent virtually the whole decade floundering from recession to recession. This hardly provided other economies with an example to follow. Nonetheless, Japan would have been placed at the top of a *U.S. News* ranking rather than at the bottom as it surely deserved.

The **placement success** measurement suffers from both types of problems. It is based in part upon a highly arbitrary formula. *U.S. News* calculates the proportion of the latest class to graduate employed full- and part-time approximately nine months after graduation but includes one-quarter of those students whose employment status is unknown and excludes those who claim they are not looking for employment. This estimate is obviously flimsy, but it happens to have major consequences. Schools that place most of their graduates locally find it easier to track them, meaning they will have fewer graduates fall into the "unknown" category, thereby giving a boost to these schools that is not readily available to those schools that place their graduates across the world (and thus find it hard to keep such close track of them). Also, numerous schools have hired their graduates for make-work positions ("coffee, anyone?") to boost their score on this measure.

The methodological difficulty in calculating an accurate placement success figure is dwarfed by another consideration: It is simply not a suitable statistic for distinguishing among the very top schools. This is admittedly a statistic that can be very helpful for applicants choosing between two lower-tier schools. If only 68 percent of Golden Gate University's graduates are employed nine months after graduation but 89.6 percent of Chapman University's are, potential applicants are likely to find this very important to their decision-making. On the other hand, if the relevant figures for Virginia and Northwestern are 99.1 percent and 99.6 percent, respectively, it is hard to imagine that anyone should choose Northwestern over Virginia on this basis.

Each of the other measures used by *U.S. News* also suffers from substantial problems similar to those discussed above. In addition, numerous schools have been severely economical with the truth (not to say that they have lied!) at various times. None of these criticisms mean that the rankings are valueless; instead, you should be careful not to place undue weight upon them in deciding to which schools you will apply.

MEDIAN SALARY

Methodology. *U.S. News* collects information about the private sector salaries accorded the most recent graduates of law schools. Thus, it provides the 25th and

75th percentiles (the midrange) of such salaries. (It does not, however, use the information in its own rankings.) The data for the chart was compiled by taking the middle of these two figures. Thus, if a school's 25th and 75th percentiles were $95,000 and $125,000, the median was considered to be $110,000.

Advantages of this approach. Many applicants to law school look to land high-paying jobs, so knowing where they're to be found is of obvious interest. Insofar as the highest-paying jobs are associated with prestigious private firms, which can be choosey about where they recruit, they are also an indication of the quality and reputation and schools' graduates.

Limitations of this approach. Not everyone cares about landing a high-paying private firm job, so the question for some may be whether government agencies, nonprofits, and the like value schools in a similar fashion. In other words, does attending a school favored by Wall Street firms make it easier to get a plum job with the ACLU or Greenpeace? This data does not answer the question.

Also, there are obvious regional biases to salary data: they are higher in New York and Chicago than New Orleans or Billings. There is no cost of living adjustment to this data. Neither is there an adjustment to account for the fact that students who opt for a school in a major metropolitan area are both more accessible to recruiters from that area and more likely to wish to settle there, making it all the more sensible for recruiters to target them.

U.S. *NEWS* PEER ASSESSMENT

See the discussion under *U.S. News & World Report*.

LSAT SCORES

Methodology. The average of the 25th and 75th percentile LSAT scores reported by the law schools was the basis for this ranking.

Advantages of this approach. LSAT scores are widely used as predictors of law school performance and, at least implicitly, as measures of intelligence. Given that much student learning results from interaction with and observation of other students, sharing the classroom and hallway with smarter rather than less smart students provides a greater learning opportunity.

Limitations of this approach. LSAT scores probably reflect native ability more than willingness to work hard during law school. Similarly, they do not reflect knowledge and experience relevant to law school classes.

BERKELEY AND TEXAS MATCHING PROGRAMS

Methodology. For some years, the University of Texas and the University of California at Berkeley (Boalt Hall) Law Schools have had a financial-aid matching program in place. They have guaranteed admitted applicants that they (the law schools) would match the financial aid offers of peer law schools so that the applicants would not have to pay more to attend Texas or Berkeley than to attend a peer school. Both schools still have this program in effect, although Texas has recently ceased to name what it considers peer schools for this program. It prefers the flexibility of being able to match offers in some but not necessarily all cases. Nonetheless, the chart above provides what Berkeley and Texas (formerly) have deemed their peer schools. The N/A designation is used to show that each school itself is precluded from showing up in its own chart. (Texas, however, is given the benefit of the doubt: for purposes of calculating the top 15 in the chart above, it is treated as though it made its own list.)

Advantages of this approach. Law schools are surely insiders when it comes to determining which schools are or are not their peers. Similarly, they are well aware of which other schools applicants consider attending.

Limitations of this approach. To some extent, the designation of peer schools may reflect which schools applicants consider rivals—schools they would attend if given a better financial package. Thus, a quality school overlooked by applicants might not make the list while a somewhat lesser school, favored by applicants, could.

Berkeley's list fails to include three schools that might otherwise be expected to be on it: UCLA, Texas, and Northwestern. Each might be considered a special case. In the case of UCLA, an in-state rival, it would be inappropriate to use taxpayer dollars to fight for an applicant who would otherwise attend another California state school. Texas, on the other hand, has traditionally had very low tuition so it has not offered (or needed to offer) substantial financial aid to attract applicants. Northwestern, on the other hand, was not much of a rival when the program was instituted. Perhaps it (as well as Texas, now that its tuition has jumped) will be included in a future edition of the list.

Another problem is that the two schools do not describe how they determined which schools to include on their lists, making it hard to evaluate their criteria.

SUPREME COURT CLERKSHIPS

Methodology. The number of Supreme Court clerkships for the period 1994–2007 was totaled for each school. This figure was adjusted according to the number of students attending each school, to produce a per capita ranking.

Advantages of this approach. A Supreme Court clerkship is one of the most prestigious honors to be bestowed on a law student. Supreme Court justices can have essentially whomever they want as clerks, and they are presumably knowledgeable consumers of legal talent, so the law schools from which they choose clerks are presumably where the very top graduates are to be found.

Limitations of this approach. This measure obviously focuses on just a relative handful of graduates, which means that it may have limited applicability to those graduating some distance from the top of their classes. Another issue concerns the appropriate time period to consider. The data is very lumpy (i.e., the number of clerks taken in one year is small, so adding one clerk from a given school could alter the school's rank enormously), which suggests that looking at only the last year or two would be inappropriate. On the other hand, the further back one goes the less relevant the data becomes. Also, it is apparent that the current clerks are highly influential in the selection process, thereby potentially adding a school-specific bias.

THE RANKINGS CONTROVERSY

Several years ago the deans of most of the leading (and also-ran) law schools in the country signed a vicious, and breathless, letter attacking the ranking of law schools. Because the rankings were not perfect, went their argument, no rankings should be published. (*U.S. News* was the intended target of this attack because of its predominance in this field.)

This was hysterical, of course, even in ways they did not intend. First of all, the tone of the letter was a caricature of all the worst qualities of lawyers. It was whining, outraged, and immoderate, the product of downtrodden victims. Second, it treated the users of rankings as small children who would never be able to extract value from a ranking without being misled to their detriment. (What an interesting view these deans have of their future students.) Third, the deans themselves often play up these same rankings whenever they are not about to be quoted in the press. One marvelous example: Stanford's Dean, Paul Brest (a signatory of the notorious deans' letter), upon his retirement, sent a valedictory letter to Stanford Law alums. His first substantive comment bragged about how well Stanford had recently done in the *U.S. News* rankings, while joking that the rankings were flawed insofar as they had failed to place it first.

Even though the *U.S. News* rankings are open to criticism, as this chapter amply demonstrates, the law schools are poorly situated to criticize them. After all, many of these same law schools admit a large part of their classes on the basis of just two numbers (candidates' LSAT and GPA). *U.S. News* at least has the good grace to consider a dozen inputs in making its decisions.

A more reasonable response to the *U.S. News* rankings would be to encourage various publications that routinely rank business schools and other educational programs to rank law schools along lines favored by the schools. Having a full set of different rankings available in the marketplace would presumably provide a better rounded view of the schools and lessen the impact of any one approach to rankings. Few leading figures at these schools have yet taken such a proactive view of how to respond. Instead, they remain locked in the complaint culture of American law.

In fact, there is an even more troubling aspect to the deans' conduct. They treat the *U.S. News* rankings as though they are a major, avoidable tragedy. Unfortunately, they quite miss the point. Going to Michigan instead of Berkeley—or vice versa—due to a misplaced reliance on some rankings is highly unlikely to destroy someone's life. What is tragic, however, is the dirty little secret the deans fail to acknowledge: So many people who enter law school end up desperately unhappy in the profession. Thus, the critical choice applicants make is not between two high-ranked law schools, but between attending law school and doing something else altogether.

The deans do not wage any protests about this, or write outraged letters to editors. Indeed, they do not even study the fate of their own graduates. How many longitudinal studies correlating graduates' happiness with the number of years worked before law school, the nature of that work, the field that the graduates entered after law school, the nature of their employer, and so on have the deans commissioned?

The career services directors at the schools are very clear that a substantial minority of graduates are sorry that they entered law. Why are they not on the admissions committees at the law schools? Why do the applications not require, as business school applications do, that applicants demonstrate that they have explored their career options and thought seriously about them?

U.S. News may have a case to answer, but so do the deans.

**ADMISSIONS DEANS DISCUSS THE
"DEANS' LETTER"**

Although almost all deans sign the letter criticizing the *U.S. News* rankings, many of those deans tout their school's success in rising up the rankings "food chain" in annual letters to alumni, when recruiting faculty candidates, and, in some cases, with brightly colored stickers slapped on the cover of the admissions bulletin. I suspect that at a great many law schools, the long-range plan uses the *U.S. News* ranking as the benchmark for success. *Susan Palmer, Virginia*

The reality is that they [the rankings] aren't the only sources candidates use in making decisions. The deans' letter was a bit paternalistic in assuming that candidates would use the rankings and no other information. *Don Rebstock, Northwestern*

I think it was an important step in trying to educate applicants about the rankings, but I don't believe it's had much impact as to the amount of weight applicants place on rankings. *Rob Schwartz, UCLA*

MORE RANKINGS

Obviously, the published rankings do not necessarily cover all of the issues and concerns you might have about law schools. This leaves you with room to make your own rankings, tailored to whichever criteria you deem to be most important. Following are a few of the "rankings" you might consider helpful.

DEPARTMENTAL RANKINGS

If you are farsighted enough to have decided what type of lawyer you aim to be, it would be wise to consider not only overall school rankings but departmental ones as well. *U.S. News*, for instance, ranks schools in eight specialties, ranging from dispute resolution to tax law. Besides consulting published departmental rankings, be sure to talk to employers in the particular field. Ask them to give a rough ranking of schools offering concentrations in that field.

JOINT-DEGREE RANKINGS

If you are considering getting a joint degree, pay attention to the ranking of the other program. Depending on your intended career path, the reputation of the non-law program may be the more important of the two.

JUDICIAL CLERKSHIPS

Many law school graduates want to get a judicial clerkship, some for the prestige, others for both the prestige and the learning opportunities. It is clear that Yale sends a much greater percentage of its class to clerkships than do other top schools:

Yale	51%
Stanford	26
Harvard	25
Chicago	21
William & Mary	20
Minnesota	19
Duke	18
Virginia	16
Georgetown	15
UC Berkeley (Boalt Hall)	14
Columbia	14

Northwestern	14
Boston College	13
Cornell	13
Michigan	13
NYU	12
Penn	12
Vanderbilt	11
UCLA	10
George Washington	10
Southern California	10
Texas	10

As is usually the case, however, this data is not unambiguous. Is Yale more successful in garnering clerkship laurels for its graduates, or do its graduates disproportionately seek clerkships? Clerkships are a natural halfway house for those intending to litigate or to teach—or to avoid committing to a real job for another year or two. Those intending to be transactional lawyers, on the other hand, will less often seek a clerkship because they are likely to learn little that will be of direct relevance to doing deals. Yale certainly produces a lot of graduates who would like to do public interest litigation, work for the government in litigation-related fields, or teach law. They also have a lot of graduates who are still uncertain what they want to do in the long run, which is fitting for a school that prides itself on taking a more intellectual (and thus less preprofessional) approach to the study of law than do most of its counterparts. This attracts a lot of people who want their graduate study to resemble their undergraduate work—to be a continuation of a liberal arts education.

NUMBER OF RECRUITERS ON CAMPUS

It is a simple matter to divide the number of employers visiting the campus by the number of students graduating. The higher this number, of course, the more employment opportunities are likely to be on offer for the school's students. This is certainly valuable as a very rough and ready guide. If one school has only one and a half employers per student whereas another school has ten employers visit for each graduating student, it is a reasonably safe bet that students at the latter school will have more employment offers from which to choose.

As with most such figures, however, this one should not be pushed too far. The difference between having eight employers and ten employers recruiting each student is hardly likely to be meaningful. After all, you can only work for one. As a means of comparing disparate schools, this too faces limitations. It is not clear whether a school with ten employers per student is twice as good as a school with five employers per student, or just marginally better. For instance, imagine that both you and your closest friend applied to the same ten law schools. You got into all of them and decided to attend Harvard; your friend was accepted only by Harvard (being denied by the other nine), and decided to attend Harvard. Did you do ten times as well as your friend in this situation, somewhat better, or only very marginally better?

NON-LAW EMPLOYERS RECRUITING ON CAMPUS

If you think you might want to work outside of law, you probably should not attend law school. If you remain determined to go to law school, though, you should consider attending a school that has successfully placed graduates in the nonlegal field you are considering. Similarly, you should check to see whether these employers recruit from a given school. For someone interested in strategy consulting, for example, it would be sensible to see how many of the prestigious strategy consulting firms (Bain, Booz-Allen, Boston Consulting Group, McKinsey) recruit on campus; note, too, how many they hire. If you are interested in

---

SHOULD DATA BE GIVEN IN ABSOLUTE OR RELATIVE TERMS?

One of the methodological issues for which there is no definitively "right" answer is whether to adjust data from absolute numbers to per capita—or proportional—figures. For example, should the number of Supreme Court clerks per school be given as a total or adjusted for the number of graduating students per school? Consider a hypothetical example, with only two schools to choose from. If Harvard had 20 clerks and Yale 10, but Harvard had four times the graduating class size of Yale, what would be the "correct" figures?

	TOTAL CLERKS	NUMBER OF CLERKS PER 100 STUDENTS
Harvard	20	3.33
Yale	10	6.67

A case can be made for either measurement. If you want to attend the school with a higher percentage of future clerks, you would opt for Yale (assuming that past performance was an accurate indicator of future results). You might figure that more of your time would be spent around one or another of these paragons than in a school in which they were more dispersed across the student body. Or you might assume that this figure was an indicator of the school's overall quality.

Under some circumstances, however, you might prefer Harvard. You might want to get to know the greatest number of future clerks so as to have the best network later in life, or because you planned to write an exposé of the Supreme Court and wanted the greatest number of sources. You might also believe that future clerks would be likely to identify one another and stick together, thereby giving you the greatest concentration of them at Harvard rather than Yale—presuming, of course, that socializing or intellectualizing with them was your primary goal for law school.

This is by no means the most intractable of methodological problems—that distinction may belong to the question of how different variables should be weighted to produce an overall ranking. But by realizing how a simple matter is open to differing views, you can understand just how complicated ranking schools really is.

investment banking, check how many of the bulge bracket firms recruit there, as well as how many they hire—and repeat the exercise for whatever boutique firms or specialists are of interest to you. The same exercise can be performed for whatever field or fields interest you.

MANAGING PARTNERS

The *Law Firms' Yellow Book* collects data from some 800 large law firms. The law school from which each firm's managing partner graduated is noted. The idea is that making it to the top of a large firm (and thus to the top of the legal profession) requires some combination of determination, managerial skill, interpersonal abilities, and perhaps a valuable network. Knowing which law schools these lawyers attended might suggest where such talents (and assets) are developed. The limitations of this approach, however, are clear. This is another measure that focuses on just a handful of graduates. In this case, nearly all of them graduated decades ago, making it all the harder to be sure that what benefited them will continue to benefit those who come some thirty or forty years later. In addition, the summary data is unadjusted for size of schools' graduating classes.

OTHER POSSIBLE RANKINGS

The rankings discussed in the first part of this chapter use various means to arrive at their results. They could use any number of other approaches. Nothing stops you from ranking schools on the basis of what most interests you. For example, you might choose any one or more of the following:

■ Percent men (or women, or minorities, or Asian-Americans, or foreigners)

■ Percent of incoming students with more than five years' experience (or over the age of 30)

- Number of books used by other top schools produced by faculty of a given school (perhaps adjusted by number of faculty)

- Citation index: number of citations (in the leading journals) of articles written by a school's faculty (perhaps adjusted by number of faculty)

- Percent of graduates entering a specific field (law teaching, public interest, environmental, tax, criminal, and so on)

- Number of courses in your chosen field (or percentage of courses offered in that field)

Each of these could be a valid measure for what you most desire. The first two measures, for instance, are means of determining whether you will have class-mates who are most like you—or most unlike you, if you look to learn from those who least resemble you—whereas the next two measures can be used to assess the scholarliness of the faculty. There are innumerable other possible bases for rankings, depending upon what you seek from your law school education.

CONCLUSION

It is impossible for a ranking to assess (accurately or otherwise) the large number of concerns, requirements, and questions that every conscientious law school applicant has. As an *approximate* gauge of a school's reputation, however, the rankings—taken together—can be useful indicators. Their rough and ready nature, however, suggests that they indicate the broad class to which a school belongs rather than the precise ranking it should enjoy.

Ultimately, whether the rankings *determine* reputation or *measure* it ceases to be the issue. The school considered "best"—by whatever standards—will generally attract the "best" students and "best" employers. Because you are bound to benefit as much from your peers as your professors, and are undoubtedly concerned primarily about your job opportunities, reputation is an extremely important factor to consider.

ADMISSIONS DEANS DISCUSS THE RANKINGS

WHAT IS WRONG WITH THE RANKINGS

We analyze undergraduate performance from a multivariate perspective. We consider such factors as grade inflation patterns (which vary significantly across the universe of undergraduate colleges), the rigor of the applicant's course of study, and the selectivity of the college attended. Of the more than two thousand colleges in this country alone, there exists a remarkable range of selectivity (and resultant student quality). That not all colleges are equal in terms of their selectivity and student quality is widely known, but, for reasons I have never been able to understand, an educational reality ignored by many law schools as they undertake their own student selection. Similarly, *U.S. News & World Report* (which accords 40 percent of its selectivity to UGPA) fails to recognize these contextual realities in weighing median grade-point average. *Jim Milligan, Columbia*

What is dangerous about the *U.S. News* rankings, I believe, is that while they appear to be purely objective and factually grounded, they are in reality largely subjective. First, the reputational component of the rankings—which accounts for 40 percent of the rankings formula—are purely subjective, and are based on relatively small statistical samples. . . . Second, I caution prospective students that *someone*—other than themselves—made a judgment about how much to weight each of these categories. If a particular prospective student feels that job placement success is more important than the median GPA and LSAT score of his classmates, then he should recognize that the rankings weight it less heavily. And, there are factors most students find important that are not factored into the rankings at all. How about cost, for example?

I also worry that too many students think that "the rankings" originate with some official educational institution. I have students insist that they come from the ABA, for example. *Susan Palmer, Virginia*

There are a large number of problems with them. For instance, placement success is of critical importance to prospective law students, but the rankings simply report the percentage of students employed (which could include those pumping gas) instead of focusing on the nature of their employment. The vast majority of the top law schools report over 95 percent employed, so choosing a school on the basis of tiny differences in placement statistics makes little sense to me. *Rob Schwartz, UCLA*

U.S. News is probably wrong in failing to adjust acceptance rates for class size. The applicant pool for top schools is largely fixed; inevitably, therefore, larger programs accept a higher percentage of applicants. *Jim Milligan, Columbia*

What Is Right with the Rankings

It's a little too "holier than thou" to object that since we're institutions of higher learning, it's foolhardy, misleading, and sinful to rank us. We have consumers like any other business. It isn't the worst thing possible. It is, for the most part, OK and mirrors the reality of law schools' quality. *Andy Cornblatt, Georgetown*

The rankings perform a useful function by keeping schools from becoming complacent. They need to work hard to keep their rankings. Our deans didn't sign the "deans' letter" protesting the use of rankings because they are a reality of our society and because—if you look at the groupings within those rankings—they tend to be pretty accurate reflections of how the public views the schools, which is highly relevant to the decision of which school to attend. *Don Rebstock, Northwestern*

How You Should Use the Rankings

Don't try to quantify the nonquantifiable; just get a good overview picture of the schools. *Joyce Curll, Harvard*

The rankings are most useful for applicants at the beginning of the search process, to get the lay of the land regarding what schools are considered most seriously. They can help to develop a general understanding of the law school landscape and applicants can assess their chances of admission to a particular school. *Jim Milligan, Columbia*

Most admissions folks find the rankings a bit unfortunate in that applicants take them too seriously. It's very difficult to quantify and portray a large number of relevant factors and combine them into a single measure of quality. *William Hoye, Duke*

To a certain extent, the law school world created the rankings. For a long time we all claimed to be all things to all people. There was thus a need for some reasonably objective approach to give applicants some sense of the relative quality of different programs. The problem is that applicants rely too much on the rankings, which should be no more than a starting point for them. *Elizabeth Rosselot, Boston College*

The rankings are useful in giving you a sense of the general reputation of a school. However, they tend to give an impression of precision that misleads more than it helps. They make what should be a complex and subtle decision appear very simple. *Rick Geiger, Cornell*

Once you're accepted by several schools, you shouldn't decide which one to attend based upon a one- or two-point difference in their rankings. Of course, if the schools are ranked in entirely different tiers, the disparity in their reputations may make a difference to you. *Megan A. Barnett, Yale*

Use them with caution. Make sure you understand how they are calculated before determining how much reliance to place on them. *Rob Schwartz, UCLA*

You can use the rankings as a starting point: they give you an idea of what schools will be within your reach. But I'd strongly discourage you from selecting a school based solely on a rank simply because the rankings can change rapidly without much really changing at the law school in any given year. *Chloe T. Reid, USC*

The rankings are a good tool with which to start. They offer a good way to assess the lay of the land. You can get a general idea of the reputation of a school—how it is viewed by others. But what makes a great law school great isn't the rankings.

You have to determine what's most important to you. If it's the faculty, look at the faculty rankings for student-to-faculty ratio as a start. Then delve further: examine the backgrounds and scholarship of faculty in fields of interest to you. Then find out how they relate to students, how well they teach, how accessible they are. If it's placement that's important to you, start with the rankings for placement statistics. Then delve further. Find out where students are placed geographically, what types of practice they enter, and find out how the career placement staff assists its students. *Derek Meeker, Penn*

No one looks at *U.S. News* and thinks their rankings are insane. In fact, in a broad-brush way, they're quite helpful. However, you shouldn't delegate your decision to *U.S. News*. After all, whatever set of factors they choose—and the weights they assign them—are unlikely to be the set (or weightings) you'd choose. *Sarah C. Zearfoss, Michigan*

How the Rankings Affect What Law Schools Do

The rankings have changed the admissions profession, perhaps irrevocably. What used to be a private, school-centered, professional practice has become a highly public one. Because the rankings so heavily focus on median LSAT scores, acceptance percentages, and the like, many law schools, regrettably, pay inordinate attention to quantifiable factors. At many American law schools, the role of the admissions professional has changed, sad to say, from one of counselor and student advocate to that of a salesperson or agent. *Jim Milligan, Columbia*

There are many opportunities to fiddle with the numbers we are meant to provide *U.S. News*. Do schools provide the average LSAT score, the highest score, or the most recent score? Do they give the cumulative GPA or just the GPA at the degree-granting institution? At least one school is rumored to put its low-number candidates into the part-time program, because *U.S. News* does not include the part-time program's numbers in its rankings. *Susan Palmer, Virginia*

The schools play to the rankings, of course, which then hurts the applicants. Schools now manage their yields, wait-listing qualified students or denying them if it seems that they probably would not attend the school. It means that schools now make the decisions for the applicants rather than letting the applicants themselves decide. For example, I've heard that some Midwestern schools seldom accept Ivy League candidates since they tend not to go to the Midwest rather than the coasts. Because of the way the rankings are constructed, it's hard to reconcile what is best for the institution with what is best for the applicant. *Elizabeth Rosselot, Boston College*

They give us measurable goals, and provide useful pieces of information to prospective students; however, the factors upon which the various rankings are based are not necessarily the only factors by which we would like to be judged. *Anne Richard, George Washington*

5

THE ADMISSIONS PROCESS

— EXECUTIVE SUMMARY —

Schools put enormous effort into considering each person's application.

Most schools use rolling admissions and a fairly standard admissions model.

Understand the criteria that law schools evaluate: brains, legal potential, and personal attributes.

—Remember that admissions professionals, mindful of
the need to fill classes with human beings
rather than data points, seek to understand who you are
as well as what you have accomplished.

The top schools also value diversity in their classes.

This chapter describes the mechanics of how schools make their admissions decisions and who makes them. In most cases, a school's admissions professionals will determine whether to admit you or not based upon the whole of your application folder—your job histories, educational achievements, extracurricular and community involvements, honors and awards, personal statement and other essays, recommendations, and interview evaluations. Not every admissions officer will weight the different elements in the same way, or for that matter grade them in the same way, but the *process* is consistent for each and every applicant to a school. Although the admissions process at different schools varies somewhat, it varies much less than might be expected—partly because admissions officers at the various schools talk with one another about procedures—but probably owing more to the desire schools have to be thorough in their evaluation of candidates. Schools go to great lengths to be sure they have given every applicant a fair chance.

"ROLLING" ADMISSIONS

Most of the top law schools adhere to a rolling admission process, in which applications are evaluated as they are submitted. The school begins to accept applications sometime in the fall (often October 1, but occasionally as early as September 1 or as late as December 1) and will continue to accept them for several months (usually through February 1 or 15). Applicants will generally learn of the school's decision within a month or two (or three) of the completion of their files, although there is considerable difference in the speed at which various schools respond.

Note that your application will receive no attention from admissions officers until it has been completed, meaning that *everything* that is required has been received by the school. Thus, if your second (but still required) recommendation has not yet been submitted, the admissions secretarial staff will keep your file open until they receive the recommendation, at which time they will indicate to the admissions officers that your file is now ready.

THE STANDARD ADMISSIONS MODEL

WHO ARE THE ADMISSIONS DEANS?
The dean of admissions is typically someone who has worked in law school admissions for some years. At the top schools, this generally means someone who

has had at least five years' experience as a more junior admissions officer at the same school, or an equivalent amount of time in charge of admissions at a less prestigious school.

WHO IS ON THE ADMISSIONS COMMITTEE?

Generally, the admissions committee includes four to seven faculty members who have been selected either by the dean of the law school or the dean of admissions. The appointment of faculty members to the committee is on a rotational basis. The selected professors are most often tenured, and come from all different fields at the school. The school's admissions director may sit on the committee; if not, he or she will be utilized as a consultant to it. In addition, a number of schools now include students on the admissions committee. They may be voting members or just advisors.

HOW ARE DECISIONS MADE?

There are several models for making admissions decisions. One that is commonly used has the dean of admissions be the first reader of all files. She will then immediately accept those she feels are outstanding, reject those who are clearly below the school's quality cutoff, and forward a modest number in the "middle group" to the admissions committee. The faculty members on the committee will, among themselves, come to a consensus about which of these files to admit.

A variation on this model has each of several admissions officers give a first reading to various files, with each person having the power to accept or reject the obvious winners and losers but, once again, referring those on the margin to the whole admissions committee (or to other admissions officers). In this variation, it is common for the admissions dean to cast a quick glance over the various files he or she has not been assigned, just to make sure that nothing is amiss in the process.

Another approach has two admissions officers give a "blind" reading to an applicant's file, meaning that each one reads without knowing what the other officer has decided. If both admissions officers rate the applicant as an "accept," then no more work needs to be done: The applicant is accepted. Similarly, if both admissions officers rate her as a "reject," the applicant is rejected. On the other hand, if they disagree about her, or both rate her as an "uncertain," then her file will be considered further. At this point most schools have the admissions committee decide as a group.

Thus, the role of the admissions committee is typically to decide the hard cases, generally with the input of the admissions dean or other senior admissions officer—or to add perspective to the reading of a file when one or another of its members has specialized knowledge that can help illuminate a candidacy. For example, a faculty member on the committee who has taught in Italy may be able to interpret an Italian academic record more expertly than can an admissions officer.

THE CRITERIA

Chicago has explained what it looks for in candidates: "Our task is to select those candidates who appear to demonstrate exceptional academic and professional promise and, at the same time, put together a stimulating and diverse entering class."

Strong academic promise. "We seek indications that an applicant has the discipline and ability to handle a demanding program. The overall quality of the undergraduate school attended and its grading practices will often be important considerations in interpreting the GPA."

Professional promise. "We will review the transcripts . . . to determine the difficulty of the courses taken and whether the college record has given the applicant an opportunity to demonstrate analytical skills and the ability to speak and write with precision, fluency, and economy."

Diversity among students. "We make special efforts to ensure that each entering class contains students from a variety of racial, ethnic, educational, and geographic backgrounds. Such diversity provides students with new perspectives on the law and promotes informed discussions inside and outside the classroom. We are particularly interested in receiving applications from women and minority candidates, two groups traditionally underrepresented in the law."

Other schools look for similar qualities. One easy way to learn what the top law schools want is to look at the recommendation forms they use. These often ask a recommender to comment on specific qualities or to check boxes in a grid, indicating whether the applicant's analytical ability, for example, is in the top 2 percent, 5 percent, 10 percent, 25 percent, 50 percent, or bottom half of those the recommender has seen at similar stages in their careers. Leading schools ask recommenders to evaluate similar qualities. Consider Cornell and Columbia, both of which have particularly detailed forms. Using the Cornell criteria as a starting point, and "mapping" Columbia's onto it, reveals how similar are their interests:

CORNELL	COLUMBIA
Academic Performance	Academic Motivation
Quality of class participation	Effectiveness of oral communication
Native Intelligence	Overall Intelligence
Analytical powers	Analytical skills
Rigor of thought	Problem-solving skills
Critical faculty	
Reasoning ability	

(Continued)

CORNELL	COLUMBIA

Independence of Thought
    Originality
    Imagination
    Creative intelligence
	Independence of Thought
	    Originality

Writing Ability	Effectiveness of Written Communication

Industry and Motivation
    Persistence
    Self-discipline
    Study techniques
	Industry and Academic Motivation
	    Persistence
	    Personal initiative
	    Organizational skills

Judgment and Maturity
    Conscientiousness
    Common sense
	Judgment and Emotional Maturity
	    Self-confidence

Leadership Ability	Leadership Ability
Cooperativeness; Concern for Others	Concern for others

The picture that emerges suggests that these two schools are looking for candidates who are very similar to the Chicago profile. That profile could be summarized as: brains, demonstrated potential for the rigors of legal study, and outstanding personal characteristics.

THE EVIDENCE SCHOOLS EXAMINE

	PRIMARY SOURCES	SECONDARY SOURCES
BRAINS	Undergraduate record LSAT scores	Work experience Additional coursework Essays
LEGAL POTENTIAL	LSAT scores Work experience	Essays Extracurriculars
PERSONAL ATTRIBUTES	Essays Recommendations Interviews	Extracurriculars Additional materials

THE CRITERIA TRADE-OFF

The question inevitably arises: How do admissions deans determine whom to accept, given that some applicants will have outstanding job records or extracurricular credentials but unimpressive grades and LSAT scores, whereas other applicants will have the reverse set of strengths and weaknesses? In other words, how do admissions directors trade off the different admission criteria? There is no set answer to this. There are, however, three considerations to keep in mind.

First of all, it is important to understand that the top schools do not need to make many such trade-offs. The Yales, Stanfords, and Harvards are in the enviable position of having many applicants with sterling undergraduate records, impressive work experience, and significant extracurricular achievements, which negates the need to trade off criteria.

Second, schools will weight criteria differently depending upon the applicant. For example, someone who is still in college and has had one part-time job at a restaurant can expect to have his undergraduate record, extracurricular activities, and LSAT scores count very heavily. Someone with seven years of work experience can expect that somewhat less weight will be placed on the academic measures; her extensive experience provides a great deal of information about her, making her experience a much more important indicator of her potential than it was for the man still in college.

Third, different schools will have different priorities, causing them to apply a somewhat different set of criteria, and criteria weighting, to the process. Northwestern, for instance, is taking fewer and fewer students straight from college; it values the depth and nature of work experience more than do other schools.

THE IMPORTANCE OF DIVERSITY

Law schools believe strongly in the values of diversity. They feel that a mixture of races, nationalities, educational experiences, and job backgrounds in their student bodies enhances the learning process and also makes for a more attractive group of graduates, given that employers need a wide range of potential recruits. Schools express their desire for diversity partly by marketing intensively to hard-to-attract groups, partly by adjusting admissions standards for those it most desires (especially African-Americans and Latinos). Schools' desire for diversity inevitably influences how they evaluate their applicants.

WHO YOU ARE IS IMPORTANT

Admissions officers have a lot of information about you when it comes time to make their decisions. Most applicants assume that the admissions process is devoted *only* to weighing applicants' grade-point averages and LSAT test scores and they therefore make a fundamental mistake. Admissions offices are made up of human beings, generally those who have chosen to work in a human resources capacity, and consequently they are particularly interested in admitting real human beings rather than a set of statistics. You will find it hard to gain admission if you are just so many data points on a page. Applicants who can make themselves real, that is, human, are more likely to gain supporters among the admissions officers and committee members. You should therefore take every opportunity to distinguish yourself from the mass of the applicant pool and make your human qualities apparent. The reason it takes so much time and effort to accept or reject a given applicant is because admissions officers try very hard to understand the person, not just to glance at the test scores.

THE USE OF INDEX NUMBERS

The most important differences in various schools' decision-making processes concern the use of index numbers. See the sidebar for more information.

INDEX NUMBERS

Many schools use an "index number" to aid their selection process. This number is constructed by applying a formula to an applicant's undergraduate grade-point average and LSAT score. One school's formula recently has been:

$$(4.159 \times UGPA) + (.24 \times LSAT) + 2.0 = Index$$

An applicant with a 3.0 undergraduate GPA and an LSAT score of 170 would have an index number of approximately 55.3. An applicant with a 3.6 and 160 would have a roughly equivalent index number (approximately 55.4). (Thus, each LSAT point equates to about .06 GPA.)

These formulas are constructed by the Law School Admission Council (also called LSAC or Law Services) for the schools that choose to use them. The schools provide Law Services with the LSAT, undergraduate GPA, and first-year law school grades of the most recent first-year class. Law Services then determines what weighting of the LSAT and undergraduate GPA would have best predicted the first-year law school grades of that year's class. Because the calculations are revised annually, and differ according to school, the weights accorded to the LSAT and GPA results can vary substantially.

Consider the case of three Washington, D.C., law schools. Their index formulas at one time were:

	GPA	*LSAT*	*CONSTANT*
American	4.580	0.576	20.220
Catholic	3.163	0.548	−13.190
George Washington	0.420	0.043	−5.252

Imagine two candidates applying to each of these schools. Martha has a high LSAT score (170), but a low GPA (2.64). George has a middling LSAT score (160), but a high GPA (3.90). Crunching the numbers reveals the following results for them:

	MARTHA'S INDEX NUMBER	GEORGE'S INDEX NUMBER	RANKING
American	130.2	130.2	Two are Equal
Catholic	88.3	86.8	Martha #1
George Washington	3.2	3.3	George #1

In the year when these schools had the formulas above, one would have ranked Martha and George as equal, another would have ranked Martha first, and the third would have ranked George first. In other words, the differences in their formulas produced every possible result.

The lessons from this are several. Knowing the formula a school uses (and its relative emphasis on LSAT vs. GPA) can tell you a great deal about your chances. Martha benefited from formulas giving more weight to LSAT scores, whereas George benefited from those favoring GPAs. In fact, the greater the difference between your LSAT and GPA, the more impact the relative weighting of LSAT and GPA will have. (This was true of our candidates: Martha, for instance had widely different LSAT and GPA numbers.) And yet, no school's formula gives GPAs as much weight as it gives LSAT scores. In the example above, George's very high GPA never accounted for as much as 20 percent of his score, even at the school that valued GPAs most highly, George Washington. In other words, the LSAT accounted for more than 80 percent.

That is not the end of the story. The ways in which schools use index numbers vary almost as much as the formulas they use. The devotees of easy decision-making use them as their primary decision-making tool. Those applicants with index numbers above a chosen cutoff are accepted; those below it are rejected.

Some schools use a refined version of this system. They adjust the GPA component of the index number for such things as the quality of school attended, the grading policy of the school, and the difficulty of the specific curriculum followed. Thus, someone who did mechanical engineering at the United States Military Academy (Army)—a very demanding major, at a top-quality school, with a very tough grading policy—would be treated quite differently from someone who majored in criminal justice at a local college. A 3.0 GPA for the former student would be impressive; a 3.0 for the latter would not be.

Other schools use an index number to select students for part of their class and a file-by-file analysis to fill the rest of it. Hastings, for example, has traditionally filled approximately half of its class using an unadjusted index number;

it fills the other half by looking closely at people's applications, not just their GPA and LSAT data.

A very common way to use index numbers is to consider people above a specified index number to be "presumptive admits"; people below a certain cut-off are considered "presumptive rejects"; and people with scores between these two will require a close, individualized look at their files. The files of the presumptive admits are examined to make sure there is nothing amiss—no trouble-making at college, no choosing the easiest courses on campus, no felony convictions, and so on. The vast majority of those in this category will be accepted. The same is true, in reverse, of those in the presumptive reject category. Their files are examined to see whether there are hidden talents and experiences. If not (true for the vast majority in this category), they are rejected.

Another, very common way to use an index number is to sort people's files by index number, but not to rely on the number for decision-making purposes. Some schools using this approach read all files of a given index number at one time; they are trying to compare "like" with "like." Others assign applicants' files to admissions officers on the basis of their index number. One officer, for instance, will be given the top sixth of files (based, of course, upon their respective index numbers).

Two factors account for most of the variation in the use of index numbers. In general, the more prestigious and higher ranked a school, the less it will rely on an index number in its decision-making. (Many of the top-ranked schools make no use at all of index numbers.) State law schools, by the same token, are more likely to rely on index numbers in their decision-making than are private schools. Given their greater need to justify their decisions—to legislatures as well as applicants—using an index number confers a spurious precision and fairness to their decisions, making them more readily defensible.

Behind the use of index numbers, of course, lurks the specter of the *U.S. News & World Report* rankings, which place such inordinate weight on LSAT and GPA data. (See Chapter 4 for a further discussion of rankings of law schools.)

The grids displayed in the *ABA-LSAC Official Guide to ABA-Approved Law Schools* (showing what number of students with a given LSAT score and GPA apply, and how many are accepted) give a rough picture of the way various schools value LSAT score relative to GPA.

ADMISSIONS OUTCOMES

There are four different outcomes to admissions deliberations. You can be admitted or rejected, of course. You can also be put on a wait-list. If the committee feels it needs more time in order to accurately assess a specific application, however, it may place the application in a "reserve" or "hold" category. This is most likely to occur to someone who has applied early in the application season and whose credentials put him or her on the margin.

THE LAW SCHOOL DATA
ASSEMBLY SERVICE

Almost all of the American Bar Association–approved law schools require applicants to subscribe to the Law School Data Assembly Service (LSDAS). LSDAS is administered by the Law School Admission Council (LSAC), a nonprofit corporation established to coordinate and streamline the law school admission process. All law schools approved by the ABA are LSAC members.

For each law school to which you are applying, LSDAS prepares a uniformly formatted report. The report contains information that schools use, in conjunction with the individual application and personal statement, to evaluate your file. The information contained in the report includes:

➤ An undergraduate academic summary

➤ Copies of all undergraduate, graduate, and law school/professional school transcripts

➤ LSAT scores and writing sample copies

➤ Copies of letters of recommendation processed by LSAC

The Law School Report, compiled by the LSDAS, must be received by law schools in order for your application to be deemed complete. This report provides officers with a standardized version of many elements in your file, including a summary of all academic transcripts (see below) and scores. Additionally, the report contains what is called the admission "index number" (discussed in detail previously) for schools that use indices and request them from LSAC.

GRADE CONVERSION

LSDAS simplifies your grades into a standard 4.0 system to make it easy to compare candidates. A common set of numerical values has been selected to represent the various grading systems used by different colleges. LSDAS does not attempt to assess the value of grades earned at each college. Along with the converted grades, copies of all transcripts are included. It is important to note that only undergraduate grades are represented in the index number. Grades received in graduate and other programs do not affect it.

	GRADE CONVERSION TABLE*				
LSDAS CONVERSION			**GRADES AS REPORTED ON TRANSCRIPTS**		
4.0 SCALE	**A TO F**	**1 TO 5**	**0–100**	**GRADES**	**GRADES**
4.33	A+	1+	98–100	Highest passing grade (4.0)	Highest passing grade (4.0)
4.00	A	1	93–97		
3.67	A–	1–	90–92		
3.33	B+	2+	87–89	Second highest passing grade (3.0)	Middle passing grade (3.0)
3.00	B	2	83–86		
2.67	B–	2–	80–82		
2.50	BC				
2.33	C+	3+	77–79	Third highest passing grade (2.0)	Lowest passing grade (2.0)
2.00	C	3	73–76		
1.67	C–	3–	70–72		
1.50	CD				
1.33	D+	4+	67–69	Lowest passing grade (1.0)	
1.00	D	4	63–66		
0.67	D–	4–	60–62		
0.50	DE or DF				
.00	E and F	5	Below 60	Failure (0.0)	Failure (0.0)

*Grades Excluded from the Conversion:
- Classes from which you have withdrawn
- Classes receiving an "Incomplete" grade which the school has deemed to be nonpunitive
- Grades awarded after the undergraduate degree was received
- Grades assigned no credit
- Passing grades from systems of one or two passing grades (e.g., Pass/Fail)
- A No Credit grade not signifying failure, and for which no attempt at credit was made

For a complete description of the nuances involved in this conversion process as well as the other elements of the report, consult the information given in the *LSAT & LSDAS Registration & Information Book*, provided by:

Law School Admission Council
Box 2000
661 Penn Street
Newtown, PA 18940-0998
Tel. (215) 968-1001
Fax: (215) 968-1119
Internet: www.lsac.org
E-mail: lsacinfo@lsac.org

ADMISSIONS DEANS DISCUSS
ADMISSIONS PROCEDURES

How the Process Works at Their Schools

I read all the files and send a large portion (one-quarter to one-third) of them to the faculty for a final decision. Our entire faculty is involved in reading applications; up to four faculty will read each file. Each faculty member rates a file based on the factors he or she considers important. *Megan A. Barnett, Yale*

Files are read on a rolling basis, in the order they are completed. Each file is read by at least one person (in addition to me). *Ann Killian Perry, Chicago*

We look at files only when they are complete. Two or three people screen the file and either make a decision—which I will typically review as the final reader—or, in perhaps 15 to 20 percent of cases, refer the file to the whole admissions committee. The possible decisions are admit, deny, or reserve (which means that we need to wait because we have already made as many offers of admission as we are comfortable with and need to see how many acceptances there will be). *Rick Geiger, Cornell*

A file's first reader has the option of accepting, denying, or holding the file for further review. If the file is held, it will be reviewed by a second reader and/or possibly the entire admissions committee. *Monica Ingram, Texas*

The admissions staff generally make 80-plus percent of decisions. Ten to 20 percent go to the admissions committee. *Andy Cornblatt, Georgetown*

Applications are not evaluated by our admissions committee until all required materials have been received, and are generally evaluated in the order in which they are completed. All files are read by at least two admissions officers. The Columbia system does not recognize any applicant as either a "presumptive admit" or "presumptive deny" based solely on the quantifiable indices of LSAT score and undergraduate grade-point average. *Jim Milligan, Columbia*

We do not use students in the admissions selection process. Files are read initially by admissions officers, then by faculty on the admissions committee. One or another of the readers will bring insight to the specifics of a given file, knowing that X is a hard major at that school (even though it is soft elsewhere), that grading at that school is particularly tough, or that a recommender writes very positive letters for many applicants each year. *Joyce Curll, Harvard*

After files are complete, they are reviewed by the director of admissions and then assigned to our graduate readers and the admissions committee comprised of faculty, deans, and a law student. The graduate readers read files with an eye towards looking for diamonds in the rough for which they can act as advocates to the admissions committee. *Chloe T. Reid, USC*

Every file is reviewed by at least two people on the admissions committee. If both agree that the candidate should be admitted, he or she is. If there is disagreement, the file will be reviewed by another committee member, typically the admissions dean or faculty chair of the committee.   *Rob Schwartz, UCLA*

All files are initially read by me. I will then pass certain files on to the committee for another review. There are no presumptive admits nor are there presumptive denies. I treat each individual part of an application as a piece of a larger puzzle. A careful read allows me to see how those pieces fit together.   *Faye Deal, Stanford*

The Value of Politeness in the Admissions Process

We understand that applicants are very anxious to receive their decisions, but calling and checking won't get the decision made (or communicated) any faster. Tell us once, in a polite way, if you are facing a deposit deadline at another school. It is always in the applicant's best interest to be polite to the admissions office staff. If you're rude to anyone in the office, I'll definitely hear about it. *Megan A. Burnett, Yale*

Expressing your interest in a law school is a good thing, but don't overdo it. Repeatedly sending e-mails or letters or stopping by the office at all hours will tend to be counterproductive. (You're going to be a graduate student, so having your parents intervene on your behalf is also likely to be highly counterproductive). *Rob Schwartz, UCLA*

Composition of the Admissions Committee

Our committee includes professors and faculty. The committee routinely has third-year student members, who review files and make recommendations on admission.   *Monica Ingram, Texas*

There are five faculty members, the dean of financial aid, and myself on the admissions committee. There are also two students on the committee who are involved in policy issues but do not read applicants' files due to privacy concerns. *Sarah C. Zearfoss, Michigan*

The committee consists of me and sometimes the dean of students, four to six faculty members, and several students. The students have input on matters of policy but are not involved in actual file review for reasons of confidentiality. *Rick Geiger, Cornell*

We have faculty, current students, and admissions professionals on the committee. *Rob Schwartz, UCLA*

All of the members of the admissions committee are admissions professionals. *Todd Morton, Vanderbilt*

The Use of Index Numbers

We don't use an index formula for any purpose whatsoever. We read every file. *Kenneth Kleinrock, NYU*

We have an index based on Law Services' regression analysis, which takes into account the correlation between incoming students' GPAs and LSAT scores and their grades in law school. While this is the single best predictor of first-year performance, it is too rough a gauge to rely on very heavily and is always evaluated in the context of the full range of information contained in the file. *Todd Morton, Vanderbilt*

We calculate an index number, but each file is individually read and numerous other factors are considered. Our very wide range of LSAT scores (25th to 75th percentile) indicates that we look at many factors beyond the index number. *Rob Schwartz, UCLA*

There are no index numbers or formulas used in our decisions. I would say that, in general terms, GPA is roughly equal to one-third of the decision (by the way, there are multiple components to a GPA), LSAT is one-third, and personal and other factors are one-third. If each applicant is trying to jump over a bar, the GPA and LSAT together serve to set the height of the bar: The rest of the application needs to be however good or OK to get over the bar at that height. Everybody gets to jump; everybody has to jump. *Andy Cornblatt, Georgetown*

We have no automatic admits. Ninety-ninth percentile LSAT and top GPAs are still not automatic admits. *Faye Deal, Stanford*

Although we do use index numbers, we make subjective adjustments to them. For engineering and science courses, for example, we expect lower GPAs. Thus a 3.6 in Political Science is comparable to a 3.2 or 3.3 in Engineering. People who attended the top colleges get a little added "star"—although you can't quantify it—because they have faced tougher competition. *Don Rebstock, Northwestern*

We don't use an index anymore. An index can become a tool of convenience. It's especially problematic regarding GPAs. Taking GPAs at face value doesn't make sense given that some schools suffer from varying degrees of grade inflation, plus applicants follow very different curriculums. We want to take into account the breadth, depth, and rigor of each applicant's curriculum. *Derek Meeker, Penn*

We used to use an index number to sort files, but we no longer do. *Susan Palmer, Virginia*

The process is driven by the index numbers. We separate candidates into three groups on the basis of their numbers. The top group is assumed to be admissible. We read their file primarily to see if something is wrong. For example, did they take only soft courses. We examine their personal statements and recommendations, looking less to see if they are academically qualified than to see if there is some other reason to deny them. The bottom group is assumed to be inadmissible, unless something special is found in their applications. The middle group is where we put much of our effort. We look here to diversify our class in terms of geography (American and international), undergraduate major, race, ethnicity, and religion.   *Elizabeth Rosselot, Boston College*

WHAT DIVERSITY MEANS TO THEIR SCHOOLS

I try to craft a class that is balanced along numerous dimensions: political ideology, socioeconomic status, ethnicity, age, gender, geographic origin, undergraduate school and focus, professional interest (type of law to be studied and practiced), type of work experience, international (versus just domestic) experience (whether study, work, or origin), and more.   *Susan Palmer, Virginia*

When you craft a class you have to think of diversity in its broadest sense: geographic, cultural, ethnicity, work experience, socioeconomic background, undergraduate major, and so on. The objective is to seat a class where there is going to be a dynamic and engaging classroom conversation.   *Renée Post, Penn*

Diversity for us incorporates ethnic and gender diversity, sexual orientation, and many other things that make people unusual and interesting, thus enriching our educational environment. We look for candidates who reflect the broad and rich diversity of our society. For instance, one who grew up in a military environment or one who worked in an unusual capacity after college or one who has overcome personal adversity would all constitute diversity in our class. *Chloe T. Reid, USC*

We are committed to diversity, with "diversity" defined broadly. We seek to recruit individuals of different ages, backgrounds, and professional experiences, as well as individuals who have overcome personal hardships and challenges. Thus, we have people who have been out of college ten, twenty, or thirty years mixed in with students coming straight from undergrad. For us, diversity means a great deal more than just a matter of race and ethnicity.   *Anne Richard, George Washington*

THE VALUE OF DIVERSITY

Because students learn as much from each other as from professors and casebooks, it's important that we have people with diverse knowledge and experiences in the class.   *Megan A. Barnett, Yale*

The law school classroom isn't a lecture environment. If it were, it wouldn't matter who will sit next to you. Instead, there's lively discussion and debate, challenge-and-defend. People approach things very differently according to who they are and what they've experienced, so the more we can put different types of people in a classroom, the better the resulting discussions will be and the more each person will learn. *Susan Palmer, Virginia*

Having a diverse student body is unquestionably an important part of law school pedagogy—it's valuable to have interesting, different voices in the classroom. Diversity in this sense encompasses a large number of factors; it's by no means limited to just race or ethnicity. *Sarah C. Zearfoss, Michigan*

We want people from all over the country, in part to spread our reputation across the country. *Don Rebstock, Northwestern*

Law students can learn as much from their classmates as from faculty. That learning is maximized when a great depth and breadth of backgrounds is present. Study groups are great when they have a twenty-two-year-old and a forty-two-year-old working together. One of the advantages of attending a school with both a full-time and a part-time program is that the latter ensures there are a large number of established professionals in classes. *Anne Richard, George Washington*

The reality of law school is that much of the learning occurs through the discussion and exchange of ideas. Having a wide range of talent and experience in the class is highly desirable. The benefit of challenging others' beliefs, and having your own challenged, is heightened when your classmates have had substantially different life and work experiences. *Renée Post, Penn*

6

THE APPLICATION TIMETABLE

— EXECUTIVE SUMMARY —

Apply as early as you can consistent with doing
the best possible application.

The top law programs basically use one type of admissions decision format, the "rolling admissions" cycle. With rolling admissions, officers evaluate applicants on a "first-come, first-served" basis. A number of top schools modify this basic format by considering the strongest applications (read: those with the strongest index numbers) first, and then so on down the line, or by offering an Early Application option to applicants. Early Application policies grant early notification of decisions to those applying by, say, November 1. For almost all schools, there is a cutoff date after which no new applications will be read. Be aware that this comes as early as January 15 for some schools.

WHEN SHOULD YOU APPLY—EARLY OR LATE IN AN APPLICATION CYCLE?

The application cycle refers to the period of time during which a school accepts applications for a given class. In other words, a school might accept applications from October 1 through February 15 for the class beginning in September. This raises an important question. Should you apply early (in November, for example) or late (in January or February) if you wish to maximize your chances of getting in?

WHAT ARE THE BENEFITS OF APPLYING EARLY IN THE APPLICATION CYCLE?

There are several benefits to applying early in the application cycle. Assuming that the application is well written, an early application suggests that you are well organized. It also suggests that you are serious about getting into law school rather than applying on a whim. Another benefit can accrue if the school underestimates the number of applications, or quality of applicants, this application season will bring it. If this is the case, early applicants will have the bar over which they must leap set lower than will later applicants.

Certain types of applicants, of course, can benefit (from applying early) more than others. If you are a "cookie-cutter" candidate, with excellent credentials but no unusual qualities or experiences, your file will be less likely to inspire yawns if yours is one of the first of its kind read. For example, the person who is applying direct from college, a political science major with a junior semester abroad in England, will certainly wish to apply very early. A second type of candidate who stands to benefit from applying early is someone who has a complicated message and who therefore must give the admissions committee the time and mental energy to read his or her application carefully. Admissions committees tend to lack this time and lose energy as the application season progresses.

BINDING VERSUS NONBINDING EARLY DECISION

Numerous schools now offer a so-called early decision option: Apply, for example, by November 1 and you will be notified of the decision by mid-December. Most of these policies differ little from regular admissions insofar as the acceptance is *nonbinding:* Successful candidates are free to keep open their already submitted applications to other schools or, indeed, to apply to additional schools in the future. Several schools, however, have instituted early-decision policies similar to those used at the undergraduate level. These require that accepted candidates immediately withdraw applications to other schools and forgo applying to any additional schools—upon pain of losing their early acceptance. In other words, these programs are *binding*.

The nonbinding programs are well worth noting. Applying early, as described above, offers an improved chance of admission under many circumstances. In addition, early notification for the successful candidate may eliminate the stress of waiting to hear from schools and the need to apply to a greater number of schools, thereby potentially saving time, effort, and money.

Most of the binding programs sweeten the pot a bit more by giving a slight admissions edge to those applying early decision. Does this mean that if you know you want to attend, say, Columbia, you should automatically apply early decision? No. If financial aid will be a prerequisite for enrolling at a given school, apply either under the regular application or early action (if available) regimes. Do not apply for a binding early decision because you may end up locked into a school that will not give you the necessary aid. This will become apparent only when the financial aid awards are announced, which is after the application deadlines of other programs.

Whether applying early action, early decision, or just early in the regular application process, note that you may need to have taken the LSAT no later than the prior June.

SOME SCHOOLS OFFERING EARLY *APPLICATION* OPPORTUNITIES

	APPLICATIONS DUE	NOTIFICATION SENT	BINDING?
Boston College	Nov. 1	Mid-Dec.	No
Cornell	Nov. 1	Late Dec.	No
Fordham	Oct. 15	Dec. 15	No
Georgetown	Nov. 1	Dec. 15	No
Minnesota	Nov. 15	Dec. 31	No
Notre Dame	Nov. 1	Dec. 15	No
NYU	Nov. 15	Late Dec.	No
Texas	Nov. 1	Late Jan.	No
Virginia	Nov. 15	Dec. 17	No

SOME SCHOOLS OFFERING EARLY *DECISION* OPPORTUNITIES			
	APPLICATIONS DUE	NOTIFICATION SENT	BINDING?
Chicago	Dec. 1	End Dec.	Yes
Columbia	Nov. 15	Late Dec.	Yes
George Washington	Dec. 15	Jan. 15	Yes
Hastings	Nov. 15	Late Dec.	Yes
Illinois	Oct. 31	Dec. 15	Yes
Michigan (Summer term only)	Nov. 15	Mid-Dec.	Yes
Penn	Nov. 1	Dec. 17	Yes

Note that early decision policies and dates change substantially year on year, so check with each school of interest to you what their policies are for this year.

For example, if you left college after your sophomore year to become a stage actress for five years—only to decide that what you *really* wanted to do was finish your degree and become a welfare counselor (your current career), your unique and complex profile needs special attention. Someone in this category should definitely apply early to ensure that his or her application is given appropriate consideration. (International students should seek to apply as early as possible because international credentials generally add complexity to their applications.)

WHAT ARE THE BENEFITS OF APPLYING LATE IN THE APPLICATION CYCLE?

There is only one substantial benefit to applying late in the cycle: An applicant has the opportunity to continue to build her credentials during the few months involved. This can be significant for someone with the potential to transform her application. An applicant who expects to finish a major project—and is hoping to achieve impressive results—might wish to apply after the project is finished rather than before. This could provide wonderful material for an optional essay or a glowing recommendation. Similarly, someone still in college who expects fall semester grades to add substantially to the application's appeal should consider waiting to apply until the grades are posted.

A second potential benefit can occur if the school has misjudged its popularity and finds that fewer good applicants have applied than it expected earlier in the cycle, resulting in reduced admissions criteria for those applying later. This is an unpredictable factor and not likely to happen to any substantial degree, however, particularly at the very top schools.

SO, WHAT SHOULD YOU DO?

Most people will benefit, if only slightly, by applying early in the admissions cycle. In general, the most important timing criterion is to get the application done well as soon as is practicable. The earlier it is started, the more opportunity there is to rewrite and reconsider, to allow recommenders to finish their work—and even to have others help out by reading the finished product. Plus, aiming to apply in the latter half of the cycle can kill your chances if something goes wrong, because you may lack the time to set it right. Thus, the only group that should purposely apply late in the cycle consists of those who can substantially improve their credentials in the meantime.

So, unless you are in the small minority expecting such credential improvement, apply as soon as you can finish a truly professional application.

HOW LONG WILL IT TAKE TO DO YOUR APPLICATION?

Most applicants underestimate the amount of time that a good application requires, thinking that they can do one in a long weekend or two. The reality is that many of the necessary steps have a long lag built into them. For example, the process of approaching a recommender, briefing her on what you want done, giving her time to do a good recommendation for you, and ensuring that she submits it on time calls for months rather than days of advance notice. This is all the more true when you apply to eight or ten schools rather than one; you have more application forms to get, more essays to write, and more recommendations to request. Although work does not increase proportionally with the number of applications, the increased complexity as well as the number of additional things you need to do will inevitably increase your efforts.

The application process should start at least one and a quarter years in advance of when you would like to start law school. Thus, if you wish to start a program in September, you should start work in May of the preceding year. This may sound excessive, but the timetable in this section makes it clear that this is an appropriate time to get serious about the process. One of the reasons this process takes so long is that schools generally require that applications be submitted six to seven months (at the very minimum) in advance of the start of the program, meaning that you will have about ten months to complete the process if you start at the suggested time.

Starting the application process late, or failing to work seriously at it until deadlines approach, leads to the typical last-minute rush and the inevitable poor marketing job. It could also mean that by the time your application gets to the committee, they have very few spots left to fill. This book presents an enlightened approach devoted to the idea that applicants can dramatically improve their admission chances if they do a professional job of marketing themselves. This timetable is meant to reinforce the message that time is required for a successful marketing effort.

It is useful to establish your own timetable for applying. Ideally, you will be able to start about 15 months before you begin your JD program. Do not panic if you can't, because many people will, like you, need to condense their work efforts. It is useful, however, to make sure you use whatever time you have to your greatest advantage. Be sure you note the dates that are fixed and immutable:

- LSAT (and TOEFL) registration deadlines and test dates
- Application deadlines themselves

APPLICATION TIMETABLE

The following is an appropriate schedule for someone applying to schools that begin in September, with application deadlines in February. It is intended not as an exact time line for you to follow, but rather as an illustration of the tasks and deadlines you will want to track.

EARLY SPRING

More than 15 months in advance of the program, you should:

- Start considering specifically what you want from a law program, and whether a law degree is indeed appropriate.
- Develop a preliminary list of appropriate schools. Read several of the better guides, look at the most recent rankings printed in the leading law and popular magazines, scrutinize the course catalogues and websites of the schools themselves, and talk with people knowledgeable about the schools.
- Examine several schools' application forms, even if they are a year out of date, to see what the application process will involve.
- Consider who should write recommendations for you (and be sure you treat them particularly well from now on).
- Start putting together a realistic financial plan to pay for school. Research financial aid sources and your likelihood of qualifying for aid. (Identify necessary forms to be completed and their deadline dates.)
- Register for the June LSAT (and TOEFL) exam.

- Consider how you will prepare for the LSAT. Start by getting sample tests from Law Services and subjecting yourself to a sample exam under realistic conditions. If you are not a strong standardized test taker, are unfamiliar with the exam, or just want to save yourself the bother of preparing on your own, figure out which test preparation course you will take and when it will be available. International students will want to do the same regarding the TOEFL exam.

- Start filling out the Personal Organizer in Appendix IV to get a jump on the essay writing. Glance at the chapters covering what the schools want and how to write the essays so you have some idea of what will be required.

- Start planning school visits.

JUNE

- Take the LSAT.

- Read the chapters in this book regarding the essay questions, and the essay examples in Part V.

JULY

- Register for the September LSAT if you are unsatisfied with your June score.

- Get an e-mail account that will last through the whole application cycle, so that schools have an assured means for contacting you.

AUGUST

- Develop a basic positioning statement; write a preliminary essay regarding where you are headed and why you want a JD. Determine appropriate topics for additional essays.

- Start visiting school campuses based upon a "short list" of preferred schools.

- Register for LSDAS, notifying them of the schools you will definitely be applying to.

AUGUST/SEPTEMBER

- Take the LSAT again (if necessary).

- Request that transcripts from the relevant schools be sent to LSDAS.

- Establish a file folder system for each school and note specific deadlines for each.

■ Approach recommenders. (Assume the average one will take at least one month to submit the recommendations.) The more time you give a recommender, the more willing he will be to support you—and you do not want to get off on the wrong foot here.

■ Revise your essays. Have a friend (or your consultant) read them over.

OCTOBER/NOVEMBER

■ Attend law school forums.

■ Submit completed applications.

■ Confirm that your recommenders sent the necessary letters and forms.

■ Submit applications for financial aid from third-party institutions (i.e., sources other than the schools themselves).

■ Request interviews at schools that offer them. Prepare for them by reading Chapter 13 and by staging mock interviews with other applicants and friends.

DECEMBER/JANUARY

■ Submit loan applications (for school loans) and any forms necessary for institutionally based scholarships or assistantships.

■ Thank your recommenders.

■ Contact schools that have not yet acknowledged your complete file.

ONCE YOU HAVE BEEN ACCEPTED (OR REJECTED)

■ Notify your recommenders of what has happened, and tell them what your plans are. Thank them again for their assistance, perhaps by giving them a small gift.

■ Notify the schools of your acceptance or rejection of their admissions offers, and send in your deposit to your school of choice.

■ If you have not gotten into your desired school, what should you do? Consider going to your second choice, or perhaps reapplying in the future. (See the discussion in Chapter 14.)

AUGUST/SEPTEMBER

■ Enroll.

Each point made above is discussed in detail elsewhere in this book; refer to the in-depth discussions as appropriate. The timing set out in this schedule is of necessity approximate, since everyone's style of working and personal circumstances will vary. For example, if you are working in a liquified natural gas facility on the north shore of Sumatra, you will probably have to allow more time for most of the steps listed here. Using this schedule as a starting point, however, should give you a good idea of the sequence to follow, as well as the approximate timing. It should also go without saying that doing things in advance is always a good idea.

Special Notes for International Students: The application deadlines for the standardized exams (LSAT and TOEFL) are approximately two months in advance of the actual test date. Failure to observe deadlines will result in either an increased fee or the need to take the exam on a later date. LSAT test preparation is not readily available outside the United States, so check carefully to determine where and when you can take a course. Because you must provide official translations or transcripts, recommendations, and the like, you should allow extra time. The slowness and lack of reliability of international mail should also be factored into your timetable, both for tests and for the other elements of the application process.

Also notify the school you have chosen to attend as early as possible so that you can begin the student visa application process. Depending upon your nationality and individual circumstances, this process may be either short and simple or lengthy and complicated.

WHERE ARE THINGS MOST LIKELY TO GO ASTRAY?

You should be aware of three problem areas: (1) Your recommenders are busy people who, despite their best intentions, are all too likely to need prodding to get the recommendations turned in on time, especially if they elected to write them themselves. As Chapter 12 suggests, you will want to make their job as easy as possible, and then stay on top of the situation. (2) Your essay writing is all too likely to fall behind schedule, leading to last-minute rushing and poor writing. Start the whole essay writing process early and continue to give yourself time, on a regular basis, to work on them. You must be disciplined about this if you want to maximize your chances. (3) You may not get the LSAT score you expect the first time you take the test. You will be unable to retake the exam if there are no more LSAT administrations sufficiently in advance of your application deadlines.

ADMISSIONS DEANS DISCUSS APPLICATION TIMING

EARLY DECISION

There are three methods of applying to Georgetown. The first is regular admission, with a February 1 deadline. The second and third (Early Action and Early Decision) are both early admission; both have November 1 deadlines, with the file to be completed by December 1, and notification from us by mid-December. We encourage you to apply early. It gives you an admissions advantage. In addition, we can take more time to evaluate your file carefully because we are not as swamped during this period as we are later in the admissions cycle. Early Action is non-binding, whereas Early Decision is binding. If you are 100 percent sure that you want an "exclusive relationship" with Georgetown, apply Early Decision. (There is a slight additional advantage to applying Early Decision, since we are naturally more interested in those who definitely want to attend Georgetown than those who are uncertain.) If you are only 98 percent sure that you want an exclusive relationship, however, apply Early Action to give yourself the chance to change your mind. *Andy Cornblatt, Georgetown*

Penn Law's Early Decision option is designed for applicants who have thoroughly researched their law school options and determined that Penn Law is clearly their first choice. Penn Law's Early Decision program is binding. Applicants who wish to be considered for Early Decision must commit to matriculate at Penn if admitted. If admitted, you must withdraw your applications from all other law schools and refrain from initiating new applications. *Renée Post, Penn*

We now offer a binding Early Decision program. Those applying by December 15 through our Early Decision process, and who are admitted through this process, are guaranteed a full-tuition scholarship. *Anne Richard, George Washington*

We have a non-binding early application rather than Early Decision program. Those who apply by November 15 we try to give a decision by December 15. This helps with applicants' planning. *Chloe T. Reid, USC*

Columbia has a binding Early Decision program. The candidate who should apply early is one who has thought very carefully about the options for law school and has decided that Columbia is his or her first choice. By applying early, the candidate is signaling his or her desire to attend Columbia above all other institutions, which provides some strategic, though not significant, advantage in the admissions process. *Nkonye Iwerebon, Columbia*

Applying for an Early Decision, which is binding, is a clear indication that Chicago is your first choice. This can only help you. *Ann Killian Perry, Chicago*

For our summer-start program only, we offer an Early Decision option. Most of the people applying to this have Michigan as their first (or only) choice, so the biggest liability of an Early Decision option is thereby limited. We won't extend it to the regular fall program, though, since the negative aspects of forcing some-one to commit to just one school choice loom larger than the advantage of early certainty. *Sarah C. Zearfoss, Michigan*

Our (nonbinding) early action plan is very popular; out of 4,000 applications last year, 1,000 were Early Action. Applicants who complete their file by November get a decision by mid-December. This gives applicants who really like Cornell a chance to test the waters. However, we do not give an admissions advantage to early action candidates. *Rick Geiger, Cornell*

WHEN APPLICATIONS ARE RECEIVED

We get about two thousand applications in the last two weeks before our Febru-ary 1 deadline. *Andy Cornblatt, Georgetown*

With the increased volume of applications, it is particularly sensible to get your file in early. We send an e-mail out once the file is completed; it is up to the can-didate to keep on top of the process to make sure that there has been no holdup with the LSDAS report and that the letters of recommendation are sent in on time. *Ann Killian Perry, Chicago*

We receive about 25 percent of applications by the end of December. The vast majority of applications are received in January. Since we are on rolling admis-sions, it does make sense to apply early. *Chloe T. Reid, USC*

By far the strongest applications come in before Christmas. The pool gets dra-matically weaker as time goes on. You do yourself a disservice by applying late in the season, let alone in the last week (when we receive some 900 of 5,500 applications). *Sarah C. Zearfoss, Michigan*

The earlier you submit an application, the better. A real problem for late appli-cants is that they may not get their decision until late April or early May. Keep in mind that even if you submit your application on time, there are a number of other documents that need to make their way into your file (your LSDAS report, LSAT score, recommendations), so it may be another 4–6 weeks before we can even begin to review it. *Megan A. Barnett, Yale*

We get about half of our applications by January 1, the rest by our deadline of February 15. *Don Rebstock, Northwestern*

We have really encouraged applicants to get their application in by November 15. We have thus been able to advance our review process by two or three weeks. This year we received almost half of our applications by December 1. *Edward Tom, Boalt Hall (Berkeley)*

Over 20 percent of our applicants apply in the last week. *William Hoye, Duke*

THE LENGTH OF TIME IT TAKES TO RENDER A DECISION

We generally mail decisions within one and a half to two months; one month is the minimum.   *Don Rebstock, Northwestern*

We try hard to get decisions out in six to eight weeks.   *Chloe T. Reid, USC*

THE BENEFITS OF APPLYING EARLY IN THE REGULAR ADMISSIONS CYCLE

There can be benefits to applying early. For one thing, you may hear from us early on. For another, if your file turns out to be incomplete, we can notify you that a key piece of information is missing.   *Michael Rappaport, UCLA*

The standard for admission to Cornell doesn't change over time, but it's still beneficial for a candidate to know what his/her situation is early in the process.
Rick Geiger, Cornell

The benefit to applying early is that we run out of space near the end of the process, so people who would have been admitted only make it onto the wait list. There are also important financial aid considerations. We run out of our limited funds before all people have been admitted.   *Don Rebstock, Northwestern*

I think it's a good idea to apply early. When you do, you give me more time to examine your file. In general, admissions people are fresher earlier in the season. Things tend to get compressed towards the end.   *Edward Tom, Boalt Hall (Berkeley)*

The more marginal people's numbers, the longer they should give us to consider their files. For one thing, they are likely to have their folders handed to second and third readers. For another, we are more likely to give the benefit of the doubt to those who have been professional, organized, and on time (versus those who have shown up at the last minute).   *William Hoye, Duke*

There are several benefits to applying early in the process. We are fresher readers early on and more likely to take a generous view. If you are a typical applicant—a poli-sci major who did a semester at LSE—it helps if you're the first one of these we see. If financial aid is an issue, the sooner you're admitted, the more likely you are to get aid. In addition, you can visit schools before deposits are due if you are accepted early on. You basically buy yourself time by applying earlier.   *Elizabeth Rosselot, Boston College*

7

COLLEGE PRE-LAW ADVISING

— EXECUTIVE SUMMARY —

▪

Numerous factors are pushing college pre-law advising to new levels of professionalism, including:

—Increased sophistication of the application process

—Student expectations

▪

This greater professionalism is developing at uneven rates, constrained in part by available resources.

▪

Thus, some college pre-law advisors now offer sophisticated help in choosing and applying to law schools.

—Some go even further and help students evaluate law as a career option.

▪

To get the most out of your college pre-law advising service:

—Start early

—Learn what is on offer

—Also learn the individual strengths of your advisor(s)

THE NEW WORLD OF PRE-LAW ADVISING

College pre-law advising is in the midst of a revolution. In the old days, applying to law school was unsophisticated and undemanding. Colleges could therefore get away with an informal effort, often consisting of an undergraduate constitutional law professor doing little more than being available to discuss the field of law or mentioning to seniors in his or her class that LSAT and application deadlines were approaching.

Those days are gone, for a host of reasons. Applying to law school is, as this book demonstrates, a sophisticated undertaking. By the same token, many college students are more reluctant than their predecessors to enter the world of work without a highly developed career plan. They have been programmed from early on to be directed in their efforts. Not only is law school attractive to them as a next step that offers apparent certainty, but they also expect expert advice in how to get where they want to go. In fact, students expect more professionalism in all career-advising functions than they did years ago.

To cope with vastly increased demand and sophistication, pre-law advising has become increasingly professionalized. This has meant increased resources devoted to the task, with many pre-law advisors freed to perform just this one role rather than being career generalists or carrying out their pre-law duties in conjunction with significant unrelated demands. As the profession pushes forward, pre-law advisors have initiated programs and services that were unheard of not long ago. Some of these innovations include:

- **Pre-Law For-Credit Courses**

  At BYU, the University of Maryland, the University of Arizona, and a handful of other schools, students can take for-credit classes geared for students curious about careers in law. These courses are commonly taught by the pre-law advisor and are intended to expose students to what it's like to be a law student (legal research and writing exercises, mediation, opening statement delivery, etc.), substantive legal topics such as debating recent Supreme Court cases, visits to surrounding law schools to attend law classes or meet with deans of admission, and so forth. Schools that have implemented such courses find that they are extremely popular.

- **Pre-Law Student Law Journals**

  An increasingly common innovation among pre-law programs is a pre-law student journal where students can write substantive law review–type articles analyzing a legal topic of their choice. Pre-law student journals provide students with an excellent opportunity to test out legal writing and research, with the added benefit of getting published before they graduate.

■ **Law Student Mentor Programs**

For those institutions with an affiliated law school, formal mentoring programs that match pre-law students with law student mentors are an excellent way to help guide students through the pre-law process. Mentors can take students to classes and lectures, expose students to law school extra-curriculars, and guide students in the pre-law process in general.

■ **Pre-Law Office Interns**

Several pre-law advisors hire motivated pre-law students or law students at affiliated law schools to work as interns in the pre-law office. Interns advise pre-law students about basic pre-law matters, update databases and websites, and free pre-law advisors to focus on counseling students and developing useful programs.

WHO ARE PRE-LAW ADVISORS?

College pre-law advisors come from all walks of life: some have degrees and experience in psychology or career counseling, others have JDs, and yet others followed a less direct path, perhaps via academic advising. What pre-law advisor background is preferable in terms of getting the best pre-law advising services? Different backgrounds have different strengths:

BACKGROUND	LIKELY STRENGTH
Career Counseling	Exploring career interests and whether law is good fit
Legal Practice	Realistic view of legal practice(s)
Academic Advising	Application advice

The ideal counselor would, of course, combine all three backgrounds—as well as experience in other fields often chosen as alternatives to law. Sad to report, pre-law advisors are generally human and therefore do not have substantial careers in the eight or ten fields that might make them all-knowing advisors. It is unfair to expect a singe pre-law advisor to provide you with in-depth, sophisticated counsel regarding every aspect of your self-assessment, career hunt, and (possible) law school application. This is in part why pre-law advisors routinely provide students avenues of access to other sources for information, such as alumni practitioners, law students, law school admissions and financial aid officers, etc. Know at the outset that adequately engaging pre-law services will require conducting real research outside the four walls of the pre-law advisor's office.

WHAT UNDERGRADUATE PRE-LAW ADVISORS DO

Most people assume that pre-law advising services consist solely of helping students with the law school application process. Although this is of course an important part of their job, most pre-law advisors will tell you that they take a much more holistic approach to their services.

HOW PRE-LAW ADVISORS SEE THEIR ROLE

My role is a combination of helping students apply to law school and, almost more importantly, to see if law school is really for them.   *Verlaine Walker, Arizona*

Guiding students through the application process is only part of what I do. I try to help students learn about the practice of law through experiential learning—whether it's participation on the mock trial team or a legal internship with a state agency—so they can evaluate whether being a lawyer is a good fit for them. *Rob Haire, Georgia*

A big part of my job is relieving anxiety. Students interested in law tend to be a very stressed out bunch.   *Michael Gabriel, George Washington*

In general, students seem happier when they leave a pre-law advising appointment with me than when they come in. Talking with someone who has been through the process before with hundreds of students gives them confidence that they can make their way through this.   *Jeanne Ravid, Northwestern*

Helping students apply to law school is an advising role—providing information. But we see our role as much broader than mere advising. We are also very active counselors. We try to walk students through the decision-making process and talk through various options.   *Albert E. Aubin, UCLA*

HELP EVALUATE LAW AS AN OPTION

Even though some students bristle at the attempt, a good pre-law advisor will spend time at the outset considering the question of whether law is a good fit. Students often enter the process acting confident that law is the right choice, but few base the decision on solid information and self-awareness. At most schools, only 5 to 10 percent of students approaching pre-law advisors have thoroughly researched the law option and have solid reasons for pursuing law. So it is no wonder that many pre-law advisors begin by exploring whether law makes sense.

**PRE-LAW ADVISORS DISCUSS TESTING STUDENTS'
ASSUMPTIONS ABOUT LAW**

Pre-law advisors are there to expand the horizons of those who might not have considered law and also those who have considered it too exclusively. *Mac Francis, Indiana*

If someone seeking advice about law tells me they like to help people, I ask them to give me examples of when they have done so. If four or five experiences don't roll right off their lips, I advise them to spend some time soul searching to really understand who they are and what motivates them. *Consuelo Lopez Springfield, Wisconsin*

I see my role as making sure that students have a good idea of what they are getting into—reality testing. I try to gauge how much research they have done. Have they talked to lawyers, sat in on law classes, sought out internships? Unless a student has taken some of these basic steps, they should not consider themselves sold on law. *Tatem Oldham, Texas (Austin)*

I've had several students who say after more exposure to law and the legal profession, "You know, when I'm honest with myself I really hate reading, and think I would be miserable in law school" or "I definitely think I had a more glamorous picture of law than what's really out there." *Janelle Larson, Minnesota*

Students should spend time visualizing themselves as a lawyer and thinking about the kinds of things that involves doing every day. Some students love the idea of being a law student at Harvard, but they haven't a clue about what comes after. *Barbara Rayman, Penn State*

If I could offer one piece of advice to students interested in law, it would be to get out there and talk to people who have made this choice before you so you understand what you are signing up for and why you want to do it. *Catherine Gillespie, Virginia*

Students are often very solid on process issues—what they need to be doing to get in, how to apply, etc.—but less prepared in terms of having determined whether law is a good fit. *Wendy Rohleder-Sook, Kansas*

It's very tricky to challenge students' reasoning for pursuing law school. Some people are offended by those types of questions. *Dena Rakoff, Harvard*

We see our role as making sure students have thought through law—not to dissuade them—just to make sure that they are aware of the costs and benefits of what comes after law school. *Albert E. Aubin, UCLA*

Students should understand at the outset that not all pre-law advisors will be candid with them. For example, although most pre-law advisors believe that students can benefit from taking time off after college, not all of them will tell you so. There is a bright line between pre-law advisors who will actively challenge students' choices surrounding law school and those who will not. (After all, arguing with headstrong if ill-informed pre-laws is a fine recipe for migraines.)

The advisors most likely to share their views are those with JDs; the least likely are those with backgrounds in career counseling. Psychology and career counseling programs drill participants that a counselor should never tell a counselee what to do—they are trained to listen and provide reliable information only. Few if any pre-law advisors will outright tell students what to do (or not do). But some are more comfortable than others about sharing their opinion.

Tools in a Pre-law Advisor's Toolkit

Whether directive or facilitative, a pre-law advisor can point students to multiple resources to help learn about law and the legal profession. Most pre-law programs feature some combination of the following resources:

- *Handbooks*. Pre-law handbooks guide students to resources on campus and provide general advice on the topic. Especially where a pre-law advisor has been at it a long time, pre-law handbooks become a record of that advisor's methods and wisdom. If your school does not publish a pre-law handbook, there are plenty to be perused online. The site www.prelawhandbook.com collects some of the most useful in one place.

- *Pre-law binders, publications*. Pre-law binders commonly contain information on specific topics like writing personal statements, getting experience in law, etc. Some schools have created binders on particular subjects and/or containing answers to surveys distributed to alumni on topics such as impressions of law school, the legal profession, and so on.

- *Pre-law websites*. The best websites link to resources on campus and off. For example, Berkeley's pre-law website embeds multiple links to campus services and outside information within the text (underlined text indicates links):

SAMPLE FROM BERKELEY'S CAREER CENTER WEBSITE

LAW SCHOOL—IS LAW FOR ME?

Have you validated and confirmed your interest in a legal career?

Have you talked to practicing lawyers about the rewarding and challenging aspects of their careers? (Use the @cal Career Network to identify lawyers who are willing to grant you informational interviews.)

Have you had an internship or job at a law firm or law related organization? (Use CalJobs and internship resources)

Have you attended law related information panels? (check the Career Center calendar for upcoming events; sign up for the Law CareerMail list for the latest information.)

Have you observed or shadowed a lawyer on the job? (Use the @cal Career Network to identify lawyers who may let you observe them at work. Attend court hearings and trials. Participate in the Career Center's Winter Break Externship Program: sign up in late October.)

Why do you want to go to law school?

Do you want to make a lot of money? (Not all types of lawyers make the same salary.)

Are you stalling on making a career decision? (Have you talked to a career counselor?)

Are you applying to law school because "everyone else is doing it"? (The decision to attend law school is ideally based on your own criteria.)

Are you applying to law school because you feel like you have no career options? (Have you used all job search methods? Have you talked to a career counselor?)

Are you delaying entry into the work world? (Have you conducted career research or talked with a career counselor?)

Do you know what your short and long term goals are and how a law degree can help you achieve them?

- *Listservs, newsletters*. Pre-law advisors commonly produce listservs and/or newsletters to inform students about activities on campus, impending deadlines, etc.

- *Workshops, information sessions, panels*. Whether organized by pre-law advisors or by student law groups only, many schools offer pre-law events designed to help students learn about law school and practice.

TYPICAL PANEL/WORKSHOP TOPICS

With Lawyers:
How Did I Get Here?
What Do I Do Every Day?
What Do I Love/Hate about My Job?
The Myths and Realities of Practicing Law
The Realities of Getting a Big Firm (Non-profit, etc.) Job

With Law Students:
Things I Wish I Had Known Before I Applied to Law School
What the First Year of Law School Is Like

With Assorted Guests, Including Pre-law Advisors Themselves:
Should I Go to Law School
The Many Paths to Law School

Interesting Panel Participants:
Access Group (or other law school lender) about law school financial aid
Law School Financial Aid Directors about financing law school, typical
student debt loads, etc.
Law School Deans of Admissions about getting into law school
Law School Career Services Directors about law students' experiences
finding work, services they provide, etc.
Alumni lawyers about realities of law practice in certain fields many
students voice interest in (e.g., intellectual property, "international law,"
etc.)

- *Alumni databases.* At many schools, your pre-law advisor will be able to steer you toward a database of alumni law students and lawyers (see box below).

- *Inside information.* If your undergraduate institution is affiliated with a law school, chances are excellent that your pre-law advisor knows the admissions process to that law school extremely well.

ALUMNI CONNECTIONS

Alumni provide one of the best resources for finding out about law school and the legal profession. Alumni who have gone on to become lawyers are often enthusiastic about sharing their experiences with students from their alma mater, and many are willing to be contacted by students interested in the direction they've taken.

Many schools have well-developed and well-stocked searchable alumni databases that allow students to plug in search terms like geographic areas, law schools, type of practice, etc. Alumni databases are commonly accessible through career services, or sometimes directly through the school's alumni office. Some pre-law advisors maintain their own alumni databases.

Just because your school has an alumni database, do not assume that you will have unfettered access to it. Some alumni offices are wary about allowing students direct contact with alums because of bad experiences with doing so in the past (students failing to follow through, etc.) Some schools have put filters in place to make sure student contact with alumni does not interfere with the school's ability to raise funds from alumni. Others require students to sit through a short program educating them about the alumni database and how to use it responsibly. Still other schools charge a small fee to deter all but the most motivated from using the database on the theory that they will treat it with the most respect.

If your school does maintain a database, do what you can to access it. Contact with alumni is a great way to find out about law and make connections that could prove useful as you proceed. These contacts are invaluable—for informational interviewing, shadowing opportunities, and internships or employment.

PROVIDE FINANCIAL INFORMATION ABOUT LAW AND LAW SCHOOL

Given students' college debt loads and the stunningly high cost of law school, pre-law advisors are more and more often asked to address the question of how (best) to pay for law school. As Chapter 18 of this book underscores, the financial aid policies of law schools are immensely complicated and vary dramatically from one school to another. Consequently, it is unlikely that a pre-law advisor will be expert on the ins and outs of many law schools' policies. Rather than abandon the field entirely, however, many advisors routinely brief students on the basics, point them in the right direction to learn more, and/or bring in financial aid officers from the law schools to speak with students. A surprising number of students don't focus on the financial piece of the law equation. A good pre-law advisor will urge students to confront these realities well in advance and plan accordingly.

PROVIDE GUIDANCE ABOUT PREPARING FOR LAW SCHOOL

A key function of pre-law advising is to help students make informed decisions that will help their chances of getting into law school and enjoying themselves along the way. One of the most common mistakes pre-law advisors attribute to students in terms of getting the most out of pre-law advising services is not taking advantage of them early enough in college.

Pre-law advisors don't want to speak with students early in college so they can track them into law early on. Quite the contrary, pre-law advisors are interested in speaking with students early on so they can stress a few essentials that will make applying to law school easier if that's what a student opts to do down the line.

**PRE-LAW ADVISORS DISCUSS WHY THEY LIKE TO
SEE STUDENTS EARLY IN THEIR COLLEGE CAREER**

One reason I like to see students early in their college career is to advise them to develop relationships with professors. Penn State is such a large school that getting to know a professor to the point that he or she can write a meaningful recommendation requires a proactive approach. *Barbara Rayman, Penn State*

If I could offer only one piece of advice to students considering law it would be to visit your pre-law advisor early. Students so often walk in their junior year and realize there is a lot they could have accomplished had they started earlier. *Tatem Oldham, Texas (Austin)*

I like to see students early in their college career, if only to tell them there is no one path, no one set of courses, no certain summer jobs that are prerequisites for law school. Taking away the rules relaxes them in a way that makes college go better. *Dena Rakoff, Harvard*

Our office provides much assistance to students and alumni applying to law school. But we can only help those who come to us in time. I can do very little to help on matters like choice of school, financial aid, LSAT preparation, and personal statements after the applications have been submitted. *Heather Struck, Binghamton*

An important reason pre-law advisors like to see students as early as possible is to reduce the vast quantities of misinformation about the law school application process. Examples of commonly reported misinformation include:

- Taking classes or majoring in a certain area because a student has heard it is a law school prerequisite
- Taking the LSAT without preparation (a big mistake since many law schools average LSAT scores)
- Failing to focus enough attention on grades
- Failing to form close relationships with professors for recommendation purposes
- Assuming law school must follow directly after college
- Applying only to law schools well out of reach

Another reason is to suggest other career options students can explore in tandem with their exploration of law.

HELP PREPARE LAW SCHOOL APPLICATIONS

Though career, financial, and self exploration are important parts of the student–pre-law advisor relationship, its primary focus usually involves helping students navigate the application process itself. This may include providing workshops (and often one-on-one work) regarding writing personal statements, résumés, and the like. In addition, pre-law advisors can provide advice about students' admissions chances based upon their own experience of prior students applying (with similar or dissimilar credentials) to the same target schools.

Pre-law advisors have access to very detailed statistical information about how students from their institutions have fared in the law school admissions game. For example, each year, they receive a report from the Law School Admission Counsel called an "action report" that reveals how applicants from their school fared in the application process. Action report data includes LSAT scores, GPAs, ethnicity, major, accepted offers, and so on. Pre-law advisors use this information to help current advisees select appropriate schools and pattern their application to follow past successes. Experienced pre-law advisors have repeatedly witnessed the law school admissions process and can share their wisdom as it applies to your particular case.

PRE-LAW ADVISORS AND ADMISSIONS ADVOCACY

Few students are aware that law school admissions officers sometimes encourage pre-law advisors to share their thoughts about which students are worthy of attention but risk being overlooked. Though admissions officers may solicit their thoughts, pre-law advisors voice strikingly different opinions about the wisdom of doing so. Some consider it a regular part of what they do; others detest the practice.

The vast majority of pre-law programs lack the resources or institutional support to undertake individual evaluations for each student, or any other sort of advocacy efforts. At many schools, pre-law advisors are so stretched for time that such an endeavor simply is not possible. Other pre-law advisors are unwilling to advocate for particular students because they are completely opposed to the concept.

Lest students start barraging their pre-law advisors with gifts and sweet talk, note that pre-law advocacy is a comparatively rare occurrence.

PRE-LAW ADVISORS DISCUSS ADVISOR ADVOCACY ISSUES

Admissions directors encourage pre-law advisors to clue them in about particular students that might fit well at their institution or were somehow misrepresented by aspects of their application.   *Rodia Vance, Emory*

Law school admissions directors regularly invite comment about particular students. But those pre-law advisors that do it all the time find that at a certain point they stop listening.   *Dena Rakoff, Harvard*

I don't feel that it is our role as advisors to lobby admissions officers. We want students to feel that they can open up during the pre-law advising process instead of worrying about establishing a lobby-worthy relationship with their advisor.   *Nicole Moran-O'Neil, UC San Diego*

We feel that advocating for particular students is almost discriminatory—why would we do so for one student and not another? Equity issues are quite important to us.   *Albert E. Aubin, UCLA*

If I have a student that has a low LSAT or GPA but otherwise shines, I feel it is my responsibility to pick up the phone and call admissions directors to speak on his or her behalf.   *Anonymous Pre-law Advisor*

I feel it's my mission to know the law schools well and to know my students well. When I see a good match, I'll let admissions know.   *Gerald Wilson, Duke*

ASSIST IN POST-APPLICATION MATTERS

A pre-law advisor's role does not end once the application is mailed out. In fact, pre-law advising offices experience a peak in activity in the spring as acceptances, wait listings, and rejections roll in. Pre-law advisors are available to counsel students on post-application issues such as dealing with wait lists, choosing which school to attend, deciding whether to defer, and so on.

COORDINATE PRE-LAW ACTIVITIES CAMPUS-WIDE

Many pre-law advisors view their role primarily as coordinators of campus pre-law activities. Particularly at the larger institutions, where pre-law activities at different schools or departments within the university coexist, the role of the pre-law advisor is to make sure that the various events and activities are coordinated and that everyone is aware of what is on offer. The University of Wisconsin provides a good example. With a student population of some 40,000 and about 1,500 students who indicate an interest in law, coordinating among various pre-law activities on campus takes up a good deal of the pre-law advisors' time. In this context, the pre-law advisor is very much a pre-law community builder. Arizona

State provides another example. There, a loose confederation of people from different departments and schools within Arizona State are assigned pre-law advising responsibilities as one of their many tasks. With one coordinator overseeing activities across campus, these advisors meet two or three times a year to plan programs, share information, and coordinate services. With over 46,000 undergraduates at ASU, this is no small feat.

At some schools, where official pre-law programs are not as vigorous, students are often the prime actors in the pre-law scene, be it through pre-law societies or other student groups like mock trial, debate, or service organizations. Where student groups are the main source of pre-law action, pre-law advisors generally work with student groups to facilitate their events. Some pre-law advisors prefer this role and encourage student initiative.

PRE-LAW CLUBS

Many college campuses have active pre-law clubs made up of students interested in law. Student law societies serve multiple purposes depending on their mission. Some function as an arm of pre-law advising, helping with law fairs and bringing speakers to campus. Others focus on promoting various underrepresented populations in the legal field. Still others encourage substantive activities meant to develop legal skills, such as debate clubs, negotiation and mediation organizations, mock trials, and so on.

Aside from student pre-law clubs that help students develop particular skills, what do pre-law societies do? Activities run by pre-law societies typically include:

➤ Organizing panels with law school admissions officers to discuss the admissions process

➤ Inviting financial aid representatives to campus to discuss financing law school

➤ Holding brown bag lunches or dinners with a guest featuring specific legal topics

➤ Giving practice LSATs under simulated conditions

➤ Providing members a reduced rate on LSAT prep courses

➤ Producing pre-law newsletters or listservs

➤ Facilitating community service projects

➤ Putting on mock trials overseen by local judges

➤ Hosting networking events with students and alumni

Phi Alpha Delta (PAD) is a national pre-law society with approximately 150 chapters. Primarily a networking organization, PAD also leads professional and philanthropic activities, puts out a pre-law manual, and publishes a pre-law periodical (*The Reporter*). The level of activity of different PAD chapters varies widely from campus to campus.

Pre-law clubs are of highly variable quality. On some campuses, they are vital; at others, they are barely active to moribund. Because the strength of pre-law clubs depends on energized student leadership, the same pre-law club can be outstanding one year and abysmal the next. That said, at some schools, pre-law clubs have become institutions with sufficient student commitment and momentum to keep them consistently strong year to year.

WHEN TO SEE A PRE-LAW ADVISOR

IN COLLEGE

Some people seemingly go to college only as a means to getting to law school. These people show up the first week of their freshman year the moment pre-law career seminars are offered—and they sit in the front row. Others drift in around Thanksgiving of their senior year as they finally face the concept that they will graduate and have to do something with themselves.

As enthusiastic as some students may be, it is unwise to become too obsessed with law school in the early years of college. There is a big difference between being educated about the option of law and suffering from tunnel vision.

PRE-LAW ADVISORS ON THE COLLEGE EXPERIENCE

When first year students come to see me gung ho about preparing for law school, I advise them to slow down and spend time exploring what it's like to be in college, to get grounded. *Catherine Gillespie, Virginia*

Take advantage of your undergraduate education. If you spend your undergraduate years on a narrow track going towards what you think law schools want to see, you will be missing out on a lot. *Julie Givens, Arizona State*

The first two years of college should be about acclimation and discovery. Students often make career decisions prematurely. *Leslie Adelman, Georgetown*

Most pre-law programs ramp up their services for students in their junior and senior years. The traditional timeline for applying to law school had students preparing for and taking the LSAT their junior year and applying to law schools their senior year.

Because of the changing trends in the law school student median age, the more sophisticated pre-law advisors are beginning to refrain from outlining strict schedules for students that indicate interest in law. More and more pre-law advisors are letting students know that nontraditional paths to law school are not only acceptable, but often welcomed by law school admissions officers.

PRE-LAW ADVISORS DISCUSS GOING DIRECTLY FROM COLLEGE TO LAW SCHOOL

To some, the fact that law schools look favorably on applicants with experience after college is new information, and quite good news.   *Suzanne Helbig, UC Berkeley*

I often tell students, if there is anything you want to do before you are thirty, get it done before law school. Once you start law school, if you're lucky, the next ten years of your life are spoken for.   *Michael Gabriel, George Washington*

A lot of people think admissions officers will look harshly on their application if they don't apply and go to law school immediately after college. In fact, solid and interesting experiences after college do nothing but boost an application's strength.   *Sara Mock, Florida*

AFTER GRADUATION

In line with the changing timeline of applying to law school, more and more alumni contact their undergraduate pre-law advisors for assistance with the application process. Most undergraduate institutions allow their alumni access to undergraduate graduate school and career advising services. As interest in law school grows, and the range and breadth of pre-law services expand, many pre-law advisors are overwhelmed by the volume. Some pre-law programs simply do not have the resources to handle alumni inquiries on top of their responsibilities for current undergraduates. As a result, some schools limit alumni access to pre-law advising services through a variety of methods. Their techniques include:

- Not granting alumni access to any advising services
- Limiting alumni access to a certain period after graduation (e.g., six months)
- Blocking out certain times of year for undergraduate advising only (e.g., fall application season)

- Limiting certain services, such as critiquing personal statements, to under-graduates

- Charging alumni a fee (usually low) for access to counseling services

Other schools, particularly those that devote real resources to their pre-law programs, have an open door policy to all alumni at all times for all matters.

SEEKING OUTSIDE HELP

Certain circumstances may lend themselves to looking beyond undergraduate pre-law advising services to other sources on and off campus. Such instances may include:

- When pre-law advising program resources are stretched (e.g., the pre-law advisor does not have time to devote significant attention to each student)

- When you have highly specific needs that might not fit well within the pre-law program

- When you need a level of expertise that your current pre-law advisor doesn't enjoy (due, for instance, to inexperience, unfamiliarity with a particular area, etc.)

- If your pre-law advisor focuses largely on schools inappropriate for you, such as the university's own law school, local schools, too high-ranking or low-ranking schools

- If you have a personality conflict with your pre-law advisor

- If your pre-law advisor won't give candid advice, or gives too much candid advice (see above)

- For alumni, if pre-law advising services are unavailable to graduates (see above) or awkward to access

GETTING THE MOST OUT OF PRE-LAW ADVISING SERVICES

Once you know that you are interested in law as a possible career you should check in with your pre-law advising office. Find out what programs and services are available—whether as part of the pre-law or the career advising offices—to help you assess your needs and interests, whether law might be a good fit for you, and so on. An early visit will provide you with key information to guide you in decision-making throughout college, and about what to expect when and if the time comes to apply to law school.

PRE-LAW ADVISORS DISCUSS MAKING THE MOST OF PRE-LAW SERVICES

Students should not assume one trip to a pre-law advisor is enough. Pre-law advising is a continuum that starts with assessment and evaluation and ends with application only if law school turns out to be the right road. *Rob Haire, Georgia*

Books and websites provide only general information. Your pre-law advisor offers personal, one-on-one guidance you won't find in any book. *Karen Severn, Texas A&M*

Don't use your pre-law advisor to find out how many years law school is or whether there is a law school on campus. You'll be able to make the most of your prelaw advisor's expertise if you have at least somewhat of a handle on the basics. *Greg Shaffer, Maryland*

Students should take advantage of the full range of pre-law services available. This will enable them to make informed decisions about their careers and help them navigate the application process. *Elayne Mazzarrella, Yale*

Sometimes students wander into the Pre-law Center and ask how much our services cost. They are surprised to hear that all of our services are free. *Catherine Bramble, Brigham Young*

I think that students applying to law school are better informed and more sophisticated about admissions when they are actively involved in our pre-law advising services. *Kathy Wright, Stanford*

Plan to meet with a pre-law advisor often. I find it is not until the second or third visit that many advisees start asking the important questions. *Nancy Hennes, Washington*

Part II

APPLYING TO LAW SCHOOL

8

MAKING THE MOST OF YOUR CREDENTIALS

— EXECUTIVE SUMMARY —

■

Although candidates with less than stellar credentials can do well
in admissions by marketing themselves effectively,
the job is much easier for those with excellent credentials.

■

Learn how to maximize the various credentials
that admissions officers will evaluate:

—Your academic record

—Your LSAT score

—Work experience

—Extracurricular, personal, and community activities

■

You can add to the impact of your credentials
by showing that you know where you are headed.

Chapter 5 provides an overview of what the top law schools look for in their candidates: brains, legal potential, and personal attributes. Admissions committees ascertain to what degree you possess these items first and foremost from the credentials you present. Your credentials include:

- Your academic record
- Your performance on the LSAT (and the TOEFL, for international applicants)
- Your work experience
- Your extracurricular, personal, and community activities

Although even candidates with less than stellar credentials can market themselves effectively—by writing essays well, getting recommenders to write favorably about them, and interviewing well—you will make the application process easier on yourself if you start out with strong credentials. This chapter will examine each category of credentials to show you how best to develop and shape your underlying profile.

THE ACADEMIC RECORD

WHAT ARE ADMISSIONS COMMITTEES LOOKING FOR?

Your academic record refers not just to the grades you received in college, but also to the quality of your university and the substance of the classes you took. Some law schools rely mostly on the index number (computed using your undergraduate grade-point average and your LSAT score) when looking at your academic credentials, without considering that a GPA can mean many different things depending upon where it was earned and what types of classes were followed. (For more information on index numbers, see Chapter 5.) Most top law schools, however, do indeed take a closer look at your record, considering your college grades in the true context in which they were earned.

Admissions officers are accustomed to examining undergraduate transcripts with a practiced eye. A given grade-point average is more impressive if achieved at a top school in demanding courses, with the better grades received in the junior and senior years. A candidate with high grades in introductory courses and low grades in more advanced courses will be considered less favorably. Similarly, high grades earned at a college (even a top one) notorious for grade inflation will mean less than outstanding marks at a college known for its rigorous grading patterns.

Your specific major matters less than the *type* of major you choose. It does not matter whether you opt for physics rather than chemistry, for example, or history rather than political science. What matters is that you choose a serious major. Schools are leery of pre-professional subjects, such as business, and those that reward performance talents, such as acting. Any subject that requires serious analytical work and dedication, and attracts at least a reasonable percentage of the best and brightest, will meet with approval.

Assuming that you have chosen a suitably demanding and reputable major, consider also taking undergraduate classes that will provide you with substantive knowledge for use in a future law field. If you intend to practice family law, for example, classes in psychology as well as those in tax and finance will help you down the road. For those planning to practice environmental law, classes in the life sciences and economics are helpful; for commercial litigation or securities law, knowledge of accounting, statistics, finance, and corporate strategy is particularly useful. Note, too, that all future lawyers can benefit from courses that develop writing, research, negotiation, analysis, and public speaking skills.

Perhaps more important than the substance of your classes is that you excel at whatever academic endeavors you pursue. Quality work and serious involvement are the most important things to demonstrate in your university studies. It is best if you also evidence interest in your studies by taking extra courses in your major or in complementary fields, as well as writing a thesis.

The ideal undergraduate record would thus exhibit all of the following:

- Top-quality school
- Demanding courseload (i.e., no path of least resistance); advanced work in a second, unrelated (to your major) field is particularly helpful
- Top grades throughout (with few courses taken pass/fail), but especially in the junior and senior years
- Courses requiring substantial reading, strong writing ability, good research skills, and analytical prowess
- Courses developing useful substantive knowledge for your future legal field

HOW IMPORTANT IS IT?

Admissions officers view your undergraduate record as a key indicator of your intellectual ability and your willingness to work hard, making this a proxy for your academic potential in law school. The less work experience you have, the more important your college record will be. A strong undergraduate record earned at a leading university will demonstrate that you can make it through law school, especially if you have had a mixture of courses requiring abstract reasoning and courses demanding substantial amounts of writing. Law schools want people with strong analytical skills, who can cover and quickly absorb an immense amount of material, write well, and are motivated to learn.

IF YOU ARE STILL IN COLLEGE

If you are still in college and serious about going to law school, follow the suggestions in the sections above to assemble the strongest possible undergraduate record. Keep in mind, too, that getting strong professorial recommendations is of great value. Therefore, try to take multiple advanced courses with each of two or three professors to lay the foundation for standout recommendations. (Consult Chapter 12 for more about getting the most out of recommendations.)

MAXIMIZING THE VALUE OF YOUR ACADEMIC RESULTS

Admissions deans are unlikely to know everything about the ins-and-outs of your program. Consider having a professor (or dean) describe in her recommendation the nonobvious, laudatory aspects of your efforts, especially if you:

➤ Selected professors or courses notorious for low grades

➤ Took a particularly demanding course load

➤ Pursued a major that attracts the school's best and brightest students

➤ Wrote a thesis requiring highly problematic or in-depth research

➤ Worked long hours (twenty-five plus?) to pay tuition

IMPROVING YOUR UNDERGRADUATE RECORD AFTER THE FACT

If you have already graduated and do not possess a sterling record, is it too late for you to do something to help your candidacy? Not necessarily. You may not be able to do anything about the grades you got as an undergraduate, but you can always take courses (at night or on weekends, presumably) to provide another set of grades—more recent and potentially more reflective of your current ability—for law schools to consider. Admissions officers call this "building an alternative transcript." Note that there is no unanimity on the effectiveness of this strategy. Some schools will allow positive results from additional classes to turn an otherwise questionable record into a favorable one; other schools, however, are more reticent to let new grades wipe out the sting of past errors. Check with individual law schools to determine how they regard a second set of grades.

Those schools that are willing to overlook past performances when a new and better transcript is provided will need help in doing so. Although the law schools are capable of interpreting the meaning of good grades received in courses at a well-known, demanding graduate-degree program, they may not know how to interpret your record in coursework from lesser-known programs. Be sure to do all you can to help them understand what your new record means (assuming, of course, that you have performed well in a highly regarded program).

Taking additional courses provides you with an excellent opportunity to cultivate a professor to be a recommender. This is of particular value for those who failed to do so in their initial degree program as well as for those who attended college long ago and whose recommenders have forgotten their performance or have died.

Law schools will value your efforts more highly if you take a series of courses showing in-depth investigation of a subject. Merely sampling a few classes here and there is not as likely to help you in your efforts to redeem an earlier weak undergraduate record. Furthermore, you should try to remedy the specific weaknesses in your original record. For example, if you have not taken any writing or writing-intensive classes (or received poor grades in such classes), you should take expository writing or a writing-intensive course at a local community college or continuing education division of a nearby university. To achieve the maximum possible benefit from these courses, you will have to receive excellent grades in them. Getting mediocre marks may show that you are interested in improving your background, but will arouse serious questions about your ability to do outstanding work in a competitive law program.

GRADUATE WORK

Law schools will want to look at the results of any graduate-degree work you have completed. Serious, well-done graduate work in a master's or other program—especially if completed in a top discipline at a top university—will always work in your favor. Remember, however, that graduate-level grades are not factored into the index number (see Chapter 5). Furthermore, admissions officers know that the grading in many graduate programs is somewhat lenient, with nearly all students receiving grades higher than a C. Although graduate-level grades are not necessarily factored as heavily into the admissions decision as undergraduate marks are, they can still be helpful to your case, especially if earned in a competitive, well-known program. Be sure to do all you can to aid admissions committees in interpreting your marks if they are not earned in a particularly well-known program by giving them as much information as possible about it. For example, have recommenders relate to the admissions committees what it takes to get into the program, the program's ranking or standing in its field, the average grades achieved in the program compared with your own grades, or even the average grades achieved course by course, if that helps to show that your record has been superb.

ADMISSIONS DEANS DISCUSS THE
ACADEMIC RECORD

WHAT FACTORS DO YOU CONSIDER WHEN EVALUATING AN UNDERGRADUATE RECORD?

Whatever the major, there should be variety, including some clearly demanding analytical courses. Thus, I'm glad to see a sociology major who has taken some tough statistics courses. There is no set preparation for law school, but some majors may be of less value than others (for example, pre-law). I examine the undergraduate transcript very closely. I look at what an applicant has undertaken in his or her major and I look at what they've done outside of their major. *Faye Deal, Stanford*

We spend a lot of time combing through an applicant's transcript in order to get a real sense of the kind of student this person would be at Columbia. We consider the types of courses taken and further evaluate the trend in grades (upward, downward, or consistent). We look for someone who has followed a curriculum of real breadth, depth, and challenge. We also pay attention to the amount of time and effort used toward extracurricular activities or work while in college. *Nkonye Iwerebon, Columbia*

When looking at an undergraduate record, we consider where you went to school, how you ranked within your class, the extent of grade inflation (we can see both the LSAT and GPA averages at the school through the LSAC report), and more. We consider the trend in your record, hoping that you have peaked in your senior year rather than long before. Since law school is all about writing, we look for expository writing ability. We also look at how long it took you to graduate. If you went through in just two-and-a-half or three years, we consider whether you will lack the maturity necessary for law school. On the other hand, if it took you much more than four years, then we may ask if it was because you had to work to support yourself of did you simply opt to take a light course load. *Chloe T. Reid, USC*

We really want to see demanding courses, especially in the junior and senior years, rather than courses in golf or human sexuality. *Anne Richard, George Washington*

There is no pre-law educational requirement or even a specific recommended course of study for admission to Penn Law. Strength of character, breadth of knowledge and intellectual maturity constitute the base upon which our legal education builds. As such, Penn Law seeks to enroll individuals who have demonstrated outstanding academic success, who are intellectually curious, and who possess superior writing, oral communication, and analytical skills. The evaluation includes understanding the trend in grades and the progression of course work. One thing we don't want to see is a fluff course senior year. *Renée Post, Penn*

You may have a person who started out college very ill-prepared, who was coaxed into going the pre-med route, and then halfway through realized he or she was a philosopher and changed majors. In that case, I would pay more attention to later grades. . . . It's not a lock-step kind of analysis we go through.   *Edward Tom, Boalt Hall (Berkeley)*

If an applicant has worked successfully for several years—performed well and progressed—and has done well on the LSAT, the undergraduate record will receive much less emphasis.   *Don Rebstock, Northwestern*

The GPA number is just a starting point. Our first concern is how rigorous the courseload has been. We look at academic letters of recommendation, which are particularly helpful if they address the difficulty of the courseload and, for example, the grading policies of professors from whom the applicant took multiple courses. Another factor we examine is whether there were substantial barriers to performance, such as the need to work many hours per week.   *William Hoye, Duke*

There are a whole host of things that can go wrong in the first year or two of college, such as picking the wrong school or major. Therefore we read transcripts backwards, starting with the most recent work.   *Elizabeth Rosselot, Boston College*

To interpret a GPA, we take into account the trend of grades, the quality of the curriculum followed, the school, when the applicant attended school—both because grades have inflated over time and because grades matter less if you went eight years ago, since you have done other things more recently.   *Andy Cornblatt, Georgetown*

It can be useful for us to know about a department or program that consistently issues lower-than-average grades. Send proof that the grading is outside the norm in order to put your performance in the appropriate context.   *Don Rebstock, Northwestern*

In general, we like to see people writing a senior thesis. It requires commitment and self-discipline. It gives them a sense of intellectual ownership of a topic. The process engenders real growth and development.   *Jim Milligan, Columbia*

I'm always impressed when a person has taken upper division electives in other departments; it's a good indication that the person is intellectually curious (and fearless).   *William Hoye, Duke*

We look at undergraduate records to see whether candidates have demonstrated strong performance while taking tough courses and generally challenged themselves.   *Don Rebstock, Northwestern*

Does It Matter What a Candidate Majors In?

People should major in what interests them, then do well in it. They should challenge themselves with demanding courses and seminars that require intensive research and writing. *Anne Richard, George Washington*

The major in and of itself is not as important as the nature (i.e., challenge and difficulty) of courses taken. We do, however, like to see non-liberal arts majors take a few courses that develop or expose their research and writing abilities. *Nkonye Iwerebon, Columbia*

For the most part we don't care what someone majors in as long as I see he or she is intellectually curious and has demonstrated academic excellence—especially with their analytical and writing skills. *Chloe T. Reid, USC*

If you major in a hard science or in business, be sure to take a few classes that involve lots of writing, as well as some that involve reading and interpreting texts. *Megan A. Barnett, Yale*

Students should favor a curriculum that requires them to read dense, complex, primary source material, analyze it closely, and present reasoned conclusions in writing. *Susan Palmer, Virginia*

Weak majors vary by institution, but in general I do not favor narrowly vocational, non-academic majors. Thus, I obviously worry about physical therapy, culinary arts, hospitality management, and the like, but I also worry about some accounting and engineering programs that allow little opportunity to develop skills in reading and writing at a sophisticated level. *Susan Palmer, Virginia*

Can Post-graduate Work Make Up for a Relatively Poor Undergraduate Performance?

Graduate school is only one of at least three possibilities that might overcome weak undergraduate work: (1) the passage of time; (2) an explanation for the weak performance; and (3) either good performance in graduate school or successful work experience. *Rick Geiger, Cornell*

Graduate work can certainly help to make up for a weak undergraduate record. A graduate degree has value for us because it demonstrates that you are intellectually mature enough to do sustained work at an advanced level. It is also closer in time to the application than the undergraduate work is. However, many graduate programs grade on a B+ curve, so graduate grades are not to be considered directly comparable to undergraduate grades. Thus, the graduate GPA is not factored into the LSDAS grade report. *Susan Palmer, Virginia*

Completing a graduate degree can certainly help you overcome a weak undergraduate record, but you should recognize that graduate grades are generally inflated, so you need to make sure you can distinguish yourself in the program. *Chloe T. Reid, USC*

If the postgraduate work supports a candidate's intellectual or professional pursuits, it can help. If it's clearly just a course or two meant to demonstrate the candidate can do graduate work, it won't help as much. *Renée Post, Penn*

We like people who are interested in the world of ideas, as graduate students tend to be. Also, good performance as a graduate student helps to make the case that the poor undergraduate performance won't recur. Graduate school grades aren't particularly meaningful, though, given that they aren't standardized and they're so high that we can't distinguish between different people's performance. On the other hand, graduate study generally allows someone to get more meaningful and insightful recommendations than were available in college insofar as graduate students usually work more closely with a key professor or two. *Rick Geiger, Cornell*

Strong post-graduate work can help redeem you and validate your story if you were immature or studying the wrong thing as an undergraduate. Obviously, though, there are limitations to the amount of redemption this can provide. *Sarah C. Zearfoss, Michigan*

Graduate work can help your cause; any kind of experience that involves analytical thinking and writing is always very important. *Edward Tom, Boalt Hall (Berkeley)*

It's hard to evaluate courses taken in a continuing education program. I don't know who's in the classroom or how stiff the grading might be. As a result, this won't rehabilitate a weak undergraduate record. I have more confidence in the process and product at a serious master's program. A letter of recommendation from a professor that lets me see the candidate's mind at work, her determination and spirit, and her intellectual curiosity, will be very valuable. *Jim Milligan, Columbia*

A master's degree, particularly if it's from a rigorous graduate program, can help make up for lackluster undergraduate results. This is not always the case, of course, but the master's performance, while not quantified, is at least another element to consider. *Kenneth Kleinrock, NYU*

Taking courses after you have graduated can be beneficial to your admission chances, but it depends heavily upon the rigor of the courses and the grading: graduate courses at a leading institution versus introductory undergraduate courses at a community college. *Andy Cornblatt, Georgetown*

Overcoming a Weak Undergraduate Record

A person with a mediocre undergraduate record should note two things. First, you'll need solid work experience to rehabilitate your situation. Second, taking additional courses after your undergraduate program can also help. The courses should be part of an in-depth, prolonged program at a serious school. This is usually found with master's-level (or higher) work but can sometimes include a non-degree program of study.   *Faye Deal, Stanford*

Strong letters of recommendation can certainly help. So can an honest, genuine explanation of what prevented getting better grades. A weak record may also argue for delaying an application in order to get some distance from it and to establish a record of successful achievement in the professional world along the way.   *Renée Post, Penn*

Strong performance in a graduate degree program can help to balance weak undergraduate performance, but grading patterns in graduate school don't separate out high performers very well. As a result, it's hard to say how much difference a graduate degree will make. On the other hand, lifelong learning and successful work experience can certainly make a difference.   *Todd Morton, Vanderbilt*

Performing well on the LSAT is the best thing someone can do to make up for poor undergraduate performance. Doing graduate work may help, but note that the more demanding a degree is, the more forgiving of a weak undergraduate record we will be—so a Ph.D. can certainly help. In addition, given sufficient time, strong performance in the professional world can help. In general, the further away an applicant is from his or her undergraduate years, the less meaningful the undergraduate grade point average will be to admissions committees. *Anne Richard, George Washington*

There are two ways to compensate for a mediocre undergraduate record: an outstanding LSAT and some significant experience out in the world. These can serve as useful counterweights to the college GPA.   *Jim Milligan, Columbia*

THE LSAT

What Is It?

The Law School Admission Test (LSAT) is a three-and-a-half hour examination created and administered by the Law School Admission Council (also known as Law Services or LSAC) and required by every ABA-approved law school.

There are two closely related purposes of the exam: to predict which candidates will do well in law school and to assist schools in ranking applicants. It is, according to LSAC, a standard measure of acquired reading and verbal reasoning skills. The LSAT does not, however, attempt to measure your legal competence or knowledge.

The test consists of five 35-minute multiple-choice sections, separately timed, followed by a half-hour essay portion that is not scored. A short break is given after the third multiple-choice section. The exam, including preliminary administrative matters, typically lasts from 8:30 A.M. until about noon, making for a very long morning.

The five multiple-choice sections vary in order for each test taker, but they include: one Analytical Reasoning section, two Logical Reasoning sections, one Reading Comprehension section, and a wild card section, which could be any of the above. This (wild card) section is used only to assist LSAC in experimenting with new testing methods and questions and is not scored. (Note that test takers do not know when taking the exam which section is the wild card and will not be scored.)

Analytical reasoning. This section gives questions that require you to make deductions from a set of statements, rules, or conditions. Often called the "games" section, a typical analytical reasoning question would give you information about the eight people seated at a circular table. You might be informed that Harold never sits facing due south, George always sits facing north (including northeast or northwest), Lisa always sits two seats away from Harold, Martha always sits opposite Lisa, and so on. You will be asked, for example, in which seat Harold must sit if Martha is not in a seat facing due north or due south.

Logical reasoning. These questions evaluate your ability to comprehend and analyze arguments that are contained in short passages. Test takers must be able to evaluate the strength of the evidence, and logic of the reasoning, as well as detect the assumptions in these arguments and draw reasonable conclusions from them.

Reading comprehension. These questions are based upon four sets of reading passages, designed to test your reading and reasoning abilities. Passages are drawn from a variety of subjects within the fields of arts/humanities, law/policy, sciences, and social science. You may not be familiar with all of the subjects, of course, but all the information needed to answer the questions can be found within the text. These questions require you to analyze the logic, structure, meaning, and details of densely written material, and to draw inferences from it.

Writing sample. This section requires that you choose one of two stated courses of action to best resolve the situation it describes. There is no right or wrong answer. Instead, you are meant to demonstrate your ability to develop and maintain a well-reasoned argument. This section is not scored, but schools to which you apply are sent a copy of your response.

HOW TO REGISTER FOR THE LSAT

There are three options for registering for the LSAT: online, by telephone, or by mail. Information about each of these options, and about the test in general (test dates, sample LSATs, etc.) is available at the Law School Admissions Council (LSAC) website at www.lsac.org.

Inquiries can also be directed to:

Law School Admissions Council
Box 2000
662 Penn Street
Newton, PA 18940-1001
(215) 968-1001
LSACinfo@LSAC.org

The exam is given in June, September, December, and February of each year. To be sure that you will be able to take the exam at the site you prefer, plan to register several months before the actual test date.

YOUR SCORE

Your score is now available approximately three weeks after you take the exam by TelScore. Otherwise, you will get the score by mail, from Law Services, approximately five weeks after the exam. This score will remain valid for five years.

Your score is based strictly on the number of questions answered correctly; any incorrect answers will not affect your score. Scores are reported on a scale from 120 to 180. Thus, the lowest you can score is 120, the highest 180. You will also receive a percentile rank, which shows the percentage of test takers who perform (above and) below you. (Remember that the essay you write is not scored, but simply forwarded to your chosen schools.)

What Are Admissions Committees Looking For?

Top schools generally have average scores in the mid-to-high 160s or low 170s, meaning that their students are typically in the top 10 percent of test takers. The range of scores is substantial, however, so a score in the low- to mid-160s need not necessarily be cause for despair. To evaluate yourself, check out where

	25TH PERCENTILE	75TH PERCENTILE
Boston College	162	166
Boston University	163	166
UC Berkeley (Boalt Hall)	163	169
UCLA	162	169
Chicago	169	172
Columbia	169	174
Cornell	166	168
Duke	165	169
Emory	162	166
George Washington	163	166
Georgetown	167	171
Harvard	169	175
Iowa	158	163
Michigan	166	170
Northwestern	166	172
Notre Dame	164	167
NYU	168	172
Pennsylvania	167	171
Southern California	165	167
Stanford	167	172
Texas	162	168
Vanderbilt	164	167
Virginia	167	171
Washington Univ. (St. Louis)	162	167
Yale	170	176

your score falls in relation to those of first-year students at some of the top schools. In the chart above, for example, only 25 percent of NYU's first-year students scored lower than 168 and only 25 percent scored above 172. If your score is a 170, you can infer that, although you are no shoo-in, your LSAT score is unlikely to be a barrier to admission at NYU.

Although no admissions officers are silly (or courageous) enough to be quoted on the subject, the average scores of minority admittees tend to be below the overall averages. As a rough rule of thumb, African-Americans average 10 points below, Hispanics 5 points below, and American Indians 3–5 points below. Thus, it is important to interpret schools' LSAT averages in light of your own circumstances. If you are African-American, for example, a score equal to a school's 25th percentile is likely to help rather than hinder your chances.

HOW IMPORTANT IS IT?

Admissions officers pay close attention to the LSAT score. Chapter 5 discusses the index number (a combination of the LSAT score and GPA), which, at some schools, is the very first thing a committee member sees and evaluates.

There is no getting around it: The LSAT score is important. Yet the degree to which admissions officers rely on it varies according to each particular situation (and school). They tend to rely on it most when analyzing students from unusual backgrounds, or when comparing people from substantially different backgrounds. If you went to a university not well known to the admissions officers, for example, you can expect extra emphasis to be placed on your LSAT score. The LSAT score will likewise be used to compare someone at the top of her class at a weak university with an applicant who did moderately well at a leading university.

The essay portion of the LSAT is read by admissions officers at some schools, and ignored at others. It is worth your while to take it seriously. Not only may it be regarded in its own right, but it may also be used to put your personal statement in context. If your personal statement is a brilliant piece of literature, but your LSAT writing sample is disturbingly shoddy, the discrepancy may be noted by the committee. They may question whether you actually wrote your personal statement.

HOW TO PREPARE FOR THE LSAT

COURSE SELECTION

Taking a good range of challenging courses during college is a good idea for many reasons. There is some thinking that logic courses, in particular, help develop the test-taking skills required on the logical reasoning sections of the LSAT. There is no need to go overboard, though. Contrary to the suggestions of one (unintentionally) hilarious book (which gives a long list of undergraduate majors and the average LSAT scores of people listing those majors), your choice of majors does not determine your LSAT score. (The author of that book hasn't mastered introductory statistics (or logic): correlation is not the same as causation; i.e., those who choose to major in physics or math (average LSAT 157.6) presumably do better on the LSAT than those who major in education (average LSAT 148.2) because they are, on average, smarter and thus better test-takers, not because physics labs turned them into multiple-choice test whizzes.)

EXAM-SPECIFIC PREPARATION

It is not easy to prepare for the LSAT at the same time you are investigating schools and preparing your applications. To avoid this problem, and to give yourself the time to prepare properly, try to take the exam before you intend to apply. Besides avoiding scheduling conflicts, you will have the chance to prepare better and retake it if necessary.

You have two options if you wish to prepare seriously for the LSAT. You can prepare on your own using specially designed preparatory books or you can take preparatory classes. Self-preparation has several substantial advantages. It is (relatively) low cost, offers complete flexibility of schedule, and allows you to tailor your preparation to suit your own needs. On the other hand, preparatory classes also offer several advantages. They force you to start preparing in earnest well in advance of the exam, they guide you through the mass of potential preparatory material, they offer you an expert on call when you have questions, and they give you the opportunity to study with other people (and compare yourself with them). Finally, their price and inconvenience will be outweighed for some people by the higher scores they are likely to produce as a result.

The appropriate choice for you will depend upon the kind of person you are, your financial resources, your goals, and other variables. Those who almost certainly should take a prep course are those who:

- Have not taken similar tests before, or have not done so in many years
- Tend to test below their overall ability level
- Lack the self-discipline necessary to prepare on an individual basis
- Need substantial help on one or more parts of the exam, such as those who have let their logic muscles atrophy

ACCOMMODATED TESTING

Law school applicants with learning or physical disabilities may be able to take the LSAT exam under circumstances suited to their own situations. At one extreme, this may mean permission to bring a pillow to the exam site (for someone with a broken tailbone); at another, it may mean extra time to complete one or more sections of the exam. LSAC provides substantial discussion of what is required to qualify for special conditions on its website (www.lsac.org). In general, you will be required to provide suitable explanation and evidence of your condition. Although the LSAC site does not so state, the general rule is that the greater the potential advantage you seek (such as extra time, rather than a softer seat), the greater the proof (expert diagnoses, documented history) you must provide of your disability.

In years past, the fact that someone took the test under an accommodation was not brought to law schools' attention. As a result, test-takers had every reason to try for an extra-time accommodation. Now that LSAC notifies schools when an applicant takes the exam under an accommodation (although the reporting does not specify the type of disability or accommodation), many applicants fear that admissions committees will view an "accommodated" score skeptically. As a result, many who would qualify for such an accommodation do not seek one. Their LSAT scores, consequently, are often far below what they could have been with extra time. According to one LSAC study, test-takers exhibit close to a nine-point increase when they repeat the test under accommodated conditions. Because law schools almost invariably consider accommodated scores as equal to scores achieved under standard test conditions, applicants who fail to seek an accommodation for which they qualify hurt their admissions chances.

MOST COMMON FORMS OF ACCOMMODATION

➤ Extra time

➤ Alternate (non "scantron") answer sheet

➤ Use of a reader or scribe

➤ Breaks between sections

➤ Sitting/standing with a podium

➤ Wheelchair access

If you think you qualify for an accommodation, by all means apply for it. Note, however, that finding and accessing the right experts, giving them suitable time to diagnose you and submit their findings, and allowing LSAC sufficient time to evaluate your submissions can require months. Thus, you should start the process well in advance of the regular exam registration deadlines.

ADMISSIONS DEANS DISCUSS ACCOMMODATED TESTING

IMPACT OF ACCOMMODATED SCORES

I always encourage disabled applicants to do their best to get the necessary accommodation for their disability. I have never encountered a case in which getting an accommodation hurt a person's application chances. We are interested in judging applicants on the basis of their ability, not on the basis of their disability. The accommodated score provides a more accurate description of their ability. *Edward Tom, Boalt Hall (Berkeley)*

We believe that if you think you might qualify for an accommodation you should request it from LSAC. We don't evaluate an accommodated score any differently from one achieved under regular conditions. *Monica Ingram, Texas*

We take accommodated scores at face value: we don't discount them at all. *Chloe T. Reid, USC*

When someone first takes the LSAT without an accommodation and then again with an accommodation, we use only the accommodated score; we don't average them. *Edward Tom, Boalt Hall (Berkeley)*

If you think you might qualify for an accommodation, I strongly urge you to apply for it. I treat accommodated scores just like regular scores. *Sarah Zearfoss, Michigan*

OTHER ISSUES

I always urge people to seek an accommodation on the LSAT if they think they have a condition warranting one. *Susan Palmer, Virginia*

You don't have to supply to law schools the documentation you used to get the LSAT accommodation, but in many cases it would be helpful to your prospects to do so. *Todd Morton, Vanderbilt*

Be sure to start the process early, because LSAC is very precise and demanding in what it requires, which is a lot of documentation. *Chloe T. Reid, USC*

GETTING THE MOST OUT OF YOUR SELF-PREPARATION

If you decide to follow the self-study route, make sure you do two things. First, buy and use several of the popular prep books, because no one book on its own contains sufficient discussion of the strategies, techniques, and fundamentals required. Second, be sure you practice on past LSAT exams rather than on the very different exams created by the various prep book authors. Old exams are available from Law Services; you can order them when registering.

You will need to keep to a regular review schedule, such as spending two hours a night twice a week, and six to eight hours on weekends, for six to eight weeks before the exam. Having a study partner can ease the strain and provide you with someone who can explain something that mystifies you (and vice versa). The best partner is likely to be someone with the opposite strengths to yours. Thus, if you are strong in reading comprehension, find someone who is excellent in logical reasoning.

CHOOSING A TEST-PREP COURSE

Test-prep courses tend to cost a lot of money, so be sure you will get what you pay for. The best value, and best instruction, may not come from the largest firms. Look carefully at their smaller competitors before handing over the $1,000 or more that the name-brand companies demand.

There are several reasons to look at the full range of test-prep companies rather than opting for the default choice of one of the famous providers. First, the major companies' claims that they have ultra-sophisticated materials, embodying the otherwise unknowable secrets of the exams, are spurious. For one thing, employees of each company, large and small, monitor the efforts of their competitors and readily incorporate their best ideas. Second, although the major companies can boast enormous libraries of materials on which to practice, few students utilize more than a modest fraction of these materials. Third, the major companies inevitably (given the huge numbers they employ) take on many instructors of less than stellar intellect (including out-of-work actors, waiters, and so on), provide them with limited training, and suffer from high instructor turnover. The best of the smaller companies can avoid this difficulty.

RETAKING THE EXAM

If, upon completing the LSAT, you are sure you did not perform well, you have the option to cancel your score—by either filling in the score cancellation section on the answer sheet or sending a written cancellation request to Law Services within five days. If you do so, you will not receive a score or your answer sheet.

Ideally, you should take the LSAT only once. If you opt to retake the test after receiving your first score, all scores will be reported to schools by LSDAS. Before deciding that this is necessary, however, you should analyze your application to see whether your LSAT score will actually handicap you significantly. Note that some people with scores in the mid-160s or below got into top programs because they marketed themselves well (and had something worth marketing). You may be better off applying the time you would otherwise spend studying for the LSAT working on your essay or improving your other credentials. Additionally, Law Services prohibits you from taking the exam more than three times within a two-year period.

Schools are now torn between averaging your scores and using only the highest ones. Most believe that an average is the best indicator of your ability. On the other hand, they need only report your highest score to *U.S. News*, so your lesser scores do not affect their own ranking. This frees them to consider only the highest scores, if they so choose. At the moment, a substantial majority use the average whereas a minority use the highest score when evaluating applicants.

GENERAL TIPS ON PREPARING TO ACE THE LSAT

➤ Familiarize yourself with the tests by taking plenty of sample exams. Be sure to practice on actual prior LSATs available from LSAC. Review the answers you miss. Make sure, at the very least, you know exactly what to expect in terms of a test's format—what each section asks you to do, how long each section is—before going in. That way you will not waste time reading directions (or panicking), and will be able to concentrate on your performance.

➤ Take care of your health. Get substantial rest for at least two nights before taking the exam.

➤ Be organized on the day of the test. Give yourself enough time to have a leisurely breakfast and prepare yourself. If the site is not familiar to you, be sure you have precise directions to it and know exactly how long it will take to get there, allowing for traffic or unexpected delays. Arrive at the testing site early so that you have time to go to the restroom and calm yourself.

➤ Do not wait until the last possible administration of the exam to take it. You may fall ill and be unable to take it, or you may need to retake it to boost your score. For regular admissions that means taking the exam no later than October (and preferably in June). For Early Action or Early Decision, taking the exam in February is recommended, although June is also acceptable.

➤ A dirty little secret of LSAT test administration is that many centers are noisy and filled with uncomfortable seats and desks. Check with prior test takers to determine whether your chosen site is suitable. If not, find one nearby that is.

FOR INTERNATIONAL APPLICANTS ONLY: THE TOEFL

The TOEFL (Test of English as a Foreign Language) is a test administered by Educational Testing Service (ETS) to non-native English speakers to measure English proficiency. Some law schools require TOEFL scores from overseas students (except native English-speaking American citizens living overseas) and those who have lived in the U.S. for fewer than a given number of years. Often, the admission materials do not specify whether or not the test is required, so it is advisable to call and ask.

Unlike the LSAT, the TOEFL is not a complicated test. If you are comfortable speaking and reading English, it should pose little problem for you.

The current electronic TOEFL format tests all four language skills: reading, writing, listening, and speaking. Five scores are given:

Reading	0–30 Points
Writing	0–30
Listening	0–30
Speaking	0–30
Total	0–120

The top law schools are generally looking for a minimum score of 100, but higher scores are greatly preferred. (The equivalent of a 100 on the older versions of the exam was 250 on the computerized exam or 600 on the paper exam.)

Note that your TOEFL score is valid for only two years, unlike your LSAT score, which is valid for five years.

TO REGISTER FOR THE TOEFL

To find out more about the TOEFL exam or register for it, contact:

TOEFL
Educational Testing Service
P.O. Box 6151
Princeton, NJ 08541-6151
USA
(609) 771-7500 or (877) 863-3546
toefl@ets.org
www.ets.org/toefl/contact.html

ADMISSIONS DEANS DISCUSS THE LSAT

HOW MUCH DECISIONAL WEIGHT IS PLACED ON THE LSAT SCORE?

For those with relatively mediocre academic records, a strong LSAT is very important. If we're looking at a candidate with a weak LSAT, we'll only discount it if the rest of the file has no weaknesses. (The same thing is true in general: If any one aspect of the file is weak, the rest of the file should be strong enough to compensate.) Incidentally, in general we care more about the four years of sustained academic work than the LSAT. *Faye Deal, Stanford*

The importance of the LSAT score varies, of course, according to the nature of each applicant's candidacy, but its importance is due in part to its being a statistically validated predictor of (first year) law school performance. *Susan Palmer, Virginia*

It's an important factor, as is the GPA. Law school is an educational endeavor; therefore our evaluation process attempts to predict one's ability to excel academically and, specifically, at Columbia, which both the LSAT and GPA address. *Nkonye Iwerebon, Columbia*

Everything we know suggests that small differences in scores matter very little in predicting performance, but some schools act as if they matter a lot. *Rick Geiger, Cornell*

The amount of decisional importance accorded the LSAT score depends somewhat upon the nature of the applicant. It receives more weight for those from a softer school or program. On the other hand, it receives less weight for second-language English speakers or for older applicants, for whom we have more to look at and each piece of their application is therefore less significant. *Sarah C. Zearfoss, Michigan*

If standardized tests have not been a good predictor of your academic performance in the past, be sure to make this clear. Thus, if you had a 1000 SAT combined score but then got a 3.9 in a tough major at Johns Hopkins, we will take your under-testing into account. *Susan Palmer, Virginia*

LSAT performance matters most for someone with a GPA below our mid-point. *Don Rebstock, Northwestern*

How Do You Use the LSAT Writing Sample?

Some faculty read the writing sample and compare it to the application essays. Among other things, they look to see whether they are of similar quality to be sure that the applicant actually wrote both essays. *Megan A. Barnett, Yale*

My advice is to take the LSAT writing sample seriously, because we do. We regard it as an important source of information about your writing ability (which is critical to success in law school and beyond). *Rob Schwartz, UCLA*

If you do not write a substantial amount, the admissions committee may draw one of two conclusions. Either you are unable to draw any conclusion from the facts presented in this relatively simple "either-or" scenario, which does not augur well for your ability to handle the complex and nuanced problems you will confront in law school, or you blew it off, which suggests something about your attitude. Neither is good. The LSAT writing sample also gets particularly close scrutiny in some cases, such as that of a science student with little evidence of having done substantial writing in college or a non-native English speaker who struggles somewhat with the language.   *Susan Palmer, Virginia*

The LSAT writing sample is important in our decision-making. Some members of the admissions committee read it first, to get a clear sense of a candidate's writing ability. We want to know whether you can put together a sentence, a paragraph, an argument.   *William Hoye, Duke*

We do not pay much attention to the LSAT writing sample. Instead, we consider the personal statement to be an applicant's main writing sample.   *Don Rebstock, Northwestern*

How Do You Interpret Multiple Scores?

We average LSAT scores if a candidate takes the test more than once. Don't take the exam unless you have prepared for it; it's meant to be taken once. Cancel the score if something goes radically wrong during the exam or if you feel that you haven't been at your best.   *Kenneth Kleinrock, NYU*

We look at all of the scores. Unless the applicant beats the standard deviation (about eight points), we use the average score. There is one exception, however. If the person took the test before finding out a learning disability, and then took the accommodated test, we would use the second score. We would also, of course, look at the rest of the file to see if they were accommodated in class.   *Edward Tom, Boalt Hall (Berkeley)*

For reporting purposes, we use the highest score. For admissions purposes, however, we generally average the scores—unless there is a 7-plus point differential.   *Chloe T. Reid, USC*

We now consider the highest score. *Anne Richard, George Washington*

We look at all of the scores, recognizing that the single best predictor is likely to be the average.   *Todd Morton, Vanderbilt*

If you take the LSAT more than once, all scores and their average will be considered. If there are circumstances that you believe affected your performance on a prior test, we encourage you to provide an additional statement with your application explaining those circumstances. The Admissions Committee will consider such information and may, at its discretion, evaluate your application based on the higher or highest LSAT score.   *Renée Post, Penn*

We take everything into consideration: the number of times an applicant took the exam, the amount of improvement, and the reasons for retaking it.   *Nkonye Iwerebon, Columbia*

Sometimes there is a very wide discrepancy between the scores, in which case the applicant should provide an explanation for the discrepancy. *Kenneth Kleinrock, NYU*

Our interpretation may depend upon the other information the application presents. We may consider the amount of time between the two tests, whether there were any particular circumstances that may have had an impact on the applicant's ability to perform, like illness or poor testing conditions, the "point spread" between the two tests, and which of the two scores appear to be most consistent with the applicant's overall record. The greater the disparity between the scores, the more likely we are to conclude that the average is not the best predictor. *Susan Palmer, Virginia*

If you have widely divergent LSAT scores, you should include a short (one paragraph) appendix explaining the discrepancy in the scores. *Megan A. Barnett, Yale*

SHOULD A CANDIDATE TAKE THE LSAT MORE THAN ONCE?

It is a good idea to retake the LSAT if you feel that you underachieved the first time; this shows that you have done everything you can to present the best possible file. This is especially worthwhile if you can improve by more than the standard error of measurement (three points). *Don Rebstock, Northwestern*

I don't think it's a particularly fun experience, so I'd suggest you think back to the first exam. When you walked out, did you feel you had done well? If so, retaking it may not make sense. On the other hand, if you felt it had gone badly wrong, it may well make sense to retake it. *Todd Morton, Vanderbilt*

Approach the test with the mindset that you are only going to take it once. *Renée Post, Penn*

WHICH IS MORE IMPORTANT, THE UNDERGRADUATE RECORD OR THE LSAT SCORE?

The top law schools generally consider both academic indicators—the undergraduate record and the LSAT—important. The most competitive schools in fact have so many fantastic applicants that they do not need to make substantial compromises by accepting students who have either excellent grades or excellent scores, but not both. In other words, it is best if you compare favorably with others on both accounts.

Still, the top law schools differ slightly in their messages about which is more crucial, a great undergraduate record or a great LSAT score. The basic story from all of the most competitive schools is that you cannot completely override a poor LSAT score with a great college record, just as you cannot completely compensate for poor college grades with a strong LSAT. Both count for something and, depending upon which schools you apply to, they vary in their value.

You can determine how some law schools value the undergraduate record versus the LSAT score by examining the various formulas they used to calculate index numbers for their applicants. The LSAT is generally weighted at three to six times the weight accorded the GPA. In other words, a candidate's LSAT score generally counts substantially more than her GPA at these schools. For one thing, law schools see the LSAT score as the best indicator (at least in the absence of anything better) of raw intellectual talent; no school wants students who will have to struggle to do the more demanding work that a rigorous law curriculum requires. For another, law school deans and admissions directors have become highly aware of the inordinate impact LSAT scores have upon their *U.S. News* rankings.

That said, strong test scores and a poor college record suggest that, though a student might be intellectually gifted, he is lazy and lacks determination to succeed. No law school—and no law school professor—is looking for apathetic candidates. (Remember that most law schools are largely run by and for the faculty.) Law schools generally figure that hardworking undergraduates will continue to work as diligently in law school and that those who are lazy in college will continue to be so in law school. Therefore, at the margins, some schools will prefer good collegiate performers over good test takers—especially good collegiate performers who can show that they tested poorly on the SAT and other college-entry exams, yet still achieved good grades at a strong undergraduate institution.

At all law schools, generally speaking, the importance of the LSAT score versus the college record changes according to the applicant's age. The longer a candidate has been out of college, the more important the LSAT score becomes; similarly, the significance of one's undergraduate GPA shrinks over time, especially for those with particularly valuable work experience.

ADMISSIONS DEANS DISCUSS HOW THEY INTERPRET MIXED (GRADE AND LSAT) DATA

We look carefully when we see disparate predictors: someone who has a 3.9 but a mediocre LSAT. If they can prove that their SAT score was similarly mediocre, we will put more weight on the GPA. An applicant with a high LSAT but a low GPA, on the other hand, does not have as strong an argument. We know that you can take a prep course, etc.   *Edward Tom, Boalt Hall (Berkeley)*

Someone who is weak in one important area may not be able to make up for it with strength in another area. Thus having good work experience may not make up for a lackluster academic record or LSAT results.   *Kenneth Kleinrock, NYU*

When someone has excelled on the LSAT but not in college, we examine and weigh carefully the circumstances of the college record. For instance, was it a matter of adjustment troubles early in college, an illness, the pursuit of a major for which the applicant was not naturally suited, or simply due to lack of effort. The reverse is also true: the low LSAT score could be the result of many factors, including illness, poor preparation, anxiety, or a history of poor performances in standardized tests. Whatever the case, we review the application holistically and make a decision accordingly.   *Nkonye Iwerebon, Columbia*

Faculty members on the admissions committee tend to react negatively to candidates with high LSAT and low GPA numbers. They sometimes view them as slackers who can't sustain commitment to studying. This sort of candidate therefore needs to explain convincingly the reason for the low grades. The candidates with low LSAT and high GPA numbers face a different scrutiny. We look carefully at how they were able to earn the high grades, considering the school they attended, their majors, the grading policies at the school, etc. We want to understand whether (and how) their academic performance would make them a standout student in law school.   *Chloe T. Reid, USC*

For people with a very strong GPA and weak LSAT, we look at their course selection. In particular, we look for academic success in more than one field. For example, does a sociology major do well in economics, statistics, and logic courses. *Elizabeth Rosselot, Boston College*

One can help make up for the other. The LSAT is probably a bit more important on average, but the relative importance of the two depends upon the whole package; I can think of examples in each direction.   *Sarah C. Zearfoss, Michigan*

A weak LSAT score combined with a high GPA in a nonacademic major at a weak school is by no means compelling. On the other hand, a 2.9 GPA combined with a 170 LSAT may be OK if an external factor drove the poor grade performance, assuming that it won't do so in law school. If someone had to raise two preschoolers while attending college, but has them safely ensconced in school now, we may pay much more attention to the potential implicit in the LSAT result than the GPA. We are most likely to overlook weak undergraduate performance when someone has matured substantially, such as through a number of years of work. *Susan Palmer, Virginia*

We take all factors into account in making admissions decisions. If one element of your application is particularly weak, you may want to include a separate, brief—certainly not more than a page—addendum.   *Megan A. Barnett, Yale*

When someone has a strong LSAT and weak undergraduate performance, we want to understand what was going on in college that he or she will turn around in law school. The LSAT score is probably not the best evidence that the person can thrive in an academic setting. When someone has a weak LSAT and very strong undergraduate performance, the situation is inherently more complex. In general, we believe that the candidate's overall record is likely to determine our decision. We've seen enough cases of people doing well without a great LSAT that we won't let it be the determinative factor.   *Rick Geiger, Cornell*

WORK EXPERIENCE

WHAT ARE ADMISSIONS COMMITTEES LOOKING FOR?

Although it is not required for applicants to have had significant work experience, more and more students are arriving at law schools having already worked full time for a year or more. Many have had accomplished careers, often entirely unrelated to the law. Law schools find this quite appealing. Columbia notes in its admissions materials that, "Our school has been strengthened by a maturity and experiential enrichment that older students bring to their classmates and faculty." Many schools are even willing to deemphasize a less-than-exemplary academic record if an applicant has performed well in a demanding—or unusual—industry.

The amount of work experience tends to be much less important than the nature and quality of the experience. Those applicants whose undergraduate performance was comparatively weak, however, should consider working a little longer in order to lessen the currency of grades and course selection, and to increase the amount of positive work-related information to show to the admissions committee.

THE NATURE OF THE EXPERIENCE

Many successful candidates take the tried-and-true path to law school by working as paralegals. Although they get to see what actually goes on in a law firm (thereby learning a bit about law, which many applicants have little or no knowledge of) while simultaneously proving that they truly know what they are getting into, this is not necessarily the best pre-law work route to take. For one, admissions committees know that few paralegals develop real skills; most paralegals spend the majority of their time at the Xerox machine or filing documents rather than learning anything substantial about the law. It is difficult, in fact, for the law schools to judge many candidates' paralegal experience. Because even leading law firms (unlike strategy consulting firms and investment banks) do not recruit only the best and brightest college graduates, excelling against such indifferent competition is not necessarily impressive. For another thing, it is difficult to differentiate yourself from the pool of applicants as a paralegal. You have a far easier time positioning yourself when you have gained substantial and relevant skills in a more unusual profession.

Thus, working in a law firm is by no means the best or only route to law school. Accepted students are successful journalists, engineers, playwrights, teachers, businesspeople, and graphic artists. Do not assume that admissions committees will penalize you for having devoted a piece of your life to pursuing an ambition that has little or nothing to do with law. On the contrary, this experience makes you an attractive, somewhat unusual candidate—assuming you market yourself well. Remember, too, that there is a big difference between simply doing a job for one to two years and becoming a true professional at something, with three or more years of work experience. This, of course, does not mean you have to work at something for three or more years before going to law school; but your efforts at selling yourself on the basis of your work experience will generally be more easily digested when your commitment to and accomplishments in a field are substantial. Note that you must also show a law degree makes sense in your life and that you have a bright-looking future; in other words, there is a point at which the value of your years of experience begins to decline. Do not squander time in a job just for the sake of appearing to have career depth in a previous field; gain relevant skills, contacts, knowledge, and credibility—and then move on to your law studies.

ACHIEVEMENT AND IMPACT AT WORK

The key to impressing admissions officers with your work experience is not a matter of your specific job or industry, or even of how long you have worked. What you accomplish is the key. Admissions officers want to see people successfully take on responsibility, perform complicated analysis, wrestle with difficult decisions, and bring about change. They want people to progress in their jobs and develop relevant skills, with consequent improvements in responsibilities, salary, and title. People who meet these criteria will be highly valued no matter what industry they come from.

To impress admissions people with your work experience, see that you can demonstrate as many of the following as possible:

- First and foremost, you have been successful at whatever your job involves.
- You have worked well with other people.
- You have developed substantial leadership ability and experience.
- No matter what your job has required of you, you have done more (and exceeded your boss's expectations).
- You have had a wide range of experiences, each one requiring different skills.
- You have done a better job than anyone else in a similar position.
- You have achieved meaningful results.
- You have gained in-depth analytical skills.
- You have gained substantial writing (and oral presentation) experience.
- You have acquired substantial skills in your job—and if they are applicable to legal study and work, all the better.
- You have learned (via close observation if not practice) what field of law best fits you.

Another good reason for acquiring substantial work experience is that it will enable you to write a substantive essay that will likely have more depth than a college senior's essay. Even if your job is a low-level one, you have the possibility of writing about "getting your hands dirty" in the real world. If your work experience gives you little to write about, you face an uphill battle in your applications. If this is the case, consider waiting a year and devoting that year to making an impact in your job. Focus on developing your skills, assuming new and different responsibilities, and impressing one or more potential recommenders to maximize your chances of success when you do apply.

ADMISSIONS DEANS DISCUSS WORK EXPERIENCE

DOES WORK EXPERIENCE "COUNT" IN ADMISSIONS?

Employers love law students who have had real work experience before law school. *Faye Deal, Stanford*

The benefits of having substantial work experience (by which I do not mean waiting tables, etc.) include developing interpersonal and relational skills, the discipline of having to show up and work hard every day, plus learning to juggle multiple tasks. We have found both for the first semester and overall, GPAs were higher for those with substantial work experience than for those without. The additional experience also plays very well with recruiters. *Don Rebstock, Northwestern*

At Columbia, we believe that people should attend law school when they feel ready to do so. That could mean going "straight through" or after working for a year or more. That said, those who work before law school have the potential to make great contributions in the classroom and to have a beneficial impact on the experience of their class mates. *Nkonye Iwerebon, Columbia*

Work experience is not required, but it can certainly add to the strength of an application. If an applicant has several years of work experience in which they progress through the company before applying, the Committee is much more likely to be forgiving of a weakness elsewhere in the application. *Renée Post, Penn*

An applicant can offset a lack of extracurricular involvement as an undergrad by having substantial work experience after college. This goes toward demonstrating the maturity of a candidate; it also helps develop critical interpersonal skills. *Don Rebstock, Northwestern*

Those who have worked in jobs that have challenged them bring much more to a class than they otherwise would have had they come directly from college. In addition to working, they may have traveled, practiced their language skills, and developed their people skills. For example, they have learned about leadership, negotiation, and so on. *Kenneth Kleinrock, NYU*

Work experience "counts" on a number of levels. It is valuable to us if you've developed substantive expertise in a field. Insofar as you have to make an affirmative decision to leave a field in which you are a success, choosing to attend law school generally suggests that you are making a thoughtful decision. It can also help to make up for undistinguished undergraduate performance, particularly when it demonstrates that you have developed focus and maturity. *Susan Palmer, Virginia*

We like people who have experienced real life, dealt with real people and real situations. This cannot but help people in law school and afterwards. Over 60 percent of our incoming class has had experience. *Rick Geiger, Cornell*

Some faculty members consider work experience very important and care a lot about it; others are less concerned with it. *Megan A. Barnett, Yale*

Work experience can help make up for other elements of an application that are somewhat weak, but only if someone has really proved him- or herself and achieved something noteworthy. To help overcome the damage done by a weak undergraduate record requires at least two years, preferably more, of strong work performance. *Sarah C. Zearfoss, Michigan*

We try to put together a group of students who can learn from one another as well as from professors. This can't happen by just taking people on the basis of their GPAs and LSATs. We value having a union organizer with ten years of experience, even if this person might have a mediocre undergraduate record and LSAT relative to some other applicants.   *Faye Deal, Stanford*

HOW IMPORTANT IS IT THAT CANDIDATES HAVE EXPOSURE TO LEGAL WORK BEFORE APPLYING?

I prefer to see business related experience rather than work in a law firm. In consulting and investment banking, for example, the demands on the person are great, whereas the responsibilities in a law firm tend to be less challenging. Thus the former carries more weight, although we do look at both.   *Don Rebstock, Northwestern*

Law firm work can give you the opportunity to see the work of lawyers—which is largely about writing, something many candidates don't understand, but it has limited admissions value. At the very most it indicates an interest in law. *Chloe T. Reid, USC*

Exposure to law can be very helpful regarding deciding whether to apply, but not in improving the chances of admission.   *William Hoye, Duke*

Law interacts with the world, so it is better that someone learn about the world (before coming to law school) than work in law.   *Don Rebstock, Northwestern*

WHAT KINDS OF WORK EXPERIENCE DO YOU LIKE TO SEE?

The specific kind of job is not as important as what you make of it. Did you take on challenges and stretch yourself? Did you excel in the job?   *Megan A. Barnett, Yale*

Paralegaling at a large firm is sometimes not helpful in developing useful skills or demonstrating your abilities. In fact, I find very interesting work experience that is far removed from law. In general, I like to see high-powered professional work, such as consulting or investment banking, public interest employment, or something in science and technology.   *Sarah C. Zearfoss, Michigan*

A student who once heard me say that the specific job you hold is less important than the extent to which you learn and grow from the experience responded by saying, "Yeah, as long as you don't work at McDonald's or something." I think that if a year at McDonald's gives you some insight into what it is like to earn a living in the lower level of the service economy and teaches you to communicate with people who are less well-educated and less sophisticated than yourself, then that will have been a pretty powerful experience.   *Susan Palmer, Virginia*

Categories of applicants who have had interesting jobs or experience that make them highly desirable include Olympians: they have shown discipline and commitment; they are interesting as classmates; military officers: their comments on international trade and treaties can be valuable; business owners; Rhodes scholars; authors of books; Capital Hill people: they can really comment on bills they have worked on. *Andy Cornblatt, Georgetown*

We like to see any sort of work in which the candidate was productive—not selling Popsicles on the corner. *Chloe T. Reid, USC*

The Committee likes to see anything substantive—where applicants can demonstrate expansion of their skill set or progression in their responsibilities and position—or anything requiring decision making, critical or analytical skills, or writing ability. Of course, it can be difficult to do such work immediately after college; it may take a couple of years to reach a position of such responsibility. *Renée Post, Penn*

An impressive career in business, government, the military, or elsewhere will certainly enhance an application. That said, we also like unique job experience—we look to incorporate a broad range of experience in our classes. *Anne Richard, George Washington*

WHAT PERCENTAGE OF CANDIDATES NOW HAVE WORK EXPERIENCE BEFORE APPLYING?

Ninety percent of our class has full-time, substantial work experience, not the waiting tables sort. Our long-term goal is for everyone to have had at least two years full-time work experience. We still admit a number of college seniors, but not without an interview. *Don Rebstock, Northwestern*

There is an increasing percentage of applicants with several years of work experience. *Edward Tom, Boalt Hall (Berkeley)*

Fewer than 15 percent of our candidates have prior full-time work experience. However, many have numerous internships which expose them to the work environment. *Chloe T. Reid, USC*

Sixty percent enter Penn with work experience, although a majority of them have two years or fewer *Renée Post, Penn*

HOW IMPORTANT IS IT THAT A CANDIDATE BE SUCCESSFUL IN HIS OR HER JOB?

It's not a matter of what job someone has. Instead, in any field, it's a matter of demonstrating achievement, success, and growth in that field. *Jim Milligan, Columbia*

It's important to see success in their jobs; I like to understand why they chose that field. It's also valuable to understand how it led to an interest in law, and how it will benefit a person in studying law. *William Hoye, Duke*

How Do You Evaluate the Quality of a Candidate's Work Experience?

One of the key things we look for is the amount of responsibility you have taken on, in whatever position(s) you've had. We prefer you being in the trenches doing real work rather than just Xeroxing files.   *Faye Deal, Stanford*

The jobs we like to see are those that help prepare applicants for law school work. For example, some jobs require enormous amounts of analytical effort and training, where the workload is enormous. Some jobs have associated training programs and require a person to make it through one selection process after another. Some jobs are very difficult to get. Some investment banking and consulting jobs, for example, require a person have very good analytical, writing, oral communication, and presentation skills, and handle themselves effectively in person. Other jobs give opportunities to interact with a broad range of constituencies. We take all of this into account in evaluating people. People should do whatever work they are interested in doing. We like a lot of different things; we prefer to have a class with people who have a wide range of background and experience.   *Kenneth Kleinrock, NYU*

We look to see whether the candidate has succeeded and advanced on the job. We consider whether the candidate has been promoted or been given additional responsibilities; had a positive impact on people and projects at the organization; and developed important skill sets. Not surprisingly, we also look to see whether the candidate has demonstrated a strong work ethic, which we can discern from the candidate's track record and employer's recommendation. *Nkonye Iwerebon, Columbia*

It can be difficult to assess what people have actually done in their jobs. We can't necessarily tell from their résumé (especially given the puffery in some) or from the name of the company they worked for. If you have done work that was qualitatively different than others, have your supervisor write a recommendation that addresses this. It has more credibility coming out of someone else's mouth. *Rick Geiger, Cornell*

ADMISSIONS DEANS EVALUATE THE IMPACT OF AGE AND EXPERIENCE UPON ADMISSIONS DECISIONS

Evaluating Older Applicants

We don't take academic risks. Everyone taken here is capable of doing very well academically. We are, however, willing to take someone who is at a different level of development than he or she was in college—someone who underperformed years ago but who has accomplished a lot in recent years. *Joyce Curll, Harvard*

We expect more career focus—a better sense of where they are headed after law school—from older applicants. *Faye Deal, Stanford*

Oftentimes they don't have as strong a GPA as a younger applicant because of the grade inflation that has occurred since then. So for them the LSAT and their work experience will be more important in our evaluation. *Anne Richard, George Washington*

The first thing we want to understand is why they are coming to law school at this time in their life. While we would like to have more older students in our student body because they add to our diversity, we are a bit paternalistic because we know what law school will demand of them and of their families. We want to ensure their success and therefore we will also want to be convinced that they will be able to cut it academically after having been out of school for years. Do they still have the perseverance and stamina to succeed in law school? *Chloe T. Reid, USC*

I look at each person as being at a given state of development. The more experience they have, the more you can see where they will get to. For those with real accomplishment, the less you look at the indicators of potential (undergraduate record, LSAT, etc.). Similarly, the less the accomplishment (for older applicants), the more it counts against them, no matter what the initial indicators say. *Joyce Curll, Harvard*

Undergraduate grades are less valuable as predictors after a number of years. With older applicants we look more at the LSAT, graduate work (if any) or additional undergraduate course work undertaken after graduation, and, of course, the nature of his or her work experience. *William Hoye, Duke*

A twenty-two-year-old poli sci major is likely to have the decision based upon his undergraduate record and LSAT score. But if you're a thirty-year-old, you've been out of school for some time and we'll evaluate your application differently. Your undergrad record will count for less. We will, instead, focus on what you could add to the classroom; we'll consider your motivation for law study carefully. You need to address these matters in your personal statement. *Elizabeth Rosselot, Boston College*

For younger applicants, we tend to give less weight to comments they make about what they intend to do in the future. Learning about the plans of older applicants is much more important. They should make it clear that they have thought about their future careers. Failing to do so—giving me the sense that they are not fully aware of where they are headed and how they intend to get there—harms their chances. *Sarah C. Zearfoss, Michigan*

For older applicants, particularly those who have already had successful careers, the question in the minds of file readers will be "why are you switching careers at this point?" Include an explanation; don't make us guess what the answer is. *Megan A. Barnett, Yale*

We particularly want to know your motivation, why you want to go to law school. It's highly appropriate to add an explanation to your file. *Ann Killian Perry, Chicago*

EVALUATING COLLEGE SENIORS

For those applying when seniors in college, we generally focus even more on the academic record than for someone who's completed their undergraduate record and been out working. *Kenneth Kleinrock, NYU*

The demands of law school are enormous, so we want to see that applicants are prepared to balance the competing demands they'll face. Thus, time management skills matter. We want to see academic excellence, but we prefer that applicants also be involved in the community (whether that be the university or the larger community) or working, too. *Renée Post, Penn*

They generally do not have a significant track record in anything but academics, so we pay greater attention to their academic performance. (Having internships or a year of work experience doesn't constitute a track record—much as we like to see these things for what they say about someone's drive.) *Anne Richard, George Washington*

EXTRACURRICULAR, PERSONAL, AND COMMUNITY ACTIVITIES

WHAT ARE ADMISSIONS COMMITTEES LOOKING FOR?

Extracurricular, personal, and community activities include all the nonacademic endeavors to which you have devoted yourself during college and since leaving the academic environment. These include team and individual athletics; artistic, dramatic, or musical performance; private activities such as playing chess or reading; religious activities; involvement in various clubs and organizations; newspaper or other editorial work; and community service.

Extracurricular and community activities are important to admissions officers for many reasons. First, your activity credentials help show that you interact with others on a regular basis. Law schools generally prefer sociable types (especially leaders) to loners, although most schools will take some candidates who appear a bit antisocial if they are strong enough in other regards. Extracurricular, personal, and community activities also show how you choose to spend your time away from school and work; demonstrate leadership, initiative, special talents, and honed skills; provide evidence of personality and character traits; and complement ideas presented within your academic profile about how you will fare in a law career. In sum, they give admissions officers an idea about how you might contribute to the law school environment if accepted. Extracurricular achievement is thus particularly important for those with little or no work experience.

A law school would much rather see that you have put many hours of valuable effort over several years into two activities than joined every group in college, playing very limited roles. Admissions officers do not share Nikita Khrushchev's view (regarding nuclear weapons) that "quantity has a quality all its own." In fact, a long list of activities merely dilutes the overall impression that your nonacademic profile gives an admissions officer or encourages skepticism about your candidacy.

The admissions officers are not looking for any particular activities on a student's palette of involvements. They do not much care whether you are editor in chief of the yearbook or director of your company's environmental and recycling team. They are, however, looking for students who have been involved in a few activities for a good length of time, showing commitment and passion. A bit of a balance is usually ideal, so that a student does not appear one-dimensional, but in general commitment and focus is better than being the "all-around" type.

Remember that anything and everything can "count" as part of your profile here. Let us assume, for example, that you are interested in a certain period in American history and have spent time at antique shows and auctions augmenting your collection of furniture and other pieces from the era. This way of spending your Saturdays can certainly become fodder for "extracurricular" material, whether it be merely mentioning it on an activity list or résumé or incorporating it into your essays somehow.

GETTING MAXIMUM VALUE FROM EXTRACURRICULAR AND COMMUNITY ACTIVITIES

Although it does not really matter what activities you choose, keep in mind the following important points about your extracurricular and community record:

▶ *Depth of involvement:* You want to be able to show that you have been committed to one or more activities for a length of time, preferably three or more years. Show that you have advanced within at least one activity and consistently devoted substantial time to it over several years.

➤ *Leadership:* Show that you have taken on an important leadership role in at least one activity. This means founding a club or group, becoming an appointed or elected high officer of a group, or directing a group's efforts in one area. Show that you can motivate others around you to contribute their best efforts to a common cause.

➤ *Something unusual:* Not everyone has the talent or resources to do something really out of the ordinary. But everyone can find a way to use his or her abilities to get involved in something that stands out from the usual student council/yearbook/varsity sports activities that show up frequently on law school applicants' résumés. Doing something a bit unusual can be beneficial because it will expand your own mind, exposing you to something you might not have run into without special effort, as well as make you a bit more memorable to the admissions officers. Training Seeing-Eye dogs, leading nature hikes, becoming a glass-blower, joining a "neighborhood watch" association to fight crime, or playing in a Korean drumming ensemble are examples of activities that are distinctive, but within reach.

➤ *Possession of at least two dimensions:* You want to present yourself as a focused individual with a memorable profile, not someone who dabbles in everything without much commitment to any one particular activity. But avoiding the tag of "well-rounded individual" does not mean you should become one-dimensional. Be sure there is at least one activity you can point to that stands out as not fitting into your main marketing scheme.

THE IMPORTANCE OF COMMUNITY SERVICE

Most law school applicants should be sure to have some sort of volunteer, community, or civic service to show for their four years in college or life beyond academia. As an exception to this general rule, those who come from very low-income families or are required to work a great deal to help support the family should not feel they need to add community service to their activity lists. If your application makes clear that you spend a substantial amount of energy working for wages necessary for your (or your family's) survival, you will not be expected to have donated your limited free time to charity work.

Other applicants, however, should at the very least have on their activity lists (or work experience lists) a mention of running an event at a Special Olympics function or raising money for a local charity. As with other areas of one's nonacademic profile, more depth in a community service project is always better than these kinds of single instances of volunteerism. Thus, it is much better if you can show that you worked for a cause for a length of time rather than showing up for one Saturday or participating in a single week-long campaign.

WHAT KIND OF COMMUNITY SERVICE?

It is not particularly important what group or cause you help with your time and effort. An admissions committee will be impressed whether you have helped blind children to learn Braille, contributed to an effort to save the seals, helped disadvantaged families with their income tax preparation, or served on the local school board. Of course, committing yourself to a particular activity could substantially help your positioning efforts if you plan to enter a field where your volunteer service could provide you with relevant experience. A candidate proclaiming an interest in family law, for example, would help himself by having worked at a free urban family law clinic for several years.

You should try to be as directly involved in your cause as possible rather than performing work that is only attached to the cause indirectly. Volunteer to work with patients at a hospital rather than shuffling papers in the administrative office, for example. Being directly involved with the people who need your help or in fashioning efforts to solve a community problem will teach you much more (in terms of both hard skills and life lessons) than raising money to support a cause or doing office work for a community organization. Try to allot at least some of your volunteer time for hands-on experience with the "service" component of the work.

Community service can also be used to show leadership, interest in (and aptitude for) the law, initiative, drive, creativity, or an entrepreneurial spirit. Your volunteer efforts in a service project will be that much more powerful and useful to you in law school admissions if you can go beyond the standard effort to contribute more meaningfully to a cause. For example, rather than merely joining a group that protects the natural habitat in your community's park systems, you might consider going one step further by spreading the group's efforts to the next town, thereby becoming the head of the task force for another community. Or you might create a new program for the existing service organization—perhaps a monthly educational meeting for community residents or a kids' task force, to encourage young children to join the service. You might even create an entirely new organization by taking something in which you have helped a single individual and spreading the impact to many others. One applicant we know had helped an elderly woman in the nursing home in which he volunteered learn how to use e-mail to communicate with her grandchildren. When the applicant saw how effective he had been in helping one woman to improve her life, he decided to take the effort a step further. He founded an organization to teach senior citizens how to use e-mail and make computer systems available for such purposes at libraries, community centers, and nursing homes.

What counts most with community service is that you prove your commitment to caring about something other than yourself. Community service can help demonstrate compassion, appreciation for one's own fortunes, maturity, humanity, and spirit.

USING COMMUNITY SERVICE OUTLETS TO RECRUIT RECOMMENDERS

Doing volunteer work is an excellent way to develop good references. You will be working in a hand-picked activity in which you will be able to control your environment. You can choose a position that is just right for you and your talents, or you can create a position that offers some benefit to an established organization. Charitable organizations know that they are highly dependent upon volunteer workers; consequently, their managers are extremely grateful to anyone who makes a difference. Your involvement in community service can be the ideal place in which to find an appreciative, enthusiastic recommender who can also comment substantively on your talents, initiative, skill, and aptitude for a law career.

THE IMPORTANCE OF COMMUNITY SERVICE FOR FUTURE PUBLIC INTEREST LAWYERS

If you intend to be a public interest lawyer, or are applying to a school's public interest program, you will be viewed with suspicion if you have not been involved in substantial community activities.

THE IMPORTANCE OF COMMUNITY SERVICE FOR ADVANTAGED APPLICANTS

A commitment to community service is especially important if you come from a wealthy (or even moderately well-off family) and have never had to work for paid wages. If it is evident that you have enjoyed many advantages in your life, you should make an effort to find a service or cause that excites you and devote substantial energy to it before applying to law school.

USE YOUR ACTIVITIES TO HIGHLIGHT YOUR PERSONAL SIDE

Your extracurricular, community, and personal activities can also be used to highlight the personal side of you. As Chapter 5 noted, you should show who you are, not just what you have accomplished. Many applicants use their application essays simply to retell the elements of their professional résumé, or brag about their accomplishments, without ever reaching beyond such matters to let admissions officers understand who they really are. This is generally a mistake. If you come across as just another self-centered, win-at-all-costs individual, your credentials will sell at a substantial discount. No school will go out of its way to take such an individual. Take the opportunity to win over these people-oriented officers; show them you have the warmth, generosity of spirit, and concern for others that will make you a truly valuable member of the incoming class (and of the legal profession thereafter). Show your leadership and team-working skills; show that you have a positive impact that reaches well beyond your own narrow interests. By doing so, you will cause admissions officers to interpret your credentials in a positive light—and your credentials will sell at a premium.

ADMISSIONS DEANS DISCUSS EXTRACURRICULAR AND COMMUNITY ACTIVITIES

GENERAL COMMENTS

We look for evidence of public spiritedness—a willingness to give substantial time and energy on campus, or in the wider community. *Susan Palmer, Virginia*

Get involved in activities you genuinely care about, not those you think you should because they're typical "pre-law" activities. I care less about the particular activities you choose than I do about the degree of leadership and commitment you demonstrate in them. *Megan A. Barnett, Yale*

On the personal level, they give us insight into candidates' interests and how they engage with their communities. They also demonstrate candidates' skills, including leadership and teamwork skills. *Todd Morton, Vanderbilt*

We don't want to see applicants participating in a dozen activities at the expense of their academic performance. We prefer to see someone doing well in school while taking active/leadership roles in two or three activities. *Anne Richard, George Washington*

We would rather see an applicant do one or two things in real depth than see someone with twenty-five things on his or her résumé. Positions of leadership are valuable, but one need not be the president of an organization to be a leader. What we value most is the leader or innovator who gets the activity or organization off the ground or takes it to the next level.   *Renée Post, Penn*

Demonstrating Leadership and Teamwork

We want to see leadership and a strong teamwork ethic. Learning how to lead while also being a good team member is important. Community service is one good way of showing this. For example, some of our applicants have received awards for community service leadership.   *Joyce Curll, Harvard*

Leadership skills matter a lot to us. We don't care how many organizations they've joined, for example; we care about the depth of involvement and leadership demonstrated in them (or elsewhere).   *Faye Deal, Stanford*

For us, a real sense of ethics and a sense of concern for others, plus a desire to make a real impact in the community, may be more important than raw intellect or academic dedication. When we see someone very decent—with a strong moral compass, compassion and passion, too—this often goes together with a strong sense of leadership. This may be seen in leadership roles or insofar as people look to him or her for leadership. This comes out in the letters of recommendation primarily, but it may come out in the personal statement or even in choices they've made.   *Joyce Curll, Harvard*

I look above all for two things in extracurricular activities: leadership and commitment to service.   *William Hoye, Duke*

What Particular Activities Do You Value?

"Professional joiners" are a turn-off.   *Elizabeth Rosselot, Boston College*

We prefer to see that an applicant has been deeply engaged in one thing than superficially in ten things. In particular, a leadership role in an activity demonstrates that an applicant has commanded the respect of peers, based in part upon a willingness to work hard and an ability to get others engaged.   *Susan Palmer, Virginia*

As a Jesuit institution, we do like to see humanitarian efforts: the Peace Corps, Teach for America, and so on. Things on the same line at the undergraduate level are also valued highly. Candidates with a demonstrated commitment to public services are the ones that the faculty on the admissions committee are most likely to get excited about.   *Elizabeth Rosselot, Boston College*

What Role Does a Candidate's Roster of Activities Play in the Decision?

It is really important to us that someone has been active in extracurricular pursuits at college. We look for evidence of well-roundedness and leadership. We are more impressed by leadership of community activities/service organizations, student government, and athletic teams than by leadership of academic organizations, since the latter tend not to involve as much interaction, coordinating of people's efforts, dealing with conflicts, and the like. We are a more cooperative school than most and want to encourage interaction amongst students, so we look for those who won't end up with their noses buried in books in the library. *Don Rebstock, Northwestern*

Someone with a long list of extracurricular activities, even impressive ones, who has a low GPA shows not public-spiritedness but misplaced priorities. *Susan Palmer, Virginia*

Extracurricular involvement can be important, assuming that someone can articulate in a fresh and compelling way why he/she was involved, how he's grown and learned as a result, and, perhaps, how it's prepared him for law school. *William Hoye, Duke*

The Importance of the Personal Side

Admissions is an art, not a science. We're not just looking at people as numbers, letters (i.e., grades), types, or categories. *Joyce Curll, Harvard*

Our policy states that weight is placed heavily on quantitative measures. But we also hold the belief that numbers don't tell us everything. I admit human beings, not numbers. For this reason, I look at the personal statement first, then at the quantitative measures. *Edward Tom, Boalt Hall (Berkeley)*

It's very important to us to try to glean the personality of the applicant. We want to understand their leadership qualities, work ethic, degree of determination and innovation. To be a successful attorney requires that one have substantial interpersonal skills. For instance, it's important to be able to argue a point but it's just as important to listen to the other side. (This is also critical in law school, where want to form a true community). We look closely at the recommendations with this in mind. *Renée Post, Penn*

Personal Qualities They Value

I really like optimists, who take whatever happens to them and see it in a positive light. They take real advantage of the opportunities available, or overcome obstacles that would have prevented others from succeeding. I see such people as a good match for this school. They can take advantage of what we have to offer. For example, we have eighty-five student organizations, twelve journals, and a variety of other opportunities of which our students can take good advantage and greatly enhance their experience here. *Joyce Curll, Harvard*

We really like to see that a person is passionate about something, whatever it might be, and engaged with their community, whether large or small. The key words for us, therefore, include interest, passion, commitment, dedication, and persistence. We read between the lines in the application to see whether an applicant has these qualities. *Nkonye Iwerebon, Columbia*

We value leadership as well as commitment to service. These traits come out clearly in good letters of reference. *Chloe T. Reid, USC*

Being able to work with others, as well as having leadership abilities, we consider very important. We also look for people with a real generosity of spirit—which we tend to see through the personal statement and the types of extracurricular activities in which they have been involved. We tend to look with disfavor on those who lack integrity and maturity or who demonstrate arrogance in their applications. *Anne Richard, George Washington*

We want to see an interest in other people: sincere concern about the well-being of others, maturity, and good listening skills, among other traits. This is important for the fit with Northwestern. *Don Rebstock, Northwestern*

"Distance traveled" matters a lot to me. Overcoming great adversity and obstacles, perseverance and commitment—all show character. *Faye Deal, Stanford*

I look for superior intellect—it's the engine—and high levels of energy and industry, which are the fuel. I also want people who have values and integrity, some kind of guidance system. *Edward Tom, Boalt Hall (Berkeley)*

SHOW WHERE YOU ARE HEADED

If you have a clear idea of where you are headed, and why, you can add substantially to the value of the credentials you possess. Imagine two different candidates. Lisa has a degree in economics and has worked for three years as an analyst in an investment bank. She intends to return to the investment banking world, working in-house as a transactional lawyer. George, on the other hand, has a degree in general studies and has worked a series of odd jobs for the last few years. He states that he wants to be a lawyer in order to help others, although he gives no specifics for how he intends to accomplish this. Imagine that

Lisa and George have similar LSAT and GPA results (indeed, their academic records look comparable if you ignore George's lack of focus). Which of the two would you take? In fact, Lisa is surely the stronger candidate. Admissions officers will readily understand her candidacy and implicitly award her "bonus points" for having explored her career options in advance of law school. They know that she will make effective use of the possibilities their school offers because she understands what will be valuable to her in her chosen career. Similarly, her prior work in the field and her continuing career focus suggest that she will be a valuable contributor at law school. In addition, it is clear that she will be readily marketable once she finishes because she has already gotten involved in the field that she intends to work in after law school.

Similarly, a clear path forward can help you take the sting out of a messy past. If you learned a lot about who you are and how you fit into the world of work, you can plausibly claim that you benefited from stints in a variety of positions and industries.

ADMISSIONS DEANS DISCUSS THE CAREER DIMENSION

The Value of Knowing Where You Are Headed

It's always good to see an applicant who knows what he or she intends to do in the future, based upon solid evidence. For example, he has already worked in the field he will practice law in. This is certainly of help in gaining admission. *Andy Cornblatt, Georgetown*

The question we're always asking ourselves when we read their files is, "Why law school?" If we don't have a clear understanding of why, it is difficult to make a strong case for admission. Even for older applicants, there can be a lack of a clear reason. If we don't understand why law school, and why now, that admissions offer may not come since we are looking for clarity and focus at this point. This is true even for someone with a very strong undergraduate record and 99th percentile LSAT scores. *Faye Deal, Stanford*

The failure to demonstrate a serious interest in law inevitably hurts applicants' chances. It makes me nervous when people apply simply because it's a professional degree. We ask about this in the interview. If they say, "It's in the family," that is simply not a good enough answer. They should be able to logically project their interests to a field of law, even if they don't know much about the practice of law. They should have at least started to give this serious consideration. *Don Rebstock, Northwestern*

If you are still in college, we take statements about your serious interest in law and your career aspirations with a grain of salt.   *Megan A. Barnett, Yale*

It's certainly valuable to be able to show you know what you want to do, but it is not credible unless you are able to connect all of the dots. You need to have a sophisticated view of your future career, compelling evidence that you have the tools to get where you want to go, and a sincere desire to do so.   *Sarah C. Zearfoss, Michigan*

Evaluating Candidates on the Basis of Their Career Futures

We don't just look at how someone will perform at law school. We're very interested in assessing what people will do after law school, what impact they'll have. For the person to be a leader, a world changer, is very desirable to this law school.   *Joyce Curll, Harvard*

We do not admit people just on the basis of their expected law school GPAs. We're looking for future leaders of the country, in both the private and public sectors. It's rare that we know someone will be a star in the future, but when we see such a person we admit him or her.   *Sarah C. Zearfoss, Michigan*

We look to admit those who will be the best law students and who will enhance the intellectual life of the school as well as contribute to its diversity based on their experience, viewpoints, and background. Relatively few applicants are judged on the basis of what they might accomplish after law school.   *William Hoye, Duke*

It's good for candidates to have thought through where they are headed, even if they change their minds in law school. Thinking about their futures helps them learn about themselves, what will suit them as well as what to avoid, and so on. This ultimately informs the choices they do make. Plus, it shows a level of maturity on their part to be trying to map out and manage their careers before they jump into law school.   *Anne Richard, George Washington*

Each year, we turn down a few people with 180 LSATs because we don't think they will add much to the class. On the other hand, we take the occasional candidate with a relatively low GPA or LSAT because we believe she will bring something special to the school or to the legal profession.   *Megan A. Barnett, Yale*

ADMISSIONS DEANS SUMMARIZE
WHAT THEY ARE LOOKING FOR

We're looking at many people who are almost indistinguishable in terms of their ability to do the work here. These are people who are truly talented. The key question is who will bring the most to the learning experience of others. *Joyce Curll, Harvard*

The three most important factors for us are the LSAT score, GPA, and personal statement. The next most important are activities, professional experience, and accomplishments, and personal accomplishments. *Anne Richard, George Washington*

Penn Law seeks to enroll individuals who have demonstrated outstanding academic success, who are intellectually curious, and who possess superior writing, oral communication and analytical skills. Importantly, we also seek individuals who will positively contribute to the Penn Law community, and ultimately, to the legal profession, based on their diverse backgrounds, their personal and professional experiences, and any challenges or obstacles that they may have overcome. *Renée Post, Penn*

There is no single quality that characterizes the ideal Columbia Law student. We would like students who are academically talented, curious, leaders, and who are looking to make a difference in some way. *Nkonye Iwerebon, Columbia*

In the final analysis, I am looking for people who have been able to take full advantage of the resources and opportunities available to them, particularly in the professional and educational realms. *Todd Morton, Vanderbilt*

We most want people who will engage on more than one front, with both academics and activities. There are many ways for students to excel at Harvard Law School and we look for excellence in a variety of ways. *Joyce Curll, Harvard*

We rate everyone versus seven categories: Interpersonal and communication skills; Career progression; Intellectual ability; Extracurricular and community involvement; Leadership potential/demonstrated skills; Motivation for Northwestern; Career focus. Although intellectual ability is certainly important, we won't admit someone with very high numbers who lacks the other pieces. *Don Rebstock, Northwestern*

FOR INTERNATIONAL STUDENTS

This section is designed to provide students from outside the United States with information about the special difficulties they face when applying to American law schools.

ADMISSIONS POLICIES

Most of the top law programs require that students have a minimum educational background roughly equivalent to an American bachelor's degree. The following list gives a rough indication of what level of education is likely to be deemed acceptable. Be sure to double-check with each institution you are interested in, because substantial differences in criteria do exist.

Australia and New Zealand. See United Kingdom and British-styled systems.

Canada. Four-year bachelor's degree from English-speaking provinces or three-year bachelor's degree from Quebec are generally acceptable.

Central America. See Spain and Latin America.

China (People's Republic). Bachelor's degree requiring four years of study at a university is generally acceptable.

Denmark. Academingenior or Candidatus are generally acceptable, even in the case of Candidatus degrees requiring only three years of study.

French and French-styled systems. Degrees (*diplomes* or *maîtrises*) that require a Baccalauréat plus four years of further study from a university or *grande école* are generally acceptable.

Germany. Magister Artium, Staatsexamen, or University Diplom are generally acceptable. Fachhochschulen graduates may or may not be eligible.

India, Pakistan, Myanmar, Bangladesh, Nepal. Bachelor's or master's degrees requiring at least four years of study are generally acceptable, but B.A., B.Com., and B.Sc. degrees alone are often unacceptable.

Indonesia. Sarjana or Sarjana Lengka awarded after five years of study is acceptable, but the Sarjana Muda (requiring only three years of study) is not.

Hungary. Oklevel requiring at least four years of study is generally acceptable.

Mexico. See Spain and Latin America.

Netherlands. The following are generally acceptable: Doctorandus, Ingenieur, or Meester. Kandidaats, Propaeseuse, and H.B.O diplomas are often considered unacceptable.

Philippines. Bachelor's degree requiring either five years of undergraduate study or four years of undergraduate study and one year of graduate study is generally acceptable.

Poland. Magister, Dyplom, and Inzynier are generally acceptable.

Russia and former states of the U.S.S.R. Diploma requiring five years at a university or institute is generally acceptable.

Scandinavia. A university diploma awarded for four or more years of study is generally acceptable.

Spain and Latin America. Licenciado, Licenciatura, or Bacharel is generally acceptable.

Switzerland. Diplom, Diplome, and Licence, requiring at least four years of university study, are generally acceptable. The following are often considered unacceptable: Betriebsokonom, HWV, Econ. ESCEA, Ingenieur ETS, Ingenieur HTL, and Ingenieur STS.

United Kingdom and British-styled systems. There is no general rule in effect as to British-styled education, although a number of schools require an honours bachelor's degree.

ACADEMIC RECORDS

Many international applicants will not be able to have their transcripts accepted by LSDAS, so they will have to send them directly to the law schools. If the transcripts are not in English, they must be accompanied by an authorized translation. Many schools specify the translation firm they prefer be used.

GRADES

The grading systems in use in your country may or may not be familiar to the admissions staff at U.S. law schools to which you are applying. If you have any doubt about this, be sure to have your school send an explanation of the grading system (in English), showing especially the percentage of students who typically get each mark. For example, if your school uses a 20-point system, the top 5 percent of students might have averages of 13–15 points. It is important to point this out, because a poorly informed admissions officer might try to translate your grade of 14 into a 2.8 average in the American style 4.0 system (by simply dividing by 5). The resulting 2.8 is a very mediocre grade, likely to place a student in the bottom half of his or her class. Your 14, on the other hand, might put you in the top 5 percent of your class, something you should want a school to know.

Showing your class rank can thus be very helpful. Another matter of concern to admissions officers is the overall quality of your school. Having your recommenders place it in appropriate context, or having your school note its usual place in the pecking order of local schools, can be helpful, at least if your school is generally well regarded.

9

MARKETING YOURSELF

— EXECUTIVE SUMMARY —

■

Understand how you compare with the competition.

■

Learn how admissions officers will view your candidacy based upon their expectations of people from your field and educational background.

■

Position yourself well, capitalizing on your strengths while minimizing your weaknesses, in light of schools' expectations.

■

Use themes to focus your marketing effort.

■

Learn how to use a special case status to your advantage.

The first part of this chapter shows you how to determine what you should emphasize in your application. Your areas of emphasis depend upon several factors: what the top law schools want, what your competition offers, and your relevant strengths and weaknesses compared with other applicants. The second part of the chapter begins the discussion of how to capitalize on your strengths and make the strongest possible argument for your acceptance. This discussion continues throughout the following chapters, which explore the marketing vehicles you need to master: the essays, recommendations, and interviews.

INDIVIDUAL CONSULTING AND WORKSHOPS

I recognize that readers may find it difficult to apply the concepts of this book to their own cases or may just want the extra admissions (or career consulting) edge that is possible through *individualized assistance*. Those desiring individual consulting are welcome to contact me through my website (www.degreeofdifference.com) or at (415) 273-1782.

I also offer small-group *workshops* that some readers will find to be attractive alternatives or supplements to individualized consulting. These are described briefly on page *xviii* in the introduction, or in more detail on my website (www.degreeofdifference.com).

CREATING A MARKETING STRATEGY

YOUR STRENGTHS AND WEAKNESSES VERSUS THOSE OF THE COMPETITION

Chapter 8 explains what schools seek in their applicants. Reading that chapter will give you a reasonable idea of what your own strengths and weaknesses are. This, however, is not really enough; at this point you should go one step further in determining how you stack up versus the competition.

Start your analysis of the competition you face by getting the summary data schools provide about their entering classes. Columbia, for instance, provides the following information about its entering class:

CLASS OVERVIEW

Applicants	7292	
Matriculants	371	
Women	177	(48%)
Total Minority Enrollment	123	(33%)
Asian	64	(17%)
African American	38	(10%)
Hispanic	20	(5%)
Native American	1	(<1%)
International Students	26	(7%)

REGIONAL BREAKDOWN

Mid-Atlantic	29%
West	23%
South	13%
Midwest	12%
New England	12%
International	11%

40 States, District of Columbia, Puerto Rico, and 21 foreign countries represented.

AGE BREAKDOWN

20 or younger	3	(<1%)
21–25	273	(73%)
25–28	80	(22%)
29 or older	15	(4%)

34% begin law school directly from college.

COMMON ADVANCED DEGREES

MA	22
MS	14
MPP	3
Ph.D.	3
MBA	2
MFA	2
MPhil	2

Matriculants with at least one graduate degree: 55 (15%)

UNDERGRADUATE MAJORS

Poli Sci/Government	86	(23%)
History	42	(11%)
Literature/English	39	(10%)
Humanities	39	(10%)
Economics	36	(10%)
Science/Eng./Math	31	(8%)
International Relations	26	(7%)
Social Sciences	26	(7%)
Philosophy	18	(5%)
Psychology	12	(3%)
Finance/Acct./Business	9	(3%)
Policy Studies	7	(2%)

Undergraduate institutions represented: 105

LSAT AND GPA

LSAT Median	172
LSAT Mean	171
LSAT 25/75 Percentile	169/174
UGPA Median	3.70
UGPA Mean	3.68
UGPA 25/75 Percentile	3.56/3.81

Other schools provide data similar to that in the chart above. In addition, you can always ask the school itself for further information. Many collect and collate more than is provided on their websites, such as the number of students coming from each undergraduate feeder school, the number of Fulbright and other fellowship winners, and the professional backgrounds of entrants with substantial work experience. With these data in hand, it is a simple matter to determine how you stack up relative to the prior year's successful candidates in terms of your academic credentials, LSAT score, amount of experience, and so on.

A SHORTCUT TO THE STRENGTHS AND WEAKNESSES ANALYSIS

Each person will be more than just a member of a category; a person who happens to be a paralegal will not—one hopes—be the same as all other paralegals. By the same token, knowing what category you fall into can help you determine how you are likely to be viewed by admissions officers. Admissions officers, like everyone, make various simplifying assumptions about the world. Not all astrophysicists and brain surgeons will be extremely smart, intellectually driven, and so on, but most of us assume this is the case unless given evidence to the contrary. Understanding how your "type" is perceived—absent any other evidence—and about how others in your category will also be perceived is valuable. (Knowing how your most direct competitors—those who most resemble you—will be viewed is an important part of developing your marketing strategy.)

The following chart is intended to make this process of identifying where to focus your efforts a bit easier by showing the presumed strengths and weaknesses of different categories of applicants. If you are a member of one of the most traditional categories of applicants to JD programs—for example, a recent graduate of an undergraduate university with no work experience—recognize that just having the strengths noted here will be insufficient reason to admit you. You may need to be demonstrably stronger than others in the same category (and perhaps even free of the category's typical weaknesses). The chart shows what are presumed to be weaknesses unless evidence proves otherwise.

The first five categories are the broadest, addressing—on the simplest level—the basic "types" of applicants: the 22-year-old, in his last year of college; the graduate student, who has pursued one or more advanced degrees; the "taker of time off," who has been out of college for a year or two, traveling or otherwise soul-searching; the "do-gooder," who has spent her time volunteering for numerous organizations and causes; and the experienced professional, who has devoted years to building knowledge and experience in a specific industry. One can, of course, fall into more than one category; be sure to pay attention to the pros and cons of each.

CATEGORY	LIKELY STRENGTHS	LIKELY WEAKNESSES
Applicant Types		
College Student	Still in study mode	Immature
	Energetic	Driven to law school by parents
	Idealistic	Postponing real career and life decisions by getting a JD
		Lacks concrete skills
		Similar to too many other applicants with interchangeable skills!
Graduate Student/Ph.D.	Bright	Ivory-tower thinker
	Accustomed to demanding academic work	Afraid to leave academia, but disillusioned about academic job market
	Knowledge of chosen field	Limited knowledge of real world
Time Off: Soul-Searcher/ Solitary	Contemplative	Cultural misfit
	Headstrong	Aimless
	Worldly	Lacks drive
	Has thought seriously about future	Romantic dreamer
Do-Gooder	Altruistic/idealistic	Not cut out to be a hardened lawyer
	A "people person"	Likely to be disappointed with realities of legal practice
		Likely to change career focus upon encountering real world
Experienced Professional	Knowledge of specific industry	Questionable interest in law
	Hardworking and determined	Possibly lacks patience for serious, independent study
	Willing to share experiences	Unable to work with younger students as equals
Profession		
Paralegal	Already exposed to the "dirty work" reality of lawyering	Possibly undynamic
	Possessing sincere interest in law	Likely to possess little substantive knowledge of any one field
Legislative Aide	Understands how laws drafted	Parents' connections (not their abilities) may have gotten them their jobs
	Knowledge of substantive field(s)	
	Research skills	At some (D.C.) schools, over-represented in applicant pool
	Communication skills	

CATEGORY	LIKELY STRENGTHS	LIKELY WEAKNESSES
Functionary/Secretary	Hardworking Capable of tedius work	Unable to think independently Needs authority Lacks industry knowledge Lacks drive, ambition
Teacher	Hard worker Good social and interpersonal skills Diplomatic, a good negotiator	Overly idealistic Needs constant interaction and feedback Lacks drive, ambition
Public interest	Willing to work hard for low pay Altruistic	Unable to tolerate opposing views Immature, naive
Consultant	Bright Understands business Strong communication skills Strong research and analysis skills Leadership skills	Questionable interest in law Lacks patience for tedious legal study
Finance/Banking	Understands business Research and analysis skills	Lacks writing, communication skills Inclined to do deals rather than help others do them
Accountant	Understands accounting Seriousness of purpose Exposure to numerous businesses and industries Quantitative skills	Undynamic; not a leader Lacks writing, communication skills
Computer Programmer	Bright Technologically up-to-date Quantitative skills	Lacks interpersonal skills Lacks leadership skills Unwilling to develop "soft" skills
Engineer	Quantitative skills Technologically up-to-date Used to rigorous academic setting Highly marketable	Lacks outside interests Lacks communication and interpersonal skills Unwilling to joust in class
Military Officer	Good leadership training Determined Team oriented	Unable to think independently A cultural misfit in (some) law schools Lacks written communication skills
Scientist	Bright Good analytical skills Very marketable	Possessing questionable interest in law Lacks communication skills Perhaps unwilling to joust in class

Category	Likely Strengths	Likely Weaknesses
Human Resources	Social and interpersonal skills Team player	Questionable interest in legal problems (perhaps just interested in people's feelings) Lacks analytical skills
Sales	Communications skills Interpersonal skills	Lacks analytical skills Short-term focus
Writer, Journalist	Research and writing skills Independent thinker	Lacks ability to lead others Romantic dreamer
Photographer/Artist	Unusual perspective Creative problem-solving skills Conceptual thinker	Unable to work with others A cultural misfit Lacks analytical skills
Undergraduate Major		
Political Science	Bona fide interest in law Knowledge of law and government	Similar to too many other applicants Tending to think of law as a grand affair rather than a practical profession Attending law school by default
History	Understanding of government, the principles behind laws Used to lengthy readings	Similar to too many other applicants Attending law school by default
Economics	Understands business Familiar with key tools for analyzing various areas of law	Lacks patience for "soft skills" Lacks writing skills Possibly preferring business school, but unwilling to work for 2–4 years before applying
Mathematics/Engineering	Disciplined Analytical and quantitative skills Extremely marketable	Unable to read between the lines Lacks writing skills Questionable people skills
Psychology	Knowledgeable about human behavior	Lacks patience for independent study May place too much emphasis on "soft skills"
Philosophy	Argumentative thinker Accustomed to analyzing formal logic, language	Lacks people skills Lacks career focus
Literature	Research skills Strong writing ability Ability to analyze language carefully	Ivory-tower thinker Not used to reading dry texts Particularly lacking in knowledge of law as career

CATEGORY	LIKELY STRENGTHS	LIKELY WEAKNESSES
Language	Aware of other cultures/ viewpoints	Lacks analytical skills
	Willing to spend long hours studying	Few scholarly interests

Note: The perception of you with regard to your undergraduate major can change if you have devoted substantial effort to more than one area of study. If you have a history major with a math minor, for example, you will be viewed as having a rather unusual, broad set of skills.

Age

Older [Early thirties or older]	Experience and industry knowledge	Lack of energy
	Likely calming influence on younger students in cohort	Unable to work with younger student as equals
		Impatience with theory

Background

Disadvantaged	Strong work ethic	Unprepared for rigors of strong academic program
	Underrepresented perspective	Might have difficulty fitting in
Wealthy/Advantaged	Rich experiential knowledge	Arrogant
	Future success all but assured	Weak work ethic
		Spoiled
Recent immigrant	Knowledge-hungry	Unpolished, unprofessional
	Strong work ethic	

CAPITALIZING ON YOUR STRENGTHS, MINIMIZING YOUR WEAKNESSES

Once you have analyzed your situation and recognize where you stand, you should be aware of what an admissions officer is likely to see as your strengths and weaknesses. Your job is now to capitalize on this understanding.

First, you will want to support any of the strengths you do indeed have. You can relate stories in your essays that show you, for example, as an effective leader. Just as important, you can (and should) have your recommenders provide supporting examples.

Second, do whatever you can to minimize your weaknesses, or, better yet, show that you do not suffer from them. Once again, it is a matter of addressing them through each of the vehicles at your disposal: the essays, the recommendations, and (for some schools) interviews. In other words, you should maximize your reward/risk ratio. Schools want students who will make major contributions to their programs—who will provide a reward for accepting them—without involving substantial risks of academic and other types of failure. The higher the reward/risk ratio, the better your chance of appealing to a school.

The tasks facing people with different profiles will, of course, be different. A legislative assistant to a congressman faces a very different task from that of a commercial photographer in trying to maximize the reward/risk ratio. The legislative assistant is likely to be regarded as being quite bright and determined, with strong research and analysis skills, and a good understanding of law, without being much of a risk to the program. After several years' work, she knows enough about how law is practiced that there is essentially no danger that she will fail out of the program, or lose interest in law, or be unplaceable in a good job upon graduation. She therefore looks like an easy admit because she brings good experience and qualities to the program without any risk. The problem for her, however, is that she is but one among congressional aides and others involved in the legislative process, many of whom bring similar qualities. To improve her chances of admission, she must show that she is quite different from those other assistants in terms of her range of work, the depth of her understanding of a specific area of law (or two or three), her success to date, and/or how she intends to employ her law degree in the future.

The commercial photographer is in a nearly opposite situation. In his case, the problem is not what he brings to the program. He is likely to be the only photographer applying, so he has considerable uniqueness value to start with. His problems involve the risk side of the ratio. An admissions director is likely to worry that he will be unable to handle the program's grueling academic demands and that he will fail out of the program early on. Similarly, she may worry that he will lose interest in law and simply go back to photography midway through the program. She will probably also worry that his lack of work in a traditional field may make the employers who recruit at the school reluctant to hire him. To improve his chances of admission, he needs to address each concern. He may, for example, want to take several courses that show he has the ability to do analytical, research-intensive work prior to applying. By doing this he also shows that he is sincerely interested in law, is not applying on a whim, and is likely to complete the program. Last, he will want to show where he is headed with his JD and how he intends to get there. This will involve explaining what skills and experiences he already has, plus showing how he will acquire other relevant skills and experiences during the law school program.

COMBATING A PRIVILEGED IMAGE

Do:

➤ Participate in/lead substantial community service activities.

➤ Show that you have taken advantage of all opportunities.

➤ Demonstrate that you have crossed social and other divides or experienced the plight of (and sympathize with) others less fortunate.

Do Not:

➤ Discuss expensive trips you have taken or glamorous events you have attended.

➤ Describe your parent as managing director of Wall Street's fanciest investment bank—"banker" will do.

➤ Sound arrogant, spoiled, or unappreciative of your opportunities. World-weary cynicism does not play well with admissions directors.

➤ Act as if you hit a triple when you were actually born on third base (as one critic had it of former President Bush). In other words, do not make a big deal out of having gone to a fancy prep school or having managed to make money performing mundane services for your parents' wealthy pals.

PERSONAL STATEMENT EXAMPLE

The personal statement written by Heather, below, provides a good example of how to capitalize on a category's strengths and minimize certain obvious weaknesses. Heather graduated from the University of California at Santa Cruz with a degree in Psychology. Although she graduated with honors, Santa Cruz's lack of a grading system at the time left her to battle the admissions process without a GPA or an index number. Additionally, an LSAT score of 160—a score below the average of her ideal law schools—was a hindrance. On the surface, Heather was obviously in a precarious position. Her numbers, and the fact that she did not attend a top-flight undergraduate institution, necessitated a strong marketing job. On the other hand, the fact that she spent the last five years working for social service and criminal justice agencies—work she describes intelligently and convincingly—was commendable. She showed that she was truly determined (and, perhaps more important, *prepared*) to work for the public interest. She proved herself to be mature: an independent thinker and a persuasive advocate. These are all qualities law schools look for when choosing among applicants.

Albert was born and raised in California. Our similarities end there. Albert is a crack addict with AIDS who was physically abused and abandoned by his parents at age twelve. He became a sex worker and, when he needed a quick fix, he would burglarize homes. At age 26, he had just been convicted on his third "strike" and was facing 25 years to life in prison.

His public defender had hired me, a sentencing specialist at the Center on Justice, to advocate on Albert's behalf and to develop an Alternative Sentencing Plan. When I first met this client, he was wearing the standard-issue orange sweat suit provided by the Los Angeles County Jail and he looked relatively healthy. As he told me his life story, including the numerous offenses of which he had been both victim and perpetrator, I began to formulate a strategy to persuade the judge that a rehabilitative sentence was warranted.

I went back to the office to begin my research on the resources available to HIV-positive drug-addicted offenders. I began by looking into the services offered in the California Department of Corrections (CDC), since the likelihood of my client being sentenced to prison was very high. I learned of the deliberate neglect of HIV-infected prisoners and the dearth of experienced medical staff in the prisons. The situation for the treatment of substance abuse was equally grim: less than 1% of the 105,000 addicts in the CDC receive drug treatment. With this knowledge I began to research community-based alternatives that would address the needs of my client.

Two weeks into my research, my work was interrupted by an emergency. I went to interview Albert a second time, but he was in no condition to talk. His lips were cracked and his face was marked with lesions. Pain radiated from where he had been injected that morning with Pneumovax, a vaccine against pneumonia. The day after my visit, after complaining of a fever and delirium for over twenty hours, the nurse finally felt his forehead. He had a temperature of 105 degrees caused by the contaminated serum the jail medical staff had given him. He was rushed to Los Angeles General Hospital.

One day after he was admitted to the hospital, Albert called me in a panic because his doctor had stopped giving him Indinavir, the protease inhibitor he had been taking for several months to combat his AIDS. From having worked with other clients with AIDS, I recognized the danger of interrupting his medication; he could develop a resistance to this and perhaps other protease inhibitors if his treatment was not resumed immediately. I called San Francisco General Hospital—a leading AIDS research institution—and was told that they did not have Indinavir. I suspected that Albert was being discriminated against due to his inmate status. I contacted his doctor and expressed my concern that it appeared my client's medication had been withheld. Ten minutes later, Albert called to thank me. The nurse had just given his first dose of his medicine. With that obstacle behind us, I resumed the development of my argument to the judge with renewed enthusiasm.

I succeeded in convincing Miller House, a respected substance abuse program for HIV-positive offenders, to accept Albert into their residential care program. In order to dissuade the judge from sentencing Albert to prison, I described in my report the grossly inadequate resources available in the California Department of Corrections to address his needs. I outlined his social history and argued that in order for Albert's cycle of crime to cease, his addiction and medical needs would have to be aggressively treated. I suggested that a term of imprisonment was, in fact, a death sentence. In conclusion, I recommended that the Court strike Albert's priors as permitted under state law, and sentence Albert to the aggravated term, to be suspended with five years of probation and mandatory participation in the Walden House residential program for one and a half years.

The judge accepted my recommendations in full. After the judge announced the sentence, Albert's public defender turned to me and said, "You saved his life." The incredible feeling I get from knowing I have helped alter the course of someone's life in a positive direction is what motivates me to want to practice law.

I have been working for social service and criminal justice agencies for the past five years and I am committed to continuing to serve historically underrepresented individuals in a broader role as an attorney. It is important to me to study law in a school that emphasizes serving the public interest and values diversity. Boalt Hall impressed me as such a school as evidenced by its strong clinical program and the wide range of courses offered that focus on public interest.

Heather chose to attend her first choice, Boalt Hall at UC Berkeley, a school that prides itself on its public interest emphases.

FIT IN–STAND OUT

Another way to think about the reward/risk ratio is, as many admissions directors put it, a "fit in–stand out" problem. *Fitting in* means you are accepted by your classmates as belonging in the program rather than being regarded as an oddity. If you can do the course work, subscribe to the program's goals, and get on well with the other students, you will fit in. *Standing out* means you bring something unique to the program, something that distinguishes you from the other students.

The trick, obviously, is to fit in and stand out at one and the same time. It is not sufficient to do just one of these things. Saying that you really fit in, that you look like a composite of all the other students, gives the school no reason to want you there, because you bring nothing different and therefore nothing special. Saying that you really stand out, that you do not resemble any of the other students in any relevant way, is similarly useless because you may be seen as too risky to have in the program. The way to straddle this apparent divide is to fit in regarding certain key dimensions and be different regarding other specifics. Most people will tend to fall more on one side of the divide than the other. The paralegal need not worry that she will fail to fit in; her problem is showing how she stands out. The photographer need not worry about standing out; his problem is showing that he fits in. (The recent college graduate, in contrast, may need to worry a little bit about both.)

FASHIONING YOUR MESSAGE: POSITIONING

Positioning is a marketing concept that is meant to deal with this problem of too many applicants trying to capture the attention of admissions directors who are overwhelmed by the onslaught. To cut through all of this communications haze, you must have a very sharp and clear image that is readily noticed and understood and valued.

Let's look at an example that is dear to my heart. There are many types of whiskey, even of scotch whiskey—and even of single-malt scotch whiskey. Nonetheless, there are a number of products that are distinctively positioned in the market for single-malt scotch. For example, Laphroaig is a single-malt scotch with a peatier, more iodine taste (and "nose") than its competitors. Its unique attributes allow it to market itself to consumers who consider themselves beyond the "beginners'" scotches and who want the strongest possible taste they can find. Macallan, on the other hand, is exceptionally smooth and even bears a certain resemblance to cognac. It tells consumers that its product is aged in old sherry casks, which impart a distinctive hint of sherry in the nose.

These two products compete in the high end of the scotch market, yet each is positioned to be completely unique. Their marketing efforts aim to make it very clear what key attributes they possess, and they are very successful. Both are held in extremely high regard by serious malt scotch whiskey drinkers, although they are considered virtually unrelated to one another. The result is that each can claim a price premium for its distinctiveness that would be impossible were they positioned to compete head-to-head.

APPLYING THE CONCEPT TO YOURSELF

How does this apply to you? You must distinguish yourself from others in the applicant pool who may apply to the same schools you do. Law school applicants are not all the same; your job is to show your uniqueness. You increase your value by appearing unique. After all, if you are the same as 2,500 other applicants, what school will really care if it gets you rather than one of the other 2,499? You also make yourself more memorable by making yourself unique. Remaining anonymous will not help you. Far better if an admissions committee remembers you, perhaps even having a shorthand expression for use in discussing you. Being "the woman who was a private investigator in Miami" means that you are remembered and can be discussed as a unique person. Contrast this with the sort of person who is discussed as "Which one is she? Really? Could I see that file again? I don't remember reading that one before."

GENERAL POSITIONING VERSUS SPECIFIC POSITIONING

To what extent should your positioning be different for each target school? Since no two schools are exactly the same, you might want to position yourself differently for each school. On the other hand, doing a markedly different application for each school is a lot of extra work. Not only do you need to write your essays differently, but you also need to have your recommenders write each recommendation differently. For example, if you intend to apply to Berkeley for its International and Comparative Legal Studies Program and to Northwestern for its Taxation Program, you will face the difficulty of being a persuasive applicant for both. (If you have identified the path of your future career, of course, this problem should not arise.)

   Take a modified approach; have a general positioning strategy that you can fine-tune as necessary to fit the needs of specific schools without making major changes in your application. Emphasize different aspects of your experience for a given school; don't try to recreate yourself for it. (Note that any positioning approach you take must be something you can reinforce via specific, powerful examples.)

THE MECHANICS OF POSITIONING: USING THEMES

Positioning is meant to provide a method for presenting a very clear picture of you. A simple way to achieve this is to use one or two themes to organize your material. When writing your essays, for example, relate all or at least most of your material to your chosen themes. Your positioning will be very clear and easy to grasp if your material is organized around these themes.

   The organizing themes you choose will be those that are appropriate to you. The essays in Part V show some examples of what kinds of ideas others have chosen; look at several of them from this perspective. Here are a few of the many possible themes around which one can organize parts of the application, and some idea of who might make use of them.

■ *Altruist:* You have spent the last three years working for the Peace Corps, distributing medicine and food in French West Africa.

■ *Polyglot:* You speak five languages fluently, with substantial knowledge of multiple cultures.

■ *Survivor:* You grew up in a remote, poverty-stricken area of Appalachia, and were the first member of your town to go to college.

■ *All-around synthesizer:* As an architect, you have had to bring together the work of various types of engineers, designers, lawyers, accountants, and city planners.

■ *Dedicated toiler:* You spent your last year of college holed away in an archive, deciphering the handwritten notes of Alexis de Tocqueville.

■ *From an unusual background:* Because of your father's job as a jail minister, you grew up on the compound of a notorious prison.

■ *Risk-taker:* As a journalist, you thrive when culling information from dangerous situations and analyzing it in light of historical fact.

■ *Crusader:* In your volunteer work for Planned Parenthood, you have organized a group of abortion-rights activists.

THE MARKETING VEHICLES

You have three primary vehicles for getting your message across to law schools: the essay(s), recommendations, and possible interviews. You will need to be consistent within and across these three vehicles to gain the maximum positive impact. The following chapters will show you how to make the most of them.

CONCLUSION

The penalty for failing to capitalize on your strengths and to prepare a powerful application is, all too often, rejection. Schools have plenty of qualified applicants who took the time to figure out the process and complete a good application. Failure to do these things suggests that you are not able to do so, or at least do not care to. In either case, you are unlikely to be viewed as having top law school potential, at least at the moment.

ADMISSIONS DEANS DISCUSS HOW YOU SHOULD MARKET YOURSELF

The Importance of Marketing Yourself Well

I have been known to say no to applicants with extremely high numbers, simply because they had nothing to say, nothing to offer. *Edward Tom, Boalt Hall (Berkeley)*

We have so many highly talented applicants we would love to accept that there are very few we feel *compelled* to take. This means that selecting from a large pool of well-qualified people often comes down to a matter of which ones have marketed themselves well and thereby gotten the most out of their credentials and circumstances. *Sarah C. Zearfoss, Michigan*

It is important to market yourself well, particularly with the increase in the volume of applications. If you do not put together a well-thought-out application, we assume that you are either not yet ready for law school or are not taking the process or Chicago seriously. This suggests that you are not meticulous and conscientious, as a lawyer should be. *Ann Killian Perry, Chicago*

The whole application process is a good test of legal advocacy. You are called upon to marshal evidence and make decisions about what to include or exclude in pleading your case. *William Hoye, Duke*

A strong presentation is quite common among those applicants who are admitted. *Joyce Curll, Harvard*

Just the way a person organizes the application materials reveals something, pro or con, about the person. *Elizabeth Rosselot, Boston College.*

Few Applicants Market Themselves Well

It's very important to market yourself well, but no more than 10–20 percent of applicants do a strong job of presenting themselves. *Susan Palmer, Virginia*

Only a very small number of applicants—no more than 2 percent—market themselves well. Too many applicants look alike in this process, even though we give you plenty of opportunity to show yourself to advantage. For example, we ask how you might contribute to our community in any number of ways, but many applicants leave these questions blank. *Rob Schwartz, UCLA*

Show Your Interest In/Fit with the School

The older and more experienced you are, the more useful it is to show the fit between your prior work and educational efforts and the curricular and programmatic offerings of your chosen law school. *Susan Palmer, Virginia*

It's easier to submit applications now, so people have taken to just sending them off to a large percentage of the top twenty-five schools. If someone looks like he/she sought out our school and tailored the application to us, that gives the person an edge. We are inevitably impressed by people who have done their homework and determined that our program fits their needs. *Elizabeth Rosselot, Boston College*

We want people for whom Harvard Law School is a good match. Does this look like a candy store (with all its options and possibilities) or a scary place? Someone with real interest and experience in East Asian studies, Islamic law, or alternative dispute resolution, for example, would be of particular interest to us. *Joyce Curll, Harvard*

Successfully showing how the school fits your interests and needs is of great benefit to you and to us. Ideally, Columbia wants a community of people who have chosen to attend Columbia because of the many opportunities and resources it offers, and not simply by default. *Nkonye Iwerebon, Columbia*

It's enormously valuable to show that you are interested in our school and would fit well here. Institutions are like people in wanting to see that you are interested in them. (This is particularly important, by the way, for those on the wait-list.) *Rob Schwartz, UCLA*

BE SURE YOUR MESSAGES ARE CONSISTENT

Presenting yourself accurately, honestly, and thoughtfully is critical. It's important that the messages we get from the different pieces of the application are consistent—that the letters of recommendation match the personal statement, which matches the extracurricular profile, etc. This makes the picture comprehensible and credible. *Joyce Curll, Harvard*

When an applicant mentions the type of law he or she intends to practice in the future, our first instinct is to check the related data. We want to see whether she can back it up—has she been active in groups related to this field, for example. If she can back it up, it's great: She definitely helps her candidacy. At the extreme, this might mean a family therapist intending to practice family law. *Elizabeth Rosselot, Boston College*

I look for the connection between people's stated interests and their demonstrated commitments and accomplishments. *Kenneth Kleinrock, NYU*

Think of your application as a complete package. In particular, decide what qualities and experiences you want to emphasize. Each piece of your application should contribute to the picture that you want to present. For example, you can give your recommenders suggestions about what to emphasize in order to fit in with your overall approach. *Megan A. Barnett, Yale*

Don't raise questions you fail to answer in the application. We don't have the time to pick up the phone to find out about gaps or inconsistencies in your record.   *Elizabeth Rosselot, Boston College*

Any seasoned admissions officer knows well that any applicant may compose an application essay laying claims to strong character, sound values, noble ideals, and impressive achievements. And many do. At Columbia, however, we are sure to place any professional claims of an application essay in the context of the rest of his/her application . . . indeed, in the context of his/her life. We study how the applicant has actually chosen to use his or her time, energies, and talents. We look at the choices applicants have made in their academic lives, in their work place and in planning their careers, in their communities, in extracurriculars, perhaps in their political and/or religious lives.   *Jim Milligan, Columbia*

Consistency is definitely a virtue. You are telling your story—which has not only a beginning, middle, and end, but also multiple pieces and perspectives—and inconsistent pieces raise questions about the basic message. Sit back and consider your whole application as if seeing it for the first time. Be sure it presents an integrated and consistent picture of who you are and where you are headed. *Todd Morton, Vanderbilt*

Appendix III

Special Cases

MINORITIES AND OTHER TRADITIONALLY UNDERREPRESENTED GROUPS

If you are a minority interested in law school, there is a lot you can do to enhance your application to law school even if your undergraduate grade point average is relatively low and your LSAT score is not as high as you would like. There are many resources available to you and specific strategies you can apply that will help you overcome these and other obstacles to gaining admission to law school.

It is important to say at the outset that minority applicants should not consider this to be the only part of this book they need read to get into a good law school. Quite the contrary, topics and advice found throughout this book apply equally to minorities and non-minorities alike.

Just who qualifies as a "minority" is a tricky question in itself. Traditionally, for the purpose of law school admissions, five groups were considered minorities: Native Americans, Asian/Pacific Islanders, Blacks, Hispanics (of any race), and women. That has changed drastically in the past few decades. Women and Asians now apply and are accepted to law school in sufficient number that they are no longer considered minority applicants (though they are still regarded as minorities in many statistical surveys on the subject of minorities in law school and the legal profession). Today, most law schools consider "minorities" to be Native Americans, Blacks, and Hispanics. (Whether gay, lesbian, bisexual, and transgendered candidates will come to be included as a minority group is unclear.) In addition, given the trouble law schools have faced in the courts in targeting minority students for preferential treatment, some schools have to begun favor "applicants from economically disadvantaged backgrounds" instead of members of specific ethnic or racial groups. Still, for the foreseeable future it is unlikely that most law schools will entirely ignore race in admissions decisions.

For a variety of reasons that go far beyond the scope of this book, many minority candidates have had inferior academic opportunity when compared to the general applicant pool. The result is often lower grades, lower LSAT scores, and/or attendance at a lower quality undergraduate institution. Each of these factors counts heavily against applicants to law school. If this is the situation you face, you will need to craft an application strategy to overcome these obstacles.

REASONS MINORITIES RECEIVE DIFFERENTIAL ADMISSIONS TREATMENT

Minority applicants are often treated differently than are non-minority applicants. The explanation for the differences in treatment is simple: Law schools have substantial reasons for wanting minorities, but have too few minority applicants that meet the same admissions standards as non-minorities. As a result, schools admit minorities with, on average, lesser credentials than non-minorities have.

There are a host of reasons law schools want minorities, including:

➤ *Representation*. Law schools generally take seriously their stated obligations to educate future advocates for otherwise underrepresented groups. Advocacy can mean legal representation or, more broadly, involvement in politics, journalism, and so on.

➤ *Diversity*. Law schools believe that learning is maximized in environments in which a wide range of people, experience, and views are present in class.

➤ *Role models*. Law schools want to graduate students who can serve as role models for younger minority group members, whether via community involvement or simply via visible professional success.

➤ *Politics*. Law schools face political pressure from constituencies inside and outside their law school communities to admit a substantial number of minorities each year.

PRE-LAW PREPARATION PROGRAMS

Many programs have sprung up in recent years to address the under-representation of minorities in the legal profession. Many law schools and law-related organizations now offer part-time or summer programs for minority students that focus on providing information about law school and law and building critical-thinking, reading, and writing skills in preparation for law school. Such programs commonly offer application assistance, too. Consult the following list for a representative sampling of pre-law preparatory programs targeted at underrepresented applicants:

- Charles Hamilton Houston Law School Preparatory Institute
- Chicago-Kent College of Law Summer Pre-law Undergraduate Scholars Program
- Cornell University School of Continuing Education and Summer Sessions— Pre-law Program
- Florida State University Summer for Undergraduates Program
- Kentucky Legal Education Opportunity (KLEO) Program
- Ohio State University—Oxford University Pre-law Program
- Santa Clara University School of Law Pre-law Undergraduate Scholars Program (PLUS Program)
- Pace Law School Summer Program
- Seton Hall University School of Law—The Summer Institute for Pre-legal Studies
- Pre-law Summer Institute for American Indians and Alaska Natives
- Tennessee Institute for Pre-law at the University of Memphis Cecil C. Humphreys School of Law
- University of Denver Academic Achievement Program Summer Prep Program
- University of Iowa College of Law Philip G. Hubbard Law School Preparation (LSAC/PLUS) Program
- University of Missouri
- University of Nebraska-Lincoln College of Law Pre-law Summer Institute
- University of Texas at El Paso Law School Preparation Institute
- Villanova University School of Law/Lincoln University Pre-law Undergraduate Scholars Program (PLUS)
- William Mitchell College of Law Summer Partnership in Law Program

Some undergraduate institutions have such programs aimed at their own minority students interested in law. At UCLA for example, participants in the Law Fellows Outreach Program attend a series of weekend "academies" focusing on substantive skills and taught by law school professors. Participants are assigned a law student mentor with whom they interact throughout the year. Everyone who successfully completes the program receives a scholarship for an LSAT preparation course, and receives substantial assistance in the law school application process.

Another place to look for such pre-law preparatory programs is through the Council on Legal Education Opportunity (CLEO). CLEO, sponsored by the American Bar Association, offers a variety of free pre-law services for minority students, including six-week rigorous pre-law preparatory summer institutes at various ABA-accredited law schools.

Finally, the Law School Admissions Council "MILE Project" (Minorities Interested in Legal Education) is another good resource for minority students. MILE offers regional law school forums and other events targeted at minorities interested in law, access to advice (via e-mail) on the law school admissions process, and assistance with preparation for the LSAT, among other benefits. Consult the following for further assistance:

- ABA Commission on Racial and Ethnic Diversity in the Profession (www.abanet.org/minorities/links/students.html)
- ABA's Presidential Advisory Council on Diversity in the Profession (www.abanet.org/leadership/councilondiversity/home.html)
- NALP Diversity Initiatives (www.nalp.org/content/index.php?pid=55)
- "For Future Black Law Students" (www.forfutureblacklawstudents.com)
- "For People of Color" (www.forpeopleofcolor.org)

STRATEGIC OVERVIEW

The following discussion of strategy is designed to help minority applicants with academic weaknesses. (Minority students without academic weakness—175 LSAT score, 3.8 GPA at a leading college, for instance—are in a strong position and can safely forgo this section's advice.) A useful starting point is to understand where such applicants should focus their efforts.

Consider the application priorities confronting two applicants. One is a non-minority political science major applying as a college senior. He (or she) has a strong LSAT score as well as a high GPA, achieved at a highly reputable college. The second is a minority political science major, also applying as a college senior. She has a weak LSAT and GPA, achieved at a low- to middle-tier college. For the sake of this example, assume that neither has a strong extracurricular profile or substantial work experience. The chart below, using the reward-risk framework developed in the chapter, shows that the two face completely different challenges:

As the chart suggests, the non-minority applicant faces the problem of being one among many similar applicants, only a modest percentage of whom will be selected by leading law schools. They are not concerned about whether he

| | CANDIDATE | |
CATEGORY	NON-MINORITY POLITICAL SCIENCE MAJOR	MINORITY POLITICAL SCIENCE MAJOR
REWARD (to a law school for accepting applicant)	*Low*: Many other applicants with similar credentials available	*High*: Schools want minority students for multiple reasons
RISK (to a law school for accepting applicant)	*Low*: Good performance at good college suggests ability to do law school work	*High*: Low academic indicators suggest high likelihood of academic trouble
APPROPRIATE STRATEGY	Differentiate candidacy	Work to lower real or apparent risk

can do the work (i.e., the risk of taking him is low). Instead, they are wondering why they should accept him rather than any of dozens quite like him (i.e., the reward for taking him is low). Generally speaking, his focus should be on the reward side of the equation: showing in what ways he will be of value to the school.

The minority applicant faces the opposite problem of being highly valued, but a high risk (of struggling throughout law school). She should probably focus on the risk side of the equation: showing that she is unlikely to encounter academic problems. The next section describes and categorizes possible strategies she can employ.

APPLICATION STRATEGIES

Application strategies can be usefully separated into those that address the reward or the risk side of the admission equation. You can certainly adopt more than one strategy. Thus, you can have a recommender demonstrate your ability to research and write on a difficult subject, while you do post-graduation courses to demonstrate your academic ability and commitment. Your choice of strategies will be a function of two variables:

- The challenge (low reward? high risk?) facing your candidacy
- The credentials and accomplishments you already possess, plus your willingness to develop others

Some likely strategies are classified below.

STRATEGIES THAT ADDRESS (PERCEIVED) RISK

- Highlight the good academic work you've already done. Get detailed recommendations from relevant professors. (Workplace recommendations can be valuable, too, but they will generally be less persuasive of your academic abilities and performance.) In order to get strong recommendations, consider taking additional courses from professors who have a high regard for your work.

- Take the LSAT seriously. Take a proper prep course. Take the exam a second (or third) time, if necessary. Even though schools generally average your scores, any improvement will still work to your benefit. You will have demonstrated your commitment and given the admissions committee reason to believe that you are in fact improving your overall performance over time.

- If still in college, make your last terms count: get strong grades; do a thesis if possible. If already out of college, consider taking graduate or continuing education courses, preferably at a highly reputable school, to show that you can handle serious academics. Note that these efforts can also generate appropriate academic recommendations for you. Recognize, though, that graduate and continuing education work is often difficult for admissions committees to evaluate, so the burden is on you to demonstrate its seriousness.

STRATEGIES THAT ADDRESS BOTH RISK AND REWARD

If your grades and/or LSAT scores do not demonstrate your ability, tell the admissions committee why either in your personal statement or in an addendum to it. Did you work through college to support your family? Were there personal setbacks along the way that you were forced to put in front of academics or LSAT preparation? The admissions committee wants to know about these circumstances, *and how you handled them*. Demonstrating maturity and commitment despite adverse circumstances is always impressive. Show you have these attributes in abundance. After all, you must convince the admissions committee that although circumstances may have prevented you from achieving up to your true potential in the past, they do not represent barriers to success in law school and beyond.

Note that admissions committees constantly hear people argue that their academic credentials do not reflect their abilities. Candidates who manage to wait until they have, at least for some period of time, lived up to their claimed potential are more impressive candidates than those who apply before doing so.

- Emphasize leadership experiences, nonacademic interests and successes, or vision and dedication in other areas of your life that would enrich the law school community.

- Highlight true commitment to serve an under-represented group. Note that this type of career focus can help a borderline minority be treated like a minority. Asians, for instance, do not generally receive minority treatment in law school admissions. A Hmong candidate with strong community ties and an intention to return to serve her community, however, might boost her chances by demonstrating her commitment. After all, she (or he) might persuade an admissions committee that she would indeed provide valuable representation to an otherwise overlooked group. The longer and more focused her service to this community, of course, the more persuasive her candidacy will be.

CONCLUDING THOUGHTS

This is an all too touchy subject. Unlike other parts of this book replete with commentary from law school admissions deans, you will notice none of that here. Admissions deans and other senior law school personnel are almost uniformly reluctant to be forthright in print about the subject. Correspondingly, there is very little hard data in this area as well. What this means for students affected by these issues is that they must make an extra effort to inform themselves and to take advantage of special opportunities available.

Recognize, though, that there are indeed many resources available—and that you have many people on your side hopeful for your success and ready to help.

RESIDENTS

Public law schools—i.e., law schools at state-funded universities—generally give preferential admissions treatment to their own state's residents. The degree of preference varies from school to school. Hastings, for example, gives no preference, Michigan gives very little, and North Carolina, Texas, and Virginia give substantial preference. Texas, for instance, appears (on rough calculations) to give residents a preference equal to 0.2 undergraduate grade points and 1–2 LSAT points. In some states, the residential preference is more finely honed. Thus, Texas gives particular preference to those from disadvantaged areas of the state.

Given the admissions impact—plus the lower tuition at state schools (see the discussion in Chapter 18)—it is well worth exploring the possibilities of becoming a resident, either before or after you apply. If you become a resident

ADMISSIONS DEANS TALK ABOUT RESIDENCY

THE IMPACT OF RESIDENCY UPON ADMISSIONS

We are limited to matriculating no more than 20 percent non-residents. Recently the 25th and 75th percentile scores for residents have been 160–166, for non-residents, 161–167. These numbers reflect a one-point differential, but in some years the disparity may be as high as two or three points. The difference between cumulative grade point averages last year was greater. The middle 50 percent range for residents' GPAs was 3.37–3.79, whereas non-residents' GPAs ranged from 3.61–3.92.   *Monica Ingram, Texas*

About 25 percent of our class are residents. We don't look as hard at the soft factors for residents—interesting extracurriculars, for example—and consequently don't eliminate them as readily on these factors as we do non-residents. By the same token, there is no statistically significant difference between the quantitative credentials (LSAT, GPA) of residents and non-residents. For example, the LSAT scores of residents are never more than one point below those of non-residents and are often equal. This was quite different fifteen and more years ago, when we had 45–50 percent residents, leading some non-residents to perceive residents as less qualified.   *Sarah C. Zearfoss, Michigan*

Forty percent of our seats are for residents, 60 percent for non-residents. We recently had 900 resident applicants; we accepted 200 and enrolled 150. We had 4,600 non-resident applicants; we accepted 700 and enrolled 200. The residents' LSAT scores were one point lower than those of the non-residents, but the GPAs were as high.   *Susan Palmer, Virginia*

Although about 70 percent of our students are California residents, that simply reflects our applicant pool's composition. We don't focus on residence in the admissions process; it's not an advantage.   *Rob Schwartz, UCLA*

BECOMING A RESIDENT

Becoming a resident after a year is fairly easy. You register to vote, get a California driver's license and a bank account, and establish and maintain physical presence. It's tantamount to giving yourself a $10,000 scholarship.   *Edward Tom, Boalt Hall (Berkeley)*

Residence is determined on the basis of your status for the twelve months prior to enrollment, looking at where you live, pay taxes, vote, are licensed to drive, and register your car.   *Susan Palmer, Virginia*

Essentially no one who enrolls as a non-resident will manage to convert to resident status during the course of the program.   *Sarah C. Zearfoss, Michigan*

> Generally Texas residency must be established twelve months prior to enroll-ment. Students may not change their residency status from non-resident to res-ident after enrollment in the Law School. *Monica Ingram, Texas*

before applying, of course, you can reap both the admissions preference bene-fit and the lower tuition; if you become a resident only after applying, perhaps during a deferral year, you will stand to gain only the tuition advantage.

States generally take a number of factors into account in determining resi-dency. You are likely to be considered a resident if you attended high school in the state, your parents were and remain state residents, and you have not left the state for any substantial, full-time purpose other than education or military ser-vice. To become a resident, on the other hand, expect some or all of the follow-ing to be considered:

- Where you are registered to vote (and have voted)
- Whether you have a state driver's license (or identity card, if you do not drive)
- Which address you designate on school, employment, and military records
- Where you register your automobile
- Whether you pay state income taxes as a resident
- Where you reside (and for how long each year), and where your belong-ings are kept
- Whether you return to your prior state of residence on a regular basis

It will be necessary to provide documentary evidence of the relevant factors.

You will have difficulty establishing residence in a state if you are consid-ered a dependent of your parents and they live elsewhere, because this single factor will tend to give you the same state residence as they enjoy. To be con-sidered financially independent of your parents requires at a minimum that you not be claimed as an income-tax deduction. Some states will also con-sider your age, whether you are married, whether you have dependents (other than your spouse), and whether you are financially self-sufficient.

To be sure of your status, check with the law school's admissions depart-ment to find out who at the university can advise you. (This is a function gener-ally handled on a university-wide basis.)

Note that in some states (California, in particular) it is easy to convert from nonresident to resident status during your time in law school; in other states, this is all but impossible while you remain a student.

LEGACIES

Being a "legacy"—i.e., related to someone who attended a given school—can greatly improve your chances of admission to college. (Colleges value legacies because admitting them encourages alumni to contribute to the school. It also adds to the class students likely to be active in school affairs and, in general, pleased to be there.) At the graduate-school level, however, the situation is different. First of all, schools tend to pay little attention to "legacies" from any other school within the university. In other words, if your mother attended North-

---

ADMISSIONS DEANS DISCUSS LEGACIES

WHAT COUNTS AS A LEGACY

Sons and daughters of UVA Law graduates definitely count as legacies. They are evaluated against the resident applicant pool. Grandchildren and siblings, just like relatives of those who attended another part of the university, are also given a more careful look.   *Susan Plamer, Virginia*

Our application asks whether any relatives attended Vanderbilt Law School. We are also interested, albeit to a lesser degree, in whether any attended another part of Vanderbilt.   *Todd Morton, Vanderbilt*

Anyone with a relative who has attended any school at USC counts as a legacy. Applicants need to point this out, however, because we don't ask it on our application.   *Chloe T. Reid, USC*

The only thing that qualifies as a legacy here is having a parent who attended Boston College Law School.   *Elizabeth Rosselot, Boston College*

THE IMPACT OF LEGACY STATUS

If an applicant's parent is a Columbia Law graduate, the legacy factor serves as a factor in our decision-making but not a highly influential one. Consider it as a feather on the scale, but one significant enough to make a positive difference if the applicant is close to admission based on his/her own merits. The legacy factor plays such a role only a few times each admissions season. The legacy factor exerts considerably less impact on law school admissions decisions than within the undergraduate realm. Expectations to the contrary, when applied to highly selective law schools, are outdated and grounded more in hope than reality. *Jim Milligan, Columbia*

We pay some attention to "development" cases, but there are very, very few of them. I get some pressure from development staff, but I respond by telling them I'm not qualified to determine the degree of institutional interest represented by that development matter. So I report back to them only on the merits and chances of admission for the applicant in question. *Jim Milligan, Columbia*

Being a legacy does not give you a leg up—even if you are the son or daughter of faculty. *Edward Tom, Boalt Hall (Berkeley)*

Legacy status is unlikely to have any substantial impact upon the admissions decision, but it may give the applicant a chance to come in to speak with us about his or her candidacy. *Chloe T. Reid, USC*

Given that we are blessed with many more strong applicants than we can admit, legacy status can sometimes tip the scales in someone's favor. *Todd Morton, Vanderbilt*

As a state school we don't advantage legacies in the admissions process. *Rob Schwartz, UCLA*

Legacies are given a special look and primarily are treated a bit differently (after their applications have been rejected) by our counseling them about possible reapplication or transfer opportunities. *Jim Milligan, Columbia*

Legacy status is given only to relatives of Michigan Law School alumni. Legacies are treated for admission (but not tuition) purposes as in-state applicants, which means they benefit from the slightly more limited scrutiny we apply to Michigan residents. *Sarah C. Zearfoss, Michigan*

western Medical School, Northwestern Law School will not consider you a "legacy" at all. Even those applicants with relatives who attended the law school itself seldom receive much of a leg up in the admissions process.

There are three factors that tend to determine the effect a legacy will have:

- The closer the relationship, the better. If one of your parents attended the law school, the impact will tend to be greater than if an uncle were the alum.

- The more active in alumni and school affairs, and the more the relative has donated to the school, the better.

- Private schools tend to put slightly more weight on legacy status than do state schools, due largely to the latter relying traditionally on public rather than private funding.

INTERNATIONAL APPLICANTS

International applicants represent a small but rapidly growing segment of the JD market. As the legal market itself has become more and more global, so too has the admissions game at American law schools. It is, of course, testimony to the positive reputation American law schools enjoy that so many non-Americans are applying. In the past, of course, international applicants generally did a bachelor of laws degree (a first degree) in their home countries, worked for some years, and then applied to an American school for an LLM. They continue to do so, but many foreign applicants now look to do a JD in the United States instead of doing a first law degree in their home countries, or in addition to such a first law degree.

The reasons for a foreign applicant to do an LLM are clear. The traditional reason was to learn about American law, so as to go back to the home country and be a better informed lawyer, professor, diplomat, or government administrator. Of course it did not hurt to add the cachet of a Harvard or a Georgetown or a Columbia degree to a curriculum vitae, either. A new reason has been added in recent years. Many international candidates for LLM degrees at the leading American law schools have come intending to practice in America after finishing their degrees. Candidates with just an LLM degree can be admitted to the bar in states such as California and New York.

Why, then, do foreign applicants consider doing a JD in the United States? Some may have done a non-law first degree, thereby necessitating about three years of study, whether in the home country or in the U.S. Similarly, some may want to practice in an American state, such as Illinois, that does not admit candidates to the bar with only an LLM. Others may want to undergo the rigorous training of an American JD degree, preferring it to their home degree options. Still others may wish to have the built-in marketing opportunities afforded by being at an American school for three years (they are able to pitch themselves to potential American employers throughout their stint) or by virtue of earning the most well-understood of American law degrees.

ATTRACTIVE OPTIONS FOR FOREIGN APPLICANTS

Northwestern offers foreign applicants who already have a first law degree the opportunity to complete a JD in just two years. One year's credit is given for prior legal study.

Duke also offers a year's credit for prior legal study, thereby making a two-year JD or three-year JD/LLM program possible.

Several things are different for international applicants whether applying for a JD or an LLM. American law schools often find it difficult to understand the nature and quality of the university work done by applicants educated abroad. The same is true for work experience, extracurricular and community activities, and so on. As a result, foreign applicants need to make their credentials clear and

---

ADMISSIONS DEANS DISCUSS ISSUES RELEVANT TO INTERNATIONAL STUDENTS

THE LSAT

In many ways, LSAT performance is more important for international applicants than for Americans. Non-native English speakers need to understand the subtleties of English, which is what the LSAT demands. Also, it is hard to equate GPAs from foreign schools with American GPAs, for one thing. As a result, I really worry if an international applicant does poorly on the LSAT. *Susan Palmer, Virginia*

The rough equivalent to an American scoring 165 on the LSAT would be a German (i.e., someone from a country where English is hardly unknown) scoring 163–164 or a Chinese from interior China (whose exposure to English is very limited) scoring 161–162. (We will look closely at foreigners' essays to see whether they have command of the English language.) *Andy Cornblatt, Georgetown*

An LSAT score of 162–164 for a Chinese applicant would be fine. *Faye Deal, Stanford*

We are aware that a standardized test may not be as predictive for a non-native speaker, but it's still an important factor in the process. *Rob Schwartz, UCLA*

We expect LSAT scores comparable to Americans', but since our LSAT scores cover a very wide range it's not particularly critical in the process. *William Hoye, Duke*

THE TOEFL AND LSAT

We ask applicants to submit TOEFL results if they earned their undergraduate degree at an institution at which English is not the primary language of instruction. *Susan Palmer, Virginia*

We don't require the TOEFL. *Rob Schwartz, UCLA*

My principal concern is that someone be able to speak English *now*. It's best if they've already lived in an Englsih-speaking environment. This is more important than a TOEFL score *Sarah C. Zearfoss, Michigan*

CREDENTIAL EVALUATION

We use the LSDAS ("JDCAS") credential evaluation service for international applications.   *Rob Schwartz, UCLA*

It can be very difficult to assess the undergraduate records of international applicants. It helps if they provide information regarding the grading system in use. If we can evaluate their performance, and it has been strong, we might give them a bit of a break on the LSAT. On the other hand, lacking good understanding of their undergraduate performance, we'll put a lot of weight on their LSAT score. *Don Rebstock, Northwestern*

GENERAL COMMENTS

It's difficult to get in as an international student. You have to meet the same criteria as everybody else. We may give you a very small break in terms of the LSAT because we know English is your second language, but it's still hard to be admitted as an international student.   *Edward Tom, Boalt Hall (Berkeley)*

These are harder files to evaluate, so anything an applicant can do to make accomplishments clear (and impressive) the better. Be sure to explain your experiences, institutions, etc. . . . Try to choose recommenders who can write well in English. It's particularly valuable if you can have an American professor who was teaching abroad at your school address your ability to handle an American legal education.   *Rob Schwartz, UCLA*

For foreign applicants who haven't done a lot of work in English, we'll check their personal statements carefully no matter how strong their LSAT score is. This is because law school grades are generally based solely upon the performance on a single, time-pressured written exam. Any inability to write English is magnified by that situation.   *Faye Deal, Stanford*

readily understood. Thus, it can be very helpful to show how exclusive (in meritocratic terms) a given university is; the way a grading system works, in full detail; the hiring policies of a firm; and so on.

Your rationale for studying in the United States will inevitably matter. At the JD level, it is particularly valuable to show that you will be able to handle the rapid flow of idiomatic English, plus the need to read large volumes of detailed materials, and to discuss them in a sophisticated manner.

One curiosity about the international application process: For a JD, a TOEFL score is not generally required but an LSAT score is; the opposite is true for an LLM.

MISCONDUCT

Some applicants to law school are faced with the potentially difficult challenge of overcoming past misconduct. Examples of misconduct that can affect admissions decisions include being convicted of a crime or being disciplined by a school. (Misconduct, in this sense, does not include getting poor grades at some point in your academic career.) The range of possible misconduct is great: from being written up by a dormitory resident advisor for making noise after hours to being convicted of murder.

Admissions deans are seldom concerned about a single minor incident that occurred some time ago. The greater the severity, or frequency, and the more recent the incident(s), however, the more concerned deans are likely to be.

Beyond notions of severity and timing is the issue of what the misconduct says about you. Being a "minor in possession" of alcohol during your sophomore year may say little negative about your character. Having seven or eight minor-in-possession convictions is a different matter, suggesting that you have (or had) a drinking problem or an inability to conform to the rules of your environment. And, of course, even one armed robbery conviction is likely to say a great deal about your character.

Even if you have had a string of offenses, you may not be beyond redemption. For example, one of my clients ("George") had a large handful of felony convictions and many more misdemeanors and dismissed charges (for driving under the influence, drunk and disorderly, resisting arrest, aggravated assault, and so on) resulting from a severe drinking problem. He also had a dreadful transcript for his early college years. He managed to get sober, though, and pulled his life together. George not only excelled in his last years of college, but also helped others through his passionate involvement with Alcoholics Anonymous. He counseled others, including those in prison, over the course of the nearly seven years before he applied to law school. He was admitted to numerous top twenty programs in spite of his serious criminal record.

In preparation for applying George was careful to contact all of the jurisdictions where he had lived, studied, worked, or partied, to get a complete record of his prior run-ins with the law. He also studied his transcript and contacted his college administration to make sure that he was aware of all his college transgressions. Having a complete record of his earlier mistakes, he then revealed absolutely everything to the law schools to which he applied.

As part of his admissions effort George also checked with the bar associations of the states in which he thought he might want to practice, to make sure that his record would not preclude his admission to the bar. He took detailed notes on these conversations and then shared the conclusions with the law schools. He made it clear that his lengthy rehabilitation period had cleared the way for him to be admitted (absent any later trouble).

FAILURE TO OVERCOME A MISCONDUCT INCIDENT

One student ("Mark") had what appeared to be a less involved record of misconduct to overcome than did George (discussed in the text, above). Unlike George, however, he failed.

Mark, a political science student at a top twenty undergraduate university, failed a course in the spring term of his junior year, having been found to have cheated on a paper. Despite good advice to the contrary, he decided to apply to law school in the fall of his senior year. He applied only to leading schools—consistent with his GPA, undergraduate university reputation, and LSAT results—without regard to the impact his misconduct would have on admissions decisions. He was rejected everywhere he applied. He was unable to convince admissions committees that he was a different, better person than he had been months before when he cheated.

Given that immaturity was his strong suit, he compounded his problems by sulking about the rejections. His grades dropped in his senior year. He also failed to take the job hunt seriously, so he did not land the quality of job he might otherwise have managed. He also badgered several of the law schools that had rejected him, thereby effectively destroying his chances as a possible reapplicant to these schools. He did gain admission to a law school the following year, but one that was ranked in the bottom half of accredited schools: hardly a victory for someone aiming for a top ten or twenty program initially.

Had Mark been more mature he might have approached the situation differently. He could have acknowledged the severity of his mistake and tried to make up for it to some extent by doing volunteer work with his school's honor council to help keep others from making such a mistake. He certainly would have been wise to wait to apply until at least one year (and preferably two or three years) later. Had he gotten good grades his senior year, and then done some additional course work after graduation, he could have had strong recommendations from professors who would have instructed him after the cheating incident. They could have addressed his ethics as well as his performance. These steps, plus the simple passage of time, would have helped lessen the impact of his cheating.

Mark could also have given law schools a positive reason to want him by excelling in his first post-college job. As a college senior, he was yet another political science major applying to law school. As a nearly fungible member of a large part of the applicant pool, schools had no need to take him rather than someone who was nearly identical (except for not having misconduct issues with his or her candidacy). As a successful young professional, however, he would had given schools a reason to want to accept him—a reason to hope that his ethical issues were indeed behind him.

Although alcoholism and the violence it engendered in George's case are hardly trivial matters, they could be overcome in the admissions process with the passage of time and appropriate behavior. It is harder to overcome problems that strike at an applicant's integrity. Being guilty of identity theft, for instance, would be much more troublesome for most admissions deans than alcohol or drug offenses. By the same token, academic cheating—whether on the LSAT, course exams, papers, or otherwise—automatically puts an applicant's integrity at issue. As Mark discovered (see box), the later in someone's academic career this happens, the worse it is. Not only is it then going to be closer to the time the person will apply to law school, but it also will mean that the person has less time to perform in an academic setting with a clean record. Many admissions deans will worry that someone who cheated in a class as a senior would not encounter similar temptations thereafter when out in the work force. As a result, even a clean record post-college may not be persuasive evidence that the person has changed his or her behavior. (Even if the person continued in education without another incident of cheating, admissions deans worry that he or she simply didn't get caught.)

Note that failure to admit your misconduct can be much more serious than the initial misconduct. Even a trivial misconduct episode, if concealed, raises issues about your integrity. Some applicants think that they can (or must) hide misconduct, only to have a school discover it anyway. Schools increasingly do spot checks on applicants' records, checking anything that seems a bit odd. Recommenders, employers, thesis advisors, college administrators, and others may be called. (If a school determines that an applicant has been guilty of misconduct in his or her application to that school, the matter may well not end there. Instead, the school is likely to communicate its finding to the Law School Admissions Council, which will then pass the information to all schools to which the person applies.)

It is not just law schools that check applicants' records. Bar associations notoriously do a detailed check of aspirants' application details. Many bar associations check applicants' bar application against their law school applications to make sure that they jibe. Some go so far as to check the law school applications of every law school to which an applicant applied, including those they decided not to attend (or to which they were not admitted).

The worst result for a candidate with a misconduct problem may not be getting rejected by a law school. Instead, if someone gets into law school and applies to be admitted to the bar during his (or her) last year, he could be found out as having failed to report something three or four years before when applying to the school. The bar association would notify the school in that case, whereupon the individual would face being thrown out of law school just before graduation. He would have no license to practice law, not even a law degree—but plenty of law school debt.

When in doubt, disclose anything that seems even passably relevant to the ethics questions law schools ask in their applications.

SUGGESTIONS

If you are in the "misconduct" category, by all means:

- Acknowledge your fault rather than blaming others
- Apologize to those affected (and make restitution as appropriate, either to individuals or society as a whole)
- Show that you have dealt with any underlying problem
- Demonstrate in as many ways as possible that you have learned your lesson and moved on
- Allow enough time to elapse to overcome the nature and severity of the incident(s)
- Address the problem frankly, in detail, in your application. Consider adding a separate addendum to do so, rather than cluttering your personal statement
- Give schools a reason to accept you by excelling in every other way you can

---

THE ADMISSIONS DEANS DISCUSS MISCONDUCT

THE NATURE OF THE MISCONDUCT

I feel differently about drinking than I do about academic cheating. For one thing, you can show that you haven't been drinking, through AA involvement and the like. It's harder to show that you have reformed if your offense was cheating. If you are in school after being caught cheating, having a clean record thereafter may just mean that you haven't been caught. If you are out of school, you aren't faced with the same temptations. There are more ways to show you've changed if the issue is drinking.   *Sarah Zearfoss, Michigan*

The most common misconduct we see is misrepresentation of their academic history. For instance, they fail to tell us about being put on academic probation their freshman year. Simply reviewing their transcript prior to applying might eliminate such problems. *Ann Killian Perry, Chicago*

One "minor in possession" violation is unlikely to have an impact upon our admissions decision, but a pattern of violations might. It could suggest that the applicant lacks maturity or good judgment. *Monica Ingram, Texas*

I am less concerned with infractions due to immaturity—such as underage drinking or traffic infractions—than those that are due to a lack of honesty or integrity, traits fundamental to the functioning of the judicial system. *Todd Morton, Vanderbilt*

Abuse of positions of trust and lack of integrity are real problems—for example, using a roommate's credit card without authorization, shoplifting, honor code violations, etc. *Anne Richard, George Washington*

Acknowledging the Problem

We need to see that someone has accepted his responsibility and recognized what will be necessary to cure the underlying issue. For example, someone with a drinking problem getting involved with AA helps his chances. That is far better than producing excuses, arguing that something is someone else's fault. *Susan Palmer, Virginia*

The first hurdle you need to get over is to understand how completely unacceptable misconduct is in the community you are about to enter. *Sarah Zearfoss, Michigan*

Evaluating the Misconduct

We review misconduct on a case-by-case basis within the context of the rest of the file. We consider whether the applicant has overcome the negative circumstances, which usually can't be done without the passage of time. We want to see how much distance applicants have put between who they are today and who they were then. *Edward Tom, Boalt Hall (Berkeley)*

Several factors determine how comfortable readers may be with misconduct. If the candidate argues that he wasn't really at fault rather than accepting responsibility, readers may be uncomfortable. If the incident(s) took place recently, readers may be uncomfortable. And if the candidate failed to learn a lesson from the experience, readers may be uncomfortable. *Todd Morton, Vanderbilt*

Even egregious cases of misconduct may not stop you from gaining admission to a law school, if you can convince the admissions committee you've turned your life around and have the potential and determination to succeed. *Rob Schwartz, UCLA*

There is no bright-line test, or cut-and-dried rules: we look at each application on a case-by-case basis. *Monica Ingram, Texas*

TIMING

Assuming that whatever happened was more than a couple of years ago and wasn't a major violation, we will usually overlook it. This assumes that you have learned from the experience and have done good things since then. If the violation was more recent, however, we are much less likely to overlook it. You won't be able to demonstrate that you've learned from it, improved yourself, and moved on. *Don Rebstock, Northwestern*

A significant passage of time between the misconduct and your application is important. The passage of time should be proportionate to the nature of your misconduct. *Susan Palmer, Virginia*

APPLICATION VEHICLES

If the misconduct is really egregious, it might make sense to address it in the personal statement. If it's less serious, it's probably more appropriate to handle it in an addendum. So, for most people, it should be in an addendum. *Rob Schwartz, UCLA*

Discussing the misconduct in a separate addendum is generally a good idea. It is more easily highlighted for the reader when it's not part of the personal essay and it gives the applicant a better opportunity to provide complete disclosure. *Edward Tom, Boalt Hall (Berkeley)*

IMPORTANCE OF FULL DISCLOSURE

Declare whatever you did. Think hard about all the ways you can show us you have changed. If you don't declare something and I find out about it in some other way, I'll withdraw you immediately and there won't be a second chance for you. *Sarah Zearfoss, Michigan*

Disclose, disclose, disclose. If you have any doubt about whether to disclose something, we urge you to err on the side of disclosure. In most cases the failure to disclose would be far more serious than the conduct involved. (In one case, an applicant failed to disclose his conviction for urinating on the beach. Urinating on the beach wouldn't have kept him out of law school, but failure to disclose it did.) *Susan Palmer, Virginia*

Read the application question closely. Some specify that you need to disclose even matters that have been sealed or expunged from your record. People get into trouble when they don't disclose information on their applications. This becomes especially troublesome when they sit for the bar exam and the bar examiners learn that they failed to disclose something when they applied to law school. *Rob Schwartz, UCLA*

Applicants often worry about the law school application process when they should be worrying about the bar application process. Be sure to disclose everything, fully, with all the circumstances. Failing to do so often causes more trouble in the bar application process than the original infraction does. *Todd Morton, Vanderbilt*

There is a continuing duty to disclose possible misconduct up until the time you matriculate here. Even though you are not obligated to disclose dismissed, purged, and expunged items, you probably are wise to do so. Such items won't be disclosed to law schools, but they will be to law enforcement officials. (The Board of Bar Examiners is considered a branch of law enforcement, so when you apply to take the bar the misconduct is likely to be discovered.) *Susan Palmer, Virginia*

POLICING THE SYSTEM

I do checks of anything that looks amiss. I will call recommenders and employers, for example, if I don't fully trust what is presented to me. *Sarah Zearfoss, Michigan*

We learn about misconduct through the dean's letter, transcripts, recommendations, and so on, as well as by doing our own checks of what applicants assert in their personal statements. *Ann Killian Perry, Chicago*

If we discover someone has omitted relevant information in applying here, the Dean of Students determines the sanction. We take this process very seriously. We recently dismissed a student who was about to graduate for a serious omission in his application. *Anne Richard, George Washington*

Many schools now do spot checks—verifications of the information supplied in résumés and applications. *Rick Geiger, Cornell*

Many boards of bar examiners look at *all* of your law school applications and check that you were truthful in them. *Susan Palmer, Virginia*

The Texas state bar does an exhaustive background check that includes looking at your law school application. Failure to disclose something in your law school application can hinder your admission to the bar. *Monica Ingram, Texas*

The requirement for disclosure doesn't end with the application to law school: that's just the beginning. The bar examiners will ask the same questions we ask and check every answer—including the ones you've given us. You're much better off disclosing something now since you'll have to disclose it later on, anyway. *Andy Cornblatt, Georgetown*

General Advice

It's a good thing to assume that you enter the legal profession once you first apply to law school, not when you take the bar exam. You need to pursue your admission to law school, as well as your law school studies, with complete honesty and integrity.   *Edward Tom, Boalt Hall (Berkeley)*

If you're serious about going to law school and have had some minor infractions, don't let that stop you from pursuing your dream.   *Rob Schwartz, UCLA*

Appendix IV

PERSONAL ORGANIZER

Age:

Marital status:

Children:

GROWING UP

Where were you born? Where did you grow up? Where have you lived?

Where were your parents born? What is their ethnic/racial/religious background?

What are your parents' educational levels and occupations?

Was your childhood or adolescence affected by divorce? Poverty?

Describe the neighborhood in which you grew up:

Describe the culture of your high school. How did you fit in there?

What was your favorite high school class? Why?

What did you want to be when you grew up?

Where did you spend (summer) vacations?

If you have siblings: How old are they? What do they do? How are they different from you?

COLLEGE EDUCATION (Repeat as necessary for graduate programs)

School:

Did you transfer? From where? Why?

Degree: Date Received:

Grade-point average: Major/Concentration:

Minor: Relevant additional course work:

Substantial papers written:

Honors, Awards and Scholarships:

How did you finance your education?

Why did you choose this school? In retrospect, was it a good decision? Why or why not?

(Repeat for choice of major.)

What was your favorite college course? Why?

Your most challenging course?

Describe any significant academic problems:

How did you spend your Christmas and spring breaks?

Describe the culture of your college. Did you fit in there?

What was the best part of your college experience?

What surprised you the most about your college experience? What disappointed you the most?

WORK EXPERIENCE

Start with your most recent job and work backward chronologically. If you had more than one job with the same employer, fill out separate data fields for each. Include all part-time as well as full-time jobs.

Employer:

Dates employed: From: _____ To: _____

Location:

Title/Position:

Beginning salary: Ending salary:

Key responsibilities:

Whom did you manage? To whom did you report?

Key accomplishments (quantify whenever possible):

Key skills that enabled you to accomplish these things:

Superiors' reviews (excerpts):

Reasons superiors feel this way about you (think in terms of your achievements, skills, actions, attitude, etc.):

Reasons for taking the job:

Reasons for leaving the job:

Ways in which the job met your expectations:

Ways in which the job did not meet your expectations:

Important stories illustrating your leadership, teamwork, analytical, and communicative abilities:

What sources (including people) are there for developing further information about each story?

PROFESSIONAL ACCOMPLISHMENTS

Copyrights: Patents:
    Title: Title:
    Date: Date:
    Publisher/Publication: Number:

Professional certification:
    Organization certifying:
    Date certified:

Professional honors and awards:
    Name:
    Date awarded:
    Organization awarding:
    Reason for the award:

EXTRACURRICULAR (AND POST-GRADUATION) ACTIVITIES (artistic, athletic, community, fraternity/sorority, religious, political, social, etc.)

Activity: Dates of involvement:

Offices held/responsibilities/achievements:

Was this a voluntary position or one to which you were elected/appointed? If elected or appointed, by whom?

Reasons for your involvement:

How does it relate to your other activities and interests?

PERSONAL QUESTIONS

What are the four or five things you most admire in others? (In whom and why?)

What is the most useful criticism you have received?

What are your four or five most memorable experiences, whether great or small?

Have you ever lived or worked with unusual people? Describe:

What was your greatest success, and what did you learn from it?

What was your greatest failure, and what did you learn from it?

What fear have you overcome? (How and why?)

What is the biggest risk you've taken? How did you make your decision? What was the outcome?

Have you ever mentored anyone? Describe:

Give an example of a strongly held belief that has changed over the course of your life. What happened?

What is the hardest decision you've ever had to make? How did you handle it?

Give an example of a situation in which you failed. How did you handle the failure?

Is your sexual orientation other than heterosexual?

What do your friends most like (and dislike) about you?

What are the four or five (or more) key words that would describe you? What on your résumé demonstrates this?

Do you have a personal motto or something that you frequently quote?

What languages do you know? How well? Have you traveled abroad?

Have you ever been arrested? Convicted? Disciplined at college? Explain briefly:

LEISURE TIME

What are your favorite books? Why? What have you read most recently?

(Repeat for favorite movies.)

What newspapers and magazines do you read regularly?

What do you like to do when given the time? Why? What do you most enjoy about it?

YOUR FUTURE CAREER

What interests, skills, values, and goals impel you toward law school?

Where do you want to be and what do you want to be doing five years after you graduate from law school?

What are your career goals? What do you hope to accomplish in your life?

LAW SCHOOL

In three sentences or fewer: why do you want to go to law school?

Would you consider deferring admission for a year if you were admitted? What would you do during that year?

Have you ever applied to law school before? Where? When? With what results?

Are you considering applying to other graduate programs (besides law school)?

PULLING YOUR INFORMATION TOGETHER

At the conclusion of this exercise, list your major accomplishments in each category.

Work:
1.
2.
3.

Education:

    1.

    2.

    3.

Personal:

    1.

    2.

    3.

Which events or activities represent inflection points in your life (i.e., when you changed direction)?

In what ways are you different from a year ago? Why? (Repeat for five years ago.) Think in terms of your personality, interests, personal and professional goals, and values.

How have your various experiences helped you to grow? What do they show about your abilities? What do they show about your interests?

Which of your experiences demonstrate the following characteristics?

Characteristic	Relevant Experience
Intellectual Ability	
Analytical Ability	
Imagination and Creativity	
Motivation and Initiative	
Maturity	
Organizational Skills	
Ability to Work with Others	
Leadership Potential	
Self-Confidence	
Ability in Oral Expression	
Ability in Written Communication	
Sense of Humor	
Career Potential	

10

Understanding Your Essay Options

— EXECUTIVE SUMMARY —

■

You will be evaluated on your choice of topic as well as the substance and the style of your writing.

■

Choose your topic carefully.
—Use themes to further your positioning effort through the essays.

■

Learn how the typical applicant approaches an essay topic and how to develop a more effective approach.

■

Include supplemental essays (if necessary) and a polished résumé, especially if you have substantial work experience.

Yale Law School's admissions information says of the personal statement requirement: "Faculty readers look to the required short essay to evaluate your writing, thinking, and editing skills, as well as to learn more about such qualities as your intellectual concerns or passions, your humor, or your ability to think across disciplines." And, if you read the fine print, in 250 words or fewer—no small feat.

With few exceptions, the top law programs in the country require a personal statement from each applicant. The essay offers you the chance to show schools who you really are. Take advantage of this opportunity. Recommenders can show only a *part* of who you are, since most of them are instructors or employers and have thus seen you in only one context. Many schools do not offer everyone the chance to interview as part of the admissions process. In addition, interviews are not under your control to the same extent as the personal statement, which can be rewritten and re-examined to make sure that the "real you" is presented.

Your personal statements can and should present a clear picture of you, but they do not need to tell all. Sketching in the main points with appropriate stories will show who you are. In fact, whenever possible, try to tell a story rather than write an essay.

This is your chance to choose which parts of your past (or your future) and yourself to highlight, and to determine how people should view them. This is a precious opportunity; take full advantage of the chance to color your readers' interpretations.

CHOICE OF TOPIC

When it comes to the personal statement section of the application, most schools leave the question open-ended. This is Columbia's:

> . . . a statement may provide the Admissions Committee with information regarding such matters as: personal, family, or educational background; experiences and talents of special interest; one's reasons for applying to law school as they may relate to personal goals and professional expectations; or any other factors which you think should inform the Committee's evaluation of your candidacy for admission.

Often, several topical suggestions will be offered, but even these suggestions will be quite broad, if not exceedingly vague. This open-endedness is both opportunity and trap. The law schools are being deliberately inexplicit. Having left *you* to make the decisions, they expect those who are insightful about themselves, the process, the competition, and the rest of the relevant factors, to make good use of this freedom. By the same token, they expect the average applicant to be upset by the degree of freedom on offer, just as they expect him or her to flub the opportunity.

So don't. Just because you *can* discuss every semi-important aspect of your life containing possible relevancy to the study of law does not mean you *should*. Chicago, which does not require an essay, nevertheless shares this bit of advice in their catalog:

> In reviewing the personal statement, the Committee looks for information that gives insight into the nonacademic contribution you would make to the class. In general, a statement with a narrow focus on some personal attribute or experience is far more helpful to us than either a broad statement about the law and its connection to your goals or a narrative restatement of the credentials described in other components of your application.

TIPS ON CHOOSING A PERSONAL STATEMENT TOPIC

Remember that an essay does not exist in a vacuum. Instead, it is part of the whole application and should be answered in the context of how you wish the whole application package to read, and, thus, how you will maximize your reward-risk ratio (see Chapter 9). Your choice of topic for a personal statement for a given school will therefore depend upon these factors:

➤ *Your desired positioning.* (For a discussion of this and the following points, see Chapter 9.)

➤ *Your choice of organizing themes.*

➤ *Circumstances specific to a given school.* For example, the University of Pennsylvania currently asks you to write two essays, one of your choosing and one about your reasons for wanting to attend Penn. Under this circumstance, it would be peculiar to write both essays on the subject of "Why Penn?" By the same token, if your usual personal statement discusses how you will contribute marvelously to courses about health law, you will probably want to change topics if this particular school offers no courses on the subject.

➤ *The subject about which you are asked to write.* A given school may constrain your choice by specifying a subject.

➤ *The number of essays you are invited to write.* For example, if Michigan offers you the chance to write two optional, shorter essays (about how you will contribute to the school's diversity, for one, and something that reveals how you think, for another), you will want to consider how best to balance the impression the whole set of essays will make.

➤ *Permitted length.* Some topics can be handled in 250 words; others need much more space.

➤ *What your recommender can address.* Focus on something, perhaps the personal side of you, that your recommenders cannot address.

➤ *The stories you have to tell.* If you have filled out the Personal Organizer (see Appendix IV), you will know what sort of material is available to you. Be sure to examine the personal statements in Part V to see what your competition writes about in order to generate your own ideas. In choosing stories, try for those that:

—Are interesting

—Are unusual (and thus memorable)

—Reveal something not fully described elsewhere in your application

—Show you to have leadership and teamwork skills and experience

—Demonstrate your maturity and judgment, compassion, determination, and/or sense of humor

—Make clear your analytical and/or communication abilities

—Demonstrate your mastery of a subject or field

—Are ones that you should tell, rather than those a recommender should tell

➤ *Your age and experience.* Few candidates who are still in college will benefit from writing about why they want to be a lawyer, whereas few older candidates at mid-career will be able to avoid discussing this. In the former situation, few college seniors can say anything both interesting and credible. Nearly all college seniors reveal themselves to be naive about the law and lacking in real self-knowledge, particularly concerning career direction, when writing about this topic. In the latter situation, admissions directors will consider it crucial to understand why someone wants to change careers. In particular, you will be expected to show that you know well what you expect to find in a legal career that you have not found in your current career. (See the following discussion regarding "Why do I want to be a lawyer?")

Each of these types of applicant can consider writing a second, smaller essay about other matters. Thus, young applicants who are truly well versed about their career futures can address this in a second essay, whereas experienced applicants who discuss their reasons for changing careers in their first essay can delve into something compelling and interesting about themselves in a second essay.

➤ *Applying to second-tier schools.* If applying to a school below the top tier, one essay should probably focus on your future career. Demonstrating that you will be readily employable will substantially improve your chances of admission.

The next section of this chapter will assist you in breaking apart and analyzing your essay options. After reading the analysis of each topic—and after having filled out the Personal Organizer (see Appendix IV)—it should quickly become apparent which are most suited to you and your application on the whole.

INDIVIDUAL CONSULTING AND WORKSHOPS

I recognize that readers may find it difficult to choose the appropriate topics for their personal statements and other essays or to write with the sophistication and impact they might wish. Those desiring *individual consulting* on these and other matters are welcome to contact me through my website (www .degreeofdifference.com) or at (415) 273-1782.

I also offer small-group *workshops* that some readers will find to be attractive alternatives or supplements to individualized consulting. These are described briefly on p. xviii in the introduction, or in more detail on my website.

VARIOUS ESSAY TOPICS ANALYZED IN DETAIL

It is often easiest to write a personal statement if you feel you are being asked to answer a specific question rather than to fill up several blank pages. Consider what question you wish to answer. For example, what are your greatest strengths and weaknesses? Or, why have you chosen law as a career? These questions represent organizing themes for your essay. The following discussion of typical themes will highlight how others will approach the same topic, as well as what you should do to get the most out of your essay.

DESCRIBE YOUR CURRENT JOB

THE TYPICAL APPLICANT

Most applicants treat a discussion of their jobs as a matter of simply rehashing their résumés, albeit with full sentences in place of phrases. The context in which they perform is absent, making it difficult to understand the significance of what they have done and what talents were required.

A BETTER APPROACH

There are usually numerous elements to a given job. Start by figuring out and listing the many things you do. Next, determine which are the most significant parts of your job and which are most consistent with the position you are attempting to communicate, and then characterize them as favorably as possible. The following should help you with this process.

Is your job important? Most people would say so only if they are egotists or are making a lot of money and enjoying a very impressive title (Senior Executive Vice President for Marketing and Strategy, perhaps).

Assuming you are not in this situation, does this mean your job is unimportant and you will have to be apologizing for it? No, of course not. A job is of real importance under a number of different circumstances. In particular, work gains significance whenever two things are true about it. First, the degree of uncertainty (regarding which course of action would be best) is high, and second, the potential impact upon the firm's success is great. In other words, is there a fair likelihood that an average-quality performer in your job would make a hash of things? If so, would that really affect your firm's performance, or that of one of its components? If the answer to both of these questions is yes, then your job certainly is of importance.

What must you do to perform successfully? In other words, what challenges do you face? For example, if you are an analyst in a consulting firm, you probably work on two different teams. The managers of each team act as if you are meant to devote 100 percent of your time to their team, leaving you to work around the clock or fight the time allocation battle. You are also probably asked to do work that has never been thoroughly explained to you, and for which no formal training was provided, which requires that you seek out the experiences of others who have suffered before you to learn the essentials of what you are meant to do. Thus, in addition to having to do serious analytical work—which might range from in-depth financial analysis to developing sociograms to understand an organization's political dynamics—you have to master the internal politics of your own organization.

Perhaps you are an engineer in a matrix structure, reporting to the regional manager and an engineering director. Your greatest challenge may be satisfying two different bosses with two completely different agendas. The regional manager is probably concerned with making money today, and wants everyone to work as a team without regard to functional specialties. The engineering boss, on the other hand, wants her people to maintain their specialized skills and the prestige of the engineering department. Working on cross-functional teams without taking time out for updating technical skills may strike the former as standard practice and the latter as anathema. To perform your job well may require balancing these conflicting desires.

Or you may be a paralegal in your first job who is effectively being asked to work as the "second chair" in a case that started before you even joined the firm. Not only do you have to learn what a second chair does in litigation, you also have to get up to speed on an involved case—as well as integrate into the firm and learn how to deal with the partner handling this case, who has no time to babysit you as you acclimate.

If the last two occupants of your position were fired, say so. This will make your performance look all the more impressive. On the other hand, the *positive* fate of prior occupants of your job may be relevant. If the last occupants were promoted high in the organization, the job will appear to be one given to high-fliers, thereby increasing its significance. The more senior the person you report to, the more important a job will look.

What is the nature of your work? There are many different types of work. A market researcher is generally doing analytical work. A financial analyst generally does quantitative analysis, although the position may also call for doing extensive write-ups, such as those an equity analyst provides the financial community. A brand manager is likely to be doing a combination of analytical work and influence work insofar as she must analyze the factors for the brand's relative success or failure in different markets and competitive conditions in her country, and then try to influence the manufacturing, packaging, or whatever department, to take the action she wants in order to address these factors. She typically will have no power over these departments and will have to rely on her influence skills (personality, reasoning, expertise, etc.) instead. A restaurant manager will probably be most concerned with managing people, whereas a technical manager may be most concerned with the management of physical processes. An administrative assistant to a senator will have to manage the boss's calendar as well as juggle the competing interests of various constituents, lobbyists, campaign workers, other legislators, the senator's family, and so on.

Many other aspects of your work can also be characterized. Is your job like being in the army: crushing boredom interspersed with brief moments of sheer terror? Are you expected to perform at a steady pace to a predictable schedule or do you work like a tax accountant, 50 percent of whose work may take place in ten weeks of the year? Are you supposed to be the steadying hand for a bunch of younger employees? Are you supposed to be a creative type who will respond flexibly to each new situation rather than simply refer to the corporate manual?

Do you supervise anyone? How many people, of what type, are under your supervision? What does this supervision consist of? For example, are you in charge of direct marketing activities, necessitating that you monitor the phone calls of your direct reports and also analyze their performance versus budget and various economic and industry factors?

Do you have control of a budget? If so, what is the amount you control, and what amount do you influence?

What results have you achieved? Results can be looked at from many different perspectives. From a strategic perspective, what have you achieved regarding the market, customers, and competitors? From a financial perspective, what have you done regarding costs, revenues, and profits (not to mention assets employed, etc.)? From an operational perspective, what have you done regarding productivity of your unit, or of your direct reports, or of yourself? What have you done regarding the percentage of items rejected, or bids that fail, and so on? Similarly, from an organizational perspective, have you taken steps such as altering the formal organization or introducing new integration or coordination mechanisms? Provide numbers and tangible details whenever possible to buttress your claims.

How has your career evolved? Did you have a career plan in place before graduating from college or university or soon thereafter? If so, did you pursue it wholeheartedly? Did it include a focus on developing your skills and responsibilities? What, if anything, has altered your original plan? What was your reaction to events that altered or affirmed this plan? When dealing with the development of your job with a given employer, be sure to note the employer's *reasons* for promoting, transferring, rewarding, or praising you as well as the *fact* of these things.

How does your career progress compare with that of your peers? Sometimes the easiest way to show your success is by comparing your progress with others who entered your firm, or others in the industry, at the same time. Have you reached a more senior position? Been given more responsibilities? Earned a higher salary?

ADVANTAGES OF THIS APPROACH

Your past and current jobs are of inherent interest to law schools. They will want to know what you have done (and are doing), and with what success, because that suggests a great deal about your talents and interests, and the way your employer views your talents and attitude. Taking a broad view of your job enables you to put the best light on your responsibilities and performance.

DESCRIBE YOUR CAREER TO DATE

THE TYPICAL APPLICANT

Most applicants simply list what they have done in the past without showing what has driven their career choices and changes. The result is a list in which the elements appear nearly unrelated to one another. This is what admissions directors term the "résumé" approach.

A BETTER APPROACH

Look at our discussion of the "Job Description" essay. Then think in terms of telling stories rather than simply listing events dryly. A good story has conflict; that is, it has obstacles placed in the way of the hero. The hero may be unable to overcome each obstacle, but she tries hard and is unwilling to give up.

One possible approach is as follows. Find a theme that unites the elements of your job history. For instance, you show how you responded to challenges that were initially daunting. You tried hard and learned how to do what was required. You started to take more initiative as you learned better how to do the job. In fact, once you mastered your initial responsibilities, you understood them in a broader context. Having done so, you moved up to the next level of responsibility.

The telling of your career story should focus upon where you have come from and where you are now headed. If you have changed your direction, explain what happened to change your direction. If you have had your decisions reaffirmed by experience, describe them and how they convinced you that you were on the right track.

(This essay is closely related to the "Reasons for Getting a Law Degree" essay.)

ADVANTAGES OF THIS APPROACH

Telling stories that focus on obstacles and the attempt to overcome them makes this essay interesting to read. Focusing on your personal development in response to challenges is well aimed for an audience of educators. They are preconditioned to appreciate your developmental capabilities.

This approach also sets up your need for a law degree. You have been overcoming obstacles by learning how to perform new jobs, and you have acquired new skills and knowledge; now you need to take another step up.

WHAT ARE YOUR STRENGTHS AND WEAKNESSES?

This question is meant to elicit your opinion of yourself. Modest people, and people from cultures less egocentric than that of the United States, have a hard time responding because it apparently asks you to brag a little. Less self-assured applicants find it hard to be honest and to mention their shortcomings. This topic provides a good gauge of how self-confident (or arrogant), accomplished (or boastful), decent (or manipulative), mature, self-aware, and honest you are.

THE TYPICAL APPLICANT

Most applicants list a large number of strengths and no weaknesses. If they do include a weakness, it is generally a strength dressed up as a weakness ("I am too much of a perfectionist." "I work too hard.").

A BETTER APPROACH

Start by choosing two or three primary strengths. Use these to organize your essay by grouping other strengths around them. For example, if you claim you are very *determined*, you might discuss your *patience* in working hard for a long time in order to achieve something important as related to this determination. The problem is not generally finding something good to say about yourself. Usually the problem is limiting yourself to a manageable number of strengths. You want to have few enough that you can discuss them in a persuasive fashion rather than just list them. Using two or three as central organizing devices (i.e., themes) helps to achieve this.

Remember that simply listing strengths is a very weak way of writing. Use illustrations to make your strengths credible and memorable. Instead of bragging about being determined, note your five-year battle to overcome childhood leukemia.

The bigger problem, however, is deciding which weakness to discuss. Simply calling a strength a weakness is not sufficient. This tactic is used by countless applicants, and its insincerity is nearly guaranteed to repel those reading your essays. Instead, discuss an actual weakness that will make your discussion of your strengths more believable, show you to be mature enough to admit your lack of perfection, or present you with an opportunity to show how you have worked to reduce the impact of that weakness or eliminate it altogether. (Do not carry a good thing too far, though, and discuss huge flaws such as your drug addictions.)

Allocate space on a three- or four-to-one basis, strengths to weakness. You will note that I say "weakness," because you should discuss only one or two weaknesses. When doing so, do not dwell on your descriptions of it, or of the problems it has caused you. Do so briefly, thereby limiting the effect the specifics will have upon admissions officers. Then note what steps you take, or have taken, to overcome it.

You want to describe yourself as having numerous strengths that relate well to your positioning effort, without sounding arrogant.

ADVANTAGES OF THIS APPROACH

Grouping your strengths in an organized fashion will give you the chance to cover a lot of ground without taking a scattershot approach. Emphasizing strengths is obviously appropriate, but discussing a weakness may be a good idea, too. Writing with appropriate illustrations will make your strengths memorable; this will also make your claims realistic rather than boastful.

WHAT ARE YOUR MOST SUBSTANTIAL ACCOMPLISHMENTS?

This obviously gives you a chance to "blow your own horn." You can brag a bit about what you have accomplished in life. Moreover, you have the chance to put your own spin on what you have done. A particular accomplishment is all the more impressive when you explain the obstacles you had to overcome in order to succeed.

The topic also allows schools to learn more about you insofar as you discuss why you consider something to have been a substantial accomplishment. Some accomplishments are of obvious significance. Winning the American Book Award for History is obviously significant; you probably do not need to elaborate on the fact of having won it. Other accomplishments are much more personal. For example, if you had stuttered as a youth and finally ended your stuttering in your twenties, this might be an extremely significant accomplishment for you personally. You have probably done things that have had more impact upon the rest of the world, but for you this accomplishment looms larger. You may well want to talk about it as an example of your determination and desire to improve yourself.

This topic gives you an opportunity to discuss matters that are unlikely to be listed on your data sheets or mentioned by your recommenders. Even if you just discuss accomplishments of a more public nature, you can personalize them in a way in which just listing them on a data sheet (or having a recommender talk about them) does not do.

THE TYPICAL APPLICANT

Most applicants use the whole of their personal statement to demonstrate that their accomplishments are impressive; they focus on their accomplishments and not on themselves. Another mistaken tendency is to list a string of things rather than to explain one or two in detail.

A BETTER APPROACH

The first step is to determine which accomplishments you will discuss. Your criteria for choosing appropriate accomplishments will be familiar. Which ones will help your positioning effort? Which will be unusual and interesting for admissions committees to read about? Was this accomplishment truly important to you?

The following criteria are also helpful guides:

- You had to overcome major obstacles, showing real determination in doing so.
- You learned more about yourself.
- You came to understand the need for further skill development and thus, perhaps, a JD.
- You used real initiative, perhaps by pushing a bureaucracy to respond or bypassing one altogether.

- Your success was unexpected.
- You worked extremely hard toward a clear goal.
- Your impact can be clearly seen (i.e., you were not simply tagging along with someone else who did the real work).

If you are trying to show that you have had relevant real-world experience despite being only 23, you will probably want one (or preferably more) of these accomplishments to concern your post-college life, especially your professional life. Not every accomplishment will fulfill all of our criteria, but you should be able to include most of them in the course of the full essay.

A PROFESSIONAL PROJECT THAT CHALLENGED YOUR SKILLS

To write about your professional accomplishments, consider discussing a project you have undertaken. Projects lend themselves to essays insofar as they tend to have definite starting and end points, specific goals, and so on. Follow this approach to develop your essay:

1. Start by determining what your professional skills are.
2. Look at the most challenging professional project you have faced, preferably one that was successful for you, or one that taught you valuable lessons.
3. After trying to remember it in real detail, abstract exactly which skills you used (or should have used, but have only come to appreciate since then).
4. Remember the attributes your readers are looking for: analytical ability, communication skills, interpersonal skills, leadership ability, dedication, integrity, and so on.
5. Which of these attributes can you illustrate via one of your projects? Which are most important to your positioning effort? Which will be the most interesting to read about? Which can you get someone else to back up in a recommendation?

In writing the essay, go into sufficient detail to bring the events to life, but do not stop there. Discuss why you consider this a substantial achievement, why you take pride in it, and what you learned from it. Did you change and grow as a result of this? Did you find that you approached other matters differently after accomplishing this?

The admissions committee will read this for more than a brief description of the items you list on your data sheet. It will want to learn more about these and the private you, if you discuss significant accomplishments of a personal nature here. It will want to know what motivates you and what you value. It will also want to see how you have developed as a person and as a professional.

ADVANTAGES OF THIS APPROACH

This topic gives you a lot of latitude, as our criteria suggest. Using it to show more of the real you will help you to avoid the usual problems people create for themselves on this essay. You do not want to restate the facts you have already listed on your data sheet; you want to show that you have been ready to face challenges, determined to overcome obstacles, and able to accomplish things that have mattered to you.

WHAT HAVE YOU DONE THAT DEMONSTRATES YOUR LEADERSHIP POTENTIAL?

Top schools expect to produce leaders in law and other fields. They are looking for applicants who have already distinguished themselves as leaders, since past performance is the best indicator of what people will be like in the future.

THE TYPICAL APPLICANT

All too often, applicants discuss being part of a group that achieved something noteworthy without making it clear that they themselves were truly leaders in this effort. Or they discuss leading a group effort as if the other members of the group did not exist, thereby undercutting their credibility (did they really shoulder so much responsibility?) and causing readers to view them as sheer egotists.

A BETTER APPROACH

This question is deceptively similar to the "Substantial Accomplishment" topic, which, as explained earlier, asks you to describe a real achievement (and what it means to you). The "Leadership" essay, on the other hand, is not looking so much for an "achievement" as it is for an understanding of how you led an effort to achieve something. In other words, your emphasis should be upon your leadership rather than the achievement.

To write this essay, you must understand what leadership is. One obvious example is managing people who report directly to you. Less obvious examples involve pushing or inspiring nonsubordinates to do what you want done. This could be a matter of leading by example, using your influence as a perceived expert in a relevant field, influencing through moral suasion, or influencing by personal friendship. You might have led people through direct management or through influence. Describe your methodology. What strategy did you employ? Why? You may not have been deliberate or extremely self-aware in your actions, of course, in which case you might wish to discuss what you did and why it was or was not a good choice. What problems did you confront? What did you learn about managing or influencing people? Would another strategy, or different actions, have been better choices? Why? Do you have a philosophy of leadership?

You should emphasize that your leadership qualities are the sort that describe a future attorney general or CEO rather than a high school football hero. Thus, such qualities as maturity, thoughtfulness, empathy, determination, valuing other people's input, the ability to influence or manage very different types of people, the ability to integrate disparate inputs into a unified perspective, and integrity are highly desirable.

You are free to choose something from your professional career, but you might wish to choose something from your extracurricular or private life, too.

ADVANTAGES OF THIS APPROACH

Viewing this topic as concerning your understanding of leadership, and the ways in which you yourself lead, will result in an essay with the appropriate approach. It is not your achievement that is paramount here; it is your method of approaching and resolving leadership issues that concerns the admissions committee. If you show yourself to be aware of the leadership issues inherent in your situation and extract some suitable comments regarding what worked or did not work, and why, you will have the core of a good essay.

DESCRIBE AN EXPERIENCE IN WHICH YOU DID NOT REACH YOUR OBJECTIVES (AND WHAT YOU LEARNED FROM THIS)

THE TYPICAL APPLICANT

Most applicants focus on the mistake they made, or failure they suffered, rather than what they learned from it. Similarly, they fail to recount any more recent successes to show they have indeed benefited from an earlier mistake.

A BETTER APPROACH

You have a great deal of latitude in choosing your failure or mistake. Several factors should govern your response. (1) Try to further your positioning effort. If you are trying to present yourself as a worldly international negotiator, you might wish to show how you flubbed your first negotiations with people from another culture due to your lack of understanding of how they valued different components of a deal. (You can then go on to explain that this started you on the path of investigating the values and beliefs of your negotiating partners and opponents in all future deals, something you believe has underpinned much of your success since then.) (2) Show that you have truly learned from your mistake. One implication of this may be that you will want to choose a failure from your more distant past, not last week. You will not have had much of an opportunity to learn from a recent failure, whereas a failure from two or three years ago may have afforded plenty of opportunity to learn (and to have compiled a run of relevant successes bearing this out). The reason is that you generally need some time to reflect upon matters in order to benefit fully from them. (3) If you choose a distant failure, you are not saying that you are currently making such mistakes.

Having chosen your failure, do not belabor your description of it. Remember that it is what you learned from this failure that is critical here, not the failure itself. Consider what you learned from the experience concerning yourself, your job, your company, your industry, how to manage people, and so on.

ADVANTAGES OF THIS APPROACH

The emphasis here should be upon your development. We learn more from our mistakes than from our successes. A willingness to admit mistakes and then try to learn from them is one hallmark of a mature adult. It is also the trait of someone who will benefit from more formal education.

DISCUSS AN ETHICAL DILEMMA YOU HAVE FACED

The ongoing debate over the proper role of lawyers in society means that ethics is an important issue in a lawyer's training, as well as in the admissions decision.

THE TYPICAL APPLICANT

Most applicants tackling an "ethical dilemma" preach about the virtues of their position rather than recognizing that both sides may have much to offer. The stridency of their approach makes it look as though they are unable to analyze issues with finesse and subtlety.

A BETTER APPROACH

The toughest part of this is to find a suitable subject. Here are some possible topics:

- *People versus profit.* For example, should you fire the Hispanic researchers working for your firm now that the initial products aimed at the Hispanic market have been launched? What were their expectations in taking the job initially? What promises were made to them? What other jobs will be open to them if they are fired? What will be the consequences to the firm if they are retained (or if they are fired)?

■ *Your career versus someone else's.* When your thesis advisor publishes your work under her name, what should you do? What were your expectations? Was there an explicit (or implicit) agreement that in return for sponsoring your work, your advisor could take credit in public for the results? Did you lose opportunities for failing to get credit? Or did your protests over the injustice cost you in some other fashion?

■ *Taking advantage of someone's lack of knowledge or opportunities.* Should you sell a product to someone who does not know that it will be inappropriate for his needs? By the time he figures this out, you may have moved on to a new division in the company so you will not face his fury or the long-term consequences of having an angry customer.

Note that you can also write about something that happened in your private rather than your professional life. In fact, such dilemmas are common, so you probably have a wealth of material available.

You will want to show that there was truly a dilemma, at least on the surface. You will probably want to show that you explored and investigated the nature of the problem, since you were no doubt reluctant to make a snap decision when it appeared that any decision would have substantial adverse consequences. In describing what you did, show that you explored every option and did your best to minimize the adverse consequences.

The tone of your essay is another minefield. If you sound like an innocent seven-year-old who believes that it is always wrong to lie, you will not fit in a world of tough senior managers and lawyers who constantly need to make hard decisions with rotten consequences for somebody. On the other hand, if you sound like Machiavelli, for whom the only calculus depends upon personal advantage, and for whom the potential suffering of other people is irrelevant, you will be rejected as a moral monster. You need to be somewhere in the middle, someone who recognizes that the world and the decisions it requires are seldom perfect, but that it is appropriate to try to minimize adverse consequences as best one can. Only in extreme circumstances would it be appropriate to walk away from the decision (and the job).

ADVANTAGES OF THIS APPROACH

It is critical to find a subject you can get your teeth into. Our examples may help you find a subject, one with layers of detail and dilemma. If you go into depth in exploring it (without sounding like a naive child or a cynical manipulator), turn it about and examine it from different angles, and weigh the various options thoughtfully, you will show yourself to be serious lawyer material.

WHY DO I WANT TO BE A LAWYER (OR, WHY DO I WANT TO GO TO LAW SCHOOL)?

THE TYPICAL APPLICANT

Too many people write on this topic. *Young applicants,* especially those still in college, have little to say that will not sound naive to a hardened admissions officer. This is particularly true for those essays devoted to how you will save the environment, represent society's unfortunates, help your ethnic group (which up until now has been woefully underrepresented), and so on. Admissions officers know how easy it is to say—and even to believe—such things at twenty-one; they also know that the majority of the people espousing such views in the admissions process head off to corporate law firms upon graduation.

Another losing approach is to show how much you look forward to attending law school, making it sound as if law school is going to be merely a continuation of your liberal arts education, rather than preparation for a serious career. Once again, this is a hallmark of a young applicant—and one who has yet to think carefully about her future career.

The typical *mid-career applicant* applies to law school because he is desperately unhappy with his current job. Too many of these applicants have no idea of where they are going, just what they are running from or avoiding. Consequently, their approach to this topic tends to show that they do not have a realistic career plan. They describe their hoped-for job in vague, rosy terms, saying they hope to fight for the rights of the people or they look forward to an intellectual career. They often demonstrate as little knowledge of law as the applicant still in college.

A BETTER APPROACH

College-aged applicants seldom have an in-depth understanding of law, so they should generally avoid this topic. (Exceptions are those who have done substantial part-time work in a legal environment.) They should look for topics that will allow them to show themselves in a positive light, rather than parading their ignorance. The top schools' admissions directors are remarkably unanimous on this point.

Mid-career applicants, however, will need to address the question of why they want to be lawyers. They may do so in any number of different ways.

1. *Fixing the Legal System/Public Interest Law.* If, and only if, you have substantial personal experience with some portion of the legal system—or have worked in a field related to your future law career—should you even consider writing about a failing of the legal system and how you will help to remedy it. Similarly, you should proclaim your interest in public interest law only if your

employment and personal histories provide abundant support for your claim that you will go this route. If you wish to represent battered women in custody fights, for example, you will sound like a marvelous candidate if you have been working for years as a counselor in a battered women's home. If you have merely volunteered once a month for the last six months (about the time you have been thinking about putting together law school applications, perhaps?), your essay will fall flat. For this essay, the context is everything. You need to demonstrate convincingly that you have a very substantial, ongoing connection with your chosen field to address this topic convincingly.

2. *Law as a Natural Career Progression.* Another favorite topic within this category concerns why law (school) represents a natural progression for the applicant. All too often, a political science major still in college writes that law school is exactly what he has been aiming for his entire college career. This is simply to state the obvious, of course; this applicant would be better off choosing another topic. This topic is a good one, on the other hand, for someone who has already had substantial career experience in a field related to law. For example, look at the personal statement in Part V written by Sacha M. Coupet, who worked as a psychological consultant for the Michigan Child Welfare Law Resource Center at the University of Michigan Law School prior to law school. Such an applicant can be very convincing about why law school truly is right for her.

To the extent possible, show that you are not running away from your prior job. Doing so suggests that you are desperate and therefore not in a suitable frame of mind to make a sensible decision about your next career. It also suggests you may have failed at this career insofar as people tend to like jobs they are good at, and dislike jobs they do not do well. If you can, show how law represents simply a further step in a process that is already well under way. Talk about your future job as being clearly related to your experiences, strengths and weaknesses, likes and dislikes. In other words, your future is based solidly upon the foundation of your prior job.

This is a particularly easy essay to write for someone, like Sacha, who has had directly relevant experience for the career she envisions, knows well what lawyers in the field actually do, and has worked with such lawyers. The same would be true for an analyst in an investment bank who works with securities lawyers, or an accountant who handles tax matters alongside tax attorneys.

ADVANTAGES OF THIS APPROACH

Young applicants, especially those still in college, are likely to fare better by writing about another subject. Mid-career applicants, though, can potentially use this topic to their advantage.

Law schools want to make sure you have given substantial thought to your future career. They want to see that a JD fits with the future you envision for yourself. Tackling the subject of "career objectives" in your essay shows that, unlike many applicants, you are aware that law school is not an end in itself.

BRIEF NOTES ON ADDITIONAL TOPICS

FORMATION OF CHARACTER ESSAYS

Because many applicants to the top schools have similar credentials and few experiences that directly indicate a passion or qualification to study law, essays that discuss aspects of the applicant's character and background are often suggested, by the law schools, as the most helpful.

The *typical applicant,* however, fails to isolate which facets of his life (and character) are distinctive. First, he claims that his parents have instilled in him a strong work ethic. Next, he says this is bolstered by an unquenchable desire to learn everything he possibly can. He concludes by proclaiming, suddenly, that only at Harvard Law School will he be able to satisfy this hunger for knowledge. Ultimately, the typical applicant does little to distinguish himself from the crowd of other applicants.

To succeed with this type of personal statement, the applicant must step back and take a good, objective look at his life. Of the qualities he would like to emphasize, which can be linked to his background, to the influence of mentors, to circumstantial events? How is he different from his peers? How would he be valuable to a top school's student body?

Everyone knows we are shaped by where, and who, we came from. Law schools, especially, know this. They want to learn how you have been affected by all sorts of circumstances, even (or especially) those that are out of your control. That does not mean, however, there are no dangers in using personal background as the sole factor in distinguishing oneself. The typical applicant holds it up like a red flag and expects the waters will part for him. This is not so. Certain backgrounds can be advantageous to have, but you need to show you are more than just a category.

THE HARD-LUCK STORY

Although the members of any admissions committee are a jaded bunch, numbed by thousands of pleading personal statements, they are still human. So do not assume they will immediately scrap your application because you have chosen to discuss unfortunate circumstances that formed your life. This category of essay, however, is for applicants who have encountered supreme disadvantage—whether it be poverty, a tragedy, or a life-altering accident. Yet, even more than this, the applicant has overcome it. The hard-luck story can be used to demonstrate stamina, perseverance, and savvy. You (if this is you) have worked harder than most other applicants and are more likely to continue to do so. It may also explain certain weaknesses in your application.

The risk is that you will end up sounding plaintive, self-righteous, and stuck in the past. For this essay to be successful, you must show that this disadvantage was not something that happened to you, but something that you conquered. How is it an inextricable part of you? What are the long-term (positive!) results of this travail?

Ethnic Background

The same is true for personal statements about one's ethnic background. Be sure to do more than claim membership in a group, even if that group is much sought-after by the school to which you are applying. Make your story interesting and detailed. Show that you have ultimately gained something important—and which will be of value in law school and beyond—from your upbringing or later circumstances.

Handicapped

Applicants who are (or were) physically or otherwise handicapped should follow the same approach as suggested above. There are two potential problems of which you need to be aware. You will face a backlash if you overplay your hand. Do not exaggerate the problems you faced. For example, if you walk with a limp, do not make your tale into a grand tragedy. Approaching your story in a very matter-of-fact, even understated, fashion, will tend to work best. The other potential problem is that you may (inadvertently) suggest you will be unable to get through law school. If this is a problem, attach whatever documentation (or recommendations) necessary to dispel this notion.

Unusual Childhood or Background

If you had an unusual childhood—lived on an American naval base in the Indian Ocean until you were ten; or you spoke Polish to your mother, German to your father, French at school, and English in the neighborhood; or you were raised by a lesbian couple—you have an opportunity to show you have been shaped by highly unusual factors of locale, language, or circumstance. The committee will notice and remember you, particularly if you show how this unusual start to your life has had an important effect upon your current capability, character, goals, and so on.

Similarly, if you have another unusual dimension to your life, consider whether it should be highlighted in your application. For example:

- Are you from an unusual part of the world: Ajaccio, Chengdu, Luxor, Tampere?

- Have you worked with unusual people? (If you are an opera singer, your work colleagues probably qualify as unusual by law school standards.)

- Do you have knowledge of an unusual industry? (The circus, for example, or the paper industry.)

- Have you been employed in unusual work conditions? (If you, an American, managed a Tex-Mex restaurant in Paris, supervising Albanian and Greek chefs, reporting to a Dutch owner who makes his real money from running drugs, and trying to satisfy a persnickety French crowd, you have the makings of an interesting essay about organizational dynamics, influence strategies, and so on, in a highly unusual situation.)

- Have you performed an unusual job? (Responsible for preventing the theft of fuel from tankers in southeast Asia, for example.)

- Do you have rare personal qualities?

- Do you have unusual outside interests? (A person who has published a successful book, been nationally ranked in squash, started a successful part-time business, or whatever, has something unusual to talk about.)

Note that you will not want to discuss your unusual dimension simply because it is unusual. Instead, you will want to discuss it if you can make yourself interesting, appealing, and meritorious in some fashion. For example, if you are talking about your job (trying to prevent the theft of tanker fuel), do more than describe the job. Show how it requires you to deal with some of the world's savviest and most dangerous thieves, in a culture that is not your own, and thus in a situation in which you could make a truly fatal mistake all too easily. Show the data gathering you did and how you did it. Show the analyses you performed in trying to understand who was involved in the thievery—your company's ship captains, contract employees working the fueling operations in Singapore, the financial controller, or someone else? And so on. In other words, get more mileage out of the situation than just showing that your job is out of the ordinary. (If you are unable to do so, consider trying a different topic.)

ESSAYS ON AN IMMERSION IN THE UNKNOWN

For applicants who have lived/studied/worked in a "foreign" environment, an essay about what they learned may be valuable. The term "foreign" in this context need not be confined to another country. A rich suburbanite who has spent several years teaching in a downtrodden, dangerous public high school can take the same approach as someone who has worked in Bangkok. Similarly, a poor urban kid who has just managed the kitchen or taught tennis in a wealthy country club has also been in a foreign environment.

Be leery of choosing this topic, however, because it backfires on the vast majority of those who write about it. If you have spent a junior semester or year abroad, for example, you almost certainly will write a disastrous, simple-minded, only-scratching-the-surface, personal statement about your learning that people are really the same everywhere despite their superficial differences. Or you will exclaim that you now have an in-depth knowledge of this second culture (despite, perhaps, attending classes in a program designed solely for Americans, or despite failing to become truly fluent in a second language). The same danger exists for others who failed to get to grips with this other culture. Backpacking through Europe or India may have been fun, but you are not likely to get much mileage out of your experiences unless you can bring a sophisticated sensibility to bear. In fact, an additional risk you run is that you will come across as a spoiled brat rather than one who offers real value in a law school setting.

The kind of experience that is likely to prove much more valuable is akin to the urban kid working in the wealthy country club. For example, if you worked for two years in a tire factory outside Clermont-Ferrand alongside French and Algerian workers, speaking only French (or Arabic) with them, you will have a much more interesting story to tell than does the applicant who did her semester at the LSE and was so mesmerized by pubs, the changing of the guard, and the fact that the English drive on the other side of the road (!).

The deeper your understanding of the other language and culture, the more extensive your experience, and the more you got off the beaten path followed by well-to-do American dilettantes abroad, the better your chances of success with this topic.

ESSAYS ON A RELATIONSHIP WITH A MENTOR

For applicants who feel a great debt to a mentor (or even a historical figure), an essay about what they learned from this relationship may be a good topic. There are potential advantages to this choice of topic. Given that law schools are in the education business, it does not hurt to show that you are an active learner. Demonstrating yourself to be mature enough to be receptive to the knowledge of those (presumably) senior to you is a nice touch, particularly for younger applicants. You can also show a real warmth to your personality via your relationship with this other person.

The danger inherent in this topic is that you may end up talking more about this influential person than about *you*. Use this person as a foil—the person should, ideally, reflect what is most impressive about your interests, your achievements, and your goals. Or show that you developed as a result of your interaction with this person, but keep the focus on *your* development.

ESSAYS THAT SHOW HOW YOU THINK

Each year a small number of applicants choose to write personal statements that make absolutely no claims, no clarifications, and no declarations of intent. Instead, they hope to demonstrate excellent writing skills and sensitively (if obscurely) chosen themes to imply who they are. Often, the essays have nothing to do with law or the applicant's credentials. Essays that fall into this category can be philosophical, anecdotal, or analytical. In the best of these essays, the reader comes away with a strong sense of the applicant, but the reader arrives at these conclusions himself. The writer skillfully articulates himself indirectly and subtly, rather than in an expository manner.

> The personal statement can be an opportunity to illuminate your intellectual background and interests. You might do this by writing about a course, academic project, book, artistic or cultural experience that has been important to you. (Harvard)

These are high-risk essays by their very nature. Admissions officers are very busy and have a limited amount of time to devote to an individual applicant's file. They are also unlikely to share a passion for whatever specific matter you are exploring in your essay. These factors make it clear that if the piece is not particularly well-written, you risk a very negative evaluation, indeed. Do not choose this strategy unless you are sure of your writing ability. Similarly, make sure several other people, including virtual strangers to you, read it. If people who do not know you understand the (indirect) point you are trying to make, then you at least have a fighting chance of this working.

EXPLANATIONS OF POOR PERFORMANCE

Many applicants use their personal statement to address a shortcoming in their application. They attempt to explain why their LSAT is not a true indicator of their ability, for example, or why they have not been promoted in the last four years. It may make sense to explain such matters, but it seldom makes sense to use the personal statement to do so.

Virtually every school will accept a brief addendum in which you explain a gap or weakness in your record. They strongly prefer that you *not* use your all-too-valuable personal statement to do so. (Instead, use your personal statement to highlight positive aspects of your candidacy.)

The rules are very simple in writing an addendum to address a gap or weakness. Explain the circumstances briefly, in a matter-of-fact way. Do not whine or complain. Offer any supporting proof, if necessary, such as the fact that you were indeed hospitalized with a high fever for three days preceding the LSAT exam. If you think better indicators of your performance exist, cite them. For example, if you had weak grades in your first three semesters, but strong grades for the following five semesters, note this. Explain that you did not enjoy chemistry (your initial major), but "found" yourself when you switched to physics.

ADMISSIONS DEANS TALK ABOUT PERSONAL STATEMENTS

THE ROLE OF THE PERSONAL STATEMENT

The personal statement frames the application. It's the one opportunity for people to tell me their story, to show me the voice they've developed, what they bring to the table.   *Edward Tom, Boalt Hall (Berkeley)*

Good writing gives us confidence that a candidate can write well; that she can handle the work in law school; and, that she can and will contribute to the intellectual life and diversity of the school.   *William Hoye, Duke*

The role of the personal statement is twofold. First, most law schools don't have the resources to interview applicants, so the statement is a way to get to know the applicants. Second, writing is an important skill for success in law school and in the legal profession. The personal statement provides a sample of the applicant's writing ability (as does the LSAT writing sample).   *Rob Schwartz, UCLA*

The personal statement gives us a basis on which to judge someone's writing ability and gives us insight into the person—as a person.   *Anne Richard, George Washington*

It's your opportunity to tie together all the various parts of your application and to tell your story. It can help the reader understand how your academic training, the ways in which you engaged with your community, your intellectual development, and professional experience relate to where you are going—and the part law school plays in that.   *Todd Morton, Vanderbilt*

The applicant's personal statement is accorded significant decisional weight. In the absence of evaluative interviews, it is the opportunity for a candidate to: educate or inform our admissions committee why they have chosen to pursue legal training; show that this choice is consonant with their personal values and professional goals; demonstrate, if their record does not do so itself, that they possess the intellectual power and have developed the academic skills necessary to negotiate well the exceptional rigor of our program; describe how various conditions and experiences in their lives—advantages as well as disadvantages, opportunities as well as obstacles—have combined to shape their view of the world and a sense of their place in it; to communicate to us how and to what extent they have strengthened (through exercise) their values and achieved their personal, academic, and professional objectives; to share with our committee their understanding of the responsibilities, not only of the benefits, that obtain to membership in the legal profession. *Jim Milligan, Columbia*

THE IMPORTANCE OF THE PERSONAL STATEMENT

Huge! The personal statement is the piece of the application most consistently undervalued by applicants. We will get thousands of applicants with credentials that are perfectly acceptable but not compelling—162–168 LSAT, 3.2–3.8 GPA— and both the substantive information and the writing skills demonstrated in the personal statement will determine who from this group is admitted and who is not. *Susan Palmer, Virginia*

We require a 250-word essay and give you the option to include an additional personal statement. Most successful applicants do both. *Megan A. Barnett, Yale*

It's very, very, very important. The personal statement should demonstrate an applicant's superior writing skills, which are so important to the succcessful completion of one's legal education. In addition, it is an applicant's main tool to communicate key information that he/she wishes the admissions committee to consider. A personal statement can make or break an application. *Monica Ingram, Texas*

As a lawyer myself, I believe that being an excellent writer is critical to being a good lawyer. It's rare that you find an excellent lawyer who isn't also an excellent writer. In practice, at the top firms and in the higher echelons of government, you separate the wheat from the chaff on the basis of writing ability. *Sarah C. Zearfoss, Michigan*

A personal statement is often a make-or-break component of an application. It should add a dimension to an application; however, it cannot add all dimensions. In other words, it should be focused rather than try to do too much. Longer does not usually make it better. *Joyce Curll, Harvard*

The bottom line is that people can write their way into law school—or out of it. *Elizabeth Rosselot, Boston College*

What I do is tantamount to building a new family each year: Would you want to know about their backgrounds, their failures? Yes, you would. *Edward Tom, Boalt Hall (Berkeley)*

GENERAL ADVICE ABOUT PERSONAL STATEMENTS

When I read an essay I ask myself, "What does the applicant know about himself and about law that leads him to think that this is the direction he wants to go in?" I want to be sure that choosing law has been a thoughtful decision, not a reflexive one ("I don't know what I'll be doing with my life so I guess I'll apply to law school"). *Jim Milligan, Columbia*

We want to learn what applicants will bring to our community and to the legal profession. Applicants should not use the personal statement to make excuses for weaknesses in their applications (they can use an addendum to explain a weak LSAT score or a bad semester in college). Applicants also should not use the personal statement to tell us how great our law school is. The personal statement should be about the applicant; it should be positive; it should illustrate how an applicant is unique; and it should show the admissions committee that the applicant will be a valuable addition to the law school and to the profession. *Anne Richard, George Washington*

Be yourself. If you try to be something or someone you're not, you'll probably fail. Why not think of this as being your interview: discuss the things you'd like the admissions committee to know about you. *Rob Schwartz, UCLA*

The personal statement has a different role for us since we interview. Applicants can use it a bit differently: to push their accomplishments, leadership, work experience, motivation, and to show that they have done their homework and know the school well. *Don Rebstock, Northwestern*

Treat your essay like a short interview: don't bite off more than you can chew. Stick to one or two important themes you want to develop and leave with the reader. Don't resort to contrivance, such as writing your essay as an obituary (after having supposedly graduated from Cornell Law School and eventually served with distinction on the Supreme Court), as a court document, or in rhyming couplets. *Rick Geiger, Cornell*

The first test of a personal statement is whether it rings true—is it an accurate portrayal of the applicant. Others include: whether I understand their motivations, why he'll be fun to teach, and how he'll be a good student. *William Hoye, Duke*

Choosing a Topic

Don't think in terms of covering the waterfront. Consider the personal statement like an interview that you control: Ask a question that you want to answer. Use one organizing theme to pull together your material; keep it focused. Avoid artifice and any kind of gimmick. A simple, straightforward statement that gets across your message is fine. *Joyce Curll, Harvard*

We are most interested in what they've done and accomplished. It's also good to see what's impacted them, helped them develop as a person, what struggles they've had. It's appropriate to focus on one item from the data forms—flesh out its significance, demonstrate what they achieved. The most important thing is that it's well written. *Don Rebstock, Northwestern*

Consider writing about experiences that have been meaningful to you. For instance, many LDS (Mormon) candidates write about their missions; applicants who have been in the Peace Corps or who have studied abroad often discuss those experiences. *Anne Richard, George Washington*

Make it about who you are and what you are going to bring to the class. Take advantage of the opportunity to introduce yourself to us. Let us really get to know what your experiences have been and thus what you will bring to classroom discussions. Don't just regurgitate your résumé.   *Ann Killian Perry, Chicago*

The salient characteristic of a personal statement is that it should be *personal.* This is your opportunity to give us some insight into who you are.   *Susan Palmer, Virginia*

If you have been through something rough, by all means consider sharing that. But recognize that there is a fair amount of suffering in the world, so show some perspective on your own situation. For example, the divorce of your parents may have been difficult for you, but recognize that this is a common topic. If you choose to write about it, you need to offer some insight that will distinguish your essay from others.   *Sarah C. Zearfoss, Michigan*

TOPICS TO AVOID

Many candidates feel that they need to write about a hardship they've overcome. These sorts of essays can be useful, and can give us a real insight into applicants, but they are certainly not necessary. Don't feel that you need to manufacture a "hardship" in order to write a successful essay.   *Megan A. Barnett, Yale*

Avoid things in questionable taste: anything that will make me blush. Also, be careful about anything meant to be funny. It's wonderful if it works, but it seldom does. Reread it after putting it aside for some time to make sure that it's funny.   *Sarah C. Zearfoss, Michigan*

I really don't like vague essays on the American system of justice (a "civics" essay), repeating my view-book back to me, or cute essays such as fake legal pleadings.   *Susan Palmer, Virginia*

Avoid talking about what kind of lawyer you'll be unless you've had experience in that field already. Remember that this is another writing sample, so avoid cute little poems.   *Ann Killian Perry, Chicago*

Nothing is off limits. However, I advise students to be cautious when writing on controversial topics about which they are passionate: you can offend file readers if you go over the edge.   *Chloe T. Reid, USC*

I'm not a fan of haiku, obituaries ("Lisa, a graduate of GW, was general counsel of such-and-such organization before her appointment to the Supreme Court five years prior to her death"), or briefs in support of someone's application. *Anne Richard, George Washington*

One topic that never works is a chronology which repeats what is in the data forms: it's a waste of time.   *Don Rebstock, Northwestern*

Certain essay approaches are usually not successful. Sometimes applicants try to be very creative or cute, but this seldom works. Poetry is not usually a good idea.

Humor is good only if a wide variety of people will appreciate it. Giving a litany of excuses for poor academic performance never works. Do not use the personal statement for cathartic purposes; use judgment regarding what personal details you share with someone who does not know you, and then do so in a dignified way. *Kenneth Kleinrock, NYU*

Some topics seldom work well. For example, travelogues (my summer vacation on a train across Europe), epic poems, or a list of activities. Be careful about "creative" approaches, too. They get my attention, but not in a good way. *William Hoye, Duke*

Select a topic more interesting than "why I want to go to law school." It's OK to connect your topic, in the conclusion, with why you want to attend law school. *Kenneth Kleinrock, NYU*

Avoid the words "LA Law" or "Perry Mason." Do not do a paragraph form of your résumé. Do not explain every weakness: just playing "good defense" will not cut it. In fact, it's better to submit a separate essay regarding weaknesses rather than use the personal statement for that purpose. *Andy Cornblatt, Georgetown*

Tailoring Your Statement to a School

My pet peeve is generic personal statements clearly sent off to a bunch of schools. I like to see that a statement has been tailored to us.   *Don Rebstock, Northwestern*

It helps a great deal to show you have researched the school and can connect what it is about Vanderbilt that particularly attracts you in light of where you've been and where you're headed. Doing so can have a very positive impact on an application. *Todd Morton, Vanderbilt*

It's helpful to tailor your statement to a school to whatever extent you can. Schools like to know that you understand and value their programs, communities, etc. *Rob Schwartz, UCLA*

Plenty of people make obvious mistakes. They assume we offer a course we don't, for instance. *Elizabeth Rosselot, Boston College*

    Do not gild the lily: Going on too long risks calling overly much attention to your weakness.

Undergraduate Performance

Feel free to point to your grade trend, strong performance in your major, good performance for all but one term, and so on. Do not offer your immaturity as an explanation for poor performance. Limit such explanations to stronger stuff: your need to work nearly full time while carrying a full load, tragedy in the family, or your lack of recognition of your dyslexia.

LSAT SCORE

This is a tricky matter, since law school is full of tests. If you were very ill during the test, consider discussing the matter. Better yet, discuss it in the context of why a later LSAT score is a better indicator of your actual ability. If you had low SAT scores relative to your college performance, note this.

GAPS IN EMPLOYMENT HISTORY

Law schools are not generally very concerned with how you have spent every week of your adult life. If you spent three months after college hitchhiking across Canada, do not feel you should apologize for this. On the other hand, if you are an older applicant, be sure to indicate why you have substantial gaps in your employment history. Similarly, be sure to explain any career shifts you have made.

OPTIONAL ESSAYS

As the box "Extra Essay Opportunities" demonstrates, the majority of the country's top law programs require one personal statement. There is generally no specified topic. Consequently, an applicant can produce one good essay and, with a minimal amount of tailoring, use it for all his or her applications.

If you read your chosen schools' admissions information with a fine-toothed comb, however, you will notice that there do exist numerous opportunities for you to provide additional information. A large number of the top programs state directly that one or two optional essays may be submitted, hint that in certain situations it may be appropriate to include information not found elsewhere, or allow that an attached sheet may be used to answer a short-answer question. All of these are opportunities best taken advantage of. Rather than cramming as many topics as possible into one, densely packed statement, you can—and should—use these hidden essay opportunities. The benefits are clear: First, you demonstrate to admissions officers that you are motivated and perceptive; and second, you show that you are a multidimensional person. Using the extra essays allows you to increase the number, or enhance the quality, of themes (and stories) in your application.

Writing optional essays is especially advantageous for schools that severely restrict the length of the *required* personal statement—such as Yale. In 250 words, you can effectively address only one or two themes; it is almost impossible to discuss your character, your uniqueness, your ambition, the reasons why

Yale Law School is a good match for you, and other matters all at the same time. Fortunately, there are two other opportunities to articulate yourself. Question 10 in Yale's application, which has no length restriction, provides some hints:

> *Optional:* Please add to this application whatever additional material you believe will enable admissions readers to make a fully informed judgment on your application. Many applicants include the personal statement they have prepared for other law school applications. Examples of issues you might choose to address are: personal goals, history of standardized testing, or special circumstances involving your educational development and achievement. The admissions file readers especially welcome statements that enable them to understand the contribution your personal background would make to the student body at Yale Law School.

EXTRA ESSAY OPPORTUNITIES

	1	2 OR MORE
Boston College		x
Cornell	x	
Duke	x	
Fordham	x	
Georgetown	x	
Michigan		x
Northwestern		x
NYU	x	
Penn		x
Stanford	x	
Texas	x	
Tulane	x	
UCLA		x
USC	x	
Vanderbilt	x	
William & Mary		x
Yale	x	

Obviously, to ignore this question would be to imply to the admissions committee that you have either very little to say about yourself, you are lazy, or that getting into Yale is not your top priority.

ADVICE TO KEEP IN MIND

- In the short-answer section of a school's application, notice when you are asked to "list and describe" something—rather than just "list." If you are allowed to answer the question on a separate sheet of paper, this can be transformed from a spartan 20 words into a paragraph—i.e., a short essay.

ADMISSIONS DEANS DISCUSS WRITING
OPTIONAL ESSAYS AND ADDENDA

The personal statement is not the place to explain your poor testing history. We do want to know if the SAT dramatically underestimated your college performance, but this does not belong in the personal statement but rather in an addendum. *Kenneth Kleinrock, NYU*

We ask for an addendum as to any factors you'd like to share regarding your academic and LSAT performance. In addition, make sure to answer any question an admissions committee would likely have about your application. For instance, if you took a year off during college, or you got a poor grade in a particular course, or there is a significant trend to your grades, you should explain matters, share the circumstances. Similarly, if you faced substantial obstacles, let us know about them. But don't overdo it. After all, we need to read thousands of applications. *Rob Schwartz, UCLA*

It's fine to write an additional essay. This is particularly appropriate if you want to explain a personal situation affecting your performance, your reasons for wanting USC, how you became interested in law, or your involvement in community service. *William Hoye, Duke*

I'm all for adding an addendum if there is something you need to explain. Put your explanation there rather than using your personal statement for it. Similarly, if there is something you strongly feel should be added to your personal statement, add another page. Be careful not to load up the file, though. *Ann Killian Perry, Chicago*

Addenda are perfect for confronting a weakness in your application. Do so openly and honestly, without groveling. *Susan Palmer, Virginia*

We're surprised that so few applicants take advantage of our offering them the opportunity to explain their GPAs and LSATs. *William Hoye, USC*

- Read applications very carefully. Often, tucked inconspicuously into the last page of a brochure somewhere, you will read that "additional information may be provided" if the applicant strongly feels an issue needs to be addressed.

- Save negative subjects (your performance in a particular semester, etc.) for an addendum.

- Do not write an optional essay simply for the sake of doing it. Unless you have something pertinent and important to say, admissions officers will feel you are wasting their time.

- Be respectful of schools, such as Michigan, that permit you to submit additional materials—such as synopses of publications, theses, or dissertations. Be considerate and concise. Do not send in 100 pages of your dissertation on the Civil War. You will be remembered—but not appreciated.

11

WRITING PERSUASIVE ESSAYS

— EXECUTIVE SUMMARY —

■

Plan before beginning to write.

■

Follow this chapter's advice in order to maximize the impact of your essays.

■

There is no excuse for basic foul-ups: misspellings,
grammatical mistakes, factual errors, or
inserting the wrong school's name into an essay.

■

Allot substantial time to reorganizing and redrafting. Remember,
"There is no such thing as good writing, just good rewriting."

■

See Part V for actual application essays written by a
variety of candidates to the top schools.

In the words of Yale Law School's brochure: "Faculty readers look to the required essay to evaluate your writing, thinking, and editing skills, as well as to learn more about such qualities as your intellectual concerns or passions, your humor, or your ability to think across disciplines." If you intend to rely on your "numbers" to get you admitted, you will be missing the opportunity to dramatically improve your chances. In fact, the better the school, the more likely it is that the objective data in your application will not determine your fate and that the essays in particular will weigh heavily in the decision.

Admissions officers will judge you on the basis of what your essays reveal about your writing ability (including your ability to persuade, structure, and maintain a well-reasoned argument, and communicate in an interesting and professional manner), honesty and maturity, understanding of what the program offers and requires and how well you would contribute to it, and clear ideas about where you are headed. They will want to learn what you have accomplished, who you are as a person, and how well you can communicate. Admissions officers never take the approach of teachers who said, "I'll grade this on the basis of the content, not your writing style."

This chapter is designed to help you actually write your essays. You have learned from prior chapters the types of things you are likely to want to say, but not how to say it; this chapter addresses that need. In addition to reading this chapter, however, learn about successful essay writing by examining some of the many examples contained in this book (see Chapter 9 and Part V).

GETTING STARTED

BEFORE WRITING

Before starting to write, let's review what we know about your audience and its decision criteria.

Who is your audience? Your audience is the set of admissions officers and professors who will read your application. They are conscientious but nearly overwhelmed by the volume of material they are required to read. They are highly familiar with the determinants of law school and career success. Thus, they will examine your application for convincing evidence of your intellectual ability, potential in the field of law, and individual personal characteristics. Being in the education business, they want applicants who clearly value learning and education. They will also like evidence that a person makes the most of opportunities, whether these be great or small.

By communicating effectively—presenting your material in an organized and concise fashion, and not exaggerating or lying—you will gain credibility as a reliable source of information about yourself and as an appropriate candidate. Remember that as important as it is to be sure you are addressing the committee's concerns, your essays should reveal yourself and convey a true sense of who you are as a person. This may, in fact, be your only chance to do so.

What are the top law schools looking for? The three principle criteria mentioned earlier—your intellectual ability, professional promise, and personal characteristics—are commonly sought by all of the top schools. (For more detailed information, see Chapter 5.)

What does a particular school look for? All schools look for certain traits, such as analytical ability. Yet not every school is looking for exactly the same sort of candidate. Some will concentrate slightly more on finding applicants focused on public service, for example, whereas others want those who are technologically oriented. If you are aware of what a given school is looking for, you can emphasize those aspects of your candidacy that are most suited to its needs. The starting point for learning about a school's specific interests, as discussed in Chapter 3, is to read the material it publishes about itself and speak with its current students and recent graduates.

This chapter focuses on writing individual essays successfully, but bear in mind that each essay is part of a whole application package, consisting of required and optional essays, résumé data, recommendations, and possibly an interview evaluation. To ensure that you put together a well-integrated, consistent package, do not try to finish any one essay until you have done at least a rough draft of all the essays for a given school, and planned the other parts of your package as well.

PLANNING

DEVELOPING YOUR MATERIAL

All too many essays sound the same. The poor admissions officer who has to read 5,000 essays, or many more, gains no understanding of an applicant who writes a personal statement that could have been written by any of another 500 applicants to the same school. Few applicants take the time to ask what makes them unusual or unique (or valuable). *Your goal is to develop materials that will help you write stories unique to you, which no one but you could tell.*

Failing to develop your material or examine yourself thoroughly will lead to dull generalities and mark your application with a deathly sense of unsophistication. You will not do yourself any favors by writing, "My travels broadened my horizons by exposing me to different cultures" or "The experience taught me that with hard work and determination I can reach my goals." Statements like these do not merit space in your essays if you want to dazzle the admissions committee.

Pulling together the relevant material for your application essay (or essays, depending on what your particular case may be) will take substantial effort, especially if you have been working for a number of years at different jobs. The material that might be relevant to the essays could come from virtually any time in your life, and be from any episode or experience.

The best way to start the process of generating material is to fill out the Personal Organizer in Appendix IV in Chapter 9. As you can see at a glance, there are numerous things to note. Try to fill this out over a period of time, because you will be unlikely to remember everything this calls for in one sitting. Referring to your résumé should be helpful. In fact, you might find it helpful to refer back to earlier versions of your résumé, if you still have them. You may also want to look at your transcripts to refresh your memory.

Consider keeping a notebook handy for jotting down ideas, stories, or details about your past or your goals for the future. Reading this book and the many examples in it may also spur your memory. I encourage you to take personal notes in the margins regarding your own experiences.

When you have completed the Personal Organizer, you should have far too much material to use in your essay(s). This is as it should be. You should feel that you have a wealth of material from which you can pick the most appropriate items.

ORGANIZING YOUR MATERIAL

Once you have generated your raw material, what will you actually say? If you have already read Chapter 9, you may have determined what your main themes will be. Now is a good time to recheck that they still make sense in light of the information you have available. Do you have good stories to tell that illustrate your being a fervent historian? Have you the right grades in the most closely related courses to claim this? If not, now is the right time to reconsider your positioning. Think in terms of what would be appropriate organizing themes given the information you do have.

After you have generated your information, you must organize it. There are many methods for doing so. One is to determine the core of your messages. In other words, what key points are you trying to make? If you can state these, the next step is to group your supporting material according to the appropriate points.

To organize your thinking effectively, it is generally a good idea to outline your essay. This will save you time because the outline will make it clear whether you have too much or too little material. It will also allow you to make changes early in the process rather than work on something that will be eliminated because it does not belong. In other words, it is a check on your thinking.

HOW TO MAKE AN OUTLINE

There are several outlining methods commonly used, including the following:

INFORMAL OUTLINE, USING BULLETS AND DASHES:

➤ Primary idea
  —Subordinate idea
  —Subordinate idea
   —Sub subordinate idea
➤ Primary idea
  —Subordinate idea
  —Sub subordinate idea

FORMAL OUTLINE, USING ROMAN NUMERALS, LETTERS, AND NUMBERS:

I. Primary idea
  A. Subordinate idea
  B. Subordinate idea
    1. Sub subordinate idea
    2. Sub subordinate idea
      a. Sub sub subordinate idea
      b. Sub sub subordinate idea
    3. Sub subordinate idea
II. Primary idea
  A. Subordinate idea

It does not particularly matter which outlining method you use. It only matters that it can perform the important functions needed: pulling together related material, showing how idea groups relate to one another, and showing which ideas are primary and in what ways supporting ideas are to be subordinated. You may find that you start with an informal outline and progress to a more formal one as your ideas become clearer.

REVIEWING THE ELEMENTS OF GOOD WRITING

It is usually a good idea, especially for those who are not accustomed to writing anything more than short memos, to review the elements of good writing style. Peruse Strunk & White's *The Elements of Style*, paying special attention to the stylistic principles in Part V. It is a good idea to have a book like this on hand as you write and rewrite, in case you need to check up on your grammar or word usage.

In particular, note the following tenets of good writing:

- *Simplicity.* Every sentence should be stripped down to its basic components. Every word that is redundant or does not add meaning should be removed. Writing improves when you pare it down and eliminate unnecessary words or phrases. For example, "a very good friend of my mother's" is better as "my mother's friend." "Hideously ugly" is better as simply "ugly" or "hideous."

- *Precision.* Be as detailed and specific as possible at all times. Details bring authenticity to your writing. If your readers see the word "car," their minds are left with a fuzzy, forgettable image. But if they read "rusted-out, pea green '78 Dodge," they are left with an indelible picture.

- *Show rather than tell.* Rather than tell readers what a situation is like, show them the situation (i.e., describe it in detail) and they will sense on their own what you want them to feel. For example, do not tell readers, "I was very sad when my older brother moved to Bangkok." Instead, describe the twisted feeling you had in your stomach as you sat on his bed while he packed his things; recall the last few minutes of nervous conversation the two of you had before he slipped out the back door; describe the tears you shed as you watched the car pull away for the airport; talk about sitting at the breakfast table all alone with your parents after his departure; explore the feelings of abandonment you sensed when he called home but never asked to speak to you. By showing the situation, you will more powerfully convey to your readers how lonely and sad you really were.

- *Choose your words carefully.* Do not follow the masses; avoid clichés and common phrases whose "understood" meanings could be conveyed more effectively using different words. Clichés will dull your reader and make you sound unimaginative or lazy. Phrases such as "blind as a bat" or "it was like looking for a needle in a haystack" can be better and more precisely conveyed in your own original words.

- *Stick to one style and tone.* Decide before writing what kind of style and tone you will employ, and stay with it throughout the entire essay. If your tone at the beginning of an essay is light-natured and humorous, do not switch to a somber or stern voice midway through the piece. If your essay is meant to be fashioned as a personal diary entry, do not suddenly start preaching to an outside audience.

- *Alter the lengths, styles, and rhythms of your sentences for variety.* Your writing should contain some long sentences as well as some especially short ones for greatest effect. You should not rely too heavily on any one or two sentence constructions, but weave many different sentence forms and structures into your essays.

- *Forget what you learned in grade school.* Not every essay needs to have the kind of "introduction," "body," and "conclusion" that you learned about as a kid. Your writing does need to be organized and unified, but organization and the development of ideas take on more sophisticated meanings once you have mastered the basics of writing. Your introduction does not have to have one single "topic sentence," nor does it have to summarize everything that will follow in the body of the essay. Your conclusion does not have to restate the topic sentence. Using the first person ("I") is entirely appropriate and necessary for law school essays. Throw out the old rules of thumb if you have not already done so.

GET YOUR CREATIVE JUICES FLOWING

There are many ways of triggering your creativity if you know you have trouble writing crisp and energetic prose. First and foremost, you must read! Reading the works of talented authors, especially those who have produced what we might call "creative nonfiction," will prepare you to let loose your own creative juices for the sake of writing your college essays. Here are a few suggestions if you would like to read brilliant personal memoirs or autobiographical accounts: Ernest Hemingway's *A Moveable Feast*; Zora Neale Hurston's *Dust Tracks on a Road*; Jill Ker Conway's *The Road from Coorain*; Vladimir Nabokov's *Speak, Memory*; Penelope Lively's *Oleander, Jacaranda*; Maxine Hong Kingston's *The Woman Warrior*; Andre Aciman's *Out of Egypt*; Vivian Gornick's *Fierce Attachments*; any autobiographical essay by Calvin Trillin, John McPhee, or Christopher Hitchens.

There are many books on writing that can suggest a variety of exercises and strategies for unleashing your creativity. Consult, for example, Natalie Goldberg's *Writing Down the Bones* or Anne Lamott's *Bird by Bird* for ideas.

THE ROUGH DRAFT

The next step in the writing process is to produce a rough draft. Be sure you are not too demanding of yourself at this point. Even though you want to do a good job, here "the perfect is the enemy of the good." If you are unwilling to write down anything that is less than final-draft quality, you are highly likely to be unable to write anything at all. Rather than take this perfectionist approach, be sure to limit your goal to that of producing a rough draft that incorporates most of the basic points you want to make. Do not be concerned if the order you had planned to follow no longer seems to work well, or if you cannot quite express your thoughts, or if your word choice is awkward. Get something reasonable down on paper as a starting point.

Writers use any number of different strategies when they start writing. No one method is recommended above others. This is very much a matter of personal preference. You can use any of the following methods. Choose the one (or invent one of your own) that gets you started on the road to producing a reasonably complete draft.

- *Start with the conclusion.* Writers who use this method feel they cannot write the body of the essay until they know what they are leading up to.

TWO WAYS TO AVOID WRITER'S BLOCK

Many people find themselves "blocked" when they try to write. They sit and stare at the paper or computer, and it stares back at them. To avoid this, do not put pressure on yourself to do too much at once. When you are in the early part of the writing process, try simply to get the basic elements of your thinking about each subtopic down on paper. Do not worry about the quality of what you are writing until you are editing.

Technique One. After you have thought about an essay, try to write down on index cards phrases that convey your various ideas. (Or, of course, use a computer to do the same thing.) Don't plan for too long; just write down the phrases as they occur to you. Then organize the cards into related groups of ideas. Write paragraphs expressing these ideas, perhaps trying to link the related ones together. Then see if you can place these paragraphs into a reasonably logical order. Next, put this structure into a proper outline to see if it makes sense. If it does, link the paragraphs with appropriate transitions. If it doesn't, try reordering the paragraphs.

Technique Two. Involve a friend in the process if it is still too difficult to get rolling with this method. Explain to your pal what you are trying to convey. Have her take notes on what you are saying. Organize those notes into a logical order, with her help, and then explain yourself to her again, being sure to follow your notes to keep things in order. If you can record this, and transcribe your recording, you will have a solid rough draft, which you can start to edit.

- *Start with the introduction.* When an introduction lays out clearly what will follow, it in effect controls the body of the paper. Some writers like to start with the introduction in order to make sure they have a grip on the body of the paper before trying to write it.

- *Start with any of the paragraphs of the body.* Some writers like to pick any self-contained part of the body of the paper and write it up, them move on to another part, and then another. These writers like to build the substantive parts of the paper first, and then provide an introduction and conclusion based upon this substance.

- *Write several different drafts, starting in different places.* This approach involves taking one perspective or starting point for writing a draft, plowing through the entirety, then doing the same thing from another perspective or starting point. Later, the writer can choose one draft or another, or cut and paste using pieces of each.

A majority of people use the third method—writing paragraphs of the body of the paper. They typically write them individually, then place them together in their predetermined order, and only then develop an introduction and conclusion. They take this approach because they know certain aspects of the subject well and can write about them easily, but require more thought to fill in the remaining pieces, such as the introduction and conclusion.

EDITING YOUR ROUGH DRAFT

Remember that "the only good writing is rewriting." You are doing your first part of this rewriting when you start to edit your rough draft.

One of the most important aspects of the editing stage is its timing. Editing without a break between the drafting and the editing stages will limit your insight into the flaws of your draft. You will not see where you skipped a needed transition or explanation because you are too close to the original writing. If you can take a break, preferably at least a night, or better yet, a week, you will be better able to read your draft from the perspective of an outsider.

Make sure you have edited your draft for substance—for what points will remain and what points will be eliminated—before you start editing the language. Otherwise, you will devote time and effort to improving the wording of material that might be discarded. (Even worse, you are likely to keep it in your draft if you have gone to the trouble of making it sound good.) This section assumes that you will revise your essay three times. In fact, if you are a good writer and have taken the time to think through an essay before doing your first draft, you might well need to edit it only once or, more likely, twice. By the same token, if you are struggling with an essay, it might require more than three revisions to sort out the problems.

One warning: Do not view editing as taking the life out of your essay. Editing's role is to eliminate the deadwood, making your points stand out as clearly as possible.

REVISING YOUR FIRST DRAFT

The initial revision should focus on the essay as a whole.

Do you accomplish your objective? Does your essay directly answer the question? Is your main idea clear?

Revise for content. The typical rough draft may have too little and too much material, all at the same time. It will have touched the surface of some portions of the essay, without providing explanation or convincing detail. At the same time, it may have discussed things that do not contribute significantly to your major points.

A good essay eliminates extraneous material while including all the information necessary to your point. Your reader needs sufficient evidence to accept what you are saying, so be sure you have adequately developed and supported your main idea. Material that does this belongs, but material that is unrelated to the main idea should be eliminated.

Revise for organization. A well-organized essay will group similar ideas together and put them in the proper order. If it is easy to produce an outline from the draft, and there is a clear logic to the flow of the material, you can be reasonably certain that you have a well-ordered essay. Otherwise, reorder your material.

Revise for length. Is your essay approximately the right length? If it is substantially longer than the stated limit, consider how to reduce the supporting material. Many schools leave the issue of length up to the applicant's discretion—but be wary of this freedom, especially if you have the tendency to write verbose, rambling manifestos. Adhere to a self-imposed limit and, unless addressing a topic that needs lengthy explanation, stick to it.

You probably need more depth if the essay is significantly shorter than the suggested length. You might consider rethinking your choice of topic if you feel you have nothing more to say.

REVISING YOUR SECOND DRAFT

Assuming you have successfully revised the first draft of the essay and the content is as you wish it to be, turn your attention to the components of the essay: the paragraphs, sentences, and individual words.

Revise paragraphs. A paragraph should not be an arbitrarily formed entity. It should, to some extent, revolve around an idea, a central point, a theme. Isolate a paragraph at a time and make sure it sticks together and is not merely a bunch of unrelated statements slapped together.

Look next at the length of your paragraphs. Most writers tend to one extreme or the other: Either all their paragraphs are very short or all are very long. A mixture of lengths is a good idea. The reasons for this are simple: Too many short paragraphs make you look simple-minded, unable to put together a complex idea or group related ideas together, whereas absurdly long paragraphs will discourage reading by any but the most conscientious reader. Use short paragraphs for emphasis; use long paragraphs for discussion of complicated points or examples.

The three methods you can use to develop your main idea are to provide examples, explanation, or details. Writing without these three components tends to be unsatisfying and unconvincing. Generalities ("I am a morally driven person") are unconvincing unless supported with specific examples and explanations.

Revise for flow. Even when you have well-written paragraphs placed in the correct order, your writing may still be difficult to read because it lacks suitable transitions between ideas or other means of showing how the ideas relate. For our purposes, the most important method of relating ideas will be using transition words and phrases. Some typical transitions include:

One other easy way to connect paragraphs is to have the beginning of one paragraph follow directly from the end of the prior paragraph. For example, if you have just said "I needed the chance to show what I could do without over-

PURPOSE	TYPICAL TRANSITIONS
Amplification	besides, furthermore, moreover, in addition
Cause and effect	therefore, consequently, as a result, accordingly
Conclusion	as a result, therefore, thus, in conclusion
Contrast	although, but, despite, however, on the one hand, on the other hand
Example	for example, for instance, specifically
Sequence	first, second; former, latter; first of all

bearing supervision" at the end of one paragraph, the next one could start out "My opportunity to prove myself came with the founding of a new office in Toronto." In this example the relationship between the two paragraphs is ensured by having the second grow organically from the end of the first.

Be sure each sentence follows logically from the prior sentence.

Check your introduction. Make sure it not only introduces your subject but also grabs the audience. A good introduction is interesting as well as successful at conveying your main points. It should appeal to the reader and set the tone for the whole essay. There are many effective openings. You can state an important and interesting fact, refer to something currently in the news, refer to a personal experience, ask a question that you will answer in your essay, or simply state your general point of view. Do not restate the question, if there is one; it wastes valuable space and is a weak, plodding way to begin.

Check your conclusion. A good conclusion does one or more of the following:

- Pulls together different parts of the essay
- Rephrases your main ideas (without repeating anything word for word)
- Shows the importance of the material
- Makes a recommendation
- Makes a forecast
- Points toward the future—showing, for example, how you will make use of something you have learned
- Gives a sense of completion

It should not make a new point that belongs in the body rather than the conclusion, nor should it sound tacked on. The concluding paragraph should develop "organically," if you wish, from the material that preceded it.

Revise sentences and words. Most essay writers pile on one long sentence after another. Avoid this by breaking up some of the longer sentences to provide variety. Use short sentences to make important points; long sentences to explain complex ideas or develop examples. Also use a variety of sentence structures to maintain reader interest. Do not, for example, use a "not only . . . but also . . ." structure in every other sentence. Eliminate sentences that sound awkward or choppy when read aloud.

Edit your sentences to eliminate imprecise or wordy language. For example, use "although" instead of "despite the fact that." Add vigor to your writing by eliminating clichés, using fresh and interesting descriptions. Try to write as much as possible with nouns and verbs, rather than primarily with adjectives (which slow the pace and reduce impact). Similarly, write in the active, not the passive, voice.

Revise for tone. Your tone can be assertive without being arrogant. Your essays should sound confident, enthusiastic, and friendly. Be sure to avoid pleading ("I'd give anything if you would just let me in") and whining ("I never do well on those awful standardized tests; it's so unfair that schools even look at the results").

One way to check the tone of your paper is to read it aloud. Read it first to yourself and then, once it sounds appropriate to you, try reading it to a friend. Ask him how easy it is to understand, what the strong and weak points are, whether there are any mistakes in it, and whether it sounds like you. Does it reflect your personal style? The ideal essay should sound just like your voice, but with repetitious and awkward phrasings and use of such filler as "you know" and "like" eliminated. It should sound relaxed rather than formal, but still flow smoothly.

Some applicants, remembering a high school textbook, try to avoid writing in the first person. In fact, it is not only appropriate to use "I" when writing your essays, it is essential that you do so. You are being asked to give personal statements, so do not write in the distant and aloof third person.

REVISING YOUR THIRD DRAFT

Three revisions is not a magic number, but will be a minimum for most people. There is nothing wrong with putting your work through more revisions.

Revise again for style. See the earlier comments.

Revise for grammar, punctuation, and spelling. The way to spot grammatical mistakes and faulty punctuation is to read your essays slowly, preferably after having put them aside for some time. Reading them aloud can also help this process. Even if your sense of grammar is keen, however, consider having a friend whose grasp of grammar is extremely good read each essay. Spellcheck the final product.

Check the length (again). One of the key factors affecting most of the essays you will write is that the law schools generally prescribe their maximum length. Failing to observe this constraint raises questions about your willingness to pay attention to the rules that will apply in other situations, so avoid going over the limit. They have established these limits to provide a level playing field for the applicants; someone who exceeds the limits is trying to assert an unfair advantage.

GIVING YOUR ESSAYS TO SOMEONE ELSE TO CRITIQUE

After you have edited the essays to your own satisfaction, or gotten stuck, hand them to several people whose views on writing you respect. They can provide you with an objective view you may not be able to bring to the essays yourself. They can be particularly useful in determining whether your attempts at humor are working, whether the essays convey a true sense of who you are, and whether you have left out important connections or explanations.

Make sure, too, you have people who do not know you well read your essays; they will be able to tell you if something is clear or not. Be open-minded about their criticism, but do not give up control of what are, after all, your essays, not theirs. Do not let them remove the life from your essays.

PROOFREADING

Why proofread your paper if you have been careful in composing the final draft? No matter how careful you have been, errors are still likely to crop up. Taking a last look at the essay is a sensible precaution.

What are you looking for? Basically, the task at this point is no longer to make sure the structure is correct; it is to spot any errors or omissions in your sentences and individual words. Errors tend to show up most often where prior changes were made. Combining two paragraphs into one, for example, may have resulted in the loss of a necessary transition phrase. Grammatical mistakes can also live on.

As with any task that is essentially a matter of editing, your timing is of the essence. Wait until you have already finished what you consider to be your final draft. If you can then put down this draft for a few days, you will be able to give it an effective last look. If not, you risk being unable to see mistakes because you are still too close to the writing. Another useful precaution is to have a friend proofread your essays.

SOME TIPS FOR GOOD WRITING

DO:

➤ *Give yourself the time to do the essays right.* Start early; it will take time to do the essays. The results will also be better if you take time between steps rather than try to finish an application in a hurry. Expect to spend 10 to 20 hours getting organized for the effort, and then averaging perhaps 5 to 10 hours per essay, with the most difficult (and first) efforts taking longer.

➤ *Use humor, but only if it works.* Few people can write humorous prose, or recount humorous stories effectively, but if you can manage it, you will definitely distinguish yourself. To check whether you are succeeding, have several people of different ages and backgrounds read your material to make sure it works on paper as well as it would if you were to tell it. Be sure it is not vicious or off-color humor, as this has no place in a law school essay.

➤ *Keep the focus on you.* For example, do not get carried away in describing a particular facet of an unsavory law without showing how this relates to you and your efforts.

➤ *Explain events whenever appropriate.* Many of the things you have done are mainly of interest because of what you learned from them, what you thought about them, and why you did them.

➤ *Favor a full description of one event rather than a listing of several.* It is generally better to describe one event or accomplishment at some length rather than mention a number of them without explaining why you undertook something, what it meant to you, and what you learned from it.

➤ *Be specific.* The more specific you make your writing, the more you personalize it and the better the chance that it will be interesting. Generalizations, without specific information and examples, are weak and not necessarily believable.

➤ *Find someone to edit your work.* Explain what you are trying to accomplish and who will be reading your essays, so that your "editor" can both determine whether you are meeting your objectives and correct your grammar. The test of your writing is what the reader understands, not what your intent may have been.

Do Not:

➤ *Start to write until you have determined what your most important contributions to this program will be.* Reread the school's brochure and the other materials you have gathered on it and remind yourself of why you are applying to it (beyond its high ranking or reputation). Read the recommendation forms the school uses to see specifically what this school wants in its applicants.

➤ *Use limited space to recite information that is available elsewhere* in the application, such as listing your part-time jobs or mentioning your LSAT results.

➤ *Give superficial answers.* Take this application seriously and work accordingly.

➤ *Pretend to be someone other than yourself.* It will not be supportable with your own history and will sound phony.

➤ *Lie or exaggerate.* Doing so causes all of your assertions to be doubted.

➤ *Think that a personal statement limit also defines the required amount to write.* No one has failed to get into a law school for failure to write the maximum number of words on a personal statement. When you have said all that you intend to say, stop.

➤ *Use a miniscule type size or borders to shrink a personal statement to a given space.* Remember that your readers have to read literally thousands of essays and will not appreciate being forced to squint or use a magnifying glass.

➤ *Start by saying,* "In this essay I will write about . . ."

➤ *Use cute or "meaningful" quotations* unless they fit perfectly and do not make people wince when they read them. Too many people seem to have been taught to start everything they write with a cute epigram, regardless of the fact that it may not fit the subject well and all too often does not match the desired tone of the essay. Shakespeare, Napoleon, Churchill, and Twain all said a lot of marvelous things, but that does not necessarily mean you should quote them.

➤ *Use a definition to begin your essay.* This is too often a sophomoric way to begin, so avoid using this crutch.

➤ *Use only bullet points.* Writing an essay requires that you use full sentences.

➤ *Discuss your low grades,* poor LSAT score, or other weak aspects of your record here, unless you have a very good reason for doing so. In general, these explanations are likely to be best placed in a separate addendum rather than in your personal statement.

➤ *Bore the reader.* A fresh and well-written personal statement will aid your application effort.

➤ *Use fancy vocabulary for its own sake.* Use the simplest possible language to explain your meaning precisely. Using "legalese," unless you are already working in a legal field, is particularly likely to strike admissions officers as presumptuous and arrogant.

ADMISSIONS DEANS DISCUSS HOW TO WRITE THE ESSAYS

WHAT CONSTITUTES EFFECTIVE WRITING

Clear, concise, focused writing is best. Convey the idea of who you are and what is important to you or motivates you as concisely and clearly as possible. This should give us a three-dimensional view of you, as well as showcase your writing ability. *Nkonye Iwerebon, Columbia*

The first sentence is critical: it has to tell me the essay will be interesting. We have so many files to read that some will get more attention than others. *Anne Richard, George Washington*

Effective writing is honest writing, in a style—and on a topic—with which the applicant is comfortable. It is easy to identify those applicants who are mistakenly writing about something they think the admissions committee wants to see versus those who are writing honestly about themselves. *Renée Post, Penn*

Use active voice primarily. Develop an appropriate rhythm, mixing shorter sentences with longer sentences. Don't overdo it: Don't make it overly dense, with inappropriately complicated vocabulary. I don't want to have to reread it to figure out what was intended. There is certainly no room for grammatical errors or typos. Don't substitute "Cornell" for Northwestern. If they do this, my response is to wish them well at Cornell. *Don Rebstock, Northwestern*

Too many personal statements lose you after the first paragraph; they're not organized, they ramble on—we don't know what you're writing about. We deliberately have many of the legal research and writing faculty on the admissions committee, because we want applicants who have a true facility with the language and care about how they craft their written work. After all, the study of law is in some sense the study of language. *Elizabeth Rosselot, Boston College*

Trying to use every big word you've ever learned doesn't necessarily work; it comes off as affected. *Kenneth Kleinrock, NYU*

Essays should be clear, direct, concise, and in active voice, but unself-conscious—not sounding like you wrote it with a thesaurus at your elbow. *Susan Palmer, Virginia*

TONE

Display a sense of humor if you have one, but don't force it. *Elizabeth Rosselot, Boston College*

It is very tough to write a personal statement that shows who you are and the significance of your achievements without blatant self-promotion. *Susan Palmer, Virginia*

Someone who sounds self-absorbed and arrogant has basically disqualified himself from consideration. *Sarah C. Zearfoss, Michigan*

Try to avoid writing in a satirical, humorous tone, because without the context a reader is likely to miss the humor. Also, watch out for those opening sentences which are meant to catch our attention, but instead offend our sensibilities. *Chloe T. Reid, USC*

ATTENTION TO DETAIL

We want people who are bright, well-rounded, and able to write. You would not believe how poorly written many personal statements are: full of grammatical errors and wrong law school names (Harvard rather than Stanford, for example). Remember that this is an application for graduate work and forget the cutesy gimmicks—no green ink, please. *Faye Deal, Stanford*

A trained file reader will tend to spend about twenty minutes with an application. Grab that reader's attention, then don't blow it with grammatical and spelling errors, and so on. Attention to detail shows whether you are serious about the school. *Elizabeth Rosselot, Boston College*

Proofread carefully. In particular, make sure that you send the right essay to the right school—essays about your lifelong dream to go to Stanford are not likely to help you here. *Megan A. Barnett, Yale*

I read files with a pencil in hand, and I circle errors in grammar, spelling, and punctuation. If I see a lot of circles when I'm finished, you have a big problem. For a lawyer, attention to detail counts. *Susan Palmer, Virginia*

The personal statement is assumed to be the best work an applicant is capable of. Lots of mistakes in it indicate inattention to detail, which will be a major problem for a lawyer. Don't substitute Michigan for Duke in the concluding "I very much want to attend ____" sentence. *William Hoye, Duke*

There is nothing better than being able to write well, to form a good sentence. Common mistakes are grammatical errors, misspellings, bad sentence structure. The misplacement of a comma even can make a big difference. *Edward Tom, Boalt Hall (Berkeley)*

Attention to detail is very important. Unlike the LSAT writing sample, the personal statement offers an opportunity to refine a piece of work—to check the grammar, consider word usage, and do more than a cursory spell-check. We just read an essay yesterday and my associate director shouted out, "Misplaced comma in the first sentence, misplaced comma in the first sentence." Needless to say, that was the end of that application. *Renée Post, Penn*

SHOULD YOU EVER EXCEED THE WORD LIMITS?

(NOTE THE DIFFERENT VIEWS ON THIS TOPIC.)

We don't specify a page limit to the personal statement, but the focus should be on quality, not quantity. (Of course, someone who's led a long and full life should probably write a longer essay than someone fresh from college.) *Elizabeth Rosselot, Boston College.*

Be the audience and the writer at the same time. I read 12,000 of these so length matters: Say what you have to say and then be quiet. For most people two pages will do the trick. *Andy Cornblatt, Georgetown*

We have no limit to the length of personal statements, but extraordinarily lengthy statements seldom show good judgment. Two to three pages would be typical. *Kenneth Kleinrock, NYU*

We do not have a word limit, so you are free to structure your essay as you see fit, understanding though that conciseness is a virtue. *Susan Palmer, Virginia*

Our optional essays have specified limits, which should not be greatly exceeded. Our personal statement, however, has no stated limit. This requires that you exercise judgment. If you choose to write twenty-six pages, you will have revealed a great deal more to me than was contained in the substance of your essay. *Sarah C. Zearfoss, Michigan*

Only if it's *absolutely* necessary. *Renée Post, Penn*

A LAST WORD

Try giving a draft of your statement to someone who doesn't know you. Have him describe you back to you. If the person has a hard time articulating much, you've got work to do. *William Hoye, Duke*

REUSING YOUR PERSONAL STATEMENTS

Law schools want to learn similar things about their applicants, so a personal statement written for one may provide the basis for an essay for other schools. This is good for you to the extent that you can reuse your essays and cut down on the amount of work you have to devote to additional applications.

On the other hand, few things annoy admissions officers more than to receive personal statements that were obviously written for another school, particularly if the other school's name was left in them. It is possible to recycle your essays as long as you do so intelligently. The reason for doing so—to save time and effort—is compelling enough that almost everyone will try to use the best material in more than one application.

Expect to make more changes than just switching school names. This will be especially true in the following situations:

- Your positioning for a particular school is different from your usual positioning.

- You are applying to schools with various numbers of allowed essays. Applying to a school that permitted just one personal statement may have required you to pack brief descriptions of several events into that essay. When writing for a school that has more essay questions, you may want to spread out these events and use them in several essays. This could also involve lengthening your description of the events. (The reverse process would be appropriate when changing from an application with several questions to an application with just one.)

■ You are applying to schools with very different essay length requirements or expectations.

—To lengthen an essay, you may wish to include more examples, elaborate the examples you have already used, or even add additional points.

—To shorten a long essay, keep your major points but reduce your elaboration of them.

FURTHER READING

Stuart Berg Flexner, ed., *The Random House Dictionary of the English Language*

Joseph M. Williams, *Style: Ten Lessons in Clarity and Grace*

William Zinsser, *On Writing Well*

William Strunk, Jr., and E. B. White, *The Elements of Style*

William Safire, *Fumblerules*

Patricia T. O'Conner, *Woe Is I*

The Chicago Manual of Style

Appendix V

WRITING RÉSUMÉS, FILLING OUT FORMS, INCLUDING EXTRA MATERIALS

WRITING RÉSUMÉS

Some schools, including Chicago, Duke, and Texas, require a résumé; most of the others welcome one. It is generally advisable that you submit one, particularly if you have had substantial work experience. A résumé allows you to frame how your experience and progress are viewed, so take advantage of the opportunity. For law school purposes, there is nothing magical about one style of résumé versus another. As long as you convey the right information in easily readable (and skimmable) form, you will be fine. Keep a few rules in mind, then examine the two examples that follow for further tips.

BASIC RÉSUMÉ RULES

■ Assume that people will spend only 30 seconds on your résumé. Therefore, keep to one page, unless you are an academician doing a CV or have already been secretary of state.

■ Emphasize important points rather than try to list everything you have ever done. Less tends to be more for résumé purposes; it shows that you can prioritize and organize.

■ Emphasize achievements, providing quantitative or tangible proof of your results whenever possible.

■ Show the progression of your career in terms of promotions, increased responsibilities, and the like.

- For jobs you wish to describe in detail, consider separating responsibilities (which you can put in an introductory paragraph form) from your achievements (which you can list as bullet points).

- Use "résumé-speak"—phrases rather than full sentences.

- Make sure your résumé is visually appealing: It should not be so crammed with material that it puts someone off.

- The space devoted to a topic should reflect its importance.

SAMPLE RÉSUMÉS

Examine carefully the two résumés that follow. Both do a good job. It is easy to skim for the key points in each: The essential information is readily apparent. Note the stylistic similarities. The relevant categories, such as education and experience, are easy to pick out. The schools and employers, in bold and all capitals, are emphasized more than are the jobs or degrees, in italics. The flow of each person's career to date is easily tracked, given the clear posting of the relevant dates.

Furthermore, the addition of "personal" information helps make each résumé unique. Personal data is highly relevant for law school purposes since admissions committees are keen to compose classes of students with diverse backgrounds and interests. They want to know as much as possible, so share anything interesting that sheds light on who you are outside of your work and education experiences.

The substantive differences of the two résumés, on the other hand, are also instructive.

- Garth puts education first, which is generally appropriate only for those who have limited full-time experience. This is indeed the case with Garth. Paul leads with experience, which is highly appropriate for someone with seven years' experience, all of it impressive.

- Garth devotes substantial space to education, even including his high school record. Only when a high school record is truly impressive, as is the case here, does it belong on a professional school application. Paul, on the other hand, limits his discussion of education, but does note his professional development efforts.

- Garth, who had only two years of work experience prior to law school, devotes substantial space to his part-time jobs, whereas Paul, with seven years of experience, does not even bother to list his. Once again, given the difference in their situations, each one made the correct choice.

- Garth lumps all of his jobs—in education as well as urban economic development, part-time as well as full-time—in one category. Paul, in contrast, splits his work into manufacturing and military categories. Within each of these, he sets up two subcategories: manufacturing and engineering for the former, peacekeeping and combat operations for the latter.

■ Garth emphasizes his academic achievements; Paul, his work achievements. Garth is easily able to show outstanding academic work by noting his honors and awards, but has relatively few concrete work achievements of similar strength. The opposite is true for Paul, who has very substantial and easily demonstrated work achievements, but fewer academic honors to note. In other words, each applicant did a fine job emphasizing his strongest suit.

■ Garth could have improved his résumé somewhat by providing several missing pieces of data. His years of involvement on the varsity soccer team and as a tutor while at Yale should be included. His work for the Democratic Coordinated Campaign should highlight any budget control he exercised. Similarly, his work for the Philadelphia Empowerment Zone should have included tangible demonstration of his successes. Paul, on the other hand, does a very effective job of making clear his success in tangible, quantitative fashion.

■ Garth does a slightly better job of formatting his material than does Paul. Garth's placement of dates, justified to line up with the left margin, and location names, justified to line up with the right margin, provide a crisp look. This format also makes it easy to see at a glance what he has done, when, and where.

Consult "Describe Your Current Job" in Chapter 10 for more information on the best ways to describe your past and current positions.

ADMISSIONS DEANS DISCUSS THE USEFULNESS OF RÉSUMÉS

A one-page résumé is often helpful. Be sure to explain whatever isn't obvious; we don't always know about the "Smith Prize" or the "Alpha Society." *Megan A. Barnett, Yale*

We ask for a résumé. One page should suffice, unless you have had a lot of work experience or activities. Be careful about submitting extra pages, though, because they are often not essential. *Ann Killian Perry, Chicago*

Résumés should *never* be more than one page. They should show the impact you've had, quantifying what can be quantified, making clear what isn't obvious. Don't embellish; don't "puff." *Anne Richard, George Washington*

__GARTH HARRIES__   101 Main St., Menlo Park, CA, 90000

                                                            (415) 555-5555 gharries@xxx.com

Education

2001–2005   __YALE UNIVERSITY__   New Haven, CT
                 B.A. in Ethics, Politics and Economics; focus on Urban Affairs. Course work included multi-variable calculus, intermediate physics, data analysis, and corporate strategy.
                 Honors: *Summa Cum Laude* with Distinction in Major
                                Phi Beta Kappa (elected junior year)
                                Heinz Fellow and Richter Fellow (summer 2003)
                                Men's Soccer Academic All-Ivy Team (2004)
                 Activities: Men's Varsity Soccer. Tutoring and classroom assistance. Ultimate Frisbee, Northeast regional champions (2005). Research assistant to School of Management professor (fall 2004).

1997–2001   __PHILLIPS EXETER ACADEMY__   Exeter, NH
                 Honors: Awarded the Yale Cup for general excellence, a Coxe Medal for top five scholastic rank, a National Merit Scholarship, and other academic prizes.
                 Activities: Student Judiciary Committee (chair). *Exonian* Editorials Editor.

Experience

2007   __PHILADELPHIA EMPOWERMENT ZONE__   Pescadero, PA
                 Special Projects Coordinator, Economic Development Office. Facilitated, designed, and/or directed a variety of high-priority economic development projects in disadvantaged neighborhoods of Philadelphia. Significant projects included:
                 • Planning for a worker-owned apparel factory, including creating a successful $500,000 grant application with business plan
                 • Initial analysis of a major retail/entertainment development proposal
                 • Research into economic development programs of comparable and/or competing cities and new business creation in the Zone
                 • Program design for a Zone-wide job matching and counseling system

2006   __DEMOCRATIC COORDINATED CAMPAIGN__   Scranton, PA
                 Field Coordinator. Responsible for Democratic State Party campaign activities in the 10th Congressional District. Directed campaign office, recruited and managed over 200 volunteers, organized events and voter outreach, and coordinated with other campaign organizations.

2005–2006   __VAIL MOUNTAIN SCHOOL__   Vail, CO
                 Teacher. Coed K–12 private day school. Taught Algebra and History to 9th, 10th, and 11th graders. Advised 10th grade homeroom and high school backcountry club. Coached 7–12 boys' soccer team to an undefeated season.

Spring 2005   __OFFICE OF BUSINESS DEVELOPMENT__   New Haven, CT
                 Part-time intern. Helped rejuvenate and organize merchants' association along commuter corridor.

Summer 2004   __DEPT. OF HOUSING AND URBAN DEVELOPMENT__   Washington, DC
                 Intern. Empowerment Zone/Enterprise Community Taskforce. Policy interpretation and implementation, office coordination and management, and review of urban applications.

Personal   Avid soccer player, telemark skier, and hiker. Backpacked through Africa and Australia.

PAUL SIMPSON

123 Center Ave., Long Beach, CA 91234   (310) 555-0000 ps@isp.com

MANUFACTURING EXPERIENCE

LEVI-STRAUSS   Los Angeles, CA   2004–Present
Supervisor/Project Engineer—Responsible for manufacturing operations. Manage capital projects for world's third largest blue jeans assembly plant.

Manufacturing
—Supervise 100 employees from three unions; represented Company during union negotiations, which resulted in a four-year contract.
—Reduced inventory levels by 60% through automation of materials management system, with cost savings of $1.8 million per year.
—Partnered with outside vendors to improve cleaning system efficiency by 15%.
—Implemented operator maintenance program that increased production efficiency, resulting in $2.0 million annual revenue increase.

Engineering
—Designed and supervised installation of two production lines, increasing output by 15%.
—Implemented strategy that ensured ERP implementation six months ahead of target date.
—Led process improvement team that reduced water usage by 30,000 gallons/day, saving over $200,000 annually.

MILITARY EXPERIENCE

U.S. ARMY CORPS OF ENGINEERS   Bosnia & Los Angeles, CA   2000–2004
Captain—Coordinated range of projects for construction and combat applications. Responsible for deployment readiness of engineering equipment and combat training for 60 soldiers.

United Nations Peacekeepers
—Initiated Civic Assistance program while in Bosnia. Completed 24 projects by working with Bosnian gov't, humanitarian groups, and military personnel from six countries.
—Directed the construction of a multilane bridge, which enabled UN access to southern Bosnia to deliver emergency medical and food supplies.
—Supervised construction of living quarters for 1200-member, multinational UN organization.

Combat Operations/Readiness
—Integrated engineering strategy into overall combat operations plans for a 1500-soldier interdisciplinary force.
—Developed and implemented a program to monitor equipment readiness and repair status for 415-vehicle fleet, decreasing processing time by 60%, and clerical errors by 75%.
—Supervised on-time rail transportation of 600 vehicles during base deployment to Bosnia.

EDUCATION

DARTMOUTH COLLEGE   *Bachelor of Science in Civil Engineering*   1996–2000
—Captain of ice hockey team (1999–2000); selected to All-Ivy Team.
—Ranked in top 10% nationally in ROTC class; supervised training program for 250 cadets.
—Designed and fabricated Formula 1 car as part of independent project team.

PROFESSIONAL DEVELOPMENT

—Licensed Professional Engineer in California.
—Additional coursework (Financial Accounting, Managerial Finance, Negotiations, Leadership Communication Strategies) at UCLA Extension School.

PERSONAL

—Mediator and Project Coordinator, Orange County Community Mediation Program.
—Led United Way fund-raising drive (2006); doubled annual contributions.
—Married; enjoy furniture restoration, skydiving, golf, and early detective novels.

FILING APPLICATIONS

There are numerous ways to submit an application. Paper applications are generally available within the brochure sent out by the law school or downloadable off the school's website. You can also download applications from the LSAC website at www.lsac.org. Many law schools now prefer (or even require) online application—either through their own website, or through an online application mechanism on the LSAC website. More and more, law schools encourage online application because it makes the information they receive easier to capture and sort and reduces many of the inefficiencies associated with paper applications. Those schools that prefer online application generally note their preference in their application materials; some also lower the fee for online applications. The LSAC website also lists each school's preferences.

In an effort to streamline the application process, the LSAC has created an online application system whereby students can create and submit applications to multiple law schools through its site. The system uses a combination of a "common application" with information gathered by all schools (name, educational history, LSAT score, and so on) and a school-specific application collected from schools themselves. This saves applicants time by allowing them to enter the otherwise repetitive data just once. In addition, for users of this service LSAC waives the fees for sending LSDAS reports to schools.

ADMISSIONS DEANS DISCUSS FILLING OUT THE APPLICATION FORMS

People shouldn't feel compelled to fill out every blank in the application. We don't expect someone to be president of the student body, editor-in-chief of the school newspaper, have done multiple internships, have a 4.0 GPA, and work thirty-five hours a week during college.   *Kenneth Kleinrock, NYU*

Never simply refer to attached sheets of paper. We want to give every application a thorough reading (and every applicant a fair shake), but that requires that we have everything before us when making a decision. It's never a positive thing when an applicant fails to assist us by making relevant information readily available.   *Todd Morton, Vanderbilt*

I'm often surprised that so many applicants simply fail to follow directions. They'll not answer a question and say, "See attachment," despite being told not to do so. You get one opportunity to present yourself. If you don't do it in a thoughtful, careful manner—and the file is laden with typos, misspellings, etc.—what does that say about you? *Kenneth Kleinrock, NYU*

Follow the directions! And use the LSAC service. *Chloe T. Reid, USC*

Be sure to read the instructions on our forms carefully. There are only a few questions, but we want them filled in carefully. Don't just say, "see résumé." *William Hoye, Duke*

Any unexplained gaps in an applicant's history raise red flags. You need to show what you were doing at each point. It's OK if you spent the year traveling the world, but it needs to be stated. *Kenneth Kleinrock, NYU*

ADMISSIONS DEANS DISCUSS WHAT OTHER MATERIALS YOU SHOULD SUBMIT

We don't have time to read lengthy materials. If you send a one-page CV or résumé, and two or three letters of recommendation, that's fine. If someone sends in an article just because their name is on the masthead, or a CD of their band . . . I just don't have time. *Edward Tom, Boalt Hall (Berkeley)*

Leave the ninety-page thesis out—the admissions committee can always request it if it will serve a purpose. Send only things that will fit into a file folder. *Susan Palmer, Virginia*

We get all kinds of things, but few help candidates. Don't bother to send in a video of yourself or your Ph.D. thesis. *Sarah C. Zearfoss, Michigan*

A good résumé organizes a great deal of information in a useful way. It takes a lot of time to do so, which is why they are so valuable. I always encourage applicants to provide one. *Todd Morton, Vanderbilt*

Applicants routinely underestimate the value of a résumé. It gives us a quick snapshot of who you are and what you've done. It shows your interests and passions. For example, did you have to work twenty-five hours a week at a demanding job in order to pay your tuition? In addition, we use it when evaluating candidates for awards or scholarship opportunities. . . . Don't supplement the application with lots of other materials. If there is something you are not sure about submitting, call us to ask whether or not you should include it. You should include supplemental statements to further explain issues which the average reader might have questions about (i.e., low GPA, poor first LSAT score, gaps in academic record, etc.), but be brief. *Chloe T. Reid, USC*

It's a good idea to include a résumé, whether one page or two. Applicants are free to provide other items, but they should recognize we have a lot to read. Therefore, it's an advocacy challenge to determine how much information, and of what type, to include. At a minimum it should be clear, concise, and compelling. It's impressive when someone achieves the right balance.   *William Hoye, Duke*

Applicants should understand that the admissions committee will evaluate them on the basis of all that they choose to submit. I think that applicants who submit an eighty-page thesis are making a mistake of judgment. I would not necessarily object to reading a thesis abstract if a person felt that it was vital to understanding what they've done. A one-page summary would be fine. Sometimes less is more.   *Kenneth Kleinrock, NYU*

Submitting a résumé makes sense, but submitting a thesis probably does not. A thesis synopsis, along with a letter of recommendation evaluating it, would be a better choice.   *Elizabeth Rosselot, Boston College*

12

RECOMMENDATIONS

— EXECUTIVE SUMMARY —

■

Choosing the right recommenders—whether they be professors, employers, or other types—is critically important.

■

Approaching potential recommenders must be done carefully.
—Give them a chance to say no.
—Explain why you want a law degree, and why you have chosen the schools you have.
—Explain how important their recommendations will be.
—Brief them fully regarding what they should write.
—Emphasize telling relevant, rich stories.

■

Make their job as easy as possible.

■

Consider whether you will benefit from supplemental recommendations.

For those of you who view the recommendations as little more than a bother-some formality—akin to the Deans' letter—this chapter should quickly convince you otherwise. Applicants complain that recommendations are a waste of time because "all applicants can find someone to say something good about them." These applicants are right to believe that most people can find a supporter, but they are wrong about the importance of the recommendations.

WHY ARE RECOMMENDATIONS REQUIRED?

To understand how crucial a recommendation can be, let us compare two applicants, John and Laura. They both went to well-known schools of Ivy League caliber and have high LSAT scores. Both are 25 and have been working for three years. Both presented solid essays; both are in the running for admission. As is often the case in law school admissions, officers might be faced with two such students but only one slot. In such a situation, when all else is equal, a recommendation can be the distinguishing factor in an acceptance. Compare and contrast these two letters of recommendation:

Recommendation for John:

I had the pleasure of teaching John two different classes: his freshman writing seminar (required of all students at the college) and a course on Southern African-American authors that he took during his junior year. I occasionally had coffee with John during his years as an undergraduate here and have kept in touch with him since he has left. I thus feel well qualified to address his candidacy to your law school.

One look at John's grades (and his LSAT score) and you will see why he graduated in the top 10% of his class. He is bright, thoughtful, and articulate; he often stimulated discussion in the classroom; he has a wonderful command of language. He never received below a B+ on a paper in my class (I am considered the toughest grader in the English department). I feel confident in John's ability to succeed academically at a law school such as yours.

Recommendation for Laura:

Laura undoubtedly belongs in your next class of promising future lawyers.

A student like Laura comes around only once or twice in a professor's entire career. I have been teaching at the college level for 21 years and have seen such a student only once before I met Laura. (That former student, by the way, is now on the Philosophy faculty at UC Berkeley, a star in his field, and also sits on several boards of directors of major corporations. If my view of Laura is anywhere near correct, you can assume that she is also headed toward great successes in life.) I taught two classes to Laura before becoming her senior thesis advisor, for which I spent the better part of an academic year working closely with her. We keep in close touch today, even seeing each other occasionally. I feel well qualified to write this recommendation on her behalf.

Recommendation for John:

Knowing how active and curious he is, I'm sure he will contribute to your various journals and even make law review.

John is also quite a soccer player. Although I don't follow soccer very closely (fencing is my thing), I went to a few games when John was on the team here, and was always impressed with his athletic prowess and his team cooperation skills. I know that he was highly regarded by his teammates and coaches while here; in fact, he even won the "Spirit Award" during his senior year.

Truly, I can't say enough good things about John. He would be a wonderful addition to your school.

Recommendation for Laura:

Laura excelled well beyond other students in both classes I taught her. In the first, "The History of the Industrial Revolution in America," she wrote with such extraordinary insight on a number of topics in the mid-term exam that I approached her about the possibility of her doing research for me on an upcoming book. (This kind of thing is all too rare. Never before had I sought out a particular student to perform research for me.) Accordingly, Laura did a superb job collecting and analyzing materials for me on western railroad development and its effect on Native peoples. She unearthed several unstudied documents showing that seven members of a particular tribe in Wyoming were actually *promoters* of the railroad companies and their plans for expansion. Always curious and up for a challenge, Laura chose Indian collaboration with white settlers on rail development as the topic of her thesis. I applauded her choice; it was novel and would require much original research, not something that every college senior is ready or able to tackle.

As soon as she began her preliminary studies, Laura ran up against two enormous obstacles, which I believed even she would not be able to surmount. First, the Library of Congress had not declassified certain documents that Laura needed to access in order to complete her study successfully. Second, a well-known Native American professor in our department heard of Laura's research and tried to persuade her against pursuing it, believing that her findings might jeopardize the strong perception that the particular tribe under study was particularly recalcitrant, often able to halt or even reverse the white man's progress. This particular professor, as part of the History Department's thesis

Recommendation for Laura:

committee, would be one of the faculty members responsible for reviewing and approving Laura's thesis at the end of her senior year. Although I obviously disagreed with my colleague's position—I was in fact outraged that a faculty member would try to stop honest and valuable research from taking place because of his own contemporary agenda—I also believed that, realistically speaking, going against his wishes was ill-advised. Looking at these two ominous obstacles, I actually suggested to Laura that we find another topic. But she decided, against all odds, to persist with her original topic.

Laura managed to overcome both problems thrown in her way, although neither was easy to do. First, she petitioned the Library of Congress to declassify the specific documents she needed. She wrote a persuasive letter explaining the historical value of her research and the new light it could shed upon many different aspects of America's past. The maturity she demonstrated in writing her plea and then campaigning about the campus to get prominent research faculty (as well as students and administration members) to sign the petition on her behalf was remarkable. I have never seen someone go after a goal with such ardor. She eventually accumulated over 1,000 signatures before she set off for Washington, D.C., to present the petition in person and argue her case, if necessary. The student newspaper wrote a feature article, and several updates, on Laura and her cause. The entire campus was impressed by her efforts. The Library consented and she was allowed access to the documents she wanted to study.

In the second case, Laura played her cards well and, again, showed great matu-rity in dealing with my colleague. She wrote him a letter laying out the reasons she believed her topic to be worthy of study. She also explained that she was personally a defender of Native rights and culture, in no way wanting or intending to do harm to the tribe's legacy. By highlighting her own contributions to Native study, she showed my colleague that she indeed had no evil agenda to pursue. She convinced him that the research was merely in pursuit of the truth, and convinced him that it was unlikely it would harm the reputation of contemporary Natives. My colleague, though of course still wary, appreciated Laura's attention to his concerns. Although a tough questioner in all thesis presentations, he judged her fairly. In the end, he was very impressed and pleased with her work. He even showed up at the graduation party her parents gave for her, indicating that the two had indeed become friends after the disagreement. Laura's interpersonal skills are clearly well developed. She holds her own, yet is appreciative of others' opinions and stakes, always giving attention where it is due. She is certainly stubborn, but she is also sensitive.

Laura's thesis was the best I have ever supervised. Although she entered a completely new area of study, meaning that there will long be unanswered questions and more room for research, she covered a lot of territory. She made convincing conjectures about the motives of the seven natives who supported the expansion of the western line, the exact nature of their collaboration with the white man, how their collaboration with the enemy affected their relations with fellow tribe members, and how it affected the future of the tribe. Her thesis required both an enormous amount of original

Recommendation for Laura:

research and a keen ability to analyze sparsely recorded data to come up with an accurate picture of history. Her writing, too, is better than that of most of our junior faculty. Moreover, and particularly important to her future in a law career, her passions about Native rights and culture today did not cloud her judgment or her ability to look accurately at the historical record. She was an impartial historian, willing to face up to evidence that she would have preferred to have been different.

Laura is not just an intellectual powerhouse (though that she is). She is also simply one of the finest young people I have ever had the pleasure of knowing. Her fire and enthusiasm in academics is matched by a similar zest for life in her other endeavors. She is thoughtful and warm, ready to share her emotions or lend an ear when it is needed. She became a very close friend of my family's during her senior year, and my kids (who still see Laura now and then) miss her baked treats and her skill as the best kick-the-can player they've ever known. She became so endeared to my wife and me that we used to leave our children with Laura when we went away. I miss being able to go on vacation knowing that my children are with someone responsible, mature, fun, and smart.

Please do not hesitate to contact me if you need any more information about this wonderful candidate.

Which one—John or Laura—would you select? Laura wins out easily, appearing to be the stronger candidate if we compare the two letters of recommendation. She may not even, in fact, be the stronger candidate, but this finely executed recommendation tips the balance well in her favor. Although John got his recommender to say good things about him, Laura got a lot more mileage out of her recommendation. She chose the right person—someone who could share classroom as well as personal experiences about her, and offer compelling as well as interesting anecdotes. Furthermore, Laura influenced the professor to include the right information to support her own positioning effort. The letter offers insight that goes well beyond regurgitating already known facts and assumptions.

The rest of this chapter is devoted to analyzing how to get your best supporters to do the same for you.

**WHAT ADMISSIONS DEANS SAY ABOUT
THE IMPORTANCE OF RECOMMENDATIONS**

Most letters will be positive, but not many will be substantive. On the other hand, a very large percentage of successful applicants will have had substantive letters of recommendation.   *Joyce Curll, Harvard*

A negative recommendation can certainly break an application, so applicants need to choose their recommenders carefully.   *Anne Richard, George Washington*

Letters from professors can add a lot to the picture of your academic performance. They know the kinds of things that law schools and law faculties will be interested in. They can show what kind of student you are, what your strengths (and weaknesses) are. For instance, they can describe in detail your writing ability and analytical skills. They can also discuss your class demeanor—your conduct and civility in class are incredibly important when it comes to assessing the contribution you are likely to make in law school. Professional recommendations, on the other hand, can show your impact on the organization and those around you. They can also show in what way, and to what extent, you are a team player.   *Todd Morton, Vanderbilt*

WHAT ADMISSIONS COMMITTEES LEARN FROM RECOMMENDATIONS

YOUR CLAIMS ARE TRUE

Recommendations are examined first for the extent to which they confirm and support your claims and your positioning. If your essay states that you are an indefatigable scholar, tirelessly researching both sides of an issue, the admissions officers reading your file will look closely to see if your Philosophy professor backs this up.

YOU HAVE MANY QUALIFICATIONS

Recommenders are asked to rate you in many areas, from written expression to initiative, from analytical thinking to maturity. Recommendations are an opportunity to provide more information about you, preferably illustrative rather than merely factual. Ideally, they function as a mirror image of the personal statement—a different (but equally positive) view of the same person.

THERE IS MORE TO LEARN ABOUT YOU THAN WHAT IS COVERED IN THE ESSAYS

Because you are limited in what you can include in your personal statement, it is difficult to present everything that might make you a desirable candidate. Therefore, it is important that your recommendations fill in the gap. By collaborating with your recommenders, you can use their letters to elaborate on areas of your candidacy that you were not able to cover in your portion of the application.

YOUR ACCOMPLISHMENTS HAVE IMPRESSED OTHERS

A recommender's positive comments show the admissions office that you have made an impression on others and ensure that your own self-descriptions are valid.

YOU ARE NOT HOPELESSLY INTROVERTED

Law schools prefer optimistic, extroverted candidates. A good recommendation can show that you are at ease in various social settings and are able to develop healthy relationships with others.

YOU CAN GET WHAT YOU WANT—SUBTLY

You must decide who should write on your behalf, determine what you want said about you, and get your recommenders to say what it is that you want said. Furthermore, you must make sure the letters are sent in on time. Typically, these are people over whom you have no authority, so you will have to use influence rather than command. The recommendation process, therefore, is a test of your ability to persuade.

THERE ARE SPECIAL CIRCUMSTANCES THAT INFLUENCE YOUR ACADEMIC OR EXTRACURRICULAR PERFORMANCE

Recommendations are a good place for shedding light on certain anomalies or special circumstances that might negatively influence your record. A professor can note that you are the only person in his tenure at the college successfully to handle taking a difficult language from scratch while also playing varsity sports and majoring in mechanical engineering. Thus your modest GPA should be viewed in this abnormal context.

YOU CAN ACCURATELY EVALUATE OTHERS AND THEIR PERCEPTIONS OF YOU

If you end up choosing someone who writes a mediocre recommendation, you will be doubted on many counts—including your judgment. It may even be assumed that you simply could not find two people who would say something good about you. This assumption is likely to kill your chances of admission.

> *One of the telltale signs that an applicant is not strong enough, or has too little experience, is that the recommenders and the applicant himself all tell the same stories. This suggests that the applicant has had only limited success.*

WHO SHOULD WRITE YOUR RECOMMENDATIONS?

Selecting appropriate recommenders involves sifting many factors. In general, you will be expected to submit recommendations from people who know you and are well placed to address the key issues concerning your candidacy. You will want them to state that you have the appropriate intellectual ability, self-discipline, and character to succeed at School X. The obvious choice—which any school's admission information will quickly tell you—is a professor who knows you well. (There are exceptions to this rule, which will be discussed in the next section.)

If there is not a wealth of obvious candidates, then your choice is relatively easy. However, it is to your advantage to be able to pick and choose. For those of you who are reading this ahead of the game, and have not yet forged relationships with two or three talented professors, start now. After selecting a professor as an ideal supporter for you, make sure to be in several of his or her classes over a period of time. Sign up for office hours. Make yourself known as an intelligent—but not obnoxious—presence in class.

AN ADMISSIONS DEAN DISCUSSES CULTIVATING RECOMMENDERS

Particularly early in college it's good to think about whose courses you want to take—and then about your conduct in those courses. As a general rule, the best recommendations come from professors who have taught you in several courses and worked with you over a sufficient period of time to be able to offer real insights into you and your performance. *Todd Morton, Vanderbilt*

Having done this, it should be simple to follow these rules:

1. ***Choose people who know you well.*** Do not choose the Nobel Prize–winning chair of the English Department if all he is going to say is that you sat

in the front row and seemed to be paying attention. Instead, choose people who can make the recommendation credible and powerful by illustrating the points they make with anecdotes that show you at your best. Need we say it? The people who will be able to do this are those who know you well.

2. ***Choose people who genuinely like you.*** Why? People who like you will take the time to write you a good recommendation. This is impressive in its own right. A recommendation that looks as though it took only five minutes to write suggests that that is exactly how much time the recommender felt you deserved. In contrast, a recommendation that looks carefully done and well thought out suggests that the recommender is committed to helping you. One other reason for choosing someone who likes you: She or he will try to put a positive spin on things, choosing examples that show you in a good light and describing them as positively as possible. Someone who does not much care may well write the first thing that comes to mind.

3. ***Choose people who can write well.*** Do not assume that all professors are created equal, particularly when it comes to articulating themselves. Pay attention, for example, to the written comments your professors leave on your papers. How eloquent—and pertinent—are their critiques? The last thing you want is a recommender who, being unable to express himself well, is consequently unable to convey his strong, positive view of you.

4. ***Choose people from a range of fields and backgrounds.*** If you are sending schools more than one recommendation letter, be sure to choose people who will be able to provide different—complementary—profiles of you. Selecting two English professors who specialized in Chaucerian literature, for example, will very likely make for two dangerously similar letters. Law schools will wonder about the depth and breadth of your skills and interests, and if you are capable of interacting with more than one type of person.

   If you have been out of school for some time, consider submitting a combination of professorial and employer recommendations.

5. ***Choose people of different genders.*** This is particularly true if you look like someone who may not do well under the supervision of people of a certain gender (if you are a male army lieutenant, for example, consider having the female captain write a letter of recommendation). This rule is not hard and fast, however; only select on the basis of gender if it is otherwise a close call.

6. ***Choose people who can address one or more of the key subjects: your brains, your character, your professional success, or your leadership skills.***

Brains. The ideal person can address the following:

- Academic achievement
- Analytical ability
- Quantitative skills
- Originality
- Healthy skepticism
- Imagination and creativity
- Communication skills (written and oral)

- Capacity for independent work
- Research skills
- Effectiveness in class discussions, debates, meetings, and so on
- Problem-solving skills
- Thoroughness
- Ability to synthesize material

Obviously, not just any professor or employer will do. Choose someone who has seen your abilities in more than one format. A thesis advisor, for example, fits the bill perfectly—someone who knows your writing intimately, and has heard you defend it verbally; someone who has watched you pull together a brilliant project; someone who knows your ability to digest a large amount of material. If it has been a long time since you have been in school, or your thesis advisor disliked you or passed away, you may have to find a substitute. Anyone who has seen you work on difficult intellectual challenges is a possible recommender. This might be someone who taught several courses you have recently

Character. The ideal person can address the following:

- Dependability
- Motivation and sense of initiative
- Honesty and integrity
- Sense of humor
- Self-discipline
- Energy
- Perseverance and work ethic
- Independence
- Potential for growth

- Open-mindedness
- Responsibility
- Leadership
- Maturity
- Judgment
- Concern for others
- Social commitment
- Concern for justice
- Interpersonal relations

taken to improve your knowledge in a field related to your career, someone who has taught seminars to your department, or even a manager under whom you have done intellectually challenging work.

One or both of the people you have chosen to recommend you on issues of professional success and brains should be able to address the character issue, too. In other words, you do not need a spiritual or moral leader to address issues of character. The person you select, however, must have seen you in a large number of different circumstances to be able to address these broad issues; his or her knowledge of you may have to be deeper than that required to address your intellectual abilities, for example.

Professional success. The ideal person can address the following:

- ➤ Overall work habits
- ➤ Self-confidence and poise
- ➤ Creativity
- ➤ Thoughtfulness
- ➤ Ability to acknowledge valuable inputs
- ➤ Ability to work with others
- ➤ Ability to motivate others
- ➤ Ability to make wise decisions
- ➤ Ability to retain self-control ` under stressful conditions

- ➤ Communication skills
- ➤ Negotiation skills
- ➤ Conflict-resolution skills
- ➤ Organizational and planning abilities
- ➤ Ability to manage a budget
- ➤ Leadership qualities
- ➤ Ability to analyze difficult problems
- ➤ Overall potential for a career in law

The person most likely to be able to assess your professional success—and therefore potential—is your current employer, preferably one who has seen you in operation over a period of time. You may not be able to use your current employer, however. If not, your next best choice might be a prior employer, someone to whom your boss reports (and who has seen your work on a number of occasions), a client, or even a competitor or rival (such as one of your peers). If you do not choose your current boss, or someone else who is an obvious choice, it will be helpful for you to explain why you have chosen not to have the obvious choice write on your behalf.

The leadership attributes might be evident in your professional success, as

Leadership skills. These may be evident from your professional success, as high-lighted above, or in a school or extracurricular setting.

- Achievement in elected or appointed positions
- Ability to motivate others
- Decision-making ability
- Team-building ability
- Responsibility to subordinates
- Priority-setting ability
- Goal-setting ability
- Ability to adapt to and lead change
- Ability to develop subordinates (and others)

- Embodiment (and encouragement) of values
- Ability to develop a sense of value and purpose in work
- Commitment to a vision
- Integrity
- Internal drive
- Maturity

highlighted above, or in another setting. Thus, you might choose to have an employer, head of a charitable organization for which you volunteer, or faculty advisor to a club you ran at college emphasize your leadership qualities.

IS IT ACCEPTABLE TO USE EMPLOYERS AS RECOMMENDERS?

Yes. Although admissions directors often state that they prefer to receive letters of recommendation written by professors, law schools are slowly shifting toward a professionally oriented model. More than half of the top schools state very explicitly in their admissions information that they accept, and find value in, recommendations from employers. Columbia, for instance, requires that those working full-time submit a letter from their employer (or commanding officer). Given that law is much more of a *business* than ever before—in conjunction with the fact that the age of the average law student is rising—an applicant's professional success is highly relevant. Firms desire mature people with real-world experience and savvy; consequently, law schools are seeking older applicants who possess these qualities and experiences. What all of this amounts to is an increase in the value of employer recommendations.

**MAKING THE MOST OF AN
EMPLOYER RECOMMENDATION**

Employer recommendations are particularly valuable when they address what law schools value most: analytical skills, teamwork and leadership abilities, and written and oral communication skills. (For a discussion of what makes your job performance noteworthy, consult "Describe Your Current Job" in Chapter 10.)

Depending on the results you have achieved in your line of work, a recommendation written by an employer may very well be superb—and, in some cases, necessary. There are two reasons for this. First, your most recent accomplishments can lessen the sting from undergraduate mistakes. Second, you **want** to highlight a job that provided excellent preparation for a legal career. If you feel your employer has a keen understanding of your intellectual abilities and capacity for law school work, then his or her recommendation may make all the difference in your application.

There are other notable reasons why a letter by an employer may be necessary. The older you are, the less likely a professor will remember you enough—if at all—to write a detailed, sensitive critique of your intellect, analytical skills, and potential as a lawyer. Additionally, the greater the breach between college and law school, the more likely it is that you will have matured into a very different person, with honed skills and altered goals. In fact, if you have worked for five or more years outside of college, and have no letter from an employer regarding that part of your life, it is likely to look suspicious.

OTHER CRITERIA IN CHOOSING A RECOMMENDER

1. ***Choose someone able to support your positioning.*** If you claim to be a hard-core philanthropist and public interest advocate, at least one of your recommenders should be able to discuss your serious commitment to the public good. Failure to choose an employer, colleague, or client who has seen this type of work over a reasonable period of time would raise a major red flag.

2. ***Choose someone able to address any potential weak spot in your application.*** If you are an engineer worried that the admissions committee will presume you to be humorless, as we discussed earlier in the book, this is your chance to prove what an engaging and funny fellow you really are.

3. ***Beware the naysayers!*** Certain personal characteristics suggest that a person will be effective in their support. Someone who is exuberant about life in general will be a good choice as she is likely to describe an average

---

THE DEAN'S LETTER

A throwback to the time when college deans were expected to know a good deal about the students assigned to them, the "dean's letter" is still required by some law schools. They do not expect to learn much from it, given that deans seldom know much of value about their students; instead, schools generally use it to make sure applicants have not misbehaved at college.

ADMISSIONS DEANS COMMENT ON DEANS' LETTERS

Often a registrar fills this out. We want to make sure that there has been no trouble during college. It's also meant to be a check on what applicants say about their record. It's rarely a detailed letter based upon close knowledge of the applicant.   *Faye Deal, Stanford*

Few deans have personal relationships with their students now, so they seldom provide in-depth evaluations to us. Therefore, the dean's letter functions only as a disciplinary clearance—an assurance that an applicant hasn't been in trouble at college.   *Susan Palmer, Virginia*

We don't require a dean's letter unless there has been an academic or disciplinary problem. In such a case, we need to understand what happened. We also require a statement from the applicant about it in addition to the dean's letter. *William Hoye, Duke*

We don't require a dean's letter.   *Todd Morton, Vanderbilt*

---

performer as marvelous, whereas a dour complainer might describe the performer as terrible. Similarly, an articulate person is likely to write a more impressive recommendation than a poorly spoken one.

4. ***Seek out the voice of experience.*** Be wary about choosing someone who is not obviously more senior, since it will look strange to have someone junior to you writing on your behalf.

5. ***Timeliness counts.*** Choose someone who is reliable and therefore likely to complete your recommendations on time.

6. ***Where did the recommenders go to school?*** People who themselves graduated from a top college and, preferably, a top graduate or professional school as well can speak convincingly about your relative abilities.

ADMISSIONS DEANS GIVE ADVICE ON
WHOM YOU SHOULD CHOOSE AS A RECOMMENDER

GENERAL COMMENTS

Recommendations from employers are useful after a couple of years of work, not after six months. *Joyce Curll, Harvard*

We require two letters. We prefer one to be from an academic; if someone is coming straight from college, then both can be from professors. If someone has been out of school five-plus years, it's OK to submit only (or primarily) work-related ones. Most applicants, by the way, submit three recommendations. *Faye Deal, Stanford*

The best recommender is likely to be a professor or someone who has attended a strong law school. I do like to see serious letters from businesspeople, of course, which is to say letters that are detailed in regard to the candidate's analytical and business prowess. *Elizabeth Rosselot, Boston College*

We prefer recommendations from professors of upper-level, rather than introductory, courses. The best recommendations come from professors you've worked with closely and extensively, such as a thesis advisor or someone for whom you did a substantial research project. They can evaluate your work and also make more personal comments about you. The least helpful kind of recommendation is from a famous person who is friends with your parents (e.g., the senator who writes that "[Applicant] comes from a well-respected family . . ."). *Megan Barnett, Yale*

Find a professor you connect with: someone who can not only talk about you in an academic context but can also put a human face on the application for us. This may mean choosing a TA instead of a famous professor, because the TA has read your papers, graded your exams, seen you in a small section, and had all those informal conversations with you. *Chloe T. Reid, USC*

If someone says, "I'll get to it in a few weeks," it's a red flag showing he or she doesn't want to write for you. *Anne Richard, George Washington*

I like to get letters from BC law students. This is more powerful than having a student just drop by to praise someone, given that it takes more time and effort to write a letter—and these students have precious little time. *Elizabeth Rosselot, Boston College*

We get a lot of letters from politicians. It's more helpful if a person you worked for directly on the politician's staff can comment. Similarly, in a large course a graduate assistant who knows your work well from a recitation section is sometimes a better choice than the course professor might be. *Kenneth Kleinrock, NYU*

Must You Use a Professor?

If you are coming directly from college, we greatly prefer to see two letters from professors. If you have been out of college for two years or more, we still want to see at least one letter from a professor. If you have been out of college for several years, though, a professorial recommendation is less relevant to your candidacy. *Derek Meeker, Penn*

Former professors, especially those within an applicant's degree field, provide greater insight into an applicant's academic strength, analytical ability, and ability to perform well in a competitive graduate level program. On the other hand, if an applicant has taken a lot of large classes, and has limited ability to develop a strong relationship with his/her professor, it is appropriate to have a graduate assistant or T.A. provide a recommendation. *Monica Ingram, Texas*

It is important to use a professor. We need to judge how well you will do in a new, rigorously academic environment, which your prior professors are uniquely placed to help us do. *Ann Killian Perry, Chicago*

Advice for Older Applicants

If someone has been out of college for only a few years it is usually still possible to get an academic recommendation, although it's not absolutely critical. For someone who has been out longer, I would expect a letter from a current employer— or former supervisor if you can't reveal that you're thinking of leaving. *Kenneth Kleinrock, NYU*

Letters from professors are preferred; the second best are from employers or colleagues. The balance shifts the older someone is. *Edward Tom, Boalt Hall (Berkeley)*

It is not at all necessary that a thirty-year-old applicant submit a recommendation from an undergraduate professor. *Don Rebstock, Northwestern*

If you use recommendations from the workplace, ask that they give concrete examples that will help us predict your academic performance in law school. For example, your participation in meetings might suggest how you would engage in classroom discussion. *Megan A. Barnett, Yale*

Recommenders to Be Avoided

People assume that the bigger the name, the better the recommender. This is by no means true. We want to see the nitty-gritty details of what he/she knows about you. *Faye Deal, Stanford*

It's a rare circumstance when a high school teacher's recommendation will help you. Your relatives have to like you, so their comments are also seldom of much value. *Kenneth Kleinrock, NYU*

We're pretty good at reading between the lines—when recommenders have felt compelled to write on someone's behalf without being able to really support them. *William Hoye, Duke*

Regrettably, a common mistake made by applicants is to solicit recommendations from individuals, often in high places in the worlds of business, politics, and academe, who are unable to comment meaningfully about the applicant because their relationship with the applicant has been limited in time and by little direct contact, much less real interaction with the candidate. Often, in fact, the "celebrity" recommender knows the applicant's family better than the applicant himself or herself. *Jim Milligan, Columbia*

One of the classic mistakes is to choose a famous professor despite having only taken his or her large lecture course. *Todd Morton, Vanderbilt*

Applicants need to choose recommenders carefully. For example, I see a lot of letters saying that the applicant should apply to a school a tier below Stanford, or that Stanford would be a real stretch for him. There are also quite a few saying that they don't recommend the applicant. *Faye Deal, Stanford*

HOW MANY RECOMMENDERS?

Most of the top law programs in the country require two letters of recommendation. (See chart on following page.) Michigan, NYU, and UCLA require one; George Washington, Hastings, and Texas do not require any. Numerous programs state both the required and the maximum number. Chicago, for example, requires two but will accept as many as four. Thus, almost every program encourages recommendations, extra or otherwise. If you are applying to Hastings, by all means submit one or two letters. It would be a missed opportunity if you did not do so—unless you really have no one to say something positive about you.

Of course, it can be dangerous to go overboard. If the extra recommendation you are considering reiterates points that have been made elsewhere, do not submit it. On the other hand, if your recommender can add a truly different and important perspective on your candidacy, consider submitting it, but only if it is done in the right way. Approach your extra recommender and explain the circumstances. Then ask that he include with his recommendation a letter that you have written stating clearly that the other recommendations are meant to be read first, and that this additional recommendation is to be considered only if the school would consider it appropriate. In other words, you offer this recommendation as helpful additional material to be consulted at the discretion of the admissions committee.

	RECOMMENDATION REQUIREMENTS		
	0	1	2
Boston College			x
Boston University			x
UC Berkeley (Boalt Hall)			x
UC Davis			x
UCLA		x	
Chicago			x
Columbia			x
Cornell			x
Duke			x
Georgetown		x	
George Washington	x		
Harvard			x
Hastings		x	
Illinois			x
Michigan		x	
Minnesota			x
Notre Dame			x
Northwestern		x	
NYU		x	
Pennsylvania			x
Southern California			x
Stanford			x
Texas	x		
Vanderbilt			x
Virginia			x
Wisconsin			x
Yale			x

ADMISSIONS DEANS CONSIDER HOW MANY RECOMMENDATIONS YOU SHOULD SUBMIT

We require two but accept up to four recommendations. Make sure that each extra recommendation offers an additional, different insight about you. *Ann Killian Perry, Chicago*

You need to make sure that any recommendations you submit are strong ones. Request a copy of each so that you can be sure of their strength because even people who mean well can end up not helping your candidacy. *Monica Ingram, Texas*

A twenty-two-year-old applicant would be wise to keep to two recommendations. Someone who has been working for three or four years might want to give us three if, for example, he or she has two faculty recommendations on file and also submits one from an employer.   *Elizabeth Rosselot, Boston College*

We require one letter; people often give us two or three. But, there is a point at which you may be demonstrating poor judgment in submitting too many. *Kenneth Kleinrock, NYU*

APPROACHING A POTENTIAL RECOMMENDER

Ideally, you should start the process about three months before the recommendation deadline. Begin your overture to a potential supporter by scheduling a 30- to 45-minute conference with her. (You will get a better response by having this meeting in person rather than by telephone.) Run it as a proper business meeting, with a typed agenda and outline of each matter you want to share. Explain briefly where you wish to go in your career and what it will take to get there. Explain how you plan to fully take advantage of a law degree. Then tell her what is required in the application process, being careful to explain how important the applications are, including the recommendations. Tell her that you have been considering having her write on your behalf.

Now comes one of the critical parts of the recommendation process. Make sure each recommender is going to write a very favorable recommendation for you. The way to be sure of this is by giving the person a chance to beg off if she is unable to write on your behalf. If she is uncomfortable about writing for you, because she knows that honesty would require her to be less than highly favorable, she will take this opportunity to suggest that someone else might be more appropriate. If she gives this kind of answer, do not press her. Thank her for her time and move on.

If, on the other hand, she is encouraging, give her a further briefing. Tell her how much work will be involved, noting that you will make the process as painless as possible for her, thereby limiting her involvement to something under three hours. (If time is a major issue for her, suggest that you write a first draft that she can then quickly "adapt." See the discussion below in this regard.) Tell her which schools you are considering, and the reasons for each. Explain how you are trying to position yourself in general, and note any differences as to positioning for particular schools if necessary. Show her what questions she will need to answer about you, and how these relate to your desired positioning. Suggest stories she can tell about you, and how these will fit in with the questions. Provide her with plenty of detail.

MAKING YOUR RECOMMENDER'S JOB EASY

Try to do as much of the work as you can, since your recommender is undoubtedly busy. Give her plenty of time to write the recommendation. Be sure to give her:

➤ The deadline for each application

➤ Stamped, addressed envelopes

➤ Several copies of each form, with the objective data (your name, address, etc.) already filled in

➤ Copies of your own essays, and a description of your positioning strategy

➤ If she is writing recommendations for all of your target schools, tell her which main points to discuss to satisfy the requirements for each school in one general letter (although she will still need to fill in the grid ratings for each school). Note that this requires you to know precisely to which schools you are applying

➤ Samples of the work you did for her

➤ A list of your recent (and past!) activities, including why you undertook them, in light of your interest in and suitability for law school

➤ An outline of what you wish her to discuss

➤ "Canned" descriptions of the stories you want her to tell

➤ Your résumé (CV)

➤ Your transcript(s)

Be sure the recommender understands what is important and how to write convincingly—i.e., using appropriate stories.

Suggest that the recommender write a general letter addressing each question asked by the schools to which you are applying. Your outline material should provide her with the basis for writing this letter; leave this material with her. You will have thus saved her a great deal of work. The letter can be made user-friendly by placing the topic addressed in each paragraph in bold print, so that readers can quickly pick out the points that are of greatest interest to them. Hint that it would be beneficial for your recommender to explicitly compare you with others who have gone to this or another comparable school. Have her quantify her claims whenever possible. For example, instead of "intelligent," have her write "one of the three most intelligent people I've ever taught."

If your recommender is extremely busy, yet another possibility exists for you. She may suggest that you do a first draft of the recommendation, which she will presumably alter to her taste later on—or she may ask that you write it, and she will simply sign it. This technique, however, can be risky. To assume the perspective and tone of someone in your recommender's position—whether that be academic or professional—requires experience and perspicacity. Chances are, you will end up sounding timid, stilted, and totally one-dimensional.

Generally, writing your own recommendations is safe only if you have a thorough understanding of what your recommender's expectations were, and why you fulfilled them. You are more likely to possess this knowledge if you have been out in the "real world" for a year or two. It is easier to step into the shoes of an employer than a professor; the former's expectations, standards, and judgments are more self-apparent. Penetrating the world of academia is a difficult task, particularly while you are still in it.

Whether your recommender writes your recommendation or has you do it, this well-thought-out approach to the matter will prove helpful in a number of ways. First, this approach minimizes the chance that you will end up with a lukewarm recommender. Second, your approach will have been highly organized and professional. If you had followed the nervous, pleading approach, why should she tell Harvard that you are an effective communicator, destined for litigating greatness? Third, you know in advance what stories she will tell. This means you will retain control of the admissions process insofar as you have a number of stories you want told about yourself, without undue repetition. Fourth, following this process means you will have a well-written recommendation. If your recommender writes it, she will almost certainly use your outline, just as she will treat the matter seriously because you have done so. If you write the recommendation, you can certainly manage to put together a good statement. Fifth, your professional approach means your recommender is likely to improve her opinion of you, meaning she will be a better resource for your future career than she otherwise would have been.

TIPS ON HANDLING DIFFICULT ISSUES

➤ If you find yourself in the position of writing all your own recommendations, formatting them differently and making them sound as if each recommender was the actual author will help camouflage their authorship. For example, you can format one as a letter and another in the question-and-answer format. Similarly, you can use different typefaces and font sizes.

➤ If you went to a second-rate or unknown university, or had mediocre grades even at a top school, you should have recommenders take every opportunity to discuss your analytical skills and intellectual leanings.

> ➤ If you are unable to get a recommendation from someone the admissions committee would expect to write on your behalf, be sure to explain why either in the optional essay question or in a separate note.

> ➤ Schools are required to allow applicants to see the recommendations written on their behalf unless the applicants waive that right. You should waive that right: Schools will interpret this as a move on your part to encourage honest expression. In fact, you should work together with your recommender on the recommendation, so you will be privy to it as it is being created, meaning that you have little to gain in any event by having the right to get the school to furnish a copy.

ADMISSIONS DEANS DISCUSS HOW YOU SHOULD HANDLE YOUR RECOMMENDERS

There are three things you should give a recommender: time, a copy of your transcript, and a résumé. In addition, let them know what you are trying to do and how you are going to do it.   *Joyce Curll, Harvard*

Give the recommender a lot of lead time; otherwise they can't do a thoughtful job and resort to boiler plate. Just because it's your deadline doesn't mean it's their deadline.   *Kenneth Kleinrock, NYU*

You need to sit down and talk with them to make sure they'd like to write for you. Then provide them with a transcript and a résumé, and possibly a personal statement. Make sure they won't contradict anything you are submitting.   *Anne Richard, George Washington*

We place more faith in recommendations when applicants have waived their rights to see them (and nearly all do waive their rights).   *William Hoye, Duke*

You have the duty to help a recommender remember why you are so impressive. Give your recommender whatever help you can, including information regarding the context in which you performed. You might photocopy the top page of a paper (containing the professor's comments) and provide a copy of your résumé and your transcript.   *Kenneth Kleinrock, NYU*

INCREASING THE VALUE OF YOUR RECOMMENDATIONS

A good recommendation should show you are an outstanding individual, one who is an appropriate candidate for a top law school by virtue of having the appropriate intellectual potential. It should also support your individual positioning strategy.

The following are true of an effective recommendation:

- It is well written. It is grammatically correct and reflects the thinking of a well-educated person.

- It reflects substantial thought and effort. In other words, the person cares enough about you to spend the time to be as helpful as possible.

- It shows you to be a distinctive candidate. The use of examples will aid this considerably.

- The writer knows you well enough to provide several highly specific examples to illustrate her points. These should not be the same examples you use in your essays or that other recommenders note. As with your essays, the use of illustrative stories and examples will make the recommendation credible and memorable. This will also show that the recommender knows you well, thereby showing that you did not have to "shop" for one.

- The recommender does not mention things best handled elsewhere in your application, such as your LSAT score.

- The writer discusses your growth and development over time. Your drive to improve yourself, in particular, is worth comment because your interest in learning and improving is part of what will make you a desirable student.

- The recommender explicitly compares you with others who have gone to this or another comparable school. Have her quantify her claims whenever possible. For example, instead of "intelligent," have her write "one of the three most intelligent people ever to work for me" (or, even better, "one of the three most intelligent of over one hundred grads of Ivy League schools to work for me").

- The person shows how you meet the requirements, as she sees them, of a top lawyer.

The general impression should be that a person of a very high caliber wrote a well-thought-out, enthusiastic recommendation for you.

ONE-SIZE-FITS-ALL RECOMMENDATIONS

In an ideal world, all recommenders would take the time and energy to fill out each recommendation form for applicants' many target schools. Of course, in an ideal world, each day would contain 36 hours and each week eight days. Thus, reality dictates that many recommenders simply write one comprehensive letter to be sent to all of an applicant's target schools.

For the sake of efficiency, it is generally fine for a recommender to write a single letter of recommendation and attach it to the recommendation form for each school, *as long as it answers all of the questions that a school poses.* In other words, recommenders should not feel they have to reinvent the wheel for each of your target schools, but they must be thorough and complete in performing their task. It is important that all recommenders realize the importance of explicitly answering all questions asked by each school. They must also fill out any required grids or checklists (concerning your qualities and abilities) that a school provides as part of its recommendation form if they choose to attach a one-size-fits-all recommendation letter.

In addition, there may be special cases in which a particular school should receive a slightly modified or amplified version of a recommendation letter. For example, if your positioning efforts are different for one of your target schools, you will want to ask your recommenders to keep this in mind (if it is appropriate, given their knowledge about you) for that school. Or if your recommender herself attended one of your target schools, she will want to make note of that in the recommendation.

**AN ADMISSIONS DEAN DISCUSSES
ONE-SIZE-FITS-ALL RECOMMENDATIONS**

It is absolutely acceptable for a recommender simply to check the grid and attach a general letter. *Andy Cornblatt, Georgetown*

HOW LONG SHOULD THE RECOMMENDATION LETTER BE?

The recommendation forms may provide limited space for a given response, but your recommender may want to write more. Should you or your recommender treat such space limitations as the ultimate authority? No. Recommenders are given some latitude in choosing how best to write a recommendation. This is one reason why it is perfectly appropriate to use the one-size-fits-all recommendation, which does not even try to fit into the provided format.

Typically, single-spaced letters of recommendation are at least one page in length, more often two or three.

ADMISSIONS DEANS DESCRIBE WHAT A GOOD RECOMMENDATION DOES

Frankly, I like a detailed recommendation. A flat recommendation, such as the following, is of no value. "John Smith received the highest grade in my class. He appears to be very bright. I know of no problems in his record. I think that he would make a very good lawyer." In this case, it's like not having a recommendation. This student clearly asked the wrong person for a recommendation. *Faye Deal, Stanford*

People mistakenly think recommendations are about adjectives: He's great, smart, etc. The information contained often matters more than the description. With mixed indicators, show why the positive one is the better indicator. For example, if someone has a strong LSAT and mediocre grades, show why grades were lower because of the applicant's excellent extracurricular efforts—and therefore that the LSAT is the better indicator. *Andy Cornblatt, Georgetown*

Relatively few recommendations are good, detailed letters that cause me to see candidates differently. *Elizabeth Rosselot, Boston College*

Most recommendations aren't very helpful because they are so general. They should be backed up with examples and specifics, yet only 10 to 15 percent are. *Don Rebstock, Northwestern*

A good letter may include weaknesses, and especially how they were overcome. *Faye Deal, Stanford*

Through recommendations we hope to learn how well the applicant learns and works collaboratively. This proven ability to learn from and teach one's peers, to appreciate as well as challenge others' points of view, to know how and when to lead a discussion, or to allow (indeed, encourage) others to lead are traits our committee values highly in a candidate because they are indispensable to enriching learning while in law school, and to working effectively thereafter. *Jim Milligan, Columbia*

Your recommenders should include specific examples illustrating their general statements. It is also helpful if the recommender can place the applicant in a larger context: "She is one of the top ten students I've seen in twenty years of teaching" or "He is comparable to the Student X, who was accepted last year." *Megan A. Barnett, Yale*

Recommenders can show what is not obvious from someone's credentials or résumé. For example, a professor can help a candidate by showing in what respects she thinks his numbers understate his potential. To argue that he will be a wonderful lawyer, despite a soft LSAT or GPA, though, requires demonstrating that he performed well in a way that such numbers don't capture. Perhaps he was a real asset in class. In that case, how did he get the most out of other students in the class—by encouraging their comments, helping them develop their ideas, and so on? Perhaps he tackled a paper topic that spurred useful discussions and inspired others to tackle better topics than they might otherwise have done. Or maybe he helped edit the professor's book manuscript and offered thoughtful comments in doing so.   *Sarah C. Zearfoss, Michigan*

A good professor's recommendation comes from someone who has taught you in a situation in which he or she could make an individual judgment about the quality of your work. Get a professor willing to talk about you as a classmate: how you treat your classmates; how you respond to challenge and criticism, which are the key to law school. I'm very interested in how a person reacts when his ideas are challenged, whether he gets defensive or overly aggressive. To be a good classmate you have to be able to mix it up, in a positive way.   *Rick Geiger, Cornell*

Recommendations are extraordinarily important in the application process. What a recommender says about an applicant can truly make or break on application. Recommendations can corroborate what we see elsewhere in the file, assist in explaining a weakness or problem, or shed additional light on something that is just touched upon elsewhere in the application.   *Renée Post, Penn*

The most effective recommendations attest to your academic strengths, reasoning skills, and ability to complete successfully a rigorous program. (For those who have been working for a number of years, a supervisor who can evaluate the nature and quality of your work is a good recommender, too.) The least effective recommendations are those that just attest to your good character and do not offer any insights into your academic strengths or other abilities.   *Monica Ingram, Texas*

The letter of recommendation that is most helpful to our committee and to an applicant's candidacy is one where the author can speak meaningfully about the applicant, because the author has been in a position, over a significant period of time, to personally observe the applicant's intellect, character, and personality in action, and perhaps in different settings (e.g., work, play, athletics, individual or group tasks), and perhaps in the same setting but under various conditions (e.g., stress, pressure of deadlines, dealing with difficult peers or clients, or with situations requiring subtlety, tact, diplomacy, discretion).   *Jim Milligan, Columbia*

I wish more people would compare candidates with others who have attended the law school. If the comparison is to a recent enough student, it's really helpful because we'll remember that student. This also says something about the recommender, that he/she knows his/her students well. It's also helpful if a professor ranks a student versus all students taught—for example, "this is one of the top ten students I've taught in twenty-three years." *Faye Deal, Stanford*

It's great if recommenders can compare an applicant with others attending top schools. *Elizabeth Rosselot, Boston College*

THE MECHANICS OF SUBMITTING RECOMMENDATIONS

There are a variety of ways to submit recommendations. The recommenders can send them directly to the law schools or they can send them in sealed envelopes to you, for you to forward them to the schools. Professors can submit to your college's recommendation service, where they are kept on file until you request that they be sent to schools. Or recommenders can submit them to LSDAS (the Law School Data Assembly Service, discussed in Chapter 5), which will copy and submit them to schools you specify. In general, schools will accept recommendations submitted via any of these methods, but many prefer that you use the LSDAS service.

Not everyone can or should use the LSDAS service, though. International applicants, for reasons discussed in Appendix VI, may or may not be able to use it. In addition, applicants applying early action or early decision may need to have their recommenders submit their recommendations directly to the law schools to meet the October or early November deadlines.

MAKING SURE RECOMMENDATIONS ARE SUBMITTED ON TIME

The law schools (or LSDAS, if you use its recommendation service) can keep you informed as to whether a given recommendation has arrived. If it has not arrived and time is getting short, contact your recommender and ask very politely how her effort is progressing and whether you can be helpful by giving her more information. This will tend to prod her into action without being annoying.

THE FOLLOW-UP

Be sure to send your recommender a thank-you note for her efforts and state that you will keep her informed as to your progress. This is simply good manners. If you need extra encouragement to do so, remember that you may need her services again if schools turn you down this time.

If you manage your recommender well, the chances are that she will submit your recommendations not long after. What should you do, however, if you call your schools and learn that a recommendation is missing? You can certainly call your recommender to encourage her to submit it soon. On the other hand, you can take a subtler approach and send her a follow-up note explaining that you have completed the application process and are currently awaiting schools' decisions. If she has not yet submitted the recommendation, this should spur her into action. If this does not work, contact her again and see if you can help the process along in some way, such as by writing a draft of what she might say.

Keep her informed as to each school's decision. Also be sure to tell her at the end of the process what you have decided to do, such as attend school X and turn down school Y, and why. At this point it would be highly appropriate to send her a small thank-you gift. Very few people do this. It is not a terribly expensive gesture, but you can be sure that you will gain greatly in her estimation for having done it.

Do your best to stay in touch with her as you go through law school, even if this means nothing more than dropping a short postcard or e-mail to her with a few comments about your progress. Staying in contact shows further sincerity in your appreciation of her efforts, and also assures that you maintain contact with a supporter and possible lifetime career advisor.

Remember that your recommender is in a position to help your career for years to come and has already shown a distinct willingness to do so. You should do your best to reward her helpfulness. One sound reason for going to a top law program is to take advantage of the networking possibilities it offers. It would be silly to throw away a very good contact prior to arriving at law school by failing to treat your recommender appropriately.

SPECIAL NOTE FOR INTERNATIONAL STUDENTS

If you have a potential recommender who is not able to write well in English, you can help matters greatly by writing up some stories or even the full draft of a recommendation for her. To the extent that you write well in English, your recommender will be all the more likely to use what you have written rather than struggling with the language on her own. Be sure, also, to provide the recommender with an appropriate editor who is a fluent, native speaker of English. This can be a colleague with whom you are both acquainted, or anyone else about whose editing and grammar skills you feel confident.

EMPLOYER RECOMMENDATION EXAMPLE

The beginning of this chapter features a valuable, well-written academic recommendation by a professor for Laura. The following is yet another example of a successful recommendation, this time from an employer. (It is longer than would normally be appropriate, but the recommender has a lot of highly relevant information to share about a very strong candidate.)

Recommendation for Steve:

I hired Steve as an analyst to the media division of SB Bank (for which I am Managing Director) four years ago and I have worked with him daily since that time. Steve has taken initiative in his own career and has matured into an accomplished self-educator, finance analyst, "intra-preneur," and project manager. In fact, he has become the one person I rely on most to help me manage my division of our company.

I hired Steve because of his academic success, particularly in economics, and his intense desire to come to Wall Street in order to decide whether he wanted to follow a path in corporate law or corporate finance. He was honest with me from the beginning about the fact that he was not certain whether his talents and interests would push him farther into business or eventually to corporate law. I appreciated his honesty. I did not see a problem with this kind of ambiguity from a youngster, since a stint as an analyst at our bank is compatible with both goals. As Steve's inclination toward law has grown, he has taken several measures to ensure that he remains as tuned in to legal matters as possible. He has befriended our in-house counsel, having lunch with her often and even moonlighting for her as a research assistant on several occasions. He tries, when his time allows, to attend all of our drafting sessions with lawyers, even though it is not routine for those at the analyst level to be at such meetings. As a result, he has gained a fine command of much of the legal code (and thinking) involved in M & A, IPO, private equity, and LBO transactions.

As with most of my assistants, I gave Steve a trial by fire when he first arrived four years ago. I put him in charge of running my prospective client operations without giving him any training. I do this as a way to test a new hire's raw intellectual firepower and ability to think on his feet and deal with the unexpected. I was more than pleased with Steve's performance. He immediately figured out that the key to any busy corporate employee's job is prioritization. He developed his own system for handling our pitch calls by the target companies' sizes, time zones, financing needs, and levels of previous contact with us. The immediate result of his effort was an incredible 30 percent increase in new deal work; we began to acquire one new deal per month, each bringing in anywhere from $40,000 to several million dollars in fees. Steve's system was so effective that I asked him to make it a formality, incorporating it into our best practices efforts and teaching everyone in the office what it was all about. This system—which we nicknamed "SS" for "Steve's System"—still helps us to get appointed as the lead bank in deals. Our income generation has continued to set new records, due in no small measure to his brilliant plan.

Steve is not just excellent at managerial tasks: He is also a superb financial analyst. His M & A work, for example, is characterized by a thoroughness that exceeds that demonstrated by our MBA hires. He understands and applies the relevant financial theory, whether that be simple Capital Asset Pricing Model use of comparables or sophisticated valuation of real options. Similarly, he has a useful understanding of the accounting and tax treatment of business combinations. Finding a young analyst with this range of understanding is a treat, but Steve actually goes far beyond this in his work. He routinely excels in understanding the likely operational difficulties that will be experienced by a combined entity. For instance, one bank acquisition was initially pitched on the basis of proposed cost savings that would be made possible by combining systems and reducing retail branches. Steve's highly detailed analysis, based upon an in-depth understanding of the actual costs of combining the specific systems the two banks had in place and the locations of their branches, showed that the likely cost savings would be only 50–60 percent of the total and would take an extra eighteen months to be realized. (His analysis was, of course, all the more impressive for being outside his usual field.) This changed our advice to our client and dramatically altered the actual purchase price.

Steve's value has extended beyond our local office, too. Since realizing Steve's public speaking capabilities, I have taken him on the road with me when I deliver seminars to investment banking employees in other branches of SB (we have branches in San Francisco, London, Singapore, Shanghai, and Buenos Aires). I have shared the floor with him on numerous occasions; his contributions have always been well prepared and his answers to spontaneous questions insightful. He was once pressed by an important high-level executive attending one of our sessions to admit that the reason our biotech division is so financially successful is that we aim to become the secondary (rather than the lead) bank on most of our transactions. This type of practice concerns many executives of SB Bank because, although it may help the bank's finances in the short term, it jeopardizes our reputation in the banking world, making it a bad long-term strategy. SB has been warning all of our divisions to stay away from developing this kind of reputation, and has thus encouraged our division to take on more lead banking positions; we have often been scrutinized on this account. Steve handled the man's questioning exceptionally well, explaining our particular difficulties in securing the lead position on biotech deals (which represent a relatively new field for us) and the ways in which biotech banking is different from banking in other industries. Even at only twenty-five years of age, Steve has remarkable composure.

Steve is one of our firm's best assets. As I think you can see from the stories I have recounted here, he has intellectual smarts, sales ability, project-management ability, interpersonal skills, oral and written communication skills, creativity, and initiative. He is also a good guy, very well liked by everyone. Much of this is because he is humble about his talents and often tries to include others in his successes, so that they may benefit and grow and share the glory with him. In my experience, when a new, hotshot youngster joins a firm and starts making waves with all of his accomplishments, others tend to form a backlash against the person, perhaps in jealousy but also perhaps due to the newcomer's own inability to deal well with success. This is certainly not the case with Steve.

I wholeheartedly recommend Steve for your program. Please do not hesitate to call me if you have any questions or want to discuss his candidacy further.

Appendix VI

RECOMMENDATION BRIEFING OUTLINE

(The material below is meant to provide an outline to illustrate how you can structure briefing sessions with your recommenders to get them to provide you with the kind of recommendations you need.)

- My ultimate goals:
- How a law degree would help me to reach these goals:
- Why I should get a law degree now (or intend to do so later on):
- Which law programs best suit me:
  —Why/how:
- My positioning/ marketing for these schools:
- How he/she can help me:
  —Does he/she want to help me?
  —Total time required:
- Show application forms/explain that only "ticking the boxes" and writing a general letter is required.
- Take recommenders through outline of an appropriate letter.
  —Include details of stories, copies of reports, and so forth.
- Discuss style and form of the master letter.
- Deadlines:
- Explain the advantages of completing/submitting the applications early.

13

INTERVIEWS

— EXECUTIVE SUMMARY —

■

Establish your objectives:
—Convey a good impression.
—Impart your strengths.
—Demonstrate your knowledge.
—Gain information.

■

Prepare yourself:
—Learn the most likely questions.
—Know yourself and your qualifications vis-à-vis those of others.
—Know the school.
—Formulate your own questions.

■

Know what to expect from different types of interviewers:
—Admissions officers
—Alums
—Students

■

Practice via mock interviews, videotaping them if possible.

■

Familiarize yourself with the dos and don'ts of interviewing.

More and more schools are interviewing a significant number of the applicants they seriously consider admitting. One reason for this is that a person's interviewing ability is a very good indicator of how attractive he or she will be to employers during and after law school. An applicant with good "paper" credentials will be unattractive to a school to the extent that he or she is likely to be regarded negatively by employers later on. Another reason for interviewing is that schools can market themselves better by meeting individually with applicants. This is particularly relevant for the elite schools, which tend to feel that they are all chasing the same few thousand absolutely outstanding candidates. These schools welcome the chance to get a jump on their rivals by better assessing candidates and by promoting themselves to their top choices. A third reason is that an interview offers a school a unique opportunity to determine whether the applicant is likely to attend the school if admitted. This is of great importance to schools concerned about the impact of "yields" (the percentage of those accepted who enroll at the school) upon their *U.S. News* rankings.

Interviews offer schools the chance to learn much more about applicants. Some things are not readily determinable without a face-to-face meeting. These include your appearance, charm, persuasiveness, maturity, presence, and potential as an attorney. Interviews also provide an opportunity to probe areas insufficiently explained in the application.

ADMISSIONS DEANS DISCUSS WHOM THEY INTERVIEW

We offer and sincerely encourage interviews as an option for anyone interested. In addition, there are a number of people we'll call—if we want more information regarding any part of the file. It may also be that we're unsure of their awareness about the school. (We want people to apply as informed consumers. There is a tendency in the law school process for applicants to just ship off a bunch of applications without researching or thinking about each.) For some top candidates it may be that we want to undertake some pro-active marketing to them. *Don Rebstock, Northwestern*

We reserve the right to call an applicant in for an interview. We do it fairly often, especially as to those on our waitlist. *Rob Schwartz, UCLA*

We look to interview everyone we can—and are building our capabilities to interview all of our applicants. We are starting with on-campus interviews. Anyone visiting the school will have the option to interview, whether with an admissions officer or a student. We will then add off-campus interviews, with admissions officers, in places where our applicants are concentrated. We are also looking to develop an alumni network of interviewers across the country. When an in-person interview is not practical, we will use telephone interviews. *Todd Morton, Vanderbilt*

We look to interview those applicants we would like to get to know better. Maybe we have questions about items in their file, or there are mixed indicators. *Ann Killian Perry, Chicago*

Applicants apply, in writing, on a first-come, first-served basis. They are eligible to request an interview after their file is complete and before it has been handed over to the committee for a final decision. *Monica Ingram, Texas*

We interviewed 3,500 candidates out of some 4,700. *Don Rebstock, Northwestern*

We interview three different groups of students. The first group consists of about 50 students we have specific questions about. These interviews focus on the particular matter that concerns us. The second group consists of about 150 candidates that we select as a random cross-section of the group of promising applicants. We want to get a "flavor" or "feel" from them rather than more in-formation on a specific, preselected topic of concern. The third group consists of wait-listed applicants. All wait-listed applicants are entitled to an interview, which is provided at their request. About one-third to one-half of our wait-listed applicants request interviews. *Rick Geiger, Cornell*

We recently started to interview those on the wait-list. Each interview is held on campus and lasts for 25 minutes. The interviewer has read the candidate's file thoroughly and focuses the interview on the critical issues facing his or her can-didacy. *Elizabeth Rosselot, Boston College*

I interview a very small number of applicants a year, usually at the request of the admissions committee. Most often it's to have the candidate explain a specific is-sue from the past raised in the application, to make sure that it's been overcome. *Kenneth Kleinrock, NYU*

Nevertheless, the interviewing policy of schools is not uniform. Northwest-ern, for example, tries to interview all its applicants and Texas allows its appli-cants to request an interview, whereas Harvard and Michigan interview none of theirs. Other schools interview only those applicants who are borderline candi-dates—with strong enough credentials that they warrant a close look, but not so strong that they will be admitted without an interview.

Some schools use only admissions officers to conduct their interviews, whereas others use alumni extensively, and still others use third-year students. The schools that rely on admissions officers alone are obviously unable to do in-person interviews with all the applicants they might otherwise wish, due to the time and logistical constraints. For example, there is the problem of interviewing the candidate who is immersed in a round-the-clock project at a remote site in Alaska. Some get around this by doing telephone interviews; others simply evaluate the candidate on the basis of the written file alone.

SHOULD YOU INTERVIEW IF GIVEN THE CHOICE?

Most people feel they interview quite well, but the reality is that most do not. To become a good interviewee, you need to understand in advance what points you want to put across, what questions you are likely to be asked, and how to maximize your presentation to satisfy your needs and those of your interviewer. The keys to doing this are to analyze what you will confront and then to practice performing under realistic conditions. Doing this will help you to avoid going blank, letting slip things you intended to avoid, forgetting to mention important points, or being unable to keep the interview flowing in a comfortable fashion.

If a school permits you to request an interview, it is generally to your advantage to do so: You demonstrate initiative and show yourself to be a serious, conscientious applicant. Obviously, you go the extra mile and have nothing to hide in your background.

SHOULD YOU INTERVIEW IF REQUESTED TO?

If a school requests that you interview with it, it is in almost all cases a mistake not to do so. Failing to interview may be taken as an indication of a lack of interest in the school or a tacit acknowledgment of the weak points in your application. It is also an indication that you do poorly in one-on-one situations due to shyness or nervousness (or worse). There are often logistical considerations, of course, and schools are aware that it may not be realistic to expect you to travel 3,000 miles for a Wednesday morning interview, since it might necessitate your missing several days of work or class. The logistical barrier is not as great as it once was, however, now that schools have their representatives travel to most major cities and regions on a regular basis, or occasionally use alumni representatives on their behalf.

Although it is generally appropriate to interview, if you are sure to make a poor impression, either improve your interviewing abilities or maneuver to avoid an interview. The people who should avoid an interview are those who are pathologically shy, whose language abilities will crack under the strain, or who are so contentious that they will inevitably get into a verbal battle with their interviewers.

ADMISSIONS DEANS CONSIDER WHETHER YOU SHOULD INTERVIEW IF GIVEN THE OPPORTUNITY

We think that interviewing is critical when it comes to applicants on the borderline. The same is true for those on the wait-list: We tend to admit only those who interviewed really well. *Don Rebstock, Northwestern*

Anyone offered the opportunity should take it: it shows interest in Vanderbilt as well as giving a chance to put across their personal qualities. If someone declines the opportunity we will try not to read anything into that decision, but we obviously will be aware of it when making admissions decisions and will have less information about them. *Todd Morton, Vanderbilt*

Two types of candidates should try to get an interview: those who are below the 25th percentiles for LSAT scores and GPAs, and those who present themselves better in person than on paper. *Monica Ingram, Texas*

If you are interested in Chicago, this is another chance to highlight what you have to offer as well as to explain things that could use explaining. If you are invited to interview, we understand that the expense of coming to school may be too great for you to bear, so we won't hold failure to come here against you. *Ann Killian Perry, Chicago*

Some applicants think that an interview will surely help them; that is by no means the case. At a minimum you need to be able to express yourself well and show your educated curiosity about the school. *Kenneth Kleinrock, NYU*

If an applicant lives in close proximity to Northwestern and doesn't choose to interview, a red flag goes up. *Don Rebstock, Northwestern*

People who have difficulty interacting one-on-one maybe should avoid interviewing. But if that's the case, you should think about something other than law—reconsider the whole enterprise. *Albert R. Turnbull, Virginia*

BEFORE THE INTERVIEW

ESTABLISHING YOUR OBJECTIVES FOR THE INTERVIEW

The interview is important for all-too-obvious reasons. The fact that the school emphasizes the interview means that you have the opportunity to market yourself in a format in which most people do very little good for themselves. Some candidates are afraid of the interview and set themselves hopelessly limited objectives for it. They hope to get through it without embarrassing themselves. Or they hope that the interviewer likes them. You have the chance to make a very positive impression that will further your marketing efforts, so it is up to you to seize it. Do not simply hope to survive the interview; be determined to achieve positive results. Use it to reinforce all of your other positioning efforts.

You already have a marketing strategy in place, so go back to it when you are considering what you hope to accomplish in the interview. If you have positioned yourself as a civil rights crusader, for example, this positioning strategy will help you think through the interview and how to prepare for it.

Ask yourself the following questions at the start of your preparations:

1. How do you want the interviewer to think of you? What specific impressions, and information, do you want her to carry away from the interview?

2. How can you reinforce your strengths and address your key weaknesses?

3. How can you convey any important pieces of information that may not receive full attention (or any attention at all) in the written application?

4. How can you show that you know a great deal about the school—that you are well prepared for the interview?

5. How can you learn whatever you need to know to decide which school to attend?

Consider whether you would accept an offer of admission from this school. If so, tell your interviewer. No school wants to waste offers on people who will go elsewhere.

PREPARING FOR THE INTERVIEW

You should be mentally prepared to deal with four aspects of any interview. The first is understanding the format of a typical meeting as well as what to expect of your interviewer. You also must know what your objectives are, what the school offers, and what questions your interviewer is likely to ask.

TYPICAL FORMAT

No matter what type of interview is involved, the format is likely to include:

- Welcome
- A few easy "ice-breaker" questions, perhaps about how you are, whether it was easy to find the location, and so forth
- Some comments about the school
- Detailed questions, tracking your educational and then work history, or your responses on the school's application form
- The chance for you to ask questions
- Conclusion

The Interview Format

A typical interview will last between 30 and 45 minutes. The first few minutes of an interview may not involve substantive discussion, but they are still important in forming the interviewer's general impression of you. Therefore, do your best to appear confident and relaxed when answering these questions, before reaching the heart of the interview. Doing so will give you confidence and momentum to carry you through the following parts of the interview.

THE INTERVIEWER

You can expect different things of an interviewer depending on whether he is an admissions officer, an alum, or a student. Here are some guidelines on what you are likely to encounter with each type of interviewer.

INTERVIEWS WITH ADMISSIONS OFFICERS

An interview with an admissions officer is likely to be the most formal, although not necessarily the most difficult, of the three types of meetings. Admissions officers will conduct themselves in a gracious and poised manner—their job is not only to find out more about you, but also to leave you with positive impressions of their schools. They are thus likely to consider an interview as much a public relations opportunity as anything else. Admissions officers have plenty of experience interviewing and socializing, so they should not leave you feeling uncomfortable or lead you astray in your discussions.

ADMISSIONS DEANS DISCUSS THEIR INTERVIEW FORMATS

Telephone interviews are for about 30 minutes, in-person interviews for about 45 minutes. *Rick Geiger, Cornell*

Our interviews are scheduled for 30 minutes, but sometimes last longer. The interviewer will have seen the file. Most of our questions will be specific to the applicant, to the issues his or her candidacy raises. *Ann Killian Perry, Chicago*

Our interview lasts for 30 minutes, which includes a 15-minute writing exercise where the applicant produces a writing sample for critique. All of our interviews are conducted at the law school at the applicant's expense. *Monica Ingram, Texas*

Our interviews are conducted at the school. They're one-on-one, generally about fifteen minutes long. *Rob Schwartz, UCLA*

Because interviewing applicants is a significant part of an admissions officer's job, you can be sure he will be well-prepared and thorough. This does not mean, however, that he will spend a great deal of time with you. On the contrary, an admissions staffer's busy schedule will probably keep an interview short rather than allowing it to run overtime, whereas alums and students may have more leisure time to spend with you.

An admissions officer will want to gain some definite opinions about how your past experience and career goals suit you for his school's program, but that does not mean he will be uninterested in your personal life or in getting a feel for your general demeanor. Do not become a straight-and-narrow bore in front of the admissions folks! Be serious, but not overly so. They are concerned about filling their programs with lively candidates who offer more than just good grades and admirable future goals.

An admissions representative will obviously have the most thorough knowledge of the "official" aspects of the school, such as its strongest fields of law. But he will not necessarily know much about what life in the graduate dorms is all about.

INTERVIEWS WITH ALUMNI

An interview with an alum is likely to be the most relaxed and easiest of the three kinds of meetings. (Obviously, this is not *always* the case. An occasional alum will approach her role with a hard-nosed determination to let only the best applicants shine—perhaps she is one of those who remembers "the halcyon days" of her alma mater with pride and wants to ensure that her school maintains high standards. Similarly, you may simply run into a personality clash with an alum, as with any other type of interviewer.) In most cases, however, alums who volunteer their time to interview applicants do so because they are personable, friendly types who like to meet new people and are basically interested in promoting their schools.

Alumni interviews generally take place in the alum's home, in the alum's office, or at a public meeting space such as a café. Interviews that are conducted in an alum's home tend to be more relaxed and perhaps a bit longer than those that take place outside the home. Interviews with alums in their offices might seem more formal because of the setting and the interviewer's naturally more serious demeanor while at the workplace (especially if it is a law firm).

Although the alum will probably have received some information about you, her knowledge of you and your candidacy will almost surely be sparse. You should inquire of her or of the school's admissions office before the interview exactly what information she will have received so that you can bring appropriate materials with you to the interview to share and leave with her. You might want to bring a copy of your application or your résumé for her. She will probably not have seen enough of your application to know what your weaknesses are, and thus will not challenge you on these points. By the same token, she will not know your strengths and positive attributes, so to make a good impression you might have to talk at length about ideas you have already expressed in your essays and supporting materials. It is certainly fine to ask your interviewer, if she does not offer the information herself, how much background material she has been given so you know what to talk about and what not to repeat.

Alumni interviewers are instructed to follow certain guidelines, so they will definitely ask some crucial questions—but most will not be as meticulous or sharpshooting as an admissions officer or student interviewer. Alums tend to be chattier, more relaxed, and more interested in selling their beloved schools (or recounting their glory days for you) than they are in grilling you or using hard-ball tactics. Alums will tend to give you more of their time than an officer of the school would, making it a more relaxed, unrushed conversation.

One drawback of having an alumni interview is that your interviewer will not be present in admissions committee meetings to push your case personally and, furthermore, might not know how to formulate a winning position to support your application. Although schools that use alumni interviewers take their opinions seriously, an alum can convey her opinion about you only through a written evaluation that she sends to the admissions office after your meeting. Even with a favorable impression of you, if she is not an effective or convincing writer, her evaluation might not exude the necessary enthusiasm to make a serious impact upon the admissions committee when it sits down to review your file. She may be relatively unpracticed in the art of admissions and might not know what it takes to push an applicant from reject to wait-list status, or from wait-list to admit status. A professional admissions officer interviewer, on the contrary, will not only know how to convey a proper argument for a candidate, but might also be able to argue his case in person at an admissions committee session.

Another drawback of having an alumni interview is that those who have not been part of the school for some time will know the least about it. In other words, if you are hoping that your interview will provide a great opportunity to learn more about a school's program and how it compares with others, an interview with an alum who has been out of law school five years or more might leave you unsatisfied. Even if an alum graduated fairly recently, it is likely that certain aspects of the school have changed since her time or are currently in the process of revision. If the alum graduated quite some time ago, she probably understands the current atmosphere and curriculum very little, even if she is active in the alumni association and tries to keep up-to-date from the outside.

INTERVIEWS WITH CURRENT STUDENTS

Student-led interviews are not yet common, but several schools are using them (and several more look likely to begin using them). As rookies, students tend to be less smooth in their interviewing tactics. They may or may not be well prepared, despite training in interviewing techniques. (If the busy law school student is faced with the choice of finishing her law review "cite check" or preparing for an interview of a prospective student, how do you think she will spend her time?) A student interviewer may have trouble keeping the conversation flowing or thinking of things to say, in which case your job will be that much more difficult. She may even be just as nervous and ill-at-ease as you are (!) because of the responsibility and newness of her role. Of course, this is not usually the case. The students whom admissions offices recruit to conduct interviews of applicants are selected in part for their good communication skills and comfort acting as representatives of the school.

Students often ask applicants very tough questions. Sometimes they simply do not have enough perspective and life experience to realize what is and is not important. Furthermore, because they are so steeped in the intricacies of the law school experience, they naturally have a lot of interview material at their immediate disposal. They know what life at the school is like, and thus can come up with very directed questions, maybe even ones that are so specific that they seem useless for obtaining relevant "big picture" information about you. This might especially be true if you and your interviewer have something in common, such as an interest in environmental law. When this is the case, your interviewer has even more interview material at her disposal. She might thus be tempted to ask you an extraordinary question such as, "Our renowned Professor So-and-So, as you probably know, just argued a major case before the Supreme Court. Do you agree with his principal arguments?"

There is no way to prepare for this kind of treatment. If this happens in your interview, just try to relax, appear calm and confident, and probe the interviewer for further explanation if the question is confusing or entails an understanding of theories or issues about which you know nothing. The interviewer is probably just trying to impress you (or herself) with her seasoned knowledge. Do not let it get to you; just tackle it as best you can and move on.

This, of course, does not always occur. Some student interviewers are likely to be as bouncy, friendly, and relaxed as alums—people with whom you will feel at home, with whom you could imagine becoming friends. You are fortunate if this is the case, but remember to be alert and serious; do not let your guard down just because you see a welcoming face in front of you. You want to match your interviewer's demeanor, but do not forget that this interview "counts," which means that you must sell yourself and why you should be admitted to the school. Selling yourself to a current student is a bit tricky, because you do not want to appear cocky or obnoxious. It is easier to market yourself aggressively with a more official administrator whose job it is to be impressed with you than it is to someone on a peer level. (This is somewhat like being able to proudly share good grades with your parents in a way that might be inappropriate with your best friend, who would find you arrogant and conceited for bragging to her about your success.)

An interview with a student is likely to be the most useful for your own fact-finding purposes. Because students are themselves involved in the day-to-day operations of the school, they will be able to give accurate answers to many of your most detailed questions. You will probably feel more at ease asking them about the nonacademic side of law school life as well, thus discovering more than you might have wanted to know about the quality of the food in the cafeteria or how often you can expect to get away to hit the ski slopes. But be astute about the types of questions you ask—by the end of the interview you will probably be able to sense whether or not your student interviewer will welcome the kinds of casual or odd inquiries that you would probably not dare to ask an admissions officer. If a student interviewer, for example, jokes with you about how wonderful he found the Pass–Fail option to be when he realized he was not doing well in a Contracts class, it is probably fine to ask him how many times a student is allowed to use the Pass–Fail option; on the other hand, if your interviewer seems particularly serious about academics or mentions that he thinks the grading scale is too lax, it is not a good idea to ask him this kind of question.

ADMISSIONS DEANS TALK ABOUT WHO DOES THE INTERVIEW

Virtually all of our interviews are done by one of our professional admissions staff. *Rick Geiger, Cornell*

Our interviewer might be me or another admissions officer, one of 20 current students, or one of 500 alumni volunteers. There is no need to seek an admissions officer, let alone me, as the interviewer because all interviews are accorded equal weight in the admissions process. *Don Rebstock, Northwestern*

Previously, we hired a UT Law graduate to conduct the interviews. This year, however, a member of the admissions office staff will conduct the interviews. *Monica Ingram, Texas*

Admissions professionals—those on my staff as well as myself—conduct the interviews. *Rob Schwartz, UCLA*

Members of the admissions committee, usually admissions officers, conduct the interviews. *Ann Killian Perry, Chicago*

INTERVIEW EVALUATION FORMS

Northwestern uses the interview evaluation form on pages 353–354. It lays out the areas that are of interest to the school and thus the qualities you will want to show. This evaluation form may not capture everything that could be relevant in a candidate, but certainly captures enough to show you the way in which a school will assess you. Other schools, of course, have their own approaches, but they tend to be similar to the one shown here. The primary differences are that some schools use much briefer forms.

KNOWING THE SCHOOL

Chapter 3 examines criteria relevant to choosing the right school for you. It also details how to find the information necessary for making a well-informed decision. Let's assume you have read that chapter and followed its advice prior to applying. Now that you are preparing for school interviews, it would be a good idea to review the information you assembled for any school with which you are likely to interview. In particular, you should be extremely familiar with the information that the school publishes about itself. If you tell the interviewer that you plan to specialize in admiralty law, but the program offers no such specialization, you will look foolish.

If you are going to interview at the school itself, try to spend several hours in advance exploring the school and its environs. Talk with people in the cafeteria or lounge, paying attention to the attitudes they evince. Are they generally pleased with the school? Do they respect most of their professors? Do they think the placement office is doing its job? Are there any particular problems concerning the facility itself, such as crime or lack of late-night restaurants, that might matter to you? It always impresses an interviewer to see that you have taken the time and effort to examine the school up close rather than just reading some materials on it. Knowing what type of housing is available, or from which professors students maneuver to take classes, is the sort of thing that shows you to be both determined and resourceful. It also helps you to develop good questions to ask the interviewer without sounding artificial. Even if you are not interviewing on campus, take advantage of any opportunities to visit schools for precisely these reasons. (Interviewers invariably spot the applicants who have done their homework by visiting the school and learning what its program is really like.)

NORTHWESTERN UNIVERSITY'S INTERVIEW EVALUATION FORM

Applicant's Name: _____ Date of Interview: _____

SS No.: _____ LSAT Score & Date: _____

Undergraduate/Graduate Institution(s): _____

Undergraduate GPA: _____ Degree(s) & Major(s): _____

Please complete the applicant evaluation grid below.
Using a sliding scale, position an "X" in the appropriate column
for each category.

	Outstanding	Strong	Average	Below Average	Poor
N/A	Top 5%	Top 25%	Middle 50%	Bottom 25%	Bottom 5%

M _____

SCFO _____

LS _____

IA _____

CP _____

CF _____

XC _____

LP _____

NUM _____

OVERALL _____

Interviewer's Name: _____ NUSL Class: _____

Daytime Phone: _____ E-mail: _____

Employer and Position: _____

Interview Quality: Good _____ Fair _____ Poor _____

If fair or poor, please elaborate: _____

The Admissions Committee is concerned with assessing the candidate's interpersonal skills, intellectual ability, career progress, clarity of post-degree career plans, extracurricular involvement, leadership potential, and interest in Northwestern University School of Law. Using the space below, please comment on these characteristics as well as any other observations which may be of interest to the Committee. Cite specific examples if possible.

M—MATURITY (poise, confidence, presence, self-awareness): _____

SCFO—SINCERITY & CONCERN FOR OTHERS (politeness, interest in well-being of others, not self-centered): _____

LS—LISTENING SKILLS (attentiveness, pertinence of responses, appropriate length of responses): _____

IA—INTELLECTUAL ABILITY (analytical skills, communication, creativity, curiosity, thinks well on feet): _____

CP—CAREER PROGRESSION (professional, career-oriented internships or post-undergraduate experience): _____

CF—CAREER FOCUS (motivation for law school, clarity of post-degree goals): _____

XC—EXTRACURRICULAR BREADTH (well-roundedness of interests and activities): _____

LP—LEADERSHIP POTENTIAL (initiative, contribution beyond expected responsibilities in extracurricular and/or work activities): _____

NUM—MOTIVATION FOR NORTHWESTERN (knowledge of and enthusiasm for Northwestern University School of Law): _____

OVERALL IMPRESSION/OTHER OBSERVATIONS: _____

If you find out which specific person will be interviewing you, ask people you know who interviewed with the same school to see how the interview was conducted. How formal or informal was it? How rapid-fire? How long? How much was the interviewee expected to initiate, rather than just respond to, questions? How friendly was the interviewer? You will be able to prepare more specifically if you know how this person likes to conduct interviews.

The advantages of knowing the school thoroughly include:

- ■ You will know that you are prepared, enabling you to relax somewhat during the interview.

- ■ You will be able to ask intelligent questions about the school, thereby impressing the interviewer, and helping you to choose the appropriate school for you.

- ■ You will show yourself as being highly motivated, concerned about your career, and in possession of the right work ethic, which will impress your interviewer.

ANTICIPATING THE QUESTIONS

The interviewer is likely to have two types of questions to ask you. One type is the set of questions she uses for everyone, such as, "Why do you want to attend School X?" The other type will be a direct response to your file. If you have claimed to have had some marvelous successes, she may wish to probe to make sure you have not exaggerated the results. Or she may wish to probe for gaps or weaknesses in your undergraduate education. For example, one of the standard

---

THE MOST LIKELY QUESTIONS

➤ Tell me about yourself.

➤ What are your greatest achievements?

➤ What are your strengths? Your weaknesses?

➤ What are your personal and professional goals?

➤ Why do you want to go to law school? (How much do you know about the practice of law?)

➤ In what field of law do you intend to practice? Why?

➤ To what other schools are you applying?

➤ Why do you want to attend this school?

➤ How have you learned about the program?

➤ Why should we accept you?

➤ What would you add to the program?

➤ Discuss [whatever legal issue is in the news].

➤ What questions do you have?

things to seek in a résumé is a period of unaccounted-for time. If such a gap exists in your application, expect to be asked what you were doing then.

The easiest question to prepare for is, "Do you have any questions?" Most interviewers will give you the opportunity to ask a few questions. You should be ready with several questions that reflect your concerns about the school. Keep these in your head rather than on paper, because having to look at your notes will slow down the interview and make it look as though you cannot remember even a few questions.

THE INTERVIEW QUESTIONS

In general, two types of approach are common. In the first, you are asked more or less directly about the trait or competence in which the interviewer is interested. For example, when trying to get a handle on your degree of independence, the direct interviewer might ask simply, "How much supervision and direction do you prefer?" The second approach tries to elicit information that will also allow the interviewer to determine whether, for example, you "strive for leadership positions," but in a much less direct fashion. In this case, the interviewer is likely to focus on various aspects of your past and current experience—in terms of your education, career, and personal life—to see how much supervision and direction you have had in various projects and whether that amount suited you. The questions that generate this information are likely to be more general, along the lines of, "Regarding that thesis project, what sort of relationship did you have with your advisor? What did you like and dislike about this relationship?"

These more open-ended questions, in which the focus is not made so obvious, are by now standard interviewing procedure. The more experienced the interviewer, and the more time she has available, the more likely she is to use the indirect approach.

You can prepare for both approaches by examining the following list, which covers the most common questions asked on each major topic—education, career, goals, and personal life. Of course, other questions may be asked, but if you are prepared to respond coherently and consistently to each of the following, you will be ready for just about anything else you will encounter as well. Preparing for the following will force you to think through the main issues that are of interest to law schools.

LEGAL ISSUES

Is the expense of trial by jury sensible for civil trials?

Should the U.S. switch to an English system of civil litigation (where the losing party must pay the attorneys' fees and court costs of the winner)?

When is jury nullification appropriate?

Is capital punishment ever warranted?

What is the relationship between law and morality?

Do you favor euthanasia?

Should criminals be forbidden to sell their stories?

Do you agree with the right to silence? Should it ever be restricted?

Should drugs be legalized?

Under what circumstances should abortion be permitted? Is this a legislative or judicial matter?

What type of affirmative action, if any, should the U.S. adopt? Should this be limited to governmental organs or extended to private concerns as well?

Do you support the recent series of Supreme Court decisions giving more power to the states? To what extent do you believe the federal government has usurped power within what is supposed to be a federal, not centralized, system?

Should Congress or the courts determine gun-control policy for the country? What should that policy be?

At what age should minors be tried as adults for serious crimes? For what crimes?

Should tobacco companies be liable for damages to those who smoke (or once smoked) cigarettes? Does your answer change if the plaintiff began smoking after health warnings were put on cigarette packages? Or if the plaintiff knew smoking to be dangerous? Should meat packers be liable for obesity?

Should gays be allowed to marry? To adopt children?

Should Internet service providers (ISPs) be held liable for whatever they disseminate over the net?

Should large political donations to candidates be prohibited? To politically active organizations?

Under what circumstances is Congress justified in turning down a presidential appointee?

What standards are appropriate for considering a prospective Supreme Court nominee?

Should the United States support the International Criminal Court?

Is the United States a leading advocate, or leading subverter, of international law?

To what extent should accused terrorists be afforded lesser rights?

How would you define justice?

What is (should be) a lawyer's role in society?

Do you feel a lawyer is obligated to be "moral" or to be impartial?

General Tips Regarding Legal Issues

1. The most likely questions regarding legal issues are either the old stand-bys, such as abortion or capital punishment, or whatever is in the headlines at the moment.

2. To prepare to discuss whatever issues are in the headlines, read *The Economist*, *The New York Times*, *The Washington Post*, *The New Republic*, or other major publications on a regular basis—but particularly for the two months before interviews. (I strongly favor *The Economist*; be sure to read the "leaders" to be ready to discuss current issues, legal and other.)

3. When discussing a legal issue, try to support your point of view while also acknowledging the merits of the opposing viewpoint. This is particularly true regarding the most emotional issues, such as abortion, to demonstrate that you are capable of analyzing any issue dispassionately. You should sound like a reasonable person able to engage in spirited but civilized discussion. In other words, do not just spout your personal beliefs. Instead, discuss the issues in a legal framework.

4. Be ready to discuss the top dozen legal issues in the news; know the main arguments on each side, and be prepared to choose a side.

5. If any of this proposed preparation strikes you as too much trouble, you should forget about law school.

COLLEGE EDUCATION

(Repeat for graduate programs as appropriate.)

Which school did you attend?

Why did you choose that one?

(If you attended a lesser quality school) Don't you worry that you will be overwhelmed by the quality of students attending our program?

What factors most influenced your choice?

In hindsight, are you glad you chose that school? What would you change now if you could? Why?

What was your major? Why?

In hindsight, are you glad you chose that major? What would you choose instead if you could do it over again?

How many hours each week did you study?

In which courses were you most successful? Why?

In which courses were you least successful? Why?

Do your grades reflect your abilities? If not, why did you not do better?

In what ways did your education prepare you, or fail to prepare you, for your career to date?

What did you most enjoy about college?

What did you least enjoy about college?

What extracurricular activities did you participate in? What was your role and contribution in each?

How did you pay for your education?

How would you describe yourself as a college student? Is this still true about you?

General Tips Regarding College Education

1. Avoid portraying your college days as a social experience rather than an intellectual one if at all possible.

2. If your record is poor, show that you have since gotten serious. If there is any acceptable way to explain a poor record without sounding whiny or childish, be prepared to explain briefly.

3. Show that you were committed to learning, whether for its own sake or for the sake of your career.

4. If you changed your goals or interests several times, show that you have been serious about at least one of them while pursuing it.

5. Portray both your academic interests and your extracurricular activities in terms of their contribution to your current (or then-current) career interests.

6. Discuss your leadership experiences.

7. If you are interviewing for admission to a part-time program, do not try to excuse a mediocre undergraduate performance by explaining that you were unable to focus well due to the need to work part-time as well as study. This combination of work and study will be your fate once again in the part-time program, so you will appear unable to handle the responsibilities.

WORK EXPERIENCE

(Repeat as appropriate for different companies and jobs held.)

Why did you choose this profession?

What is your job title? To whom do you report?

What are your key responsibilities?

What have been your major successes?

What resources and whom do you manage directly?

What are the skills required of you in your job?

What are the key challenges of your job?

What do you do best/worst in your job? Why?

How could you have improved your performance?

What have been your major successes?

What have you done that best shows your willingness to work hard/take initiative/innovate/exceed expectations?

Describe a failure on the job.

What are you doing to address your failings?

What do you like most/least about your position? Why?

How do you see this work experience preparing you for the study and practice of law?

GENERAL TIPS REGARDING WORK EXPERIENCE

1. When discussing your boss, your description of what was good and bad about him will probably make it clear what you need, and also what you cannot tolerate, in a boss. This also says a lot about your own strengths and weaknesses, so be careful here.

2. Even when describing what you did not particularly like about your job, try to focus on the positive aspects; otherwise, you risk sounding like a malcontent.

3. Any job change should have been motivated by a desire for more challenges, more responsibility, the chance to grow, and so on. In other words, emphasize the positive, forward-looking reasons for making the change. Avoid the negative, backward-looking reasons for the change, such as being unappreciated, underpaid, or disliked by your boss.

4. If you were fired, confess to this fact if necessary, but be sure to note what you learned from the experience.

5. Working fewer than 50 hours per week may suggest that you are insufficiently motivated. A good answer will establish that you work as hard as necessary to achieve your objective.

6. Try to bring out the ways in which you demonstrate the key skills and aptitudes valued by law schools: analytical, communication (written and oral), teamwork, and leadership.

INTEREST IN LAW/YOUR GOALS

What inspired you to apply to law school? How long have you had this in your plans?

What in your experience (educational and professional) has prepared you for legal study?

What interests you about the legal system?

Which undergraduate courses gave you a grounding in legal theory?

What research have you done regarding law school?

What do you expect to be the largest challenges you will face in law school?

What type of law do you want to be practicing in five years? Ten years? Twenty years?

(If you profess an interest in public interest law) How will you reconcile your desire to practice public interest law with your debt repayments and desire to earn a good living when you graduate?

What do you want to accomplish in life?

How have your goals changed in recent years?

What do you expect to learn in law school?

Which other schools are you applying to?

How did you choose these schools?

What will you do if you are not accepted at a top school?

GENERAL TIPS REGARDING YOUR INTEREST IN LAW AND YOUR GOALS

1. Showing that you have thought long and hard about your future career demonstrates your seriousness of purpose.

2. Regarding your long-term goals, do not say that you want to retire as early as possible and lie on a beach in Cancun. Saying this would show you to be lazy or overly stressed, hardly ideal attributes for someone trying to get into a challenging law school. Discuss instead how you arrived at your chosen goal in light of a consideration of your relative strengths and weaknesses, what you most enjoy, your backgrounds and desires, etc.

3. You want to show that you are committed to career success, however you define it.

4. Be sure not to sound as if law school is a default choice rather than something you have actively sought out.

5. If you claim that you will go into public interest law, you will need to do everything possible to sound credible. (A large majority of those who profess this interest do not actually enter the field; this is especially true of those who have not worked for an extended period after college.) If you can support this position with examples of personal sacrifice and work in a relevant field, do so. If you cannot, reconsider your goals—and what you pitch to the law schools.

PERSONAL

Tell me about yourself.

Who most influenced you when you were growing up? How?

What publications do you read regularly? Why?

What books have you read recently? What impressed you about them?

What have you done to keep yourself current, or to develop your skills, in your particular area of interest?

How do you feel about:

—China's advent upon the world stage?

—African internecine warfare?

—(Anything else on the front pages, especially if it relates to your home region or that of the school?)

How do you spend your time outside of work?

Is your current balance among career, family, friends, and interests the right one for you over the long term?

What would you do with the extra time if days were 28 hours long?

What activity do you enjoy the most? Why?

Who are your heroes? Why?

General Tips Regarding Personal Questions

1. When describing yourself, or what your long-term goals are, be sure a large part of your response focuses upon your career. You want to appear career-oriented, albeit not lacking in personality or other interests.

2. Take every opportunity to show you are highly achievement oriented, and do what you can to develop both personally and professionally.

3. At the same time, show yourself to be a sensible and well-balanced person with compelling outside interests, including (but not limited to) family and friends.

4. When talking about your reading interests, it does not much matter whether you read science fiction, monographs about the Napoleonic wars, or locked-room mysteries, as long as you show that you are knowledgeable and enthusiastic regarding whatever you pursue.

5. These questions provide a natural opportunity to subtly strengthen your chosen positioning.

RECOLLECTING YOUR THOUGHTS DURING THE INTERVIEW

Remember your pre-interview objectives during the interview session. Ask yourself whether you have put across your major points. If you have not, mention briefly but persuasively the points you wished to make, along with the supporting examples or illustrations you intended to use.

PREPARING TO DESCRIBE KEY EVENTS

You should be ready to discuss major and minor milestones in your personal, educational, and professional life. Some interviewers prefer to ask very general, open-ended questions to learn how well you can develop an organized, intelligent response. Questions of this nature often revolve around major events interviewers glean from your résumé or application. Prepare yourself by reviewing the relevant aspects of each event you expect to discuss. In the case of a successful business or research project, you would want to recall:

SOUNDING EDUCATED AND ARTICULATE

There is nothing more annoying to a highly educated professional than someone (younger) who fails to use proper English grammar in speech. Many interviewers are exasperated by the fact that even the most educated applicants these days cannot seem to put a sentence together without making some unbearable mistake. Make sure you refine your speech habits before embarking upon your law school interviews, especially regarding the following common (yet not at all excusable) mistakes:

➤ Know the difference between "good" (an adjective) and "well" (an adverb). If you are describing a noun, use "good": "My grades last year were very good." If you are describing a verb or an adjective, use "well": "This year is going really well." Your year cannot ever "go good."

➤ Do not use objective pronouns (as in "me," "her," or "him") as subjects of a sentence. In other words, "Me and my parents went to Italy" is entirely incorrect. Would you ever say "Me went to Italy"?

➤ Do not use words or phrases if you are not 100 percent certain how to use them correctly. Know the difference between "imply" and "infer." Remember that "irregardless" is not a word.

➤ Similarly, expunge "you know," "like," "as if," "uhh," "whatever," and other annoying verbal tics from your conversation.

■ The project's initial objective

■ Who originated it

■ Who was in charge

■ The resources available

■ The timetable

■ The activities undertaken

■ What you did well and poorly, and why

■ What skills you used (including teamwork and leadership skills)

■ What you would do differently in retrospect

■ Other people's roles

- The results
- What went right and what did not, and why

In the case of a successful thesis or advanced study project, you would want to recall these factors:

- The initial proposition or hypothesis that you aimed to prove
- How you formulated the concept
- What research you undertook to prepare
- Who your advisor or mentor was
- The resources available
- The timetable
- The texts consulted
- The activities undertaken
- The methods applied
- The conclusion or results of the project
- What you did well and poorly, and why
- What you would do differently in retrospect

It is a useful exercise to write down on an index card the half dozen most important incidents you expect to discuss, using this sort of approach for each. Carry these cards with you for reading when you are waiting or have a spare moment. Learn them well enough that you can produce a well-organized, apparently spontaneous summary of each of them at the drop of a hat, but do not memorize the stories by rote. Be prepared to be interrupted by the interviewer, and be ready to carry on with the story smoothly once you have answered his question.

WHAT DETERMINES THE LIKELIHOOD OF A GIVEN QUESTION BEING ASKED?

Questions are not generally asked without a reason. Some interviewers believe that certain questions should be asked of anyone, no matter what the person's circumstances. In interviewing for law programs, the most likely questions concern why you want to get a law degree, why at this school, what other schools you are considering, what you think you will contribute while at School X, and what you intend to do professionally in the near and long terms.

The other determinant of questions is, of course, you. Your background invites questions that may be quite different from those that would be asked of someone else. If you are in a field that seldom produces JD candidates, you can expect questions concerning why you want a JD. If one of your credentials is relatively weak, you can expect questions about it. If you are the resident of a non–English-speaking country, and attended a foreign institution, you can expect to have your English skills probed.

**ADMISSIONS DEANS DISCUSS HOW THEY
CONDUCT INTERVIEWS**

When I interview people, I try to ascertain whether a person has a sense of perspective, is comfortable discussing controversial matters, and does not take criticism of an idea personally. I also want to understand how they will interact with their classmates. I want to be sure that they are comfortable tossing ideas around. *Rick Geiger, Cornell*

Our interview process is currently set up for the applicant to present his or her case for admission to the interviewer. It is not a question and answer session where the interviewer extracts information from an applicant. Ideally, the applicant should provide information in addition to what he/she has submitted in the original application. After the allotted 15-minute interview, the applicant selects one question from five pre-written questions to write a brief essay. *Monica Ingram, Texas*

Our interviews are 30 minutes. Typical subjects include their educational experience, work experience, goals, what they do in their free time, extracurriculars, nature of their interest in attending school here. We try to do it in a relaxed setting, since that is where you get the most useful perspective on them. We do throw in a few questions to make them think on their feet. *Don Rebstock, Northwestern*

A good interviewer, and often even a bad interviewer, will try to use the interview to learn as much relevant information as possible about you. Given that most interviewers will not have read your application in depth, you can expect them to ask many of the same basic questions that appear on the various applications. One way to influence the course of an interview with someone who knows little about you is to take a résumé along. Most interviewers will use it as the basis for their questions, so they will ask about the items you choose to list on your résumé. They will also probe for internal inconsistencies as well as checking things that sound inherently unlikely.

The other items an interviewer will probe are things you and she have in common, or about which she is simply curious. ("I see you worked for Senator so-and-so; what do you think of his policy about such-and-such?") The more an interviewer takes this approach, the easier the interview is likely to be. Discussing interests you share is likely to provide an opportunity to share enthusiasms, which is generally easier to handle than responding to probing questions about why you dropped your thesis project after six months. Be sure, however, to keep your own objectives. You can still make the impression you want by being articulate and well organized, even when just discussing your summer in Geneva.

PRACTICE

There are two ways you can practice your interviewing skills and responses. The first is by doing mock interviews with others who are applying, or someone else who appreciates what is involved. This is a good first step to understanding what an interview will be like. The quality of the experience will depend in large part upon how prepared your interviewing partner is. If you can find someone who is willing to read your application carefully, and perhaps even read this chapter, then you are likely to get a good interview. The ideal person to team up with would be someone who is applying to the same schools, but has a very different background from yours, and who is willing to be tough when necessary in the interview. It can be difficult to find the right person, of course. (It is partly for this reason that Degree of Difference regularly does mock interviews with clients—if necessary by phone—to give them a realistic view of what to expect.) It is not only fair, but also good for you, to switch roles with your partner. If you have to read her essays and data sheets with an eye to seeing what her strengths and weaknesses are, what she will contribute to the program, and the like, you will more readily understand how someone else will do this with you.

Your interview partner can tell you which responses were convincing and which were not (and why). Be persistent and force your interview partner to be specific in noting what worked and what did not. After all, the point is not what you say but *what your interviewer hears* that determines the success of your interview. In fact, simply saying things out loud will often cause you to hear what is not right. Speaking out loud often makes it clear that you are wandering instead of staying focused, trying too hard to excuse some prior mistake, staying too stiff, or pleading rather than persuading. Tape recording your practice sessions will make this apparent.

The second means of practicing is to be sure that, if possible, you interview first with a school that matters less to you. This allows you to develop and refine your pitch and get rid of your first interview nerves without too much at stake.

It is a good idea to use both of these approaches intermittently if you can. Maximize the potential benefits by debriefing your partner after an interview, or reviewing the experience yourself, to be sure that you understand what worked and what needed more thought, and why.

PHYSICAL PREPARATIONS

PHYSICAL ENERGY
- Get plenty of sleep the two nights before the interview.
- Eat a solid breakfast or lunch on the day, so that you do not run out of energy.

APPEARANCE
- Arrive at the actual site slightly before the allotted time so that you do not need to rush and get nervous as a result. Find the restroom and check your appearance.

MEN:
- Make sure your hair is combed, and your tie is straight and completely covered in back by the collar of your shirt.
- Consider carrying an extra tie or perhaps even a shirt, in case something is spilled at lunch.

WOMEN:
- Make sure your lipstick is not smudged or on your teeth.
- Consider carrying extra stockings, in case of a run.

LOCATION
- Be sure you know where the interview will take place and how to get there (and where to park).

OTHER
- Take several copies of your résumé and a copy of your application.
- Take a copy of the law school's brochure and other relevant information about the program to review if you get there early.
- Take the name and telephone number of your interviewer in case you need to telephone her to notify her of a delay in your travel.

STAYING RELAXED

A modest degree of nervousness is good because it gives you the energy to perform at your best. If you tend to be too nervous, try one of these techniques to keep yourself relaxed:

➤ Remind yourself that you have prepared thoroughly (assuming that this is the case) and that this preparation will see you through.

➤ Acting positive, by using the appropriate body language, will help you to feel the way you are acting. Positive body language involves keeping your head up, shoulders square, and eyes forward. Your body should be still (avoid swinging a leg or drumming your hands on the table) but not stiff.

➤ Breathe slowly and deeply.

➤ A great friend of mine, to give himself confidence before exams and cross-country races, used to go off by himself and keep repeating, with concentration and intensity, "I am King Kong, I am King Kong."

➤ Remind yourself that failing to get in, or failing to get in this year, is not the end of the world.

ADMISSIONS DEANS GIVE ADVICE ON HOW TO PREPARE FOR INTERVIEWS

Make sure that you dress professionally, such as in a suit and tie. (Some fail to do this.) Research the school; be ready to talk about it in a knowledgeable way. Read the admissions catalogue and more. Come prepared to talk about examples of what you have accomplished and how it relates to the qualities you think you have. *Don Rebstock, Northwestern*

If applicants are in college, they should be prepared to talk about what they are doing now—for example, what classes they are taking. . . . In general, they should remember that they will not have the chance to cover everything they want to so they should have in mind a kernel or two that they make sure they leave with us. We do give them the chance to highlight what they wish, so they should have a main theme that they try to develop. *Rick Geiger, Cornell*

The interview is, in part, an opportunity to give us another personal statement, so consider what you want to highlight about your candidacy. In addition, try to determine whether Vanderbilt offers the kind of community you're interested in: small, noncompetitive, and collegial. Determining whether Vanderbilt is a good match for you is one of the key things we hope to assess and we hope you will discover through the interview. *Todd Morton, Vanderbilt*

If you are called in for an interview, you should be able to figure out why. If not, ask. Think about why you'd be a good fit for the school, know the school's programs, and when asked why you want to attend it, say something more than you like the location.   *Rob Schwartz, UCLA*

Read through what you've already presented to us in your application. Then consider what you want to present to us that is not in your application, because if all you try to do is to rehash your application, you will have wasted an opportunity. "Package" your information as you would do for any oral presentation. Particularly if you are not a good presenter, practice your presentation and presentation skills. In addition, make sure that you are ready to write an essay, because that is the other part of our interview format.   *Monica Ingram, Texas*

In addition to being ready to talk about your candidacy, review what you can about the law school so that you are ready to ask some questions of your own. *Ann Killian Perry, Chicago*

DURING THE INTERVIEW

A considerable degree of the impact you have in an interview is achieved nonverbally; nonverbal messages may constitute over half of the message you deliver. As a result, it is highly appropriate to consider such factors as dress, physical comportment, and the like in order to maximize the chances of interview success.

DRESS
RULES FOR MEN:

- Wear clean, neatly pressed clothes and highly shined black shoes.
- Be sure your clothes fit well. Be sure your clothes do not look as if you are wearing them for the first time, but they should not be so worn that this is noticeable.
- Avoid wild colors or styles.
- Men will never go wrong wearing a conservative dark blue or gray suit with a white or blue shirt, or moderately striped shirt, and a conservative tie.
- Comb your hair and wear no cologne.
- It should go without saying that your shirt should be 100-percent cotton, long-sleeved, professionally cleaned, and heavily starched. The tie should be pure silk and extend to the middle of your belt buckle.

- Be sure your fingernails are clean and well groomed.
- You should be clean shaven. If you have a mustache or beard, that is fine; but if not, you should avoid the five o'clock shadow look.

RULES FOR WOMEN:

- Women should wear a suit (skirt or pants) or a simple dress, and no more than a modest amount of jewelry, makeup, and perfume. Jewelry should not rattle or otherwise distract.
- Women have more leeway than men in choosing appropriate lengths, colors, and cuts of clothing. Your appearance may alter with changing fashion trends but do not go wild; be especially wary of skirts that are too short or blouses that are too low-cut.
- Try not to bring both a briefcase and purse because it is difficult to be graceful when carrying both.
- Wear panty hose (no matter how hot the weather) and eschew bare arms.

RULES FOR MEN AND WOMEN:

- Do not wear such ostentatiously expensive clothes that you might offend your interviewer. For example, leave the Hermes tie in the closet, if it is obvious where it came from.
- Do not wear a hat or cap.
- Be sure you have invested appropriately in mouthwash, deodorant, and other hygienic necessities.
- You want to be remembered for what you said, not for what you wore (or failed to wear).

BEHAVIOR

PHYSICAL BEHAVIOR

Your goal is to be considered self-confident and relaxed. You can show this by remaining poised and thoughtful throughout the interview.

- Greet the interviewer with a smile, an extended hand, and a firm handshake (matching the interviewer's pressure).
- Look the interviewer in the eye.
- Do not sit down until invited to do so.
- Do not put anything on the interviewer's desk.
- Do not smoke, drink, or eat anything even if invited to do so—not even if the interviewer herself does. This can distract either you or the interviewer,

perhaps showing you to be clumsy or worse, without any chance of improving her opinion of you. If the interviewer offers you a cigarette, decline politely but not judgmentally by saying, "No, thank you."

- Do not chew gum.

- Make sure your cell phone is turned off.

- Maintain a moderate amount of eye contact throughout the interview, perhaps 40–60 percent, but do not stare.

- Gesticulate moderately to make points, but do not go overboard.

- Remain physically stationary, without fidgeting. Interviewers often check your response to a tough question to see if you are exhibiting signs of nervousness (or lying).

- Maintain good rapport with the interviewer by being warm and smiling often. Do not, however, smile idiotically without stopping for the entire interview!

- Sit up straight, but not rigidly, and lean forward slightly. This will show that you are interested in what the interviewer has to say, and that you are professional.

- Listen carefully, and show that you are listening by nodding, or saying, "uh-huh," "I see," or "right" occasionally.

- Avoid crossing your arms, or folding your arms behind your head.

- Keep your voice well modulated, but alive. Speak at a normal speed; do not rush.

ATTITUDES

- *Be upbeat.* Be sure to emphasize your strengths. Do not discuss your weaknesses in any detail unless pushed to do so. Never complain about anything that has befallen you. No complaint about a low LSAT score, or personality conflict with a boss or professor, can improve an interviewer's opinion of you.

- *Flatter the interviewer, subtly.* Although a good interviewer will have you do 75 to 80 percent of the talking, that does not mean you will be excused for failing to listen to her.

    Adopt an attitude similar to the interviewer's. If your interviewer is deadly serious, avoid joking. If your interviewer is lighthearted and jocular, do not sit deadpan. In the first instance jocularity will make you seem frivolous, whereas in the latter instance seriousness will make you seem unintelligent.

    Maintain more formality if your interviewer remains behind her desk throughout the interview, without even coming around to greet you initially.

■ *Treat the interviewer respectfully, but not too respectfully.* Treat her as an equal, albeit one who temporarily is allowed to set the direction of the interview. Do not behave submissively. Do not, however, use the interviewer's first name unless and until told to do so.

■ *Relax and enjoy yourself.* The relatively few people who enjoy interviews are those who view them as a chance to discuss important matters with an equal who happens to be interested in the same subjects. They view the interview as a time to learn more about the school as well as a chance to explain themselves.

   A little nervousness is to be expected, but exhibiting substantial nervousness works against you insofar as a strong candidate is meant to believe himself well suited to interact at this level.

■ *Make sure it is a conversation.* A good interview resembles nothing so much as a conversation. If there is a pause in the conversation, consider whether:

— You have answered the question fully enough. If you suspect not, ask whether the interviewer would like you to add to the answer.

— You should follow up with a question of your own related to the same subject.

— You should simply sit quietly, without tension, with a pleasant smile.

   Ask the interviewer questions to follow up on what she has said. This helps to build rapport and puts you on a more equal footing with her by getting you out of the role of interviewee answering questions. It is also the way normal conversations work, trading back and forth.

■ *Avoid sounding like a robot.* If you follow this book's suggestions and prepare thoroughly for your interviews, you run the risk of sounding preprogrammed rather than spontaneous. It is good to sound as though you have given thought to the relevant issues, but not as though you have memorized answers.

   How can you avoid this problem? There are three keys: (1) Avoid a robotic monotone, or appearing to be reaching into your memory for what comes next in your rehearsed response. (2) Focus upon your interviewer. You should be able to remain relaxed, given that you know you are well prepared, and this will allow you to stay focused upon how your interviewer is reacting to you. (3) Occasionally pause before you speak, as if to get organized before starting.

■ *Look interested.* Avoid looking at your watch. Do not stretch in your chair. Do not appear bored, no matter how long the interviewer is speaking.

■ *Do not ramble on.* If your answer has gone on too long, cut your losses by briefly restating your main points.

HOW TO READ THE INTERVIEWER

The interviewer's demeanor will help to reveal her reactions to the interview. Smiles and nods clearly suggest she agrees with what you are saying, in which case, think about what you are doing right so you can do more of it. Perhaps your interviewer likes the fact that you are backing up your abstractions with solid examples. Maybe you are keeping your cool when being asked very tough questions.

Looking away from you, frowning, or constantly fiddling with papers or pens may reveal disagreement or a lack of interest. If you sense you are losing the interviewer, try to get back on track by asking the interviewer a relevant question or making comments that are sure to be winners, such as some self-deprecating humor or mention of the incidents you feel show you in your best light.

It is important to keep in mind whatever the interviewer says in her opening remarks, because they may give you good clues as to what she values.

If you are talking too much, your interviewer is likely to start looking away, looking at her watch, or asking such questions as "Could you just summarize this part?"

YOUR QUESTION TIME

A failure to ask questions if invited to do so risks leaving the impression that you either did not do your homework or do not particularly care whether the school admits you. Asking questions gives you the opportunity to show how knowledgeable you are about the process and the program as well as that you are taking a proactive approach to your career future.

If you are asked what questions you have, do not rush into asking them. If you have not yet had the opportunity to make one or two key points, ask whether it would be acceptable to go back to the earlier question and then mention what you have just accomplished (or whatever). Even if these points are unrelated to any prior question, feel free to say, "I am glad to have the opportunity to ask you a couple of questions, but I hope you will forgive my wanting to mention two things that have come up since I applied. I think they might be relevant to the school's decision making, after which I will continue with my questions." Briefly mention the one or two points. Then go on to your questions.

Try to avoid questions that call for a yes or no response. To understand an area in depth, plan to ask several questions about it. One good way to do so is to ask your interviewer to compare, for example, her school and a major competitor (one that you are actively considering). She will probably mention several points, after which you can ask about one or more of them in greater detail, or ask her why she did not mention subject X.

If you think that the interviewer harbors major objections to you, try to get her to confess what it is she is concerned about, so that you can address her concerns, assuming that you have not yet had the opportunity to do so.

Some appropriate questions, in case you are stuck for something to ask, include:

- How do you expect the school to change in the near future?
- Has the character of the school changed in recent years? How? Why?
- What distinguishes students at this school from those at its principal rivals?

If one reason for attending the school is that a certain professor teaches there, by all means ask whether the interviewer knows him or her, and, if so, what he or she is like as a professor.

Do not try to baffle the interviewer with questions you know she won't be able to answer. If she is an alum of the school, for example, she will not be privy to the school's rationale for its recent decision not to offer tenure to assistant professor X. Similarly, do not ask unintelligent questions, or ones that can be answered with a glance at the school's application materials (such as "What is the usual class size?") just for the sake of asking a question.

After asking several questions, if necessary you can fall back on the old standby: "I had a number of questions when the interview started, but you have covered them all."

Being asked if you have any questions signals that the interview is coming to an end, so do not take too much time.

ENDING THE INTERVIEW

Be sure to smile at the interviewer, shake hands, and thank her for seeing you, and leave with an energetic, confident demeanor. (Do not ask your interviewer how you did at the end of the interview. This will put him on the spot and make you seem immature, lacking tact, or unable to wait for a decision to be made in due course. It will not do anything to improve your chances of success.)

Be careful not to be taken in by an old trick. Once you feel the interview is over, you may be asked a potentially revealing question as you are being shown out, on the assumption that you may have let down your guard at this point. Or the office assistant may be instructed to ask a question such as, "How do you think you did?" in hopes of eliciting a telling comment. Assume that the interview is really over only after you have left the premises.

INTERVIEW WRECKERS

➤ Criticizing your undergraduate institution, boss, or company intemperately. (You do not need to be so upbeat as to have no real opinions whatsoever, but negative comments should not evince uncompromising hostility; be sure you have, and express, reasonable grounds for any negative remarks.)

➤ Being too nervous to look the part of a successful, confident lawyer

➤ Appearing blasé about attending the school at hand

➤ Asking no questions

➤ Whining about past grades, low LSAT scores, and so on

➤ Blaming others for weaknesses in your profile

GENERAL RULES FOR INTERVIEWS

The following advice is good no matter what type of interview or interviewer you encounter:

Do not criticize others without good reason. Even if you have good reason, do not let the focus of more than a small part of the interview be on your criticisms. Otherwise you may be viewed as a chronic malcontent. Remain positive.

Assume that alumni interviewers do not have your file memorized. In fact, for schools at which you requested the interview, most interviewers will not even have seen your file. You can therefore expect to be able to make good use of the same incidents you discussed in your essays.

Be truthful. Do not lie in answering questions. Being honest, however, does not mean the same thing as being blunt, so do not volunteer negative information if it can be avoided.

Be yourself. Do not pretend to be someone other than yourself to impress your interviewer. Very few people are able to act well enough to carry it off successfully. Focus instead on presenting the best aspects of your own personality.

Never be less than highly courteous and friendly to the staff. The staff is generally in charge of all of the logistical elements of your candidacy, so do not alienate them. The admissions officers may also ask them to give their impression of you, so make sure it is a positive one.

Do not try to take over the interview, but take advantage of opportunities to make your points. Interviewers want to feel they are in charge of an interview, since they need to feel confident that they will be able to get what they consider information relevant to their decision making. Taking over the interview may allow you to make the points you want to make, but the risk is far too great that your interviewer will react very negatively to this and resent your aggressiveness. Use of polite phrases in a confident tone of voice can keep your interviewer from fearing that you are trying to take over the interview: "Perhaps you wouldn't mind . . ."; "I would find it very helpful if you could . . ."

Stay relaxed. A good interviewer takes the following as possible indications that you are lying, being evasive, or hoping that he will not follow up on a point:

— Fidgeting (such as twirling your hair, drumming your fingers, bouncing your leg up and down, or picking at a part of your body or clothing. Many people have a tic of which they are completely unaware. Use your mock interview partner or videotape to find yours, and then stop doing it.)

— Speaking much faster or more slowly

— Avoiding eye contact

— Lengthy, convoluted responses

— Desperately looking for a drink of water

— Coughing at length before staring a response

Remain calm even in the face of provocation. An interviewer may be trying to annoy you to see how you respond. A successful litigator, it should go without saying, is unlikely to be easily ruffled.

Answer questions concisely. Do not ramble. Do not take more than two or three minutes for any but the most involved, important questions. In fact, three to five sentences is an appropriate length for the majority of answers.

Structure your responses. Because you have prepared thoroughly (if you have taken this chapter to heart), you are in a position to respond with structured answers to most questions you will be asked. You do not need to start every response by saying "I did such and such for five reasons. Number one was . . . ," but having coherent and well-organized responses will be impressive. Summarize any particularly lengthy answers you give.

Listen well. Be sure you have understood what the interviewer is asking. If uncertain, ask for clarification of the question. Answering the question you thought was being asked, or the one you anticipated being asked, rather than the one she really did ask you, will annoy her and suggest that you are either dim or not paying attention. Listening well means more than paying attention to what is being said. It also requires that you encourage the interviewer by appearing interested. In addition, you should be able to sense the feelings behind the comments made.

ADMISSIONS DEANS DISCUSS WHEN INTERVIEWS ARE CONDUCTED— BEFORE OR AFTER FILES ARE COMPLETE

An interview can take place at any point in the process, before or after applying. Our interviewer has generally not read the applicant's file prior to the interview. We ask the applicant to bring a résumé and complete some basic demographic information sheets. We do the interviews "blind" in order to eliminate potential, pre-formed bias.   *Don Rebstock, Northwestern*

Our interviewer may or may not have examined the file before conducting the interview.   *Monica Ingram, Texas*

In all cases, we have carefully reviewed the file before we interview someone. *Rick Geiger, Cornell*

We interview applicants after their file is complete and it has been preliminarily reviewed.   *Rob Schwartz, UCLA*

Our interviews could be either before or after the file is complete, but in general the interviewer will not have access to the file. We want the interviewer's judgment to be independent of what is in the file so that we get another, unbiased view of the applicant.   *Todd Morton, Vanderbilt*

Assume that anyone at the office may be an interviewer. Sometimes a junior employee will chat with you while you wait for the real interview to start, trying to get you to give your real reactions to the school or your own qualifications as though a junior person should be on your side rather than the school's. Expect any information you give away to be fed into your file immediately, maybe even given to your real interviewer prior to your upcoming interview.

SPECIAL TYPES OF INTERVIEWS

STRESS INTERVIEWS

Stress interviews are not much in evidence anymore, but they still pop up often enough to merit comment. The idea underlying any form of stress interview is that applying enormous stress to an interviewee will cause him to reveal his true nature and likely performance under stress in the future. A failure to remain poised will reveal a person's supposed lack of confidence in himself.

What exactly is a stress interview? It can take many forms. You may be put in a position in which bright sunlight will be directly in your eyes (think of the movies you have seen in which detectives grill a suspect under a bright light) or your responses may be met by long silences. The tendency in this case is to try to fill up the awkward moments by adding to a response, thereby revealing information you would have been better advised to keep from view.

More likely you will be given too little time to answer questions. As you start to answer a question, your response may be ignored or cut short and taken out of context, and the next question tossed at you as fast as possible. The interviewer may dispute what you are saying and challenge you very aggressively. Your weaknesses may be pointed out at every turn. The interviewer can also be obviously hostile and rude. This will continue for some time, until you react, most probably by becoming angry or resentful that you are not being allowed to get your full answers out.

The key to this situation is to recognize it for what it is. If you know that it is a game, you can respond with suitable bits of gamesmanship. Once you know that you are deliberately being pressured, you have the opportunity to take control of the situation. (This is one of the few circumstances in which it is appropriate for you to take control.) If the sun is shining directly into your eyes, excuse yourself and move your chair to a more comfortable location. If you are being subjected to the silent treatment, respond by smiling at the interviewer and simply waiting for her to ask another question. If, on the other hand, you are being pressured verbally, start by leaning back, smiling, and not saying anything for a few seconds. Then restate the last question, "You have asked me whether this project was really successful." Go on to explain that there are, let's say, four parts to your response. Once you have done this it will be all but impossible for the interviewer to interrupt you until you have finished all four. Be sure to start each portion of your response by saying, "first," "second," and so on.

If you are interrupted again, lean back once more, smile again, and say that this approach seems a bit much, and invite the interviewer to share information instead.

FRIENDLY CHATS

One type of interviewer will come on as extremely friendly and casual. She will chat away about recent football results or the interviewee's favorite foods. When she shifts to legal matters, she will be completely unthreatening and will agree with anything and everything you say. The danger is that she will lull you into totally dropping your guard so that you end up volunteering information that you would be better off keeping to yourself. You are inclined to consider a person who finds you agreeable, fascinating, and invariably correct to be on your side. Resist this temptation; your interviewer may just be using a technique to get you to open up about yourself.

SPECIAL INTERVIEW SETTINGS: RESTAURANTS

➤ Do not sit until the interviewer invites you to be seated.

➤ Consider the menu when the interviewer invites you to. Pick something mid-priced, and do so without lengthy deliberations. Make sure you choose something familiar and easy to eat. Avoid things that splatter or require eating with your fingers.

➤ If the interviewer orders a drink or first course, follow suit by ordering at least some mineral water so that you will have something to occupy yourself with while she is drinking or eating.

➤ Do not order too much, since this suggests lack of discipline.

➤ It is usually a good idea not to drink alcohol at all before or during an interview.

➤ Do not criticize the décor or the food.

➤ Treat the servers and busboys very politely.

➤ Wait for the interviewer to begin the "business" end of the discussion. She may prefer to wait until after the drink or first course has been consumed.

NON-INTERVIEWS

Some schools do not so much interview you as invite you to meet with an admissions officer and then, rather than ask you specific questions, simply wait for you to explain why you should be admitted. Surprisingly few applicants are ready for this most basic question. Assuming that you have prepared adequately, you should be able to address both (implicit) parts of the "question." The more important is how the school will benefit from your presence (and your later alumni involvement), but do not neglect an explanation of how well the school fits your own requirements.

HOW TO DEAL WITH THE INCOMPETENT INTERVIEWER

What marks an incompetent interviewer? Examples are: talking too much, going off on tangents, failing to maintain control of the interview, dwelling on inconsequential matters, and failing to pay attention. Here are some tips for dealing with the most common problems:

He talks too much. The more an interviewer talks, the less information he can get about you. Build rapport with him by providing nonverbal encouragement. You do not want to offend him or be rude, but you still want to get some points across. Do so by appearing to agree with him, following up on one of his comments by immediately saying something like, "In fact, one of the things that first got me interested in school X was . . ." And, of course, take advantage of the break he gives you at the end of the interview when he asks you if you have any questions. Phrase your questions as questions, but make sure they are really short advertisements for yourself. For example: "I believe I would be an asset to your

---

**ADMISSIONS DEANS GIVE ADVICE ON
HOW TO HANDLE YOURSELF IN AN INTERVIEW**

Follow general professional etiquette. Make eye contact. Do not fidget. Be comfortable, and appear comfortable: Do not worry about whether to fold your hands or have them at your side. Exude energy and enthusiasm; otherwise it can get dry. You need to show that you're very interested in being here. *Don Rebstock, Northwestern*

Be prepared to be proactive; there's too little time for us to work at drawing someone out. You have a limited amount of time to make the argument for why you should be admitted. In fact, my first question is likely to be "give me some sense for why you're here." *Elizabeth Rosselot, Boston College*

One common mistake interviewees make is not being straightforward—being vague and evasive about a difficulty. *Rick Geiger, Cornell*

In the interview itself, allow us to lead the actual interview. One fellow came in and made the mistake of talking for 20 minutes before I got my first question in. *Don Rebstock, Northwestern*

Dress professionally. Act professionally. People do the strangest things in interviews. One guy pulled his chair up to my desk and leaned as far over it toward me as possible and never stopped staring at me. Be on time; get there early. *Rob Schwartz, UCLA*

program, with my background: a master's in psychology and a lot of counseling experience. Can you tell me more about what opportunities I would have to teach (or share) these skills and experiences to (with) others? Would I be able to participate in workshops or counseling internships, for example?"

She goes off on tangents. If you want to get the discussion back on track, use such phrases as: "Let me be sure I understand this correctly" (and then repeat the couple of key points briefly); "Could we go back to that first point, such and such"; "In our remaining time, I hope we will have the chance to touch on the following points that are particularly important for me: X, Y, and Z."

She constantly interrupts. Make a note of where you are in a conversation when the interruption occurred and recall this for the interviewer's sake when the interview recommences. She will be impressed that you have kept your focus while she was losing hers.

AFTER THE INTERVIEW

First, debrief yourself regarding what went well and what went poorly, and why. This will help you with later interviews for other schools; you will be able to anticipate, for example, what you might be asked concerning an apparent weakness.

INTERVIEW CHECKLIST

- Clothing: My dress was/was not appropriate and comfortable.
- My entrance, including handshake and greeting, was/was not positive.
- My physical actions (smile, eye contact, body language, avoidance of fidgeting) were/were not appropriate.
- Attitude: I did/did not appear confident, enthusiastic, and friendly.
- Questions I handled well (list each, with what was good about your answer):
- Questions I handled poorly (list each, with what was bad about your answer, and suggestions for improvement):
- General Comments:
  —I spoke too much/too little.
  —I did/did not establish rapport quickly and easily.
  —I did/did not stay on a more or less equal footing with the interviewer.
  —I did/did not impress the interviewer without bragging.
  —I did/did not balance sincerity and humor appropriately for this interviewer's style.

ADMISSIONS DEANS' FURTHER COMMENTS
ABOUT INTERVIEWING

WHY DOES YOUR SCHOOL INTERVIEW?

We are a small school, so a slight change in the mix of students can be critical to the dynamics of the class. Interviewing helps us to get the right balance. *Rick Geiger, Cornell*

The law is a very interactive profession; communication skills are critical to succeeding in it. They are number one or two on the list of what is most important. Developing client relationships depends upon communication skills, as does representing a client well. A law firm won't hire someone without an interview, so why should we? *Don Rebstock, Northwestern*

We owe applicants who have gone to the trouble of filling out an application and paying an application fee the greatest possible opportunity to present their arguments about what they have to offer as well as what they think about Vanderbilt. Simply put, we want to get to know them as best we can. *Todd Morton, Vanderbilt*

I like to explore their interest in the school and in any particular areas of law. I also look to probe any areas of concern to us, whether that be academic performance, misconduct, or something else. *Rob Schwartz, UCLA*

Our interviews are designed to assess someone more as a prospective professional than as a prospective law student (which much of the rest of the file addresses). In other words, it will focus on "Would you hire this person" kind of questions. Thus, we'll look at issues of leadership, decision-making, response to adversity, the nature of someone's impact on colleagues and community, and so on. *Todd Morton, Vanderbilt*

Interviews are designed to yield additional information that couldn't be presented, or was overlooked, in the written application. *Monica Ingram, Texas*

We have certainly encountered people with very high (LSAT and GPA) numbers who floundered in the interview; we do not admit them. *Don Rebstock, Northwestern*

WHAT INFORMATION DO YOU FIND INTERVIEWS YIELD?

It gives you a sense of the person's character, her interest in the school, the impression she makes, and how well she expresses herself—a vital skill for an attorney. *Rob Schwartz, UCLA*

It shows their presence, demeanor, and articulation. Hiring partners at law firms would say these are critical to the practice of law. They are also critical to performance in law school and in one's development as a professional. *Todd Morton, Vanderbilt*

Interviews can yield a sense of a candidate's communication skills, engagement, thoughtfulness, how broadly read they are, and how committed they are to law school and a legal career. *Susan Palmer, Virginia*

We assess maturity, interpersonal communication skills, the way they conduct themselves in a professional setting. This is more of a question for those lacking substantial or impressive work experience after graduation. Another thing we look for is leadership potential, especially for those lacking a leadership track record. . . . Only 10 to 15 percent of applicants do a really good job in the interview. Perhaps 45 to 50 percent do an acceptable job, whereas 20 to 25 percent do a poor job and 15 to 20 percent do a truly awful job. *Don Rebstock, Northwestern*

Comments from Schools Not Interviewing on a Large Scale

Our biggest concern with interviewing is that it's so time consuming. It would help weed out the few people we would just as soon not have gotten, but there are so few that it's not clear interviewing is worth the effort. For example, one recent grad had a very difficult time getting a job. He had an enormous sense of entitlement, he whined, and of course he didn't interview well. He blamed everyone around him instead of himself for his trouble. We don't get many like him, thank goodness, but interviewing might well have eliminated him. *Faye Deal, Stanford*

We do not interview for reasons of equity and logistics. It would be challenging for us to meet all the over 7,000 applicants and unfair to expect everyone who is interested to be able (and have the financial resources) to come to New York. *Nkonye Iwerebon, Columbia*

Interviewing on a large scale would mean accommodating candidates from all over the country and from outside the country. Keeping the playing field level is difficult from the outset, and we would need to facilitate interviewing for all eligible candidates. Most schools pre-select who will be interviewed. Even with that approach, the task is enormous if we are to do it well and fairly, and doing it well and fairly is essential for it to be useful. *Joyce Curll, Harvard*

- My ending questions were/were not appropriate (and sufficient).
- My exit was/was not smooth and upbeat.
- I was/was not appropriately knowledgeable about the program (and the school).
- Interviewer's likely impression of me:
    —Personal:
    —Professional:

Second, send a brief thank-you note to your interviewer. Note something that occurred during the interview to make it clear that this is not a form note. You can mention, for example, that you were glad to learn that it will be very easy to get moderately priced housing near the campus. The one absolute requirement of the note is that you get the interviewer's name and title correct, so be sure to get her business card during the interview. If you do not, call the school to determine that you have correct information.

Appendix VII

HIDDEN INTERVIEWS

Many law schools do not interview their candidates, but their admissions committees often wish they had the kind of information good interviews can provide (as discussed at length in the body of this chapter). These schools may be unwilling to undertake a formal interviewing program, whether because they lack the resources to do so or fear that not all candidates will have an equal opportunity to interview. Yet that does not mean they must forego entirely the benefits an interviewing program could provide. After all, there are many opportunities to conduct "hidden interviews" with candidates.

Admissions directors and other admissions officials have innumerable contacts with applicants. Some of these are perfunctory, such as answering a question about whether their school offers an international human rights clinic, but others involve substantial discussion. For instance, when visiting a "feeder" college or manning her law school's stand at a law school forum, an admissions officer may spend five or fifteen minutes with an applicant discussing his goals, why he believes he is a good candidate and so on. Even at schools that do not (officially) conduct evaluative interviews, notes from this conversation are likely to be made part of the candidate's file and thus part of the admissions decision. Although this can certainly help the thoughtful, articulate candidate who presents himself well, the average candidate is more likely to harm his chances in these circumstances. He does so by:

- Asking inane questions readily answered by a quick glance at the school's website ("Do you offer any international law courses?")

- Rambling on about his credentials rather than giving a well-organized, one minute "elevator pitch"

- Revealing he has not yet given any serious thought as to where he is headed in his life or his career

- Showing he is feckless: a one-afternoon effort at pounding nails for Habitat for Humanity has led him to believe he should be a lawyer for a non-profit organization

- Being rude to other participants (including by monopolizing the admissions officer's time)

- Showing he is an overly entitled whiner

- Using "like" twelve times a minute

- Badgering the admissions officer regarding his chances of admission

- And so on

Keep in mind that in applying to a professional program, it pays to act like a professional. In any interaction with law school personnel—not just the admissions officers—there is a good chance you will be either helping or hurting your chances of admission.

ADMISSIONS DEANS DISCUSS HIDDEN INTERVIEWS

We have many interactions that give us useful information about prospective students. If that information is particularly positive (or negative) it is likely to come into play in the selection process. For instance, if someone has done serious research about the school and is making a serious effort to consider whether to become a student here, we are likely to be impressed by this.   *Todd Morton, Vanderbilt*

A lot of law schools are looking at interviewing and we may end up going down this road in the future. For the moment, it's unusual for us to conduct a formal interview. On the other hand, I do meet a lot of candidates—and make notes about them—and keep what I've learned about each candidate in mind when reading his or her file.   *William Hoye, Duke*

We have extensive contacts with many applicants. Even though we don't officially conduct interviews, anytime admissions professionals have substantial contact with an applicant they are likely to make notes about the interaction.   *Anne Richard, George Washington*

Applicants call all the time. If they speak with me, I may put a notation regarding my impressions of that conversation in their files.   *Faye Deal, Stanford*

We give people the opportunity to come and visit us. Positive and negative interactions can have an effect on the application. Phone calls, e-mail correspondences and personal visits all can impact the applicant and can in some ways constitute hidden interviews.   *Chloe T. Reid, USC*

Most applicants have more interaction with our staff than with us (the admissions professionals). If an applicant is particularly horrible to a staff member, make no mistake that the admissions committee will hear about it. We're dedicated to building a law school community that is engaged, thoughtful, and respectful—and such a person will not be welcome. *Renée Post, Penn*

We do not interview. We have considered doing so but the logistical constraints are substantial. On the other hand, if you stop by (for an informational interview) and the staffer likes you, he or she may make a note. This becomes a part of your file and will be taken into account in our decision-making. *Andy Cornblatt, Georgetown*

Part III

ON THE ROAD TO LAW SCHOOL

14

RESPONDING TO WAIT-LISTING, DENIAL, AND OTHER DISAPPOINTMENTS

— EXECUTIVE SUMMARY —

■

To optimize your chance of being accepted from a wait list,
bring relevant new material to the attention of the admissions office.

■

When reapplying to a school, start by understanding the reasons
for your initial rejection.

—Recognize that you will need to address these deficiencies
to warrant reapplying.

If you have followed our suggested approach, you have applied to six to ten schools. Only one or two of them are in the "likely" category and several others are very likely to turn you down. Prepare yourself for rejection by some of your choices. (In fact, if you get into every school, perhaps you have not aimed high enough.)

Nonacceptance comes in many forms. You may be put on an administrative hold, wait-listed, told to apply again at a later date after you have remedied a specific deficiency, or just rejected outright.

Your reaction should depend upon which of these categories applies and which school is in question. If one of your stretch schools says no, for example, you will probably react differently than if one of your likelies says no. Do not overreact, however, to any single school's decision. The vagaries of the admissions process and the differences between schools mean that one school's decision has limited predictive value in terms of what another school will do. (This is one of the reasons that we suggest applying to so many schools.)

RESPONDING TO AN ADMINISTRATIVE HOLD

An administrative hold means that the school was unable to make a decision on your candidacy within the typical four to eight weeks, so your application will be held over until a later (often, significantly later) date. This suggests that your candidacy is strong, but the school will not know if you are quite strong enough until it has seen more of the applicants.

Take the opportunity to send a short note reaffirming your interest in the program if the delay is scheduled to extend for more than about a month. If you have strong new information available—such as a promotion or a published thesis—by all means, communicate it to the admissions office.

RESPONDING TO WAIT-LISTING

Being wait-listed generally means that you will be admitted to the program only if someone who has been accepted chooses not to come. In fact, schools know that a certain percentage of their admittees will choose other schools or decide to wait a year or two, so they routinely admit more students than they can actually take. The "excess" number admitted, however, is often not sufficient to make up for all those who decline admission. The wait list is used to manage this situation.

WAIT-LIST EXCEPTION

There is an exception to the general rule that a wait-listed candidate will only be admitted if a space in the class opens up. Some schools wait-list candidates they suspect will choose to go to another school. By so doing, the schools eliminate the likely impact on their "yield" statistics—the percentage of people who, having been accepted, actually enroll at the school. (Managing a school's yield is part of playing the rankings game—controlling the school's admissions statistics to get the highest possible *U.S. News & World Report* ranking.) The strongest candidates to the school, along with those whose personal ties or academic interests point to another school, thus sometimes receive wait-list treatment.

Do not despair if you happen to fall into this category. For one thing, schools that play this game are delighted to find that they have been overly cautious and that you actually want to attend their school. By communicating to them that you do indeed wish to attend their school, you are likely to be admitted forthwith. For another, by wait-listing you even though your credentials are strong, the school has indicated that it believes you will get into another top school.

The trouble with being wait-listed is that you may not get off the wait list and into the school until very late in the game. It is not uncommon for schools to call people on the wait list only days before the program's start or, indeed, some days after the start. The lower down the candidate preference (ranking) list a school is, the more it is at the mercy of the wait list decisions made at other schools, and thus the later it makes its own final decisions. Schools atop the list, such as Harvard, Yale, and Stanford, in effect make the first moves in this game. When they take people off their wait lists, many of these accepted candidates withdraw from the schools they would otherwise have attended (and at which they had already put down deposits). This second group of schools then goes to their wait lists, causing the third group of schools to lose some of their accepted candidates. This ripple effect does not conclude until classes are under way in the fall.

Your situation will be complicated by the fact that most law schools will give you no indication as to where you fall on the list. In fact, most schools do not rank wait-list candidates. This is because admissions officers realize how many variables will not come into play until later in the game. There is no way for them to accurately assess how many—and which types of—wait list applicants they will need. Depending on the initial yield, the wait list may not even be tapped at all. In another scenario, law schools may find that they are "short" in one particular category of student (say, economists or international students) and utilize the wait list only to fill in such gaps. Another reason wait lists are not ranked has to do with the priorities of the wait-list candidates themselves. Many will be accepted at other schools and drop completely out of sight. Admissions officers are often uncertain as to how many wait-list candidates are still actively interested.

It is for precisely this reason that you, as a wait-list candidate, must not remain silent. By making yourself a presence to the admissions committee, you dramatically increase your chances of being one of the lucky few they "tap" in June, July, or August. As you are likely to continue to augment your list of responsibilities and accomplishments during this lengthy waiting period, you should communicate them to the admissions office.

The information you will want to impart to the admissions officers might become available at different times. Thus, it is acceptable to send them more than one update for your file, but it is wise to limit your contact to two (or three) instances, unless you know for certain that they welcome your constant attention. Find out from the school at which you are wait-listed how it suggests you carry out your contact—whether it wants to receive one or two notices from you or whether it enjoys continuous updates and inquiries from its wait-listed applicants.

What information will be relevant to this process? How should you communicate your new information? Any new information should show you to be even more the dynamic leader, thoughtful and mature decision maker, and so on, that the earlier chapters showed you how to portray. The one thing that makes your task easier at this point is that, having gone through all of the applications, you probably have a pretty good idea of where your applications were weakest and thus what sort of new information would be most helpful to your case. Knowing where your applications were initially weak means that you can be clever about bolstering these weak points in the months between the initial application and your follow-up communiqués. For example, if you know that one weak point is that your involvement in community and/or extracurricular activities has been virtually nonexistent, there is no time like the present to expand them.

A sound strategy, whether or not you have dramatic new information available, is to send a short letter to the admissions committee that provides any useful additional information you have—and that also restates why you think you would be a valuable contributor to their program, and emphasizes that you still very much wish to attend it. When a law school goes to its wait list, it wants to be able to make one call per available spot and fill that spot. It does not want to have to contact ten people to find someone still hopeful of attending that school. Neither does it want to have to track someone down, so be sure that you remain readily contactable throughout the summer.

ADMISSIONS DEANS DISCUSS THE
KEY ISSUES CONCERNING WAIT LISTS

THE ADDITIONAL MATERIALS YOU SHOULD SUBMIT
WHEN WAIT-LISTED

Wait-listed applicants definitely should interview if they haven't already. They should also submit a letter of interest, detailing as clearly as possible why they want Northwestern. Additional recommendation letters seldom help because they tend to be pretty redundant. Consider retaking the LSAT in June; we have admitted several applicants due to significant score improvements. *Don Rebstock, Northwestern*

Sometimes I'm swayed by information about what competitors you got into. (We do like to beat them!) Of course, we check this if it's hard to believe, so don't lie to us. *Admissions Director who wishes to remain anonymous*

It's helpful if a wait-listed applicant submits a new recommendation that covers recent months. *Elizabeth Rosselot, Boston College*

It is certainly appropriate to update your transcripts, if you are still in college, or to add letters of recommendation. *Ann Killian Perry, Chicago*

If you are still a student, submit your most recent grades. If you have worked extensively with another professor since applying, a recommendation from him or her is a good idea. We offer wait-listed candidates a chance to interview, which we think is a very good idea. Interviewing shows an interest in Cornell as well as offering another vehicle to get to know you. *Rick Geiger, Cornell*

THE NEED TO STAY IN TOUCH

It is helpful for someone to show that he or she is still interested by maintaining contact, but be sure not to stalk us. *Sarah C. Zearfoss, Michigan*

Although it is helpful to keep in touch to show you are still eager to attend Yale, please do so in writing. Be sure to bring important new developments—such as new grades or a prize received at graduation—to our attention. *Megan A. Barnett, Yale*

Come August 1, many people who had said they were interested may no longer be, so expressions of continuing interest are important. It's therefore appropriate to contact us two or three times during the summer. *Rob Schwartz, UCLA*

Not all schools feel this way, but I value contact. Stay in touch, send e-mails, and submit additional materials as appropriate. *Anne Richard, George Washington*

Go beyond sending a postcard. Assuming that you're interested, show it by being proactive—within reason. *Rick Geiger, Cornell*

There's a balance to be struck: you need to remain in touch, so as to indicate continuing interest and to show that you are easily contactable, but should not contact us daily.   *Ann Killian Perry, Chicago*

The Importance of Your Desire to Attend Their School

It certainly doesn't hurt to say this is your first choice, assuming that is the case. We benefit in two ways. For one, someone who wants what we have to offer will be a positive, engaged student. For another, we only need to make one offer to fill each place, which is a key consideration during the compressed time period when we are going to the wait list. Knowing that this is your choice will not trump someone with decidedly better credentials, but it really helps versus those with comparable credentials.   *Susan Palmer, Virginia*

You should know that many applicants on the wait list make their enthusiasm for Yale very clear. It certainly does not guarantee their admission, but it never hurts.   *Megan A. Barnett, Yale*

It's critically important. When we go to the waitlist, we go first to those we think will come if admitted. The goal is to admit one and get one.   *Anne Richard, George Washington*

I suggest that you send us a fax or note every three weeks or so. It's never a bad idea to help us understand your continuing interest in attending Duke. We review each wait-list candidate periodically, and take into account any new information.   *William Hoye, Duke*

New information is less important than other things:

—Make sure that we know how and where to find you during the summer, even if you are on the road or vacationing. We don't have three weeks to wait to hear from you.

—At that point, we are trying to gauge the level of interest of 50 applicants we are having trouble tracking down. Find a way to let us know that Georgetown is your number one choice (assuming that it is true). We want to make 20 offers to get 20 students, not 60 offers.   *Andy Cornblatt, Georgetown*

No law school wants to extend several offers to fill each remaining spot during the late spring or summer, because it negatively affects their acceptance rates and yield ratios and, as a result, their selectivity profile in the rankings world. And all schools want to enroll students who have manifested a sincere and particular enthusiasm for enriching their community.   *Jim Milligan, Columbia*

WAIT-LIST TIMING

We start out with at least 500 on the list and cut it down progressively to 75 or 100 in early July. We may keep a list of 15–25 right up until the start of school. *Anne Richard, George Washington*

We review wait-listed applicants in early June, then again in early July, and finally in August. *Nkonye Iwerebon, Columbia*

We will probably never be able to go to our wait list before mid-June and quite possibly not until August, even though for many of these candidates the notice is terribly late. *Monica Ingram, Texas*

We only take candidates from the wait list when someone in the class gets sick or is otherwise precluded from attending. This is not predictable: it can happen at any time, including late in the summer. *Megan A. Barnett, Yale*

It's particularly useful to keep in touch with us—and show that you remain available—at the end of the summer, when things happen quickly but most candidates cannot actually arrange to attend. *William Hoye, Duke*

Schools have a different sense of time than the candidate does. Serious wait-list activity for us occurs near the start of school. Candidates give up on the process by then, but should stick it out. We're playing musical chairs at this point. Many candidates deposit at more than one institution; summers are the time things are sorted out. We're like the airlines deciding how much to over-book. The closer we get to the time the plane takes off, the more we know about who'll board the plane. *Elizabeth Rosselot, Boston College*

THE WAIT-LIST NUMBERS GAME

We have two wait lists, our priority list and our regular list. In an average year, 450 to 500 are offered places on our priority list, and 25 to 50 are admitted from it. Similarly, 200 are offered places on our regular list, and 10 to 20 admitted. Of course, the numbers admitted from our wait lists vary dramatically from one year to the next. *Andy Cornblatt, Georgetown*

We intend to put fewer than 100 on the list and expect to accept between 0 and 15 in any given year. *Megan A. Barnett, Yale*

In some years, we may take 40 or 50 off the waiting list; in other years, none. *Susan Palmer, Virginia*

We waitlist between 150 and 250 students. We admit anywhere from 0 to 25 students off the wait list depending upon the year. *Monica Ingram, Texas*

We invite from 200 to 300 to be on our list. We have accepted between 0 and 50 in recent years. *William Hoye, Duke*

We usually have about 300 on the wait list; in recent years, we have accepted be-tween 45 and 50.   *Don Rebstock, Northwestern*

The number of waitlisted applicants varies from year to year, depending upon the competitiveness of the pool. We begin wait-listing applicants in February. We invite several hundred to join the wait-list. We have accepted as few as zero and as many as fifty from it.   *Renée Post, Penn*

We offer wait-list status to as many as 500, but some will decline it. In recent years we've taken between 30 and 100, generally starting in mid-May and end-ing in mid-August.   *Rob Schwartz, UCLA*

In recent years, we've had about 150 ask to stay on the wait list. We cut the list down throughout the summer as the class firms up. At the end of the summer, we might have 20 left on it in case we have to go to the wait list during the first week of class. (In some years we've taken as few as zero, in other years as many as 20.) *Faye Deal, Stanford*

RESPONDING TO DENIAL

The first thing to do when confronting a denial is to ask yourself how significant it really is. If you have already been accepted by a school you favor, the rejection is truly insignificant. If this is a school you very much wish to attend, however, a different reaction is appropriate.

SHOULD YOU EVER APPEAL A DENIAL?

If you have no truly dramatic new information to bring to the table, do not raise your blood pressure and that of the admissions committee by appealing a rejec-tion. Admissions committees go to great lengths to give applicants a sympa-thetic reading of their files—with even the most marginal file being read by at least two and often three people—so you can count on the school's having con-sidered your application material fairly.

Some schools, on relatively rare occasions, will be willing to reconsider an application based upon presentation of important new information. If you have such information and wish to appeal, contact the admissions office and explain the situation. See whether they will entertain an appeal. If so, be sure to present convincing new information, reiterating that you do wish to attend this school and will contribute greatly if admitted. (If you are not absolutely certain that this is your number-one choice, do not even consider putting busy admissions people to the trouble an appeal will involve.) Recognize, however, that the odds against being admitted will be very long indeed.

ADMISSIONS DEANS COMMENT ON APPEALS

The best reason to appeal is if you have new, objective information that the committee didn't have when it made its decision, such as a new LSAT score or a change of residence to Virginia. Curiously, it's people with credentials far from our norms, such as a 153 LSAT and 3.0 GPA, who most often appeal. *Susan Palmer, Virginia*

We have an appeal process in place. You need to submit a written appeal within 30 days of receiving notification of your rejection. But unless you can provide significant new information that was unavailable when you first applied, the initial rejection will be upheld. *Monica Ingram, Texas*

Often they look to bring new information to the table. They may ask us to consider them for the part-time program after we've denied them for the full-time program. However, we rarely change the initial decision—although it does happen once or twice each year. *Anne Richard, George Washington*

Although it is possible to appeal a rejection, only 1 percent of the time does it turn out to be worthwhile. If something truly significant has changed since applying, it is possible to turn a rejection into a wait-listing (never an acceptance). *Don Rebstock, Northwestern*

SHOULD YOU REAPPLY IN THE FUTURE OR SETTLE FOR A LESSER SCHOOL?

The question of whether to reapply is of course a complicated one. If you got into one of your top choices, you might wish to attend it this year, instead of waiting, hoping that you will get in next year to your very first choice. The situation is more difficult if you got into your eighth choice, but none of your first seven choices. If you realistically think you will be a stronger candidate in the near future, then it might be a good idea to wait and reapply with your improved credentials.

The important thing here is to analyze in what way you will, or could, be a stronger candidate. Cast a critical eye over your file. Look at it from the perspective of this book, analyzing each component fully. Was the component a relative strength or weakness for you at School X, given what the competition was probably like? If it was a glaring weakness, can you do something to improve it?

Chapter 8 analyzes in detail what you could do to improve your credentials. If the fault in your application was not the application itself, but your credentials, consider what strategy you will employ to improve them. Ask yourself whether a successful effort will significantly change the nature of your candidacy. Also ask yourself whether you are being realistic in thinking that you can do what you are contemplating.

ADMISSIONS DEANS DISCUSS REAPPLICATIONS

DEBRIEFINGS

If an unsuccessful applicant writes us between June and September, we will discuss the strengths and weaknesses of their files. *Don Rebstock, Northwestern*

Our time is limited, so we can't respond to all requests for feedback. To the extent that we have time in August, we will give some general feedback about a file, but we cannot give specific suggestions as to what should be done differently. We cannot tell rejected applicants why they were rejected. *Megan A. Barnett, Yale*

I'll review a file with a denied applicant; we're pretty open-door about this—anytime other than our February through April crunch period. *Anne Richard, George Washington*

We're always willing to discuss a decision we've made. Ours is a holistic rather than a formulaic approach, however, so we are unlikely to say that "according to our algorithm, you need to add five points to your LSAT score to get in next time." *Todd Morton, Vanderbilt*

I am happy to talk with someone after the season is over to help an applicant identify areas he or she might improve. *Susan Palmer, Virginia*

I am happy to speak with denied applicants after our season has ended. I review each element of the application, comparing them with the norms of both the entering and previous year's class. Where applicable, I suggest areas which can be improved. *Monica Ingram, Texas*

I try to help counsel them, especially regarding reapplying. Of course, it's rarely just one thing that was lacking in their application. *William Hoye, Duke*

DOES A REAPPLICANT START WITH A BLANK SLATE?

Reapplicants do not have to overcome a prior application: They simply face a blank slate. *Rick Geiger, Cornell*

We bring forward last year's file, but there's no strong presumption based upon last year's judgment. *Susan Palmer, Virginia*

If an applicant has applied within the last two years, we include the old application in the file. *Megan A. Barnett, Yale*

We don't hold it against people that they didn't get in when they first applied. We focus on this year's application: We rarely scrutinize closely the prior year's material. *Sarah C. Zearfoss, Michigan*

There is no black mark against them. They start with a clean slate. *Anne Richard, George Washington*

Reapplicants start with a completely blank slate. Their previous application has no bearing on a current application. *Monica Ingram, Texas*

When looking at a reapplication, we use the original application to help us focus on what has changed in the meantime. For example, perhaps there has been a change in job, title, responsibilities, etc. We keep old files on applicants for three years. Reapplicants should interview if they didn't last time. *Don Rebstock, Northwestern*

The decision we make on your file this year has no bearing on future decisions. Most people, however, don't do anything to change their applications. *Edward Tom, Boalt Hall (Berkeley)*

WHAT MUST A REAPPLICANT DO TO SUCCEED?

We suggest you take a good look at the timing of your application: applying late in the process could put a candidate at a strategic disadvantage. Next, look at the application itself: does it convey who you really are? Fine tune the aspects that are not suitably reflective of you. But do not stop there. Look to improve whatever substantive areas you can: revise or redraft the personal statement; if a new recommendation letter will convey new information, the candidate should consider including an additional recommendation; update us on what you've been doing. *Nkonye Iwerebon, Columbia*

They should approach the process with a 100 percent clean slate. They should generate a new personal statement, secure additional letters of recommendation, update their resumes, and provide any additional academic credentials. Without saying so, they should make the case as to why their application should be successful this time (whereas it wasn't last time). *Renée Post, Penn*

There are three ways to improve your chances. You need to transform yourself or your application—or apply earlier in the process. *Andy Cornblatt, Georgetown*

Reapplication is certainly possible, but it is interesting how few people make major changes to improve their chances. Perhaps five people in this year's first-year class are successful reapplicants. *Don Rebstock, Northwestern*

> We receive many reapplications, but few reapplicants have substantially improved their credentials in the interim. Admissions committees are relatively consistent in their judgment, so people who haven't improved their candidacies will again be denied. *Elizabeth Rosselot, Boston College*
>
> It is rare to go from a no to a yes, not so uncommon to go from wait list to a yes. *Andy Cornblatt, Georgetown*

Then consider the application itself. Did you write polished, persuasive essays? Did your résumé highlight your achievements and career progression in a highly readable format? Do you have reason to doubt that your recommenders wrote assertively and well on your behalf? If you interviewed, did it go well? If the answer to any of these questions suggests that you have an opportunity to improve your application substantially, what will you do to make the improvements? Are you being realistic in thinking that you will put in the necessary time and effort?

Do not be lazy if you choose to reapply. Rewrite your personal statement(s) and other essays to take advantage of your performance since your initial application, in light of what you have learned was wrong with that application. Consider using new recommenders, based upon their knowledge of your recent performance. If you use the same recommenders, have them rewrite their recommendations, incorporating new information about you to the extent possible.

OTHER OPTIONS

If schools that you want to attend have rejected you (for the moment), do not give up on getting a law degree. If you seriously want a law degree, there are probably a number of schools that can help you meet your needs. Most people who have investigated schools carefully, including those who produce the school guides and rankings discussed in Part I, sincerely believe there are 50+ quality law programs in the country. So even if you applied to an unrealistic set of schools this time around, cast your net a bit wider or reapply to schools you narrowly missed this time.

For those of you who are positively determined to attend your preferred schools—and cannot be convinced to go elsewhere—there are a few other tactics you may wish to employ. The following chapter will discuss them in some depth.

15

TRANSFER AND OTHER OPTIONS

— EXECUTIVE SUMMARY —

If you do not get into one of your top-choice schools, consider:

—Transferring to one of your top choices after a year at another law school.

—Attending a foreign law program for one or more years.

—Becoming an exchange student or third-year matriculant at one of your top-choice schools.

—Taking advantage of law schools' reciprocity policies to use another school's career services facilities.

Come summer, you may find that you have been rejected by all of the law programs from which you had most hoped to hear positive feedback. Although this is hardly an ideal situation to be in, there are still several paths— *other than waiting to reapply for entry into the first-year program*—by which the determined applicant can reach her goal: to benefit from the resources of a top program.

TRANSFERRING FROM AN INSTITUTION WHERE YOU *HAVE* BEEN ADMITTED

Each year, the top law programs' admissions offices receive applications from law students wishing to transfer to their institutions. Some of these students have discovered that they are unhappy with their current program—for reasons including unsatisfactory curricula, career services, or location—or have simply realized that their ultimate goals have changed. Most, however, are simply hoping to attend a school with a more impressive reputation than the one at which they first enrolled.

Until recently, most schools took in very few transfers. They did so only to "top up" their second-year classes, to make up for the (minimal) attrition from the first-year class. As the chart suggests, some schools still operate in this fashion, but others do not. Many top schools have determined that they can profit from a policy of accepting substantial numbers of transfer students—up to 10 percent of their second-year classes. There are several important reasons for these schools' changed policies. There are always some applicants for the first-year class who have substantial strengths but also present substantial academic question marks. These applicants can transform themselves into very attractive candidates, without such weaknesses, upon highly successful completion of a year of law school. Another reason for the schools to have changed policies is that transfer students' GPA and LSAT numbers do not count in the *U.S. News* rankings. Thus, schools can get students whom they value highly (due to their work experience or personal characteristics, for instance) without having to pay a price in terms of their median GPA or LSAT numbers (and thus their *U.S. News* rankings). Those schools that do not provide generous financial aid to transfer students have yet another reason to value them. (See Chapter 18 for a discussion of schools' financial treatment of transfers.) In addition, transfer applicants function as the ultimate wait list: Schools can use transfer students to adjust a class's composition after its first year.

	RECENT TRANSFER NUMBERS	
	NUMBER APPLIED	NUMBER ACCEPTED
Boston College	100–110	15–20
UC Berkeley (Boalt Hall)	200–225	40–45
UCLA	250	50
Chicago	120	12–15
Columbia	350	45–60
Cornell	150–200	10–20
George Washington	350–400	100
Harvard	200	25
Michigan	125	20–30
Northwestern	225	30–45
NYU	400–425	50
Pennsylvania	180	20–25
Southern California	175	25
Stanford	80–100	5–10
Texas	50–75	15
Vanderbilt	80–100	20–25
Virginia	250	35
Yale	100–140	8–14

EVALUATING TRANSFER APPLICANTS

Schools examine one or more of the following when evaluating transfer applicants:

- First-year law school grades and class rank
- Law school professors' recommendations
- Quality of the law school
- LSAT score(s)
- Undergraduate performance
- Rationale for transferring:
  —Professional/academic
  —Personal
- Work experience, extracurricular and community pursuits, and so on; i.e., the rest of your file

All schools consider first-year law school grades (better stated as your rank in class) to be the single most important criterion when evaluating transfer applicants. Some, in fact, consider nothing but this one factor. Some consider the quality of the law school at which you earn those grades, but others, remarkably, do not.

Some schools take into account one or more of the other criteria listed above. Thus, some schools will consider you in much the same way that they would have (or did) when you first applied to law school. They will consider your undergraduate performance (grades, grade trend, strength of curriculum, quality of school, and so forth) as well as your LSAT score. They will also evaluate your professional experience to date, and so on.

Other schools will evaluate your reasons for wishing to transfer. Some demand that you have a professional or academic reason for doing so. For instance, you may have decided that you want to practice international tax law but your current school offers no courses in this, whereas your target school offers several. Other schools care little about such professional interests and require instead that you have personal reasons for wishing to transfer. One such reason would be that your spouse will attend the medical school of your target law school's university, thus requiring that she move to its location.

CHOOSING THE SCHOOL YOU WILL TRANSFER *FROM*

If you intend to go to law school only if you get into a top school, you may wish to avoid over-committing to law at this stage. If you have (or can obtain) a fine job, consider attending law school part-time. This will allow you to continue to make money, bolster your nonacademic résumé even as you are attending classes, and even to out-work your classmates for top grades (given that few attending part-time programs will be particularly concerned about maximizing their GPAs). If you decide that law is not for you, or if you do not fare well enough in GPA terms to transfer into a top program, you can walk away from the field without having suffered unduly. After all, your career will not have been on hold and you will have sharpened your reasoning, writing, and research skills while developing some substantive knowledge of law.

If your situation lends itself only to a full-time program, you are faced with a difficult choice. On the one hand, you can select a much lesser school in the knowledge that it will be easier to rank in the top 10 percent of a weak class than of a strong class. This will make it easier to get into schools that consider rank in class of paramount importance. The problem with this is that you risk being saddled with the weak school on your résumé if you fail to transfer to a stronger school. On the other hand, you can opt for the best school you have gotten into. In this case, your chances of finding your way to the top of the class will be diminished, but your résumé will not be a disaster if you end up graduating from this school.

In general, if you feel that you are good enough to merit acceptance at the top schools, you should be able to get top grades at any (lesser) school. Thus, you are likely to favor attending the strongest school to accept you.

RULES FOR PLAYING THE TRANSFER GAME
ONCE YOU ARE IN LAW SCHOOL

➤ Get the most out of your first year.
  —Your rank in class will be critically important, so do all that you can to maximize it. (See Chapters 16 and 17 for discussions of how best to do so.)
  —Be sure to impress two professors deeply, particularly those teaching you in smaller courses or multiple courses. You will want each of them to write a highly detailed recommendation about your dynamic class performance, marvelously researched and written papers, and sterling exam. Put your discretionary time into preparing for their classes.
  —Pick up any academic awards that you can. For example, moot court at many schools is regarded as something of a chore by most students, but it offers a fine opportunity to bolster your legal résumé.

➤ Analyze your target schools.
  —Make sure they admit sufficient numbers of transfer applicants to warrant your efforts.
  —Speak with their admissions officers to determine which criteria they employ in evaluating transfer applicants. Do so at the appropriate time— when they are least busy. If you applied for first-year admission, contact them the summer following your application. If you are going to be applying to the school for the first time as a transfer, discuss matters in late spring (when first-year applications have been largely wrapped up).

➤ Analyze your appeal to the school.
  —Are their needs consistent with the profile you can present? Examine information about the first-year class when it becomes available. This will help you to see how you can position yourself to fill gaps in a class's composition.

➤ Upgrade your credentials as appropriate.
  —If your target schools will consider your LSAT score(s), you may wish to retake the exam.
  —See the discussion in Chapter 8 regarding how to improve your other credentials.

➤ Market yourself according to the advice in this book's second section (Chapters 8 through 13).

—Emphasize in particular the work you have done in your first year of law school.

—Emphasize any professional or academic reasons for wanting to transfer. (See Part V for a sample transfer essay and our critique of it.)

—Do not underestimate the importance of your personal needs. When writing your transfer personal statement, do not hesitate to address personal reasons for your desire to transfer to School X. If, for instance, your spouse is transferred to a location in the vicinity of your dream school—and a long flight from the one you are currently attending—be sure to bring this to the attention of the admissions officers.

➤ Understand that some law schools try to make it difficult for you to transfer out. They do this by neglecting to provide you with a transcript in time for you to apply or by pressuring professors not to give you a good recommendation. Although it is understandable that a law school would not wish to lose its strongest students, it is reprehensible that some schools would stand in the way of your bettering your opportunities. By all means ask friendly professors and/or administrators for help if you encounter such a situation.

—If these requests for help do not work, consider taking the following steps: (1) let your law school know that you might contact the LSAC about this behavior; (2) contact your college prelaw advisor and urge him or her to contact the law school (with the implicit threat that future classes at the college will be warned against applying to this law school); or (3) threaten to post suitable warnings on chatrooms or blogs (but be very careful about the legal implications of doing so).

—Unfortunately, I have to intervene several times each year on behalf of clients facing this type of problem.

➤ Be prepared to wait for an answer on your transfer applications until late in the summer after your first year.

—Schools do not make decisions about transfer applicants until they have second-semester (third-quarter) grades available. As a result, expect to hear no earlier than mid-summer whether you have been admitted.

➤ Recognize that this is a policy area in flux.

—Many schools are likely to increase the number of transfer students they accept. Schools in the midst of such a change are likely to be temporarily easier to get into than would otherwise be the case.

—Most schools are likely to change their admissions policies to a substantial extent over the next few years. For example, fewer schools are likely to consider only first-year law school performance in evaluating transfers. (Schools are likely to make a full file review the standard.) Make sure you know what each school *currently* considers relevant.

Several factors, however, may shift the balance in your decision of what school to attend for your first year:

- Consider the criteria employed by your likely target schools. If most of them emphasize the quality of law school attended, go to the best school you can. If they do not place much weight on this factor, however, you may still wish to consider a lower-tier option.

- If you have an inexpensive state school nearby or near where you wish to locate, by all means consider the financial aspects of your decision. In this case, your target transfer schools will likely understand the financial reasons for your choice of a less-than-stellar initial law school.

- A school that has one or more very small first-year classes (15 to 30 students, say) makes it easier for you to get to know and impress at least one professor than a school that features only classes of 100 or more. (This will make it easier to get a strong, detailed professorial recommendation when you do your transfer application.)

- A school that has very limited offerings in an area that is likely to interest you may give you an academic/professional rationale for looking to transfer. (Of course, you will need to show that you discovered this interest after your initial applications to law school.)

PREPARE BEFORE LAW SCHOOL

The importance of your first-year grades and other aspects of your law school performance means that you should do everything possible before school starts to get a jump on the process. See Chapter 16 for a thorough discussion of how best to do so.

Ultimately, it will be up to you to use and adapt the marketing skills you have already learned in this book and apply them to your second application process. All sorts of unpredictable factors may make you a desirable transfer student. If a school yielded an unexpectedly low number of students in a particular category—female students, black students, or students interested in public service, for example—they may see you as a way to boost their poor statistical showing. Use this to your advantage.

ADMISSIONS DEANS DISCUSS TRANSFERRING

EVALUATIVE CRITERIA

Our emphasis is upon how well they've done in law school. We look for stars in other law schools. Our assumption is that they want to move up, not that they are looking to do a specific program.   *Faye Deal, Stanford*

We look primarily at a transfer applicant's performance in law school and the strength of the school. Only at the margins do we look at other factors. Our goal is to get people who will rank in the top half of our graduating class.   *Sarah C. Zearfoss, Michigan*

We examine the first-year law school grades, taking account of the quality of the law school at which they were earned, plus a recommendation from a law school professor. We also examine the rest of an applicant's credentials, including undergraduate performance, work experience, and so on.   *Ann Killian Perry, Chicago*

We look at many of the same factors as we do for applicants to the first year class, such as involvement in extracurricular activities and leadership experience. A significant part of the evaluation is dedicated to grades in the first year, as well as recommendations received from law school professors.   *Nkonye Iwerebon, Columbia*

The primary consideration is first year law school performance and recommendations from law faculty. However, as the transfer applicant pool has grown, we also look at academic interests. What about Penn Law appeals to them? What will they study here? In particularly close calls, the undergraduate record will also be examined.   *Renée Post, Penn*

We primarily look at first year law school grades. Our secondary concerns are the reasons someone wants to transfer to Vanderbilt. What has attracted them and will be beneficial to their intellectual or professional development and/or is there a personal reason for them to be in Nashville?   *Todd Morton, Vanderbilt*

The key is first year law school performance, but we look at everything: undergraduate performance, LSAT score, work experience, and the reason they want to come here.   *Anne Richard, George Washington*

We have a twofold process. Candidates have to have done very well in their first year of law school, but they also need to have been strong enough candidates before law school to have been admitted as a first-year student here.   *Monica Ingram, Texas*

We consider a full year of actual law school performance to be a better predictor of future law school performance than undergraduate grade point average and LSAT score. We pay close attention to the quality of competition at the law school, so being in the top 15 percent at a relatively strong school will impress us more than being in the top 10 percent of a weak school.   *Susan Palmer, Virginia*

First-year grades and recommendations from their law schools are by far the most important credentials. The LSAT is much less relevant at that point. *Andy Cornblatt, Georgetown*

We don't emphasize the LSAT or undergraduate GPA as much as the first- and second-term law school GPA. *Edward Tom, Boalt Hall (Berkeley)*

GENERAL COMMENTS

Most law schools are now accepting more transfer applicants. They are very enthusiastic members of the community. *Andy Cornblatt, Georgetown*

Think long and hard about why and where you want to transfer. Be sure to develop strong relationships with several faculty members (who will ultimately be called upon to write your recommendations). *Renée Post, Penn*

If you know the law school you want to attend but are given a no the first time you apply, don't despair. You can go to the best law school that admits you and prove yourself in your first year. There are a number of top law schools that will be happy to look at you as a transfer applicant. Georgetown, for example, admits 45–50 transfer applicants each year. *Andy Cornblatt, Georgetown*

We receive about 250 applications. Those that are not completed in time typically lack first-year transcripts. Some schools are so dilatory in getting grades out that it effectively eliminates a student's opportunity to transfer. *Susan Palmer, Virginia*

We have few first-year students fail to return for their second year. Our admission of 20 to 30 transfer students is because we like to get an infusion of new blood. This gives a second chance to those who did not get in here before or got in and were unhappy with the school they chose. *Sarah C. Zearfoss, Michigan*

BEGIN A DEGREE ABROAD

If you are not accepted at a top program of your choice, rather than attend an American law school, you could study law abroad for a year (or more). This could be done in a Commonwealth country, such as England, which enjoys a common law heritage similar to that of the United States. Or you could study in a very different legal system such as the civil code system of Western Europe and Latin America. (The American system is slowly shifting to incorporate more of the civil code system, just as the civil code systems are incorporating more of the common law approach. But even though the two systems are coming closer together, the differences remain marked.)

Studying law abroad offers you the chance to show that you are definitely interested in law. It also gives American schools a set of highly relevant grades to examine to determine whether you are academically up to snuff. In addition, you can add to your admissions profile by learning about a foreign legal system and culture.

As the study of law becomes more and more global, American law schools have placed a higher value on foreign legal study. This can work to your advantage in the admissions game. Note, however, that there is tension between the goal of maximizing your admissions opportunities and getting credit for prior work done.

If you choose to study in a common law system, you will have more limited uniqueness value when it comes time to apply to American programs. (For example, a not insubstantial number of Rhodes, Marshall, Fulbright, Rotary, and other scholarship winners go to England to study law and then enroll in American law schools.) Yet at the same time, it is fairly easy to receive credit for up to one year of course work done abroad due to English (and Commonwealth) common law's similarity to American law.

On the other hand, if you choose to study in another system, such as a civil code system, you will have more uniqueness value when you apply to American programs because such study is less common. (It generally involves studying in a

---

STUDYING LAW IN BRITAIN

A Bachelor of Laws, the law degree in Britain, is a three-year program. Although the program is geared to prepare students to practice law in England, many of the first-year "common law" courses are similar to American first-year courses. (Foreigners often do just one or two years of study, intending to learn about law but not necessarily wanting to stay the whole three years.) The first year at The London School of Economics, for instance, features these courses:

➤ English Legal System
➤ Public Law
➤ Law of Contracts and Torts ("Obligations")
➤ Criminal Law
➤ Property I

The tuition for LSE, as with other leading British schools such as Oxford and Cambridge, is somewhat less expensive than tuition at private law schools in the United States.

language other than English, making it difficult for many potential applicants to pursue.) The result is that you will improve your admissions chances substantially, but risk not getting credit for as many courses as you might have had you studied in a common law setting.

Studying abroad will appeal most to those who are likely to have a substantial international aspect to their practice. The list of practices involving such an international dimension continues to increase. No longer do just a few people at New York or Washington firms, or working for the State Department, need (or wish) to understand foreign law. Even in family law, formerly a true backwater, there are now attorneys who specialize in divorces for those whose spouse lives abroad or is a foreign national, just as there are attorneys whose practice is devoted to child custody cases involving spouses domiciled abroad. Others who will be attracted to foreign legal study include those who wish simply to have the opportunity to live abroad for the period of study.

The tuition for foreign schools—not just British schools—is generally substantially less than tuition for American programs.

TRANSFERRING TO AN AMERICAN PROGRAM AFTER A YEAR OR TWO ABROAD

Most American law schools require that those studying law abroad apply for admission as a first-year and, once admitted, petition for advanced standing. The dean or a faculty committee will evaluate your individual case and decide for which courses to give you credit. (A few schools, including Yale, do not give credit for work done abroad.) Obviously, this can be a slightly risky undertaking, depending upon the policies of the school you ultimately attend. The school in America, after having seen your exemplary performance at a prestigious school such as Oxford, may admit you—but may not give you a full year's credit. Check your target school's policies and determine how recent admittees with similar backgrounds have been treated before assuming that your foreign course work will receive full (or any) credit.

**ADMISSIONS DEANS DISCUSS
STUDYING LAW ABROAD**

We really like to see someone who has studied law abroad, such as at the top English law programs. This provides a sophisticated training that few entering students have. *Sarah C. Zearfoss, Michigan*

> Doing law in England after your bachelor's degree can help you in two ways: It shows seriousness of purpose and it also gives us a set of relevant grades that will be a factor used in making the admissions decision.   *Elizabeth Rosselot, Boston College*

COMPLETE A DEGREE ABROAD

There is another approach available to those intending to study law abroad. You can complete a degree abroad, which will typically take about three years, then apply to an American program for an LLM degree, which can be finished in one year. With an LLM you can practice in some, but not all, states.

When it comes time to get a job, however, it may be difficult to convince a top firm, company, or agency that your education stacks up to that of your competition. If your law degree is from a well-known, highly regarded foreign school, you will reduce this risk somewhat. Similarly, if your performance at the American program is compelling, you may make it easier to get a top job. (Some LLM programs require that LLM students do course work separate from JD students. This will work against you. Try, instead, to compete directly—and successfully—with JD students, who are, after all, your competition for jobs.)

This approach to getting a job in the United States is too risky for most candidates to consider. Only those who are likely to have a very substantial international dimension to their practices are at all likely to profit from it. (But see the box "Canadian Law Schools" for a potentially attractive option.)

AN ALTERNATIVE APPROACH

Some foreign law schools permit their students to do a year abroad (and receive full credit for it). This opens up the possibility of doing two years abroad, then a third year in an American JD program—and then an LLM degree at this or another American law school. Doing two years in an American program will basically eliminate the problem of being taken seriously by leading American employers. (Many serious observers of the American legal scene believe that law school should not be more than two years, anyway.) As a result, this approach may appeal to a segment of those intending to become well-versed in international law or hoping to have a practice that focuses on more than one country or region.

CANADIAN LAW SCHOOLS

The combination of low tuition (generally a modest fraction of that at American law schools), common law curriculum (in most programs), and geographic proximity makes Canadian law schools a potentially appealing alternative to American programs. For some time, there have been accepted routes to bar admission in some American states. Massachusetts and New York accept Canadian law degrees from ABA-approved law schools as the equivalent of ABA-approved American law schools. Other states are less permissive, however, requiring either that you have practiced for a given period of time, in another American state or (perhaps) in a Canadian province, or have pursued further legal education in the United States, such as an LLM. (For detailed information about the educational credentials necessary to sit each state's bar exam, consult www.abanet.org/legaled/publications/compguide2005/chart10.pdf.) What has made Canadian schools a more attractive option in recent years is that leading American law firms have started actively recruiting at some of them, notably British Columbia, McGill, Osgoode Hall, and Toronto. (This recruiting is primarily to stock American, not Canadian, offices of these firms.) Also noteworthy is the number of London-based law firms recruiting at the top Canadian programs. These firms find Canadian graduates' global outlook—and bilingualism, in some cases—particularly attractive.

Application to Canadian common law programs greatly resembles that for American programs, down to the requirement that candidates register with LSDAS and take the LSAT. Note, however, that even at the leading Canadian programs the LSAT results fall short of those at leading American programs.

PARTICIPATE IN AN EXCHANGE PROGRAM OR BECOME A THIRD-YEAR MATRICULANT (VISITING STUDENT)

Each year a small number of law students study for one or two semesters at an institution other than their own. The courses they take are credited toward the degree they will receive at their "home" institution. This can be done in one of two ways: as an exchange student or as a "third-year matriculant." A number of schools have established official exchange programs with each other (the Harvard–Berkeley Exchange is one notable example), thereby allowing students at one to take courses at the partner school. The other option is to become a third-year matriculant at a leading school. Most of the top schools permit a handful of third-year matriculants. Columbia, for example, accepts five to ten visiting students each year.

BENEFITS OF BECOMING AN EXCHANGE STUDENT OR THIRD-YEAR MATRICULANT

Job opportunities. Attending a prestigious law school for your second or third year is an excellent way to gain access to recruiters who otherwise might have passed you by. At most schools, exchange students are allowed to use the career placement tools, programs, and facilities. Although prospective employers will no doubt notice that you will be receiving your degree from a school other than the one you are now attending, your résumé will nevertheless be substantially enhanced. You can expect prospective employers to take notice if you perform well at the stronger institution.

The improvement in your job prospects may also be a matter of the school's location. If you want to get a job in Chicago but are currently attending a school in Kansas, doing a year at Northwestern could obviously improve your contacts with your desired job market.

Access to influential professors. The professor in your taxation seminar probably will not know—or care—that you are an exchange student or third-year matriculant. Use this to your advantage. Build professional (even personal) relationships with influential professors: Impress them in class, do outstanding papers and exams for them, and so on. If you outperform the students from this school, you may well be able to get recommendations, job referrals, and other professional assistance.

The possibility of getting a degree from your target school. At several schools, there is a tiny loophole that allows some hardworking, ambitious exchange students to earn bona fide degrees. Taking a double load of courses, and thus getting approximately two years' worth of course credit in your one year, may entitle you to a degree from this school rather than your home school. The chances of pulling this off are slim, indeed, but a few people have managed it.

MAXIMIZING YOUR CHANCES

Admission to a prestigious law program as an exchange student or third-year matriculant is highly competitive. Although to some extent dependent on the fluctuation of student body size and your performance to date in law school, your chances of admission will rise dramatically if you can show the committee that you have a genuine need to be at their particular school. Committees are not often swayed, however, by your desire to seek employment in their area or by your declaration that you must attend their school because they are the only program on the planet to offer an Abused Animal Clinical Program. They are more likely to treat your application favorably if you demonstrate the necessity of your being in Chicago or Philadelphia or New Haven, rather than your need to attend Chicago, Penn, or Yale Law School. The reason could be a family illness, a spouse's personal situation, or anything else that would have a serious effect on the way you live your life.

ADMISSIONS DEANS DISCUSS THIRD-YEAR MATRICULANTS

About 20 to 30 people apply for 5 to 8 spots. We only admit people with a compelling need to be here. That does not mean a specific kind of law that we offer courses in; it's much more on the personal side, such as having a spouse transferred. *Edward Tom, Boalt Hall (Berkeley)*

We take quite a few: 12 or 13 for this fall. We look at their law school performance and other credentials to make sure they won't have trouble here. We do our best to accommodate them: they're usually coming for important personal reasons. *Anne Richard, George Washington*

We enroll two to four visiting students each year. Those applicants ordinarily have compelling academic or personal reasons for wanting to visit Penn Law. *Renée Post, Penn*

USE ANOTHER LAW SCHOOL'S CAREER PLACEMENT OFFICE

Nearly every ABA-approved law school in the country allows law students from other programs to use its career services facilities (but not to take part in the on-campus recruiting of its students). The practice, referred to by career services directors as "reciprocity," can be useful—especially for those students attending lower-tier schools.

Each school's policy differs slightly from the next. The more rigid policies adhere to a quid pro quo, one-to-one basis. In order for a student at Wisconsin to use the career placement office at Harvard, for instance, there must be a Harvard student with a desire to use Wisconsin's. This seems to be a rule that is honored more in the breach than in the observance, however, at least as long as the number of students requesting such service at the given school remains small.

Limitations to be aware of:

- Some schools grant reciprocity only to law school graduates, *not* to current law students. This presents a problem, of course, if you are in your first year at School X and are dying to access the career placement office at School Y in order to get a summer job.

■   Some schools will not grant reciprocity during the busy months of their on-campus interviewing program.

■   A general rule is that students cannot use services of a school within the same area as the one they are currently attending. An American University student, therefore, will probably not be permitted to use Georgetown's career placement office. Similarly, in areas well populated with law schools, students from out of the area may be limited to using the services of only one school.

■   Even at the most welcoming of schools, some services will not be available. Thus, counseling and résumé review are seldom on offer.

16

WHAT TO DO ONCE YOU ARE ACCEPTED

— EXECUTIVE SUMMARY —

◼

Congratulations!

◼

Consider deferring law school,
especially if you are not absolutely certain that law is for you.

◼

Take the necessary steps to reserve your place at your chosen school.

◼

Leave your job in a professional manner.

◼

Do all that you can to be ready for law school. At a minimum:
—Upgrade your writing skills.
—Learn how to take law school exams.
—Gain a solid understanding of several first-year courses.

◼

If you have additional time, upgrade your knowledge in other areas as well.

Two things should be true if you have followed the advice of this book. First of all, you have applied to law school in the knowledge that you are headed in the right career direction. You analyzed your own interests, goals, and talents, and considered them in light of what a career in law involves. Second, you have applied to an appropriate range of schools—and did so in a professional manner. As a result, you now have one or more acceptances in hand.

If both of these are true, you are ready to head to a fine school—so skip the next section concerning "deferral" unless you have a question about when you should attend, now or in the future. On the other hand, if you are not yet sure that law and law school are for you, read the following section with care.

DEFERRAL

Once you have been accepted to one of your top-choice schools, you need to decide how to handle the offer. Before sending in your deposit, consider whether you should attend school now, or whether you would be better off postponing it for one or more years.

The majority of schools have generous deferral policies, in part because they recognize that many people who apply to law school should not attend. These policies, however, are by no means uniform. At some schools, it is simply a matter of making your request in a timely fashion. (This basically means applying for a deferral in the spring rather than the summer.) Some other schools grant only a set number of requests, often in the order in which they are received. As a result, the timing of your request may be all important. At still other schools, you will be granted a deferral as long as your reason for wishing one is not regarded as frivolous.

Your reason can be either a personal or professional matter. Gaining a prestigious scholarship for study abroad would certainly suffice; so, too, would the opportunity to manage an important project. Given that your value to law schools and employers will generally increase with development of your skill set and experience, consider carefully what you stand to gain via an opportunity. Most applicants who defer—even for frivolous purposes, frankly—end up glad in retrospect that they did so. On the personal side, taking care of a dying parent would pass muster, as would other, less dramatic matters.

Different schools place the bar you must get over at different heights, so be sure to inquire of your chosen school exactly what its standards are. There are, moreover, a handful of schools (including UCLA and Virginia) that rarely grant deferrals. These do not penalize you, however, if you choose to reapply in the future.

ADMISSIONS DEANS DISCUSS DEFERRALS

HOW READILY DO YOU GRANT DEFERRALS?

We grant one- and two-year deferrals quite readily because of our philosophy that people should attend law school only when they feel ready to do so. *Nkonye Iwerebon, Columbia*

Quite readily. It's very rare that we turn down a request for a deferral. *Todd Morton, Vanderbilt*

We grant deferrals provided that candidates have a good reason for their request, which a majority do. An exceptional opportunity that is not likely to be available three years later, such as a major fellowship, would qualify. So, too, would true family hardship or the need to continue working in a department that depends upon you due to recent layoffs or departures. *Monica Ingram, Texas*

Deferrals are not readily granted in most years (i.e., unless we are over-subscribed). I want to be sure that you will do something important in the interim, that you are likely to show up after the deferral period, and that you are a strong enough candidate that you would be admitted anew even in a more competitive year. *Sarah C. Zearfoss, Michigan*

Provided they apply before June 30, we routinely grant one-year deferrals without serious scrutiny. Those applying for more than one year, however, are scrutinized more carefully. Our theory is that we want candidates to be here when *they* want to be here. *Rick Geiger, Cornell*

FOR WHAT PURPOSES (AND WHEN) DO YOU GRANT DEFERRALS?

I'm usually fairly generous, until about June 1. I'm generous with people who have some amazing academic opportunity. If they just want to go to Europe to play, I'll think twice, although I may still grant it. Personal reasons, of course, may also come into play. *Edward Tom, Boalt Hall (Berkeley)*

Deferrals are by no means automatic. In general, we grant them only for foreign academic fellowships (such as the Rhodes and Marshall scholarships) and extremely interesting, once-in-a-lifetime opportunities. *Megan A. Barnett, Yale*

Our one-year deferral policy is very liberal. We have a June 1 deadline to request deferrals, so timing can become a factor. Any number of reasons will qualify: a personal situation, employment experience, study abroad opportunity, public service (such as Teach for America)—with the possible exception of working simply to earn a few dollars. *Renée Post, Penn*

We are much readier to grant a deferral if someone has a substantial reason for waiting, such as having received a Fulbright scholarship, rather than simply being uncertain about whether to attend law school. *Chloe T. Reid, USC*

We grant deferrals on a case-by-case basis. We like to see that the reason for the request is for a chance-of-a-lifetime experience or a strong personal need. *Ann Killian Perry, Chicago*

We grant two types of deferral requests: for employment opportunities and for personal or family issues the applicant needs to deal with. The request should be made by June. By the way, we strongly prefer that people take time off to get real-world work experience, so having a younger applicant wish to defer to take advantage of a solid job opportunity strikes us as quite sensible. *Don Rebstock, Northwestern*

We are very flexible in granting one-year deferrals, as long as we know by about July 1. After that date, we are a bit tougher. More than one year is a different matter. We'd consider granting a longer deferral for a serious scholarship, but in general, the longer the deferral people want, the less likely they are to come. In fact, only one-half of deferred applicants eventually come. *Andy Cornblatt, Georgetown*

May Deferred Applicants Apply to Other Schools?

We preclude deferred applicants from applying elsewhere during the interim. We don't use deferrals to let a person keep an option open while considering whether law school (or Duke) is the right choice for him. *William Hoye, Duke*

Deferred applicants have to pay their deposits to hold their place in the class, but they are not precluded from applying to other schools in the interim. *Susan Palmer, Virginia*

We ask deferred students for a moral commitment to us—that they withdraw other applications and not apply elsewhere in exchange for a guaranteed place here. *Rick Geiger, Cornell*

Deferred applicants are obligated not to apply to any other schools during the deferral period, but I know that many do so. *Monica Ingram, Texas*

I don't have any control over this. If someone isn't sure she wants to come here, she should explore other options. I don't believe that law schools should try to impose restrictions ("we'll defer your admission for one year, but you have to promise not to apply to any other law schools and you have to promise that you will come to our law school next year") on individuals who are making the very important decision of which law school to attend. *Anne Richard, George Washington*

Yes; we don't require any commitment other than a tuition deposit. *Todd Morton, Vanderbilt*

Deferred applicants may not apply to other law schools. The deferment contract we have them sign prohibits deferred candidates from applying to other law schools (in exchange for maintaining a guaranteed seat in a future class). *Nkonye Iwerebon, Columbia*

Deferred applicants must agree not to apply to other schools in the interim. *Andy Cornblatt, Georgetown*

GENERAL COMMENTS

Applicants should not apply fully intending to defer their enrollment if they are admitted. Their application may in fact be stronger if submitted in a subsequent year. *Kenneth Kleinrock, NYU*

We give substantial deference to a prior year's acceptance, whether a person requested a deferral or not, or even if a deferral was not granted. *Susan Palmer, Virginia*

If you are not certain that law school—and the practice of law—are right for you, by all means defer. If you are unable to defer, trust that you will be able to gain admission again in the future if you so choose—and turn down the offer of admission. *Do not attend law school unless and until* you have ascertained that it is the right career move.

ACCEPTING YOUR OFFER

If you do not face any questions about whether and when to attend law school and you are accepted by your top choice, be sure to send in your deposit to reserve your place in a timely manner. If you are accepted by one of your secondary choices before you have heard from your number-one school, you may face a dilemma if you are required to send in a deposit immediately. Most schools have become so quick about responding to applications, however, that this quandary is no longer common. If you do encounter it, ask the school that has accepted you whether you can delay sending your deposit for a short time, and also ask your first-choice school to speed up its decision making, explaining the situation politely. It is probably wise to refrain from mentioning what your alternate school is, especially if it is of obviously lower caliber or is a very different kind of program.

The one time when this is still likely to be a major problem is if you are accepted by a secondary choice and wait-listed by your first choice. You may not get off the wait list, or be definitively turned down, until the start of school. You may have to send in a deposit to your second choice, risking losing it if you are eventually accepted by your first-choice school.

International students. As soon as you have chosen the school you will attend, begin the student visa process. This means getting a certificate of eligibility (I-20) form from the school, which verifies that you have the appropriate credentials, language skills, and financial resources to attend the program. This form, along with the accompanying financial documents, must be submitted to the local U.S. Consular office to request the actual visa. This process is all too often delayed by either the school or the consular office, so it is important to begin it as soon as possible.

ADMISSIONS DEANS DISCUSS ADMISSIONS ETIQUETTE

Even after being accepted, you still need to exhibit good professional behavior—you don't want to risk your reputation at a school before classes have even begun. Being rude or nasty to someone in the admissions or financial aid office can come back to haunt you when you need a favor later. Especially at a school as small as Yale, word gets around about which students are particularly nice and which are anything but.   *Megan A. Barnett, Yale*

Throughout the application process we try to gauge an applicant's judgment. We consider their choice of personal statement topic, whom they ask for recommendations, and their behavior when trying to get our attention. There is a fine line between being proactive and becoming a pest. Law school is a professional endeavor so applicants should treat the application process in the manner of the professionals they look to become.   *Renée Post, Penn*

LEAVING YOUR JOB

Leaving your current job may fill you with joy, sadness, or a mixture of the two. No matter which, it is important to resign in a highly professional manner. Once you have decided to leave, step carefully. Do not pop into your boss's office and wax ecstatic over your newfound freedom. Instead, think about how much notice you should give. You will obviously give at least as much as is called for in your employment contract. Whether you should give more depends upon a balance of several factors:

- Are you likely to be regarded as a traitor or spy or bad influence? If so, you may be ordered to clean out your desk immediately.

- How difficult and time-consuming will it be to transfer your knowledge and responsibilities to a replacement? Must you be the one to train your replacement?

  —If you will be involved in an in-depth training process, you may want to leave enough time to provide the appropriate support.

- How has the company treated others at your level who have resigned?

- What is your relationship with your boss?

  —If your boss is truly reliable, perhaps you can tell her in advance of an official announcement in order to give her time to make appropriate adjustments, without jeopardizing your paycheck.

- Does your company know that you have applied to law schools?

  —If so, you should tell them sooner rather than later.

- How much do you want to continue working?

  —If you would just as soon have more time off before starting school, you do not need to worry about being dismissed too quickly.

RESIGNING

Schedule a meeting with your boss on a Friday afternoon, so that she will have the weekend to reconcile herself to your decision. Explain what you have gained from your job and from her. Think in terms of what you have learned about your industry, analytical aspects of your job, written and oral communication skills, and so forth. Then explain why you are going off to get a law degree. (If your boss wrote a recommendation for you, all this can be done briefly, of course.)

To leave the best possible impression, be sure to:

- Complete any pending projects.

- Turn over all your files, with detailed explanations regarding how you would suggest your replacement proceed.

- Train your replacement yourself, if possible.

- If you have people working under you, give them one last review.

- Ask for a concluding review of your own performance, assuming that your boss is not angry about your leaving.

- Consider mentioning what aspects of your position vis-à-vis the company could be improved, but only if you think your boss would be pleased to receive this input.

- Consider scheduling a telephone call with your replacement one week after she starts work to help her out (and volunteer to call a second time at her discretion).

- Make every effort to stay on good terms with your former colleagues. Remember that they may well be your future recommenders or clients.

FINISHING COLLEGE

If you still have a few months left of your last semester, do not assume that it is harmless to neglect your courses and party the rest of your time away. Make sure you graduate with the best grades possible, particularly in key classes—those that demand substantial research, analysis, and/or writing. It is not unlikely that, during your search for summer employment after your first or second year of law school, a prospective employer will examine your undergraduate grades along with your first set or two of law school grades. B's and C's in your last term of college give a very different impression to employers than do straight A's. An exemplary record throughout college demonstrates you are self-motivated, that you always give your best. If you have the chance to make Phi Beta Kappa or graduate summa cum laude, do your best to achieve this. Furthermore, get any departmental prizes you can.

If you have a full semester of college left, be sure to take courses that will help you in law school. These include: intensive writing courses, courses in your expected field (accounting if you are considering tax law, ecology if you are considering environmental, and so on), and courses that would allow you to complete a second major. Write a thesis or major paper that will give you credibility in the future; in order to enhance your visibility—and your credentials—see if you can get this published in a journal or scholarly magazine, or even a local newspaper.

In addition, start thinking about your future career. How can you best utilize your school's services, organizations, and alumni to get a leg up in advance? Discuss the areas of law you are most interested in with your career office's dean or pre-law advisor, if there is one. Contact alumni who have attended the law school at which you will matriculate; focus on the ones who practice in your area of interest. These people are a gold mine of networking possibilities. Tell them that you will attend school X in the fall, and that you would love to chat with them about the world of family law or intellectual property law or whatever. When it comes time to search for your first-year summer job, these will be extremely useful contacts.

Think about joining organizations that may be useful to you in terms of developing specific skills. Participating on the debate team, for example, may assist you in conquering some of your fears about the Socratic Method. If another senior is slacking off in the presidency of a relevant organization, volunteer to take over. Approach a professor with whom you have developed a good rapport and find out whether she needs any assistance for an article she is working on.

PREPARING FOR LAW SCHOOL

RATIONALE FOR STARTING THE PROGRAM WELL PREPARED

If you are ambitious enough to seek a top law degree, you are probably also eager to do well in the program.

The easiest way to do this is by starting the program well prepared. The poorly prepared student is likely to struggle in the crucial first term and get poor grades in the first set of courses. The redemption process is not likely to start, if ever, until after the core courses have been completed. Only at that point will he be able to compete on somewhat equal ground with other students.

At that point, however, it may be too late to retrieve the situation entirely. After all, the students who performed well initially have been piling up points with professors and students, demonstrating over a lengthy period of time that they are capable analysts and persuasive advocates. This will be reflected in the summer job offers to students. These often lead to permanent offers (i.e., offers for employment upon graduation from law school). In any event, these initial jobs have an impact upon how other law students, professors, and potential future employers perceive you. As if this were not bad enough, at many law schools membership in the law review is partially or totally dependent upon first-year grades.

Starting law school well prepared will not only contribute to a stronger first-year performance; it will also alleviate—if not eliminate—the overwhelming level of stress that takes hold of some 1Ls and refuses to let go.

THE ELEMENTS OF GOOD PREPARATION

Learning the law school game is difficult if you have to master every element at one time. You need to learn, among other things:

- Legal writing (of case briefs, memoranda, moot court briefs, and exams)
- Substantive law in a host of fields
- Legal reasoning—i.e., what is relevant and what is not, and how to analyze the relevant facts

- Legal research methodology
- A new vocabulary
- How to survive classroom confrontations with professors (when they hold all the cards and, in some cases, believe that threatening you with public humiliation is the hallmark of the caring professor!)

Far better for you if you have familiarized yourself with substantial parts of this game before you have to play it for real.

SKILLS: THE BARE MINIMUM

LEGAL WRITING

Writing is essential to the careers of most lawyers. It is certainly relevant to law school performance. Despite this, very few people are good writers when they enter law school. This is as true for the English literature majors as it is for the engineering majors. Frankly, most law schools do a poor job of teaching students to write, despite the schools' protestations to the contrary. Even if they did teach writing well, there is no reason to enter the program as a particularly weak writer. No improvement in writing skills before you enter the program will be wasted.

You have two ways to go about this. First, you can develop your general writing skills. If you are not yet a strong writer, be sure to put in the necessary work before law school. Consider taking a writing course, or a copyediting course, at your local university's extension division. Whereas a writing course will have you doing your own writing, a copyediting course will force you to analyze, critique, and edit other people's writing. Either approach can be very helpful. The key is to take something rigorous.

Second, once your writing is at an appropriate level, you can take a course in legal writing. Harvard Summer School, for example, offers a course called "Legal Writing," described as follows in the course catalog:

> This course is designed for law students, students considering law school, or writers who wish to improve their analytical writing. It is based on the assumption that good legal writing communicates well-considered ideas clearly, concisely, and accurately. Students use the elements of good writing to construct legal arguments, to argue from precedent and principle, and to use facts effectively. They draft a variety of basic legal documents that may include a case brief, a complaint, an answer, an opinion letter, a legal memorandum, and a statute. Course materials are based on contemporary social issues drawing on the areas of constitutional due process, criminal law, domestic relations law, and the right to privacy.

TAKING LEGAL EXAMS

In law school, although other types of writing matter, exams are of ultimate importance. During the first year, in particular, your grade for an entire course will be based solely on the end-of-the-semester exam. Because law school exam performance is so vitally important—and woefully neglected as a part of teaching—you should prepare in advance for it. Some of the general legal writing courses of the type described above may show you how to play the law school exam game. (The UCLA extension course "Writing for Law School," for example, focuses as much on writing legal exams as it does on other types of legal writing.) If you are unable to take such a course, however, consider one of the following strategies during the months prior to matriculation:

Attend an exam-writing seminar. Various companies offer seminars on the skills needed to do well on legal essay exams. You can attend their seminars or buy their seminar tapes. It is actually wiser to buy the recorded tapes because you can listen to them at your own pace, and repeat them as appropriate. These seminars and tapes demystify the all-important law school exams and identify the methods needed to conquer them.

Attend a law camp. Recently, several companies have begun to offer five- to ten-day programs intended to immerse students in all aspects of law school. The structure of the programs is modeled after a first-year curriculum, and the courses are taught by law school professors. These "boot camps" are pricey affairs but they can provide good training in many areas, including:

- Legal analysis
- Briefing cases
- Oral argumentation
- Essay exam writing

Some of them also feature overviews of the American legal system and discussions of possible careers in the legal profession. Thus, they are of potential value both for those headed for law school and those who are considering whether or not to apply.

SUBSTANTIVE LAW IN A HOST OF FIELDS

So much for the preliminaries; now let's look at the substantive core courses. The key here is to avoid shouldering a full slate of first-year courses for which you are not adequately prepared. If you have no preparation in the basics of at least several of them, you will be in for a tough time. Be sure you have gained a very solid overview of at least two of the fall courses. There are several ways in which you can prepare.

Enroll in a bar review course. Bar review courses are designed to prepare law school graduates to pass the bar exam. More than half of the preparation is devoted to the first-year material, which the bar exam tests heavily. Many of the bar review courses allow you to enroll for their courses while you are in your first year of law school for a small down payment (approximately $50–200). You receive a book of outlines for all the subjects you will study during your first year and are allowed to attend the lectures that pertain to first-year subjects. This will consist of approximately ten classes, each two or three hours in length. Additionally, you are permitted to attend the Final Exam Lecture Series. This is a very sensible method of preparation; you will begin law school having already become familiar with each of the first-year subjects. Many of these courses allow you to use tapes of the lectures; this allows you to do the work when your schedule permits. Yet if you are in an area where your chosen course is running at times convenient to you, consider going to the lectures. You will start to soak up the law school atmosphere and law student attitude by being immersed with those facing the bar exam itself. This will likely spur you to greater effort in your own studying.

Read overview materials. One good option is to purchase a commercial outline. Gilbert, Emanuel, and the Sum and Substance series all produce quality products. Read only the introductory outlines, however, rather than the whole book. These introductions (ranging from 35 to 90 pages!) will provide you with a sense of the subject's structure. Reading the whole outline, totaling several hundred pages, will tend to immerse you in too much detail for your first look at a subject. Another alternative is to read the Nutshell books. These are, however, somewhat too long and involved to provide an easy tour of the subject, so they will work best for those prepared to devote substantial effort. You will need to read your chosen material more than once to develop some understanding of how the subject is structured, which is the key to good preparation.

LEGAL REASONING, RESEARCH METHODOLOGY, VOCABULARY, AND CONFRONTATIONS WITH PROFESSORS

The suggestions discussed above will stand you in good stead in many regards. In fact, if you follow them diligently, you will develop at least a reasonable understanding of legal reasoning, research methodology, and, as well, a substantial legal vocabulary. Taken together with your knowledge of the first-semester courses, you will even be well armed for any confrontations with old-style, difficult professors.

ADDITIONAL PREPARATION

If you have extra time, consider developing your knowledge in any of the following areas:

- Courses you will take in the second term.

- Legal research: If you want to learn more about the particulars of legal research, courses are often available at institutes that train paralegals.

- Microeconomics: Microeconomic thinking has become a standard part of the legal tool kit for discussing contracts, torts, antitrust, and a variety of other courses.

- Accounting: Anyone headed into corporate law or commercial litigation of any sort will find accounting knowledge invaluable. The same is true, surprisingly enough, in many public interest fields.

- Whatever will help you in your future career: If you are heading into family law, for example, any course work or reading you undertake in psychology, accounting, taxation, or finance is likely to be very helpful.

Do not undertake these additional preparations, though, until you have readied yourself for the writing you will do in law school and prepared for the (first-term) substantive courses.

SOME PROSPECTIVE STUDENTS SHOULD
PUT IN EXTRA EFFORT BEFORE SCHOOL STARTS

Several types of beginning law students should pay particular attention to preparing as well as possible. These include:

- Those intending to transfer. Given the importance of first-year grades to their chances of transferring successfully, potential transfers should make every effort to be ahead of the curve upon entering law school.

- Those intending to work for employers that demand top law school grades (and law review experience).

- Foreign students. Non-native speakers of English obviously need to get their English language skills up to snuff, preferably by living, working, and studying in an English-speaking environment for an extended period prior to the start of law school. It is especially useful for nonnative speakers to study the material described above, to improve both their grasp of English (including in a legal context) and their understanding of the American legal system. Those raised in the American legal system, and exposed daily to various disputes arising within it, have a substantial advantage over those who assume that the American system is probably much like their own legal system.

Those unfamiliar with the American legal system are advised to consult the resources listed in Appendix VIII.

➤ Those from weak undergraduate programs and those who are unaccustomed to doing close analysis and writing.

17

How to Get the Most Out of Law School

— EXECUTIVE SUMMARY —

■

Understand how best to manage your time.

—Learn how to study for classes and exams without investing too much time.

■

Think broadly about career development.

■

Recognize that law school is about more than classwork.

■

Keep stress under control.

■

Take advantage of the networking and social opportunities.

To get the most out of law school, be ready to start working hard—and smart— from the beginning of the first class. There are three keys to this. The first, discussed at length in Chapter 16, is to be up to speed on the basics before you start classes. This means having a good overview knowledge of the courses you will take in the first semester. It also means understanding how to prepare for and take law school exams. The second key is learning how to use your time effectively. To do so requires that you ignore the traditional panic around you during your first term at law school. The third key is to think sensibly about your career development.

TIME MANAGEMENT MATTERS

Law schools deliberately give you more work to do than most people could manage to do thoroughly—at least not without giving up on life as human beings know it. You must learn how to prioritize your assignments. The potential work facing you greatly exceeds your time available to do it. Determine what is most important for each course and focus on precisely that, doing additional work only as time allows.

Falling behind is the biggest trap you face. If you fail to keep up, you will face ever increasing problems. Falling behind results in a downward cycle: You have trouble following today's lecture because you hadn't prepared for it, so you must do extra work to make up for your lack of understanding of the lecture, meaning that you will never have time to get ready for tomorrow's lecture, underpreparation for which will mean that even more work is required to be able to make up for your lack of understanding of it, and so on.

Time management extends to your whole law school experience. You should learn how to do your classwork efficiently, and also decide in advance how you will spend your free time. Arrange your schedule to make time for the key activities you value most highly, and limit your involvement with other matters. You might have time to participate actively in two clubs, a sport, and a volunteer group, along with attending various career services workshops and special lectures that interest you, but you are unlikely to be able to participate in six or eight clubs and play as many sports, too.

CUT TO THE CHASE

There are too many reading assignments in law school, and they are far too long, to do all of them completely and well. The key to keep from being overwhelmed is to learn how to do the essential work first, and the inessential later (or, perhaps better yet, not at all).

The typical student. To work effectively, you must learn to see the forest rather than the trees, the big picture rather than only the details. This is contrary to the way that courses are taught, particularly first-year courses. Most students, even those who have been advised by second- and third-year students to get the "big picture," lack the courage of their convictions and spend too much time on the details. They believe the professors who urge them to read the cases (and ignore the commercial outlines and such). They try to read and brief the assigned cases, and may top this up with a look at a commercial outline or other outside material. They end up overwhelmed. As a result, they sacrifice what they regard as the optional efforts—reading the outline for overall perspective and doing practice exams—in order to be able to spend more time reading cases. They work all the time and are consumed by stress.

A better approach. The better approach is a strictly disciplined one. Pick one course for which you will (try to) do all the readings, brief each case, and so on. That will be more than enough practice at the traditional law student efforts. (Pay attention to how much more work this requires than do your other courses, without consequent increase in learning.) For all of your other courses, read relatively few cases. Instead, read two other outside materials. Read a canned brief of each case—a summary of the case. *Legalines* and *Casenote* are well-known publishers of such briefs. This will prepare you to follow the day's classroom discussions.

More important, read and re-read a commercial outline. These outlines, from Gilbert, West, Siegel, Emanuel, and so on, offer a (relatively) easy-to-understand guide to the important aspects of a subject. As with the canned briefs, they are keyed to the specific casebook you are using, so it is easy to understand which portions will be relevant to the upcoming week's assignment. Read these, and then re-read them. You should make it through the relevant section more than once before a class, and more than once in the weeks immediately after class. (Another possibility is to use a bar review outline.)

A sensible alternative. There is another sensible approach to courses for which a student outline has already been done. Check with second- and third-year students to find out whether anyone in their year produced an outline for any of your first-year courses as taught by the same professor you have. If such an outline is available, highly regarded as an accurate record of the course, and sufficiently detailed (such as 100+ pages, single spaced), feel free to rely on it as your primary source for the course. Make a copy of it to use for your daily note-taking in class. Then, at the end of each day, reread the relevant parts of the outline and your notes, and put any notes that pass muster onto your master outline (the relatively pristine original).

The bottom line is simple: If you are putting in more than four or five hours a day outside class, you are being inefficient (and possibly wearing yourself

CHAPTER 17

down). Stay disciplined; working smart is more valuable than working hard. Extra time spent is unlikely to equate to better grades, just to extra time spent.

PREPARING FOR EXAMS

Take mock exams every several weeks in each course. Pick questions relevant to whatever you have already studied. Have a study partner aid you in assessing your performance; examine, too, the model answer provided by the commercial outline you are using. Doing this will serve many useful functions, among them:

■ You will become accustomed to taking law school "exams," so you will not tend to panic when you must do so for real.

■ You will learn the nature of law school exams. Spotting issues and giving a quick overview of the relevant legal standards, along with a very quick discussion of the relevant facts, is far different from the undergraduate exams you remember. (It is also vastly different from other graduate schools' exams.) Taking such exams calls for a different mind-set than you developed for undergraduate exams.

■ You will understand that a very good overview of a course is critically important, but knowing the details of all the many cases you were assigned is of limited value, indeed. This will cause you not to get overly interested in or overwhelmed by the details of these cases, or by the desire to take excessive notes in class.

MORE EXAMSMANSHIP

Gaining a good understanding of what a professor is likely to test is a valuable skill. Consider four important sources of information:

➤ The emphasis within the course itself. Examine the amount of time devoted to each subject.

➤ Examine the professor's old exams (often found on file in the library), or ask second- and third-year students what they remember of this professor's exams.

➤ Find out what the professor has written about and is currently researching. Similarly, find out what work he or she is doing on behalf of clients.

438

> ➤ Keep an eye on the recent decisions being handed down in the field.
>
> Although many professors eschew the teaching of "black letter" law (i.e., what the rules are) in favor of discussions of policy matters, most test students largely on black letter law.

Mock exams are available from several sources. The same publishers that offer commercial outlines and canned briefs also offer exam questions, in some cases included in these booklets, in other cases sold separately. The other source of mock exams is the school library. Many schools keep files of prior exams. If your professor's exams are on file, by all means use them. Even if the only examples are from other professors, use them as a viable second choice. Using several sources for exams will keep you from becoming too fixated on any one aspect of the subject.

THINK ABOUT YOUR CAREER DEVELOPMENT

Presumably, one of your primary reasons for being at law school is to propel your career forward. If you do nothing other than work hard for your classes, however, you will miss a large part of what law school offers in terms of career advancement potential. Several nonacademic parts of the law school experience are ideal for career enhancement, as are specific courses. Discuss with potential future employers and the career services office which skills you should master and experiences you should gain during the program. Some suggestions:

- Take advantage of the opportunity to get to know your *classmates*. You will learn a lot from the more experienced ones, and will profit from these friendships in the future, including in your career. Staying in touch with them will provide you with important career advice and information.

- Get to know *faculty* members, especially in your chosen field. You will learn a lot more about a field if you spend time with the faculty members who are doing research in it, consulting about it, and so on. They will also be able to put you in touch with good industry sources to discuss the field and potential employers or specific job prospects. You do need to avoid the appearance of trying to cozy up to them simply to improve your grades or to benefit from their largesse without giving back as well. A sincere and active interest in learning about the field, on the other hand, will meet with a positive response.

■ Join *student organizations* that are relevant to your likely future career. For example, if you are interested in environmental law, join the environmental law society. You will have a chance to get to know the other members, who are themselves interested in environmental law. They will be valuable contacts in the future for information about the industry, job opportunities, and so on. In addition, advocacy organizations and the like, which involve members working on behalf of clients or causes, will give you an opportunity to practice your skills—analysis, presentation, negotiation, communication, and so on—in a relatively relaxed setting.

■ Take advantage of the professional services offered by the *career services office*. Take their résumé preparation and interviewing workshops, have them tape a presentation and several mock interviews, and, most important, consult them about your career plans. Take the career assessment tests they give; have them analyze your personal and professional goals; ask for their perspectives on where you are most likely to derive both satisfaction and frustration in your chosen field. These experts are a source of knowledge you would have to pay a great deal to consult outside of law school, so be sure you do not waste an opportunity to get their input free of charge.

■ Future employers will value *skills that go beyond substantive knowledge of law*. Your ability to speak in front of large groups, your negotiation skills, your writing abilities, and your knowledge of how to handle clients will, in total, be likely to have as much impact upon your future as will your technical legal knowledge. Therefore, gear your academic efforts to develop a broad range of relevant skills. Consider taking courses outside the law school to do so. In particular, look at the business school's course offerings.

■ Join the local or national *bar association*. Become active on a relevant committee if you wish to meet lawyers active in your field. In order to establish yourself as knowledgeable about your field, contribute to the association's periodical. You have an opportunity to develop your skills and reputation along with your Rolodex (Palm Pilot) without anyone viewing you as a potential rival (yet).

■ Join the local or national *industry association(s)* relevant to your field. For example, if you are a biotech person, joining a relevant biotech association will give you access to people throughout the industry. You can join a relevant committee or help out in some other way. Note, too, that it is particularly easy to get published in most relevant industry periodicals. If you are clever, you can develop relationships with those who will be your future clients (or employers). It is notoriously hard for young associates in law firms to develop their own clientele. This is one way to start the process early and get ahead of the game.

■ For those expecting to practice in the same area as the one in which the law school is located, make contact with *practitioners* in your field. Local alums are likely to be the most receptive to your advances. Even before you start school you can solicit their advice regarding which courses and professors to take, what special skills are most likely to be in demand, and so on. If you keep in touch with them as your law school career progresses, you may well find them offering you part-time work, or keeping you in mind when others are looking for help. They will also be helpful after you graduate, when having a strong local network will be of great value to you.

KNOW WHERE YOU ARE HEADED

Potential employers will compare you with other members of your class, and those at comparable law schools. Before committing yourself to an all-consuming effort to get top grades (and be editor-in-chief of the law review)—which will generally come only at the expense of many of the other benefits and pleasures law school can offer—figure out where you want to go and what it will take to get there. Talk with the career services professionals to determine what GPA, course selection, extracurricular pursuits, and so on will make you an attractive candidate for your chosen (type of) employer. If you intend to work for a major corporate firm, for example, you will need to get better grades than if you intend to open your own firm (where your GPA will be next to irrelevant). But even the most grade-conscious employers do not look just at grades, so make sure you understand how the rest of the package you offer will work for or against you.

The optimal mix of courses, grades, extracurricular pursuits, prior work experience, part-time work experience in law school, and so on will vary by field. For example, a Ph.D. (in addition to a JD) may be considered all but essential to teach antitrust at a top law school, whereas it may be considered nearly valueless in other arenas. Similarly, being a law review editor will be of great value in going the large firm route, but of modest value in many other contexts. For instance, if you want to practice family law you are almost certainly better off making good connections in the field in your chosen city of practice than writing a law review note.

The better you understand in advance of attending law school what you hope to do afterward, the better able you will be to chart your law school path effectively. Thus, where two- and three-course sequences are concerned, you can avoid discovering too late that a course vital to your future has prerequisites you failed to take in time. Consider very carefully—before or early in your law school education—what will most benefit you in light of your choice of legal field and employer, as well as your background and interests. The following chart looks at where people with different career interests might put their efforts. This is, of course, a very rough-and-ready view, meant more to highlight the fact that people headed in different directions will be wise to emphasize different matters during law school than to prescribe specific activities. In fact, within any field (including those below) there will be substantial variations regarding the specific practice desired, and, as a result, the most appropriate mix of law school efforts. For instance, within the "family law" category, George may want to do international child custody work whereas Martha might want to represent clients in financially complex divorce cases. George will need to take international litigation courses as well as those covering child custody. He may want to take child psychology courses if he has not yet done so. He will also benefit from perfecting his second or third language, and should consider doing a term or more of legal study abroad. Martha, on the other hand, would benefit little from these courses. She will, instead, focus on developing as much knowledge as possible about accounting and finance (in addition to the typical divorce, litigation, and mediation subjects). For example, she will want to become knowledgeable about forensic accounting—the tracking of assets.

NETWORKING

One of the most valuable assets you will have upon graduation is your network of contacts from your JD program. This network can help you to get jobs and even, through knowing whom to call for information and assistance, help you in your current job. The key to building an appropriate network is of course to make friends, avoid making enemies, be more cooperative than competitive, and impress as many people as possible. The impression you should make is of being clever, hardworking, a great team player, dependable, sensible, and comfortable working under pressure. In other words, your performance at law school will have a major bearing upon the network—as well as the skill base— you develop. Do not go to extremes in trying to network, though, because people trying to curry favor rather than develop relationships will always run the risk of annoying people.

   The networking opportunities law students are most likely to overlook, however, are not those within the law school, but those outside: alums, local practitioners (and judges), businesspeople (who hire lawyers), business school students (who will soon be hiring lawyers), and so on.

HOW TO SPEND YOUR ENERGY IN LAW SCHOOL,
GIVEN YOUR SPECIFIC CAREER GOALS

DESIRED EMPLOYMENT:	LITIGATOR (LARGE CORPORATE FIRM)	FAMILY LAW (SMALL SPECIALIST FIRM)	LAW PROFESSOR	PUBLIC INTEREST	START OWN FIRM
ACTIVITY:					
Maximize GPA	++		++	+	
Law Review	+		++	+	
Other Publication		+	(+)	+	
Courses Outside Law School		+			
Local Contacts		+		+	++
Student Organizations		+		+	
Clinical Courses	++	+		(+)	+
Cultivate Relationship with Professor(s)			++	(+)	(+)
Part-Time Work		(+)		+	++

(+) Potentially important
+   Important
++ Very important

KEEP STRESS UNDER CONTROL

The first months of law school are loaded with stress. You will probably be in an unfamiliar environment, surrounded by people you do not know, and be expected to produce more work faster than you have before. In addition, you may be competing with people of a higher quality than you have ever encountered before. This, combined with your high expectations for your own performance, can generate tremendous pressure.

Such pressure can be good or bad. Pressure can motivate you to work hard in a focused fashion. On the other hand, too much pressure can paralyze you and leave you unable to work or concentrate.

To avoid being overwhelmed by stress, *be aware of the signs.* If you feel panicked about not meeting your goals, or enraged about what is being asked of you, or you are feeling the physical symptoms of stress (such as digestive problems; compulsive consumption of food, alcohol, or cigarettes; or tightness in your neck and shoulders), you may well be suffering from excessive stress.

Then *recognize what is causing your stress.* This is likely to be a combination of two things. First, you are demanding too much of yourself. You are expecting to read each case down to the minutest detail, and be able to respond correctly to each and every interrogation in class. You are also probably expecting to get through the whole program without falling flat on your face a few times. Be realistic; disappointments and mistakes are a normal part of the learning experience. Second, you are failing to appreciate that law school programs deliberately give you more work than anyone can do in the time available.

This can be a rotten combination. You need to learn, as noted earlier, how to digest the important elements of courses without wasting unnecessary amounts of time on them. You must carefully and firmly prioritize what you will do and what you will skip.

In addition, keep your everyday life under suitable control:

- Get regular exercise. Pick a sport you enjoy and devote half an hour or an hour to it at least five days a week. This will provide you with a suitable outlet for your anxiety, anger, and frustration.
- Eat properly. Too many late-night pizzas, or burgers wolfed down minutes before class, will eventually sap your energy and health.
- Get a reasonable amount of sleep, and make sure that once a week you get an extra couple of hours to help make up for your overly demanding schedule.

If you feel overwhelmed, by all means seek counseling, which law schools make readily available.

DON'T FORGET THE SOCIAL EXPERIENCE

Get involved in school life. Join several clubs, participate in a sport or two, and get to know your classmates and your professors. If you are married, involve your spouse in as many activities as possible, because it will enrich your experience to be able to share it with someone who truly understands what is involved, and he or she will enjoy the time rather than resenting your new and all-consuming lifestyle.

FINANCING YOUR LAW DEGREE

— EXECUTIVE SUMMARY —

■

Calculate the full cost of a law degree.

■

Consider your options in terms of programs and financing alternatives.

—Schools' aid policies differ dramatically, giving you opportunities to save a lot of money.

—There are many financing strategies available, but few are realistic unless you start working on them early in the process.

■

Do not leap to attend a program just because it will save you money in the short run.

—Law school should be considered a long-term investment: Look for the best value, not the cheapest option.

Going to law school is a very expensive proposition. Those attending the leading private schools without grant aid can expect to spend over $150,000 for their three years. Even those attending a public school such as the University of Michigan—and paying resident tuition—may spend over $100,000. These figures represent the *direct costs* of the program, but the indirect costs are also important. The *opportunity cost*—or money foregone—is the amount of money you could have earned had you continued working (or begun to work) rather than going to law school. Similarly, if your spouse has to take a lower paying job or change careers, this also represents a potentially substantial opportunity cost.

Despite the size of these sums, the financial consequences of attending a *well-chosen* top school suggest that it can be a very good investment. It has been an extremely good investment historically, and looks to be an even better investment at the moment (given the level of private-sector starting salaries).

The question of how you will finance your law degree is nonetheless of critical importance. Whereas the minutiae of filling out financial aid forms is beyond the scope of this book, this chapter will examine the major financing strategies you can employ consistent with your career choices.

CALCULATING THE COST OF LAW SCHOOL

The financial aid you will receive for law school is based upon a simple formula:

Cost of Law School – Expected (Family) Contribution = Financial Need

The cost of attending law school is hardly a mystery. Schools are quite good about providing applicants with information about the cost of attendance (based upon the experiences of their current students) in the application materials they send out. For instance, Duke's 2007–08 academic year budget for a single student was:

Tuition	$39,960
Hospital Insurance	1,489
Health Fee (mandatory)	546
Law Bar Dues	110
Activity Fee	26
Recreation Fee	66
Transcript Fee (one time only)	40

Rent/Room	5,400
Food	3,780
Books/Supplies	1,140
Miscellaneous	2,880
Transportation	1,840
Total	**$57,277**

This estimate will not necessarily be a totally accurate one for you, of course, depending upon such things as how luxuriously you intend to live during law school, how many times you intend to visit home (and how much it will cost for each visit), and so on, so be sure to alter the bottom-line figure to reflect your personal circumstances.

In general, the direct cost of attending a school will depend mainly on its tuition rate, the living expenses in the area, and your chosen lifestyle. Annual tuition and fees can range from about $20,000 to more than $40,000, with the top private schools all charging at the high end of that range. Other costs (housing, food, books, personal expenses, etc.) for a single student can range from $12,000 to more than $24,000, as estimated by the schools themselves. (Note, however, that some schools underestimate these additional expenses.) Married students, and those with children, will pay proportionately more. A quick look at one public school and one private school reveals the range of expense involved:

	TEXAS	HARVARD
Resident Tuition and Fees	$20,632	
Non-Resident Tuition and Fees	$35,130	$39,325
Total Budget: Resident	$34,268	
Total Budget: Non-Resident	$48,766	$62,400

As is readily apparent, the total may be as little as $30,000–35,000 or well over $62,000 per year.

YOUR EXPECTED (FAMILY) CONTRIBUTION

HOW YOUR CONTRIBUTION IS DETERMINED

The "sticker price" of law school is one thing; the amount you will actually have to pay is another. You may be given a grant (scholarship), loan, or work-study assistance. Before handing out any money, however, both the law schools and the federal government—the most important sources of financial aid for law students—calculate what they will expect you to contribute.

The law schools expect you to get whatever government loan aid is available before they will kick in any funds themselves (except, in some cases, when they give out merit grants, as discussed below). Thus, the first question is what the *federal government* will lend you. Federal government lending is based upon its calculation of your financial need, which it determines through the use of the Free Application for Federal Student Aid ("FAFSA"; available at www.fafsa.ed.gov), which you may recall from your college applications. Your expected contribution will be calculated by looking at your assets (including bank accounts, home equity, automobile, and so on) and income. Your spouse's assets and earnings are included in these calculations. Annual federal loans up to $18,500 are available—depending, of course, upon your demonstrated financial need.

What if you need more than you can get from the federal government? Law schools still are not ready to help; they expect you to get *private loans* next, from banks or other lenders (see below for a list of possibilities). *Law schools expect you to take on anywhere from $21,000 to $25,000 or more in annual loans before they will give you need-based grants.* The first $18,500 will come from the federal government, the remaining thousands from private lenders.

Finally, after you have accessed the federal and private loans up to the ceiling amount expected by the particular school, you may qualify for law school grants. Now it is the turn of the *law schools* to assess your expected contribution. They follow much the same approach as the federal government, albeit with two significant differences. First, in many instances they also assess your parents' ability to pay. (In assessing your parents' ability to contribute, however, they are not mandating that your parents pay out any money. Instead, the schools will subtract your parents' expected contribution from what they consider your financial need, allowing you to try to borrow or earn that amount if you so choose in place of having your parents contribute.)

Second, the schools also require an additional application form for their own financial aid. The most commonly used form is the Financial Aid PROFILE, developed by the College Board (available at www.collegeboard.org). The other commonly used form is the Need Access application (available at www.accessgroup.org). Both of these operate in a similar fashion: You fill out the form and pay them to send it to your designated schools. As with every other aspect of the financial aid process, be sure that you proceed in a timely fashion. It can take up to one and a half months for these organizations to get your form to all of your schools.

THE LOGISTICS OF APPLYING
FOR FINANCIAL AID

Apply early for aid. For some schools, fund limitations dictate that financial aid be granted on a first-come, first-served basis. This means that if you submit your forms even a month before the deadline, you may find yourself without much assistance. This is often the case for grants, yet can also be true for need-based loans. Therefore, do not wait until you have been accepted to submit your FAFSA and supplemental forms.

File your income taxes as early as possible after January 1, because schools will require you to send a copy of your actual return and, as well, the FAFSA form requires information that is derived from your tax return. (Keep copies, too.)

Determine whether you need to declare an interest in grant aid. At many schools, all applicants are considered for merit grants. Check at each school to which you are applying, however, whether you need to declare your interest.

Note what is necessary to file for federal and law school aid. Federal funds are available on the basis of what you (and your spouse) need, without regard to your parents' financial situation. Note that your spouse's income and assets will be included in this calculation. School funds, on the other hand, may not only take account of your income and assets, and those of your spouse, but also those of your parents.

To apply for loans only (government or private), expect to submit:

➤ FAFSA form

➤ A signed copy of your most recent federal tax return

➤ A signed copy of your spouse's (if any) most recent federal tax return

To apply for other forms of financial aid, including school grant aid, expect to submit a PROFILE or Need Access report in addition to the other materials.

Expect to refer to numerous other records as well, including:

➤ Current bank statements

➤ Mortgage information

➤ Medical payments

➤ Business financial statements

➤ Stock, bond, and retirement accounts

➤ Loan information (including prior educational loans)

RUN MOCK FAFSA, PROFILE, AND NEED ACCESS CALCULATIONS

The intricacies of the FAFSA, PROFILE, and Need Access calculations are beyond the scope of this book. Instead, you are urged to gather the information necessary to fill out the practice forms on-line (at the sites noted above). There are numerous benefits to running these calculations:

■ You will learn approximately what contributions are expected of you (and your family).

■ You will have gathered the information necessary to fill out these forms "for real."

■ You can play "what-if" games to determine how to structure your finances before law school. For instance, should you sell stocks to pay down the mortgage on your condo or keep them for law school? Should you give $10,000 to your parents? Or to a sibling? (This is the maximum amount you can transfer absent tax effects.)

The former *asset-shuffling game* (paying down the mortgage) can work because most schools do not assess your primary residence. The latter game (transferring assets within the family) can work because schools assess parents' assets at a lesser rate than they do applicants' assets. These are probably the two most important asset-shuffling games but, of course, there are others. By running mock calculations, you can determine which games are open to you—and which promise the greatest benefits. (For more information on playing "what-if" games, consult www.finaid.org/fafsa/maximize.html for the helpful article "Maximizing Your Aid Eligibility.")

TYPES OF FINANCIAL AID

LOANS

The vast bulk of law school financial aid is in the form of loans. As noted earlier, for those who will receive only need-based aid (not merit aid), schools typically require that students take on a set amount of loan—typically between $22,000 and $24,000 per year—before any grant aid or work-study is offered. Given that only a minority of students at the top schools receive merit grants, this means that a substantial majority of students will indeed take on a very substantial debt load to pay for law school. (This is clear from the fact that approximately three-quarters of those who attend the top schools borrow money to do so and, for those who do borrow, the average debt upon graduation now exceeds $80,000.)

For those with good credit histories (see page 448), it is generally easy to borrow such amounts. Whether you should do so, of course, is another question. After all, borrowing influences not just your financial future, but also your career future. If you graduate with a massive debt load, you will not be able to work for the next years at a community college instructor's salary.

LOAN PROGRAMS

There are four types of loans generally on offer for law school education: Federal Perkins, Federal Subsidized Stafford, Federal Unsubsidized Stafford, and private. American citizens or permanent residents are eligible for the various federal loan programs.

- *Federal Perkins Loan.* Perkins loans are funded through a combination of university and federal funds. These long-term loans generally offer the best terms of any educational loan. They carry an interest rate of 5 percent and defer the accumulation of interest while students are in law school. (In fact, the loan is free of interest until the repayment point, nine months after the student leaves school.) To be eligible, you must be a full-time student in good standing. The amount of Perkins loan money available to each school, and thus to each student, is limited, causing schools to award Perkins loans to the neediest students. In general, the maximum amount is $6,000.

- *Federal Subsidized Stafford Loan.* These long-term educational loans are underwritten by a government guarantee, but are made by banks, savings and loans, and other lenders. They carry a variable interest rate of the 91-day Treasury Bill plus 1.7 percent (with an additional 0.6 percent increase upon graduation), capped at 8.25 percent. There is an origination fee of 3 percent, and a guarantee fee of 0–1 percent (based upon the agency). The government pays all interest charges while students are in school and during the six-month grace period thereafter. The maximum amount a law student may borrow in an academic year is $8,500.

- *Federal Unsubsidized Stafford Loan.* The costs of an Unsubsidized Stafford Loan are the same as for a Subsidized Stafford except that the government does not pay interest charges while the student is in school and during the six-month grace period. Law students are eligible for up to $18,500 annually from the Unsubsidized Stafford loan program, minus any amount borrowed through the Subsidized Stafford program.

- *Private Loans.* Various private loans are on offer from well-established educational lenders. These include Citibank, TERI, Sallie Mae (a largely private loan agency), and the Access Group. Note that all of these involve credit checks and require a satisfactory credit history. One easy way to determine whether you are likely to be approved for a private educational loan is to contact a lender, such as the Access Group, which offers a pre-approval process. Once you have provided your information, they will conduct a credit check and notify you of their decision. If you qualify, you can complete their loan application process, or simply rest assured that you will be able to qualify for a loan when the time comes.

CHOOSING LOANS

Students should borrow from lenders in the order listed above: Federal Perkins first, and to the extent that this does not suffice, Federal Subsidized Stafford. If more is needed, borrow next from the Federal Unsubsidized, and then from private lenders. Because Perkins and Stafford loans will not ordinarily cover tuition fully, students often use private educational loans to complete their funding needs.

When comparing loans, consider both the fees charged for origination or guarantee and the interest rates. Origination or guarantee fees can be charged upon disbursement of your money, or when you go into repayment. In either case, consider these fees in your calculations. Interest rates in private loan programs are seldom flat rates. Instead, they are based upon the Treasury Bill or prime rates, with an additional several percentage points tacked on. This means that the actual interest rate will fluctuate with these market interest rates. It is, of course, easy to determine the cheapest rate if the loans you are examining all use the 91-day T-Bill rate, or all use LIBOR (the London inter-bank offer rate), as the basis of their calculations. It is a bit trickier to compare rates if one lender uses the T-Bill and another uses LIBOR. To determine what will be cheaper, calculate the current rate in effect by looking up the relevant T-Bill and LIBOR rates and then adding the relevant percentage figures.

THE IMPLICATIONS OF YOUR CREDIT HISTORY

Student loans depend upon your credit history. If you have loans in default, have made late credit card payments, and so on, your ability to borrow may be limited. To make sure that you have a clean credit history, or to start the process of cleaning up your record, obtain a copy of your credit report by contacting one of the following credit-reporting agencies:

➤ Equifax (800) 685-1111, www.equifax.com

➤ Experian (formerly TRW) (888) 397-3742, www.experian.com

➤ Trans Union (800) 888-4213, www.transunion.com

Try to keep any loans you take out with the same lender as any prior educational loans you have. This will make your record keeping and repayment simple. In fact, even if you take out Federal Stafford loans, you will find that most private educational lenders also participate in this federal program. Consequently, you will probably be able to stick to the one-lender policy.

LOAN REPAYMENTS

- *Grace periods.* Most private loans, as well as Federal Stafford loans, have a six-month period after graduation during which no payments are required. Federal Perkins loans have a nine-month grace period.

- *Repayment amounts.* The following chart provides amortization data to help you determine the amount of monthly payment you will make for any given loan. To utilize it, first determine the amount of principal for each loan. (Note that unsubsidized loans will accrue interest during your period of study, meaning that the principal amount to be repaid will have increased.) Once you have the principal amount, check the chart for the duration of the loan and its interest rate. The associated figure in the chart shows how much you will repay monthly *for each one thousand dollars of principal.* For example, if you borrowed $20,000 for 20 years at 10.0 percent, you will need to repay $9.65 per thousand. Thus, you will need to repay $193.00 per month (i.e., 20 × $9.65). If you borrowed the same amount, at the same interest rate, but for *10* years rather than 20, you would need to repay $264.50 per month.

NUMBER OF YEARS	INTEREST RATE					
	5.0%	**8.0%**	**9.0%**	**10.0%**	**11.0%**	**12.0%**
5		20.28	20.76	21.25	21.75	22.25
10	10.61	12.14	12.67	13.22	13.78	14.35
15		9.56	10.15	10.75	11.37	12.01
20		8.37	9.00	9.65	10.33	11.02
25		7.72	8.40	9.09	9.81	10.54
30		7.34	8.05	8.78	9.53	10.29

To calculate the exact loan payments facing you, consult one of the following loan calculators:

www.finaid.org/calculators/loanpayments.phtml

www.salliemae.com/manage/index.html (click on "estimate your monthly loan payments")

www.accessgroup.org/calculators/loan_repay.htm

http://apps.collegeboard.com/fincalc/sla.jsp

Loan Repayment Assistance Programs (LRAPs)

Paying back student loans is no easy feat, particularly if you wish to head into a low-paying field. Because of this, many of the top schools have instituted loan forgiveness programs for students who choose relatively low-paying jobs in one or another of the following sectors: local, state, and federal government; private nonprofit organizations serving the public interest; low-wage private law practices serving underrepresented constituencies; and academe.

The key elements of Stanford's program are set forth below, to provide an overview of a typical program. Following this are a series of charts designed to show the range of differences of top schools' programs on these key points. *A few caveats are called for.* First, in order to simplify a very complex subject, these charts inevitably overlook numerous subtleties. The charts are not designed to show the workings of a specific school; instead, they are meant to show the range of policies at the leading schools in order to highlight the type of information an interested applicant needs to examine for each. Second, some top schools are not included in these charts, either because information was not available prior to this book's publication or because they do not have an LRAP program (Texas, for example). In some cases, the policy of a given school cannot be readily captured by the categories used in a chart, so it has been left out. Third, as is so often the case with financial aid at the moment, the programs are in a state of flux. Expect the weaker programs to be forced, through competition, to improve their terms and conditions.

Stanford's Loan Repayment Assistance Program

Qualifying employment. The employment must be law-related and public interest in spirit and content. The "law-related" requirement means that the position must substantially utilize the legal training and skills of the graduate. Public interest work is defined as working for a tax-exempt organization, a governmental unit (a foreign governmental unit may qualify), or a private employer—as long as at least 50 percent involves providing legal services on a pro bono, reduced, or court-awarded fee basis.

Judicial clerkships do not usually qualify. (The rationale is that the short-term commitment to clerking is designed to lead to a higher paying job after the year or two of clerking.) There is an exception for those who intend to take a public interest position after the clerkship position is completed.

Teaching does not qualify, unless it is clinical teaching (with a practical component).

Income eligibility.

ADJUSTED INCOME	LRAP POLICY
<$45,000	Loan for all monthly payments provided
$45,000–$60,000	Loan for all monthly payments provided less 15% of income over $45,000
>$60,000	Loan provided to cover need-based monthly payments less base contribution of $2,250 plus 70% of income over $60,000

Adjustments to income:

- ■ *Spouse's income:* The graduate will be considered as having the higher of his or her individual income or half the joint income.

- ■ *Dependents' allowance:* An exemption of $8,000 for each minor child is allowed.

- ■ *Seniority:* $1,000 is deducted from the graduate's salary for each year in public interest employment.

- ■ *Assets:* Any substantial physical and financial assets over $130,000 will be included as income.

- ■ *Additional income:* Any unearned income is treated as income.

- ■ *Part-time work:* Pro rata adjustment made according to hours worked. Thus, a graduate working half-time would have her salary doubled for purposes of LRAP calculations.

Qualifying loans. Financial assistance is available for need-based educational loans. ("Need-based" excludes loans taken in lieu of "student contribution.") Loans taken to meet undergraduate, law school, and other graduate-school degree requirements, as well as bar examination and bar examination preparation expenses, are eligible. Defaulted loans are not eligible for LRAP and will not be considered in determining the graduate's award.

Other eligibility requirements. Graduates may not enter the program more than five and a half years after graduation. Also, graduates cannot participate in the LRAP program if they have defaulted on their original student loans. Once loan accounts have been cleared, however, the law school will process the LRAP application.

Loan cancellation. LRAP-qualifying loans can be canceled upon sufficient length of public interest employment.

Years of Qualifying Employment	Percentage of Principal Canceled
1	0%
2	0%
3	25%
4	50%
5–10	100%

LRAP Programs at a Glance

Qualifying employment

	Legal Service Agencies	Public Defenders	District/ State Attorneys	Nonprofit Organizations	Government	Judicial Clerkships	Private Practice	Other
UC Berkeley (Boalt Hall)	x	x	x	x	x			
UCLA	x	x	x	x	x			
Chicago	x	x	x	x	x			
Columbia	x	x	x	x	x	x		
Cornell	x	x	x	x	x			
George Washington	x	x	x	x	Some		Some	Think tanks
Georgetown	x	x	x	x	x			
Harvard	x	x	x	x	x	Some	x	Academic
Michigan	x	x	x	x	x		x	Academic
Northwestern	x	x	x	x	x			
NYU	x	x	x	x	x	Some		
Penn	x	x	x	x	x		x	Nonlegal (some)
Southern California	x	x	x	x	x	x		
Stanford	x	x	x	x	x	Some	x	
Vanderbilt	x	x	x	x	x			
Virginia	x	x	x	x			x	Military
Yale	x	x	x	x	x	x	x	Nonlegal

Income eligibility

	Income Ceiling
UCLA	$45,000
Chicago	$60,000
Duke	$60,000
Northwestern	$60,000
Southern California	$55,000
Vanderbilt	$50,000

Adjusted incomes above the figures given make a person ineligible for program benefits. Note, however, that the programs differ substantially in two important regards. First, they differ as to how to consider spousal (or domestic partner) income. Some simply average the graduate's income with that of his or her spouse (or domestic partner, in the case of one or two schools). Others take the higher of the graduate's income or the averaged income of the two people. Second, the schools differ as to what they regard as an adjustment (deduction) to income. At issue are such matters as: prior educational debt payments, spouse or domestic partner debt payments, deductions for dependents, child care expenses, cost of living, and medical expenses.

Similarly, some programs increase the income ceiling according to seniority. A typical adjustment is to add $1,000 per year in the program.

Qualifying loans

	UNDERGRADUATE	GRADUATE (NON-LAW)	LOAN TYPE LAW SCHOOL (GOVERNMENT)	LAW SCHOOL (PRIVATE)	BAR EXAM	FAMILY/ FRIENDS
UC Berkeley (Boalt Hall)			x	x	x	
UCLA			x	x	x	
Chicago			x	x	x	
Columbia	x		x	x		
Cornell			x	x	x	
Duke			x	x	x	
George Washington			x	x		
Georgetown			x	x	x	
Harvard	x		x	x	x	
Michigan			x	x	x	
Northwestern			x	x		
NYU			x	x		
Penn	x		x	x	x	
Southern California	x	x	x	x	x	
Stanford	x	x	x	x	x	
Vanderbilt			x	x	x	
Virginia			x	x	x	
Yale	x		x	x	x	

- Joint-degree candidates should consider whether the loans for the non-law program will be eligible for LRAP treatment.

- Loans from family and friends are never eligible for LRAP treatment.

- Those contemplating transferring should note that loans from one school generally will not qualify for LRAP inclusion at another.

- At many schools, graduates are ineligible for the LRAP program if their principal loan balance does not exceed a given total. At Duke, for instance, it must be at least $20,000. To meet this total, educational loans to finance undergraduate or other graduate study might be included (although loan forgiveness may be available only for law school loans).

Approximate number of graduates currently participating in program

UC Berkeley (Boalt Hall)	100
UCLA	5–10
Chicago	25
Columbia	190
Cornell	25–35
Duke	60–75
Georgetown	120
Harvard	320
Michigan	90
Northwestern	50
NYU	400
Penn	140
Southern California	5–10
Stanford	115
Vanderbilt	15
Virginia	60
Yale	305

The number of LRAP participants at a given school can be very signifi-cant for several reasons. A large number of participants (adjusted for class size) suggests that the program is attractive enough to warrant participation. It also suggests that the program has been up and running for some time. In addition, it is a rough indication of the number of people who pursue public interest work upon graduation.

LRAP Programs: Conclusion

The variation in LRAP policies makes it essential that you know where you are headed (district attorney? private firm with a substantial public interest prac-tice?) in order to know which elements are likely to be most important to you. These variations, and the infinite subtleties accompanying them, oblige you to examine each program carefully, in great detail. The detail can be boggling, but this should not deter you from a proper examination (given that you do intend to be a lawyer, after all).

A note of warning: At many of the top law schools a majority of entering stu-dents claim that they will enter public interest law, yet only 2 to 10 percent actually do. Therefore, it may be unwise to place too much emphasis upon the quality of LRAP programs when choosing schools, just as it is unwise to load up on debt in the expectation that an LRAP program will rescue you from having to repay it—unless you are dead certain that you are headed into public interest law, and already have the real-world experience to make that belief a reasonable one.

Resources

Equal Justice Works (formerly NAPIL)
2120 L Street, NW, Suite 450
Washington, D.C. 20037–1541
Tel. (202) 466–3686
Fax (202) 429–9766
www.equaljusticeworks.org

HOW MUCH DEBT IS TOO MUCH?

The general rule is that the better the school you attend, the more you are likely to earn, both in your first job out of law school and throughout your career. Attending a better school thus makes a high level of debt more affordable than would be the case if you attended a lesser school.

Nevertheless, the question of how much debt is appropriate for you depends upon your individual circumstances. If you intend to take a relatively low-paying public sector job upon graduation, you may view a $100,000 debt as inconceivable. If you take a job at a leading firm in New York, on the other hand, with total first-year pay of $160,000 or more, the same $100,000 would probably look manageable. This fact could well alter your choice of jobs, which might or might not be a problem. If you have to focus on the salary and bonus of your first year in order to facilitate debt repayment, to the exclusion of all else, you may take a job that is not appealing in terms of the actual work, the particular area of law, the specific firm, the city, or your future prospects. This would be an unfortunate consequence of your debt situation.

Let's put the question of borrowing into perspective. In terms of the amounts you will have to repay, someone who borrows $100,000 for ten years at 8–20 percent interest will face a monthly (after-tax) payment of approximately $1,200 to 1,300. This would ordinarily require an annual income of at least $70,000 to $80,000, given that some $25,000 of pre-tax income will be devoted to this (depending upon your marginal—federal+state+local+social security—tax rate). This estimate is well below the starting salaries of many people graduating from top schools, excepting students who take low-paying public sector or public interest jobs. Someone borrowing $50,000 for ten years at the same 8–10 percent interest will pay only some $600–$660 per month and needs a salary of only about $50,000 to survive. These figures suggest that the size of a loan necessary to fund an average student may or may not be large relative to her post-JD earning capacity.

Equal Justice Works is an organization dedicated to the advancement of public interest law. It is a repository of information about such things as public interest internships and full-time positions in addition to scholarship and loan repayment programs. If you are interested in a public interest career, by all means take advantage of the wealth of information with which they can provide you.

The law schools themselves have, in most cases, separate booklets explaining the details of their LRAP programs.

GRANTS

Law schools offer two types of grants:

- *Need-based:* These are offered at all of the top schools. Note, however, that they are available only after a student has taken on the requisite amount of loan. Eligibility varies from school to school. For example, wait-listed students may not be eligible at some schools. (See the later discussion, under "Financial Aid Policies," for more about these restrictions.)

- *Merit:* Many, but not all, of the top schools use merit grants to attract top applicants. Schools obviously differ in what they consider a "top applicant." This will vary according to the relative standing of the schools (a top applicant at North Carolina might not be one at Georgetown), the mix of backgrounds in each school's applicant pool (former foreign service officers might be thick on the ground for Washington, D.C.–based schools but rarities for Chicago schools), the desired types of students (if Michigan were trying to beef up the biotech side of its intellectual property program, it might find a biochemist from a major pharmaceutical company to be worth paying extra for), and a host of other factors.

Many schools have both internal and external constituencies that prevent candid talk about their merit aid policies. The subject of merit aid is complicated by a number of factors:

- Even the schools that are very active in giving merit aid find it controversial among their own administration and faculty. The idea of competing for students is repugnant to some, as is taking any money out of the pot for the financially needy.

- It is handy for a school to be able to claim that it is so good, and so attractive to applicants, that it need not enter the competitive fray by offering merit aid.

- Many schools now mix merit and need-based aid together under the simple heading of "grants," without wishing to describe the extent to which merit aid is included. (This facilitates several schools' saying that they do not actually give merit aid, even though they do indeed.)

■ The merit aid policies of many schools are now very much in flux.

The net result of this situation is that you should not expect to get entirely clear (or straightforward) answers from all of the leading schools about their merit aid policies. Instead, you may learn about some of them only through the actual offers schools make to you. (For more about this, consult the "Bargaining" discussion below.)

A tip concerning merit aid: To maximize your chances of getting a merit grant, be sure that once you are admitted you go to whatever admitted students' days you can in order to demonstrate your keen interest in the school.

PUBLIC SERVICE SCHOLARSHIPS AND SUMMER GRANTS

Some schools, such as Georgetown, NYU, Stanford, and Penn, offer public service scholarships in addition to their LRAP programs (see the previous discussion regarding LRAP programs). By making it possible for graduates to incur little debt for law school, these grants facilitate taking low-paying jobs upon graduation. The programs are designed for those who have already demonstrated substantial commitment to public service. Those awarded public service grants are often required to take specific courses and participate in various activities during law school. In addition, these programs generally require a substantial post-graduation commitment to public service, typically for three or more years.

Similarly, some schools offer grants to subsidize students taking public interest jobs during the summer after their first year of law school. Harvard, for instance, offers a $5,500 grant.

OUTSIDE GRANTS

There are numerous organizations that have funded general purpose or specialized grants that may be applied to law studies. These include foundations, clubs, fraternal organizations, labor unions, and churches. (For information about such grants, see the sources listed at the end of the discussion on "Impact of Outside Grants," later in this chapter.)

PART-TIME WORK DURING LAW SCHOOL

Students who have demonstrated sufficient financial need are given a package of loans and, often, work-study job opportunities. The jobs on offer often include library work, research for professors, and so on, generally for about $10 per hour. At most schools in major urban centers, however, part-time work for local firms will offer pay that dwarfs the work-study pay. Consequently, it is only at isolated schools that work-study is likely to prove your best option for earning money. (It can be helpful to do research work for a professor, of course, but not for monetary reasons.)

THE LOCATION TRADE-OFF

In general, the schools that offer the lowest cost of living are in locations where it will be hard to earn a great deal of money working part-time during the school year. Charlottesville, for example, is a less expensive place to live than is New York City. By the same token, part-time jobs at local firms pay much better in New York than in Charlottesville. If you intend not to work during law school, you may find the University of Virginia a bargain relative to NYU or Columbia. On the other hand, if you *do* intend to work during your second and third years, Charlottesville may represent a false economy insofar as you could more than make up for a higher cost of living through your earnings elsewhere. This is, of course, yet another example of the fact that your choice of law school may be heavily conditioned by the extent to which you already know what you will do during law school.

ADDITIONAL INFORMATION SOURCES

➤ A good place to start your research is at www.finaid.org, which is the most comprehensive financial aid site and also provides links to numerous other resources.

➤ FAFSA (Free Application for Federal Student Aid) may be obtained by writing:

Federal Student Aid Information Center
P.O. Box 84
Washington, D.C. 20044–0084
(800) 433-3243
www.fafsa.ed.gov

The same organization publishes the helpful *The Student Guide: Financial Aid from the U.S. Department of Education*. Applicants can read the guide online, or download a PDF file from http://studentaid.ed.gov/students/publications/student_guide/index.html

➤ Loan programs:

    Access Group   (800) 282-1550; www.accessgroup.org

Sallie Mae	(888) 272-5543; www.salliemae.com
Citibank's Student Loan Corporation	(800) 967-2400; www.studentloan.com
The Education Resources Institute (TERI)	(800) 255-8374; www.teri.org
Key Education Resources	(800) 539-5363; www.key.com/education

➤ For information on minority scholarship opportunities:

Council on Legal Education Opportunity
740 15th Street, NW
9th Floor
Washington, D.C. 20005
(866) 886-4343 or (202) 216-4343
cleo@abanet.org
www.cleoscholars.com

LIMITS UPON TERM-TIME WORK

The American Bar Association officially limits full-time law students to 20 hours per week of work. All of the top law schools abide by this restriction and would certainly have a word with you if you were known to be exceeding this total. None of these schools, however, actually monitors the number of hours students log at local firms. Thus, the real limitations upon your work hours are your own time and inclinations, not law school or ABA policies.

FINANCIAL AID POLICIES

Financial aid policies are particular to individual schools. These policies, such as whether you are considered a resident for purposes of paying in-state tuition, can have a major impact upon your eligibility for financial aid and the amount of aid you will receive. Whether any given policy will affect you, of course, depends upon your individual circumstances. The following policies have been highlighted because they are the most likely to have a major influence upon your aid awards. Examine them to see which are most likely to affect you, then look more closely at which schools (and how many schools) have policies that might favor you.

IS THE FINANCIAL AID DECISION INDEPENDENT OF THE ADMISSION DECISION?

No top schools take account of your need for financial aid in making their admissions decisions, unless you are an international applicant. Numerous schools that wish to have foreign students, but lack the funds to sponsor them, do give preference to foreign students able to pay their own way.

ADMISSIONS AND FINANCIAL AID DEANS DISCUSS THE ADMISSIONS IMPACT OF NEEDING FINANCIAL AID

The two decisions are completely independent of one another. We do not reject applicants simply because they lack the money to pay for law school.   *Ann Killian Perry, Chicago (Admissions)*

The financial aid and admissions decisions are completely independent.   *Sarah C. Zearfoss, Michigan (Admissions)*

There is a real firewall between need-based aid and admissions.   *Katherine Gottschalk, Michigan*

CONVERTING TO RESIDENT STATUS FOR THE SECOND YEAR

Given the lower tuition that public schools charge residents, becoming a resident can reduce the tuition burden considerably. At the California schools it is very easy to enter as a non-resident student in the first year, yet be converted to resident status for the second and third years. In other states, this is very difficult to do. In fact, it often requires marrying a state resident to accomplish this conversion. As a result, to get the advantage of Michigan's, Virginia's, or Texas's resident tuition would require becoming a resident prior to law school. (See the discussion concerning residency on pages 223–225.)

PERCENT OF STUDENTS CONVERTED TO RESIDENT STATUS FOR SECOND YEAR

UC Berkeley (Boalt Hall)	>90%
UCLA	100%
Michigan	<5%
Texas	<5% (Note, however, that Texas offers 90 non-resident tuition exemptions—i.e., it considers 90 incoming out-of-state students to be "residents.")
Virginia	<5%

TREATMENT OF PARENTS

WHEN ARE APPLICANTS CONSIDERED INDEPENDENT OF THEIR PARENTS?

Schools traditionally considered law school students to be, at least in part, dependent upon parental support. This was due to the fact that the typical law school student was coming straight from college, or very soon thereafter. Now that the average age at which students start law school is approaching 25, many schools have changed their policies. Some schools always consider students independent, whereas some never consider them independent. Many take an intermediate position, but they apply a dog's breakfast of rules to determine independence. Some consider your age; others consider how many years ago you graduated from college, whether you have dependent children, or whether you have been in the military; still others consider how many years you have gone without being claimed as a tax exemption by your parents. Harvard applies several tests. It considers independent those who, during the last seven years:

- Have not been claimed as an income tax exemption by their parents
- Have not lived in their parents' home/household for more than six months
- Have not received more than $10,000 from their parents

Several schools apply a graduated approach to the contributions they expect from parents. Yale, for instance, requires a full contribution (as calculated by their financial need analysis) from parents of students under 27, a half contribution from parents of students between 27 and 29, and no contribution from parents of students 29 and above. Similarly, at Stanford the parents' expected contribution is 100 percent at fewer than three years of student independence, 75 percent at three years, 50 percent at four years, 25 percent at five years, and 0 percent at six years. Northwestern, which prefers candidates to have at least several years' work experience, has an independence policy that encourages those with substantial work experience to apply. At two years after college graduation, a student's parents are required to contribute 50 percent of the otherwise expected amount; at three years, 25 percent, and at four years, 0 percent.

Note that parents need not actually contribute the amount expected: You are always free to borrow or earn the amount yourself.

ASSESSMENT OF NONCUSTODIAL PARENTS

If your parents are divorced, some schools will still assess the noncustodial parent (unless they consider you to be independent of your parents), whereas other schools never assess the noncustodial parent. Some schools are in the middle, assessing noncustodial parents in some cases but not others. Michigan, for instance, assesses them unless the divorce occurred at least ten years ago.

DETERMINATION OF APPLICANTS' INDEPENDENCE STATUS

	APPLICANTS ALMOST NEVER CONSIDERED INDEPENDENT	APPLICANTS GENERALLY CONSIDERED INDEPENDENT	APPLICANTS INDEPENDENT ACCORDING TO CERTAIN AGE	CONSIDERED INDEPENDENT ACCORDING TO NO. OF YEARS OF INDEPENDENCE	MAJOR EXCEPTIONS
UC Berkeley (Boalt Hall)			30	5	
UCLA			30	7	Military veteran; having dependent child
Chicago	X				Age or estrangement
Columbia	X				
Cornell				6	
Duke	X				Marriage
George Washington			30		Independent 2+ years if under 30
Georgetown		X			
Harvard					Reduced parental contribution for those entering at/after 29
Michigan				5	Marriage; also, reduced contribution for those independent 1+ years
Northwestern		X			
NYU	X				Few exceptions
Penn			30		
Southern California		X			
Stanford				6	Starting at 3 years, parents' contribution reduced
Texas		X			
Vanderbilt			26		
Virginia		X			
Yale			29		At 27–28, lesser parental assessment

ASSESSMENT OF NONCUSTODIAL PARENTS

	Usually **ASSESSED** (**UNLESS APPLICANT CONSIDERED INDEPENDENT**)	**SOMETIMES ASSESSED**	**NEVER ASSESSED**
UC Berkeley (Boalt Hall)	x		
UCLA			x
Chicago			x
Columbia	x		
Cornell	x		
Duke	x		
George Washington	x		
Georgetown		x (depends upon length of time since divorce and degree of support)	
Harvard	x		
Michigan		x (depends upon whether taken as deduction in last five years)	
Northwestern			x
NYU	x		
Penn		x (assess unless divorce at least seven years old)	
Southern California			x
Stanford			x
Texas			x
Vanderbilt		x	
Virginia			x
Yale	x		

IMPACT OF OUTSIDE GRANTS

Scholarships are available from sources other than the law schools. They are most often given on the basis of residence, membership of a specific ethnic group, relationship to a relative who served in the armed forces or is a member of a particular civic organization, or interest in a particular area of law. Do not, however, count on getting an award that will materially affect your options: There are relatively few that pay truly substantial sums. In addition, some law schools deduct part or all of the scholarship from their own grant, meaning that the financial value of the award to you may be limited. Even in this case, though, the nonfinancial value may still make such a scholarship worthwhile.

Some of these scholarships will look impressive to future employers, so their résumé value alone is worth the effort of applying.

Do not, however, pay anyone to conduct such a search for you. This field is notoriously loaded with charlatans.

IMPACT OF OUTSIDE GRANT*

	REDUCES LOAN	REDUCES GRANT AND LOAN
UC Berkeley (Boalt Hall)	x	
UCLA	x	
Chicago	x	
Columbia		x
Cornell	x	
Duke	x	
George Washington	x (with some exceptions)	
Georgetown		x (after first $3200)
Harvard	x	
Michigan	x	
Northwestern	x	
NYU	x	
Penn	x	
Southern California	x	
Stanford	x	
Texas	x	
Vanderbilt	x	
Virginia	x	
Yale	x	

*A school's treatment of a grant often depends upon the grant amount. A very small scholarship grant (say, $100) will often be ignored; an immense scholarship (say, $100,000) will cause a school to eliminate all aid, including any grants. For purposes of this chart, an in-between sum of $5,000 was assumed.

Finaid's scholarships page (www.finaid.org/scholarships) is a good place to start your search for outside aid. It provides information and links to free scholarship searches, particularly the FastWeb Scholarship Search (http://fastweb .monster.com). Other scholarship searches are available at:

http://salliemae.collegeanswer.com
www.collegeboard.com
www.srnexpress.com

FOREIGN EXCHANGE PROGRAMS

If you do an exchange program abroad, for a semester or a full year, you may have to pay tuition to your home (American) school instead of to the foreign school. In some instances, the school you pay depends upon whether you are

PAYMENT OF TUITION FOR FOREIGN EXCHANGE PROGRAMS

	USUALLY PAY HOME SCHOOL TUITION	USUALLY PAY FOREIGN SCHOOL TUITION	PAY WHICHEVER TUITION IS HIGHER	OTHER
UC Berkeley (Boalt Hall)		x		
UCLA		x		
Columbia	x			
Cornell	x			
Duke	x			
George Washington		x		
Georgetown		x		
Harvard	x			
Michigan	x			
Northwestern		x		
NYU	x			
Penn			x (for non-Penn sponsored programs)	
Southern California	x			
Stanford				x
Texas				x
Vanderbilt		x		
Virginia	x			
Yale		x		

going to a school with which your home school has an exchange agreement or to a school that you yourself "found." The question of whether your home school's financial aid will "travel with you" is similarly messy—it varies in much the same way. Given that the foreign school's tuition may be higher or lower than your home school's tuition, you may find yourself much better or worse off according to which tuition you are required to pay—and whether suitable financial aid is available. Be sure to examine the fine print of your home institution and whichever exchange programs interest you.

AMERICAN EXCHANGE PROGRAMS OR THIRD-YEAR MATRICULATION

The same issues that matter when attending a program abroad are present when attending a second law school in the U.S. If, for example, you currently attend Yale but will do a term or year at another American law school, will you pay Yale's tuition or the other school's? Will your Yale financial aid travel to the other school if you pay its tuition?

This situation is most likely to arise if your spouse has a job or educational program that pulls him or her to another location, thereby inspiring you to follow. You might yourself initiate such a change for reason of the program available at the other school, perhaps via an existing exchange relationship (see Chapters 15 and 17 for a fuller discussion of this possibility). Or you might wish to shift schools in part for financial reasons. If you intend to practice law in a state with a very good state law school, which charges a very low tuition for residents (and you could qualify as a resident), you might wish to spend your last term at that school. The *potential costs* of doing so are clear:

- You might not have access to the same quality professors or courses.
- You might not have access to the same courses, journals, or organizations.
- You might miss your law school friends and feel isolated, in part because few students at the new school will be looking to make new friends in their last term.
- You might miss out on law school merit-based grants.

  The *potential benefits*, on the other hand, might prove more substantial:

- If you have already exhausted the courses likely to be most valuable to your future career that are offered at Yale, you might benefit from other courses on offer at your new school.

PAYMENT OF TUITION FOR VISITING STUDENT TERMS

	USUALLY PAY ORIGINAL SCHOOL TUITION	USUALLY PAY "NEW" SCHOOL TUITION	PAY WHICHEVER TUITION IS HIGHER
UC Berkeley (Boalt Hall)		x	
UCLA		x	
Chicago		x	
Columbia		x	
Cornell		x	
Duke			x
George Washington		x	
Georgetown		x	
Harvard	x		
Michigan		x	
Northwestern		x	
NYU		x	
Penn			x
Southern California		x	
Stanford		x	
Texas		x	
Vanderbilt		x	
Virginia		x	
Yale		x	

- You may pay much less in tuition (especially if you have relatively few credit hours left to complete and the state school charges by the credit hour, which many do).

- You may be able to work for much higher wages than you could in New Haven.

- You can get a head start on your local networking (especially valuable for those with intensely local practices, such as family law), including building your credibility within your new firm.

- Your degree will still say "Yale."

The most substantial benefits will thus accrue to those able to pay resident tuition at a fine state school and work for their new firm. Those who will be unable to pursue such a strategy are those whose obligations (law review, for example) make it imperative that they remain on campus or whose chosen future requires maintaining contact up until the last moment with the school (such as those who need a great recommendation from a professor for clerkship purposes, both now and in another year or two for a follow-up clerkship, such as at Federal Appellate Court or Supreme Court level).

ASSESSMENT OF TERM-TIME EARNINGS

Many schools will ignore term-time earnings, especially in the third year, unless they are told explicitly about them. Schools seldom actually learn about part-time earnings unless they involve work at the law school or elsewhere on campus. Michigan, on the other hand, will hold you responsible for any such earnings—if they find out about them—*unless* you tell the school about them prior to their finding you out. (Go figure.) Some schools that do not assess term-time earnings at all want to provide an incentive to students to work or they consider that students are sacrificing so much in terms of leisure time and law school activities that they should not be further penalized. Others make three-year grants when you begin school and impute some expected term-time earnings (whether you do or do not actually work, during school). The schools that ignore only third-year part-time earnings, on the other hand, generally calculate financial need on the basis of the prior academic year's earnings (so that by the time third-year earnings would be inputted, law school is over for you).

This situation gives rise to interesting possibilities. You can vary the number of course credits you take each term during your second and third years. If you wish to maximize your GPA in the second year, for instance, you could take a slightly lighter courseload, then take a heavier one in the third year. (Firms will have made final offers by December of your third year, so third-year grades are much less important than second-year grades—and only of critical importance for those going the public interest route [employers hire very late in the spring] or needing to have their grades examined once they change jobs later on.) To maximize short-term economic benefit, on the other hand, take the heaviest possible load second year, and work little or not at all. Third year, take a light load and work maximum hours (supposedly 20 per week, according to American Bar Association rules—but no one actually monitors this). Schools will already have determined your aid for the whole third year, so your actual earnings during the year (at most schools) will not subtract from it.

In the case of merit grants, many of the schools that award them do so without regard to how much you will earn during law school, so your term-time earnings will be free of financial aid implications.

This is one area in which student practice continues to evolve. At Cornell, for instance, a few students are working during the academic year, while remaining in Ithaca, for firms in New York City and Los Angeles that they had worked for during the previous summer. (It is not yet clear, however, whether cyber-commuting will become a regular feature of law school.) Some Penn students, on the other hand, are working part-time in New York City, making sure

ASSESSMENT OF TERM-TIME EARNINGS

	SECOND YEAR ASSESSED	THIRD YEAR ASSESSED	NEITHER YEAR ASSESSED
UC Berkeley (Boalt Hall)	x		
UCLA	x		
Chicago			x
Columbia			x
Cornell	x (work-study; affects loan only)	x (work-study; affects loan only)	
Duke			x
George Washington	x		
Georgetown			x
Harvard			x
Michigan			x (as long as you declare earnings)
Northwestern			x
NYU	x	x	
Penn			x
Southern California	x		
Stanford			x
Texas	x		
Vanderbilt			x
Virginia			x
Yale	x (only amount above $7,200 affects grant)	x (only amount above $7,200 affects grant)	

not to have any classes on Thursday or Friday so as to facilitate spending those days in Manhattan. One thing remains constant, however: Yale students seldom work for local firms, no doubt in part because they do not wish to remain in New Haven once they finish law school.

ASSESSMENT OF SUMMER EARNINGS

In calculating aid, many schools factor in a sum of money that you are expected to hand over from your summer jobs during law school. Sometimes this is a flat number, varying from $1,500 to $3,000, which they will impute to you even if (especially if) you have tanned yourself on the beach all summer. Given that it is now

ASSESSMENT OF SUMMER EARNINGS				
	SUMMER AFTER FIRST YEAR ASSESSED	SUMMER AFTER SECOND YEAR ASSESSED	NEITHER SUMMER ASSESSED	OTHERS
UC Berkeley (Boalt Hall)	x	x		
UCLA		x		
Chicago			x	
Columbia			x (Three-year award fixed at entry)	
Cornell			x	
Duke			x	
George Washington	x	x		
Georgetown	x	x		(Assess if >$12,000)
Harvard	x	x		(If work more than 12 weeks, "excess" weeks not assessed)
Michigan	x	x		
Northwestern			x	(Affects loan eligibility)
NYU	x	x		(Assess if >$12,000)
Penn			x	
Southern California	x			
Stanford	x	x		
Texas	x			
Vanderbilt			x	
Virginia			x	
Yale	x	x		

possible to make over $30,000 in a summer, this oversight of actual earnings can be very helpful to you. (Similarly, many of the schools that award merit grants do so without regard to how much you will earn during law school, so in such cases your summer earnings are free of financial aid implications.) Sometimes it involves an equation. Virginia, for example, requires that a student contribute 70 percent of her net salary, minus $1,500. Stanford's contribution formula requires that you contribute at least $1,000, and takes half of whatever you earn above $5,000.

Some schools will "normalize" the time you work. For instance, they will compute your earnings as if you work a ten-week summer. Gross income for the ten weeks is calculated, then taxes and living expenses (based upon a standard student budget) are subtracted. The difference is considered to be savings, applied to law school expenses. Extra weeks of work are not taken into account, but those who work fewer than ten weeks have their salary grossed up to a ten-week total. (Those who do not work at all have an average savings figure imputed to them.)

TREATMENT OF WAIT-LISTED STUDENTS

The treatment of wait-listed students is by no means uniform. At most of the top schools, they are eligible for both need-based grants and loans (government and

AID ELIGIBILITY OF WAIT-LISTED STUDENTS

	ELIGIBLE FOR GRANT	ELIGIBLE FOR GRANT BUT MONEY MAY RUN OUT	ELIGIBLE FOR LOAN ONLY
UC Berkeley (Boalt Hall)	x		
UCLA	x		
Chicago	x		
Columbia		x	
Cornell		x	
Duke		x	
George Washington		x	
Georgetown	x		
Harvard	x		
Michigan	x		
Northwestern			x
NYU	x		
Penn	x		
Southern California		x	
Stanford	x		
Texas		x	
Vanderbilt		x	
Virginia		x	
Yale	x		

private), but at some of these schools there is likely to be little money left for them by the time they are admitted. Many schools have already spent most of their aid resources on applicants they needed to entice away from other schools by the time wait-listed students are admitted.

TREATMENT OF TRANSFER STUDENTS

Some of the top schools treat transfer students just as they treat regular admits (those admitted for the first rather than second year of the program). This is by no means true, however, across the board. Some schools make no grant aid available, or make it available only in some circumstances. Schools that do not give grants, even on the basis of financial need, do not want to look as though they are luring students from their neighboring schools (many students transfer within a limited region to the best school nearby) and, furthermore, do not need to bid for these students.

The top schools have not competed actively for transfer students up to this point, but this is changing as competition for talent heats up across the board.

AID ELIGIBILITY OF TRANSFER STUDENTS

	GRANT-ELIGIBLE	GRANT-ELIGIBLE, WITH LIMITATIONS	LOAN-ELIGIBLE ONLY
UC Berkeley (Boalt Hall)	x		
UCLA	x		
Chicago			x
Columbia			x
Cornell		x (grant-eligible in 3d year)	
Duke			x
George Washington		x (grant-eligible in 3d year)	
Georgetown	x		
Harvard	x		
Michigan	x		
Northwestern			x
NYU			x
Penn			x
Southern California			x
Stanford	x		
Texas		x (but money may run out)	
Vanderbilt			x
Virginia			x
Yale	x		

TREATMENT OF INTERNATIONAL STUDENTS

International students face a different financial aid situation than do American students. Internationals are not eligible for federal loans, nor can they readily obtain private (American) loans without an American citizen or permanent resident cosigner (guarantor), except in the case of two institutions that have recently established a program with NYU allowing for foreign cosigners. (The private educational loans available to international applicants with an American cosigner include Access Group's Graduate International Student Loan, CitiAssist, LawEXCEL, PEP, and Signature Student Loan programs.) Some American schools will still make grant aid available to internationals, but note that such aid is generally available only after another $20,000-plus of loans (that may not be available) have been factored into the need equation. Only a very few schools have merit aid available for internationals. A few schools will replace the (unavailable) federal loans with their own institutional loans, but that is discouragingly rare. Some schools do have limited aid funds for second- and third-year international students, but not for first-year students.

AVAILABILITY OF INSTITUTIONAL FINANCIAL AID FOR INTERNATIONAL STUDENTS

	INSTITUTIONAL GRANTS AVAILABLE	INSTITUTIONAL LOANS AVAILABLE (TO REPLACE FEDERAL LOANS)	PRIVATE LOANS, WITH FOREIGN COSIGNER, AVAILABLE
UC Berkeley (Boalt Hall)	x		
UCLA	x	x	
Chicago	x		
Columbia	x		
Cornell	x		
Duke	x		
George Washington	x		
Georgetown			x
Harvard	x	x	
Michigan	x	x	x
Northwestern	x		
NYU	x		x
Penn	x	x	
Southern California	x		
Stanford	x		
Texas	x (merit only)		
Vanderbilt	x	x	
Virginia	x	x	
Yale	x	x	x

Thus, international students typically must be able to demonstrate their ability to pay for at least the first year of study and sometimes the whole program before a school will issue a Certificate of Eligibility for the appropriate visa. It is therefore critical that foreign students consider their financial situations carefully, well in advance of applying.

OTHER FINANCIAL AID POLICIES

Numerous other law school policies can affect your financial aid. For instance, some schools impute earnings (and thus a required contribution) to spouses, whether or not the spouse actually works. This can be particularly tricky if the spouse is remaining home with a preschooler rather than working outside the home. Another example actually concerns child-rearing expenses: Only some schools permit child-care expenses to be deducted. These are not the only such examples of other financial aid policies, but the lesson should be clear: Whatever your own situation is, be sure you understand the policies that can affect you at your chosen schools.

EVALUATING FINANCIAL AID PACKAGES—AND TRYING FOR MORE

EVALUATING AND COMPARING AWARD PACKAGES

Be ready to evaluate, compare, and perhaps negotiate financial aid packages at different schools. When evaluating an aid package, or comparing various aid packages that you have received from schools to determine which is best, there are six primary factors to consider:

- *The portions of grant versus "self-help" funding:* Two schools can offer to fill your financial need in radically different ways. One law school may give you 50 percent of your $30,000 total need in grant aid whereas another might offer only 15 percent in grant, forcing you to take on substantial debt.

- *The terms of the loan repayments:* Not all loans are created equal. Subsidized loans, for which the government or institutional lender will pay interest while you are still in school, are better than unsubsidized ones. Loans without origination fees are preferable to those with fees.

- *The treatment of outside scholarships:* Compare how each school handles outside scholarships, whether you have gained an outside grant for your first year or are hoping to get one later on.

- *The treatment of summer and part-time earnings:* Note whether such earnings are considered when granting aid, and whether they serve only to reduce loans or can also reduce grants.

■ *Whether there are performance requirements to retain aid:* Grants and loans that are not fixed for three years are generally less valuable than those that are fixed. In considering the potentially variable awards, take into account the possibility that your award amount may be reduced because you were successful in earning money during law school—or because your spouse or parents were newly successful.

In addition, consider whether a grant that is conditional upon your performance at law school will be readily placed in jeopardy. Examine the grade-point average required to keep it. Do not, however, consider this GPA in light of your college GPA. You are likely to struggle to perform as well at law school as you did in college, given the much stiffer competition, and, oftentimes, the stiffer grading policies. Instead, look at the required GPA in light of the actual distribution of grades at this school. If you are required to maintain a 2.7 GPA at a school with a mandated median of 2.85, you face a very substantial risk of losing your grant.

■ *The treatment of spousal income:* If your spouse is likely not to work for substantial periods during law school, perhaps due to caring for a young child, will the school still impute some earnings to him or her?

BARGAINING

Prior to the mid-1990s, applicants to the top schools could not successfully haggle with schools about their financial aid offers. If Penn offered you a $2,000 grant and $14,000 in loan, you took it or went elsewhere. Those days are gone.

In recent years, schools have started to bargain—rather surreptitiously—with the applicants they most wish to catch. This started with schools well below the level of the national schools, but has now reached well up the ladder to the truly top schools. A safe generalization is that any school that dishes out merit aid, rather than aid based solely on financial need, is open to some degree of bargaining. This means that Harvard, Yale, and Stanford are unlikely bargainers (although there are hints that at least one of these has been using its vast resources to pursue a few highly desirable candidates). There are few other schools resisting out-and-out bargaining, so it is safe to say that of the top twenty schools (however defined), the vast majority now engage in some degree of bargaining.

There are no rules to this new world of bargaining, except that failure to try results inevitably in failure. If Penn, NYU, Columbia, and Chicago all admit you, take the best offer you have from one and show it to the others to see whether any of them will improve their offer to you. Some of them may try to convince you that you will actually do better, financially and otherwise, with the offer they have already made to you. By all means pay attention to this perspective; it may well be right. But by the same token, see whether you can get more money out of the school (regardless of whether you believe the argument they have made).

Do not expect all schools to be equally interested in you. The higher up the list of admits you find yourself, the greater your bargaining leverage. You might be at the bottom of Penn's list of admits, yet at the top of Boston University's or Notre Dame's. As a result, Penn would be unlikely to match their offers. In fact, even if you were atop Penn's list, it might not feel compelled to match BU or Notre Dame because it might well trust that its reputation and/or program specifics would be sufficient to land you without an increase in aid.

The more schools of similar repute that have admitted you, the more your leverage with any one of these schools. (As a result, you should apply to many schools that are similar to one another.) This principle can, however, be taken too far. Do not expect Penn to pursue you avidly if you look like a great fit at another school but a poor one at Penn, because the effort to pursue you would not be worth the time of Penn's financial aid people. If you have strong ties to Chicago, for example, and no compelling interest in a program done particularly well at Penn, expect Penn's financial aid people to focus on other people rather than on you. The obvious lesson here is to show how you would be a perfect fit for the program, and vice versa, without foreclosing the reasonable possibility of your going elsewhere.

Bargaining is already important in the law school financial aid game, but it will certainly increase as more and more schools try to buy talent. Texas, until recently, was unusually frank (see the box) in its willingness to show not only that it will match or better other schools' offers, but also which other schools it regarded as rivals to be matched. (Its general policy remains in effect but it no longer specifies the schools it considers peers or rivals.) The same competitiveness exists in other leading schools, albeit without the frankness. Given the advent of bargaining throughout the undergraduate (college) world, more and

---

The general rules when trying to bargain:

➤ When the school gives no merit grants whatsoever, emphasize your poverty. Note that your expenses (rent, child care, auto repairs, and so on) will run higher—and perhaps your (and your significant other's) earnings will be lower—than the school anticipated in its aid award.

➤ When the school gives merit grants, remember that it is most likely to be willing to match another school's grant the better the other school's reputation/rankings, and the more the two are rivals due to geography or similarity of programs.

THE TEXAS FINANCIAL AID MATCHING PROGRAM

The University of Texas School of Law offers a merit-based financial aid matching program for admitted students who have received financial aid packages from peer law schools. Until recently, it specified the schools:

UC Berkeley (Boalt Hall)	University of Michigan at Ann Arbor
UCLA	Northwestern University
University of Chicago	NYU
Columbia University	University of Pennsylvania
Cornell University	Stanford University
Duke University	University of Virginia
Georgetown University	Yale University
Harvard University	

"Through this program, the University of Texas School of Law will award scholarship packages so that the admitted applicant's student contribution and educational loans for attending The University of Texas School of Law are equal to or lower than the amounts offered by the listed law schools. . . . To apply for a scholarship package through this program, please submit a copy of your Financial Aid Notification (FAN) or similar official document that reflects the cost of attendance and the amount of grants, scholarships, and loans offered from one of the law schools to The University of Texas School of Law Scholarships Committee." (*Quoted from the University of Texas's own materials.*)

more of those applying to law school will expect to haggle over law school financial offers; this will propel the competition for law student talent even further into the world of bargaining. One last note to the wise: When trying to determine which schools are most likely to put toe (and whole leg) into these waters, note that new deans of law schools are highly likely to try to improve the student profile at their schools by changing the basis for awarding aid.

FINANCIAL STRATEGIES

THE BASIC STRATEGIES

By starting the process early, you make it possible to play the financial aid game with real cunning. The key is to figure out both your career goals and, correspondingly, how you wish to do law school. Choose the school that best matches these desires. For instance, if you intend to work part-time during law school for maximum earnings, try to attend a law school that does not assess term-time earnings and that is located in a city where part-time pay is high. Use the charts on the preceding pages to understand the extent to which the relevant financial policies vary by school and choose accordingly.

Other strategies, based upon the information above, include:

1. Apply early enough to qualify for grant aid. At NYU for instance, the financial aid deadline is January 1, whereas the application deadline is February 1.

2. Save money before going to school. (This is just one more reason to work seriously before law school.)

3. Shift income away from the base year used to calculate financial aid awards, especially at the schools that make three-year grants up front. Do what you can to get a Christmas bonus the year before—or New Year's bonus the year after—the critical base year, or get paid in options rather than salary.

4. Consider shuffling your assets by transferring funds, for example, to your parents or siblings.

5. Before you file your FAFSA and other forms, reduce your cash on hand by paying off consumer debt (such as car loans and credit cards) and accelerating necessary expenses (such as purchasing a new computer).

6. Nail down any outside grants you can.

7. Consider reacquainting yourself with your parents. Their financial aid may involve fewer restrictions and qualifications than other likely sources of financing.

8. If your parents have substantial earnings or assets and you do not, consider becoming independent of your parents, or favoring schools that will consider you to be independent.

9. Become a resident in a state that has a public law school you wish to attend.

10. Attend a state law school that permits students to pay resident tuition in the second and third years.

11. Consider delaying your marriage if your prospective spouse will add to your joint assets and earnings. This is especially likely to be the case during the first years of law school, when you will be studying more than working. (You could even consider divorcing such a person, but I am loth to advise such a thing.)

12. Live cheaply during law school. You can save several thousand dollars a year by living frugally.

13. Get a grant based upon performance in law school. All of the top schools

make awards for "best performance in Corporations I," "best moot court brief," or "highest grades by a first-year student."

14. Work for as many weeks as possible during the summer, especially during your second summer, when law firms will pay you especially handsomely. Resist the temptation to live it up when the big checks roll in.

15. Given that few schools assess part-time earnings, consider logging as many hours as practicable at the best-paying (local) firms. Note that salaries differ dramatically from one location to another, so if you intend to work part-time, consider choosing a school on this basis. You are likely to be paid best for part-time work during your third year, so take a heavier courseload second year, so that you can work more hours during third year.

16. Attend a much cheaper school for your last term, or for a term abroad.

17. Enter a field before law school that makes your law school expenses tax deductible, assuming that you return to it upon graduation (see box, page 483).

Despite all of the above advice, do not believe that attending a lesser law school for a reduced price is generally a better idea than paying full freight at a demonstrably better school. You are making a long-term investment, so think in terms of value rather than just in terms of price.

KEEP YOUR SPENDING UNDER CONTROL

BEFORE LAW SCHOOL

Law schools will consider your income, not just your savings, when calculating how much money you should be able to contribute. Therefore, wasting money on frivolous purchases in the years before law school can have unintended consequences. Take a look, well in advance of applying to law school, at how schools calculate your expected contribution (discussed earlier) to make sure your current spending plans will not come back to haunt you.

Be careful, also, not to run up too much credit card or other consumer debt. Not only is it an expensive way to finance your spending, but failure to meet your payments will make it difficult or impossible to gain federal or private law school loans. Make sure, too, that you manage carefully your existing educational debt (taken on for college and, perhaps, graduate school). Defaulting on this, or even being late with payments, can also limit or eliminate your ability to get new loans for law school.

DURING LAW SCHOOL

Live as inexpensive a lifestyle as you can manage. It will allow you to live better upon graduation, when your loan repayments will be lower than they would if

THE TAX DEDUCTIBILITY OF LAW SCHOOL

Under the current tax law, every American taxpayer can claim a Lifetime Learning Credit for higher education. Some, however, will be better off claiming a Deduction for Higher Education Expenses instead. Regrettably, the two are mutually exclusive. (For a discussion of these and other possibilities, such as the impact of employer assistance upon your own taxable income, see two IRS publications: IRS 970, *Tax Benefits for Education*, and IRS 520, *Scholarships and Fellowships*.)

A few people, moreover, may be able to deduct the full cost of law school. To do so, there are two basic requirements. You need to maintain or enhance skills required by your employer, without qualifying for a new trade or business. Thus, if you were a child advocate for a public interest organization and return to this field (and perhaps this same employer), doing very similar work, albeit at a higher level, you may qualify for a deduction. Similarly, if you work before law school as a foreign trade representative for a state or as a political science professor and return to the same field, your payments may be deductible. Be sure you discuss this with your accountant or tax lawyer. The rules are complicated and the case law is very messy, so you may not get a definitive answer to whether such a deduction will pass IRS muster. In that case, your attitude toward risk may be the determining factor as to whether or not you claim a deduction.

By the way, not only may your law school expenses be deductible, but your expenses incurred getting into law school may also be deductible.

you had lived at all extravagantly during law school. In addition, the less debt you have, the more career flexibility you will retain. If your debt is $125,000, you will feel pressured to work in the highest paying private firm environment possible or in a public interest position that qualifies for LRAP treatment.

MAKE SURE YOUR FINANCING STRATEGY IS CONSISTENT WITH YOUR CAREER GOALS

When considering how to finance a law school education, be sure to think through the implications of your financing strategy. Make sure your financing approach is consistent with how you intend to do law school. Do not expect to work 20 hours a week for a local firm while also being on law review. Do not expect your earnings from summer jobs between years of law school to be massive if you intend to pile up public interest credentials (public interest positions, especially during summer internships, pay poorly). Similarly, make sure your financing approach is consistent with your post–law school goals. Thus, do not pile on $125,000 of debt if you intend to teach law at a community college.

SHOULD YOU TRADE DOWN IN SCHOOL QUALITY TO SAVE MONEY?

When should you take a merit scholarship at a lesser school instead of paying full freight at a better school? When should you go to a state law school with lower tuition than a more prestigious private school (with higher tuition)? There are numerous factors to consider:

➤ How large is the quality (and reputation) difference between the two schools?

➤ To what extent do the two schools offer the courses you want and other elements (such as location and atmosphere) you most value? (See Chapter 3 for a full discussion of these elements.) What are the earnings possibilities during summers and term-time at the two schools?

➤ What amount of scholarship is on offer?

➤ How certain are you that you will be able to keep the aid for all three years?

➤ What field do you intend to enter? How certain are you of this? If you are likely to enter a public interest area, consider the LRAP possibilities at the two schools. For other fields that do not pay much (such as teaching), note that you are unlikely to qualify for LRAP benefits (except at a program like Yale's). Huge debts may constrain your ability to enter such a field, although your attractiveness to such employers may well depend upon the quality of the law school you attend.

➤ The more likely you are to enter a high-paying field, the less importance you should attach to the debt you may carry upon graduation.

➤ How likely are you to practice near the lower-ranked school? As discussed in Chapter 3, the value of local connections can be very substantial.

➤ Note that performance pressure may be much less at the better school, oddly enough, because your rank in class may not matter much to your employment chances. At Harvard, it may be sufficient to be in the upper two-thirds of your class to get the type of job you want, whereas you may need to make law review at a lesser school to get such a job. Check with your desired employers about what it takes from each school.

To plan your financing effectively, you therefore need to have a good understanding of where you are headed: how you intend to spend your time in law school, what type of law you will practice, and for what type of employer. Do not leave your financing strategy to chance. Instead, start the process of determining how best you can finance your law school education early in the process.

Part IV

ANOTHER LAW DEGREE

19

LLM AND OTHER GRADUATE LAW DEGREES

— EXECUTIVE SUMMARY —

▪

More lawyers than ever are pursuing advanced law degrees.

▪

The increased complexity of legal systems and the related need to specialize are primary drivers of the increase in LLM and other degrees.

—There are many other drivers, however, including the increased competitiveness of legal practice and the globalization of business and law.

▪

Choosing the right LLM program can be difficult.

—Hundreds of programs, with perhaps one hundred different specialties, are now on offer.

—Relevant rankings to sort through the many programs are lacking.

▪

Admission to LLM and other advanced-degree programs is not the same as for JD programs.

—The LSAT is generally not a factor.

—Instead, law school performance and work experience take priority.

The increasing complexity of modern legal systems has pushed ever more lawyers to seek additional training. Thus, lawyers routinely take continuing legal education courses in a way that would not have been recognizable even twenty or thirty years ago. Similarly, more and more lawyers pursue advanced law degrees, especially master's degrees. The generic term for these is an LLM (Master of Laws, in Latin), although various specialist degrees have other titles, such as MST (Master of Science in Taxation) or MCL (Master in Comparative Law).

There are now LLM programs in dozens of different fields, ranging from environmental law to international taxation, offering the opportunity to study ever more specialized subjects. Thus, it is no longer necessary to take a generalist corporate law program if you want to focus on securities regulation, or a yearlong introduction to European Union law if you want to study just EU competition law and policy.

Many LLM programs offer the chance to complete the degree entirely through course work; others require a serious paper (perhaps 10,000–20,000 words) in addition to course work; and still others permit students the choice of whether to take additional courses or write one or multiple papers in their stead. There are some programs that are entirely research-based, but they remain comparatively rare.

This chapter focuses on issues likely to be of primary interest to foreign students considering applying to American LLM programs, but in so doing covers the issues relevant to Americans applying either in the United States or abroad. Indeed, it also covers (albeit indirectly) the issues likely to be relevant to non-Americans applying to non-American programs.

A DOZEN REASONS TO DO AN LLM

YOU NEED TO JUMP-START YOUR CAREER

If you are currently unemployed or under-employed, doing an LLM not only adds to your skill base but also keeps you from having a gaping hole in your CV.

If you have been out of the legal market for some time, an LLM can provide a useful combination of retraining and credential enhancement. For example, if you stepped away from the practice of law to start a company or to raise young children, you may be out of touch with current developments in your field—or have forgotten too much of what you once knew—to practice with confidence. Employers generally expect you to be productive from the first day, but law schools are more forgiving: the staleness of your credentials is unlikely to be a major issue for them.

YOU WANT TO CHANGE FIELDS

An LLM offers the opportunity to change career focus. By choosing the right specialist program, a corporate generalist can become a securities regulation specialist or a litigator can become a human rights advocate.

YOU WANT TO CHANGE EMPLOYERS

The quality of your education will be one of the determining factors in your ability to switch employers; so, too, the alumni network of both your JD (or undergraduate) and graduate law schools.

YOU FACE EMPLOYMENT UNCERTAINTIES

An LLM program can give you a useful option when facing uncertainties concerning your employer:

- Perhaps you are in the last year of your JD program and face a terrible hiring year. In this case, you might not know whether you will be hired anytime soon.

- Or perhaps you have accepted a firm's offer of employment but sense that the firm might be tempted to renege on its offer, due to its own economic difficulties.

In either case, having the option to attend an LLM program can be an invaluable way of reducing the uncertainties you face.

YOU WANT TO CHANGE REGIONS

The more well developed your skills, the further employers will go to hire you. For example, middle-tier law schools in the United States are able to market their JD graduates only in the surrounding area. Yet employers from across the country recruit graduates of their master's in taxation programs.

YOUR FIELD IS INTERNATIONALIZING

Increasing globalization means that fewer and fewer lawyers can afford to view their clients' or employers' affairs from the perspective of just one legal system. LLM programs offer the chance to learn the law, practices, and institutions of other countries.

YOU WANT TO MASTER YOUR FIELD

The further training an LLM offers can help you get to grips with a field too complex to be mastered in a first-degree program. For instance, tax law has become so complicated that even those who trained as accountants before becoming lawyers find extra instruction extremely helpful.

THE NEED TO SPECIALIZE

The increased specialization of the profession has not only reduced the role of the generalist. It has also meant that young lawyers are seldom given the time to settle into a practice—to look around for the right fit within a firm's departments, for example—before specializing. Instead, they are often expected to be specialists immediately: highly productive and billable at high rates. Therefore, those who fail to choose and master a field early in their careers may face difficult times.

YOU WANT TO WORK IN THE BIG-TIME

The possibility of getting top jobs is limited by the quality of your first law degree (as well as your grades, etc.). One way to get your foot in the door, despite a weak first degree, is to upgrade your academic credentials with a quality LLM. Similarly, you can develop specialized knowledge of value to high-end employers.

YOU WANT TO TEACH LAW

Those who wish to teach law may need an advanced degree no matter the quality of their first degree. The choice of program should differ slightly for would-be academics. Some LLM programs offer the opportunity to do a degree solely by course work or, alternatively, partly by course work and partly by completing a major research paper. The opportunity to do a major paper—especially one that can be published or provide the basis for a future book—is clearly the better option. Better yet might be doing a doctorate in law or in another, relevant field.

YOU WANT TO EARN MORE

Many of the points made above apply to those who want to earn more money. Switching fields or employers, becoming an expert in a complicated field, and so on all present excellent ways of increasing your pay.

YOU WANT GREATER STATUS

Possessing an LLM degree conjures up a different impression and reaction than being the possessor of just a JD degree. Getting your LLM from a better quality school than you received your JD from will add further status. The same is true of getting a degree abroad.

YOU SEEK AN INTERESTING EXPERIENCE

Many of the benefits of doing an LLM are intangible. For some it is a matter of seeking an intellectually challenging experience; for others, interacting with faculty and fellow students who are interested in the same professional field.

SHOULD *YOU* DO AN LLM?

The preceding section discusses many good reasons for doing an LLM. Before rushing into one, though, consider carefully whether the expenditure of time and money will pay off for you. After all, a year of full-time study will take you away from your current (or prospective) employer, when you could be earning money and, at least potentially, learning by doing. Part-time study offers the chance to earn and learn simultaneously, of course, but it too involves trade-offs (discussed in detail in Chapter 2).

Consider your alternatives carefully, whether they include pursuing another degree, such as an MBA, or furthering your career by continuing to work.

WHEN SHOULD YOU DO AN LLM?

There is no set time to do an LLM. Some people do so immediately after completing their first law degree, whereas others wait until they have been in practice for several or many years. In general, those who should look to pursue an LLM very early in their careers, perhaps right after their first degree, should know where they are headed in terms of legal subject area and type of practice or employer. They should also be clear that an LLM will be of value to their (potential) employers as well as to the development of relevant skills. And of course their finances should permit pursuing the degree now.

BENEFITS OF WORKING BEFORE AN LLM PROGRAM

Given that many LLM programs are willing to admit students straight from their first degree programs, you may face the question of whether to work before starting your master's degree. There are several benefits to working first:

➤ Your employer may pay for all or part of the program.

➤ You will be able to save some money for the program.

➤ If your tuition payments will be tax deductible, working first may give you some income against which to deduct them.

➤ And, of course, you may determine more precisely what you want in an LLM program.

If these factors are not present, consider delaying your degree until you can get the most from the experience and the credential.

CHOOSING THE RIGHT LLM

Your decision to get an LLM is an important one, so you'll want to choose the right program. The process is likely to resemble that described in Chapters 2–4, which focus on choosing JD programs. Consult them as a starting point, then consider the following discussion, which highlights factors that may differ for a graduate program.

Given that you are choosing a second law degree program, you should know well what you intend to achieve—and your goals should drive the application process. If your primary goal, for instance, is to work in an international finance center, such as London or New York, doing major merger and acquisition work, you will favor schools that are feeders to the major law firms, investment banks, and other financial services firms.

STUDENTS

The other students are likely to be more experienced and more focused than in your JD or bachelor of laws program. The composition of the student body can therefore have a major impact upon your learning experience and your enjoyment of the program. The other students should be experienced enough that you can learn a great deal from them.

On the other hand, they should not be so skilled, relative to your own level, that you will be unable to compete with them. Make sure, too, that their goals are compatible with your own. You may not want to be the only person aiming to work for a private firm upon graduation if all of your classmates will be returning to government posts. Consider, also, whether you want to have classmates drawn only from the local area or region.

LOCATION

Given that your program will last one year rather than three, its location (expense, quality of life, etc.) may matter less to you than it did for your first law degree.

PROGRAM

LLM programs' missions vary dramatically. Some are meant for those who wish to get a general introduction to a national legal system, others for those who intend to become specialists in a narrow field. Similarly, some expect their graduates to enter private practice, whereas others are geared for those headed into government service or teaching.

The specializations on offer cover a remarkably wide range. The following legal subjects, and many more at that, are offered as LLM degrees:

- Admiralty
- Agriculture
- American law
- Asian and comparative
- Banking and finance
- Comparative
- Comparative and European
- Competition law and economics
- Corporate
- Corporate governance
- Criminal
- Dispute resolution
- Energy, environment, natural resources
- Entertainment and media
- Estate planning
- European business
- European and international litigation
- European and international taxation

- European integration
- Family
- Finance
- French and European Union
- Health
- Indigenous peoples
- Insurance
- Intellectual property
- International business and trade
- International commercial arbitration
- International development
- International human rights
- Labor and employment
- Law and economics
- Legal theory
- Litigation
- Securities regulation
- Taxation
- Technology
- Trial advocacy

CAREER SERVICES

The career services function may be even more important to you than when you were considering initial law degree programs, given that you are presumably more career-focused now than you were years ago. You may also have highly specific needs that were lacking at that time, such as overcoming a weak first law degree or wanting to be hired by a specific type of employer or in a particular city. On the other hand, some LLM applicants will regard the career services function as largely irrelevant if they intend to return to their current employers or, indeed, will continue to work for them while attending a program part-time.

CHAPTER 19

SHOULD YOU DO YOUR LAW DEGREE ABROAD?

If you have decided to do an LLM to learn about another country's legal system, it is not obvious that you should go abroad for the program. After all, studying locally may provide an opportunity to do an LLM on a part-time basis and thereby continue working full-time. By the same token, more financial aid may be available locally.

On the other hand, doing an LLM abroad offers opportunities not readily available locally. For instance, if do your LLM in Germany, you can:

➤ Do all of your course work in German, and speak German outside the classroom, too.

➤ Develop your understanding of German society and culture, without which a knowledge of law is incomplete.

➤ Take courses related only to German law.

➤ Learn how German lawyers (and prosecutors and judges) are trained and how they practice.

➤ Have in-depth experience of a whole host of German legal institutions, from the local and national bar associations to various courts.

➤ Develop a substantial network of professors and students working in related fields.

➤ Make contacts with local law firms and other employers, giving you the chance to work for them (in Germany or elsewhere).

Local programs will be able to offer no more than very weak approximations of these (and other) benefits.

THE LIMITED ROLE OF LAW SCHOOL RANKINGS

In many countries newspapers, magazines, or professional organizations rank or rate law schools. However, no serious rankings of LLM programs (as opposed to first degree programs) exist. Even in the rankings-crazy U.S. market, the various rankings are for JD programs only. Another problem, for those considering LLM programs in different countries, is that no serious attempt has yet been made to compare law schools in different countries, let alone in different regions of the world. American rankings look only at American schools; Australian rankings include only Australian schools; and so on.

So although rankings of JD (or undergraduate) programs can give you a general idea of how well a law school is regarded, they cannot tell you anything about the school's LLM programs specifically. Rapid development of the LLM market—and lack of rankings—means that choosing the right course will remain a tricky proposition for the foreseeable future.

PRACTICAL DETAILS

Cost. In the United States, expect to spend $40,000–$60,000, but recognize that the range is much greater than that. For instance, at Louisiana State University, you are likely to pay about $30,000, whereas at Columbia (in expensive New York City) you will pay closer to $65,000. LLM programs abroad range from nearly free to programs that cost the equivalent of pricey U.S. degrees.

Course Design. Many LLM programs offer the opportunity to design your own program, with the exception of a required seminar or two designed to introduce you to the native country's law, legal reasoning, and research. Others require you to choose most of your courses from within a specific department, such as taxation.

Size. Although many first degree law programs are quite large, with thousands of students in total, most LLM programs are quite small. Stanford, for instance, offers an LLM with a specialization in either Corporate Governance and Practice or Law, Science, and Technology. It enrolls just ten students per year in each specialization. As a result, students can benefit from the extensive scope of such a school without sacrificing the close-knit feature of being on a program with just nine other students.

GETTING IN

Some LLM programs are substantially less difficult to get into than are the JD or LLB programs offered by the same law schools, but the leading schools tend to have anywhere from three or four to ten applicants per place. NYU, for instance, has more than 2,200 applicants for a class of 425; the University of Virginia, over 500 for a class of 50. The smaller class sizes also add a complicating element. The smaller the group, the more important diversity (of nationality, type of experience, and so on) becomes, thus making it harder to predict whether an applicant will be admitted to a particular school.

LLM programs are similar to JD programs insofar as their admissions committees hope to find the brightest students and most promising professionals for their classes. There are, however, several significant differences. LLM applicants have already had a legal education, thus providing a substantial record of the sort of law student they are (or, at least, were). Many applicants have also had post-JD work experience, thereby demonstrating the quality of jobs they were able to obtain and, via recommendations and the like, the quality of the work they have done. Given their involvement in law, and their greater age, LLM applicants are expected to be able to map out their future careers more extensively than are JD applicants.

All of this provides LLM admissions committees with a great deal of relevant information on which to base their decisions. It also means that much of what qualified you to get into your JD or LLB program is no longer as relevant as it once was. The LSAT and undergraduate grades of American applicants, for instance, pale in comparative importance relative to JD grades and the quality of law school attended. Similarly, post-JD work experience will outweigh college extracurricular involvements in all but the most unusual cases.

Therefore, your LLM application should almost surely focus more on what you have done during and after law school than on what you did beforehand. Other important differences between JD and LLM applications are summarized below.

ALL APPLICANTS

CRITERIA: WORK EXPERIENCE SOUGHT

Many schools favor applicants with at least a few years of experience, preferably legal (although corporate or government work with substantial legal exposure may suffice). There is seldom a maximum age or amount of experience, but top schools will want to see a strong career trajectory.

The Application's Components

Essay or Personal Statement

Most law schools require one essay. Some require you to discuss your career goals and/or your reason for pursuing an LLM; others leave the choice of topic to you. No matter which you face, it is essential you show you know where you are headed and how you are going to get there. Be sure to discuss your professional (and perhaps also your personal) reasons for pursuing an LLM. Explain what you are interested in studying and how this relates to your prior study, work experience, and professional goals.

It is critical that your essays be your own work. Many LLM applicants "outsource" this work—to give the practice a polite name, but the resulting essays are usually easily spotted by admissions committees. The results are predicable: many applicants are denied on the basis of their inappropriate application efforts.

Recommendations

Most schools require two or three recommendations, including at least one from a law professor. Consult Chapter 12 for an analysis of how to select and get the most out of your recommenders.

Interview

Although few LLM programs require interviews, many interview at least some applicants. The University of Michigan, for example, interviews candidates from around the globe depending upon where its professors are teaching (on a visiting basis) and thus available to interview. Interviewers for LLM programs generally focus substantial effort on understanding your career goals and how they relate to your past achievements and interests. Expect questions about:

- Your choice of your first law school
- Your course selection at your first law school
- Your relative success at law school
- Your work experience during and after law school, if any; your future career goals (legal or non-legal, location, type of practice and employer); and how the two fit together
- What skills, contacts, experience, or credentials you need to further your career
- What courses you intend to take in this LLM program
- What else you intend to do (involvement in student organizations, part-time work, other) while on the program
- What you like/dislike about this program relative to others to which you are applying
- Why you think an LLM is a smart move for you

Résumé

Résumés are by no means always required, but you should submit one anyway. Make sure that it is brief (preferably one page) rather than a multipage CV, unless you have a substantial number of publications to include (in which case a second page is permitted).

FOREIGN APPLICANTS TO AMERICAN PROGRAMS

Applicants to programs outside their home country often face difficulties insofar as matters that are well understood and accepted locally are subject to misinterpretation abroad. The quality of a local university or employer, for instance, may be obvious to locals but not to outsiders. The following discussion covers the areas in which the most problems arise.

ELIGIBILITY

All foreign candidates must hold a first degree in law from a university recognized by the American Bar Association or its foreign equivalent. Unlike many European and other LLM programs, American law schools require that candidates be law school graduates. Note that some programs are designed for American students, others for foreigners, and still others for both.

The Application's Components

TOEFL Score

A TOEFL score is generally required of those whose first law degree program was not in English. Although schools will state a minimum score (often 600 on the paper exam, 250 on the computer-based exam), the need for strong English language proficiency to participate successfully in and out of class means that schools generally favor applicants with scores substantially above their stated minimum. Although a good TOEFL score is required, many schools believe it is possible to score well without being able to speak the language sufficiently well to participate in an LLM program. As a result, look for other ways (recommendations, legal courses done in English, working for Anglophone employers or clients, telephone interviews with the school's personnel or graduates) to demonstrate your English abilities.

Undergraduate Transcript

American admissions committees may not be very familiar with your undergraduate school. By all means explain how highly ranked or regarded it is in your country (assuming it is highly ranked), with appropriate documentation such as newspaper or governmental rankings. Consider having your recommenders discuss the same issue. Explain your rank in class as well as the grading and honors systems in effect at your school, so that the admissions committee will fully appreciate your achievements.

Work Experience

If your employment is not truly self-explanatory, by all means provide the relevant context in your application. For instance, if you worked for a small but highly regarded local law firm, by all means discuss (and have a recommender discuss) its local reputation.

CONCLUSION

Whether you hope to climb the ladder in your current field or wish to change fields, you are most likely to benefit from an LLM if you know exactly what you want. By all means choose the program carefully, but then go further and understand how to get the most out of it. Know which options to choose within the program—which courses, professors, and outside activities (student organizations, career development series, and so on) will provide you the highest payoff in terms of what you want from the program.

Appendix VIII

AMERICAN LLM PROGRAMS

The United States, as an immigrant nation, has relied on law to settle disputes between people of different cultures that in other, more homogeneous countries might never have arisen. The result is an intensely legalistic culture that offers lawyers status and an opportunity to earn very substantial amounts. The result has been that many of the best and brightest American students have been attracted to law school.

Law in the United States is unusual in another important regard, too. The first degree offered by American law schools—the JD, or Juris Doctor, degree—is actually a second degree for those who obtain it. This is because JD programs are open only to holders of an "undergraduate" first degree (in a non-legal field, ordinarily). Thus, legal studies are graduate programs in the United States.

TYPES OF LLM PROGRAMS

There are two basic types of LLM degree program offered in the United States. One is offered specifically for foreign-trained lawyers. It is generally meant as an introduction to American law, with the chance to take some advanced courses in one or more fields. The other, meant more often for American-trained lawyers but frequently open to foreign-trained lawyers as well, is devoted to advanced study of a particular subject.

REASONS TO STUDY LAW IN THE UNITED STATES

In the increasingly global legal market, lawyers in more and more specialties need to master more than one legal system. Doing an LLM abroad is one way to accomplish this. Doing so in America offers many advantages for a foreign lawyer:

- A knowledge of American substantive law—and legal institutions—is helpful for those whose clients will have interests in the United States, or who will represent American clients abroad. Given America's substantial global diplomatic role, diplomats and other government officials can benefit from such knowledge as well.

- Learning common (or "case") law method and its attendant reasoning process, is particularly valuable—and surprising—for lawyers trained in civil law.

- The sophistication of the U.S. legal system makes it an influential example for those looking to redesign their own systems as well as for interpreting current laws. Knowledge of it is therefore of value to judges, regulators, practicing lawyers, and others.

- Future interactions with American lawyers are facilitated by an understanding of how they are trained.

- Studying at a top American school (such as Harvard, Columbia, NYU, Georgetown, and so on) is a marvelous addition to your CV.

In addition, the leading American law schools boast all of the supporting services that will allow you to get the most out of your experience: massive library collections; fully wired campuses, with extensive legal (and other) databases; computer technical support and instruction; professional career advice; and so on.

Appendix IX

THE GLOBAL PERSPECTIVE

Law has become a strikingly more global profession in recent years. Law firms in Europe and the United States are merging, as are those in various parts of Europe; other firms are working hand in glove across national borders and continents. Similarly, legal regimes themselves are becoming more and more international. In Europe, for example, it is routinely noted that more than 50 percent of new legislation even in highly developed EU member countries comes from Brussels rather than the individual countries. These developments mirror the needs of governments, businesses, and individuals whose affairs are increasingly international. In most practice areas you can now expect to have an international dimension that would not have existed twenty years ago.

It is perhaps unsurprising that corporate merger and acquisition specialists in sophisticated practices are likely to face deals with international dimensions. After all, cross-border acquisitions hit the headlines frequently. Yet it is not just such high-flying corporate types who face international complications. For instance, divorce lawyers with clients leading lives in multiple countries now routinely have to counsel them whether to sue for divorce in London rather than Tokyo, or New York rather than Frankfurt. These clients potentially have a choice of where (as well as whether) to seek a divorce, so the question of where to do so can be momentous, given the massively different outcomes that are likely in different places. Thus, even the most mundane practices may require knowledge of one or more foreign legal systems.

COMMON LAW VERSUS CIVIL LAW

There are a substantial number of different legal systems in the world, including the remnants of socialist systems, tribal systems, and so on. The two most influential, however, are clearly the common law and civil law systems. Given their importance, their increased interaction in the ever-more global legal world, and their growing closer together as a result of mutual influence on one another, there is a strong argument for doing an LLM focusing on whichever system is unfamiliar to you.

THE VALUE OF AN LLM

First law degrees, which are generally completed in three years, leave little time to get to grips with one legal system. In fact, most students feel they have had just enough time to become acquainted with the basics of local law and the beginnings of whatever they intend to make their specialization. There is unlikely to be sufficient time to master these basics and to travel abroad in an exchange program lengthy enough to permit mastery of a second system. For those whose practices will (or do) involve a substantial international dimension, an LLM can therefore be a very sensible next step.

It can also serve another, powerful purpose. In some countries, such as the United States, getting an LLM can qualify a foreign student to practice law in that country. (The American rules governing this, however, are complicated, not least by the fact that each of the 50 states sets its own terms for admission of lawyers to practice.)

EDUCATIONAL DIFFERENCES

Both Chapters 2–4 and this chapter discuss how to choose a suitable law school. Consult them in this regard, but keep in mind that choosing a program abroad may introduce a new wrinkle: pedagogy. The differences between common law and civil law, for instance, also have their analogues in differences in how courses are taught.

Common law programs—and courses—tend to be smaller than those in civil law jurisdictions. Perhaps partly as a result, case-oriented courses are typically more participatory than are statutory courses. In the United States, for instance, students are not generally expected to be mere note-takers during class. Instead, they are meant to be active participants, responding to professors' questions and jumping in with their own questions and views. This tends to be true in most courses, not just small seminars. The traditional continental European model, where classes are based on a professor lecturing and students passively absorbing ideas, stands in nearly complete contrast. The same is true of most Asian and Latin models as well.

PRACTICAL DETAILS

Employment. During the program, your visa will permit employment on-campus (i.e., working for the school) of up to 20 hours per week, but the rigors of the program often make this impractical.

Remaining in the U.S. Under current visa regulations, you are entitled to remain in the U.S. to receive "limited (additional) training." Most U.S. programs are not designed to help you remain, but many students manage to do so. This involves not just attracting a potential employer; you also need to pass a state bar exam (some of which are very rigorous), which will involve another six weeks of intensive study.

RECOMMENDED READINGS

Those wishing to prepare to study American law are advised to consult the following:

- William Burnham, *Introduction to the Law and Legal System of the United States*, 3d ed., 625 pages. Sophisticated treatment of American substantive law and legal institutions tailor-made for foreign-trained lawyers. Highly recommended.

- New York University School of Law (corporate author), Alan B. Morrison (editor), *Fundamentals of American Law*, 512 pages. Fine alternative to Burnham as a comprehensive introduction to American law.

- Jay M. Feinman, *Law 101: Everything You Need to Know about the American Legal System*, 353 pages. Concise yet highly readable introduction to American law, focusing primarily on the core subjects taught in the first year of American JD programs: civil procedure, constitutional law, contracts, criminal law, property, and torts. Not as sophisticated or detailed as Burnham or Morrison.

- Lawrence M. Friedman, *A History of American Law*, 3d ed., 640 pages. The standard history of American law, this book would make an excellent companion to Burnham or Morrison (or Feinman).

- Lawrence M. Friedman, *American Law in the Twentieth Century*, 736 pages.

To get further information about the books described above, along with other appropriate readings, consult my website, www.degreeofdifference.com, which also makes purchasing them easy.

Part V

APPLICATION ESSAY EXAMPLES

Twenty-two actual applicant essays are included in this book, all but one in Part V. (The other one is included in Chapter 9.) The majority of these are personal statements. The other essays include those written for a scholarship, optional pieces written for schools allowing more than one essay (including explanations for weak college performance and the likelihood of being certified for admission to the bar despite a criminal record), a reapplication essay, and a transfer essay.

Thus, you have a full menu of essay types in front of you. In fact, the range is even greater than you might yet think. The personal statements and other essays reflect the diverse experiences and interests of the applicants writing them—and a diverse lot they are. There are seven men and eight women. Four are Hispanic or African-American. Several were born and raised abroad. Their experience ranges from zero to ten years of full-time work, at jobs ranging from paralegal to journalist, investment analyst to psychologist. Several have done substantial graduate work. They applied to the whole range of leading schools. We did not indicate for which school a given essay was written—since similar essays were generally submitted to multiple schools—except in the case of those written in response to a very specific question. Some of the essays describe applicants' formative experiences, including looks at their families; some discuss their academic interests; others describe what they intend to do after law school; still others provide think-pieces about law, society, and the like.

There is no magic essay topic, so do not feel compelled to choose what one of these applicants wrote about. In fact, this wide-ranging selection of essays is meant to send an opposite message: What makes a given topic an excellent choice for one applicant is likely to make it a bad one for another. The comments that follow the essays are meant to provide assistance in this regard, pointing out what did and did not work—and why—for each applicant.

Use this section to help you find what topic will work best for you, given your experiences, interests, strengths, and weaknesses. In other words, consider the lessons from Chapter 9, "Marketing Yourself," and those that follow concerning your desired positioning, your reward-risk ratio, and so on. Keep in mind also that some topics will not need to be covered because they may already feature in your recommendations.

Not all of the essays are brilliantly written, but each demonstrates at least very good writing quality for those admitted to the top schools. If you wish to read particularly well-written essays, regardless of subject matter, consider those of Maura Wilson, Sacha M. Coupet, David P. White, Noah, and Heather (page 209).

Note how much more interesting the essays become as you proceed through this section. The essays are placed in order of the applicants' experience, with the college seniors' essays coming first, followed by those with more (and more) experience. Even though various of the essays written by inexperienced applicants are good, the lack of experience tends to shine through. The gap in experience, maturity, self-knowledge, and understanding of the career choices available—from the college seniors to those with real career experience—is dramatic.

To get the most out of this section, do four things:

- Read the best examples—those of Maura Wilson, Sacha M. Coupet, David P. White, Noah, and Heather (page 209)—to see how professionally someone can market him- or herself. These are textbook examples of good applications.

- To get a sense of how to write an opening paragraph that grabs attention—which is extraordinarily valuable given how many essays admissions officers have to read—consult the essays by Lisa, Tuan, Julie, Tori, Jon, and Antonio.

- Refer back to the discussion in Chapter 9 of overall marketing principles and the Chapter 10 analysis of specific essay topics, while looking at the essays.

- Then look at the efforts of the people who most resemble you in terms of their backgrounds, their chosen topics, and so on.

You will probably not want to read page by page through this whole section. The charts on the following pages are meant to facilitate your picking and choosing whatever is of greatest interest to you.

One last note: Some of the applicants wanted their full names used whereas others wanted only their first names used, or even wanted their identities lightly disguised by our using a different first name. The first three applicants, in fact, wanted no details given as to their identities. Thus there is no uniform policy followed here, except that of honoring the wishes of the applicants. A minority of the applicants were clients of Degree of Difference: I leave it to you to figure out which were and which were not.

Applicant	Job	Years Experience	College	Subject (Major)	GPA	Graduate Education
Lisa	N/A	0	Harvard			
Tuan	N/A	0				
Julie	N/A	0	Princeton			
Tori	N/A	2				
Jon Queen	Assistant to handicapped woman	2	Cornell	Economics	3.5	
Antonio	Paralegal	1+	Yale	Molecular Biophysics and Biochemistry		
	College counselor (for Community Organization)	1+				
Maura Wilson	Program analyst, Office of Inspector General, U.S. Department of Commerce	3	Univ. of Washington	International Studies	3.6	
Brendan	Capital markets analyst	3+	Yale	History	3.3	
Amy Crawford	Legal aide, Equity Derivatives Trade Desk	3 / 1	Univ. of Virginia	Double Major—Sociology—Afro-American Studies	3.4+	
Sacha M. Coupet	Clinical psychologist	4+	Washington University	Psychology	3.4	M.A., Ph.D., Univ. of Michigan (Psychology)
David P. White	Executive director, Community Org.	4+	Grinnell	Political Science		Oxford (Philosophy, Politics, and Economics)
James M.	Government program manager	2	Univ. of Rhode Island	Management Information Systems	3.3	
	Senior systems engineer R & D technology analyst	2+				
Oluwabunmi Shabi	Journalist, *Business Week*	6	Univ. of Chicago	History		
Bill	Religious meditator	10	Yale	Philosophy	3.6+	
Noah Pittard	N/A	0	Univ. of Georgia	Philosophy	3.0	1st year, Hastings Law

Applicant	LSAT	Essay Topics	Other
Lisa		Cultural influences	Native of South Africa
Tuan		Immigration and experiences leading to interest in law	Native of Vietnam
Julie		Experiences with injustice leading to interest in law	
Tori		Influence of grandfather	
Jon Queen	168	Experience as home aide	
Antonio	160	Talent and training in science and communications leading to interest in law	Hispanic
Maura Wilson	165	1) Interest in internationalism and international law; 2) Contribution to diversity essay: Applicant's courage and tenacity evident in breaking traditions at a young age; 3) Way-you-think essay: Benefits of "children's" literature for adult readers	
Brendan	168	Interest in Latin America and economic development	
Amy Crawford	165	Observations on discrimination and her civil rights work	
Sacha M. Coupet	161	Experience in psychology and children's advocacy, leading to interest in law	African-American (First language: French)
David P. White	158	Experience in foster parenting and as leader of community agency, tied to his interests in law and urban development	African-American (Rhodes Scholar) (Truman Scholar)
James M.	167	1) Alcoholic's journey from depths to recovery; helping others recover; career progress; 2) Contribution to diversity essay: AA membership offering valuable perspective; 3) Statement regarding interruption of studies; 4) Addendum: Fitness of character certification	Recovering Alcoholic
Oluwabunmi Shabi		Discussion of candidate's Brooklyn neighborhood as extension of herself	Reapplicant: Wait-listed year before
Bill	176	1) Discussion of applicant's study of meditation and interest in law; 2) Scholarship essay	
Noah Pittard	165	Why applicant wants to transfer to Boalt Hall (Berkeley) from Hastings	Transfer Applicant

LISA

The day will stand out in my mind for the rest of my life. I know it will because it was one of those series of moments when past and present fit together with great significance, one of those series of moments when you stop to take mental photographs so as to absorb each minute one at a time. It was at the short acceptance speech delivered by President Nelson Mandela on my campus of Harvard University only a few short weeks ago that the trajectory of my life flashed before me. I shivered with pride when Mandela alluded to his Long Walk to Freedom. Time raced backwards in my head as I thought of the long walk of my own family which began on the same soils of South Africa. As I recalled thoughts of people, places and experiences, I began to think of my life not so much as one linear road, but as a puzzle, a conglomerate of separate pieces which somehow fit together to shape the person I have become . . .

A blurry red haze hangs over the deep clay South African soil, the soil of my birth and the base of my puzzle. Emigrating at the age of one, I would learn to love another distant soil in the United States before I would understand my African roots. Time and distance erased homely smells of milliepap and damp cool air. Yet African rhythms would always ring deep in my soul. I was connected to that land somehow. My parents tried to explain to me why near the red soil of Africa, black pieces did not fit with white pieces. They too struggled to handle the stark separation. To them, Africa meant rolling mountains, blue skies, and green trees—colors and curves, not straight edge monochromatic pieces. One day the pieces would match more smoothly, they told me. Until then, Dallas, Texas would become my new home.

In Dallas, I began to discover the world through my one eyes, and in my spirit grew a Texan pride—a reciprocal love of a new home so welcoming to my family. A warm sunny climate translates to warm friendly people in the southwest, and through my progression from elementary school to high school to university, I have forged friendships of binding ties. This is because people take time for one another in Texas. These days I take time to listen to the fascinating stories of my fellow Harvard students, who come from all over the world and each have their own interesting stories to tell. In Texas I was also exposed to the beautiful Latin culture, to the soft roll of the Spanish language, to spicy Tex/Mex food, to happy mariachi music, and to a light-hearted spirit which seeks only the enjoyment of every precious moment of life!

A soft yellow glow emanates near the center of my puzzle and sheds rays of light over all the other pieces. This is the glow of Judaism represented by a symbolic pair of candles lit in my household each Friday to welcome in the Sabbath. Friday evenings in my home are special times. The house is warm with rich smells of roasted chicken and challah bread toasting in the oven, and the calmly dancing candles spread an aura of peace over the house. It is a family time, when my mom and dad, my brother and I sit round the finely decorated Sabbath table to discuss news, events of the week, our individual hopes and dreams, and our goals we hope to achieve together. Judaism touches all the pieces of my puzzle because it touches every part of my existence. My close family ties, my strong system of values and ethics, my search to elevate my life beyond the trivial and mundane, and my appreciation for beautiful things in nature, art, music and literature, in some way all find their derivation in Judaism.

My heart rang with nostalgia and longing when the full resounding voices of the Harvard Kuumba singers sang Ngosi Sikale le Africa—a song my mom used to sing to me when I was a small girl. Mr. Mandela did not see my mouth, but as his lips formed the shape of the words, so did mine. We were singing together, he and I, and I cried. As Mr. Mandela graciously accepted the award of an honorary doctorate of law with a dignified bow and an elegant smile, I smiled too as he reaffirmed for me that day, that hard work and persistence can bring the sweetest rewards.

COMMENTS

What this candidate achieves here is difficult for most applicants of similarly "exotic" backgrounds. The applicant applies a poet's touch and reveals a believable spirit that is not affected or contrived. Many applicants who might wish to convey a similar message would be unable to pull off this kind of essay, the main idea of which is nothing greater than "I am a product of my diverse inputs." The detail about each of the influences—South Africa, Texas, and Judaism—help to solidify the essay's believability and impact. In fact, it comes as a surprise midway through the essay that the applicant is Jewish; we expect her to be black, and the upsetting of that expectation adds to the essay's multicultural message.

TUAN

In the summer of 1978, on a small, overcrowded ship carrying two hundred Vietnamese refugees, a seven-year-old boy forever lost his innocence. Separated from his parents and alone with his thirteen-year-old cousin on this journey, he stood silently while the ship was attacked by pirates who robbed and raped many of the passengers. Terror struck his soul and tears filled his eyes as he witnessed bodies being thrown overboard. He simply could not comprehend the senseless killings. But the nightmare did not stop; dissatisfied with the gold and jewelry plundered from the passengers, the pirates forced everyone overboard in order to seize the ship. The sea tossed and turned as people panicked and fought one another for empty gasoline tanks and water containers to use as flotation devices—it was a quarter of a kilometer to shore. The young boy and his cousin were fortunate;

they both knew how to swim. The sight and sound of desperation and death sent chills down his spine, but all he could do was swim. To this day, the memory of a young girl calling to her drowning mother for help still haunts his dreams; and sometimes a deep sense of guilt overwhelms him for having survived when over half of the passengers perished.

I was this young boy. Two years later, I was reunited with my father and eldest sister in the United States. But life in a new country was terribly difficult. For nine years, my father, sister, cousin and I struggled to earn enough to send home to my mother and two sisters in Vietnam while trying to keep our heads above water. The situation was such that I had to sew piecework for the garment industry after school to supplement my father's small income. As a result of his perceived inability to provide for his family, my father resorted to alcohol to escape the loss of dignity and sense of shame. Racial intolerance also added to our difficulties. Derision such as "chink" and "gook" by fellow classmates induced feelings of inadequacy and self-hatred on my part; and because of my poor English skills, I responded by fighting, which further exacerbated the problem. In addition, an assault on my father by three youths who told him to "go back to China" and the subsequent burning of my sister's car forced us to move from our apartment. Such experiences reinforced my resolve to succeed in school in order to escape both poverty and the stigma of being a foreigner.

With the arrival of my mother and two older sisters to the United States in 1989, after eleven years of separation, my financial obligation to the family was eased slightly, which enabled me to concentrate more on my studies. However, the dual necessity of work and commuting to school did not allow me to take advantage of extracurricular activities provided by organizations on campus. Nevertheless, I did gain extensive experience working as a self-employed commercial artist during my undergraduate years. Unable to find a job suitable to my school schedule, I decided to put my artistic talent to work. I bought ads in local Vietnamese newspapers offering my services of designing and painting posters, signs, and advertisements at half the price of competitors. Most of my jobs are on a small scale that include painting windows and banners, and designing menus and advertisements for Vietnamese businesses. While working within the Vietnamese community, I became aware of the pressing need by small businesses as well as individuals in the community for affordable legal assistance. Because of their immigrant background, many Vietnamese lack an awareness of their rights and obligations in American society, which often lead to misunderstandings, confusion, and insecurity. Given the opportunity to attend law school, I hope to alleviate some of the friction and distrust that Vietnamese immigrants have in the law by broadening their knowledge of the legal system.

COMMENTS

This essay starts off well with a jarring story that emphasizes the applicant's background and the difficulties he has had to overcome to get where he is today. The story of the applicant's struggle against discrimination and insecurity also helps to show his attraction to the legal profession. The essay would have been substantially strengthened, however, if he had gone much further into his current work to show that his sentiments are sincere enough that he will indeed play the role he imagines, helping Vietnamese immigrants deal with the legal system. Not only could he have made stronger, more concrete connections between his experiences and observations and his legal future, but he could also have worked in nonlegal capacities to help fellow immigrants.

JULIE

Meet, first, my grandmother, Lea. She's eighty-six now and lives across the street. By leaving Germany in 1935, when the public schools of her hometown were closed to Jewish children, she escaped the Holocaust. She treasures American liberties; her favorite song is "God Bless America"; and she reminds me . . . I don't know how good I have it.

Now let me introduce you to the classmate who changed my high school campaign posters from "Vote Julie" to "No Jews." Then to the Neo-Nazis who sporadically demonstrate in front of the synagogue three blocks from my house. Next to Representative David Duke, selling *The Hoax of the Twentieth Century* in my backyard. These are some of my neighbors, and they have caused me to examine those rights which theoretically will prevent Lea's story from becoming my own.

My focus is the freedom of the press: its allotted latitude and resulting ability to shape social discourse. I observe, for example, in my research for my senior thesis, disturbing trends in the coverage of Mr. Duke's senatorial campaign. *The New Orleans Times Picayune* runs article after article on his growing support, his charisma, his nationwide sources of funding. It is only in mid-August that I read of racist and anti-Semitic comments made as late as 1989. The *Picayune*, I discover, has known of these remarks for ten months. For nine months, as the campaign gained momentum, they weren't considered newsworthy. A staunch opposer of censorship, I wonder: Should there be some guidelines for what is and is not printed?

My own journalistic experience reinforces my concern. I worked as a stringer for the Associated Press. I know that its editors will accept a story on Princeton's nude olympics and reject one on Louis Farrakhan. They realize that Farrakhan has caused one of the largest controversies on campus this year, they say, but he's doing it for the publicity. Don't cover it. I also know that *The Bridge-water Courier-News, a USA Today* subsidiary, isn't interested in the speeches of Catharine MacKinnon or of Abba Eban or of the American ambassador to El Salvador, but will pay me for ten to twelve inches on Princeton's cheerleaders.

I complement my interest in the societal influences of the media with close studies of our legal and judicial systems. My junior independent work, awarded more than once and published by the New Jersey Department of Higher Education, concludes that women should not turn to the judicial system for protection from the sadistic sexism of hard-core pornography. This semester I chair a Woodrow Wilson School policy conference that examines alternative means of dispute resolution, asking whether the current system truly provides justice. I direct the efforts of eighteen juniors toward a cohesive policy statement which we will present to the U.S. Senate Judiciary Committee.

I do not confine my analysis of the functioning of the law to the classroom. Summer work with the prosecuting office of the District of Columbia taught me that the system is easily manipulable. I answered motion after motion by defense attorneys who knew that if they delayed long enough, the case would be dropped for want of prosecution. I prepared cases with the knowledge that because they were going before Judge X* instead of Judge Y*, the fifth-offense drunk driver would be dismissed with minor penalty.

Back at Princeton, my term on the University Discipline committee offers a different perspective on justice. Four students, along with a group of faculty and administrators, hear charges of violations ranging from plagiarism to alcohol policy infractions to vandalism. I benefit from a view of, and a say in, yet another level of judicial structure.

Law school is a natural extension of these experiences. My professional goal is both to practice public interest law and to continue as a writer of social commentary. It is a goal that allows me to assure my grandmother: I not only value "what I have," but I aim to protect and to strengthen it.

COMMENTS

This candidate's approach is to paint quick portraits of her experiences with "justice," and then draw the conclusion that she belongs at law school—a natural extension of her interests and pursuits to date. This is a valid strategy. Furthermore, the initial stories she tells grab our attention and sympathy. The problem is that she over-gilds the lily. Even the first two paragraphs are rendered a bit melodramatically; they make a reader feel that the writer might be crassly taking advantage of her Jewish roots, trying to win over the admissions committee with a simplistic claim to felt discrimination. After that, Julie demonstrates a basic intolerance of others, which cannot help her cause. Even though any one of the foes she targets could be lambasted, the net effect of objecting to all of them suggests that she is a shrill, neurasthenic sort. It is one thing to object to Farrakhan, another to insist that you have the only acceptable way of dealing with him. Thus, insisting—as a journalistic intern, no less—that your paper must report his activities in full rather than ignore him sounds a bit strident. Similarly, an-

---

*Actual names were used in the personal statement, but for legal reasons I have withheld them here.

nouncing that any and all speeches of Catherine MacKinnon are newsworthy, and that pornography is sadistic sexism against women, is painting with a very broad brush, indeed.

Julie should have eliminated some of her complaints and tempered her portraits with an admission that she realizes discrimination against Jews is not actually common at Princeton (her current home) or at the top law schools to which she is applying. In addition, she could have altered her tone a bit to sound less naive or incredulous that such acts of discrimination indeed occur to this day.

Julie is all too ready to see injustice and evil everywhere, with herself all too often the victim of it. She comes across as immature and lacking in the perspective that real-world experience would provide. Compare her overdone tone, and the limited nature of what she personally has had to confront, with the personal statements of David P. White and Tuan. They faced much more substantial difficulties, weathered them with more grace, and reported them more matter-of-factly. The results are much greater reader sympathy and respect.

TORI

My grandmother says that to the day my grandfather Ted died, she could still see my cousin Anita's pink handprint smeared across his right cheek. After Ted had a stroke and a heart attack in the same week, my family and his doctors decided to let him die a peaceful death staring with a half-opened eye at a silent flickering television hanging from the hospital ceiling. Anita returned early from a European vacation just in time to witness the impending death that the rest of my family had grown to accept, and when she entered Room 204, she walked right over to my grandfather and smacked him in the face. As his face burned, Ted ate food again for the first time in days and decided not to die.

Ted lived twenty years after that slap. My family spent half of every other weekend visiting my grandmother and him, bringing them food. Many of my earliest memories are of the way my face felt against a cold vinyl backseat of a car as I slept through the Lincoln Tunnel on the way back home to New York. I would only be a fraction of the person I am now had Anita not been courageous enough to hit her uncle as the nurses gasped in astonishment.

When I was young, Ted used to tell me all the things we would do together when he recovered from his paralysis. He taught me to imagine the two of us walking through art museums and sharing blankets at cold football games. I always knew that his fierce desire to walk again was what got him out of bed every morning. Bruises and cuts were commonplace as Ted would pull himself up from his chair, take one step, then tumble forward until his face hit the cement floor. I used to wonder what he thought each time in the instant between the fall and the landing, knowing not enough of his limbs worked well enough to break his fall.

As I grew up our conversations gradually shifted from what we would someday do together to what I was doing without him. He taught me to live a life passionate enough for both of us, to perform enough good for both of us, to have enough fun for both of us. When his nightly phone call would interrupt my dinner I'd feel embarrassed if I had nothing noteworthy to tell him. When I left for college, he cried and told me to learn enough for him to feel his own enlightenment.

The summer after I graduated from college, Ted pulled himself up from his bed in his nursing home and tried one last time to walk. He fell sideways to his left, and his paralyzed left arm could not protect him from the floor. His left leg twisted grotesquely but painlessly and one of its bones snapped in half. Lying in the hospital afterwards, he no longer could convince himself that he would be able to walk again. When he died soon after, I realized that after heart attacks and strokes, diabetes and seizures, a broken leg killed my grandfather.

My favorite image of my grandfather is one I've only seen abstractly. When my mother was a girl Ted would bring her to the same park bench every night to stare at the Hudson River. Every night all the other men from their apartment building would hover around him and listen to his jokes and stories. My mother calls those his nights of holding court: they were probably the best times my grandfather ever had. In all the smiles I ever saw on my grandfather's face, the left side of his mouth fails to rise along with the right, but what I actually remember are all of my grandfather's teeth shining, big like an easel, like he smiled by the river as a painless and hopeful young man.

I saw my grandfather hold court in nursing home after nursing home. He'd sit in his wheelchair next to the nurses' station surrounded by other men and women in their wheelchairs. The other residents would hear stories about all the things he and I were going to do when he got well once more. They told me that when I wasn't there he'd talk about all the things I was doing, how I was living a life, in his words, grand enough for both of us.

The day my grandfather died, I went from the hospital to his nursing home to retrieve his belongings. Every person there, from cooks to residents to visiting volunteers, asked me how he was, and it invariably sounded like the most important question they would ask anyone that day. When I told them he died, and I saw their eyes water, I also saw my grandfather's handprint across their cheeks. I realized how profound an impact my grandfather had on everyone he met. As my cousin succeeded in doing twenty years ago, my grandfather tried to slap life into everyone around him, and I lie awake at night hoping he is no longer held captive inside a body.

COMMENTS

This is a nicely wrought essay about a rather ordinary and commonplace influence on a young person: that of a close family member. This essay helps us learn several things about the candidate: She is dedicated to her family, she is compassionate, sensitive, inspired, perceptive, lyrical, and humane, and she is capable of forging connections with and learning from others. The "handprint" theme (developed in the first paragraph and returned to in the final one) helps make this essay memorable.

Most essays that focus on people other than the candidate are failures because they do not teach us much about the candidate. This essay is a rare exception.

JON QUEEN

"Why are you not packing up my house? I am leaving tonight, and you have to pack everything up right now," Diane yells at me as I try to fade into the wood floor—not an easy task for someone six foot six and two hundred fifty pounds. Later, I will bathe her and change her clothes after she has another biological accident. It is Sunday night at the Pogson house, and I must remind myself why I remain here.

Not very long ago, I was one of a large pool of ambitious graduates with big dreams of entering law school, learning the necessary tools, and contributing something positive to this world. However, at that time the closest I had come to the pressures of real life was the semester I spent interning on Capitol Hill. I felt ready for new challenges, a proving ground other than the traditional classroom. I opted to make it on my own for a while, prove that I was self-sufficient, and recover my focus as a student. What I never anticipated was that during this time, working as a home aide for a disabled woman, I would face challenges that would define my character and test my dedication to its fullest.

I had little inkling of the emotional commitment necessary to care for an elderly lady with multiple sclerosis. I was unprepared for her dementia, incontinence, or confrontational personality. In fact, her husband had committed suicide two years earlier, and the turnover rate for her home aides was very high. Recently, her son casually mentioned that I am the one thing delaying Diane Williams from entering a home, and that touched me deeply. So every night I clean up her excrement, and listen to her disjointed commands and angry outbursts. To further complicate matters, she has been unable to compensate me for the past week due to her financial situation.

Working with Diane has taught me many important lessons. Through her, I have learned the value of a positive outlook on life. I have also learned that in life, challenges never disappear; they merely change shape. I now regard the world from a different perspective, from the viewpoint of a contributor who has faced life's harsh realities, and has done his best to shield another from them. I feel that this new insight will serve as an excellent complement to the knowledge I will gain in law school. In addition, I have proven that I have the tenacity to overcome adverse and stressful situations, a skill that will help me excel in school as well as in life.

I am two years older and ages wiser than I was as a fresh graduate. Although I found my work as an economics major meaningful, I have grown much since then. I have learned the importance and satisfaction of contributing in a real world, one of poverty and disability. After all, life provides a different kind of education, and such experiential knowledge enriches classroom study and conceptual mastery.

COMMENTS

This essay explains how the applicant has spent his time since college, and helps position him as a compassionate and mature adult with more perspective on life than the usual college graduate. Jon benefits from the uniqueness of his experience as a home aide for a disabled woman, and is wise *not* to try to grope for specific connections between his job duties and his future as a lawyer. An applicant would be hard-pressed to group the two careers into a single framework, unless he or she had had other serious exposure to working with the disabled or disabilities law, and thus was better able to forge a natural link between these pieces.

Jon illustrates that he has both the heart to try to help others and the willingness to work hard at unpleasant tasks. (Note, however, that Tori does a better job of capturing her inspiration in words.) The implicit message is that this combination can be powerful; also, that one can trust that he will indeed enter public interest law practice.

ANTONIO

Our family gatherings were always full of entertainment provided by the youngest attendees. Cousin Alby was the magician. His brother Nelson was the contortionist. Our cousin Maria from Hartford was vying to be the next Celia Cruz at nine years old. The family talent shows that would spontaneously erupt at each barbecue, christening, or birthday kept the children occupied and allowed the adults to appreciate the spoils of parenthood. My contributions did not involve pulling a rabbit out of a hat, wrangling my legs behind my head, or singing salsa songs octaves too high. I had the gift of enthralling my family members by answering correctly any scientific question posed to me.

"How many planets are in the solar system?" "Why is the sky blue?" "Name the parts of the human digestive system." These were (and still are!) the classics of my repertoire, and year after year my animated answers became a lot more entertaining than the prosaic explanations offered by textbooks and teachers. I developed a sense of identity around my ability to explain everyday observations and occurrences simply and completely. More education brought increasingly sophisticated answers to the same questions and resulted in my characterization as The Scientist. When important conversations during college invited a perspective from the natural sciences, I reveled in being able to contribute substantively.

These very conversations made me question, among other things, my identity, and compelled me to find answers by continuously striving to build community among Latinos at Yale. Much hard work was involved in overcoming the barriers to sustaining that community, and I developed an ability to assess my surroundings more critically than ever before as I became more committed to student activism. Ultimately, I turned this critical eye to the study of science, and realized the profession would not highly value or productively use some of the personality traits that I would bring to it. While Antonio the Scientist fit in well within the confines of the laboratory, Antonio the Communicator did not.

I saw that, like me, most scientists valued communication, but very few cared to interact with individuals outside their own specialty, much less with non-scientists. I lamented the absence of undergraduate scientists in the broader discourse at Yale, especially in those areas that were most important to me, such as the diversity of Yale's student body. This often made me feel isolated, and the ramifications of that feeling, once understood, prompted self-examination and the exploration of alternative career paths. I left college with a greater appreciation of how important it was for me to communicate science to non-scientists, and to urge those that I left behind in the laboratory to do the same. The maturity I gained during this process made me value the exchange between the lay and technical, not for the validation I could receive from relatives or employers, but rather for the larger impact that I could have by being the intermediary between these two groups.

Although I left Yale with the tools for life-long learning, I did not leave with a crisp personal vision. This has developed during the two years since I finished college, and is due in large part to my experience at [large Wall Street law firm]. Here, I have found that the law will allow me to be the communicator that it is natural for me to be, and that the law provides an audience that is interested in communicating about technology's growing impact beyond the laboratory. I have seen that lawyers employ an even more rigorous standard for truth than scientists that fits in well with my technical background. And I also see that the unexpected ambiguities and unanswerable questions of the law will keep things interesting.

I have not even started working as a lawyer, but I already have the feeling that my impact is significant. I have awoken several mornings in the past eight months to hear the first public announcement of the deal on which I was working the previous evening. As one of a handful of paralegals who work on intellectual property due diligence at the firm, I play a role in most "high-tech" deals for which it is necessary. Assisting with patent prosecution and litigation has given me an inside-out view of the law while enhancing the technical competency of the firm's work product. My internal sense of accomplishment has been reinforced by the feedback I have received from the attorney with whom I work, and I can confidently say that the firm looks at me with an eye to the future.

With this experience has come a renewed confidence and desire for academic success, which, in turn, leaves me with an unclouded vision of the type of impact I can make. I am excited about the prospects of taking a biotechnology start-up public, securing protection for a large pharmaceutical company that allows it to post industry record profits, negotiating licensing contracts for a university that allows it to increase the size of its financial aid awards, or acquiring the international influence to figure prominently in developing countries' enjoyment of the full promise of the AIDS triple therapy. All of these are possible in my lifetime.

To borrow a phrase from microbiology, I am in the "logarithmic-phase" of my career. That is to say, the incremental steps in my development as a lawyer over the next several years will lead to explosive leaps in ability to contribute to the profession. In the process, Antonio the Communicator will become Antonio the Advocate. Three years at [law school X] will be an ideal start to that transformation.

COMMENTS

The majority of law school applicants have backgrounds in the humanities or social sciences. Those with science backgrounds automatically stand out a bit, albeit not always to their advantage if they suffer from the archetypal problems associated with scientists/engineers: poor communication and social skills. Antonio does a fine job in positioning himself: He shows that he is indeed a scientist, whose work makes him a natural for intellectual property law (a very hot field at the time of his application). He avoids the negatives associated with his science background, moreover, by showing his desire to be part of a field that requires substantial communication skill.

Much of Antonio's writing is superb. The opening paragraph, for instance, shows him to be a minority candidate without dwelling on the subject. The penultimate paragraph is loaded with examples that lend credibility to his candidacy. The one weak part is the third paragraph, which lacks a clear message and which does not fit comfortably within the flow of ideas here.

Despite this fine effort, however, one major problem remains: It is unclear why Antonio wishes to go to law school. After all, even if he wants a career in which communication skill is crucial, he could more readily choose a field other than law. For example, he could opt for scientific journalism or biotech marketing. He could have dispelled this issue by elaborating on how much and why he enjoyed his law firm experience.

MAURA WILSON

I shifted my feet uneasily as I listened to President Reagan's "evil empire" speech. That evening my six-year-old world was dark, and the yellow glow of our kitchen light did not dent the long ominous shadows that lurked outside our windows. I slowly continued setting the table, the television flickering, and I learned to fear people half a world away, whom I had never seen. My fear made me angry because I was not used to such feelings. I was an independent, confident child, accustomed to facing my few problems directly. The fact that I could not talk to the leaders and citizens of the Soviet Union, and explain to them that Americans were really very nice, infuriated me. I wanted to make things better. I hated being afraid.

Seven years later, elation pumped my heart as I sat in that same kitchen and watched sections of the Berlin Wall come down. I had never been to Berlin, or touched that wall, but the legacy of the Iron Curtain was burned into me. Every current map that I had ever seen of Europe was half red: half feared, half evil. I never considered that it would be any different in my lifetime. Yet there, right before my eyes, concrete slabs were cut and the world swirled with change.

I became an international studies major because I was so excited by this new world we had entered. I chose to focus on United States diplomacy and security because I was intrigued by the opportunities of the post–Cold War era, and I was concerned by the many knotty problems that had emerged out of the disintegration of the formerly bi-polar world. The rules of the Cold War no longer applied, but what would the new rules be? The legacy of the decades-long standoff allowed the world to return to an era of fragmentation and militant nationalism, yet it also provided an unprecedented chance for countries to join together in positive political and economic agreement.

During college I worked for Gensler, an international architecture firm, to learn about the realities of operating a modern global operation. Gensler faced many challenges with its large Pacific Rim clientele. To open an office in Japan, it had to form a business alliance with a Japanese *keiretsu,* one of the powerful families that control economic operations in Japan. It also had to address corporate culture issues, such as altering marketing presentations for Asian clients, who prefer to see very detailed, full-color mock-ups of buildings before they will agree to close the deal. The company learned to carefully navigate the many obstacles, misunderstandings, and difficulties that are a regular part of operating a successful international operation.

After graduation I chose to work for the Department of Commerce because I wanted to help the American government operate more efficiently, especially on a global scale. Among other issues, the Commerce Department is concerned with international trade, along with world-wide problems such as the maintenance of the oceans and atmosphere. I performed in-depth research and reviews of Commerce agencies and programs to identify any operational deficiencies or violations. I reviewed a program within the International Trade Administration that helps American companies to expand their operations overseas. I also evaluated an agency that performed most of the research on the El Nino phenomenon—a topic that could not be effectively and completely examined without input from scientists around the world.

Our home planet is a much smaller place than it was ten years ago, or even ten months ago. Helping the federal government to react and adapt to the increasingly interlinked world we are creating was a very valuable experience. I now look forward to utilizing that experience in obtaining a legal education and practicing law. To ignore the increasingly international scope that law must encompass is unreasonable.

The uncharted political and economic intricacies of the post–Cold War era have created a cacophony of legal viewpoints. This confusion is compounded by the advent of the Internet age, whose international legal ramifications have barely begun to be addressed. I am so excited by the possibilities of international law. I hope that those who create and enforce it can eventually form a set of regulations, precedents and institutions, where lasting and fruitful political, social and economic understandings (instead of wars or decades-long stand-offs) can be forged.

The University of Michigan Law School offers exactly what I want: an excellent, innovative education in international law. The opportunity to meet and learn from law professors from around the world through the Center for International and Comparative Law is unmatched. The comprehensiveness of the program's curriculum expresses a deep understanding of how the future of society, economics and the law are inextricably moving towards a global society that requires international legal expertise. The University of Michigan Law School would shine with the addition of my experience, intelligence and zeal.

At a very young age, an international conflict touched my life with fear. But as the world left the Cold War behind, I left my fear with it, and emerged with a dedicated interest in international relations. The legacy of that fear sparked my concern for protecting and maintaining our efforts in forming a global community. I do not want to slip back to a time when the menace of an "evil empire" is broadcast into our kitchens. The law is a very important caretaker for this exciting, hyperlinked new world, and I want to be an essential part of shaping and caring for it.

COMMENTS

Maura does an excellent job making sense of her interest in internationalism and the law. Her opening paragraph—showing her as a young child watching Reagan's "evil empire" speech on her kitchen TV—is memorable, and helps her to set up the trajectory that would cause her to become an international studies major, work for an international corporation, perform research for the Department of Commerce, and now prepare for a career in international law. Notice the deft way that she placed her work at Gensler into this "thematic" build up. Rather than writing off that experience as unmentionable here (as some, viewing it as "architecture" or "design" work, might have), Maura realized the potential to utilize that job to further explain her understanding of our globally connected world. By the same token, her fourth and fifth paragraphs are somewhat wooden: résumé-like recounting of her experiences, told without adequate transitions.

Michigan Optional Essay #1. *"This essay should focus on aspects of your background and past experiences that will contribute to the diversity the Law School wishes to foster. This essay should offer information not included in your personal statement."*

My stomach felt like it was somewhere in the middle of my chest, and it threatened to move further up at any moment. What had I done? What was I thinking? I had chosen to attend St. Ignatius Prep, a previously all-male institution that had gone co-ed. I would be one of the 175 freshman girls, who would buck an over-century-long tradition, and mingle with the 1000 or so boys that roamed S.I.'s halls. I was terrified.

I had attended an all girls' elementary school, and not had a class with a boy since pre-school. Yet I chose to continue my education with hundreds of them, many of whom did not like the idea of females entering their enclave.

High school is tough, and my decision to go to Saint Ignatius made it tougher, but I have never regretted it. Besides being an excellent school, S.I. taught me that I could rely on my intelligence, quick instincts, and sense of humor to get me through many difficult situations. The first few weeks were the most awkward. Girls were greeted in the halls with quick, intense gazes that ranged from hostile and affronted, to amused at our novelty. I discovered that meeting these gazes directly would make my male classmates at least stop staring. With that victory, I faced the rest of my time at S.I. in the same direct manner.

I endured cat calls and whispers every time I entered my freshman science class, where, due to a scheduling glitch, I was the only girl. I discovered that consistently doing excellent work, and providing intelligent answers to questions, eventually earned me respect in that class. I had my first surprising encounter with a urinal, in the hastily converted women's bathroom, and decided they were nothing to fear. I was quietly amused that the girls' locker room was painted pink. The transition had its bumps, but by the end of my freshman year, we had smoothed the way for all the other girls to come.

At thirteen years old, I stormed a tradition, and stretched my comfort zone to unprecedented proportions. My high school experience had the usual highs and lows, but I treasure the uniqueness of my four years at Saint Ignatius. The self-confidence and maturity that I gained there will be with me for my entire life.

COMMENTS

For a white "mainstream" applicant who has had a fairly ordinary life, the topic Maura chose works well. Since she has no tales to tell about a harrowing immigration journey to the U.S. and no cultural or ethnic "tags" by which to sell herself, she is smart to focus on her courage and tenacity, especially as they were evident as she "stormed a tradition" by entering the first class of females to attend a formerly all-boys school. The little details—the pink painted walls in the girls' locker room, for example—help to make this effective. So, too, does the sense of perspective she brings to her history—the fact that she can smile about what happened, and see how she benefited from it. Her sense of humor and lack of self-pity, when combined with an exemplary use of detail, make this highly successful.

Michigan Optional Essay #2. This essay "should reveal, in a way that an LSAT score or a grade point average cannot, something about the way you think. For example, you might choose to discuss an intellectual or social problem you have faced or a book or film that has particularly affected you."

I disagree with the concept of "children's literature." A book that is well-written and compelling appeals to me, regardless of the section of the book store where one can find it. I can still curl up with E. L. Konigsburg's *From the Mixed-Up Files of Mrs. Basil E. Frankweiler* and thoroughly enjoy myself. I love reading about the exploits of Eloise or Madeline. I still get chills when I revisit *A Wrinkle in Time*. These books were my friends when I was growing up, and as an adult I have not forgotten them. Today, I have an even greater appreciation for the skill and deftness with which my favorite early writers serve their craft. They never patronize their readers, and with just a few phrases, they can translate complicated ideas and feelings into something equally meaningful to a child or an adult.

These excellent qualities are found in the increasingly popular Harry Potter series. J. K. Rowling has created a wonderful world, with complex and interesting characters. She employed the clever trick of creating a fantasy world that parallels and mixes with the world that we already know. She makes it easy to believe in witches and wizards, flying broomsticks, and a boarding school that teaches magic. Her descriptions are brief and vivid, and she always leaves her reader wanting more.

The media is shocked by how widely embraced Harry is. It is a "children's book" after all. I read a discussion of Harry in which the reviewer admitted embarrassment about reading the book in public. He kept his laptop close at hand to prove to any passers-by that he was working. I would read Harry Potter in public with pride! I have read plenty of recently best-selling, and critically acclaimed books that were boring, awkwardly written, or just plain tedious. Rowling not only entertains but also challenges her reader. Averaging around 300 pages, the books are much longer than most written for kids, the vocabulary is advanced, and the plots are complex "who-done-it puzzles," with wonderfully unexpected twists and turns.

Children and adults love the Harry books because they are exciting and funny. But adults also enjoy them because the books give them access to a kid's world. This is a world no less confusing, complex or heart-wrenching than an adult world—it is often more so—but often out of reach for adults. The fantasy, imagination and pure joy of the series inspires nostalgia in adults for their own childhoods. At the same time, adult readers can create a connection with children who are experiencing Harry Potter.

I hope that those adults who eagerly anticipate and enjoy each new Harry installment will branch out and sample some of the many other quality books that children have loved for years, and that too many adults quickly forget. These books can help adults to connect to their pasts, as well as their present situations.

COMMENTS

This is a refreshing way to write about "the way you think." Maura decided to write not on an international concern or political issue but a fairly simple idea close to her heart: adults' enjoyment of so-called "children's" literature. She is sure to remain memorable with this, since it's highly unlikely any other candidate would have written on this same topic. (On the other hand, applicants who write on the importance of human rights, feminism, and other hot issues are sure to remain unmemorable to admissions officers.) The thoughts laid out here are not particularly complex, but they are fresh and compelling.

BRENDAN

For the past two years I have lived and worked in Latin America. I have seen first-hand both the potential for development that exists throughout the region, and the mistakes that foreigners make in Latin America for lack of local experience. However, I am also deeply attached to my home state, Rhode Island, and I believe in my responsibility to development opportunity locally. My aim is to find a way to connect the opportunities that exist in Latin America to the growth of my home state.

I was one year old when I made my first visit to Latin America—traveling with my parents to Mexico's Yucatan Peninsula. That trip marked the beginning of a life-long fascination with South America. My formation as a Latin Americanist—my consciousness of the layers of society and history in the region, began within the ambient orientation of my family toward Latin America, and has been informed by my own experiences there since before I can remember.

From my earliest memories the region's language, art, food, and music were part of my growing up. As a teenager, I spent several summers in Mexico: traveling with my parents or staying with family friends in the slow, hot city of Kampuchea. When I was thirteen, my parents adopted my sister Maggie from Honduras and we spent the summer in the rainy, unrelenting poverty of Tegucigalpa. My childhood, in sum, was a steady exposure to the variety and contrasts of Latin American—the wealth of nature and ancient civilization, the poverty of the people, the army, the complexity of feeling towards the United States.

Since finishing college, I have been fortunate to experience unusual successes working in the capital markets at a time when these markets are fueling historic changes throughout the region. In the emerging markets of Latin America, the political, economic, and cultural lives of each country ebb and flow around the markets to a pronounced degree. In Buenos Aires a cabdriver can tell you where YPF's stock closed the day before. A waiter in Sao Paulo will know the daily change in the Consumer Price Index. Because of these markets' central importance, I have had a glimpse of both where these countries are coming from, and where they are going.

I have observed that three core misunderstandings mark the missteps that foreigners, particularly Americans, make in Latin America. The first is the most obvious, yet poses continual difficulties for foreigners, especially in business: Latin America is not a monolith—cultures vary as widely between Latin countries as they do between the U.S. and any one Latin country, maybe more. Differences range in subtlety from racial and gender attitudes to simple use of language. Thus, Mitsubishi wasted months of effort and uncountable brand value trying to introduce its Pajero sport utility vehicle, which had enjoyed great success in Brazil, to Argentina. The company, in its monolithic view of Latin America, didn't know that the word "pajero" has a sexual meaning in Argentine Spanish that it does not in Brazilian Portuguese.

Secondly, foreigners tend to mistake the meaning of their "rights" in Latin America. They often assume that the same ideas of contracts and obligations prevail in Latin America as they do in the first world, and that the courts occupy the same exalted place in society that they do in the U.S. They often fail to realize that in Latin America, possession is the chief determinant of ownership (thus the ferocity of land battles between peasants and landowners throughout Latin America). It follows that the prestige of the courts is often less than in the U.S. Power tends to rest much more directly in the hands of politicians and labor leaders. This has been the source of endless tension between the governments of the U.S. and several Latin countries, arising most recently with regard to the ownership of intellectual property rights. Governments in Chile and Argentina have questioned the American assertion that development of drugs and medicines connotes ownership, and that therefore cheap and easy replication by local firms should be prohibited.

Finally, Sam Rayburn's admonition to "go along to get along" holds special meaning in Latin America. The systemization of relationships that makes the U.S. a very efficient society does not yet exist in Latin America. Personality and background play a very important role in transactions ranging from social to official to professional. The importance of individual relationships, especially those arising from family background, is difficult to overstate. Personal relationships are the lubricant of business and society, and the failure to develop them is a principal mistake made by foreigners.

One of the benefits that I have derived from living and working in Latin America, and witnessing first hand the mistakes made and opportunities missed by others, is that I see how the mistakes can be avoided, and the opportunities seized. I hope that this knowledge will allow me to continue to be a part of the evolution and development of Latin America.

I have Latin America in my heart, and I have no doubt that my professional future lies in the region. However, I am from Providence, R.I., and I am strongly committed to the values of place and home. I feel bound by my family and my upbringing to the place of my childhood, and I believe deeply that opportunity is not to be followed elsewhere, but created locally.

One of the principal challenges that I foresee for myself in my professional life is to connect the dynamism and opportunity that the development of Latin America represents, to the stagnant Rhode Island economy. The way is far from clear. Rhode Island's areas of economic strength, tourism and oceanography, bear little relation to the needs of the Latin countries—infrastructure, telecommunications, financial services. As a market, Rhode Island, with fewer than 1 million inhabitants and little cultural attachment to Latin America, is too small and too remote to represent a great attraction to Latin exporters.

However, I am convinced that the flow of knowledge in the interconnection of the Americas will be two ways. Clearly, the Latin countries can learn much from the U.S. in terms of industrial and social organization, investment, etc. I believe that there are also important lessons that the U.S. can learn from the growth of Latin America as well. Examples abound of lessons learned by Latin countries during the course of their recent development that would be well applied in the U.S.

In the mid 1980s Chile privatized its state-controlled pension system. The result was fiscal havoc for the government for four or five years, but out of the chaos emerged a stable base of local capital that has financed the double-digit growth rates that Chile has experienced through the 1990s.

Similarly, in the early 1990s Mexico decided to finance the replacement of its aged highway infrastructure by selling toll-taking concessions to construction firms. In many ways the effort was disastrous (toll revenues failed to meet expectations for reasons that should have been easily avoided, and the concessionaires received a government bailout). However, a new infrastructure was built, and the government demonstrated that private capital and public need could successfully be joined for the benefit of both.

There are clear lessons for the U.S. to learn from the experience of Latin America during the heady growth of the early 1990s. I would like to see Rhode Island benefit from these lessons, and to begin to look beyond its own beverages for engines of growth. For my part, I intend to continue to seek a way of creating opportunity in my state by linking Rhode Island to the continuing development of Latin America.

COMMENTS

Overall, this is a compelling portrait of both the applicant and his passions, what makes him tick. He demonstrates substantial understanding about several topics: Latin American cultures, economic development, and so on. Similarly, his use of detail—in the discussion of the Pajero sport utility vehicle or his family's trip to Honduras, for example—brings the piece to life and helps to make him memorable. So, too, does his perceptive discussion of the different meanings attached to the word "rights" in Latin America and the U.S. There is no doubt that admissions officers will remember "the candidate from Rhode Island interested in forging connections between his home state and Latin American development." This will likely describe no other candidate in the pool.

There are, however, three fundamental problems with Brendan's personal statement. He should have spelled out how he would attempt to link Rhode Island and Latin America, rather than just express a vague ambition to do so. His essay reflects the inherent lack of linkage between these ideas; the last third of the essay seems to be almost a new essay, all too casually linked to the first part of the essay. In addition, he should have made clear that law school is indeed the right place for him. Frankly, from this essay one would think that the candidate should be planning to attend an MBA program instead. He should have explained, even in just a sentence or two, how a law degree would help him achieve his goals.

AMY CRAWFORD

I wish to attend law school in order to practice public interest law. This decision is based upon a number of influences and experiences, some of which go back to my childhood, others of which are of more recent origin.

I grew up in rural Southwestern Virginia, where my father was an attorney. My father's law practice is probably unique. It is not unusual for him to handle a divorce in exchange for a load of wood or to represent a client in a child custody case in return for having our house painted. Although my father has never been very financially successful, his work as a lawyer has always been characterized by a great and abiding generosity. Over these years I have seen in my father a genuine enthusiasm for helping people who would otherwise be shut out from the legal system.

In my hometown I also witnessed the silent divisions of our society along racial and economic lines. Why, for example, was the town's curfew only enforced in a neighborhood where the majority of the black community resided? Why did a public school divide kindergartners by their parents' social position or educational level, rather than by the children's capacities to learn? Why were students at one school offered a choice of four foreign languages for study, and students at another school, in a poorer neighborhood, offered only one? I later came to believe that these once puzzling questions are best addressed through social policy or litigation, and though shifts may seem small they can achieve profound and long-term consequences in a given community.

At the University of Virginia, I majored in Sociology and African-American Studies, with a special emphasis on the dynamic between social policy and law. I saw that the questions which had troubled me as a child in my hometown did indeed involve issues of discrimination and social and economic equality. I think that being one of the few white African-American Studies majors gave me an unusual opportunity to examine institutional biases based upon race, gender and class. While in college, I also worked in an alternative sentencing program which provided education, job training and drug abuse counseling to prison inmates. As an intern case manager, I was responsible for interviewing inmates to determine their eligibility for the program. The program was an innovative one, but it was realistic as well, and I saw the tangible benefits which the men and women who participated in it received. Just prior to graduating from college, I prepared an extensive recidivism study which was used to demonstrate to the Virginia Department of Corrections the real impact the program was having on the lives of the inmates after leaving prison and completing our program.

After graduating from the University of Virginia in 1993, I moved to New York City to work for the Legal Aid Society. For the past three years I have been a paralegal with the Legal Aid Society's Civil Appeals and Law Reform Unit. One of the first cases to which I was assigned at Legal Aid was *Jiggets v. Dowling*, a major affirmative litigation case in which Legal Aid challenged the adequacy of the shelter allowance paid to welfare recipients in New York City. The case has been pending for a number of years and has not yet been decided; however, the presiding judge granted the interim application of one family for preliminary relief while the decision is pending. Since the original grant of preliminary relief to one family, more than 25,000 families have applied for and obtained housing assistance and protection from eviction through this interim preliminary relief system.

A primary part of my work at The Legal Aid Society involves coordinating the efforts of Legal Aid attorneys and their clients to take advantage of this system of preliminary relief created by *Jiggetts* particularly in emergency situations. I am one of the individuals for the litigation team designated to contact New York State officials in Albany to ensure proper and immediate processing for relief in emergency situations. Legal service attorneys throughout New York City often ask me to assist them in applications for relief with evictions as imminent as the next day. I have conducted various seminars for Legal Aid and Legal Services attorneys, law school clinics and community based organizations on the benefits available through *Jiggetts*. I have also intervened on behalf of individual Legal Aid clients. For example, one client I worked with recently was a woman who had been a victim of domestic violence and who consequently needed help obtaining housing. First I advocated on behalf of my client pursuant to *Jiggets v. Dowling* by finding a home for her and her family—safe from the batterer. Then I was able to help her with other issues as well, such as correcting her disability payments and obtaining admission of her child to a gifted student program. I saw how the lives of this client and her children were materially improved, and it was significantly based on the judge's interim order of preliminary relief. My work with *Jiggetts* has confirmed my belief that through the legal process our society can be forced, albeit reluctantly, to confront the issues of injustice and inequality which blight the lives of so many individuals.

Another case I worked on at The Legal Aid Society which has demonstrated to me the power of the law to improve people's lives is *Rivera v. New York City Housing Authority*, an ongoing class action suit on behalf of mobility impaired tenants challenging the New York City Housing Authority's implementation of the Americans with Disabilities Act. In this case, I have been assigned to act as the informal liaison between the defendant's Law Department and Legal Aid's individual clients. I have seen first-hand how the lives of mobility impaired people and their families have been changed for the better by *Rivera*. For example, in the case of one family with a daughter confined to a wheelchair, I successfully argued that the family must be relocated because they lived in an apartment building with no elevator. This family's move to an accessible apartment improved the family dynamic by enabling the daughter to attend school independently and by granting her parents more freedom.

Outside of my work at The Legal Aid Society, I have also had to address issues of race, gender and class as a volunteer teaching a weekly class on Civil Rights and Race Relations to students in New York Civil Rights Coalition, which began in 1989 in the wake of the race riots in the Crown Heights section of Brooklyn. Volunteer teachers like myself go to public high schools in the five boroughs to initiate a dialogue about issues of racial and cultural bias with students. These discussions are frank, and range from specific experiences which students have had (e.g., what it is like to be scrutinized by a security guard in a store or to be ignored by a cab driver) to general concerns about discrimination in employment or housing. My experience as a teacher leading these classes has demonstrated to me that some of the same concerns which I had as a child in Virginia are still troubling the youth today. I hope that I have exposed students to the legal system's role in confronting their concerns.

Year by year, case by case, client by client, my commitment to public interest law has broadened and deepened. My passion is to serve disadvantaged and underrepresented people as an attorney advocating for their interests.

COMMENTS

Amy's approach is simple and direct, yet highly effective. She shows how natural it was for her to become a civil rights advocate by highlighting her interesting family background. Many candidates try to do this, in fact, but few succeed fully. The difference in her case is not that she has *written* more persuasively on this topic, but that she has *lived* more persuasively in this regard. She followed up her father's example by majoring in African-American studies, an unusual choice for a white person, as she notes here. After that, she stopped working in the corporate world after one year at Lehman Brothers in order to pursue her passion for civil rights work. In her case, the passion she expresses in this essay does not lack the necessary correlative for credibility: full-time work in the trenches.

It is easy to claim an interest in civil rights law, or other public interest fields, and even to walk that walk while in college. After all, few college students feel that they are making major sacrifices in college by spending a few hours a week in some volunteer activity. After college is when the crunch comes. Applicants who claim a great interest in lesser-paid public interest work are never entirely believable until they have indeed spent some years in the field.

Amy is particularly effective because she combines a lengthy history of involvement with an essay that conveys the nature of the lessons she has learned. The great detail she brings to the stories about her positions with the Legal Aid Society and teaching for the New York Civil Rights Coalition demonstrate both her commitment and the extent to which she will bring a well-developed perspective to the law school classroom (and clinical programs).

This is, however, an essay that suffers the faults of its virtues. It is a résumé-like recounting of her career, complete with dull introduction. It would therefore function better as an addendum (addressing "why I want to be a lawyer" or "why I want to do public interest work") then as a main personal statement.

SACHA M. COUPET

Monique is a fourteen-year-old going on forty, a survivor of incest whose delinquent behavior is a plea for help. Jamie, barely five and in foster care, insists that he should be able to take care of himself and his younger siblings as he has done, he says, since he was "little" and living with his "forever mom." Sarah, four, was rushed to the emergency room three years ago, severely bruised and minus several teeth after her mother's boyfriend attempted to "discipline" her. Today, this same mother and boyfriend plead before the court for her return. In our legal system, who speaks for these children, too young to exercise any power or to comprehend the magnitude of the decisions that concern them? What is the fate of these children who face an adolescence in juvenile detention, a childhood in foster care, or worse yet, a childhood cut short? Who acts "in the best interest" of these children in whose faces we may see our own sons and daughters? I believe we are all vested with a moral responsibility to advocate for the needs of children and am eager to lend my voice.

My decision to pursue a legal education has emerged from my collective experiences as a psychologist, an advocate, a scholar, and an observer of society. Contrary to my colleagues in psychology who suggest that my decision to study law is tantamount to a defection to "the other side," I do not feel I am abandoning my field, rather I am incorporating it into another much in the way an artist might combine two media. I am a creative person, intellectually and artistically, whether in a classroom or at a potter's wheel, and welcome the challenge of improving on traditional methods by combining the best elements of many techniques. While the theory, language, and practice of clinical psychology and law differ, I do not believe these disciplines are at odds, but rather complement one another. On a micro level, clinical psychology focuses on the transformation of the individual psyche into a structure of operating and understanding one's world. The law is an expression of a similar process on a broader scale, with a focus on the transformation of societal values into social structures. In my experience, the most rewarding challenge has been examining the interface between psychological and legal issues, identifying the points of convergence and divergence, and integrating the two.

Although I began my undergraduate study with the intention of pursuing a career in medicine and complemented my high school curriculum with a number of medical-related volunteer experiences, I broadened my focus in the helping professions one year into college. After two grueling terms in a pre-med curriculum I declared a major in psychology. The research and practice in this discipline more closely reflected the way in which I understood and preferred to work with people, particularly those with socioeconomically disadvantaged backgrounds. Years later, in my graduate research, clinical work, and teaching, I continue to develop a more comprehensive knowledge of how sociodemographic and psychological factors influence the lives of marginalized, oppressed, or underserved populations.

While I admit to a fair share of idealism, my desire to successfully integrate a background in psychology with the study and practice of law has not developed from a visionary notion to right all injustice and cure every social ill, but from a number of positive experiences I have had in the real world. As a family and child therapist, I have counseled numerous persons whose lives have been profoundly impacted by events in the courtroom. Whether working with victims of domestic violence, child abuse, divorce and contested custody, assisting adults and children during prolonged legal disputes, or serving as a representative of the court, I have learned a great deal from observing and participating in the legal process.

Increasingly, as the court becomes the arbiter of America's most intimate family decisions, judges find themselves in need of input from a number of sources. Information gathered about a variety of psychological issues, including child development, parental capacities, attachment relationships, or family functioning has become critical in such legal decision making. From the beginning of my professional training I have had many opportunities to assist the court in searching for and providing this information. My interest and involvement in the legal process has only deepened since.

As a consultant to law students in the University of Michigan Law School's Child Advocacy Law Clinic, I assisted inexperienced attorneys to develop an understanding of the psychological issues inherent in child advocacy, particularly as they relate to child protection, parental termination, permanency planning, and foster care. More recently, my work with the Child Welfare Law Resource Center has afforded me continued opportunities to share a psychological perspective with representatives of other disciplines interested in highlighting the importance of child welfare law. My dissertation research reflects this interdisciplinary theme as it combines legal and psychological issues in an examination of the impact of child welfare and foster care policy on family functioning. In addition, I continue to publish and present professionally in areas related to interdisciplinary work in child abuse and neglect.

I have faced each of these experiences within the legal system with the utmost degree of curiosity, excitement, and enthusiasm. I have grown both personally and professionally, having wrestled with philosophical elements of the law that have challenged me to think critically in my role as a psychologist and to flexibly adapt my skills to a legal context. As a psychologist in a legal arena, I felt at first like a foreigner in a new unfamiliar environment, uncertain of the climate, culture, or language. I developed a psychological index applied to the legal system that included such diagnostic categories as "adversarial angst" and "expert witness hysteria," conditions which I observed to afflict many persons whose professional obligations brought them, often reluctantly, into the courtroom. Fortunately, I was spared from such afflictions and found myself, instead, quite intrigued. While I learn from every new legal experience, each exposure has left me feeling particularly limited in my capacity to effect significant change because of my unfamiliarity with the law. Although cognizant of the changes I have helped to bring about in my work as a psychologist, I feel drawn to the broader level of change that a law degree would permit me. Having developed an extensive background in psychological theory and practice, I am now compelled to turn my efforts towards the pursuit of a legal education.

My long-term objective is to facilitate an integration of psychology and law with the goal of enhancing the lives of children and families. As an African-American female, I feel particularly invested in the plight of the growing number of poor and minority children who are over-represented in the child welfare system and intend to play a key role in developing both legal and psychological strategies to assist them. I have committed myself to remaining involved, as a community volunteer and a professional, with children and families whose opportunities in life have been much more limited than my own. While I am conscious of the fact that the course of my life has been significantly shaped by the privileges of a middle class upbringing, I am not too far removed from the experience of those for whom I seek to advocate. My parents were immigrants who left Haiti over a decade before I was born to find opportunities in the U.S. They arrived with few resources, but much determination to succeed. By their word and their example, they have instilled in me the virtues of compassion and respect for others, the importance of hard work and commitment, and an appreciation for all that I have received. With this, I feel it is incumbent upon me to give back to my community in every manner possible.

As a law student, I seek to be an active participant in an educational setting enriched by more than the practical elements of law, but also the philosophical, contextual, and social dimensions of jurisprudence. The University of Pennsylvania Law School is nationally recognized and respected for providing this kind of dynamic learning environment. My life experience, breadth of knowledge in psychology, and commitment to an interdisciplinary approach and public service would allow me to contribute greatly to the diversity and the strength of the University of Pennsylvania student body. I possess the intellectual capacity, perseverance, and maturity to meet the challenges of a legal education and a professional career and look forward to continued opportunities to work on behalf of children like Monique, Jamie, and Sarah.

COMMENTS

This is a superb essay, created from Sacha's wealth of knowledge about her former field of psychology and extensive experience with child advocacy and family law. In one coherent essay she shows:

- Her passion for serving the interests of children
- How and why she got into psychology
- The evolution of her career
- The depth of her involvement and expertise (she presents and publishes in the field)
- How she will contribute to this field in the future, with the addition of her law degree (She does a particularly good job of showing that she is not so much changing careers as adding another dimension to what she already does.)
- Her reasons for wanting to attend Penn (although these could have been better developed)

Her personal statement is well-balanced, giving the right amount of space to each aspect of her presentation. It is also easy to follow her intellectual journey; she uses detail to make her points memorable and believable, without cluttering up the flow of her material. (Note how much better a résumé-like essay she has written than Amy has; it is more subtle and much more effective.)

Sacha's statement shows how convincing an applicant with real expertise in a related field can be. There is no doubt that she really knows her field. Similarly, it is clear that she will stay in this field and make more of a contribution with a law degree than she can without. She will have no trouble finding relevant employment, given her experience to date. In addition, her experience has presented her with ample opportunity to make sure that law is the right field for her.

Not only admissions officers would find her an appealing candidate; so, too, would career services officers. After all, they know that they will not have an unemployable person on their hands in three years and, far more important, they will not have an emotional wreck to handle. Sacha has sufficient relevant experience to know what she is getting into, and to know that it is right for her.

DAVID P. WHITE

My older brother is a drug addict. On April 4, 1995—two months before I took the LSAT—this fact changed my life. After returning from my first vacation in years, I came home to a frantic phone message stating that my brother had disappeared. "What are we going to do with the kids?" my mother's message asked. As a young Executive Director of a youth and family-empowerment organization, my response was immediate: "I have room at my place—I'll take the youngest two." Now 28, I have been the physical and legal guardian to Adam, now eight, and Taylor, now five, ever since.

With the humor and insight that distance provides, those first months with the kids almost seem nostalgic. There were dirty faces to wash, walks in the park to take, stories to read and many lessons to teach to these new little people in my life. But I also remember the trauma. My agency, born of grassroots movement, nearly closed down because of my reduced work schedule. Every day, at 5:30 p.m., I went home, no questions asked. I quit playing the saxophone and I resigned from several boards of directors on which I served. Money became a scarce commodity and my non-work life was a blur of cooking, cleaning, laundry and discipline. At times, I was bitterly resentful of my brother and his ex-wife's inability to get their lives together. When asked by others, "how are you handling all this?" I used to tell them, "there are dark nights." Day after day, through laughter and pain, we trudged through.

Now, after nearly two years of heroic effort, my brother has pieced together his life and will regain custody of his children soon. Sometimes, as I sit in the nearby park cheering for Adam's soccer team or as I scold Taylor for practicing her gymnastics on our furniture, I can scarcely believe that time has moved so quickly. Our family has actually benefited from the experience. Through a collective determination to keep our children out of state custody, my oldest brother (who also took two kids), mother and extended family members have become part of a stronger family unit. Following the shock of losing his children, my brother has successfully arrested more than a decade of behavior infested with drugs and violence. Most importantly, four of my nieces and nephews have been given a chance to succeed in life without the fetters of a childhood devoid of love and commitment.

For me, parenting my brother's children has never felt extraordinary. As a student of philosophy, I have the tendency to view life's events as connected to each other, as part of a fuller mosaic where each act is understood only within the context of the whole. This belief, that somehow the storm front of my new parenting responsibilities—and the opportunities in my life which I was subsequently forced to delay—would one day make sense to me when placed within the matrix of my whole life, was often the only thread on which I could hold. This belief was also critical to my success in my first job experience. My position as Director of Y.O.U. was a major undertaking which few of my friends expected me to survive. I was chosen from a national group of 52 candidates and was by far the youngest and least experienced of the group. As it turns out, my selection was due more to my lack of political relationships and connections than to anything else; the previous two years of the agency's history had been filled with tension, closed relationships and a visible lack of progress on any programmatic front. In fact, Y.O.U. was not even an agency at the time but rather a network of community-based organizations and activists who were openly divided along racial, financial and neighborhood lines. Apparently, they wanted a fresh start and, with a 24-year-old, cherub-looking face, I represented that.

The first several months were difficult. Few members of the network showed up for the first steering committee meeting that I organized. Many of them wanted me to visit them on their own turf in order to check my "grassroots credentials" before they would accept me as their new staff person. One of those who did show up brought his morning newspaper, whose pages he flipped and read throughout the meeting. It was the first of many frightening experiences and by the third month I was so demoralized that I was ready to resign.

I did not resign, however, and instead took a bold step: I hired staff and started to construct programs. It occurred to me that we could fulfill the original intent of the grassroots movement that had established the Y.O.U. network by molding the stated priorities of the steering committee into a coherent mission statement and a set of non-traditional services. So we did. The result was both unexpected and remarkable: success. Within a short period of time, and through a combination of politics, begging, will-power and luck, we built an organization that merged together the various agendas of opposing committee members into a full-blown initiative, one that could contribute to the larger system of youth and family services in our area while providing direct services to a number of young people.

I have been with Y.O.U. for nearly four years now. During my tenure, and by working with a host of others, I have overseen the development of the following: an incorporated agency in the state of Kansas; four community-/school-based programs; a core of professionally trained staff; an active Board of Directors; and a budget that has tripled in size and that now includes funding from public, private and contractual sources. In a move that could never have been foreseen before my arrival, the original network of agencies opted to become members of a larger coalition that has grown to over 100 members. In addition to providing services to over 500 youth and families annually, Y.O.U. received an award from the Governor of Kansas in 1994 for "Outstanding Community Service" and in that same year was described by the Kansas Office for Community Service as a "pillar" in the field of service-learning. Our success has included something as large as a transportation project that successfully transported 400 youths to jobs and enrichment-related activities, to something as localized as developing an academically failing, clinically depressed youth into a frequent public speaker and school leader through the sustained guidance of our leadership programs. We have accomplished much with the simple concept that agencies make better decisions regarding their services when they work together, and that our whole community is improved when our agencies make better decisions. Ironically, this is the basic idea that stood behind the establishment of the original network long before I arrived but it took a political novice to help them achieve it.

The past four years have been a time of relentless activity and significant accomplishment. Now, looking towards the future, I believe it is time to move forward and to build new skills. I plan to do this in two phases. First, I have recently accepted a position at the Chapin Hall Center for Children, a research and evaluation agency associated with the University of Chicago, to help initiate a city-wide project that focuses on youth development through large collaborative efforts. The position is for six months only and begins in early 1997; my role will be to develop the strategy by which the sponsor organizations can implement their expansive vision. My time at Chapin Hall will also serve as a period of reflection and transition into the second phase of my plan, which is to attend law school in the fall of 1997. I have looked forward to entering law school for some time now and believe that I can significantly enhance my professional abilities through the process of earning my law degree. The method of thought, the actual content of the information taught and the chance to review the accumulated statutes and thoughts that have shaped our society—all of these are things that excite me and that will improve my ability to bring about positive change in the world around me. In particular, I want to expand my understanding of how laws are constructed, interpreted, enforced, marketed to and understood by the public in urban areas across the country. As one who expects to be intimately involved with children's issues and urban community development throughout the duration of my life, I firmly believe that my experience in law school will help me become a better advocate for issues of concern and, ultimately, a more effective man of action.

Aristotle teaches that there is a path to success in life, one that involves a constant dialogue between hardship and joy, family and career. To date, my experiences have confirmed his teachings; my joy and sense of accomplishment have been the direct fruits of a determined struggle to overcome the obstacles in my family and professional life. Now it is time to take these experiences and build on them so that I can continue to contribute to a society that, I believe, is capable of being a safe, humane place for all of us. It simply needs constant advocacy and pressure from those of us who care. I do and I look forward to the challenge of law school which I believe will provide me with the tools to continue to contribute in ways that make a positive difference in the lives of others.

COMMENTS

This essay is remarkable in several ways. First, of course, the writer's remarkable family tale overwhelms readers. Second, David succeeds in tying together his adult life history with his career to date and his future. Few applicants to law school have as interesting a personal history to relate, or as clear a professional impact to offer, let alone personal histories and professional efforts that work in concert—and that show where they will head after law school. Third, David conveys this in a matter-of-fact tone that does not ask for readers to pity him, or indeed to admit him because of unusual circumstances. His positive, understated approach actually gets the most mileage from his position. Most applicants would overplay their hands, risking a negative reaction from admissions officers in so doing.

JAMES M.

If someone had told me eight years ago that one day I would find something beneficial in the mistakes of my adolescence, I would have laughed. But with maturity came a fresh perspective that gave me the ability to see value in my darkest moments, while revealing social opportunities to which I otherwise might have been blind. My formative years are bittersweet in that they created significant obstacles for me, yet also gave me a worthy cause to champion and ultimately inspired me to pursue a law degree.

I picked up alcohol at an early age, not heeding steady warnings from my family concerning drink. As a dedicated honor student, Boy Scout, altar boy and all-star baseball player, I had a false sense of sanctuary. Conned by youthful illusions of invincibility, I lost perspective early on, putting sociability before responsible behavior. The consequences came swift and harsh, by age fifteen a debilitating lethargy replaced my dreams of being a person of energy, character, and responsibility. By seventeen, my interest in education and athletics waned at the onset of an embarrassing series of legal encounters. By nineteen, tangled amidst throes of addiction and unable to devote proper attention to my studies, I requested time away from school.

Fortunately, on January 29, 1996, I had the clarity of mind to see my malady in proper perspective. Tears of surrender welled within as my eyes focused on a sign reading "Talbot House Treatment Center." With the benefit of a supportive family and candid self-evaluation, I was able to summon the courage and humility to walk through the door of fear, embarrassment and doubt lying between me and triumph over substance abuse. I chose a life of abstinence from alcohol and drugs that day—a decision I never regretted.

I never could have imagined the absolute catharsis I was to undergo. Upon completion of Talbot House, I met with a counselor regularly and joined Alcoholics Anonymous (AA), a fellowship that supported my aspirations for change. As importantly, I met my mentor, an animated and energetic U.S. Merchant Marine officer, Ivy League doctoral student and high school teacher who overcame similar obstacles in his youth. Invigorated by a new sense of direction and focus, I reengaged myself academically and became involved with my community.

In the fall of 1996, I returned to the university, primed and finally poised for the rigors of academia. I reaffirmed my original decision to study psychology; I enjoyed the research and analytical thinking the psychology curriculum demanded and found it benefited a newfound ambition of helping misdirected youth. After a year or so back in the groves of academe, I decided a business education would be a practical supplement to my university experience. The real world applicability of economics, finance, and technology complemented the largely theoretical foundation of psychology, making for a robust education. Rallying back from my earlier poor performance, my final six semesters more accurately demonstrated my true capabilities (3.75 GPA).

At about the same time, I began volunteering at local AA church groups that supported youths recovering from substance abuse. I remember the first ride home I gave to Kenny, a gaunt, scrappy-looking character with dark leather skin, slicked back hair, and a patchy mustache. Fresh from the jailhouse, his shifty personality alarmed me enough that I kept a close eye on him, worried something of mine might make its way into his pocket. A year later, with structure and direction, he was thirty pounds heavier and as fine a specimen of integrity one could hope to meet. When I see him now, I often joke with him about the "scrawny hoodlum" I drove home that night. In the process of helping others I discovered that my own struggles made me useful to society in a capacity I never anticipated: as a tenable advocate for recovery. My two-year tenure as chairperson of a recovery group called the "Sunday Night 1, 2, 3" capitalized on this qualification while affirming my aptitude for leadership.

At college graduation, I entered the software industry, accepting a position as a Systems Engineer for the industry leader in clinical software development. I assumed complete responsibility for several multimillion dollar system integration projects in the Southeast, and was soon promoted to Senior Systems Engineer. Touted for my technical prowess, I found my real strength to be my ability to gain client confidence and trust in high stress situations; as a result I was awarded the "Technology Approach" and "Key Contributor" awards and was named "Distinguished Performer" for my leadership in challenging situations. I was actively sought by other companies and, soon after, was recruited by my current employer. Originally hired by Lighthouse Business Solutions as a consultant, I took on many additional administrative responsibilities including researching, quoting and documenting an interactive voice response system and help desk. I also developed the System Disaster Planning guide for a product quotation that was successfully marketed to General Electric. After proving my value in the private sector, I was promoted to Government and Clinical Services Program Manager, a position responsible for managing relations for all government and healthcare contracts. In this position, I enriched my management, writing, and oratory skills while formulating functional and technical specifications for government and hospital computer systems.

As my professional life flourished, my social involvement evolved and intensified. I spoke regularly at recovery meetings and rehabilitation centers all over the country, explaining how I overcame addiction. Public speaking engagements challenged me to tell stories with serious themes, something that had at one time made me uncomfortable. I enjoyed this valuable opportunity to give back to society. Also, I began visiting county correction facilities to talk to inmates. I told them about my life, the polarity between my new circumstance and my rocky adolescence, and the methods I used to change. As rewarding as this work was, it was tarnished by an ugly reality. Some of the men I spoke with claimed innocence, but could not appeal due to financial constraints and lack of county resources; the public defenders were engulfed in caseloads numbering hundreds. The men all shared two common characteristics—they were young and disadvantaged. Echoes from the steel doors clanging behind me rang long after my visits with the inmates, as did my awakening to the specter of injustice.

My work for S.T.O.P.—a prison diversionary program designed to help inmates develop structure and positive contacts upon release from jail—confirmed the presence of injustice outside of the walls. After trying to help inmates assimilate back into society, it became clear that proper legal representation played an integral role in rehabilitation. Upon release from the detention centers, the men had trouble getting jobs due to perfunctory adjudication, feeding the cycle of abjection. I watched cynicism oust enthusiasm when the only legitimate jobs they could obtain paid minimum wage. Even in freedom they dwelled behind bars of poverty and ignorance.

My experiences and respective awakenings revealed weaknesses in the justice system. Though I recognized that some of the men's claims of innocence may have been fabricated, the idea that even one had merit roused a hunger to act on their behalf. For the first time, I saw a place where my professional ability and skills could complement my personal ambitions and passions. My eyes have been opened to the power and responsibility of lawyering, yet, lacking credentials, I remain an impotent advocate. An education from George Washington Law School can give me the credibility and training I need to take action and maximize my effect of these problems.

I am fascinated by criminal law and excited about my future in it. My collective community experience has molded me into a staunch proponent of ensuring that youth and poverty do not inhibit impartial justice; my professional experience in business, government, and healthcare has honed the leadership skills and acumen needed to navigate the legal cosmos. Armed with a Juris Doctorate from George Washington, I will be prepared to pierce the dense fog of legalese for those in straitened circumstance.

COMMENTS

A résumé-like essay—"first I did this, then I did that, and next I did something else"—is a good bet to bore readers. This is particularly true when an essay covers at length everything from the applicant's college education to his whole career history, related in depth, to his extensive community involvements. This essay, however, is anything but boring. The depths to which James fell, and his subsequent rehabilitation, make this gripping and powerful. In addition, he builds a successful argument for why his personal challenges and community involvement have led him to law school.

Ordinarily this range of experience would not call for an all-encompassing résumé style essay, but James faced the need to show that his alcoholism (and criminal record) had been transformed into personal, professional, and community success over a substantial period of time. This meant that focusing on only one element of his past would be insufficient to demonstrate conclusively his rehabilitation.

CONTRIBUTION TO DIVERSITY

You could say I grew up in Alcoholics Anonymous (AA). My first exposure to it was by way of my father. He started attending when I was around 10 years old, following a devastating bankruptcy that stripped us of our vehicle and my childhood home. For years I accompanied him to the meetings. It was a jovial place, a stark contrast to the ridiculous portrayals seen on television. There were no trench coat–shrouded men, no "brainwashing" or whiney neurotics; just a group of people enjoying a better life. I watched with admiration as my father rebuilt our lives.

At age 20, I concluded that AA would benefit me. The first few months attending on my own were awkward and lonely. I had to distance myself from some lifelong friends who were not heading in the same direction as I was. To successfully turn my life around, I needed a new and solid foundation of quality people in life. I found AA to be brimming with such people, though they certainly did not take the form I envisioned.

With an average age of 35, I was by far the youngest member of the groups I attended. Initially, I had difficulties relating on an emotional level. Soon, though, I learned to appreciate the wonderfully motley crew, and found myself with a host of unique friends. Among them: a professional mountain biker, a dreadlocked Jamaican, a paralyzed art professor, an offshore fisherman who lived for Kierkegaard and Kerouac, a rocket scientist, and a fully tattooed biker, none of whom were under the age of thirty. Their grounded autonomy and open-mindedness encouraged me to re-examine my ideas on everything from calculus to karma.

I never realized my preconceptions of intelligence before my friendship with Todd. The scraggly offshore fisherman blew me away with his knowledge about literature and culture. I would never have guessed he had visited over 40 countries, owned a massive personal library of books (each of which he had read and could recall in scary detail), and could captain any boat on any ocean in the world. Al, the rocket scientist, gave me a glimpse of the realities of being homosexual. One evening, at a dinner party, a man made a crude reference to the gay pride parade. Al confronted him and said, "I'm gay, and I didn't really find that funny." Al's reddened face alongside the man's shaken composure decimated my idea that our society is "tolerant." Paul, the paralyzed art professor, gave me a graduate level lesson in handicapped accessibility. Regularly carrying him up the stairs to my house gave me a new appreciation for the railed ramps and blue signs that had grown transparent in my daily haste. These are just a few examples of how the people of AA awoke me from the sleepy social cobweb of prejudgment and complacency.

People are often confused when I explain that AA is not strictly about forsaking drink. Not drinking is just the keystone to a fellowship that promotes personal development. The transition I made was difficult but rewarding. Watching my father grow in AA exposed me to the fellowship, yet it was not until I joined AA myself that I reaped the benefits in my life. Subconsciously categorizing people and ideas expended less energy, but limited me to a monochromatic world with rigidly drawn plots and one-dimensional characters. Experience tells me that when I set aside the things I think I know, I am usually humbled before a colorful spectrum of society that was once invisible.

COMMENTS

Most diversity essays focus on someone's nationality, race, or ethnicity (or, occasionally, someone's poverty-stricken upbringing). The Alcoholics Anonymous focus of this essay is therefore quite unusual, but it certainly works. The AA perspective James brings is clearly out of the mainstream of applicants' experience, but it is hardly irrelevant. Not only has he learned a great deal from his exposure to the camaraderie of AA, but he is well placed to help others who may need to deal with their own demons during law school.

STATEMENT REGARDING INTERRUPTION OF STUDIES

During the 1995–96 school year, I requested a voluntary one-year leave of absence to re-evaluate my goals and reflect on my reasons for attending college. Prior to this, I had two years of serious academic underperformance. During these two years—fall 1993 to spring 1995—I struggled, not yet possessing the focus needed to succeed in academia. I did not truly understand the privilege bestowed upon me, and accordingly did not apply myself in the classroom. After two years of wasting the resources of the university, I decided it best to take some time to work at my family business and deal with personal difficulties. One year later, I returned to the university fortified with the clarity of purpose and scholarly ambition needed to succeed in a collegiate setting.

ADDENDUM: FITNESS OF CHARACTER CERTIFICATION

One area that surely will be of paramount concern to the admissions committee is my qualification for admittance to a state bar. This is also a source of apprehension to me, as I have no intention of making the financial, temporal, and emotional investment in three years of education, yet be unable to practice law. I desire to practice in Georgia, so I contacted the state bar to discuss my ability to be certified of fit character. The Board to Determine Fitness of Bar Applicants in Georgia stated that although each individual is handled on a case-by-case basis, and they could not guarantee membership over the phone, I *am* eligible to be a member of the bar. The bar entrance manual explicitly states that the candidate must be *currently* of fit character. As long as I am completely candid on my law school and bar applications, and am able to show rehabilitation, the board states that there is a high probability I will be admitted. Since 1977 only 31 hearings out of approximately 11,000 applications resulted in denial of certification. By the time I am finished with law school it will have been ten years since my misconduct. I am very involved with my community and have countless upstanding business and community leaders who are willing to state their support for me.

COMMENTS

James's two addenda address the fallout from his period in the throes of alcoholism. Both are straightforward and both are necessary. The "fitness of character certification" shows that he has done his homework and that he is indeed likely to be admitted to the Georgia bar if he succeeds in law school. Given his criminal record, this was by no means evident absent this explanation.

OLUWABUNMI SHABI

This time I decided to take my usual jog uphill past the tennis courts and the playground and straight to the tall obelisk that sits at the center of Fort Greene Park. Out of breath, I squatted against the monument and thought about how the array of colors of the Brooklyn/Manhattan skyline had never been seen by the soldiers who fought here during the Revolutionary war. I also wondered what the skyline must have looked like when Ralph Ellison sat in this park and crafted his novel *Invisible Man*. Focusing my eyes on the Williamsburg Bank clock tower, I realized that it was nearly 7:00 p.m. I snapped myself out of the daze and started the jog home.

I began thinking about how much the neighborhood and I have changed since my awkward and nerdy days at Brooklyn Technical High School on Fort Greene Place. The blocks that were once filled with dilapidated buildings and crack addicts are now filled with coffee bars and young black professionals. But somehow, the neighborhood has been able to maintain its indelible Brooklyn edge, which consists of one part hospitality and two parts attitude. Maybe that's why someone like Spike Lee—who could afford posh midtown digs—chose Fort Greene as his company's home base.

As for myself, I cannot say that my own transition has been as dramatic. There are the usual superficial changes that accompany the shift from adolescence to adulthood. I went from donning bright green coke-bottle glasses to sporting contact lenses. My 16-year-old size six body has become a svelte size eight (or at least I'd like to think so). And of course there are the obligatory Generation-X transitions from chocolate milk to caffe latte and from being an omnivore to being a vegetarian. But beneath the surface the changes have been much more significant. The sure-footed vigorousness, with which I used to argue black and white ideals on my high school debate team, has become an understanding and an appreciation for the complex nuances that envelop even the smallest of issues. My grasp of world politics has shed some light on why in high school my Muslim Egyptian friend and my Jewish Israeli friend were constantly at each other's throats. And my teenage cockiness and self-congratulatory spirit that were often dependent on making good grades or hanging out with the coolest kids, have transformed themselves into a self-awareness and an inner-confidence that is part of me regardless of how I do on my next exam.

Over the past couple of years, much of my worldly deliberations have taken place at a local Fort Greene coffee shop, the Brooklyn Moon Cafe. When I walk in I am greeted by friends and acquaintances. Everyone from artists and musicians to bankers and lawyers patronize the place. They muse over their existence or take a break from the burdens of work and life that await them outside this safe haven. The burgeoning writer exchanges numbers with the up-and-coming actress, and the recent MBA grad conspires with cohorts about starting up a new business. This, I think to myself as I sip my cappuccino, is the new Harlem Renaissance.

There are even times when Brooklyn Mooners can act as a very opinionated surrogate family. While sitting in the Moon after Sunday brunch, I pull out some of my pictures. I had just returned from an eight-week trip to Paris, Cairo, and Lagos. It was the first time I had left the country since I was ten years old. I talked about how my trip had opened my eyes. I discovered the extent to which millions around the world are suffering. But unlike my old days on the debate team, I had decided that my energized words must be followed by decisive action—hence, my desire to practice international human rights law. I speak about the fact that though I love business journalism, I believe the true vehicle of change lies in the law. This of course begins a dispute among dilettantes. But I can't complain. As much as I enjoyed humus in Cairo and crepes in France, there was something comforting about returning home to heated conversation over spicy fries.

But even Fort Greene is not without its own share of distress and tragedy. The neighborhood is occasionally mentioned in the news. It is the location of the funeral procession of Christopher Wallace, aka rap artist Biggie Smalls. It is the site of the electronics store that was robbed at gunpoint several times over. Fort Greene is also the neighborhood where a 12-year-old, who was molested by her stepfather, had lived. But it is also where I had my first kiss. It is the neighborhood that has the McDonald's where I spent countless afternoons with classmates. And it is, of course, where I take my daily run.

These days I see many who are fleeing the high costs of the nearby Park Slope and lower Manhattan for the more affordable Fort Greene. This neighborhood may just go from being a tree-lined haven for a young community of artists and professionals to a gentrified, watered down version of Greenwich Village. Who knows? But as with all neighborhoods and people, in another few years both Fort Greene and I will be something else. Maybe something completely unexpected or something highly predictable—but most definitely something else. As I walk home each day and acknowledge this uncontrollable spirit of change, my only hope is that some day someone will stand in front of my building as she takes a breather from her evening run and muse about what my skyline must have looked like.

COMMENTS

The applicant uses her neighborhood of Fort Greene (Brooklyn) as a lens through which to examine herself—an interesting and effective way of discussing one's self and one's own development while also making connections with larger movements and developments of local, national, or international importance.

The weakness of her effort is in claiming that she will practice international human rights law, a future that she apparently discovered during a single trip abroad. This of course is not convincing; in addition, it sits poorly with an essay devoted to her local neighborhood.

She is very perceptive about the neighborhood—and herself, as well. This, combined with her light, humorous touch, makes her someone a reader would like to meet. Her light touch serves another function as well; it camouflages the fact that she is making references (to Ellison, the Harlem Renaissance, the Revolutionary War, and Brooklyn Tech) meant to demonstrate that she is very well educated. The light touch allows her to do so without seeming to be tooting her own horn.

BILL

For between five and ten months of each of the past nine years, I have lived in Buddhist monasteries and retreats, devoting myself to the cultivation of insight and moral strength. During these periods, I have maintained silence—speaking, as a rule, only to teachers for ten or fifteen minutes two or three times each week. During these periods, I have given up many pleasures, including movies, television, and music, in order to focus more fully on this contemplative labor. I have sought the kind of wisdom that comes from looking within, from paying attention to and staying aware of the immediate experience of life, of the body, feelings, thoughts, etc. This particular type of introspection, which has been practiced in Buddhist monasteries for more than 2,500 years, has also been taught in medical centers throughout the United States, at Monsanto Company, and to the Chicago Bulls; it will soon be taught at Yale Law School. My goal has been to learn what can be learned, to develop the kind of understanding that comes from a calm and concentrated mind's studying life as it unfolds moment by moment. I have aspired to live, in the words of one famous lawyer, "with malice toward none; with charity for all."

Doing so for so long has not been easy. I have had to find the courage to live by my convictions and to follow a path seldom tread; I have not pursued wealth or prestige. I have had to endure the inconveniences of subsisting on very modest means and not having a home of my own. I have had to persevere without the support of my society's culture, the dominant American culture. I have had to find the strength to face life directly—even when it was unpleasant or boring—without distraction and without the dullness that comes from alcohol, drugs, or refusing to acknowledge the truth.

As a result of my efforts, I now more often feel happy and peaceful, more often feel good, than I did before—even when circumstances were trying. I face adversity with greater strength. Feelings of laziness, fear, and discouragement less often defeat me, less often slow me down or sway me from my course. Less often than before do I find myself the servant of loneliness, envy, or craving, acting at their behest, following their dictates. I more quickly notice my own feelings and less often am driven blindly by anger or ill will to speak or act in harmful ways. Even when provoked or insulted, I am more likely to recognize any feelings of hurt, sadness, or shame, and so retain the freedom to choose how to respond. I am less likely to become a slave of anger, immediately and unthinkingly striking back with spiteful words, for instance, heedless of the consequences. Not only do I enjoy greater self-awareness, but also I observe others more perceptively than I did before. My commitment to acting ethically is stronger than ever, and so is my ability to honor that commitment.

Some who have devoted themselves to seeking wisdom now live as monks. Others, including many Westerners, have married and now work in a wide range of fields, as professors, writers, lawyers, political activists, etc., leading dynamic lives that contribute visibly to society. I have decided to become a lawyer.

Embarking on a voyage of legal education appeals to me. I wish to exercise and further strengthen my powers of precise thinking, analyzing, and reasoning, of careful reading, and of persuasive writing and speaking. I believe that knowledge of the law will aid me greatly. I look forward to the opportunity to study and think about the resolution of conflict and the American legal system.

However, I am applying to [law school X] not only because I want a legal education, but also because I wish to have the professional opportunities that a law degree brings, because I believe that a JD will help me find work that is meaningful and satisfying to me and beneficial to others. I enjoy paying attention to detail and being thorough. I am capable of excellence in analyzing, reasoning, reading, and writing. Working as a lawyer will allow me to use my talent. Though I am not yet sure exactly which of the paths that leads from law school I will choose to take, several of them appeal to me, especially employment in the not-for-profit or government sectors.

Since high school, I have felt a strong pull towards public service. During college and after, I felt drawn in two directions to help prevent and alleviate causes of suffering and happiness, and sharing my understanding with others. In the past, my interest in political matters led to my being elected and serving as Chairman of the Liberal Party of the Yale Political Union. I spent time inviting, listening to, and questioning guest speakers about political issues and exploring and debating policy questions with my fellow students. Also in college, in a spirit of public service, I founded and directed a program to bring Yale student tutors into the New Haven public schools. I learned first-hand about education in the inner cities and succeeded in convincing dozens of Yalies to use their time and intelligence to help poor children learn. After college, I worked for Greenpeace. There I had the opportunity not only to learn to train and manage others, but also to go from door to door, from living room to living room, speaking with strangers about my concerns about the environment, informing and educating them, and persuading them to act by donating money, writing letters to their political representatives, and continuing to learn. I encountered some people who were hostile, and others who were sympathetic; I met some who were interested, and others who were not; I engaged and spoke persuasively even to some of those initially skeptical or unfriendly. More recently, I founded a religious not-for-profit corporation and organized six-week retreats with Sayadaw U Pandita, a highly respected Burmese Buddhist monk. This demanding work allowed me to make available, in the United States, opportunities to cultivate insight under the guidance of one of the world's foremost teachers in this field.

Whatever direction my legal career takes—whether I choose to safeguard the environment, protect children, or help in some other way—I will bring to my work a keen intelligence and a certain eloquence, as well as the qualities developed in my rare training: character, strength, compassion, and awareness. Much of the understanding I have is the result of a sustained encounter with, reflection on, and testing of teachings of the Buddha as well as an extensive observation of the human mind. These teachings and the particular form of introspection that I have engaged in are, to the legal profession, largely unexplored sources of knowledge and wisdom. To the discussions of a profession troubled with relatively high levels of dissatisfaction, depression, and alcoholism, I hope to bring interesting ideas, drawn from these sources among others, about which conduct and mental habits contribute to happiness and which to suffering. In a profession sometimes portrayed as dishonest, greedy, and selfish, I hope to swell by one the ranks of those who live with integrity, kindness, and altruism and inspire or convince others to live likewise. To interaction with clients, negotiations, and attempts to resolve disputes, I hope to bring a valuable sensitivity to unspoken needs and to the inner sources of conflict and disagreement. And in a society and to a profession that lavishes affluence and prominence on those who honor their duty of zealous advocacy on behalf of clients, especially rich clients, even if those advocates neglect their duty to third parties and to society, I hope to bring a strong dedication to justice, fairness, and public service.

My commitment to academic excellence is much stronger now than when I was in college, when much of my time, energy, and interest were drawn to the search that led me after graduation into monasteries and retreats. I feel ready to devote myself to the study of law. And I look forward to developing the skills, acquiring the knowledge, and earning the credentials that will help me find a position as a lawyer to help many, to share the fruits of my quiet cultivation of wisdom and virtue in action for the welfare of others.

COMMENTS

Although a bit long—a shorter statement would have been more effective—this does a good job of putting the candidate's "alternative" lifestyle into perspective. It is important for someone with big gaps in his or her employment record—in

Bill's case, the result of a commitment to Buddhist retreat practices and his philosophical quest—to explain the record to admissions committees. Bill does so by using his knowledge quest as the single most important theme in his profile. He does a good job of explaining the unique difficulties of his passion while also making it known that he is not "loony"—indeed some corporations and mainstream groups have begun to cultivate similar practices in their ranks. Incorporating his interest in public service (which is backed by significant tangible evidence of that commitment) makes sense because it is somewhat related.

After a strong first half, however, the essay runs into problems. Paragraphs five and six border on the trite, and his admission that he does not know what he will do upon graduation is worrying for someone who is already in his mid-thirties. Paragraph seven lapses into regurgitation of his résumé, and the start of paragraph eight is simply too self-congratulatory.

NYU DEAN'S SCHOLARSHIP ESSAY

Five of the opportunities available at NYU particularly interest me. First is the opportunity to study with NYU's faculty. NYU seems determined to attract outstanding law professors; I hope to feast at the table that has been—and is being—prepared. Second is the opportunity to study at a school seriously committed to public service. I expect to benefit from the Public Interest Law Center and NYU's excellent public interest faculty. I expect, too, to benefit from my fellow students. Finding like-minded classmates in an environment as demanding as law school can make the experience of school not only more enjoyable, but also richer, as a result of friendly discussion. NYU's commitment to public service, its generosity in supporting those committed to public service, and its reputation as a school dedicated to public interest law insure that NYU's class will contain more than the usual percentage of people dedicated to such work. The third opportunity at NYU that particularly interests me is the opportunity to participate in NYU's excellent clinical education program. I intend to make clinical education an important part of my legal education. Fourth, the opportunity to study the law in New York City interests me greatly. The opportunities in New York for internships and for studying with adjunct professors who are leading practitioners are unsurpassed. Much of my family and many of my friends live in New York. Also, though a JD from NYU should serve me well wherever I go, law degrees seem to be somewhat more geographically sensitive than medical or business degrees. Since I think it likely—though not yet certain—that I will settle in New York, can I do better than attend law school there? Fifth is the opportunity to receive an outstanding legal education. I would rate the likelihood of my seeking a job at Cravath as *extremely* low. Still, I know that such jobs are highly sought after. Some research revealed that an unusually high percentage of Cravath lawyers were NYU alumni. While speaking with an attorney who was once an associate at Cravath, I mentioned my discovery and hypothesized that the NYU network at Cravath was particularly strong. No, he corrected me, it is not just that the NYU network is strong. Rather, the partners found that, as a rule, NYU graduates have been trained exceptionally well. Though I expect to serve different interests than Cravath's lawyers, I do seek excellent training. NYU can provide me with that.

COMMENTS

Bill's Dean's Scholarship Essay for NYU is nicely, albeit simply, constructed. There is no room for creativity here, so it is best to state one's argument clearly and succinctly. Bill shows that he has done his homework, that he really understands NYU. A nice touch is his incorporation of the information gleaned from research at Cravath—arguably New York's most prestigious firm—despite the fact that this is a path he personally is unlikely to follow. It shows him to be active in learning about the school. It also shows him to be in touch with the real world of law, which is particularly valuable for someone who has been off meditating for the last decade (and is therefore vulnerable to a charge of not knowing much about the real world, let alone legal practice).

NOAH PITTARD

Transfer application

While I am pleased with my first-year performance at Hastings and fully aware of the advantages accruing to me as a result of it, I am convinced that transferring to Boalt Hall would create opportunities and yield benefits that are simply not available to me at Hastings.

Primarily, I would prefer to attend a smaller law school with a more intellectually driven student body. I write this not as a first-year applicant filled with brochure ideals, but as a rising "second-year" who has just completed his first year at a large, academically multifarious institution. I do not suggest that Hastings lacks bright, exceptional students; indeed, a substantial portion of my section consistently contributed to a vigorous dialectic, both in and out of class. This notwithstanding, I believe Boalt Hall's higher admissions criteria are bound to produce a materially higher percentage of students who share my interest in legal scholarship.

Secondarily, because I arrived at law school with a successful background in entrepreneurial business, as well as a keen interest in the law of commerce, I cannot overstate the appeal and value of student-level access to Boalt's nationally recognized business faculty. Although I would very much enjoy taking more classes with my first-year Hastings professors, I am more excited by the prospect of enrolling in corporations and international business classes with Professors Mel Eisenberg and Dick Buxbaum, to name but two. Furthermore, Boalt's curriculum includes a number of programs (e.g., financial services) that Hastings' does not.

In sum, my decision to apply to Boalt Hall is compelled by a strong preference to be part of a law school where interested, intelligent students, and a dynamic faculty, are the rule. This past year I learned the difference between mere competitiveness and competition, and it is the latter that I hope to find—and contribute to—at Boalt Hall. If admitted as a transfer student, I am confident that I would make as meaningful a contribution to your second-year class as I made to my own first-year class at Hastings.

COMMENTS

Noah was wise to focus intensely on a few reasons for wanting to transfer, rather than discussing each and every benefit of Boalt. Going overboard—using a laundry list approach—would have diffused his message, making him a less appealing candidate as a result. He is also smart not to insult his current school. It is better to discuss the attractions of your prospective school than to criticize your current school. For one thing, your prospective school wants to believe that you will be a full and enthusiastic supporter of it down the road.

Noah did miss one important trick, however. He is clearly attracted to business and should have used this as part of his rationale for seeking out Boalt. Hastings, his current law school, has no business school affiliated with it whereas Boalt's sister school is Berkeley's highly ranked Haas School of Business. (In fact, he later applied to Haas to do a joint JD–MBA.) His successful entrepreneurial experience would have been especially valuable in this context. He should have elaborated on it and explained exactly how he planned to take advantage of Boalt's and Haas's resources in this regard. This would have fitted well his basic argument that he was hoping to transfer to Boalt because it offered much that Hastings did not.

INDEX

Page numbers in **bold** indicate tables.

Morton, Todd, 13, 23, 54, 115, 116, 160, 167, 172, 173, 189, 198, 216, 226, 227, 235, 237, 270, 274, 304, 305, 312, 314, 323, 342, 345, 369, 378, 383, 388, 402, 412, 423, 424
rankings, 87
recommendations, **324**
transfers, **407**
Verrier, Jo-Ann (Career Services, Penn), 14
Villanova University School of Law/Lincoln University, 219
Virginia. *See* **University of Virginia**
Visas, student, 127, 426, 505
Visiting, admissions offices, 44, 75, 77–78
Visiting law schools, 75–82. *See also* Choosing right law school; Criteria for assessing schools
  admissions offices, 44, 75, 77–78
  career services, 78, 81
  classes, sitting in on, 7, 24, 44, 75, 78, 79, 80
  financial aid office, 77, 78, 82
  impressions after, 79, 80–81
  information sessions, 65, 75, 77, 82
  interviews and, 75, 76, 77–78, 354–55
  prejudices and, 78–79
  pre-law advising and, 132
  professors and, 77, 78, 80, 81
  questions for, 76, 78, 80, 81–82
  revisiting after acceptance, 76
  students, talking with, 7, 44–45, 51, 66–68, 75, 77–82
  thank-you notes, 82
  things to note, 80
  timetable for, 125
  timing of visit, 75–76, 80
  tours, 75, 76, 77, 82
Visiting students, 405, 418–19, 469–71, **470**
Vocabulary, legal, 432
Volunteer Income Tax Assistance Programs, 40
Volunteerism, 187–88. *See also* Community service; Crusader marketing theme; Do-gooder applicants

Wait-listing, 393–404. *See also* Admissions process
  acceptance and, 425–26
  admissions deans on, 397–400
  in admissions process, 111
  desire to attend school and, 395–96, 398
  financial aid and, **474**
  new information during, 393, 396, 397
  as numbers game, 395–96, 399–400
  push to admit status, 349
  reject push to, 349
  timing and, 399
Walker, Verlaine (Pre-law advisor, Arizona), 134
Washington. *See* University of Washington
Weaknesses. *See also* Gaps/weaknesses
  explanations for, xvi, 266, 269–70, 319
  minorities' academic, 217, 218, 220, 222
Wealthy applicants, 188, **206**, 208

Websites
  applications from LSAC, 304
  courses on, 7, 63
  Degree of Difference, xix
  for financing degree, 448, 452, 453–54, 462–63, 468
  pre-law, 137
  professor information on, 66
  school information on, 44, 82
West series, 437
"What if" games, 450
White, David P., 508, 509, **510–11**, 517, 536–39
White, E. B., 284, 298
Who you are, importance in admissions process, x, 108–9
Wild card section, of LSAT, 161
William & Mary. *See also* Admissions process; Law schools; Marketing yourself; Rankings
  clerkships, **95**
  essays, **276**
William Mitchell College of Law, 219
Wilson, Gerald (Pre-law advisor, Duke), 142
Wilson, Maura, 508, 509, **510–11**, 522–27
Wisconsin. *See* **University of Wisconsin**
The Woman Warrior (Kingston), 285
Women
  appearance for interviews, 368, 371
  battered, 264
  diversity and, 106
  to men ratio, 39
  as minorities, 217
Word choice, in essays, xvii, 284, 290, 294
Work experience. *See also* Credentials; Internships; Résumés
  academic record vs., 153–54
  accomplishments and, 177–78, 180–81
  achievement/impact through, 177–82
  admissions committees on, 176–84
  admissions deans on, 178–82
  admissions process and, **107**, 108
  applicants', 39
  deferring attendance for, xvi, 3, 11
  evaluation of, x
  exchange programs/matriculants and, 418
  extracurricular activities vs., 184–85, 186
  gaps in, 275
  law career and, xvi, 3, 11, 12–14, 180
  LLM degrees and, 488–91, 496, 498–99, 503–5
  marketability impacted by, 14, 46
  paralegals, 18–19, 23–24, 176–77, 202, **203**, 211, 252–53, 433
  in public interest, 33, 208–10, 471, 483
  questions on, 360–61
  self-assessment and, 11
  unrelated to law, 176
  unusual, as essay theme, 267–68
  value of, xvi, 3, 11, 12–14
Workload, in law school, 27, 33–34, 65
Workshops, pre-law, 138, 141